THE CITY
American Experience

The City

American Experience

ALAN TRACHTENBERG
Yale University

PETER NEILL
Yale University

PETER C. BUNNELL
The Museum of Modern Art

NEW YORK   OXFORD UNIVERSITY PRESS   1971

A. R. AMMONS: from *Briefings, Poems Small and Easy.* Copyright © 1971 by A. R. Ammons. Reprinted by permission of W. W. Norton & Company, Inc.

SHERWOOD ANDERSON: from *The Portable Sherwood Anderson.* Copyright 1930 by Sherwood Anderson. Reprinted by permission of Harold Ober Associates Incorporated.

MARY ANTIN: from *The Promised Land.* Copyright 1940 by Mary Antin. Reprinted by permission of Houghton Mifflin Company.

DONALD BARTHELME: from *Unspeakable Practices, Unnatural Acts.* Copyright © 1966, 1968 by Donald Barthelme. Reprinted by permission of Farrar, Straus & Giroux, Inc.

SAUL BELLOW: from *Mosby's Memoirs and Other Stories.* Copyright 1951 by Saul Bellow. Reprinted by permission of The Viking Press, Inc.

KENNETH BOULDING: from *The Historian and the City,* edited by Handlin and Burchard. Copyright © 1963 by the Massachusetts Institute of Technology and the President and the Fellows of Harvard College. Reprinted by permission of the MIT Press.

WILLIAM S. BURROUGHS: from *Nova Express.* Copyright © 1964 by William S. Burroughs. Reprinted by permission of Grove Press, Inc.

ROBERT COOVER: from *Pricksongs and Descants.* Copyright © 1969 by Robert Coover. Reprinted by permission of E. P. Dutton & Co., Inc.

HART CRANE: from *The Complete Poems and Selected Letters and Prose of Hart Crane.* Copyright 1933, 1958, 1966 by Liveright Publishing Corporation. Reprinted by permission of the publisher.

FRED DAVIS: from *American Journal of Sociology.* Copyright © 1959 by The University of Chicago. Reprinted by permission of the publisher and the author.

ST. CLAIR DRAKE and HORACE R. CAYTON: from *Black Metropolis.* Copyright 1945 by St. Clair Drake and Horace R. Cayton. Reprinted by permission of Harcourt Brace Jovanovich, Inc.

THEODORE DREISER: from *Sister Carrie.* Copyright 1927 by Theodore Dreiser. Reprinted by permission of The World Publishing Company by arrangement with the Estate of Theodore Dreiser.

W. E. B. Du BOIS: from *The Souls of Black Folk.* Copyright © 1961 by Fawcett Publishers, Inc., copyright 1953 by W. E. B. Du Bois. Reprinted by permission of Mrs. Shirley Graham Du Bois and Fawcett Publishers, Inc.

ALAN DUGAN: from *Poems.* Copyright © 1961 by Alan Dugan, © 1963, 1967, 1969 by Yale University Press. Reprinted by permission of the author and the publisher.

ROBERT DUNCAN: from *The Opening of the Field.* Copyright © 1960 by Robert Duncan. Reprinted by permission of Grove Press, Inc.

Introduction

As a culture, America seems to have awakened only recently to the fact that its way of life, its values and techniques, are predominantly urban. This awakening is often accompanied by shock and fear in the face of the serious social problems located in cities of all sizes—problems of poverty, race relations, crime, drugs, violence. No one can deny that we are indeed "a nation of cities," but few Americans seem pleased with the fact. The city today seems to affect our society as if it were the corrupting sore upon the body politic Jefferson warned against almost two hundred years ago. City has become synonymous with problems, the pressures of a competitive social order heightened and intensified by traffic, polluted air and water, oppressive housing. For most Americans the city symbolizes the disorder of contemporary life as a whole.

This is, of course, a one-sided view; it ignores the special pleasures of city life, its opportunities which constitute what we mean by civilization itself. The negative view is, however, powerfully compelling today. For this reason most readers will expect that a book on the experience of the city will deal with such specific issues as politics, economics, family structure, mental health, transportation—issues which affect the majority of the population.

This collection of writings and photographs has a different intent. It does not mean to address itself to concrete urban problems, at least not directly. We do not deal with explicit social patterns or with statistics. Our aim is to assemble materials which compose a city of the mind, of feelings and imagination, a composite city rendered from the experience of America's city people: European immigrant, black migrant, ghetto dweller, student, intellectual, worker, poet, historian, social critic, visionary planner. We wish to present the city as it has been known in America, restructured from raw experience into word and image.

The city of this book is, in short, the refracted image of individual experience. Actual cities are elusive, known and understood through the fragments of perception which form our personal experience. Moreover, what we know, about cities or anything else, depends almost entirely upon our language, just as what we see depends upon how we see, our particular point of view. The city represented in this collection is composed of a great variety of vocabularies and styles of seeing: history, sociology, autobiography, fiction, poetry. No selection is more "true" or accurate than another. Each views and reconstructs the world through its own assumptions, its own values. The level of generalization in a historical essay on urbanization will result in an account of the movement toward the city far different from a personal memoir on the same theme: the sociologist and historian will value the abstraction because it gathers into itself the typical experience of many, while the writer of the memoir will value the concrete, the unique truth of private experience.

Yet both may show evidence of sharing a cultural atmosphere. Values held in common, conventions of language, exercise a subtle control over personal response. Our aim in arranging the materials of this book has been to allow the reader to experience the individual nuance, the idiosyncrasy of style and meaning of each selection, and at the same time to recognize the force of the cultural, the aspect of each selection which links it to the others as an *American* expression. Just as the actual history of cities in America has been significantly different from that of Europe, Asia, and Africa, so the city occupies a singular place in the culture of America.

The organization of the book is designed to suggest that place. Each section designates a significant phase in the American experience of the city. **Before the city, Finding the city, Place and style, Interactions, Visions:** these titles embody characteristic moments and gestures, phases of the process by which Americans have come to recognize and deal with their urban lives. The process can, of course, be described historically, and we have included several essays which provide firm contexts in social and political fact. Our primary emphasis has been on contemporary materials. We have selected writings with an eye both to their representativeness and their intrinsic interest, and have found as a rule that the better a work from a literary point of view, the more effective it is as representative of group experience. Within each section the student will encounter multiplicity and contradiction, and he will be encouraged to discover common themes, threads which connect the selections. We stress diversity of language, of racial and ethnic points of view, of region and neighborhood, of class, and expect that patterns will emerge which conform to the actual history and structure of American cities.

Fundamental and recurring attitudes are introduced in **Before the city.** The historical fact which lies behind this section is the relative newness of American cities. As a culture we still have a memory of a condition prior to the rise of large cities. This pre-urban collective memory often appears as an active nostalgia for a simpler way of life, associated with frontier, farm, or rural town. Sentimentalized and exploited by mass media and political rhetoric, the image of a pastoral life, untroubled by complications, maintains a powerful hold upon many Americans. In movies, on television, in popular song and in advertisements, the rural life is represented as the original, the authentic American life; the city, a latecomer, is alien.

Such simplifications ignore the fact that the city has been the formative experience for most Americans for almost three generations, and in a sense, has always stood for the ideal of success. The persistence of anti-urban bias in mass culture is a peculiarity of modern American life. On the other hand, an important tradition based on country and village life is buried under the familiar stereotypes. The selections here contain elements of a positive inheritance from the pre-urban experience. Common to all of the selections is an awareness of landscape, of nature itself. The uses of landscape, the particular forms of communal adaptation to it, the value to the person in preserving it and deepening one's sense of it, differ in each case. So too do the kinds of family and village culture depicted. But the section argues that American urban society has a fund of experience outside the city which might serve as touchstone for renewal.

The act of coming to the city, of entering by gate or highway or terminal, is a typical feature of the American experience. During the great period of urbanization of the last hundred years, the city was populated by immigrants from abroad and migrants from the countryside. For this reason alone, **Finding the city** is a distinct moment in the drama of American culture. The initial experience is a conflict of values, a feeling of dislocation in the face of new demands. Newcomers are likely to lose their way, physically and morally. The big city presents itself as a mysterious maze, with its own system of signals. All cultures have the idea that the city represents sophistication and worldliness to the country's innocence and naïveté. The theme of the country innocent baffled and perhaps corrupted by first encounter with the city appears in several of the selections. Finding the city is like an initiation, at the end of which the initiate is transformed in some manner. In the popular success story, such as Horatio Alger's, the transformation appears in dress, in speech, and in accumulation of wealth and goods. Loss, however, is also a frequent theme; what the city gives with one hand it may take away with the other.

Movement through the city reveals a man-made environment, a manufactured landscape. Successive technological changes in the physical structure and appearance of the city have, in the past hundred years alone, enforced new demands upon the human sensorium. Simply to find one's way through the city, on its concrete and steel pathways, requires acclimated faculties of perception and recognition. The subliminal effects of these challenges are difficult to measure, but physical passage through the man-made space of the city is also fundamental to the drama of finding the city. In the way of life designated by the term "urbanism," topography assumes considerable importance. The outer surroundings, we see in several of these selections, become a map to an inner landscape.

The city is, in short, a demanding place, and what it demands is a style. How one presents oneself, in speech and appearance, is an accommodation to place, to surroundings, just as place frequently assumes and enforces an appropriate style of behavior. **Place and style,** then, includes essential activities of the city. The relationship between personal style and particular place has a special tone in American cities. As relatively recent places, without traditional institutions of burghership to sustain and control them, American cities have generally taken "progress," or change, as a chief value. Self-renewal rather than self-preservation, is the rule. City places are constantly changing, and developed styles of life find themselves in a backwash. To return to an old familiar place only to discover it has been replaced, is common to these selections. So is the experience of encountering a familiar place from within a new personal style, a new set of values.

A place assumes not only a personal but also a communal style, a bond among people who share its confines. Newcomers to the city tend to group together in places where old practices of social life are continued as long as possible. But the pressures of social mobility and of personal success work against the survival of such distinct places, and escape, or the wish to escape, is common. This section includes several examinations of the hold of such city places, the strength and weakness of their bonds. Other selections explore the peculiar life of such city entities as the rooming house and the supermarket.

Interactions presupposes face-to-face relations, acting upon another and being acted upon in turn; it presupposes confrontation. All cities impose certain patterns, certain codes, which minimize the expense of emotion in the multitude of transactions that occur daily. In American cities the social psychology of interaction is further complicated and intensified by several factors: race, ethnic styles, and mobile class status. These factors, together with the high-pressured effect of machines upon nerves and fantasy life, help account for the abrasiveness that marks the American metropolis. The selections here cover a gamut of feeling: from tenderness in chance meetings to antagonism and violence. The section concludes on a note which may be palliative to the rather bleak tone of much of the preceding material, with an ideal vision of urban motion and interaction.

Visions: the city and beyond recapitulates the entire volume and translates the themes of city experience into projected image and symbol. The section divides roughly between negative and positive visions, the nightmare of a cataclysmic death and the dream of a new life. The negative vision is chiefly an extension of present blight: dehumanizing forces which may engineer solutions to sewerage and smog but pollute the spirit. The concluding selections present a variety of provoking visions: new ideas about community and communication, about total design. We move in this section, where poets accompany planners, away from the explicit daily experience of American urban dwellers, toward several stunning and difficult possibilities for the future. Movement itself, the perpetual movement of the final selection, is revealed as the essential life of the city.

Alan Trachtenberg   Peter Neill
Winter 1970
New Haven, Connecticut

About the Photographs

Photography, while not an American invention, owes its perspective as a creative art to the photographers who have pursued their talents in the United States. As the most modern of all the visual arts, the evolution of photography has paralleled urban development in this country, and photographers here have revealed each step in the expansion of our awareness that we are "a nation of cities." No other visual medium is so pertinent to understanding the greatness or triviality of America's urbanism, or of such aid in demonstrating the duality of creative perception and insightful commentary. In its very abundance photography is also impressively significant. As early as 1853 the *New York Daily Tribune* estimated that three million photographs were being produced that year. Today it would be impossible even to hazard such an estimate. Not only has photography preserved the image of our physical past, but its artists have presented to us, with ever increasing sophistication, the content of our society. From a beginning wholly in keeping with the nineteenth-century American's propensity for detail and realism, photography gradually has come to be understood in terms of our visual imagination. Photographs are now seen to embody ideas which extend far beyond the actual frame of the picture itself. Today we realize that photography affects us like experience; it shows us what we see.

The photographs in this volume are presented in essays, or sequences, which parallel the divisions within the text. The individual images are not illustrations, in the usual sense, but are expressions in another medium of the views manifested in the book as a whole. Direct connections between the subjects of the photographs and the locations, incidents, or persons described in the texts should not be sought. Instead the student should find in the photographs an equivalent statement of the sectional themes which are described earlier in the introduction. Each image is by a photographer who, like the poet, social critic, or historian, has sought to state his individual experience of the American city. These particular photographs have been selected because their quality reflects the acuity of the photographer's sensibility and his exemplary use of the visual vocabulary. They should not be seen only as a series of pictures but read as essays in themselves. In this form photography is perhaps closer to literature than any other visual medium, for while it is generally assumed that the photographer is confined to a reportorial approach, the goal of the most able photographer is to explore beneath the surface to discover the significance of outer appearances.

The purpose of these photographic essays is to provide a means for the student to enlarge his understanding of the city and more readily to visualize the extremely subtle and complex aspects of the urban environment which may be lost in words alone. Each picture should be studied individually and in relation to those which precede it and those which follow it. The five portfolios taken together also form a kind of extended essay as well. The layout has been designed so that the student can approach the content of the image as a timeless referential touchstone apart from any outside data such as the place or date of the photograph. It is unimportant to know that a picture was made in New York, Omaha, Los Angeles, or Chicago, although this documentation is given elsewhere in the book. Within each essay the student will encounter diversity and contradiction, as he will in the text selections, and he should feel free to interpret the images himself and to speculate on their appropriateness.

The study of the history of photography, as with the work of the fifty-four photographers represented in this book, reveals that the concept of what is worth photographing constantly changes. Most fundamentally this change concerns the photographer's attitude toward what is significant in terms of inner meaning and symbol, more than what is eventful or newsworthy. Seventy years ago, for example, the photographers in New York, Cincinnati, Evanston, and Manchester made us realize that the interiors of tenements and hovels and factories were pertinent to everyone's life. Today the same may be said for the interiors of motels and hamburger stands, or simply empty spaces. In selecting such ubiquitous subjects photographers join the community of writers and artists who are not content that we merely be curious about our environment, but rather that we confront what is more truly our social landscape.

Peter C. Bunnell
Winter 1970
New York City

Contents

1 Before the city

2 Finding the city

3 Place and style

4 Interactions

5   Visions: the city and beyond

1
Before the city

Here nature and liberty affords us that freely which in England we want or it cost-eth us dearly. What pleasure can be more than (being tired with any occasion ashore in planting vines, fruits, or herbs, in contriving their own grounds to the pleasure of their own minds, their fields, gardens, orchards, buildings, ships, and other works, etc.) to recreate themselves before their own doors, in their own boats upon the sea, where man, woman, and child, with a small hook and line, by angling, may take diverse sorts of excellent fish at their pleasures? And is it not pretty sport to pull up two pence, six pence, and twelve pence as fast as you can haul and veer a line? He is a very bad fisher [that] cannot kill in one day with his hook and line one, two, or three hundred cods, which, dressed and dried, if they be sold there for ten shillings the hundred (though in England they will give more than twenty), may not both the servant, the master, and merchant be well content with this gain? If a man work but three days in seven, he may get more than he can spend unless he will be excessive. Now that carpenter, mason, gardener, tai-lor, smith, sailor, forgers, or what other, may they not make this a pretty recrea-tion, though they fish but an hour in a day to take more than they eat in a week? Or if they will not eat it because there is so much better choice, yet sell it, or change it with the fishermen or merchants for anything they want. And what sport doth yield a more pleasing content and less hurt or charge than angling with a hook, and crossing the sweet air from isle to isle over the silent streams of a calm sea, wherein the most curious may find pleasure, profit, and content?

John Smith
"A Call to the New World"

1
Before the city

Ansel Adams

Gertrude Käsebier

Paul Caponigro

Timothy O'Sullivan

Paul Vanderbilt

Robert Frank

John Runk

George Read

Southworth and Hawes

Robert Walch

Paul Strand

Frances Benjamin Johnston

Art Sinsabaugh

Edward Weston

Paul Strand

LEWIS MUMFORD
The Medieval Tradition

1

For a hundred years or so after its settlement, there lived and flourished in America a type of community which was rapidly disappearing in Europe. This community was embodied in villages and towns whose mummified remains even today have a rooted dignity that the most gigantic metropolises do not often possess. If we would understand the architecture of America in a period when good building was almost universal, we must understand something of the kind of life that this community fostered.

The capital example of the medieval tradition lies in the New England village.

There are two or three things that stand in the way of our seeing the life of a New England village; and one of them is the myth of the pioneer, the conception of the first settlers as a free band of "Americans" throwing off the bedraggled garments of Europe and starting life afresh in the wilderness. So far from giving birth to a new life, the settlement of the northern American seaboard prolonged for a little while the social habits and economic institutions which were fast crumbling away in Europe, particularly in England. In the villages of the New World there flickered up the last dying embers of the medieval order.

Whereas in England the common lands were being confiscated for the benefit of an aristocracy, and the arable turned into sheep-runs for the profit of the great proprietors, in New England the common lands were re-established with the founding of a new settlement. In England the depauperate peasants and yeomen were driven into the large towns to become the casual workers, menials, and soldiers; in New England, on the other hand, it was at first only with threats of punishment and conscription that the town workers were kept from going out into the countryside to seek a more independent living from the soil. Just as the archaic speech of the Elizabethans has lingered in the Kentucky Mountains, so the Middle Ages at their best lingered along the coast of Appalachia; and in the organization of our New England villages one sees a greater resemblance to the medieval Utopia of Sir Thomas More than to the classic republic in the style of Montesquieu, which was actually founded in the eighteenth century.

The colonists who sought to establish permanent communities—as distinct from those who erected only trading posts—were not a little like those whom the cities of Greece used to plant about the Mediterranean and the Black Sea littoral. Like the founders of the "Ancient City," the Puritans first concerned themselves to erect an altar, or rather, to lay the foundations for an edifice which denied the religious value of altars. In the crudest of "smoaky wigwams," an early observer notes, the Puritans remember to "sing psalms, pray, and praise their God"; and although we of today may regard their religion as harsh and nay-saying, we cannot forget that it was a central point of their existence and not an afterthought piled as it were on material prosperity for the sake of a good appearance. Material goods formed the basis, but not the end, of their life.

The meeting-house determined the character and limits of the community. As Weeden says in his excellent Economic and Social History of New England, the settlers "laid out the village in the best order to attain two objects: first, the tillage and culture of the soil; second, the maintenance of a 'civil and religious society.'" Around the meeting-house the rest of the community crystallized in a definite pattern, tight and homogeneous.

The early provincial village bears another resemblance to the early Greek city: it does not continue to grow at such a pace that it either becomes overcrowded within or spills beyond its limits into dejected suburbs; still less does it seek what we ironically call greatness by increasing the number of its inhabitants. When the corporation has a sufficient number of members, that is to say, when the land is fairly occupied, and when the addition of more land would unduly increase the hardship of working it from the town, or would spread out the farmers, and make it difficult for them to attend to their religious and civil duties, the original settlement throws out a new shoot. So Charlestown threw off Woburn; so Dedham colonized Medfield; so Lynn founded Nahant.

The Puritans knew and applied a principle that Plato had long ago pointed out in The Republic, namely, that an intelligent and socialized community will continue to grow only as long as it can remain a unit and keep up its common institutions. Beyond that point growth must cease, or the community will disintegrate and cease to be an organic thing. Economically, this method of community-development kept land values at a properly low level, and prevented the engrossing of land for the sake of a speculative rise. The advantage of the Puritan method of settlement comes out plainly when one contrasts it with the trader's paradise of Manhattan; for by the middle of the seventeenth century all the land on Manhattan Island was privately owned, although only a small part of it was cultivated, and so eagerly had the teeth of monopoly bitten into this fine morsel that there was already a housing-shortage.

One more point of resemblance: all the inhabitants of an early New England village were co-partners in a corporation; they admitted into the community only as many members as they could assimilate. This co-partnership was based upon a common sense as to the purpose of the community, and upon a roughly equal division of the land into individual plots taken in freehold, and a share of the common fields, of which there might be half a dozen or more.

There are various local differences in the apportionment of the land. In many cases, the minister and deacons have a larger share than the rest of the community; but in Charlestown, for example, the poorest had six or seven acres of meadow and twenty-five or thereabouts of upland; and this would hold pretty well throughout the settlements. Not merely is membership in the community guarded: the right of occupying and transferring the land is also restricted, and again and again, in the face of the General Assembly, the little villages make provisions to keep the land from changing hands without the consent of the corporation; "it being our real intent," as the burghers of Watertown put it, to "sitt down there close togither."

These regulations have a positive side as well; for in some cases the towns helped the poorer members of the corporation to build houses, and as a new member was voted into the community, lots were assigned immediately, without further ado. A friend of mine has called this system "Yankee communism," and I cheerfully bring the institution to the attention of those who do not realize upon what subversive principles Americanism, historically, rests.

What is true of the seventeenth century in New England holds good for the eighteenth century in the Moravian settlements of Pennsylvania; and it is doubtless true for many another obscure colony; for the same spirit lingered, with a parallel result in architecture and industry, in the utopian communities of the nineteenth century. It is pretty plain that this type of pioneering, this definite search for the good life, was conducted on an altogether different level from the ruthless exploitation of the individual muckers and scavengers who hit the trail west of the Alleghanies. Such renewals of the earlier European culture as the Bach Festival at Bethlehem give us a notion of the cultural values which the medieval community carried over from the Old World to the New. There is some of this spirit left even in the architecture of the Shaker community at Mount Lebanon, New York, which was built as late as the nineteenth century.

In contrast to the New England village-community was the trading post. Of this nature were the little towns in the New Netherlands which were planted there by the Dutch West India Company: the settlers were for the most part either harassed individuals who were lured to the New World by the prospects of a good living, or people of established rank who were tempted to leave the walks of commerce for the dignities and affluences that were attached to the feudal tenure of the large estates that lined the Hudson.

The germs of town life came over with these people, and sheer necessity turned part of their energies to agriculture, but they did not develop the close village-community we find in New England; and though New Amsterdam was a replica of the Old World port, with its gabled brick houses, and its well-banked canals and fine gardens, it left no decided pattern on the American scene. It is only the country architecture of the Dutch which survives as either a relic or a memory. These trading posts like Manhattan and Fort Orange were, as Messrs. Petersen and Edwards have shown in their study of New York as an Eighteenth Century Municipality, medieval in their economy: numerous guild and civic regulations which provided for honest weight and measure and workmanship continued in force within the town. In their external dealings, on the other hand, the practice of the traders was sharp, and every man was for himself. Beginning its life by bargaining in necessities, the trading post ends by making a necessity of bargaining; and it was the impetus from its original commercial habits which determined the characteristics of the abortive city plan that was laid down for Manhattan Island in 1811. Rich as the Dutch precedent is in individual farmhouses, it brings us no pattern, such as we find in New England, for the community as a whole.

2

Since we are accustomed to look upon the village as a quaint primitive relic of a bygone age, we do not readily see that its form was dictated by social and economic conditions. Where the village had to defend itself against Indians, it was necessary to lay it out completely, so that it might be surrounded by a stockade, and so that the meeting-house might be such a rallying center as the bell-tower or the castle was in Europe, or as the high temple site was in classic times. But in the eighteenth century the Indian figured less in the scheme of colonial life, and along the seacoast and river—as at Wells Beach in Maine or Litchfield in Connecticut —the village became a long strip upon a highroad, and the arable land stretched in narrow plots from the house to the water, so that the farmer might better protect his crops and his livestock from the fox, the wolf, the woodchuck, the hawk, the skunk, and the deer.

I emphasize these points of structure because of the silly notion superficial observers sometimes carry away from the villages of Europe or New England; namely, that their irregularity is altogether capricious and uneconomical, associated only with the vagaries of the straying cow. It would be more correct to say that the precise reverse was true. The inequality in size and shape of plots shows always that attention was paid to the function the land was to perform, rather than to the mere possession of property. Thus, there was a difference in size between home lots, which were always seated in the village, and purely agricultural tracts of land, which were usually on the outskirts; and in Dedham, for example, married men had home lots of twelve acres, while bachelors received only eight. Another reason for the compactness of the village was a decree of the General Court in Massachusetts, in 1635, that no dwelling should be placed more than half a mile from the meeting-house in any new plantation. Even irregularities in the layout and placement of houses, which cannot be referred to such obvious points as these, very often derive from an attempt to break the path of the wind, to get a good exposure in summer, or to profit by a view.

All this was genuine community planning. It did not go by this name, perhaps, but it achieved the result.

3

We have learned in recent years to appreciate the felicities of eighteenth-century colonial architecture, and even the earlier seventeenth-century style is now coming into its own, in the sense that it is being imitated by architects who have an eye for picturesque effects; but we lose our perspective altogether if we think that the charm of an old New England house can be recaptured by designing overhanging second stories or panelled interiors. The just design, the careful execution, the fine style that brings all the houses into harmony no matter how diverse the purposes they served—for the farmhouse shares its characteristics with the mill, and the mill with the meeting-house—was the outcome of a common spirit, nourished by men who had divided the land fairly and who shared adversity and good fortune together. When the frame of the house is to be raised, a man's neighbors will lend him a hand; if the harvest is in danger, every man goes out into the fields, even if his own crop is not at stake; if a whale founders on the beach, even the smallest boy bears a hand, and gets a share of the reward. All these practices were not without their subtle effect upon craftsmanship.

Schooled in the traditions of his guild, the medieval carpenter pours his all into the work. Since sale does not enter into the bargain, it is both to his patron's advantage to give him the best materials, and to his own advantage to make the most of them. If at first, in the haste of settlement, the colonists are content with makeshifts, they are nevertheless done in the traditional fashion—not the log cabins of later days, but, more probably, wattle and daub huts like those of the charcoal burners in the English forests. In some points, the prevailing English tradition does not fit the raw climate of the north, and presently the half-timbered houses of some of the earlier settlers would be covered by clapboards for greater warmth, as in the eighteenth century their interiors were lined with pan-elled pine or oak, instead of the rough plaster. No matter what the mate-rial or mode, the carpenter works not simply for hire, but for dear life's sake, and as a baker's dozen numbers thirteen, so a piece of handicraft contains not merely the workmanship itself, but a bit of the worker's soul, for good measure. The new invention of the gambrel roof, which gave ad-ditional room to the second story without raising the roof-tree, is a prod-uct of this system; and the variation in its length and pitch in New Eng-land, New Jersey, and New York is a witness to the freedom of design that prevailed throughout the work.

These seventeenth-century houses, built at first with one or two rooms, and then as luxury increased and family needs multiplied with as many as four, would doubtless seem unspeakably crude and mean to the resi-dent of Floral Heights; indeed, if our present requirements for housing were so simple it would not be quite so difficult to meet our perpetual shortage. As a matter of fact, however, these early provincial houses were well up to the standards for a similar homestead in England; and in some ways were a distinct advance. Just as all the separate courses on a restaurant menu were a few hundred years ago cooked in the same pot, so the different subdivisions of the modern house were originally com-bined into a single room, which was not merely kitchen, workroom, and living quarters, but which also, at least in winter, served as a stable for the more delicate members of the barnyard. By the time America was settled the division into rooms had just commenced among the better sort of farmer: the barn had split off from the rest of the house, and the bed-chamber was becoming a separate apartment. As the seventeenth cen-tury lengthened, this division of functions became more familiar in the provincial house.

Let us take a brief look at one of these seventeenth-century buildings; let us say, the John Ward house in Salem which still survives as a relic. As one approaches the village on some November day, when the leaves are no longer on the trees to obscure the vista, one feels the dynamic quality of medieval architecture—a quality altogether different from the prudent regularities of the later Georgian mode. It is not merely a matter of painted gables, leaded, diamond-paned windows, overhanging second stories, much as these would perhaps remind us of a medieval European town. What would attract one is the feeling, not of formal abstract design, but of growth: the house has developed as the family within it has pros-pered, and brought forth children; as sons and daughters have married, as children have become more numerous, there have been additions: by a lean-to at one end the kitchen has achieved a separate existence, for instance; and these unpainted, weathered oaken masses pile up with a cumulative richness of effect.

Every step that brings one nearer to the house alters the relation of the planes formed by the gable ends; and so one must have got the same effect in these old village streets as one gets today when one skirts around, let us say, Notre Dame in Paris, now overwhelmed by the towers at the front, and now seeing them reduced to nothing by the tall spire in the rear. So the building seems in motion, as well as the spectator; and this quality delights the eye quite as much as formal decoration, which the architecture of the seventeenth century in America almost completely lacked.

The Puritan had his failings; and this lack of decoration was perhaps the most important one in architecture. In his devotion to books and in his love for music, even psalm-music, the Puritan was not immune to art; but he was suspicious of the image, and one is tempted to read into his idol-breaking a positive visual defect, akin to the Daltonism or color blindness of the Quakers. Whereas medieval architecture had cherished the sculptor and the painter, even in the commonest vernacular work, the Puritans looked upon every diversion of the eye as a diversion from the Lord, and, by forbidding a respectable union between the artist and the useful arts, they finally turned the artist out on the streets, to pander to the first fine gentleman who would give him a kind word or a coin. Whereas Puritan buildings in the seventeenth century were straightforward and honestly bent to fulfill their functions, the Puritan did not see that ornament itself may be functional, too, when it expresses some positive gesture of the spirit. The bareness of the seventeenth century paved the way for the finicking graces of the eighteenth.

4

In essentials, however, both the life and the architecture of the first provincial period are sound. While agriculture is the mainstay of life, and the medieval tradition flourishes, the New England village reaches a pretty fair pitch of worldly perfection; and beneath all the superficial changes that affected it in the next century and a half, its sturdy framework held together remarkably well.

Consider the village itself. In the center is a common, a little to one side will be the meeting-house, perhaps a square barnlike structure, with a hipped roof and a cupola, like that at Hingham; and adjacent or across the way will be the grammar school. Along the roads where the houses are set at regular intervals is a great columnar arcade of elm trees. All these elements are essential to our early provincial architecture, and without them it would be a little bare and forbidding. The trees, above all, are an important part of New England architecture: in summer they absorb the moisture and cool the air, besides giving shade; in the winter their huge boles serve as a partial windbrake; even the humus from their leaves keeps the soil of the lawns in better order. The apple trees that cling to the warmer side of the house are not less essential. Would it be an exaggeration to say that there has never been a more complete and intelligent partnership between the earth and man than existed, for a little while, in the old New England village? In what other part of the world has such a harmonious balance between the natural and the social environment been preserved?

Nowadays we have begun to talk about garden cities, and we realize that the essential elements in a garden-city are the common holding of land by the community, and the coöperative ownership and direction of the community itself. We refer to all these things as if they represented a distinct achievement of modern thought; but the fact of the matter is that the New England village up to the middle of the eighteenth century was a garden-city in every sense that we now apply to that term, and happily its gardens and its harmonious framework have frequently lingered on, even though the economic foundations have long been overthrown.

This is a medieval tradition in American architecture which should be of some use to our architects and city planners; for it is a much more substantial matter than the building of perpendicular churches or Tudor country-houses in painfully archæological adaptations. If we wish to tie up with our colonial tradition we must recover more than the architectural forms: we must recover the interests, the standards, the institutions that gave to the villages and buildings of early times their appropriate shapes. To do much less than this is merely to bring back a fad which might as well be Egyptian as "colonial" for all the sincerity that it exhibits.

ROBERT FROST
Mending Wall

Something there is that doesn't love a wall,
That sends the frozen-ground-swell under it
And spills the upper boulders in the sun,
And makes gaps even two can pass abreast.
5   The work of hunters is another thing:
I have come after them and made repair
Where they have left not one stone on a stone,
But they would have the rabbit out of hiding,
To please the yelping dogs. The gaps I mean,
10   No one has seen them made or heard them made,
But at spring mending-time we find them there.
I let my neighbor know beyond the hill;
And on a day we meet to walk the line
And set the wall between us once again.
15   We keep the wall between us as we go.
To each the boulders that have fallen to each.
And some are loaves and some so nearly balls
We have to use a spell to make them balance:
"Stay where you are until our backs are turned!"
20   We wear our fingers rough with handling them.
Oh, just another kind of outdoor game,
One on a side. It comes to little more:
There where it is we do not need the wall:
He is all pine and I am apple orchard.
25   My apple trees will never get across
And eat the cones under his pines, I tell him.
He only says, "Good fences make good neighbors."
Spring is the mischief in me, and I wonder
If I could put a notion in his head:
30   "*Why* do they make good neighbors? Isn't it
Where there are cows? But here there are no cows.

Before I built a wall I'd ask to know
What I was walling in or walling out,
And to whom I was like to give offense.
35 Something there is that doesn't love a wall,
That wants it down." I could say "Elves" to him,
But it's not elves exactly, and I'd rather
He said it for himself. I see him there,
Bringing a stone grasped firmly by the top
40 In each hand, like an old-stone savage armed.
He moves in darkness as it seems to me,
Not of woods only and the shade of trees.
He will not go behind his father's saying,
And he likes having thought of it so well
45 He says again, "Good fences make good neighbors."

HENRY DAVID THOREAU
Where I Lived, and What I Lived For

At a certain season of our life we are accustomed to consider every spot as the possible site of a house. I have thus surveyed the country on every side within a dozen miles of where I live. In imagination I have bought all the farms in succession, for all were to be bought, and I knew their price. I walked over each farmer's premises, tasted his wild apples, discoursed on husbandry with him, took his farm at his price, at any price, mortgaging it to him in my mind; even put a higher price on it,—took everything but a deed of it,—took his word for his deed, for I dearly love to talk,—cultivated it, and him too to some extent, I trust, and withdrew when I had enjoyed it long enough, leaving him to carry it on. This experience entitled me to be regarded as a sort of real-estate broker by my friends. Wherever I sat, there I might live, and the landscape radiated from me accordingly. What is a house but a *sedes,* a seat?—better if a country seat. I discovered many a site for a house not likely to be soon improved, which some might have thought too far from the village, but to my eyes the village was too far from it. Well, there I might live, I said; and there I did live, for an hour, a summer and a winter life; saw how I could let the years run off, buffet the winter through, and see the spring come in. The future inhabitants of this region, wherever they may place their houses, may be sure that they have been anticipated. An afternoon sufficed to lay out the land into orchard, wood-lot, and pasture, and to decide what fine oaks or pines should be left to stand before the door, and whence each blasted tree could be seen to the best advantage; and then I let it lie, fallow perchance, for a man is rich in proportion to the number of things which he can afford to let alone.

My imagination carried me so far that I even had the refusal of several farms,—the refusal was all I wanted,—but I never got my fingers burned by actual possession. The nearest that I came to actual possession was when I bought the Hollowell place, and had begun to sort my seeds, and collected materials with which to make a wheelbarrow to carry it on or off with; but before the owner gave me a deed of it, his wife—every man has such a wife—changed her mind and wished to keep it, and he offered me ten dollars to release him. Now, to speak the truth, I had but ten cents in the world, and it surpassed my arithmetic to tell, if I was that man who had ten cents, or who had a farm, or ten dollars, or all together. However, I let him keep the ten dollars and the farm too, for I had carried it far enough; or rather, to be generous, I sold him the farm for just what I gave for it, and, as he was not a rich man, made him a present of ten dollars, and still had my ten cents, and seeds, and materials for a wheelbarrow left. I found thus that I had been a rich man without any damage to my poverty. But I retained the landscape, and I have since annually carried off what it yielded without a wheelbarrow. With respect to landscapes,—

> I am monarch of all I *survey,*
> My right there is none to dispute.

I have frequently seen a poet withdraw, having enjoyed the most valuable part of a farm, while the crusty farmer supposed that he had got a few wild apples only. Why, the owner does not know it for many years when a poet has put his farm in rime, the most admirable kind of invisible fence, has fairly impounded it, milked it, skimmed it, and got all the cream, and left the farmer only the skimmed milk.

The real attractions of the Hollowell farm, to me, were: its complete retirement, being about two miles from the village, half a mile from the nearest neighbor, and separated from the highway by a broad field; its bounding on the river, which the owner said protected it by its fogs from frosts in the spring, though that was nothing to me; the gray color and ruinous state of the house and barn, and the dilapidated fences, which put such an interval between me and the last occupant; the hollow and lichen-covered apple trees, gnawed by rabbits, showing what kind of neighbors I should have; but above all, the recollection I had of it from my earliest voyages up the river, when the house was concealed behind a dense grove of red maples, through which I heard the house-dog bark. I was in haste to buy it, before the proprietor finished getting out some rocks, cutting down the hollow apple trees, and grubbing up some young birches which had sprung up in the pasture, or, in short, had made any more of his improvements. To enjoy these advantages I was ready to carry it on; like Atlas, to take the world on my shoulders,—I never heard what compensation he received for that,—and do all those things which had no other motive or excuse but that I might pay for it and be unmolested in my possession of it; for I knew all the while that it would yield the most abundant crop of the kind I wanted, if I could only afford to let it alone. But it turned out as I have said.

All that I could say, then, with respect to farming on a large scale—I have always cultivated a garden—was, that I had had my seeds ready. Many think that seeds improve with age. I have no doubt that time discriminates between the good and the bad; and when at last I shall plant, I shall be less likely to be disappointed. But I would say to my fellows, once for all, As long as possible live free and uncommitted. It makes but little difference whether you are committed to a farm or the county jail.

Old Cato, whose "De Re Rusticâ" is my "Cultivator," says,—and the only translation I have seen makes sheer nonsense of the passage,— "When you think of getting a farm turn it thus in your mind, not to buy greedily; nor spare your pains to look at it, and do not think it enough to go round it once. The oftener you go there the more it will please you, if it is good." I think I shall not buy greedily, but go round and round it as long as I live, and be buried in it first, that it may please me the more at last.

The present was my next experiment of this kind, which I purpose to describe more at length, for convenience putting the experience of two years into one. As I have said, I do not propose to write an ode to dejection, but to brag as lustily as chanticleer in the morning, standing on his roost, if only to wake my neighbors up.

When first I took up my abode in the woods, that is, began to spend my nights as well as days there, which, by accident, was on Independence Day, or the Fourth of July, 1845, my house was not finished for winter, but was merely a defence against the rain, without plastering or chimney, the walls being of rough, weather-stained boards, with wide chinks, which made it cool at night. The upright white hewn studs and freshly planed door and window casings gave it a clean and airy look, especially in the morning, when its timbers were saturated with dew, so that I fancied that by noon some sweet gum would exude from them. To my imagination it retained throughout the day more or less of this auroral character, reminding me of a certain house on a mountain which I had visited a year before. This was an airy and unplastered cabin, fit to entertain a travelling god, and where a goddess might trail her garments. The winds which passed over my dwelling were such as sweep over the ridges of mountains, bearing the broken strains, or celestial parts only, of terrestrial music. The morning wind forever blows, the poem of creation is uninterrupted; but few are the ears that hear it. Olympus is but the outside of the earth everywhere.

The only house I had been the owner of before, if I except a boat, was a tent, which I used occasionally when making excursions in the summer, and this is still rolled up in my garret; but the boat, after passing from hand to hand, has gone down the stream of time. With this more substantial shelter about me, I had made some progress toward settling in the world. This frame, so slightly clad, was a sort of crystallization around me, and reacted on the builder. It was suggestive somewhat as a picture in outlines. I did not need to go outdoors to take the air, for the atmosphere within had lost none of its freshness. It was not so much within-doors as behind a door where I sat, even in the rainiest weather. The Harivansa says, "An abode without birds is like a meat without seasoning." Such was not my abode, for I found myself suddenly neighbor to the birds; not by having imprisoned one, but having caged myself near them. I was not only nearer to some of those which commonly frequent the garden and the orchard, but to those wilder and more thrilling songsters of the forest which never, or rarely, serenade a villager,—the wood thrush, the veery, the scarlet tanager, the field sparrow, the whip-poor-will, and many others.

I was seated by the shore of a small pond, about a mile and a half south of the village of Concord and somewhat higher than it, in the midst of an extensive wood between that town and Lincoln, and about two miles south of that our only field known to fame, Concord Battle Ground; but I was so low in the woods that the opposite shore, half a mile off, like the rest, covered with wood, was my most distant horizon. For the first week, whenever I looked out on the pond it impressed me like a tarn high up on the side of a mountain, its bottom far above the surface of other lakes, and, as the sun arose, I saw it throwing off its nightly clothing of mist, and here and there, by degrees, its soft ripples or its smooth reflecting surface was revealed, while the mists, like ghosts, were stealthily withdrawing in every direction into the woods, as at the breaking up of some nocturnal conventicle. The very dew seemed to hang upon the trees later into the day than usual, as on the sides of mountains.

This small lake was of most value as a neighbor in the intervals of a gentle rain-storm in August, when, both air and water being perfectly still, but the sky overcast, midafternoon had all the serenity of evening, and the wood thrush sang around, and was heard from shore to shore. A lake like this is never smoother than at such a time; and the clear portion of the air above it being shallow and darkened by clouds, the water, full of light and reflections, becomes a lower heaven itself so much the more important. From a hilltop near by, where the wood had been recently cut off, there was a pleasing vista southward across the pond, through a wide indentation in the hills which form the shore there, where their opposite sides sloping toward each other suggested a stream flowing out in that direction through a wooded valley, but stream there was none. That way I looked between and over the near green hills to some distant and higher ones in the horizon, tinged with blue. Indeed, by standing on tiptoe I could catch a glimpse of some of the peaks of the still bluer and more distant mountain ranges in the northwest, those true-blue coins from heaven's own mint, and also of some portion of the village. But in other directions, even from this point, I could not see over or beyond the woods which surrounded me. It is well to have some water in your neighborhood, to give buoyancy to and float the earth. One value even of the smallest well is, that when you look into it you see that earth is not continent but insular. This is as important as that it keeps butter cool. When I looked across the pond from this peak toward the Sudbury meadows, which in time of flood I distinguished elevated perhaps by a mirage in their seething valley, like a coin in a basin, all the earth beyond the pond appeared like a thin crust insulated and floated even by this small sheet of intervening water, and I was reminded that this on which I dwelt was but *dry land.*

Though the view from my door was still more contracted, I did not feel crowded or confined in the least. There was pasture enough for my imagination. The low shrub oak plateau to which the opposite shore arose stretched away toward the prairies of the West and the steppes of Tartary, affording ample room for all the roving families of men. "There are none happy in the world but beings who enjoy freely a vast horizon,"—said Damodara, when his herds required new and larger pastures.

Both place and time were changed, and I dwelt nearer to those parts of the universe and to those eras in history which had most attracted me. Where I lived was as far off as many a region viewed nightly by astronomers. We are wont to imagine rare and delectable places in some remote and more celestial corner of the system, behind the constellation of Cassiopeia's Chair, far from noise and disturbance. I discovered that my house actually had its site in such a withdrawn, but forever new and unprofaned, part of the universe. If it were worth the while to settle in those parts near to the Pleiades or the Hyades, to Aldebaran or Altair, then I was really there, or at an equal remoteness from the life which I had left behind, dwindled and twinkling with as fine a ray to my nearest neighbor, and to be seen only in moonless nights by him. Such was that part of creation where I had squatted;—

> There was a shepherd that did live,
>   And held his thoughts as high
> As were the mounts whereon his flocks
>   Did hourly feed him by.

What should we think of the shepherd's life if his flocks always wandered to higher pastures than his thoughts?

Every morning was a cheerful invitation to make my life of equal simplicity, and I may say innocence, with Nature herself. I have been as sincere a worshipper of Aurora as the Greeks. I got up early and bathed in the pond; that was a religious exercise, and one of the best things which I did. They say that characters were engraven on the bathing tub of King Tching-thang to this effect: "Renew thyself completely each day; do it again, and again, and forever again." I can understand that. Morning brings back the heroic ages. I was as much affected by the faint hum of a mosquito making its invisible and unimaginable tour through my apartment at earliest dawn, when I was sitting with door and windows open, as I could be by any trumpet that ever sang of fame. It was Homer's requiem; itself an Iliad and Odyssey in the air, singing its own wrath and wanderings. There was something cosmical about it; a standing advertisement, till forbidden, of the everlasting vigor and fertility of the world. The morning, which is the most memorable season of the day, is the awakening hour. Then there is least somnolence in us; and for an hour, at least, some part of us awakes which slumbers all the rest of the day and night. Little is to be expected of that day, if it can be called a day, to which we are not awakened by our Genius, but by the mechanical nudgings of some servitor, are not awakened by our own newly acquired force and aspirations from within, accompanied by the undulations of celestial music, instead of factory bells, and a fragrance filling the air—to a higher life than we fell asleep from; and thus the darkness bear its fruit, and prove itself to be good, no less than the light. That man who does not believe that each day contains an earlier, more sacred, and auroral hour than he has yet profaned, has despaired of life, and is pursuing a descending and darkening way. After a partial cessation of his sensuous life, the soul of man, or its organs rather, are reinvigorated each day, and his Genius tries again what noble life it can make. All memorable events, I should say, transpire in morning time and in a morning atmosphere. The Vedas say, "All intelligences awake with the morning." Poetry and art, and the fairest and most memorable of the actions of men, date from such an hour. All poets and heroes, like Memnon, are the children of Aurora, and emit their music at sunrise. To him whose elastic and vigorous thought keeps pace with the sun, the day is a perpetual morning. It matters not what the clocks say or the attitudes and labors of men. Morning is when I am awake and there is a dawn in me. Moral reform is the effort to throw off sleep. Why is it that men give so poor an account of their day if they have not been slumbering? They are not such poor calculators. If they had not been overcome with drowsiness, they would have performed something. The millions are awake enough for physical labor; but only one in a million is awake enough for effective intellectual exertion, only one in a hundred millions to a poetic or divine life. To be awake is to be alive. I have never yet met a man who was quite awake. How could I have looked him in the face?

We must learn to reawaken and keep ourselves awake, not by mechanical aids, but by an infinite expectation of the dawn, which does not forsake us in our soundest sleep. I know of no more encouraging fact than the unquestionable ability of man to elevate his life by a conscious endeavor. It is something to be able to paint a particular picture, or to carve a statue, and so to make a few objects beautiful; but it is far more glorious to carve and paint the very atmosphere and medium through which we look, which morally we can do. To affect the quality of the day, that is the highest of arts. Every man is tasked to make his life, even in its details, worthy of the contemplation of his most elevated and critical hour. If we refused, or rather used up, such paltry information as we get, the oracles would distinctly inform us how this might be done.

I went to the woods because I wished to live deliberately, to front only the essential facts of life, and see if I could not learn what it had to teach, and not, when I came to die, discover that I had not lived. I did not wish to live what was not life, living is so dear; nor did I wish to practise resignation, unless it was quite necessary. I wanted to live deep and suck out all the marrow of life, to live so sturdily and Spartan-like as to put to rout all that was not life, to cut a broad swath and shave close, to drive life into a corner, and reduce it to its lowest terms, and, if it proved to be mean, why then to get the whole and genuine meanness of it, and publish its meanness to the world; or if it were sublime, to know it by experience, and be able to give a true account of it in my next excursion. For most men, it appears to me, are in a strange uncertainty about it, whether it is of the devil or of God, and have *somewhat hastily* concluded that it is the chief end of man here to "glorify God and enjoy him forever."

Still we live meanly, like ants; though the fable tells us that we were long ago changed into men; like pygmies we fight with cranes; it is error upon error, and clout upon clout, and our best virtue has for its occasion a superfluous and evitable wretchedness. Our life is frittered away by detail. An honest man has hardly need to count more than his ten fingers, or in extreme cases he may add his ten toes, and lump the rest. Simplicity, simplicity, simplicity! I say, let your affairs be as two or three, and not a hundred or a thousand; instead of a million count half a dozen, and keep your accounts on your thumb-nail. In the midst of this chopping sea of civilized life, such are the clouds and storms and quicksands and thousand-and-one items to be allowed for, that a man has to live, if he would not founder and go to the bottom and not make his port at all, by dead reckoning, and he must be a great calculator indeed who succeeds. Simplify, simplify. Instead of three meals a day, if it be necessary eat but one; instead of a hundred dishes, five; and reduce other things in proportion. Our life is like a German Confederacy, made up of petty states, with its boundary forever fluctuating, so that even a German cannot tell you how it is bounded at any moment. The nation itself, with all its so-called internal improvements, which, by the way, are all external and superficial, is just such an unwieldy and overgrown establishment, cluttered with furniture and tripped up by its own traps, ruined by luxury and heedless expense, by want of calculation and a worthy aim, as the million households in the land; and the only cure for it, as for them, is in a rigid economy, a stern and more than Spartan simplicity of life and elevation of purpose. It lives too fast. Men think that it is essential that the *Nation* have commerce, and export ice, and talk through a telegraph, and ride thirty miles an hour, without a doubt, whether *they* do or not; but whether we should live like baboons or like men, is a little uncertain. If we do not get out sleepers, and forge rails, and devote days and nights to the work, but go to tinkering upon our *lives* to improve *them,* who will build railroads? And if railroads are not built, how shall we get to Heaven in season? But if we stay at home and mind our business, who will want railroads? We do not ride on the railroad; it rides upon us. Did you ever think what those sleepers are that underlie the railroad? Each one is a man, an Irishman, or a Yankee man. The rails are laid on them, and they are covered with sand, and the cars run smoothly over them. They are sound sleepers, I assure you. And every few years a new lot is laid down and run over; so that, if some have the pleasure of riding on a rail, others have the misfortune to be ridden upon. And when they run over a man that is walking in his sleep, a supernumerary sleeper in the wrong position, and wake him up, they suddenly stop the cars, and make a hue and cry about it as if this were an exception. I am glad to know that it takes a gang of men for every five miles to keep the sleepers down and level in their beds as it is, for this is a sign that they may sometime get up again.

Why should we live with such hurry and waste of life? We are determined to be starved before we are hungry. Men say that a stitch in time saves nine, and so they take a thousand stitches to-day to save nine tomorrow. As for *work,* we haven't any of any consequence. We have the Saint Vitus' dance, and cannot possibly keep our heads still. If I should only give a few pulls at the parish bell-rope, as for a fire, that is, without setting the bell, there is hardly a man on his farm in the outskirts of Concord, notwithstanding that press of engagements which was his excuse so many times this morning, nor a boy, nor a woman, I might almost say, but would forsake all and follow that sound, not mainly to save property from the flames, but, if we will confess the truth, much more to see it burn, since burn it must, and we, be it known, did not set it on fire,—or to see it put out, and have a hand in it, if that is done as handsomely; yes, even if it were the parish church itself. Hardly a man takes a half-hour's nap after dinner, but when he wakes he holds up his head and asks, "What's the news?" as if the rest of mankind had stood his sentinels. Some give directions to be waked every half-hour, doubtless for no other purpose; and then, to pay for it, they tell what they have dreamed. After a night's sleep the news is as indispensable as the breakfast. "Pray tell me anything new that has happened to a man anywhere on this globe,"—and he reads it over his coffee and rolls, that a man has had his eyes gouged out this morning on the Wachito River; never dreaming the while that he lives in the dark unfathomed mammoth cave of this world, and has but the rudiment of an eye himself.

For my part, I could easily do without the post-office. I think that there are very few important communications made through it. To speak critically, I never received more than one or two letters in my life—I wrote this some years ago—that were worth the postage. The penny-post is, commonly, an institution through which you seriously offer a man that penny for his thoughts which is so often safely offered in jest. And I am sure that I never read any memorable news in a newspaper. If we read of one man robbed, or murdered, or killed by accident, or one house burned, or one vessel wrecked, or one steamboat blown up, or one cow run over on the Western Railroad, or one mad dog killed, or one lot of grasshoppers in the winter,—we never need read of another. One is enough. If you are acquainted with the principle, what do you care for a myriad instances and applications? To a philosopher all *news,* as it is called, is gossip and they who edit and read it are old women over their tea. Yet not a few are greedy after this gossip. There was such a rush, as I hear, the other day at one of the offices to learn the foreign news by the last arrival, that several large squares of plate glass belonging to the establishment were broken by the pressure,—news which I seriously think a ready wit might write a twelvemonth, or twelve years, beforehand with sufficient accuracy. As for Spain, for instance, if you know how to throw in Don Carlos and the Infanta, and Don Pedro and Seville and Granada, from time to time in the right proportions,—they may have changed the names a little since I saw the papers,—and serve up a bull-fight when other entertainments fail, it will be true to the letter, and give us as good an idea of the exact state or ruin of things in Spain as the most succinct and lucid reports under this head in the newspapers: and as for England, almost the last significant scrap of news from that quarter was the revolution of 1649; and if you have learned the history of her crops for an average year, you never need attend to that thing again, unless your speculations are of a merely pecuniary character. If one may judge who rarely looks into the newspapers, nothing new does ever happen in foreign parts, a French revolution not excepted.

What news! how much more important to know what that is which was never old! "Kieou-he-yu (great dignitary of the state of Wei) sent a man to Khoung-tseu to know his news. Khoung-tseu caused the messenger to be seated near him, and questioned him in these terms: What is your master doing? The messenger answered with respect: My master desires to diminish the number of his faults, but he cannot come to the end of them. The messenger being gone, the philosopher remarked: What a worthy messenger! What a worthy messenger!" The preacher, instead of vexing the ears of drowsy farmers on their day of rest at the end of the week,—for Sunday is the fit conclusion of an ill-spent week, and not the fresh and brave beginning of a new one,—with this one other draggle-tail of a sermon, should shout with thundering voice, "Pause! Avast! Why so seeming fast, but deadly slow?"

Shams and delusions are esteemed for soundest truths, while reality is fabulous. If men would steadily observe realities only, and not allow themselves to be deluded, life, to compare it with such things as we know, would be like a fairy tale and the Arabian Nights' Entertainments. If we respected only what is inevitable and has a right to be, music and poetry would resound along the streets. When we are unhurried and wise, we perceive that only great and worthy things have any permanent and absolute existence, that petty fears and petty pleasures are but the shadow of the reality. This is always exhilarating and sublime. By closing the eyes and slumbering, and consenting to be deceived by shows, men establish and confirm their daily life of routine and habit everywhere, which still is built on purely illusory foundations. Children, who play life, discern its true law and relations more clearly than men, who fail to live it worthily, but who think that they are wiser by experience, that is, by failure. I have read in a Hindoo book, that "there was a king's son, who, being expelled in infancy from his native city, was brought up by a forester, and, growing up to maturity in that state, imagined himself to belong to the barbarous race with which he lived. One of his father's ministers having discovered him, revealed to him what he was, and the misconception of his character was removed, and he knew himself to be a prince. So soul," continues the Hindoo philosopher, "from the circumstances in which it is placed, mistakes its own character, until the truth is revealed to it by some holy teacher, and then it knows itself to be *Brahme.*" I perceive that we inhabitants of New England live this mean life that we do because our vision does not penetrate the surface of things. We think that this *is* which *appears* to be. If a man should walk through this town and see only the reality, where, think you, would the "Mill-dam" go to? If he should give us an account of the realities he beheld there, we should not recognize the place in his description. Look at a meeting-house, or a court-house, or a jail, or a shop, or a dwelling-house, and say what that thing really is before a true gaze, and they would all go to pieces in your account of them. Men esteem truth remote, in the outskirts of the system, behind the farthest star, before Adam and after the last man. In eternity there is indeed something true and sublime. But all these times and places and occasions are now and here. God himself culminates in the present moment, and will never be more divine in the lapse of all the ages. And we are enabled to apprehend at all what is sublime and noble only by the perpetual instilling and drenching of the reality that surrounds us. The universe constantly and obediently answers to our conceptions; whether we travel fast or slow, the track is laid for us. Let us spend our lives in conceiving then. The poet or the artist never yet had so fair and noble a design but some of his posterity at least could accomplish it.

Let us spend one day as deliberately as Nature, and not be thrown off the track by every nutshell and mosquito's wing that falls on the rails. Let us rise early and fast, or break fast, gently and without perturbation; let company come and let company go, let the bells ring and the children cry,—determined to make a day of it. Why should we knock under and go with the stream? Let us not be upset and overwhelmed in that terrible rapid and whirlpool called a dinner, situated in the meridian shallows. Weather this danger and you are safe, for the rest of the way is down hill. With unrelaxed nerves, with morning vigor, sail by it, looking another way, tied to the mast like Ulysses. If the engine whistles, let it whistle till it is hoarse for its pains. If the bell rings, why should we run? We will consider what kind of music they are like. Let us settle ourselves, and work and wedge our feet downward through the mud and slush of opinion, and prejudice, and tradition, and delusion, and appearance, that alluvion which covers the globe, through Paris and London, through New York and Boston and Concord, through Church and State, through poetry and philosophy and religion, till we come to a hard bottom and rocks in place, which we can call *reality,* and say, This is, and no mistake; and then begin, having a *point d'appui,* below freshet and frost and fire, a place where you might found a wall or a state, or set a lamp-post safely, or perhaps a gauge, not a Nilometer, but a Realometer, that future ages might know how deep a freshet of shams and appearances had gathered from time to time. If you stand right fronting and face to face to a fact, you will see the sun glimmer on both its surfaces, as if it were a cimeter, and feel its sweet edge dividing you through the heart and marrow, and so you will happily conclude your mortal career. Be it life or death, we crave only reality. If we are really dying, let us hear the rattle in our throats and feel cold in the extremities; if we are alive, let us go about our business.

Time is but the stream I go a-fishing in. I drink at it; but while I drink I see the sandy bottom and detect how shallow it is. Its thin current slides away, but eternity remains. I would drink deeper; fish in the sky, whose bottom is pebbly with stars. I cannot count one. I know not the first letter of the alphabet. I have always been regretting that I was not as wise as the day I was born. The intellect is a cleaver; it discerns and rifts its way into the secret of things. I do not wish to be any more busy with my hands than is necessary. My head is hands and feet. I feel all my best faculties concentrated in it. My instinct tells me that my head is an organ for burrowing, as some creatures use their snout and fore paws, and with it I would mine and burrow my way through these hills. I think that the richest vein is somewhere hereabouts; so by the divining-rod and thin rising vapors I judge; and here I will begin to mine.

SARAH ORNE JEWETT
A White Heron

The woods were already filled with shadows one June evening, just before eight o'clock, though a bright sunset still glimmered faintly among
the trunks of the trees. A little girl was driving home her cow, a plodding,
dilatory, provoking creature in her behavior, but a valued companion for
all that. They were going away from the western light, and striking deep
into the dark woods, but their feet were familiar with the path, and it was
no matter whether their eyes could see it or not.

There was hardly a night the summer through when the old cow could
be found waiting at the pasture bars; on the contrary, it was her greatest
pleasure to hide herself away among the high huckleberry bushes, and
though she wore a loud bell she had made the discovery that if one
stood perfectly still it would not ring. So Sylvia had to hunt for her until
she found her, and call Co'! Co'! with never an answering Moo, until
her childish patience was quite spent. If the creature had not given good
milk and plenty of it, the case would have seemed very different to her
owners. Besides, Sylvia had all the time there was, and very little use to
make of it. Sometimes in pleasant weather it was a consolation to look
upon the cow's pranks as an intelligent attempt to play hide and seek,
and as the child had no playmates she lent herself to this amusement
with a good deal of zest. Though this chase had been so long that the
wary animal herself had given an unusual signal of her whereabouts, Sylvia had only laughed when she came upon Mistress Moolly at the
swamp-side, and urged her affectionately homeward with a twig of birch
leaves. The old cow was not inclined to wander farther, she even turned
in the right direction for once as they left the pasture, and stepped along
the road at a good pace. She was quite ready to be milked now, and seldom stopped to browse. Sylvia wondered what her grandmother would
say because they were so late. It was a great while since she had left
home at half past five o'clock, but everybody knew the difficulty of making this errand a short one. Mrs. Tilley had chased the hornéd torment
too many summer evenings herself to blame any one else for lingering,

and was only thankful as she waited that she had Sylvia, nowadays, to give such valuable assistance. The good woman suspected that Sylvia loitered occasionally on her own account; there never was such a child for straying about out-of-doors since the world was made! Everybody said that it was a good change for a little maid who had tried to grow for eight years in a crowded manufacturing town, but, as for Sylvia herself, it seemed as if she never had been alive at all before she came to live at the farm. She thought often with wistful compassion of a wretched dry geranium that belonged to a town neighbor.

" 'Afraid of folks,' " old Mrs. Tilley said to herself, with a smile, after she had made the unlikely choice of Sylvia from her daughter's houseful of children, and was returning to the farm. " 'Afraid of folks,' they said! I guess she won't be troubled no great with 'em up to the old place!" When they reached the door of the lonely house and stopped to unlock it, and the cat came to purr loudly, and rub against them, a deserted pussy, indeed, but fat with young robins, Sylvia whispered that this was a beautiful place to live in, and she never should wish to go home.

The companions followed the shady woodroad, the cow taking slow steps, and the child very fast ones. The cow stopped long at the brook to drink, as if the pasture were not half a swamp, and Sylvia stood still and waited, letting her bare feet cool themselves in the shoal water, while the great twilight moths struck softly against her. She waded on through the brook as the cow moved away, and listened to the thrushes with a heart that beat fast with pleasure. There was a stirring in the great boughs overhead. They were full of little birds and beasts that seemed to be wide-awake, and going about their world, or else saying good-night to each other in sleepy twitters. Sylvia herself felt sleepy as she walked along. However, it was not much farther to the house, and the air was soft and sweet. She was not often in the woods so late as this, and it made her feel as if she were a part of the gray shadows and the moving leaves. She was just thinking how long it seemed since she first came to the farm a year ago, and wondering if everything went on in the noisy town just the same as when she was there; the thought of the great red-faced boy who used to chase and frighten her made her hurry along the path to escape from the shadow of the trees.

Suddenly this little woods-girl is horror-stricken to hear a clear whistle not very far away. Not a bird's whistle, which would have a sort of friend-liness, but a boy's whistle, determined, and somewhat aggressive. Sylvia left the cow to whatever sad fate might await her, and stepped discreetly aside into the bushes, but she was just too late. The enemy had discovered her, and called out in a very cheerful and persuasive tone, "Halloa, little girl, how far is it to the road?" and trembling Sylvia answered almost inaudibly, "A good ways."

She did not dare to look boldly at the tall young man, who carried a gun over his shoulder, but she came out of her bush and again followed the cow, while he walked alongside.

"I have been hunting for some birds," the stranger said kindly, "and I have lost my way, and need a friend very much. Don't be afraid," he added gallantly. "Speak up and tell me what your name is, and whether you think I can spend the night at your house, and go out gunning early in the morning."

Sylvia was more alarmed than before. Would not her grandmother consider her much to blame? But who could have foreseen such an accident as this? It did not appear to be her fault, and she hung her head as if the stem of it were broken, but managed to answer "Sylvy," with much effort when her companion again asked her name.

Mrs. Tilley was standing in the doorway when the trio came into view. The cow gave a loud moo by way of explanation.

"Yes, you'd better speak up for yourself, you old trial! Where'd she tuck herself away this time, Sylvy?" Sylvia kept an awed silence; she knew by instinct that her grandmother did not comprehend the gravity of the situation. She must be mistaking the stranger for one of the farmer-lads of the region.

The young man stood his gun beside the door, and dropped a heavy game-bag beside it; then he bade Mrs. Tilley good-evening, and repeated his wayfarer's story, and asked if he could have a night's lodging.

"Put me anywhere you like," he said. "I must be off early in the morning, before day; but I am very hungry, indeed. You can give me some milk at any rate, that's plain."

"Dear sakes, yes," responded the hostess, whose long slumbering hospitality seemed to be easily awakened. "You might fare better if you went out on the main road a mile or so, but you're welcome to what we've got. I'll milk right off, and you make yourself at home. You can sleep on husks or feathers," she proffered graciously. "I raised them all myself. There's good pasturing for geese just below here towards the ma'sh. Now step round and set a plate for the gentleman, Sylvy!" And Sylvia promptly stepped. She was glad to have something to do, and she was hungry herself.

It was a surprise to find so clean and comfortable a little dwelling in this New England wilderness. The young man had known the horrors of its most primitive housekeeping, and the dreary squalor of that level of society which does not rebel at the companionship of hens. This was the best thrift of an old-fashioned farmstead, though on such a small scale that it seemed like a hermitage. He listened eagerly to the old woman's quaint talk, he watched Sylvia's pale face and shining gray eyes with ever growing enthusiasm, and insisted that this was the best supper he had eaten for a month; then, afterward, the new-made friends sat down in the doorway together while the moon came up.

Soon it would be berry-time, and Sylvia was a great help at picking. The cow was a good milker, though a plaguy thing to keep track of, the hostess gossiped frankly, adding presently that she had buried four children, so that Sylvia's mother, and a son (who might be dead) in California were all the children she had left. "Dan, my boy, was a great hand to go gunning," she explained sadly. "I never wanted for pa'tridges or gray squer'ls while he was to home. He's been a great wand'rer, I expect, and he's no hand to write letters. There, I don't blame him, I'd ha' seen the world myself if it had been so I could.

"Sylvia takes after him," the grandmother continued affectionately, after a minute's pause. "There ain't a foot o' ground she don't know her way over, and the wild creatur's counts her one o' themselves. Squer'ls she'll tame to come an' feed right out o' her hands, and all sorts o' birds. Last winter she got the jay-birds to bangeing here, and I believe she'd 'a' scanted herself of her own meals to have plenty to throw out amongst 'em, if I hadn't kep' watch. Anything but crows, I tell her, I'm willin' to help support,—though Dan he went an' tamed one o' them that did seem to have reason same as folks. It was round here a good spell after he went away. Dan an' his father they didn't hitch,—but he never held up his head ag'in after Dan had dared him an' gone off."

The guest did not notice this hint of family sorrows in his eager interest in something else.

"So Sylvy knows all about birds, does she?" he exclaimed, as he looked round at the little girl who sat, very demure but increasingly sleepy, in the moonlight. "I am making a collection of birds myself. I have been at it ever since I was a boy." (Mrs. Tilley smiled.) "There are two or three very rare ones I have been hunting for these five years. I mean to get them on my own ground if they can be found."

"Do you cage 'em up?" asked Mrs. Tilley doubtfully, in response to this enthusiastic announcement.

"Oh, no, they're stuffed and preserved, dozens and dozens of them," said the ornithologist, "and I have shot or snared every one myself. I caught a glimpse of a white heron three miles from here on Saturday, and I have followed it in this direction. They have never been found in this district at all. The little white heron, it is," and he turned again to look at Sylvia with the hope of discovering that the rare bird was one of her acquaintances.

But Sylvia was watching a hop-toad in the narrow footpath.

"You would know the heron if you saw it," the stranger continued eagerly. "A queer tall white bird with soft feathers and long thin legs. And it would have a nest perhaps in the top of a high tree, made of sticks, something like a hawk's nest."

Sylvia's heart gave a wild beat; she knew that strange white bird, and had once stolen softly near where it stood in some bright green swamp grass, away over at the other side of the woods. There was an open place where the sunshine always seemed strangely yellow and hot, where tall, nodding rushes grew, and her grandmother had warned her that she might sink in the soft black mud underneath and never be heard of more. Not far beyond were the salt marshes and beyond those was the sea, the sea which Sylvia wondered and dreamed about, but never had looked upon, though its great voice could often be heard above the noise of the woods on stormy nights.

"I can't think of anything I should like so much as to find that heron's nest," the handsome stranger was saying. "I would give ten dollars to anybody who could show it to me," he added desperately, "and I mean to spend my whole vacation hunting for it if need be. Perhaps it was only migrating, or had been chased out of its own region by some bird of prey."

Mrs. Tilley gave amazed attention to all this, but Sylvia still watched the toad, not divining, as she might have done at some calmer time, that the creature wished to get to its hole under the doorstep, and was much hindered by the unusual spectators at that hour of the evening. No amount of thought, that night, could decide how many wished-for treasures the ten dollars, so lightly spoken of, would buy.

The next day the young sportsman hovered about the woods, and Sylvia kept him company, having lost her first fear of the friendly lad, who proved to be most kind and sympathetic. He told her many things about the birds and what they knew and where they lived and what they did with themselves. And he gave her a jack-knife, which she thought as great a treasure as if she were a desert-islander. All day long he did not once make her troubled or afraid except when he brought down some unsuspecting singing creature from its bough. Sylvia would have liked him vastly better without his gun; she could not understand why he killed the very birds he seemed to like so much. But as the day waned, Sylvia still watched the young man with loving admiration. She had never seen anybody so charming and delightful; the woman's heart, asleep in the child, was vaguely thrilled by a dream of love. Some premonition of that great power stirred and swayed these young foresters who traversed the solemn woodlands with soft-footed silent care. They stopped to listen to a bird's song; they pressed forward again eagerly, parting the branches,— speaking to each other rarely and in whispers; the young man going first and Sylvia following, fascinated, a few steps behind, with her gray eyes dark with excitement.

She grieved because the longed-for white heron was elusive, but she did not lead the guest, she only followed, and there was no such thing as speaking first. The sound of her own unquestioned voice would have terrified her,—it was hard enough to answer yes or no when there was need of that. At last evening began to fall, and they drove the cow home together, and Sylvia smiled with pleasure when they came to the place where she heard the whistle and was afraid only the night before.

Half a mile from home, at the farther edge of the woods, where the land was highest, a great pine-tree stood, the last of its generation. Whether it was left for a boundary mark, or for what reason, no one could say; the woodchoppers who had felled its mates were dead and gone long ago, and a whole forest of sturdy trees, pines and oaks and maples, had grown again. But the stately head of this old pine towered above them all and made a landmark for sea and shore miles and miles away. Sylvia knew it well. She had always believed that whoever climbed to the top of it could see the ocean; and the little girl had often laid her hand on the great rough trunk and looked up wistfully at those dark boughs that the wind always stirred, no matter how hot and still the air might be below. Now she thought of the tree with a new excitement, for why, if one climbed it at break of day, could not one see all the world, and easily discover whence the white heron flew, and mark the place, and find the hidden nest?

What a spirit of adventure, what wild ambition! What fancied triumph and delight and glory for the later morning when she could make known the secret! It was almost too real and too great for the childish heart to bear.

All night the door of the little house stood open, and the whippoorwills came and sang upon the very step. The young sportsman and his old hostess were sound asleep, but Sylvia's great design kept her broad awake and watching. She forgot to think of sleep. The short summer night seemed as long as the winter darkness, and at last when the whippoorwills ceased, and she was afraid the morning would after all come too soon, she stole out of the house and followed the pasture path through the woods, hastening toward the open ground beyond, listening with a sense of comfort and companionship to the drowsy twitter of a half-awakened bird, whose perch she had jarred in passing. Alas, if the great wave of human interest which flooded for the first time this dull little life should sweep away the satisfactions of an existence heart to heart with nature and the dumb life of the forest!

There was the huge tree asleep yet in the paling moonlight, and small and hopeful Sylvia began with utmost bravery to mount to the top of it, with tingling, eager blood coursing the channels of her whole frame, with her bare feet and fingers, that pinched and held like bird's claws to the monstrous ladder reaching up, up, almost to the sky itself. First she must mount the white oak tree that grew alongside, where she was almost lost among the dark branches and the green leaves heavy and wet with dew; a bird fluttered off its nest, and a red squirrel ran to and fro and scolded pettishly at the harmless housebreaker. Sylvia felt her way easily. She had often climbed there, and knew that higher still one of the oak's upper branches chafed against the pine trunk, just where its lower boughs were set close together. There, when she made the dangerous pass from one tree to the other, the great enterprise would really begin.

She crept out along the swaying oak limb at last, and took the daring step across into the old pine-tree. The way was harder than she thought; she must reach far and hold fast, the sharp dry twigs caught and held her and scratched her like angry talons, the pitch made her thin little fingers clumsy and stiff as she went round and round the tree's great stem, higher and higher upward. The sparrows and robins in the woods below were beginning to wake and twitter to the dawn, yet it seemed much lighter there aloft in the pine-tree, and the child knew that she must hurry if her project were to be of any use.

The tree seemed to lengthen itself out as she went up, and to reach farther and farther upward. It was like a great main-mast to the voyaging earth; it must truly have been amazed that morning through all its ponderous frame as it felt this determined spark of human spirit creeping and climbing from higher branch to branch. Who knows how steadily the least twigs held themselves to advantage this light, weak creature on her way! The old pine must have loved his new dependent. More than all the hawks, and bats, and moths, and even the sweet-voiced thrushes, was the brave, beating heart of the solitary gray-eyed child. And the tree stood still and held away the winds that June morning while the dawn grew bright in the east.

Sylvia's face was like a pale star, if one had seen it from the ground, when the last thorny bough was past, and she stood trembling and tired but wholly triumphant, high in the tree-top. Yes, there was the sea with the dawning sun making a golden dazzle over it, and toward that glorious east flew two hawks with slow-moving pinions. How low they looked in the air from that height when before one had only seen them far up, and dark against the blue sky. Their gray feathers were as soft as moths; they seemed only a little way from the tree, and Sylvia felt as if she too could go flying away among the clouds. Westward, the woodlands and farms reached miles and miles into the distance; here and there were church steeples, and white villages; truly it was a vast and awesome world.

The birds sang louder and louder. At last the sun came up bewilderingly bright. Sylvia could see the white sails of ships out at sea, and the clouds that were purple and rose-colored and yellow at first began to fade away. Where was the white heron's nest in the sea of green branches, and was this wonderful sight and pageant of the world the only reward for having climbed to such a giddy height? Now look down again, Sylvia, where the green marsh is set among the shining birches and dark hemlocks; there where you saw the white heron once you will see him again; look, look! a white spot of him like a single floating feather comes up from the dead hemlock and grows larger, and rises, and comes close at last, and goes by the landmark pine with steady sweep of wing and outstretched slender neck and crested head. And wait! wait! do not move a foot or a finger, little girl, do not send an arrow of light and consciousness from your two eager eyes, for the heron has perched on a pine bough not far beyond yours, and cries back to his mate on the nest, and plumes his feathers for the new day!

The child gives a long sigh a minute later when a company of shouting cat-birds comes also to the tree, and vexed by their fluttering and lawlessness the solemn heron goes away. She knows his secret now, the wild, light, slender bird that floats and wavers, and goes back like an arrow presently to his home in the green world beneath. Then Sylvia, well satisfied, makes her perilous way down again, not daring to look far below the branch she stands on, ready to cry sometimes because her fingers ache and her lamed feet slip. Wondering over and over again what the stranger would say to her, and what he would think when she told him how to find his way straight to the heron's nest.

"Sylvy, Sylvy!" called the busy old grandmother again and again, but nobody answered, and the small husk bed was empty, and Sylvia had disappeared.

The guest waked from a dream, and remembering his day's pleasure hurried to dress himself that it might sooner begin. He was sure from the way the shy little girl looked once or twice yesterday that she had at least seen the white heron, and now she must really be persuaded to tell. Here she comes now, paler than ever, and her worn old frock is torn and tattered, and smeared with pine pitch. The grandmother and the sportsman stand in the door together and question her, and the splendid moment has come to speak of the dead hemlock-tree by the green marsh.

But Sylvia does not speak after all, though the old grandmother fretfully rebukes her, and the young man's kind appealing eyes are looking straight in her own. He can make them rich with money; he has promised it, and they are poor now. He is so well worth making happy, and he waits to hear the story she can tell.

No, she must keep silence! What is it that suddenly forbids her and makes her dumb? Has she been nine years growing, and now, when the great world for the first time puts out a hand to her, must she thrust it aside for a bird's sake? The murmur of the pine's green branches is in her ears, she remembers how the white heron came flying through the golden air and how they watched the sea and the morning together, and Sylvia cannot speak; she cannot tell the heron's secret and give its life away.

Dear loyalty, that suffered a sharp pang as the guest went away disappointed later in the day, that could have served and followed him and loved him as a dog loves! Many a night Sylvia heard the echo of his whistle haunting the pasture path as she came home with the loitering cow. She forgot even her sorrow at the sharp report of his gun and the piteous sight of thrushes and sparrows dropping silent to the ground, their songs hushed and their pretty feathers stained and wet with blood. Were the birds better friends than their hunter might have been,—who can tell? Whatever treasures were lost to her, woodlands and summer-time, remember! Bring your gifts and graces and tell your secrets to this lonely country child!

W. E. B. DU BOIS
Of the Meaning of Progress

Once upon a time I taught school in the hills of Tennessee, where the broad dark vale of the Mississippi begins to roll and crumple to greet the Alleghanies. I was a Fisk student then, and all Fisk men thought that Tennessee—beyond the Veil—was theirs alone, and in vacation time they sallied forth in lusty bands to meet the county school-commissioners. Young and happy, I too went, and I shall not soon forget that summer, seventeen years ago.

First, there was a Teachers' Institute at the county-seat; and there distinguished guests of the superintendent taught the teachers fractions and spelling and other mysteries,—white teachers in the morning, Negroes at night. A picnic now and then, and a supper, and the rough world was softened by laughter and song. I remember how—But I wander.

There came a day when all the teachers left the Institute and began the hunt for schools. I learn from hearsay (for my mother was mortally afraid of firearms) that the hunting of ducks and bears and men is wonderfully interesting, but I am sure that the man who has never hunted a country school has something to learn of the pleasures of the chase. I see now the white, hot roads lazily rise and fall and wind before me under the burning July sun; I feel the deep weariness of heart and limb as ten, eight, six miles stretch relentlessly ahead; I feel my heart sink heavily as I hear again and again, "Got a teacher? Yes." So I walked on and on—horses were too expensive—until I had wandered beyond railways, beyond stage lines, to a land of "varmints" and rattlesnakes, where the coming of a stranger was an event, and men lived and died in the shadow of one blue hill.

Sprinkled over hill and dale lay cabins and farmhouses, shut out from the world by the forests and the rolling hills toward the east. There I found at last a little school. Josie told me of it; she was a thin, homely girl of twenty, with a dark-brown face and thick, hard hair. I had crossed the stream at Watertown, and rested under the great willows; then I had gone to the little cabin in the lot where Josie was resting on her way to town. The gaunt farmer made me welcome, and Josie, hearing my errand, told me anxiously that they wanted a school over the hill; that but once since the war had a teacher been there; that she herself longed to learn, —and thus she ran on, talking fast and loud, with much earnestness and energy.

Next morning I crossed the tall round hill, lingered to look at the blue and yellow mountains stretching toward the Carolinas, then plunged into the wood, and came out at Josie's home. It was a dull frame cottage with four rooms, perched just below the brow of the hill, amid peach-trees. The father was a quiet, simple soul, calmly ignorant, with no touch of vulgarity. The mother was different,—strong, bustling, and energetic, with a quick, restless tongue, and an ambition to live "like folks." There was a crowd of children. Two boys had gone away. There remained two growing girls; a shy midget of eight; John, tall, awkward, and eighteen; Jim, younger, quicker, and better looking; and two babies of indefinite age. Then there was Josie herself. She seemed to be the centre of the family: always busy at service, or at home, or berry-picking; a little nervous and inclined to scold, like her mother, yet faithful, too, like her father. She had about her a certain fineness, the shadow of an unconscious moral heroism that would willingly give all of life to make life broader, deeper, and fuller for her and hers. I saw much of this family afterwards, and grew to love them for their honest efforts to be decent and comfortable, and for their knowledge of their own ignorance. There was with them no affectation. The mother would scold the father for being so "easy"; Josie would roundly berate the boys for carelessness; and all knew that it was a hard thing to dig a living out of a rocky side-hill.

I secured the school. I remember the day I rode horseback out to the commissioner's house with a pleasant young white fellow who wanted the white school. The road ran down the bed of a stream; the sun laughed and the water jingled, and we rode on. "Come in," said the commissioner,—"come in. Have a seat. Yes, that certificate will do. Stay to dinner. What do you want a month?" "Oh," thought I, "this is lucky"; but even then fell the awful shadow of the Veil, for they ate first, then I—alone.

The schoolhouse was a log hut, where Colonel Wheeler used to shelter his corn. It sat in a lot behind a rail fence and thorn bushes, near the sweetest of springs. There was an entrance where a door once was, and within, a massive rickety fireplace; great chinks between the logs served as windows. Furniture was scarce. A pale blackboard crouched in the corner. My desk was made of three boards, reinforced at critical points, and my chair, borrowed from the landlady, had to be returned every night. Seats for the children—these puzzled me much. I was haunted by a New England vision of neat little desks and chairs, but, alas! the reality was rough plank benches without backs, and at times without legs. They had the one virtue of making naps dangerous,—possibly fatal, for the floor was not to be trusted.

It was a hot morning late in July when the school opened. I trembled when I heard the patter of little feet down the dusty road, and saw the growing row of dark solemn faces and bright eager eyes facing me. First came Josie and her brother and sisters. The longing to know, to be a student in the great school at Nashville, hovered like a star above this child-woman amid her work and worry, and she studied doggedly. There were the Dowells from their farm over toward Alexandria,—Fanny, with her smooth black face and wondering eyes; Martha, brown and dull; the pretty girl-wife of a brother, and the younger brood.

There were the Burkes,—two brown and yellow lads, and a tiny haughty-eyed girl. Fat Reuben's little chubby girl came, with golden face and old-gold hair, faithful and solemn. 'Thenie was on hand early,—a jolly, ugly, good-hearted girl, who slyly dipped snuff and looked after her little bow-legged brother. When her mother could spare her, 'Tildy came,—a midnight beauty, with starry eyes and tapering limbs; and her brother, correspondingly homely. And then the big boys!—the hulking Lawrences; the lazy Neills, unfathered sons of mother and daughter; Hickman, with a stoop in his shoulders; and the rest.

There they sat, nearly thirty of them, on the rough benches, their faces shading from a pale cream to a deep brown, the little feet bare and swinging, the eyes full of expectation, with here and there a twinkle of mischief, and the hands grasping Webster's blue-back spelling-book. I loved my school, and the fine faith the children had in the wisdom of their teacher was truly marvellous. We read and spelled together, wrote a little, picked flowers, sang, and listened to stories of the world beyond the hill. At times the school would dwindle away, and I would start out. I would visit Mun Eddings, who lived in two very dirty rooms, and ask why little Lugene, whose flaming face seemed ever ablaze with the dark-red hair uncombed, was absent all last week, or why I missed so often the inimitable rags of Mack and Ed. Then the father, who worked Colonel Wheeler's farm on shares, would tell me how the crops needed the boys; and the thin, slovenly mother, whose face was pretty when washed, assured me that Lugene must mind the baby. "But we'll start them again next week." When the Lawrences stopped, I knew that the doubts of the old folks about book-learning had conquered again, and so, toiling up the hill, and getting as far into the cabin as possible, I put Cicero "pro Archia Poeta" into the simplest English with local applications, and usually convinced them—for a week or so.

On Friday nights I often went home with some of the children,—sometimes to Doc Burke's farm. He was a great, loud, thin Black, ever working, and trying to buy the seventy-five acres of hill and dale where he lived; but people said that he would surely fail, and the "white folks would get it all." His wife was a magnificent Amazon, with saffron face and shining hair, uncorseted and barefooted, and the children were strong and beautiful. They lived in a one-and-a-half-room cabin in the hollow of the farm, near the spring. The front room was full of great fat white beds, scrupulously neat; and there were bad chromos on the walls, and a tired centre-table. In the tiny back kitchen I was often invited to "take out and help" myself to fried chicken and wheat biscuit, "meat" and corn pone, string-beans and berries. At first I used to be a little alarmed at the approach of bedtime in the one lone bedroom, but embarrassment was very deftly avoided. First, all the children nodded and slept, and were stowed away in one great pile of goose feathers; next, the mother and the father discreetly slipped away to the kitchen while I went to bed; then, blowing out the dim light, they retired in the dark. In the morning all were up and away before I thought of awaking. Across the road, where fat Reuben lived, they all went outdoors while the teacher retired, because they did not boast the luxury of a kitchen.

I liked to stay with the Dowells, for they had four rooms and plenty of good country fare. Uncle Bird had a small, rough farm, all woods and hills, miles from the big road; but he was full of tales,—he preached now and then,—and with his children, berries, horses, and wheat he was happy and prosperous. Often, to keep the peace, I must go where life was less lovely; for instance, 'Tildy's mother was incorrigibly dirty, Reuben's larder was limited seriously, and herds of untamed insects wandered over the Eddingses' beds. Best of all I loved to go to Josie's, and sit on the porch, eating peaches, while the mother bustled and talked: how Josie had bought the sewing-machine; how Josie worked at service in winter, but that four dollars a month was "mighty little" wages; how Josie longed to go away to school, but that it "looked like" they never could get far enough ahead to let her; how the crops failed and the well was yet unfinished; and, finally, how "mean" some of the white folks were.

For two summers I lived in this little world; it was dull and humdrum. The girls looked at the hill in wistful longing, and the boys fretted and haunted Alexandria. Alexandria was "town,"—a straggling, lazy village of houses, churches, and shops, and an aristocracy of Toms, Dicks, and Captains. Cuddled on the hill to the north was the village of the colored folks, who lived in three- or four-room unpainted cottages, some neat and homelike, and some dirty. The dwellings were scattered rather aimlessly, but they centred about the twin temples of the hamlet, the Methodist, and the Hard-Shell Baptist churches. These, in turn, leaned gingerly on a sad-colored schoolhouse. Hither my little world wended its crooked way on Sunday to meet other worlds, and gossip, and wonder, and make the weekly sacrifice with frenzied priest at the altar of the "old-time religion."

Then the soft melody and mighty cadences of Negro song fluttered and thundered.

I have called my tiny community a world, and so its isolation made it; and yet there was among us but a half-awakened common conscious-ness, sprung from common joy and grief, at burial, birth, or wedding; from a common hardship in poverty, poor land, and low wages; and, above all, from the sight of the Veil that hung between us and Opportu-nity. All this caused us to think some thoughts together; but these, when ripe for speech, were spoken in various languages. Those whose eyes twenty-five and more years before had seen "the glory of the coming of the Lord," saw in every present hindrance or help a dark fatalism bound to bring all things right in His own good time. The mass of those to whom slavery was a dim recollection of childhood found the world a puzzling thing: it asked little of them, and they answered with little, and yet it ridi-culed their offering. Such a paradox they could not understand, and therefore sank into listless indifference, or shiftlessness, or reckless bra-vado. There were, however, some—such as Josie, Jim, and Ben—to whom War, Hell, and Slavery were but childhood tales, whose young ap-petites had been whetted to an edge by school and story and half-awak-ened thought. Ill could they be content, born without and beyond the World. And their weak wings beat against their barriers,—barriers of cast, of youth, of life; at last, in dangerous moments, against everything that opposed even a whim.

The ten years that follow youth, the years when first the realization comes that life is leading somewhere,—these were the years that passed after I left my little school. When they were past, I came by chance once more to the walls of Fisk University, to the halls of the chapel of melody. As I lingered there in the joy and pain of meeting old school-friends, there swept over me a sudden longing to pass again beyond the blue hill, and to see the homes and the school of other days, and to learn how life had gone with my school-children; and I went.

Josie was dead, and the gray-haired mother said simply, "We've had a heap of trouble since you've been away." I had feared for Jim. With a cultured parentage and a social caste to uphold him, he might have made a venturesome merchant or a West Point cadet. But here he was, angry with life and reckless; and when Farmer Durham charged him with stealing wheat, the old man had to ride fast to escape the stones which the furious fool hurled after him. They told Jim to run away; but he would not run, and the constable came that afternoon. It grieved Josie, and great awkward John walked nine miles every day to see his little brother through the bars of Lebanon jail. At last the two came back to-gether in the dark night. The mother cooked supper, and Josie emptied her purse, and the boys stole away. Josie grew thin and silent, yet worked the more. The hill became steep for the quiet old father, and with the boys away there was little to do in the valley. Josie helped them to sell the old farm, and they moved nearer town. Brother Dennis, the carpenter, built a new house with six rooms; Josie toiled a year in Nashville, and brought back ninety dollars to furnish the house and change it to a home.

When the spring came, and the birds twittered, and the stream ran proud and full, little sister Lizzie, bold and thoughtless, flushed with the passion of youth, bestowed herself on the tempter, and brought home a nameless child. Josie shivered and worked on, with the vision of school-days all fled, with a face wan and tired,—worked until, on a summer's day, some one married another; then Josie crept to her mother like a hurt child, and slept—and sleeps.

I paused to scent the breeze as I entered the valley. The Lawrences have gone,—father and son forever,—and the other son lazily digs in the earth to live. A new young widow rents out their cabin to fat Reuben. Reuben is a Baptist preacher now, but I fear as lazy as ever, though his cabin has three rooms; and little Ella has grown into a bouncing woman, and is ploughing corn on the hot hillside. There are babies a-plenty, and one half-witted girl. Across the valley is a house I did not know before, and there I found, rocking one baby and expecting another, one of my schoolgirls, a daughter of Uncle Bird Dowell. She looked somewhat worried with her new duties, but soon bristled into pride over her neat cabin and the tale of her thrifty husband, and the horse and cow, and the farm they were planning to buy.

My log schoolhouse was gone. In its place stood Progress; and Progress, I understand, is necessarily ugly. The crazy foundation stones still marked the former site of my poor little cabin, and not far away, on six weary boulders, perched a jaunty board house, perhaps twenty by thirty feet, with three windows and a door that locked. Some of the window-glass was broken, and part of an old iron stove lay mournfully under the house. I peeped through the window half reverently, and found things that were more familiar. The blackboard had grown by about two feet, and the seats were still without backs. The county owns the lot now, I hear, and every year there is a session of school. As I sat by the spring and looked on the Old and the New I felt glad, very glad, and yet—

After two long drinks I started on. There was the great double log-house on the corner. I remembered the broken, blighted family that used to live there. The strong, hard face of the mother, with its wilderness of hair, rose before me. She had driven her husband away, and while I taught school a strange man lived there, big and jovial, and people talked. I felt sure that Ben and 'Tildy would come to naught from such a home. But this is an odd world; for Ben is a busy farmer in Smith County, "doing well, too," they say, and he had cared for little 'Tildy until last spring, when a lover married her. A hard life the lad had led, toiling for meat, and laughed at because he was homely and crooked. There was Sam Carlon, an impudent old skinflint, who had definite notions about "niggers," and hired Ben a summer and would not pay him. Then the hungry boy gathered his sacks together, and in broad daylight went into Carlon's corn; and when the hard-fisted farmer set upon him, the angry boy flew at him like a beast. Doc Burke saved a murder and a lynching that day.

The story reminded me again of the Burkes, and an impatience seized me to know who won in the battle, Doc or the seventy-five acres. For it is a hard thing to make a farm out of nothing, even in fifteen years. So I hurried on, thinking of the Burkes. They used to have a certain magnificent barbarism about them that I liked. They were never vulgar, never immoral, but rather rough and primitive, with an unconventionality that spent itself in loud guffaws, slaps on the back, and naps in the corner. I hurried by the cottage of the misborn Neill boys. It was empty, and they were grown into fat, lazy farm-hands. I saw the home of the Hickmans, but Albert, with his stooping shoulders, had passed from the world. Then I came to the Burkes' gate and peered through; the inclosure looked rough and untrimmed, and yet there were the same fences around the old farm save to the left, where lay twenty-five other acres. And lo! the cabin in the hollow had climbed the hill and swollen to a half-finished six-room cottage.

The Burkes held a hundred acres, but they were still in debt. Indeed, the gaunt father who toiled night and day would scarcely be happy out of debt, being so used to it. Some day he must stop, for his massive frame is showing decline. The mother wore shoes, but the lion-like physique of other days was broken. The children had grown up. Rob, the image of his father, was loud and rough with laughter. Birdie, my school baby of six, had grown to a picture of maiden beauty, tall and tawny. "Edgar is gone," said the mother, with head half bowed,—"gone to work in Nashville; he and his father couldn't agree."

Little Doc, the boy born since the time of my school, took me horseback down the creek next morning toward Farmer Dowell's. The road and the stream were battling for mastery, and the stream had the better of it. We splashed and waded, and the merry boy, perched behind me, chattered and laughed. He showed me where Simon Thompson had bought a bit of ground and a home; but his daughter Lana, a plump, brown, slow girl, was not there. She had married a man and a farm twenty miles away. We wound on down the stream till we came to a gate that I did not recognize, but the boy insisted that it was "Uncle Bird's." The farm was fat with the growing crop. In that little valley was a strange stillness as I rode up; for death and marriage had stolen youth and left age and childhood there. We sat and talked that night after the chores were done. Uncle Bird was grayer, and his eyes did not see so well, but he was still jovial. We talked of the acres bought,—one hundred and twenty-five,—of the new guest-chamber added, of Martha's marrying. Then we talked of death: Fanny and Fred were gone; a shadow hung over the other daughter, and when it lifted she was to go to Nashville to school. At last we spoke of the neighbors, and as night fell, Uncle Bird told me how, on a night like that, 'Thenie came wandering back to her home over yonder, to escape the blows of her husband. And next morning she died in the home that her little bow-legged brother, working and saving, had bought for their widowed mother.

My journey was done, and behind me lay hill and dale, and Life and Death. How shall man measure Progress there where the dark-faced Josie lies? How many heartfuls of sorrow shall balance a bushel of wheat? How hard a thing is life to the lowly, and yet how human and real! And all this life and love and strife and failure,—is it the twilight of nightfall or the flush of some faint-dawning day?

Thus sadly musing, I rode to Nashville in the Jim Crow car.

WALLACE STEGNER
The Making of Paths

". . . I . . . loved the trails and paths we made. . . ."

On the Saskatchewan homestead that we located in 1915 there was at first absolutely nothing. I remember it as it originally was, for my brother and I, aged eight and six, accompanied my father when he went out to make the first "improvements." Our land lay exactly on the international border; the four-foot iron post jutting from the prairie just where our wagon track met the section-line trail to Hydro, Montana, marked not only the otherwise invisible distinction between Canada and the United States but the division between our land and all other, anywhere.

There were few other marks to show which three hundred and twenty acres of that empty plain were ours. The land spread as flat as if it had been graded, except where, halfway to our western line, a shallow, nearly imperceptible coulee began, feeling its way, turning and turning again, baffled and blocked, a watercourse so nearly a slough that the spring runoff had hardly any flow at all, its water not so much flowing as pushed by the thaw behind it and having to go somewhere, until it passed our land and turned south, and near the line found another lost coulee, which carried in most seasons some water—not enough to run but enough to seep, and with holes that gave sanctuary to a few minnows and suckers. That was Coteau Creek, a part of the Milk-Missouri watershed. In good seasons we sometimes got a swim of sorts in its holes; in dry years we hauled water from it in barrels, stealing from the minnows to serve ourselves and our stock. Between it and our house we wore, during the four or five summers we spent vainly trying to make a wheat farm there, one of our private wagon tracks.

Coteau Creek was a landmark and sometimes a hazard. Once my father, gunning our old Model T across one of its fords, hit something and broke an axle. Next day he walked forty miles into Chinook, Montana, leaving me with a homesteader family, and the day after that he brought back the axle on his back and installed it himself after the homesteader's team had hauled the Ford out of the creek bed. I remember that square, high car, with its yellow spoke wheels and its brass bracing rods from windshield to mudguards and its four-eared brass radiator cap. It stuck up black and foreign, a wanderer from another planet, on the flats by Coteau Creek, while my father, red-faced and sweating, crawled in and out under the jacked-up rear end and I squatted in the car's shade and played what games I could with pebbles and a blue robin's egg. We sat there on the plain, something the earth refused to swallow, right in the middle of everything and with the prairie as empty as nightmare clear to the line where hot earth met hot sky. I saw the sun flash off brass, a heliograph winking off a message into space, calling attention to us, saying "Look, look!"

Because that was the essential feeling of the country for me—the sense of being foreign and noticeable, of sticking out—I did not at first feel even safe, much less that I was taking charge of and making my own a parcel of the world. I moped for the town on the Whitemud River, forty miles north, where we lived in winter, where all my friends were, where my mother was waiting until we got a shelter built on the homestead. Out here we did not belong to the earth as the prairie dogs and burrowing owls and picket-pin gophers and weasels and badgers and coyotes did, or to the sky as the hawks did, or to any combination as meadow larks and robins and sparrows did. Our shack, covered with tar paper, was an ugly rectangle on the face of the prairie, and not even the low roof, rounded like the roof of a railroad car to give the wind less grip on it, could bind it into the horizontal world.

Before we got the shack built, we lived in a tent, which the night wind constantly threatened to blow away, flapping the canvas and straining the ropes and pulling the pegs from the gravel. And when, just as we were unloading the lumber for the shack, a funnel-shaped cloud appeared in the south, moving against a background of gray-black shot with lightning-forks, and even while the sun still shone on us, the air grew tense and metallic to breathe, and a light like a reflection from brass glowed around us, and high above, pure and untroubled, the zenith was blue— then indeed exposure was like paralysis or panic, and we looked at the strangely still tent, bronzed in the yellow air, and felt the air shiver and saw a dart of wind move like a lizard across the dust and vanish again. My father rushed us to the three shallow square holes, arranged in a triangle, with the iron section stake at their apex, that marked the corner of our land, and with ropes he lashed us to the stake and made us cower down in the holes. They were no more than a foot deep; they could in no sense be called shelter. Over their edge our eyes, level with the plain, looked southward and saw nothing between us and the ominous funnel except gopher mounds, the still unshaken grass. Across the coulee a gopher sat up, erect as the picket pin from which he took his name.

Then the grass stirred; it was as if gooseflesh prickled suddenly on the prairie's skin. The gopher disappeared as if some friend below had reached up and yanked him into his burrow. Even while we were realizing it, the yellow air darkened, and then all the brown and yellow went out of it and it was blue-black. The wind began to pluck at the shirts on our backs, the hair on our heads was wrenched, the air was full of dust. From the third hole my father, glaring over the shallow rim, yelled to my brother and to me to keep down, and with a fierce rush rain trampled our backs, and the curly buffalo grass at the level of my squinted eyes was strained out straight and whistling. I popped my head into my arms and fitted my body to the earth. To give the wind more than my flat back, I felt, would be sure destruction, for that was a wind, and that was a country, that hated a foreign and vertical thing.

The cyclone missed us; we got only its lashing edge. We came up cautiously from our muddy burrows and saw the clearing world and smelled the air, washed and rinsed of all its sultry oppressiveness. I for one felt better about being who I was, but for a good many weeks I watched the sky with suspicion; exposed as we were, it could jump on us like a leopard from a tree. And I know I was disappointed in the shack my father swiftly put together on our arid flat. A soddy that poked its low brow no higher than the tailings of a gopher's burrow would have suited me better. The bond with the earth that all the footed and winged creatures felt in that country was quite as valid for me.

And that was why I so loved the trails and paths we made; they were ceremonial, an insistence not only that we had a right be be in sight on those prairies but that we owned a piece of them and controlled it. In a country practically without landmarks, as that part of Saskatchewan was, it might have been assumed that any road would comfort the soul. But I don't recall feeling anything special about the graded road that led us three-quarters of the forty miles of our annual June pilgrimage from town to homestead, or for the wiggling tracks that turned off it to the homesteads of others. It was our own trail, lightly worn, its ruts a slightly fresher green where old cured grass had been rubbed away, that lifted my heart; it took off across the prairie like an extension of myself. Our own wheels had made it; broad, iron-shod wagon wheels first, then narrow democrat wheels that cut through the mat of grass and scored the earth until it blew and washed and started a rut, then finally the wheels of the Ford.

By the time we turned off it, the road we had followed from town had itself dwindled to a pair of ruts, but it never quite disappeared; it simply divided into branches like ours. I do not know why the last miles, across buffalo grass and burnouts, past a shack or two abandoned by the homesteaders who had built them, across Coteau Creek, and on westward until the ruts passed through our gate in our fence and stopped before our house, should always have excited me so, unless it was that the trail was a thing we had exclusively created and that it led to a place we had exclusively built. Those tracks demonstrated our existence as triumphantly as an Indian is demonstrated by his handprint painted in ochre on a cliff wall. Not so idiotically as the stranded Ford, this trail and the shack and chicken house and privy at its end said, "See? We are here." Thus, in a sense, was "located" a homestead.

More satisfying than the wagon trail, even, because more intimately and privately made, were the paths that our daily living wore in the prairie. I loved the horses for poking along the pasture fence looking for a way out, because that habit very soon wore a plain path all around inside the barbed wire. Whenever I had to go and catch them for something, I went out of my way to walk in it, partly because the path was easier on my bare feet but more because I wanted to contribute my feet to the wearing process. I scuffed and kicked at clods and persistent grass clumps, and twisted my weight on incipient weeds and flowers, willing that the trail around the inside of our pasture should be beaten dusty and plain, a worn border to our inheritance.

It was the same with the path to the woodpile and the privy. In June, when we reached the homestead, that would be nearly overgrown, the faintest sort of radius line within the fireguard. But our feet quickly wore it anew, though there were only the four of us, and though other members of the family, less addicted to paths than I, often frustrated and irrated me by cutting across from the wrong corner of the house, or detouring past the fencepost pile to get a handful of cedar bark for kindling, and so neglecting their plain duty to the highway. It was an unspeakable satisfaction to me when after a few weeks I could rise in the flat morning light that came across the prairie in one thrust, like a train rushing down a track, and see the beaten footpath, leading gray and dusty between grass and cactus and the little orange flowers of the false mallow that we called wild geranium, until it ended, its purpose served, at the hooked privy door.

Wearing any such path in the earth's rind is an intimate act, an act like love, and it is denied to the dweller in cities. He lacks the proper mana for it, he is out of touch. Once, on Fifty-eighth Street in New York, I saw an apartment dweller walking his captive deer on a leash. They had not the pleasure of leaving a single footprint, and the sound of the thin little hoofs on concrete seemed as melancholy to me as, at the moment, the sound of my own.

SHERWOOD ANDERSON
The American County Fair

It is an odd time in a town. The fair ground commonly is a deserted place. It stands on a hill.

The land rolls away. Now the fair is being held. From the grandstand, where you sit to watch the races, you can see, over a high board fence, into distant hills.

The fair is held sometimes at the end of August but sometimes not until late October or early November. It makes a difference in the color of the hills.

Hills are at their best when white farmhouses cling to their sides. Nature untouched by man is too terrible. It is too difficult of approach. You become terrorized. The pioneers, who go into lands where man has not been, must be very brave or very dull. Perhaps they are only dull.

You are always wanting man in nature—woman in nature. You can get it at the fair. What a place for pictures. You will do well, at the country fairs, not to draw too close.

What a scene it is. Suppose you go up into the high grandstand. There is the bright grandstand, yellow in the afternoon light. The hills in the distance are blue.

Thousands of cars are parked in a great field at the rear of the grandstand. A cloud of dust arises. Nowadays people come to a fair from two or three counties.

The shows are here—in the open space between the field where the cars are parked and the grandstand. There is the snake tamer, the fat woman, the hoochy-coochy girls, the woman buried alive, the man with the web feet and hands, a calf with two heads. The gamblers are out in force.

They have all sorts of little wheels. They are shrewd-looking, hard-faced young men and they have their women with them. The women whirl the wheels while the men implore the men in the crowd, begging them to come up and win money. Win money indeed. These men and women are young but already they know a thousand foxy tricks to get money.

The fair is something special in the county. In spite of all the talk about improving agriculture, etc., it is a pagan outbreak.

See the women going about, the girls from the towns and from the farms. They walk boldly. Now is the time to get yourself a man. They all feel that. It shows in the way they walk. It is in their eyes. They will stay at the fair all day and far into the night. They are tireless.

The men all act a little puzzled. They wander aimlessly about.

The state agricultural department has brought fine cattle to be shown. Some of the rich farmers have also brought fine fat cattle, huge horses, sheep and pigs.

The older men go down to the sheds to look. They stand about and talk, spitting on the ground. The young fellows do not go and the women do not go.

The older women go into the buildings and sheds where women's work is shown. An amazing number of the older women are fat. Fat bodies rubbing against each other, fat still faces.

The children are tired, become tired early in the day. They cry. The tears make little streaks in the tiny dusty faces. The mothers carry the children into the field where the cars are parked and lay them on the car seats. They sleep there. When they waken they again cry.

Now it is time for the races. A bell rings. The judges of the races are in the judges' stand that is directly in front of the grandstand. There is a race starter who has a voice like an auctioneer. He shouts through a megaphone.

It is difficult to clear the track for the races. Thousands of people have gathered there. The starter of the races, with his megaphone, shouts, the county sheriff, a large man, appears and shouts. The people move back slowly, reluctantly.

And now, here are the horses—the trotters and pacers. This is something to wait for.

The horses are moving down the tracks, swiftly and smoothly. What has man done more noble than this?

He has developed these fine beasts.

They have been taught to go at a certain gait, the trot or pace, faster, faster, faster. They are hitched to little carts, very delicately made, and the driver sits up close to the horse. The moving flanks of the horse are almost in the driver's lap.

The drivers are young and old men. Some of them, many of them in fact, are quiet respectable men at other times during the year, excepting only in the fall when the fairs are being held. Now they shout, they lean forward over their horses.

There is no money to be made racing horses at the fairs. The horses cost too much. It costs too much to train them.

Professional trainers must be employed. There is feed to be bought, harness, racing carts and other equipment. The trainer's salary must be paid and there are grooms, in our part of the country a black for each horse.

The owners are country bankers, farmers, doctors and merchants.

The horses race for a purse of say two hundred dollars. A hundred dollars is given the winner and the other hundred is distributed between the second, third, and fourth horse.

And now the doctors, bankers, merchants, prosperous farmers have become something other than doctors, bankers, merchants, farmers. They have put on little gaily colored caps and gaily colored coats. The horses are brought out hitched to their carts.

The respectable citizen, who has become a jockey, is on the track, before the grandstand walking up and down.

Now the crowd is all attention. The shows are deserted, the band stops playing.

People crowd into the grandstand, they crowd to the fences.

The jockeys have mounted the little sulkies with the delicate bicycle wheels and the horses are being warmed up.

They dash up and down. The horses also are excited and the drivers are tense.

The drivers try to appear cool. After all this is dangerous business. These horses, so highly bred, so finely trained, sometimes lose their heads.

The horses must score down past the grandstand and the judges' stand until the race starter decides it is a fair start. Each driver tries to crowd to the front, to give his horse an advantage.

If it is not a fair start a bell rings and they must try again.

In the Grand Circuit, to which the fastest of all the trotters and pacers go, where the purses are larger, nearly all driving is done by professional drivers but at these little fairs—here the owner himself has a chance.

What would Mr. Harry Sinclair give if he could himself ride one of his beautiful thoroughbreds, or Mr. Harry Payne Whitney, or Mr. Bradley?

It can't be done. The rider of the thoroughbred must weigh almost nothing. He must be a mere slip of a boy.

On the Grand Circuit where the fastest of all trotters and pacers go the amount of money involved is large. They are racing for ten thousand dollars, not for two hundred.

But these men, these country bankers, doctors, lawyers, farmers, who are horse lovers, have also invested their money. The horses here are often but a few seconds slower than those on the Grand Circuit. Some of them are sons and daughters of great sires. At the stables, over here under that hill, you will hear names of kings bandied about "He is a son of Grayson Gravy 2.01 1/2. All the sons of that fellow go fast."

There is talk too of the art of driving. There is a certain horse you must "tuck in" until you get to the head of the stretch. He is a stretch trotter. Wait. Wait. Wait. Then ask him for it.

Ask him softly or with a gentle tap of the whip.

"Now, now, now."

Or he may be one who will take his punishment like a soldier. Give it to him. Lay the whip to him. Shout.

"Ata boy. Ata boy." A wild cry.

You have to put your own excitement into the nerves of some of the horses, make them feel it, tell them what you want.

You want all they have got, every ounce. The horse to keep his head, not to lose the smooth rhythm of the trot or pace, not to leap into the air, to keep on trotting or pacing.

The stride to be lengthened more and more, the legs to reach, reach, reach.

All the very fast ones have that smooth long rhythmical stride. They have courage too. They know what they are doing.

It is something to be the driver of such a horse. Everything is in the driver. If he is timid or weak-hearted the horse will know it now.

The horse will lose confidence, he will never win.

Something like love between the man and the horse. You feel it when you go to the stables. Watch the way that man over there, that merchant, touches his horse. It is the touch of a lover.

Do you think he touches the goods in his store that way.

And what about his wife?

A wife is a wife but a horse is a horse.

Do you think there are many wives in America as beautiful as Mary Rose, who this afternoon, at our fair, won the 2.18 trot? Will they respond as courageously when you call on them?

Why Mary Rose will not cry, she will not sulk. She is what she is. Look at her.

This afternoon, in the 2.18 trot, after she had won two heats, in the third heat that great raw-looking gray there challenged her on the back stretch.

The gray came with a terrific burst of speed and passed Mary Rose.

She was tired, tired. Already she had gone, at top speed, to win two grueling heats.

But that man there, that not-too-slender merchant from a neighboring town, who owns her, who was risking his precious neck driving her—he called upon her.

There was something pleading in his voice.

"Mary, Mary."

He touched her with the whip too.

Did you see how her ears lay back, did you hear how the breath whistled through her nostrils? Why you could hear it clear across the tracks, in the grandstand here, in the intense silence.

All these thousands of people silent, all staring.

Mary Rose seemed to get smaller. She flattened. Her body went down closer to earth. Her stride lengthened and quickened.

She went faster than she could go. That merchant sat up there and plead with her. He was like a determined, half-angry, hopeful boy.

She never went back on him though. She raced the gray through the stretch to the wire, neck and neck, and then, forty yards from the wire, she made him cough it up.

He broke his stride. Mary Rose won of course.

Can you imagine any wife doing that?

Is the man, that merchant, in love? Of course he is. He is a lover. What else?

And so the fair again. Every year a moment like that. Something pagan, everyone feeling it.

In the evenings, now-days, traveling musical comedy companies come, "Revue" they call them. Young girls come out and dance, and show their legs.

Fat comedians get off stale Broadway jokes. The people laugh, year after year, at the same jokes.

And then the fireworks.

It is best, in the evening, to go a little away, up the track, into the darkness.

See it from there, the moving lights, the moving pictures.

In the dark stables Mary Rose is resting now. It would be interesting to go there. You will find that man, that merchant, hanging about.

He is going home, to his store in another town, on the late train.

However he has come back for a last look. He goes into Mary Rose's stall, touches her once more in the darkness. She puts her head on his shoulder.

He is going away now, back to his store, but next week, at the next town where a fair is being held, and where there is racing, next Thursday he will be back again.

He will be driving Mary Rose in another race. She will not last long, three, four, five years, but perhaps she will drop a fast colt.

There is, after all, the uncertainty of this sort of thing. You have to take chances in life.

2
Finding the city

Once I pass'd through a populous city imprinting my brain for future use with its
    shows, architecture, customs, traditions,
Yet now of all that city I remember only a woman I casually met there who de-
    tain'd me for love of me,
Day by day and night by night we were together—all else has long been forgotten
    by me,
I remember I say only that woman who passionately clung to me,
Again we wander, we love, we separate again,
Again she holds me by the hand, I must not go,
I see her close behind me with silent lips sad and tremulous.

                                           Walt Whitman, 1860

William Shew

George Krause

Lewis W. Hine

Jacob Riis

Berenice Abbott

Bruce Davidson

John Spence

Rudolph Janu

Lee Friedlander

Bruce Davidson

Ralph Steiner

Lee Friedlander

Harry Callahan

Harry Callahan

Perkin-Elmer Corporation

NATHANIEL HAWTHORNE
My Kinsman, Major Molineux

After the kings of Great Britain had assumed the right of appointing the colonial governors, the measures of the latter seldom met with the ready and general approbation which has been paid to those of their predecessors, under the original charters. The people looked with most jealous scrutiny to the exercise of power which did not emanate from themselves, and they usually rewarded their rulers with slender gratitude for the compliances by which, in softening their instructions from beyond the sea, they had incurred the reprehension of those who gave them. The annals of Massachusetts Bay will inform us, that of six governors in the space of about forty years from the surrender of the old charter, under James II., two were imprisoned by a popular insurrection; a third, as Hutchinson inclines to believe, was driven from the province by the whizzing of a musket-ball; a fourth, in the opinion of the same historian, was hastened to his grave by continual bickerings with the House of Representatives; and the remaining two, as well as their successors, till the Revolution, were favored with few and brief intervals of peaceful sway. The inferior members of the court party, in times of high political excitement, led scarcely a more desirable life. These remarks may serve as a preface to the following adventures, which chanced upon a summer night, not far from a hundred years ago. The reader, in order to avoid a long and dry detail of colonial affairs, is requested to dispense with an account of the train of circumstances that had caused much temporary inflammation of the popular mind.

It was near nine o'clock of a moonlight evening, when a boat crossed the ferry with a single passenger, who had obtained his conveyance at that unusual hour by the promise of an extra fare. While he stood on the landing-place, searching in either pocket for the means of fulfilling his agreement, the ferryman lifted a lantern, by the aid of which, and the newly risen moon, he took a very accurate survey of the stranger's figure. He was a youth of barely eighteen years, evidently country-bred, and now, as it should seem, upon his first visit to town. He was clad in a coarse gray coat, well worn, but in excellent repair; his under garments were durably constructed of leather, and fitted tight to a pair of serviceable and well-shaped limbs; his stockings of blue yarn were the incontrovertible work of a mother or a sister; and on his head was a three-cornered hat, which in its better days had perhaps sheltered the graver brow of the lad's father. Under his left arm was a heavy cudgel formed of an oak sapling, and retaining a part of the hardened root; and his equipment was completed by a wallet, not so abundantly stocked as to incommode the vigorous shoulders on which it hung. Brown, curly hair, well-shaped features, and bright, cheerful eyes were nature's gifts, and worth all that art could have done for his adornment.

The youth, one of whose names was Robin, finally drew from his pocket the half of a little province bill of five shillings, which, in the depreciation in that sort of currency, did not satisfy the ferryman's demand, with the surplus of a sexangular piece of parchment, valued at three pence. He then walked forward into the town, with as light a step as if his day's journey had not already exceeded thirty miles, and with as eager an eye as if he were entering London city, instead of the little metropolis of a New England colony. Before Robin had proceeded far, however, it occurred to him that he knew not whither to direct his steps; so he paused, and looked up and down the narrow street, scrutinizing the small and mean wooden buildings that were scattered on either side.

"This low hovel cannot be my kinsman's dwelling," thought he, "nor yonder old house, where the moonlight enters at the broken casement; and truly I see none hereabouts that might be worthy of him. It would have been wise to inquire my way of the ferryman, and doubtless he would have gone with me, and earned a shilling from the Major for his pains. But the next man I meet will do as well."

He resumed his walk, and was glad to perceive that the street now became wider, and the houses more respectable in their appearance. He soon discerned a figure moving on moderately in advance, and hastened his steps to overtake it. As Robin drew nigh, he saw that the passenger was a man in years, with a full periwig of gray hair, a wide-skirted coat of dark cloth, and silk stockings rolled above his knees. He carried a long and polished cane, which he struck down perpendicularly before him at every step; and at regular intervals he uttered two successive hems, of a peculiarly solemn and sepulchral intonation. Having made these observations, Robin laid hold of the skirt of the old man's coat, just when the light from the open door and windows of a barber's shop fell upon both their figures.

"Good evening to you, honored sir," said he, making a low bow, and still retaining his hold of the skirt. "I pray you tell me whereabouts is the dwelling of my kinsman, Major Molineux."

The youth's question was uttered very loudly; and one of the barbers, whose razor was descending on a well-soaped chin, and another who was dressing a Ramillies wig, left their occupations, and came to the door. The citizen, in the mean time, turned a long-favored countenance upon Robin, and answered him in a tone of excessive anger and annoyance. His two sepulchral hems, however, broke into the very centre of his rebuke, with most singular effect, like a thought of the cold grave obtruding among wrathful passions.

"Let go my garment, fellow! I tell you, I know not the man you speak of. What! I have authority, I have—hem, hem—authority; and if this be the respect you show for your betters, your feet shall be brought acquainted with the stocks by daylight, to-morrow morning!"

Robin released the old man's skirt, and hastened away, pursued by an ill-mannered roar of laughter from the barber's shop. He was at first considerably surprised by the result of his question, but, being a shrewd youth, soon thought himself able to account for the mystery.

"This is some country representative," was his conclusion, "who has never seen the inside of my kinsman's door, and lacks the breeding to answer a stranger civilly. The man is old, or verily—I might be tempted to turn back and smite him on the nose. Ah, Robin, Robin! even the barber's boys laugh at you for choosing such a guide! You will be wiser in time, friend Robin."

He now became entangled in a succession of crooked and narrow streets, which crossed each other, and meandered at no great distance from the water-side. The smell of tar was obvious to his nostrils, the masts of vessels pierced the moonlight above the tops of the buildings, and the numerous signs, which Robin paused to read, informed him that he was near the centre of business. But the streets were empty, the shops were closed, and lights were visible only in the second stories of a few dwelling-houses. At length, on the corner of a narrow lane, through which he was passing, he beheld the broad countenance of a British hero swinging before the door of an inn, whence proceeded the voices of many guests. The casement of one of the lower windows was thrown back, and a very thin curtain permitted Robin to distinguish a party at supper, round a well-furnished table. The fragrance of the good cheer steamed forth into the outer air, and the youth could not fail to recollect that the last remnant of his traveling stock of provision had yielded to his morning appetite, and that noon had found and left him dinnerless.

"Oh, that a parchment three-penny might give me a right to sit down at yonder table!" said Robin, with a sigh. "But the Major will make me welcome to the best of his victuals; so I will even step boldly in, and inquire my way to his dwelling."

He entered the tavern, and was guided by the murmur of voices and the fumes of tobacco to the publicroom. It was a long and low apartment, with oaken walls, grown dark in the continual smoke, and a floor which was thickly sanded, but of no immaculate purity. A number of persons—the larger part of whom appeared to be mariners, or in some way connected with the sea—occupied the wooden benches, or leather-bottomed chairs, conversing on various matters, and occasionally lending their attention to some topic of general interest. Three or four little groups were draining as many bowls of punch, which the West India trade had long since made a familiar drink in the colony. Others, who had the appearance of men who lived by regular and laborious handicraft, preferred the insulated bliss of an unshared potation, and became more taciturn under its influence. Nearly all, in short, evinced a predilection for the Good Creature in some of its various shapes, for this is a vice to which, as Fast Day sermons of a hundred years ago will testify, we have a long hereditary claim. The only guests to whom Robin's sympathies inclined him were two or three sheepish countrymen, who were using the inn somewhat after the fashion of a Turkish caravansary; they had gotten themselves into the darkest corner of the room, and heedless of the Nicotian atmosphere, were supping on the bread of their own ovens, and the bacon cured in their own chimney-smoke. But though Robin felt a sort of brotherhood with these strangers, his eyes were attracted from them to a person who stood near the door, holding whispered conversation with a group of ill-dressed associates. His features were separately striking almost to grotesqueness, and the whole face left a deep impression on the memory. The forehead bulged out into a double prominence, with a vale between; the nose came boldly forth in an irregular curve, and its bridge was of more than a finger's breadth; the eyebrows were deep and shaggy, and the eyes glowed beneath them like fire in a cave.

While Robin deliberated of whom to inquire respecting his kinsman's dwelling, he was accosted by the innkeeper, a little man in a stained white apron, who had come to pay his professional welcome to the stranger. Being in the second generation from a French Protestant, he seemed to have inherited the courtesy of his parent nation; but no variety of circumstances was ever known to change his voice from the one shrill note in which he now addressed Robin.

"From the country, I presume, sir?" said he, with a profound bow. "Beg leave to congratulate you on your arrival, and trust you intend a long stay with us. Fine town here, sir, beautiful buildings, and much that may interest a stranger. May I hope for the honor of your commands in respect to supper?"

"The man sees a family likeness! the rogue has guessed that I am related to the Major!" thought Robin, who had hitherto experienced little superfluous civility.

All eyes were now turned on the country lad, standing at the door, in his worn three-cornered hat, gray coat, leather breeches, and blue yarn stockings, leaning on an oaken cudgel, and bearing a wallet on his back.

Robin replied to the courteous innkeeper, with such an assumption of confidence as befitted the Major's relative. "My honest friend," he said, "I shall make it a point to patronize your house on some occasion, when"—here he could not help lowering his voice—"when I may have more than a parchment three-pence in my pocket. My present business," continued he, speaking with lofty confidence, "is merely to inquire my way to the dwelling of my kinsman, Major Molineux."

There was a sudden and general movement in the room, which Robin interpreted as expressing the eagerness of each individual to become his guide. But the innkeeper turned his eyes to a written paper on the wall, which he read, or seemed to read, with occasional recurrences to the young man's figure.

"What have we here?" said he, breaking his speech into little dry fragments. " 'Left the house of the subscriber, bounden servant, Hezekiah Mudge,—had on, when he went away, gray coat, leather breeches, master's third-best hat. One pound currency reward to whosoever shall lodge him in any jail of the province.' Better trudge, boy; better trudge!"

Robin had begun to draw his hand towards the lighter end of the oak cudgel, but a strange hostility in every countenance induced him to relinquish his purpose of breaking the courteous innkeeper's head. As he turned to leave the room, he encountered a sneering glance from the bold-featured personage whom he had before noticed; and no sooner was he beyond the door, than he heard a general laugh, in which the innkeeper's voice might be distinguished, like the dropping of small stones into a kettle.

"Now, is it not strange," thought Robin, with his usual shrewdness,— "is it not strange that the confession of an empty pocket should outweigh the name of my kinsman, Major Molineux? Oh, if I had one of those grinning rascals in the woods, where I and my oak sapling grew up together, I would teach him that my arm is heavy though my purse be light!"

On turning the corner of the narrow lane, Robin found himself in a spacious street, with an unbroken line of lofty houses on each side, and a steepled building at the upper end, whence the ringing of a bell announced the hour of nine. The light of the moon, and the lamps from the numerous shop-windows, discovered people promenading on the pavement, and amongst them Robin hoped to recognize his hitherto inscrutable relative. The result of his former inquiries made him unwilling to hazard another, in a scene of such publicity, and he determined to walk slowly and silently up the street, thrusting his face close to that of every elderly gentleman, in search of the Major's lineaments. In his progress, Robin encountered many gay and gallant figures. Embroidered garments of showy colors, enormous periwigs, gold-laced hats, and silver-hilted swords glided past him and dazzled his optics. Travelled youths, imitators of the European fine gentlemen of the period, trod jauntily along, half dancing to the fashionable tunes which they hummed, and making poor Robin ashamed of his quiet and natural gait. At length, after many pauses to examine the gorgeous display of goods in the shop-windows, and after suffering some rebukes for the impertinence of his scrutiny into people's faces, the Major's kinsman found himself near the steepled building, still unsuccessful in his search. As yet, however, he had seen only one side of the thronged street; so Robin crossed, and continued the same sort of inquisition down the opposite pavement, with stronger hopes than the philosopher seeking an honest man, but with no better fortune. He had arrived about midway towards the lower end, from which his course began, when he overheard the approach of some one who struck down a cane on the flag-stones at every step, uttering, at regular intervals, two sepulchral hems.

"Mercy on us!" quoth Robin, recognizing the sound.

Turning a corner, which chanced to be close at his right hand, he hastened to pursue his researches in some other part of the town. His patience now was wearing low, and he seemed to feel more fatigue from his rambles since he crossed the ferry, than from his journey of several days on the other side. Hunger also pleaded loudly within him, and Robin began to balance the propriety of demanding, violently, and with lifted cudgel, the necessary guidance from the first solitary passenger whom he should meet. While a resolution to this effect was gaining strength, he entered a street of mean appearance, on either side of which a row of ill-built houses was straggling towards the harbor. The moonlight fell upon no passenger along the whole extent, but in the third domicile which Robin passed there was a half-opened door, and his keen glance detected a woman's garment within.

"My luck may be better here," said he to himself.

Accordingly, he approached the door, and beheld it shut closer as he did so; yet an open space remained, sufficing for the fair occupant to observe the stranger, without a corresponding display on her part. All that Robin could discern was a strip of scarlet petticoat, and the occasional sparkle of an eye, as if the moonbeams were trembling on some bright thing.

"Pretty mistress," for I may call her so with a good conscience, thought the shrewd youth, since I know nothing to the contrary,—"my sweet pretty mistress, will you be kind enough to tell me whereabouts I must seek the dwelling of my kinsman, Major Molineux?"

Robin's voice was plaintive and winning, and the female, seeing nothing to be shunned in the handsome country youth, thrust open the door, and came forth into the moonlight. She was a dainty little figure, with a white neck, round arms, and a slender waist, at the extremity of which her scarlet petticoat jutted out over a hoop, as if she were standing in a balloon. Moreover, her face was oval and pretty, her hair dark beneath the little cap, and her bright eyes possessed a sly freedom, which triumphed over those of Robin.

"Major Molineux dwells here," said this fair woman.

Now, her voice was the sweetest Robin had heard that night, the airy counterpart of a stream of melted silver; yet he could not help doubting whether that sweet voice spoke Gospel truth. He looked up and down the mean street, and then surveyed the house before which they stood. It was a small, dark edifice of two stories, the second of which projected over the lower floor, and the front apartment had the aspect of a shop for petty commodities.

"Now, truly, I am in luck," replied Robin, cunningly, "and so indeed is my kinsman, the Major, in having so pretty a housekeeper. But I prithee trouble him to step to the door; I will deliver him a message from his friends in the country, and then go back to my lodgings at the inn."

"Nay, the Major has been abed this hour or more," said the lady of the scarlet petticoat; "and it would be to little purpose to disturb him to-night, seeing his evening draught was of the strongest. But he is a kind-hearted man, and it would be as much as my life's worth to let a kinsman of his turn away from the door. You are the good old gentleman's very picture, and I could swear that was his rainy-weather hat. Also he has garments very much resembling those leather small-clothes. But come in, I pray, for I bid you hearty welcome in his name."

So saying, the fair and hospitable dame took our hero by the hand; and the touch was light, and the force was gentleness, and though Robin read in her eyes what he did not hear in her words, yet the slender-waisted woman in the scarlet petticoat proved stronger than the athletic country youth. She had drawn his half-willing footsteps nearly to the threshold, when the opening of a door in the neighborhood startled the Major's housekeeper, and, leaving the Major's kinsman, she vanished speedily into her own domicile. A heavy yawn preceded the appearance of a man, who, like the Moonshine of Pyramus and Thisbe, carried a lantern, need-lessly aiding his sister luminary in the heavens. As he walked sleepily up the street, he turned his broad, dull face on Robin, and displayed a long staff, spiked at the end.

"Home, vagabond, home!" said the watchman, in accents that seemed to fall asleep as soon as they were uttered. "Home, or we'll set you in the stocks by peep of day!"

"This is the second hit of the kind," thought Robin. "I wish they would end my difficulties, by setting me there to-night."

Nevertheless, the youth felt an instinctive antipathy towards the guardian of midnight order, which at first prevented him from asking his usual question. But just when the man was about to vanish behind the corner, Robin resolved not to lose the opportunity, and shouted lustily after him,—

"I say, friend! will you guide me to the house of my kinsman, Major Molineux?"

The watchman made no reply, but turned the corner and was gone; yet Robin seemed to hear the sound of drowsy laughter stealing along the solitary street. At that moment, also, a pleasant titter saluted him from the open window above his head; he looked up, and caught the sparkle of a saucy eye; a round arm beckoned to him, and next he heard light footsteps descending the staircase within. But Robin, being of the household of a New England clergyman, was a good youth, as well as a shrewd one; so he resisted temptation, and fled away.

He now roamed desperately, and at random, through the town, almost ready to believe that a spell was on him, like that by which a wizard of his country had once kept three pursuers wandering, a whole winter night, within twenty paces of the cottage which they sought. The streets lay before him, strange and desolate, and the lights were extinguished in almost every house. Twice, however, little parties of men, among whom Robin distinguished individuals in outlandish attire, came hurrying along; but, though on both occasions they paused to address him, such intercourse did not at all enlighten his perplexity. They did but utter a few words in some language of which Robin knew nothing, and perceiving his inability to answer, bestowed a curse upon him in plain English and hastened away. Finally, the lad determined to knock at the door of every mansion that might appear worthy to be occupied by his kinsman, trusting that perseverance would overcome the fatality that had hitherto thwarted him. Firm in this resolve, he was passing beneath the walls of a church, which formed the corner of two streets, when, as he turned into the shade of its steeple, he encountered a bulky stranger, muffled in a cloak. The man was proceeding with the speed of earnest business, but Robin planted himself full before him, holding the oak cudgel with both hands across his body as a bar to further passage.

"Halt, honest man, and answer me a question," said he, very resolutely. "Tell me, this instant, whereabouts is the dwelling of my kinsman, Major Molineux!"

"Keep your tongue between your teeth, fool, and let me pass!" said a deep, gruff voice, which Robin partly remembered. "Let me pass, I say, or I'll strike you to the earth!"

"No, no, neighbor!" cried Robin, flourishing his cudgel, and then thrusting its larger end close to the man's muffled face. "No, no, I'm not the fool you take me for, nor do you pass till I have an answer to my question. Whereabouts is the dwelling of my kinsman, Major Molineux?"

The stranger, instead of attempting to force his passage, stepped back into the moonlight, unmuffled his face, and stared full into that of Robin.

"Watch here an hour, and Major Molineux will pass by," said he.

Robin gazed with dismay and astonishment on the unprecedented physiognomy of the speaker. The forehead with its double prominence, the broad hooked nose, the shaggy eyebrows, and fiery eyes were those which he had noticed at the inn, but the man's complexion had undergone a singular, or, more properly, a twofold change. One side of the face blazed an intense red, while the other was black as midnight, the division line being in the broad bridge of the nose; and a mouth which seemed to extend from ear to ear was black or red, in contrast to the color of the cheek. The effect was as if two individual devils, a fiend of fire and a fiend of darkness, had united themselves to form this infernal visage. The stranger grinned in Robin's face, muffled his party-colored features, and was out of sight in a moment.

"Strange things we travellers see!" ejaculated Robin.

He seated himself, however, upon the steps of the church-door, resolving to wait the appointed time for his kinsman. A few moments were consumed in philosophical speculations upon the species of man who had just left him; but having settled this point shrewdly, rationally, and satisfactorily, he was compelled to look elsewhere for his amusement. And first he threw his eyes along the street. It was of more respectable appearance than most of those into which he had wandered; and the moon, creating, like the imaginative power, a beautiful strangeness in familiar objects, gave something of romance to a scene that might not have possessed it in the light of day. The irregular and often quaint architecture of the houses, some of whose roofs were broken into numerous little peaks, while others ascended, steep and narrow, into a single point, and others again were square; the pure snow-white of some of their complexions, the aged darkness of others, and the thousand sparklings, reflected from bright substances in the walls of many; these matters engaged Robin's attention for a while, and then began to grow wearisome. Next he endeavored to define the forms of distant objects, starting away, with almost ghostly indistinctness, just as his eye appeared to grasp them; and finally he took a minute survey of an edifice which stood on the opposite side of the street, directly in front of the church-door, where he was stationed. It was a large, square mansion, distinguished from its neighbors by a balcony, which rested on tall pillars, and by an elaborate Gothic window, communicating therewith.

"Perhaps this is the very house I have been seeking," thought Robin.

Then he strove to speed away the time, by listening to a murmur which swept continually along the street, yet was scarcely audible, except to an unaccustomed ear like his; it was a low, dull, dreamy sound, compounded of many noises, each of which was at too great a distance to be separately heard. Robin marvelled at this snore of a sleeping town, and marvelled more whenever its continuity was broken by now and then a distant shout, apparently loud where it originated. But altogether it was a sleep-inspiring sound, and, to shake off its drowsy influence, Robin arose, and climbed a window-frame, that he might view the interior of the church. There the moonbeams came trembling in, and fell down upon the deserted pews, and extended along the quiet aisles. A fainter yet more awful radiance was hovering around the pulpit, and one solitary ray had dared to rest upon the open page of the great Bible. Had nature, in that deep hour, become a worshipper in the house which man had builded? Or was that heavenly light the visible sanctity of the place,—visible because no earthly and impure feet were within the walls? The scene made Robin's heart shiver with a sensation of loneliness stronger than he had ever felt in the remotest depths of his native woods; so he turned away and sat down again before the door. There were graves around the church, and now an uneasy thought obtruded into Robin's breast. What if the object of his search, which had been so often and so strangely thwarted, were all the time mouldering in his shroud? What if his kinsman should glide through yonder gate, and nod and smile to him in dimly passing by?

"Oh that any breathing thing were here with me!" said Robin.

Recalling his thoughts from this uncomfortable track, he sent them over forest, hill, and stream, and attempted to imagine how that evening of ambiguity and weariness had been spent by his father's household. He pictured them assembled at the door, beneath the tree, the great old tree, which had been spared for its huge twisted trunk and venerable shade, when a thousand leafy brethren fell. There, at the going down of the summer sun, it was his father's custom to perform domestic worship, that the neighbors might come and join with him like brothers of the family, and that the wayfaring man might pause to drink at that fountain, and keep his heart pure by freshening the memory of home. Robin distinguished the seat of every individual of the little audience; he saw the good man in the midst, holding the Scriptures in the golden light that fell from the western clouds; he beheld him close the book and all rise up to pray. He heard the old thanksgivings for daily mercies, the old supplications for their continuance, to which he had so often listened in weariness, but which were now among his dear remembrances. He perceived the slight inequality of his father's voice when he came to speak of the absent one; he noted how his mother turned her face to the broad and knotted trunk; how his elder brother scorned, because the beard was rough upon his upper lip, to permit his features to be moved; how the younger sister drew down a low hanging branch before her eyes; and how the little one of all, whose sports had hitherto broken the decorum of the scene, understood the prayer for her playmate, and burst into clamorous grief. Then he saw them go in at the door; and when Robin would have entered also, the latch tinkled into its place, and he was excluded from his home.

"Am I here, or there?" cried Robin, starting; for all at once, when his thoughts had become visible and audible in a dream, the long, wide, solitary street shone out before him.

He aroused himself, and endeavored to fix his attention steadily upon the large edifice which he had surveyed before. But still his mind kept vibrating between fancy and reality; by turns, the pillars of the balcony lengthened into the tall, bare stems of pines, dwindled down to human figures, settled again into their true shape and size, and then commenced a new succession of changes. For a single moment, when he deemed himself awake, he could have sworn that a visage—one which he seemed to remember, yet could not absolutely name as his kinsman's—was looking towards him from the Gothic window. A deeper sleep wrestled with and nearly overcame him, but fled at the sound of footsteps along the opposite pavement. Robin rubbed his eyes, discerned a man passing at the foot of the balcony, and addressed him in a loud, peevish, and lamentable cry.

"Hallo, friend! must I wait here all night for my kinsman, Major Molineux?"

The sleeping echoes awoke, and answered the voice; and the passenger, barely able to discern a figure sitting in the oblique shade of the steeple, traversed the street to obtain a nearer view. He was himself a gentleman in his prime, of open, intelligent, cheerful, and altogether prepossessing countenance. Perceiving a country youth, apparently homeless and without friends, he accosted him in a tone of real kindness, which had become strange to Robin's ears.

"Well, my good lad, who are you sitting here?" inquired he. "Can I be of service to you in any way?"

"I am afraid not, sir," replied Robin, despondingly; "yet I shall take it kindly, if you'll answer me a single question. I've been searching, half the night, for one Major Molineux; now, sir, is there really such a person in these parts, or am I dreaming?"

"Major Molineux! The name is not altogether strange to me," said the gentleman, smiling. "Have you any objection to telling me the nature of your business with him?"

Then Robin briefly related that his father was a clergyman, settled on a small salary, at a long distance back in the country, and that he and Major Molineux were brothers' children. The Major, having inherited riches, and acquired civil and military rank, had visited his cousin, in great pomp, a year or two before; had manifested much interest in Robin and an elder brother, and, being childless himself, had thrown out hints respecting the future establishment of one of them in life. The elder brother was destined to succeed to the farm which his father cultivated in the interval of sacred duties; it was therefore determined that Robin should profit by his kinsman's generous intentions, especially as he seemed to be rather the favorite, and was thought to possess other necessary endowments.

"For I have the name of being a shrewd youth," observed Robin, in this part of his story.

"I doubt not you deserve it," replied his new friend, good-naturedly; "but pray proceed."

"Well, sir, being nearly eighteen years old, and well grown, as you see," continued Robin, drawing himself up to his full height, "I thought it high time to begin in the world. So my mother and sister put me in handsome trim, and my father gave me half the remnant of his last year's salary, and five days ago I started for this place, to pay the Major a visit. But, would you believe it, sir! I crossed the ferry a little after dark, and have yet found nobody that would show me the way to his dwelling; only, an hour or two since, I was told to wait here, and Major Molineux would pass by."

"Can you describe the man who told you this?" inquired the gentleman.

"Oh, he was a very ill-favored fellow, sir," replied Robin, "with two great bumps on his forehead, a hook nose, fiery eyes; and, what struck me as the strangest, his face was of two different colors. Do you happen to know such a man, sir?"

"Not intimately," answered the stranger, "but I chanced to meet him a little time previous to your stopping me. I believe you may trust his word, and that the Major will very shortly pass through this street. In the mean time, as I have a singular curiosity to witness your meeting, I will sit down here upon the steps and bear you company."

He seated himself accordingly, and soon engaged his companion in animated discourse. It was but of brief continuance, however, for a noise of shouting, which had long been remotely audible, drew so much nearer that Robin inquired its cause.

"What may be the meaning of this uproar?" asked he. "Truly, if your town be always as noisy, I shall find little sleep while I am an inhabitant."

"Why, indeed, friend Robin, there do appear to be three or four riotous fellows abroad to-night," replied the gentleman. "You must not expect all the stillness of your native woods here in our streets. But the watch will shortly be at the heels of these lads and"—

"Ay, and set them in the stocks by peep of day," interrupted Robin, recollecting his own encounter with the drowsy lantern-bearer. "But, dear sir, if I may trust my ears, an army of watchmen would never make head against such a multitude of rioters. There were at least a thousand voices went up to make that one shout."

"May not a man have several voices, Robin, as well as two complexions?" said his friend.

"Perhaps a man may; but Heaven forbid that a woman should!" responded the shrewd youth, thinking of the seductive tones of the Major's housekeeper.

The sounds of a trumpet in some neighboring street now became so evident and continual, that Robin's curiosity was strongly excited. In addition to the shouts, he heard frequent bursts from many instruments of discord, and a wild and confused laughter filled up the intervals. Robin rose from the steps, and looked wistfully towards a point whither people seemed to be hastening.

"Surely some prodigious merry-making is going on," exclaimed he. "I have laughed very little since I left home, sir, and should be sorry to lose an opportunity. Shall we step round the corner by that darkish house, and take our share of the fun?"

"Sit down again, sit down, good Robin," replied the gentleman, laying his hand on the skirt of the gray coat. "You forget that we must wait here for your kinsman; and there is reason to believe that he will pass by, in the course of a very few moments."

The near approach of the uproar had now disturbed the neighborhood: windows flew open on all sides: and many heads, in the attire of the pillow, and confused by sleep suddenly broken, were protruded to the gaze of whoever had leisure to observe them. Eager voices hailed each other from house to house, all demanding the explanation, which not a soul could give. Half-dressed men hurried towards the unknown commotion, stumbling as they went over the stone steps that thrust themselves into the narrow foot-walk. The shouts, the laughter, and the tuneless bray, the antipodes of music, came onwards with increasing din, till scattered individuals, and then denser bodies, began to appear round a corner at the distance of a hundred yards.

"Will you recognize your kinsman, if he passes in this crowd?" inquired the gentleman.

"Indeed, I can't warrant it, sir; but I'll take my stand here, and keep a bright lookout," answered Robin, descending to the outer edge of the pavement.

A mighty stream of people now emptied into the street, and came rolling slowly towards the church. A single horseman wheeled the corner in the midst of them, and close behind him came a band of fearful wind-instruments, sending forth a fresher discord now that no intervening buildings kept it from the ear. Then a redder light disturbed the moonbeams, and a dense multitude of torches shone along the street, concealing, by their glare, whatever object they illuminated. The single horseman, clad in a military dress, and bearing a drawn sword, rode onward as the leader, and, by his fierce and variegated countenance, appeared like war personified; the red of one cheek was an emblem of fire and sword; the blackness of the other betokened the mourning that attends them. In his train were wild figures in the Indian dress, and many fantastic shapes without a model, giving the whole march a visionary air, as if a dream had broken forth from some feverish brain, and were sweeping visibly through the midnight streets. A mass of people, inactive, except as applauding spectators, hemmed the procession in; and several women ran along the sidewalk, piercing the confusion of heavier sounds with their shrill voices of mirth or terror.

"The double-faced fellow has his eye upon me," muttered Robin, with an indefinite but an uncomfortable idea that he was himself to bear a part in the pageantry.

The leader turned himself in the saddle, and fixed his glance full upon the country youth, as the steed went slowly by. When Robin had freed his eyes from those fiery ones, the musicians were passing before him, and the torches were close at hand; but the unsteady brightness of the latter formed a veil which he could not penetrate. The rattling of wheels over the stones sometimes found its way to his ear, and confused traces of a human form appeared at intervals, and then melted into the vivid light. A moment more, and the leader thundered a command to halt: the trumpets vomited a horrid breath, and then held their peace; the shouts and laughter of the people died away, and there remained only a universal hum, allied to silence. Right before Robin's eyes was an uncovered cart. There the torches blazed the brightest, there the moon shone out like day, and there, in tar-and-feathery dignity, sat his kinsman, Major Molineux!

He was an elderly man, of large and majestic person, and strong, square features, betokening a steady soul; but steady as it was, his enemies had found means to shake it. His face was pale as death, and far more ghastly; the broad forehead was contracted in his agony, so that his eyebrows formed one grizzled line; his eyes were red and wild, and the foam hung white upon his quivering lip. His whole frame was agitated by a quick and continual tremor, which his pride strove to quell, even in those circumstances of overwhelming humiliation. But perhaps the bitterest pang of all was when his eyes met those of Robin; for he evidently knew him on the instant, as the youth stood witnessing the foul disgrace of a head grown gray in honor. They stared at each other in silence, and Robin's knees shook, and his hair bristled, with a mixture of pity and terror. Soon, however, a bewildering excitement began to seize upon his mind; the preceding adventures of the night, the unexpected appearance of the crowd, the torches, the confused din and the hush that followed, the spectre of his kinsman reviled by that great multitude,—all this, and, more than all, a perception of tremendous ridicule in the whole scene, affected him with a sort of mental inebriety. At that moment a voice of sluggish merriment saluted Robin's ears; he turned instinctively, and just behind the corner of the church stood the lantern-bearer, rubbing his eyes, and drowsily enjoying the lad's amazement. Then he heard a peal of laughter like the ringing of silvery bells; a woman twitched his arm, a saucy eye met his, and he saw the lady of the scarlet petticoat. A sharp, dry cachinnation appealed to his memory, and, standing on tiptoe in the crowd, with his white apron over his head, he beheld the courteous little innkeeper. And lastly, there sailed over the heads of the multitude a great, broad laugh, broken in the midst by two sepulchral hems; thus, "Haw, haw, haw,—hem, hem,—haw, haw, haw, haw!"

The sound proceeded from the balcony of the opposite edifice, and thither Robin turned his eyes. In front of the Gothic window stood the old citizen, wrapped in a wide gown, his gray periwig exchanged for a night-cap, which was thrust back from his forehead, and his silk stockings hanging about his legs. He supported himself on his polished cane in a fit of convulsive merriment, which manifested itself on his solemn old features like a funny inscription on a tombstone. Then Robin seemed to hear the voices of the barbers, of the guests of the inn, and of all who had made sport of him that night. The contagion was spreading among the multitude, when all at once, it seized upon Robin, and he sent forth a shout of laughter that echoed through the street,—every man shook his sides, every man emptied his lungs, but Robin's shout was the loudest there. The cloud-spirits peeped from their silvery islands, as the congregated mirth went roaring up the sky! The Man in the Moon heard the far bellow. "Oho," quoth he, "the old earth is frolicsome to-night!"

When there was a momentary calm in that tempestuous sea of sound, the leader gave the sign, the procession resumed its march. On they went, like fiends that throng in mockery around some dead potentate, mighty no more, but majestic still in his agony. On they went, in counterfeited pomp, in senseless uproar, in frenzied merriment, tramping all on an old man's heart. On swept the tumult, and left a silent street behind.

"Well, Robin, are you dreaming?" inquired the gentleman, laying his hand on the youth's shoulder.

Robin started, and withdrew his arm from the stone post to which he had instinctively clung, as the living stream rolled by him. His cheek was somewhat pale, and his eye not quite as lively as in the earlier part of the evening.

"Will you be kind enough to show me the way to the ferry?" said he, after a moment's pause.

"You have, then, adopted a new subject of inquiry?" observed his companion, with a smile.

"Why, yes, sir," replied Robin, rather dryly. "Thanks to you, and to my other friends, I have at last met my kinsman, and he will scarce desire to see my face again. I begin to grow weary of a town life, sir. Will you show me the way to the ferry?"

"No, my good friend Robin,—not to-night, at least," said the gentleman. "Some few days hence, if you wish it, I will speed you on your journey. Or, if you prefer to remain with us, perhaps, as you are a shrewd youth, you may rise in the world without the help of your kinsman, Major Molineux."

STEPHAN THERNSTROM
Urbanization, Migration, and Social Mobility in Late Nineteenth-Century America

The United States, it has been said, was born in the country and has moved to the city. It was during the half-century between the Civil War and World War I that the move was made. In 1860, less than a quarter of the American population lived in a city or town; by 1890, the figure had reached a third; by 1910, nearly half. By more sophiscated measures than the mere count of heads, the center of gravity of the society had obviously tilted cityward well before the last date.

If to speak of "the rise of the city" in those years is a textbook cliché, the impact of this great social transformation upon the common people of America has never been sufficiently explored. This essay is intended as a small contribution toward that task. It sketches the process by which ordinary men and women were drawn to the burgeoning cities of post-Civil War America, assesses what little we know about how they were integrated into the urban class structure, and suggests how these matters affected the viability of the political system.

1

The urbanization of late nineteenth-century America took place at a dizzying pace. Chicago, for instance, doubled its population every decade but one between 1850 and 1890, growing from 30,000 to over a million in little more than a generation. And it was not merely the conspicuous metropolitan giants but the Akrons, the Duluths, the Tacomas that were bursting at the seams; no less than 101 American communities grew by 100 percent or more in the 1880s.[1]

1. C. N. Glaab and A. T. Brown, *A History of Urban America* (New York, 1967), pp. 107–11.

Why did Americans flock into these all too often unlovely places? There were some who were not pulled to the city but rather pushed out of their previous habitats and dropped there, more or less by accident. But the overriding fact is that the cities could draw on an enormous reservoir of people who were dissatisfied with their present lot and eager to seize the new opportunities offered by the metropolis.

Who were these people? It is conventional to distinguish two broad types of migrants to the American city: the immigrant from another culture, and the farm lad who moved from a rural to an urban setting within the culture. It is also conventional in historical accounts to overlook the latter type and to focus on the more exotic of the migrants, those who had to undergo the arduous process of becoming Americanized.

This is regrettable. To be sure, immigration from abroad was extremely important in the building of America's cities down to World War I. But the most important source of population for the burgeoning cities was not the fields of Ireland and Austria, but those of Vermont and Iowa. The prime cause of population growth in nineteenth-century America, and the main source of urban growth, was simply the high fertility of natives living outside the city.

We tend to neglect internal migration from country to city, partly because the immigrants from abroad seem exotic and thus conspicuous, partly because of the unfortunate legacy left by Frederick Jackson Turner's frontier theory, one element of which was the notion that the open frontier served as a safety valve for urban discontent. When there were hard times in the city, according to Turner, the American worker didn't join a union or vote Socialist; he moved West and grabbed some of that free land. This theory has been subjected to the rather devastating criticism that by 1860 it took something like $1,000 capital to purchase sufficient transportation, seed equipment, livestock, and food (to live on until the first crop) to make a go of it; that it took even more than $1,000 later in the century; and that it was precisely the unemployed workmen who were least likely to have that kind of money at their command. It is estimated that for every industrial worker who became a farmer, twenty farm boys became urban dwellers.[2] There was an urban safety valve for rural discontent, and an extremely important one. The dominant form of population movement was precisely the opposite of that described by Turner.

Since scholarly attention has been focused upon immigrants from abroad, upon Oscar Handlin's "Uprooted," it will be useful to review what is known about their movement to the American city and then to ask how much the same generalizations might hold for native Americans uprooted from the countryside and plunged into the city.

Immigration is as old as America, but a seismic shift in the character of

2. Fred Shannon, "A Post Mortem on the Labor-Safety-Valve Theory," *Agricultural History*, XIX (1954), 31–37.

European immigration to these shores occurred in the nineteenth century, as a consequence of the commercial transformation of traditional European agriculture and the consequent displacement of millions of peasants.[3] Compared to earlier newcomers, these were people who were closer to the land and more tradition-bound, and they generally had fewer resources to bring with them than their predecessors. One shouldn't overwork this; a substantial fraction of the German and Scandinavian immigrants had enough capital to get to the West to pick up land. But some of the Germans and Scandinavians, and most men of other nationalities, had just enough cash to make it to the New World and were stuck for a time at least where they landed—New York, Boston, or wherever. They swelled the population appreciably and the relief rolls dramatically, particularly in the pre-Civil War years, when they entered cities which were basically commercial and had little use for men whose only skill in many cases was that they knew how to dig. Eventually, however, the stimulus of this vast pool of cheap labor and the demands of the growing city itself opened up a good many unskilled jobs—in the construction of roads, houses, and commercial buildings, and in the manufacturing that began to spring up in the cities.

That they were driven off the land in the Old World, that they arrived without resources, immobilized by their poverty, and that they often suffered a great deal before they secured stable employment is true enough. But these harsh facts may lead us to overlook other aspects which were extremely significant.

One is that immigration was a *selective* process. However powerful the pressures to leave, in no case did everyone in a community pull up stakes. This observation may be uncomfortably reminiscent of the popular opinion on this point: that it was the best of the Old World stock that came to the New—the most intelligent, enterprising, courageous. But this should not lead us to neglect the point altogether. The traits that led some men to leave and allowed them to survive the harrowing journey to the port, the trip itself, and the perils of the New World, could be described in somewhat different terms: substitute cunning for intelligence, for example, or ruthlessness for courage. Still, whatever the emphasis, the fact remains: as weighed in the scales of the marketplace, those who came—however driven by cruel circumstance—were better adapted to American life than those who remained in the village or died on the way.

The other main point about the immigrants, and especially those who suffered the most extreme hardships—the Irish in the 1840s and 1850s, the French Canadians in the 1870s, the Italians and various East Europeans after 1880—is that they appraised their new situations with standards developed in peasant society. Lowell was terrible, with its cramped stink-

3. For general accounts, see Marcus L. Hansen, *The Atlantic Migration, 1607–1860* (paperback ed.; New York, 1961); Oscar Handlin, *The Uprooted* (Boston, 1951).

ing tenements, and factory workers labored from dawn till dark for what seems a mere pittance. Children were forced to work at a brutally early age; the factories and dwellings were deathtraps. But Lowell was a damn sight better than County Cork, and men who knew from bitter experience what County Cork was like could not view their life in Lowell with quite the same simple revulsion as the middle-class reformers who judged Lowell by altogether different standards. It is not so much the objectively horrible character of a situation that goads men to action as it is a nagging discrepancy between what *is,* and what is *expected.* And what one expects is determined by one's reference group—which can be a class, an ethnic or religious subculture, or some other entity which defines people's horizon of expectation.[4] Immigration provided an ever renewed stream of men who entered the American economy to fill its least attractive and least well rewarded positions, men who happen to have brought with them very low horizons of expectation fixed in peasant Europe.

That those Americans with greatest reason to feel outrageously exploited judged their situation against the dismally low standards of the decaying European village is an important clue to the stunted growth of the labor movement and the failure of American Socialism. Working in the same direction was what might be called the Tower of Babel factor. A firm sense of class solidarity was extremely difficult to develop in communities where people literally didn't speak each other's language. Even in cases where groups of immigrant workers had unusually high expectations and previous familiarity with advanced forms of collective action— such as the English artisans who led the Massachusetts textile strikes in the 1870s—they found it hard to keep the other troops in line; a clever Italian-speaking or Polish-speaking foreman could easily exploit national differences for his own ends, and if necessary there were always the most recent immigrants of all (and the Negroes) to serve as scabs to replace the dissenters en masse.

A somewhat similar analysis applies to the migrants who left the Kansas farms for Chicago. They were linguistically and culturally set apart from many of their fellow workers; they too had low horizons of expectation fixed in the countryside and brought to the city. The latter point is often missed because of the peculiar American reverence for an idealized agrarian way of life. As we have become a nation of city dwellers, we have come more and more to believe that it is virtuous and beautiful to slave for fourteen hours a day with manure on your boots. Recently

4. For discussion of the sociological concepts of reference groups and the theory of relative deprivation, see Robert K. Merton, *Social Theory and Social Structure,* rev. ed. (Glencoe, Ill., 1957) and the literature cited there. The problem of assessing the level of expectations of any particular migratory group in the past is extremely complicated, and it is obvious that there have been important differences between and within groups. But the generalizations offered here seem to me the best starting point for thinking about this issue.

that sturdy small farmer from Johnson City, Texas, remarked that "it does not make sense on this great continent which God has blessed to have more than 70 percent of our people crammed into one percent of the land." A national "keep them down on the farm" campaign is therefore in the offing.[5] But it is damnably hard to keep them down on the farm after they've seen New York (or even Indianapolis), and it was just as hard a century ago, for the very good reason that the work is brutal, the profits are often miserably low, and the isolation is psychologically murderous. Virtuous this life may be, especially to people who don't have to live it, but enjoyable it is not—not, at least, to a very substantial fraction of our ever shrinking farm population.

This applies particularly to young men and women growing up on a farm. Their parents had a certain stake in staying where they were, even if it was a rut. And the eldest son, who would inherit the place eventually, was sometimes tempted by that. But the others left in droves, to tend machines, to dig and haul and hammer—or in the case of the girls, to sell underwear in Marshall Field's, to mind someone else's kitchen, or in some instances to follow in the footsteps of Sister Carrie.

There were some large differences between native-born migrants to the cities and immigrants from another land, to be sure. But the familiar argument that native workmen "stood on the shoulders" of the immigrant and was subjected to less severe exploitation is somewhat misleading. The advantages enjoyed by many America-born laborers stemmed more from their urban experience than their birth, and they did not generally accrue to freshly arrived native migrants to the city. The latter were little better off than their immigrant counterparts, but then they too were spiritually prepared to endure a great deal of privation and discomfort because even the bottom of the urban heap was a step up from the farms they had left behind. The two groups were one in this respect, and perceptive employers recognized the fact. In 1875, the Superintendent of one of Andrew Carnegie's steel mills summed up his experience this way: "We must steer clear as far as we can of Englishmen, who are great sticklers for high wages, small production and strikes. My experience has shown that Germans and Irish, Swedes and what I denominate 'Buckwheats'—young American country boys, judiciously mixed, make the most honest and tractable force you can find."[6]

2

The move to the city, therefore, was an advance of a kind for the typical migrant. Were there further opportunities for advancement there, or

5. *Boston Globe,* February 5, 1967.
6. Quoted in Oscar Handlin, *Immigration as a Factor in American History* (Englewood Cliffs, N.J., 1959), pp. 66–67.

did he then find himself crushed by circumstance and reduced to the ranks of the permanent proletariat? Did his children, whose expectations were presumably higher, discover correspondingly greater opportunities open to them? Remarkably little serious research has been devoted to these issues. Historians who see American history as a success story have been content to assume, without benefit of data, that the American dream of mobility was true, apparently on the principle that popular ideology is a sure guide to social reality. Dissenting scholars have been more inclined to the view that class barriers were relatively impassable, an assumption based upon generalized skepticism about American mythology rather than upon careful empirical study. Some recent work, however, provides the basis for a tentative reappraisal of the problem.

We know most about mobility into the most rarified reaches of the social order regarding such elite groups as millionaires, railroad presidents, directors of large corporations, or persons listed in the *Dictionary of American Biography.* What is most impressive about the literature on the American elite is that, in spite of many variations in the way in which the elite is defined, the results of these studies are much the same. It is clear that growing up in rags is not in the least conducive to the attainment of later riches, and that it was no more so a century ago than it is today.[7] There have been spectacular instances of mobility from low down on the social scale to the very top—Andrew Carnegie, for instance. But colorful examples cannot sustain broad generalizations about social phenomena, however often they are impressed into service toward that end. Systematic investigation reveals that even in the days of Andrew Carnegie, there was little room at the top, except for those who started very close to it.

Furthermore, this seems to have been the case throughout most of American history, despite many dramatic alterations in the character of the economy. It seems perfectly plausible to assume, as many historians have on the basis of impressionistic evidence, that the precipitous growth of heavy industry in the latter half of the nineteenth century opened the doors to men with very different talents from the educated merchants who constituted the elite of the preindustrial age, that unlettered, horny-handed types like Thomas Alva Edison and Henry Ford, crude inventors and tinkerers, then came into their own; that the connection between parental wealth and status and the son's career was loosened, so that members of the business elite typically had lower social origins and less education, and were often of immigrant stock. Plausible, yes, but true, no. It helped to go to Harvard in Thomas Jefferson's America, and it seems to have helped just about as much in William McKinley's America. There were the Edisons and Fords, who rose spectacularly from low origins, but there were always a few such. Cases like these were about as excep-

7. For a convenient review of this literature, see Seymour M. Lipset and Reinhard Bendix, *Social Mobility in Industrial Society* (Berkeley, Cal., 1959), Ch. 4.

tional in the late nineteenth century as they were earlier. The image of the great inventor springing from common soil, unspoiled by book-larnin', is a red herring. It is doubtful, to say the least, that the less you know, the more likely you are to build a better mousetrap. And in any event it was not the great inventor who raked in the money, in most cases—Henry Ford never invented anything—but rather the organizer and manipulator, whose talents seem to have been highly valued through all periods of American history.

These conclusions are interesting, but an important caution is in order. It by no means follows that if there was very little room at the top, there was little room anywhere else. It is absurd to judge the openness or lack of openness of an entire social system solely by the extent of recruitment from below into the highest positions of all. One can imagine a society in which all members of the tiny elite are democratically recruited from below, and yet where the social structure as a whole is extremely rigid with that small exception. Conversely, one can imagine a society with a hereditary ruling group at the very top, a group completely closed to aspiring men of talent but lowly birth, and yet with an enormous amount of movement back and forth below that pinnacle. Late nineteenth-century America could have approximated this latter model, with lineage, parental wealth, and education as decisive assets in the race for the very peak, as the business elite studies suggest, and yet with great fluidity at the lower and middle levels of the class structure.

Was this in fact the case? The evidence available today is regrettably scanty, but here are the broad outlines of an answer, insofar as we can generalize from a handful of studies.[8] At the lower and middle ranges of the class structure there was impressive mobility, though often of an unexpected and rather ambiguous kind. I will distinguish three types of mobility: Geographical, occupational, and property, and say a little about the extent and significance of each.

First is geographical mobility, physical movement from place to place, which is tied up in an interesting way with movement through the social scale. Americans have long been thought a restless, footloose people,

8. The main sources for the generalizations which follow, unless otherwise indicated, are: Stephan Thernstrom, *Poverty and Progress: Social Mobility in a Nineteenth Century City* (Cambridge, Mass., 1964); Merle E. Curti, *The Making of an American Frontier Community* (Stanford, Cal., 1959); Donald B. Cole, *Immigrant City: Lawrence, Massachusetts, 1845–1921* (Chapel Hill, N.C., 1963)—for my reservations about this work, however, see my review in the *Journal of Economic History*, XXIV (1964), 259–61; Herbert G. Gutman, "Social Status and Social Mobility in 19th Century America: Paterson, N.J., A Case Study," unpublished paper for the 1964 meetings of the American Historical Association; Howard Gitelman, "The Labor Force at Waltham Watch During the Civil War Era," *Journal of Economic History*, XXV (1965), 214–43; David Brody, *Steelworkers in America: The Nonunion Era* (Cambridge, Mass., 1960); Pauline Gordon, "The Chance to Rise Within Industry" (unpublished M.A. thesis, Columbia University); Robert Wheeler, "The Fifth-Ward Irish: Mobility at Mid-Century" (unpublished seminar paper, Brown University, 1967); and the author's research in progress on social mobility in Boston over the past century, in which the career patterns of some 8,000 ordinary residents of the community are traced.

and it has been assumed that the man on the move has been the man on the make: he knows that this little town doesn't provide a grand enough stage for him to display his talents, and so he goes off to the big city to win fame and fortune, or to the open frontier to do likewise. When you examine actual behavior instead of popular beliefs, however, you discover that things are more complicated than that.

It proves to be true that Americans are indeed a footloose people. In my work on Newburyport, a small industrial city, I attempted to find out what fraction of the families present in the community in the initial year of my study—1850—were still living there in the closing year, 1880, one short generation. Less than a fifth of them, it turned out—and this not in a community on the moving frontier, like Merle Curti's Trempealeau County, where you would expect a very high turnover. There the true pioneer types, who liked to clear the land, became nervous when there was another family within a half day's ride of them and sold out to the second wave of settlers (often immigrants who knew better than to try to tame the wilderness without previous experience at it). But to find roughly the same volatility in a city forty miles north of Boston suggests that the whole society was in motion.

The statistics bear out the legend that Americans are a restless people. What of the assertion that movement and success go hand in hand, that physical mobility and upward social mobility are positively correlated? Here the legend seems more questionable. It seems likely that some who pulled up stakes and went elsewhere for a new start did improve their positions; they found better land, or discovered that they possessed talents which were much more highly valued in the big city than in the place they came from. What ever would have happened to Theodore Dreiser in small-town Indiana had there been no Chicago for him to flee to?

But the point to underline, for it is less commonly understood, is that much of this remarkable population turnover was of quite a different kind. As you trace the flow of immigrants into and then out of the cities, you begin to see that a great many of those who departed did so in circumstances which make it exceedingly hard to believe that they were moving on to bigger and better things elsewhere. There is no way to be certain about this, no feasible method of tracing individuals once they disappear from the universe of the community under consideration. These questions can be explored for contemporary America by administering questionnaires to people and collecting life histories which display migration patterns, but dead men tell no tales and fill out no questionnaires, so that part of the past is irrevocably lost. But some plausible inferences can be drawn about the nature of this turnover from the fact that so many ordinary working people on the move owned no property, had no savings accounts, had acquired no special skills, and were most likely to leave when they were unemployed. They were, in short, people who had made the least successful economic adjustment to the community and who were no longer able to hang on there. At the lower reaches of the social order, getting out of town did not ordinarily mean a step up the ladder somewhere else; there is no reason to assume that in their new destinations migrant laborers found anything but more of the same. When middle-class families, who already had a niche in the world, moved on, it was often in response to greater opportunities elsewhere; for ordinary working people physical movement meant something very different.

That is a less rosy picture than the one usually painted, but I think it is more accurate. And we should notice one very important implication of this argument: namely, that the people who were least successful and who had the greatest grievances are precisely those who never stayed put very long in any one place. Students of labor economics and trade union history have long been aware of the fact that there are certain occupations which are inordinately difficult to organize simply because they have incessant job turnover. When only 5 percent or 1 percent of the men working at a particular job in a given city at the start of the year are still employed twelve months later, as is the case with some occupations in the economic underworld today (short-order cooks or menial hospital workers, for instance), how do you build a stable organization and conduct a successful strike?

An analogous consideration applies not merely to certain selected occupations but to a large fraction of the late nineteenth-century urban working class as a whole. The Marxist model of the conditions which promote proletarian consciousness presumes not only permanency of membership in this class—the absence of upward mobility—but also, I suggest, some continuity of class membership *in one setting* so that workers come to know each other and to develop bonds of solidarity and common opposition to the ruling group above them. This would seem to entail a stable labor force in a single factory; at a minimum it assumes considerable stability in a community. One reason that a permanent proletariat along the lines envisaged by Marx did not develop in the course of American industrialization is perhaps that few Americans have *stayed* in one place, one workplace, or even one city long enough to discover a sense of common identity and common grievance. This may be a vital clue to the divergent political development of America and Western Europe in the industrial age, to the striking weakness of socialism here, as compared to Europe—though we can't be sure because we don't definitely know that the European working-class population was less volatile. I suspect that it was, to some degree, and that America was distinctive in this respect, but this is a question of glaring importance which no one has yet taken the trouble to investigate.

When I first stumbled upon this phenomenon in sifting through manuscript census schedules for nineteenth-century Newburyport, I was very doubtful that the findings could be generalized to apply to the big cities of the period. It seemed reasonable to assume that the laborers who drifted out of Newburyport so quickly after their arrival must have settled down somewhere else, and to think that a great metropolis would have offered a more inviting haven than a small city, where anonymity was impossible and where middle-class institutions of social control intruded into one's daily life with some frequency, as compared to a classic big-city lower-class ghetto, where the down-and-out could perhaps huddle together for protective warmth and be left to their own devices—for instance, those Irish wards of New York where the police made no attempt to enforce law and order until late in the century. Here if anywhere one should be able to find a continuous lower-class population, a permanent proletariat, and I began my Boston research with great curiosity about this point.

If Boston is any example, in no American city was there a sizable lower class with great continuity of membership. You can identify some more or less continuously lower-class areas, but the crucial point is that *the same people do not stay in them.* If you take a sample of unskilled and semi-skilled laborers in Boston in 1880 and look for them in 1890, you are not much more likely to find them still in the city than was the case in Newburyport.[9]

The bottom layer of the social order in the nineteenth-century American city was thus a group of families who appear to have been permanent transients, buffeted about from place to place, never quite able to sink roots. We know very little about these people, and it is difficult to know how we can learn much about them. You get only occasional glimpses into the part of this iceberg that appears above the surface, in the person of the tramp, who first is perceived as a problem for America in the 1870s and reappears in hard times after that—in the 1890s and in the great depression most notably. But what has been said here at least suggests the significance of the phenomenon.

So much for geographical mobility. What can be said about the people who come to the city and remain there under our microscope so that we can discern what happened to them? I have already anticipated by gen-

9. Recent work suggesting that even the most recent U.S. Census seriously undernumerated the Negro male population may make the critical reader wonder about the accuracy of the census and city directory canvases upon which I base my analysis. Some elaborate checking has persuaded me that these nineteenth-century sources erred primarily in their coverage—their lack of coverage, rather—of the floating working-class population. For a variety of reasons it seems clear that families which had been in the community long enough to be included in one of these canvases—and hence to be included in a sample drawn from them—were rarely left out of later canvases if they were indeed still resident in the same city. A perfect census of every soul in the community on a given day would therefore yield an even higher, not a lower, estimate of population turnover for men at the bottom, which strengthens rather than weakens the argument advanced here.

eral line of argument here in my discussion of migration out of the city—which amounted to the claim that the city was a kind of Darwinian jungle in which the fittest survived and the others drifted on to try another place. Those who did stay in the city and make their way there did, in general, succeed in advancing themselves economically and socially. There was very impressive mobility, though not always of the kind we might expect.

In approaching this matter, we must make a distinction which is obscured by applying labels like "open" or "fluid" to entire whole social structures. There are, after all, two sets of escalators in any community; one set goes down. To describe a society as enormously fluid implies that there are lots of people moving down while lots of others are moving up to take their place. This would obviously be a socially explosive situation, for all those men descending against their will would arrive at the bottom, not with low horizons of expectation set in some peasant village, but with expectations established when they were at one of the comfortable top floors of the structure.

Downward mobility is by no means an unknown phenomenon in American history. There have been socially displaced groups, especially if you take into account rather subtle shifts in the relative status of such groups as professionals.[10] But the chief generalization to make is that Americans who started their working life in a middle-class job strongly tended to end up in the middle class; sons reared in middle-class families also attained middle-class occupations in the great majority of cases. Relatively few men born into the middle class fell from there; a good many born into the working class either escaped from it altogether or advanced themselves significantly within the class. There is a well-established tradition of writing about the skilled workman, associated with such names as the Hammonds, the Lynds, Lloyd Warner, and Norman Ware, which holds the contrary, to be sure.[11] This tradition still has its defenders, who argue that with industrialization "class lines assumed a new and forbidding rigidity" and that "machines made obsolete many of the skilled trades of the antebellum years, drawing the once self-respecting handicraftsmen into the drudgery and monotony of factory life, where they were called upon to perform only one step in the minutely divided and

10. The assumption that discontent stemming from social displacement has been the motive force behind American reform movements has exerted great influence upon American historical writing in recent years. See for instance David Donald, "Toward a Reconsideration of Abolitionists," *Lincoln Reconsidered* (New York, 1956), pp. 19–36; Richard Hofstadter, *The Age of Reform: From Bryan to F.D.R.* (New York, 1955). Donald's essay is easily demolished by anyone with the slightest acquaintance with sociological method. Hofstadter's work, while open to a very serious objection, is at least sufficiently suggestive to indicate the potential utility of the idea.
11. J. L. and Barbara Hammond, *The Town Labourer (1760–1832)* (London, 1917); Robert S. and Helen M. Lynd, *Middletown* (New York, 1929), and *Middletown in Transition* (New York, 1937); W. Lloyd Warner and J. O. Low, *The Social System of the Modern Factory* (New Haven, Conn., 1947); Norman J. Ware, *The Industrial Worker, 1840–1860* (Boston, 1924).

automatic processes of mass production."[12] Rapid technological change doubtless did displace some skilled artisans, doubtless produced some downward mobility into semiskilled positions. But defenders of this view have built their case upon little more than scattered complaints by labor leaders, and have not conducted systematic research to verify these complaints.

Careful statistical analysis provides a very different perspective on the matter. Two points stand out. One is that as certain traditional skilled callings became obsolete, there was an enormous expansion of *other* skilled trades, and, since many of the craftsmen under pressure from technological change had rather generalized skills, they moved rapidly into these new positions and thus retained their place in the labor aristocracy.[13] Second, it is quite mistaken to assume that the sons of the threatened artisan were commonly driven down into the ranks of the factory operatives; they typically found a place either in the expanding skilled trades or in the even more rapidly expanding white-collar occupations.[14]

As for workers on the lower rungs of the occupational ladder, the unskilled and semiskilled, they had rarely drifted down from a higher beginning point. Characteristically, they were newcomers to the urban world. A substantial minority of them appear to have been able to advance themselves a notch or two occupationally, especially among the second generation; a good many of their sons became clerks, salesmen, and other petty white-collar functionaries. And the first generation, which had less success occupationally, was commonly experiencing mobility of another kind—property mobility. Despite a pathetically low (but generally rising) wage level, despite heavy unemployment rates, many were able to accumulate significant property holdings and to establish themselves as members of the stable working class, as opposed to the drifting lower class.[15]

It may seem paradoxical to suggest that so many Americans were ris-

12.   Leon Litwak, ed., *The American Labor Movement* (Englewood Cliffs, N.J., 1962), p. 3.
13.   This is evident from aggregated census data and from my Boston investigation, but we badly need an American counterpart to Eric Hobsbawm's splendid essay on "The Labour Aristocracy in Nineteenth Century Britain," in *Labouring Men: Studies in the History of Labour* (London, 1964), pp. 272–315.
14.   So, at least, the evidence from Boston and Indianapolis indicates; for the latter, see Natlic Rogoff, *Recent Trends in Occupational Mobility* (Glencoe, Ill., 1953).
15.   The clearest demonstration of this is in Thernstrom, *Poverty and Progress,* Ch. 5. It might be thought, however, that the remarkable property mobility disclosed there depended upon the existence of an abundant stock of cheap single-family housing available for purchase. It could be that where real estate was less readily obtainable, laborers would squander the funds that were accumulated with such sacrifice in places where home ownership was an immediate possibility. It appears from Wheeler's unpublished study of nineteenth-century Providence, however, that the working-class passion for property did not require an immediate, concrete source of satisfaction like a home and a plot of land. The Irish workmen of Providence were just as successful at accumulating property holdings as their Newburyport counterparts; the difference was only that they held personal rather than real property.

ing in the world and so few falling; where did the room at the top come from? The paradox is readily resolved. For one thing, our attention has been fastened upon individuals who remained physically situated in one place in which their careers could be traced; an indeterminate but substantial fraction of the population was floating and presumably unsuccessful. By no means everyone at the bottom was upwardly mobile; the point is rather that those who were not were largely invisible. Furthermore, the occupational structure itself was changing in a manner that created disproportionately more positions in the middle and upper ranges, despite the common nineteenth-century belief that industrialization was homogenizing the work force and reducing all manual employees to identical robots. The homogenizing and degrading tendencies that caught the eye of Marx and others were more than offset, it appears, by developments which made for both a more differentiated and a more top-heavy occupational structure. Third, there were important sources of social mobility that could be attained without changing one's occupation, most notably the property mobility that was stimulated by the increases in real wages that occurred in this period. Finally, there was the so-called "demographic vacuum" created by the differential fertility of the social classes, best illustrated in the gloomy late nineteenth-century estimate that in two hundred years 1,000 Harvard graduates would have only 50 living descendants while 1,000 Italians would have 100,000. The calculation is dubious, but the example nicely clarifies the point that high-status groups failed to reproduce themselves, thus opening up vacancies which had necessarily to be filled by new men from below.

For all the brutality and rapacity which marked the American scene in the years in which the new urban industrial order came into being, what stands out most is the relative absence of collective working-class protest aimed at reshaping capitalist society. The foregoing, while hardly a full explanation, should help to make this more comprehensible. The American working class was drawn into the new society by a process that encouraged accommodation and rendered disciplined protest difficult. Within the urban industrial orbit, most of its members found modest but significant opportunities to feel that they and their children were edging their way upwards. Those who did not find such opportunities were tossed helplessly about from city to city, from state to state, alienated but invisible and impotent.

ST. CLAIR DRAKE
and HORACE R. CAYTON
Flight to Freedom

The Pottawattomie Indians who relinquished the Chicago portage to the white man in 1835 had a saying: "The first white man to settle at Chickagou was a Negro." Frenchmen—trappers, priests, and explorers—had touched this portage from time to time during the seventeenth century; and Louis Joliet and Father Marquette crossed it in 1673. But it was a French-speaking Negro, Jean Baptiste Point de Saible, described by a contemporary British army officer as "a handsome Negro well educated and settled at Eschikagou," [1] who made the first permanent settlement, some time around 1790. At "the place of the evil smell," Point de Saible erected a frontier establishment consisting of a large wooden homestead, bakehouse, smokehouse, poultry house, and dairy; a workshop and a horse mill; a barn and two stables. Here the Pottawattomie came to trade; and the English and French, exploring and fighting for dominance in the back-country, stopped to rest and replenish their stores. Reclaimed from the prairie and wrested from the wilderness, this solitary frontier settlement became the seedbed of skyscrapers and factories. Its trading post was the progenitor of the wheat-pit and its workshop the prototype of factories and mills. The canoes and pirogues that stopped here foreshadowed the commerce of after-years.

Where he came from originally—this Father of Midwest Metropolis—we do not know. According to one tradition he was from Santo Domingo, and planned to establish a colony of free Negroes near the shores of Lake Michigan. Another story would have him the descendant of a Negro slave and a French fur-trader in the Northwest Territory. We know with certainty only that for sixteen years he and his Pottawattomie wife Catherine, his daughter Cézanne, and Jean Baptiste *fils,* lived at the present site of Chicago. In 1796, for reasons unknown he sold his establishment to one LeMai, who in turn sold it to an Englishman, John Kinzie. Point de

1. From the diary of Colonel Arent Schuyler de Peyster, British commander at Michilimackinac, July 4, 1779, as quoted in A. T. Andreas, *History of Chicago from the Earliest Period to the Present Time,* Chicago, 1884, Vol. I, pp. 70–71.

Saible then moved to Peoria, where he spent most of the remainder of his life, dying in St. Charles, Missouri. Within the house he had built, so tradition says, Chicago's first marriage was solemnized, the first election held, and the first white child born.

Of Point de Saible one student of early Chicago, Milo Quaife, has written: "He was a true pioneer of civilization, leader of the unending procession of Chicago's swarming millions. Even in his mixed blood he truly represented the future city, for where else is a greater conglomeration of races and breeds assembled together?" [2]

With his departure, only an occasional Negro filtered into the city until the late Forties, when a steady, though small, stream began to arrive.

Chicago—city of refuge

The earliest Negro migrants to Chicago, like those of later years, were refugees from the bondage of America's cotton kingdom in the South. They poured into the city by the hundreds between 1840 and 1850, fleeing slavery. Some remained; others passed through to Canada and points east.

Chicago gradually became an important terminal on that amazingly ingenious combination of secret trails, mysterious hay wagons, hideouts, and zealous people that was known as the Underground Railroad.[3] Up the Mississippi, across the Ohio River, through the Allegheny gaps, over the western prairie, nearly a hundred thousand slaves were passed from farm to farm and town to town during the seventy years' operation of "freedom's railroad." Secrecy was necessary, even in Chicago, for the Illinois Black Code required every Negro who remained in the state to post a thousand-dollar bond and to carry a certificate of freedom. The federal Fugitive Slave Law of 1793 made it a criminal offense, punishable by a $500 fine, to harbor a fugitive or to prevent his arrest. Yet throughout the Forties and Fifties a few churches and homes in Chicago served as "stations" on the Underground Railroad. The "conductors"—usually church people or political radicals—were recruited mainly from the ranks of white artisans, business people, and Negroes holding free papers. The *Western Citizen,* abolitionist journal, boasted during the Fifties: "We can run a load of slaves through from almost any part of the border states into Canada within forty-eight hours and we defy the slaveholders to beat that if they can." [4]

Furious and frustrated planters in the lower Mississippi Valley fulminated at this lawless traffic in stolen property. They derisively and indig-

2. Milo Milton Quaife, *Checagou,* University of Chicago, 1933, p. 46.
3. For a full account of the Underground Railroad, see Henrietta Buckmaster, *Let My People Go,* Harper, 1941.
4. As quoted in L. D. Reddick, "The Negro in Chicago, 1790–1860," unpublished manuscript, Schomburg Collection, New York, p. 73.

nantly dubbed Chicago a "nigger-loving town." One editor in southern Illinois, a proslavery stronghold, contemptuously dismissed Chicago as a "sink hole of abolition." [5] To the slaves, however, it was a city of refuge, and once within its boundaries they jealously guarded their own illegal freedom while helping their fellows to escape.

Chicago's small group of Underground "officials" received its first open support from a wider public when the murder of the famous abolitionist, Elijah Lovejoy, by a southern Illinois mob in 1837 drew sharp protests from a number of church groups. Several antislavery societies sprang up within the next decade. They flooded the city with pamphlets, presented antislavery dramas, sponsored lectures by eminent abolitionists from the East, and tried to organize political support for the Free Soil and the Liberty parties. Gradually the slavery controversy began to affect Chicago as it had numerous other northern communities. Churches and secular organizations alike were riven asunder as radicals and conservatives divided on points of antislavery principle and tactics.

Despite the local political contests of the Forties, however, the general public had not yet become excited over the slavery issue. It was more immediately concerned with proposals for a Galena and Chicago Union Railroad, over which wheat and corn and hogs would flow in abundance, than with the human freight of the Underground Railroad. Yet no obstacles were interposed to curb the abolitionist minority, and Chicago—with a reputation even then for colorful violence—tolerated some rather rough treatment of slave-catchers who came to ferret out fugitives. More moderate antislavery sympathizers were occasionally disturbed by the activities of the Underground; and on one occasion in 1846, when a group of Negroes, armed with clubs and led by white abolitionists, rescued a slave from his captors and "paraded in triumph," they convoked a public meeting to disavow this show of force. The editor of one influential newspaper declared: "Better even is law, enforced by the standing armies of tyrants, than for a community to be the subjects of every handful of outlaws, black or white, who may choose to combine and set the laws at defiance." [6] Just four years later, however, the Chicago city council itself was setting the law at defiance; and, as for returning fugitives to the South, an influential church newspaper was insisting that "no Christian rightly understanding his duties can engage in it." [7]

This crystallization of public sentiment was due primarily to the Compromise of 1850, which gave the southern planters a revitalized fugitive-slave act in exchange for their consent to the admission of California as a free state. The amended act raised the fine for harboring fugitives to

5. Shawneetown *Gazette,* as quoted in Reddick, *op. cit.,* p. 68.
6. *Weekly Chicago Democrat,* Nov. 3, 1846, as quoted in Bessie Pierce, *A History of Chicago,* Knopf, 1937, Vol. I, p. 253.
7. *Watchman of the Prairies,* n.d., quoted in Pierce, *op. cit.,* Vol. II, pp. 382–83.

$1,000 and added a prison term of six months. A slave-catcher's affidavit became sufficient evidence in court to identify any Negro as a fugitive. Trial by jury and the right to testify in his own defense were denied the suspected slave. Magistrates were rewarded with a ten-dollar fee for ruling in favor of the master, while only five dollars was allotted for decisions in favor of the Negro. Any bystander could be deputized to assist in a capture. Federal officials who let a slave escape from their custody were financially liable for the entire value of the lost property.

A wave of indignation swept through the North when the terms of the new fugitive-slave act were announced. In Chicago, three hundred Negroes—over half the permanent adult population—met in their Methodist Church, organized a Liberty Association, and set up vigilante groups. Seven patrols of six persons each were assigned "to keep an eye out for interlopers." The Association passed a ringing resolution explaining the Negroes' stand:

". . . We do not wish to offer violence to any person unless driven to the extreme, in which case we are determined to defend ourselves at all hazards, even should it be to the shedding of human blood, and in doing thus, will appeal to the Supreme Judge of the Social World to support us in the justness of our cause. . . . We who have tasted of *freedom* are ready to exclaim, in the language of the brave Patrick Henry, 'Give us liberty or give us death.' " [8]

White sympathizers, too, were aroused, and it became evident that some justices would refuse to enforce the law. One famous case, soon after the passage of the Compromise, involved a Mr. Hinch, who arrived in town with a devoted slave to help him catch three fugitives. One day when he and the trusty were standing near Lake Michigan, even this faithful retainer deserted to freedom, by jumping aboard a steamer pulling out for Canada. A group of abolitionists threatened to tar and feather Mr. Hinch, so he appealed to a local justice for the protection of his person and for co-operation in recapturing his property. The justice advised him that "immediate flight would be his safest course."

Even the Chicago Common Council, the city's legislative body, took formal action condemning the fugitive-slave act as "a cruel and unjust law . . . [which] ought not be respected by an intelligent community." The city police were assured that they were under no obligation to assist in rounding up escaped slaves. At a mass meeting on the night of the Council's vote, a white lawyer made a fiery speech against the fugitive-slave act and closed by "defying the law and trampling a copy of it under his feet, to the delight and admiring cheers of his hearers." [9]

8. Chicago *Daily Journal*, Oct. 3, 1850.
9. J. S. Currey, *Chicago: Its History and Its Builders,* Clarke, 1912, Vol. I, pp. 415–16. See also C. W. Mann, *The Chicago Common Council and the Fugitive Slave Law of 1850,* Chicago Historical Society, pp. 73 ff.

Stephen A. Douglas, Senator from Illinois, had backed the Compromise. He was now so disturbed by this smoldering in the grass roots that he rushed home from Washington to prevent it from becoming a prairie fire. His eloquent and skillful defense of the Compromise won a resolution from his audience condemning the Chicago Council for its "precipitate action." The city fathers would not retreat completely, however. They voted to "reconsider," but refused to "expunge from the record." [10]

But neither Douglas's oratory nor the desire for an orderly community restrained the aroused abolitionists. An official of the Underground Railroad commented in the late autumn of 1850: "This road is doing better business this fall than usual. The Fugitive Slave Law has given it more vitality and activity; more passengers and more opposition, which accelerates business." [11] The Chicago *Daily Journal* had insisted since the early Forties that "every man that wears the image and likeness of his Maker should be treated as a man." Now, it advocated violent action against slave-catchers with a broad, humorous hint: "We have no doubt but those interested are upon their guard and the gentleman [i.e., slave-catchers] will return with a *flea in their ears.*" [12] The *Democratic Press,* organ of "Deacon" Bross, Chicago's most colorful civic booster of the day, declared that the Fugitive Slave Law could be enforced only "at the muzzle of a musket," and declared that "we have known of many attempts being made to take fugitives away from Chicago, but we have yet to learn the first instance in which the thing has been done." [13]

In case after case during the stormy decade between the Compromise and the Civil War, the Negroes and their abolitionist allies outwitted and outfought the slave-catchers. One of the most dramatic of these episodes involved one Eliza, an escaped slave who had found employment as a maidservant in a house of prostitution. A slave-catcher, discovering her whereabouts, came to claim his quarry, escorted by a local deputy. Eliza and a white girl companion both begged the slave-catcher not to take the girl away. They were silenced by a drawn revolver, while Eliza, kicking and screaming, was forced into a waiting hack. An angry crowd surrounded the carriage, and the captors fled into a nearby armory, dragging Eliza with them.

By this time a large group of colored men, armed with clubs and knives, descended upon the armory. The sheriff then appeared with a warrant for Eliza's arrest on a charge of disorderly conduct—a calculated stratagem to get her away from the slave-catcher. As the sheriff emerged from the armory with Eliza, the crowd wrenched her from his

10. Pierce, *op. cit.,* Vol. II, pp. 195–97.
11. *Western Citizen,* as quoted in Reddick, *op. cit.,* p. 73. The reference was not to the earlier Fugitive Slave Law of 1793 but to the fugitive-slave act embodied in the Compromise of 1850.
12. Chicago *Daily Journal,* Aug. 5, 1853.
13. *Democratic Press,* March 29, 1855, as quoted in Reddick, *op. cit.,* p. 106.

grasp and quickly spirited her away to a station on the Underground Railroad. The mob then proceeded to the house of assignation, threatening to level it to the ground in the belief that the owner had revealed Eliza's identity. The ringleaders were arrested but released the next day. Scant wonder that the Cairo (III.) *Weekly Times* was led to complain of the Chicagoans: "They are the most riotous people in the state. Mention nigger and slave-catcher in the same breath and they are up in arms." [14]

Finally, in the spring of 1861, a group of federal marshals threatened to swoop down upon Chicago and other northern cities in one last but futile gesture aimed at appeasing a South on the verge of secession. The Negro community was panic-stricken, and the Chicago *Journal,* leading antislavery daily, in a dramatic admonition advised every Negro without a certificate of freedom to "make tracks for Canada as soon as possible": [15]

Don't delay a moment. Don't let grass grow under your feet. Stand not upon the order of your going but go at once. You are not safe here and you cannot be safe until you stand on English soil where you will be free men and free women. It is folly for you to remain here an instant, for the slaveholders encouraged by their late success are making and will continue to make the most determined effort to reclaim fugitives from bondage. Strike for the North Star.

The Underground was now functioning in the open. Four freight cars were boldly chartered to carry the fugitives to an embarkation point on Lake Michigan. A *Journal* reporter was on hand to describe this exodus: [16]

All day, yesterday, the vicinity of the Michigan Southern depot was a scene of excitement and confusion. After the religious services at the Zoar Baptist Church in the morning, which was densely attended, the leave-taking commenced . . . the fugitives and their friends, going from door to door, bidding each other good-bye and mingling their congratulations and tears.—The colored clergymen of the city were also among the number, and labored ardently in extending encouragement and consolation to those about to depart. . . . In some instances, entire families were going together, in which cases there seemed to be a general jubilation; in others a few members, a wife leaving a husband, or a mother her children, amid tears. . . .

. . . All the afternoon, drays, express wagons and other vehicles were busy transporting trunks, bandboxes, valises and

14. Cairo (III.) *Weekly Times,* Sept. 9, 1857. For another famous case, see Pierce, *op. cit.,* Vol. II, p. 198. See also Chicago *Democrat,* Feb. 7, 1848; and Chicago *Daily Journal,* Feb. 5, 1848, Oct. 3, 1850, June 26, 1857, Nov. 12, 1861, and April 4, 1861.
15. Chicago *Journal,* April 5, 1861.
16. *Ibid.,* April 8, 1861.

other various articles of household furniture to the depot. The wants of the outer man had been attended to also, and a goodly store of provisions, such as crackers, bread, beans, dried beef and apples, were packed in, and a barrel of water in each car; for the fugitives were to be stowed away in the same cars with the freight, with plenty of fresh air, but no light, and in crowded unwholesome state.

As the hour of departure . . . drew nigh, the streets adjacent to the depot and the immediate vicinity of the four cars . . . were thronged with an excited multitude of colored people of both sexes and all ages. Large numbers of white people also gathered from motives of curiosity, and stood silent spectators of this rather unusual spectacle. The four cars were rapidly filled with the fugitives, numbering one hundred and six in all, and embracing men, women, youth and infants. In the rear car were two or three sick women, who were treated with the utmost tenderness. . . . The whole business of the transportation was supervised by two or three colored men assisted by several white people.

After all were aboard, . . . the immense crowd pressed up to the cars and commenced the last farewell. . . . Here and there was one in tears and wringing the hands, but the majority were in the best of humor, and were congratulated by their friends lingering behind, that tomorrow they would be free. "Never mind," said one, "the good Lord will save us all in the coming day." . . . [They were] bidding their friends write when they got to "the other side of Jordan," and not forget them in the new country. The minister of the neighborhood church where they had attended, also went from car to car bidding them to be men when they got to Canada.

The larger proportion of the fugitives were stout, ablebodied young men, many of them well dressed and some of them almost white. . . . The elder ones envinced no levity but acted like those who had been hardened by troubles, and were now suffering a lot foreseen and prepared for. . . . Quite a number of children were among the crowd, who, ignorant of the cause of such a commotion, gave the rest constant trouble by getting into the wrong cars and climbing round and between the wheels.

But all were finally stowed away, the bell of the engine sounded and the train started amid lusty cheers, many-voiced good-byes and the waving of hats and handkerchiefs as far as the eye could see. The fugitives heartily responded and the train vanished in the distance. . . .

About one thousand fugitives have arrived in this city since last fall, a large number of whom have left within the past few days.

The Great Canadian Exodus had become another step in the flight to freedom.

From city street to battlefield

Street fights between slave-catchers and abolitionists or between pro-slavery and antislavery crowds were rather common occurrences in northern cities between 1850 and 1860. They were the storm signals of that great political groundswell which culminated in the organization of the Republican party and the election of Abraham Lincoln to the presidency. Both the sporadic violence and the humanitarian agitation of the antislavery movement were gradually merged with and subordinated to political action. Chicago's antislavery forces had tried to elect a mayor in 1841 and failed. Yet, less than twenty years later, the Republican party controlled the city. Migrants from the eastern seaboard, immigrants from England, and German radical refugees from the reaction which followed the European revolutions of 1848 provided the majority which tipped the balance in favor of the Republicans.

In 1856, "Honest Abe" and Stephen A. Douglas, the "Little Giant," both came to Chicago to plead for the senatorial vote. The Democrats roared thunderous assent when Douglas declared that the government of the United States "was made by white men for the benefit of white men, to be administered by white men in such a manner as they should determine."

The next night Lincoln spoke—and with a forthrightness which he seldom assumed in other sections of Illinois. He appealed to the foreign-born, who made up over 50 per cent of the electorate, calling them "blood of the blood, and flesh of the flesh of the men who wrote the Declaration of Independence and pronounced the equality of men." He took a bold stand against the extension of slavery, declaring that "if we cannot give freedom to every creature, let us do nothing that will impose slavery upon any other creature." He made a stirring plea for national unity: "Let us discard all this quibbling about this man and the other man, this race and that race and the other race being inferior, . . . and unite as one people throughout this land, until we shall once more stand up declaring that *all* men are created equal." One eyewitness reported that as Lincoln finished his address, " 'cheers like blasts of a thousand bugles' came from the throats of his listeners." [17] Douglas won the statewide vote, but Lincoln carried the city of Chicago. He carried it again three years later when he ran for President. He carried it, too, when he sounded his call for volunteers in April, 1861.

Chicago's response to Lincoln's call for troops was immediate and enthusiastic. The native-born volunteered freely. Many of the foreign-born enrolled—in some cases under their national banners. The Hungarians,

17. Pierce, *op. cit.*, Vol. II, pp. 228–35.

Bohemians, and Slavs organized the Lincoln Rifles. The German Turner Union Cadets, the French Battalion, and the Scottish Highland Guards marched out to defend the American Union. Even the Irish, Democratic to the core and not too enthusiastic about Republican war aims, now responded to the call of their Colonel Mulligan: "RALLY! All Irishmen. . . . For the honor of the Old Land . . . for the defense of the New!" [18] The street fights of the Forties and Fifties had been transferred to a national battlefield. The flight to freedom had been replaced by a fight for freedom. Only the Negroes were prevented from answering Lincoln's call. Not until 1863 did the Union officially permit them to shoulder arms for their own freedom.

The community of the free

For many of the fugitive slaves, the flight to freedom ended in Chicago. When the Civil War began, there were about a thousand Negroes living in the city. Some were "free-born persons of color"; others had been emancipated by kindly masters or had purchased their freedom. The majority were fugitives, without legal certificates of freedom.

In the center of the city, along the banks of the Chicago River, a small community of the free had been growing since 1840. Social life centered around several small Baptist and Methodist churches which also functioned as stations on the Underground Railroad. Three years before the Civil War, the *Christian Times,* appealing to the white community for aid to one of these churches, referred to its membership in laudatory terms:

> The colored Baptist church in this city is made up of very excellent and reliable material. Its leading male members are respected and successful business men, and fully capable of directing wisely the financial affairs of the church. . . . The church is small, and though, as intimated above, some of its male members are tolerably prosperous in their business, they are not able to assume the whole burden of these payments.[19]

The antislavery newspapers often referred to the small Negro community with pride, for it seemed to justify their faith in the potentialities of the slaves. On several occasions reference was made to the orderliness of the Negroes and to their interest in literary societies, religion, and education. One editor remarked, with a rhetorical flourish characteristic of the period: "Such evidences speak volumes for the enterprize of those whose fathers dwelt long ago, where the White Nile wanders through its golden sands." [20] There were even occasional hints that certain sections

18. Lloyd Lewis and H. J. Smith, *Chicago: The History of Its Reputation,* Harcourt, Brace, 1929, p. 89. See also Pierce, *op. cit.,* Vol. II, pp. 255–58.
19. *Christian Times,* Sept. 2, 1857.
20. Chicago *Journal,* July 29, 1850.

of the white population might do well to emulate these "well informed, and peaceable citizens [who] seldom see any of their brethren grace the police calendar." [21]

That not all the Negro settlers were quiet businessmen or devotees of church and literary societies is obvious, however, from a lurid newspaper account in 1860 of a "Negro Dive in Full Blast." [22] The "excellent and reliable material" within the colored community also had to face other threats to its reputation. Old church records reveal anxious discussion over the question: "If a slave should be separated from his spouse by the master or by escaping into a free state, and should marry another, is he guilty of bigamy?" Sometimes an embarrassing scandal broke, such as the highly publicized account of a "reverend scoundrel" who, caught *in flagrante delicto* with a parishioner's wife, fled into the street, the wrath-maddened husband in hot pursuit. Even the more friendly papers could not overlook the possibilities of such a story, although one journal softened its spicy account of the minister's plight with a sober comment: "The affair has created the most intense excitement amongst the colored population who unanimously take sides against him." [23]

Negro leaders of the period were continually urging their followers to prove that ex-slaves were worthy of the city's hospitality. Typical of those Negroes who had a stake in Chicago's future was one John Jones, spokesman for the Negro community and first colored man to win an elective political office. The *Journal* carried his business advertisement in 1860: [24]

> Go to John Jones' Clothes Cleaning and Repairing Rooms, 119 Dearborn street, and get your clothes neatly repaired and thoroughly cleaned. The oldest and best establishment in the city. Your clothes will not be drawn up by steaming, nor spoiled with chemicals. Give me a trial, my prices are reasonable.

Such men had come to the city to stay.

The antislavery forces in Chicago were united in their opposition to slavery. They were willing to make their city a haven of refuge. They were not of one mind, however, on how to treat the Negroes in their midst. At one extreme were individuals such as the anti-slavery editor who stated frankly: [25]

21. *Ibid.,* August 5, 1853. Probably this thrust was directed at the large Irish population. "As in other American cities, clannishness, religion, poverty, and a distinguishing dialect held them aloof from the rest of the population. In the eyes of other groups the proportion arrested for disorderliness and roistering tended further to set them apart." (Pierce, *op cit.,* Vol. I, p. 180.)
22. *Ibid.,* February 1, 1860.
23. *Ibid.*
24. *Ibid.,* Nov. 1, 1860.
25. Charles L. Wilson, editor of the Chicago *Journal,* quoted in Pierce, *op. cit.,* Vol. II, p. 231.

I am resolutely opposed to the "equalizing [*sic*] of the races," and it no more necessarily follows that we should fellowship with Negroes because our policy strikes off their shackles, than it would to take felons to our embraces, because we might remonstrate against cruelty to them in our penitentiaries.

At the other extreme were a few persons who went all-out for integration and drew the denunciatory fire of southerners for being "amalgamationists" desirous of "mongrelizing" the white race by allowing intermarriage and "social equality."

Throughout the period prior to the Civil War, the laws of the state forbade intermarriage and voting by Negroes. Segregation on common carriers and in the schools and theaters was widespread. The abolitionists regarded these as side issues which should not interfere with the main fight against slavery. Indeed, many abolitionists hoped that once the Negroes were freed, the bulk of them would either remain in the South or emigrate to the West Indies and Africa.

When emancipation was proclaimed, there was considerable discussion in antislavery circles of how Chicago would meet a possible sudden influx of freedmen. The "colonizationists" were hopeful that even those Negroes already in the city would voluntarily leave. When only forty-seven Negroes accepted an invitation from the president of Haiti to emigrate to that island in 1865, and the bulk of the colored population openly declared its intention to remain, the editor of the *Northwestern Christian Advocate* was so incensed at what he called their "impolitic and ungrateful behavior" that he threatened to withdraw his support from a financial campaign of the impecunious African Methodist Episcopal Church.

Most of the former abolitionists and their sympathizers soon became reconciled to the prospect of a small permanent Negro community with its own separate social institutions. A pattern of enforced segregation conflicted with the high sentiments of equality and the brotherhood of man, and that there were some uneasy consciences is evident from the minutes of the Illinois Baptist State Convention of 1865. The impropriety of segregation is suggested in the same paragraph with a statement implying that such separation was to be naturally expected (the italics are the authors'):

". . . We ought to extend fraternal courtesy and kindness to individuals scattered among us *when their numbers are not sufficient to justify the formation of colored churches.* Let them know that all our churches offer them a home and a cordial welcome. *Let them not be tempted to organize churches on the basis of color* rather than of Christian Faith."

While there was outside pressure upon the freedmen to establish a separate institutional life, there were also internal forces at work: a community of interests, a group of educated leaders, and the existence of local Negro churches and lodges with national connections. The ex-slaves were proud to have what they called "something of our own." At the same time they insisted upon the extension of full economic and political opportunity, and access to all public accommodations.

Opposition to an increase in the Negro population was most pronounced among the white laboring classes. It was not the issue of social equality which fundamentally disturbed them, however, but the fear and suspicion that Negro freedmen would be used to depress the wage level. Most bitter in their opposition were the Irish, who, Catholic and poor, were scornfully referred to as "unwashed Dimmycrats" by the Protestant Republican businessmen and artisans who controlled the city and professed to champion the Negro. From time to time during the twenty years preceding the Civil War, Irish workingmen in Chicago rioted against fugitive slaves who secured employment as stevedores, porters, canal bargemen, and general laborers.

In 1864, the Chicago *Tribune* carried a long editorial on "Mobbing Negroes," which probably reflected the antagonism of the Protestant Germans and Easterners toward the Catholic Irish as much as it did sympathy for Negroes. A mob of four or five hundred Irish laborers had beaten a dozen Negroes on the lumber docks, allegedly because "it was degrading to them to see blacks working upon an equality with themselves, and more so, while their brothers were out of employment." The *Tribune* insisted, however, that work was not scarce, and that "if all the black people in the city should leave Chicago tomorrow it would not benefit the condition of the Irish a single dime." Calling them "mobocrats," "raw laborers," and "the most illogical people on the face of the earth," the editor proceeded to belabor the Irish for "biting off their own noses for the benefit of Copperhead demagogues." * "It is a little singular," he observed, "that no class of people in Chicago fear the competition of the handful of blacks here, except the Irish. The Germans never mob colored men for working for whoever may employ them. The English, the Scotch, the French, the Scandinavians, never molest peaceable black people. Americans never think of doing such a thing. No other nationality consider themselves 'degraded' by seeing blacks earning their own living by labor." The editor concluded with a suggestion that "if they must mob anybody, it should be the slaveholders. . . . If they must quarrel with the negroes [*sic*], it should be with the slave negroes. . . . They ought to

* Chicago suffered from general war weariness during 1863 and 1864. There was widespread dissatisfaction with the draft, and on one occasion Lincoln had to rebuke some of the leading citizens for their lack of co-operation. Treason itself was not unknown, and one plot was discovered which would have resulted in a *putsch* by Confederate soldiers interned in Chicago. Yet throughout the period, except for one mayoral election, the Republicans kept control of the city, and after the war the "radical" Republicans were in the saddle.

teach the slave blacks to assert their rights; to 'strike' for wages. . . . By so doing, the Irish laborer would remove the crushing, degrading competition of unpaid labor, and open to himself vast fields of employment now shut out from him by slavery." [26]

The logic of the present was more compelling, however, than this abstract theory of long-run interests. The Irish laborers remained suspicious and resentful against people who castigated them in this fashion, and they made the Democratic party the weapon for their defense. Inevitably, local policies were colored by national events, and three years after the Civil War, Irish contingents in a Democratic election parade in Chicago carried signs denouncing Republican reconstruction policies in the South: "LET THE NIGGERS PAY FOR THEIR OWN SOUP"; "NO NIGGER VOTING"; "WHITE SUPREMACY."

Chicago Republicans, their eyes focused upon the growing Irish vote, did not hesitate to openly declare their opposition to any influx of "free and untrained Negroes." There was no such influx, but by 1870 some four thousand Negroes were living in the city—one out of every hundred persons.

Five years after the Civil War the leaders of the Negro community, in conjunction with other Negroes in the state, called a Colored Convention to present grievances and "devise ways and means whereby a healthy opinion may be created . . . to secure every recognition by the laws of our state and to demand equal school privileges throughout the state." [27] The Black Code was still on the books, and, in some of the communities of southern Illinois, Negroes were as thoroughly subordinated as they were in the deeper South. Even in Chicago, as the Negro population increased, colored children were forced to attend the so-called "Black School," and when protests failed, some of the parents resorted to civil disobedience. A colored Old Settler relates the story as her mother told it to her:

> The parents—most of them—objecting to segregation sent their children right on to the nearest schools as before. The teachers declined to assign them to classes or studies.
> The children, however, attended daily, taking their seats in an orderly fashion throughout the controversy that ensued. The school board then determined that any child with no more than an eighth of Negro blood could attend the usual schools; but here again was trouble, for the wide range of complexions in the colored families soon demonstrated the impossibility in such a division. After a short time and a determined fight on the part of the colored citizens who invaded the offices of the Board of Education and the Mayor, the inglorious career of the Black School was done away with and never resumed.

26. Chicago *Tribune,* July 15, 1864.
27. Chicago *Times,* Oct. 5, 1869.

It took twenty years to create a public opinion strong enough to erase all of the discriminatory laws from the state's statute book, but by 1885 this had been accomplished. Lacking political power and appealing solely within the framework of the abolitionist tradition, democratic idealism, and constitutional rights, the community of freedmen were able to mobilize enough support to establish their equality before the law, to secure the right to vote, and to erect a set of guarantees against discrimination in the use of public facilities. To lay the ghosts that stalked in proslavery southern Illinois, the Colored Convention of 1869 explicitly stated that "[we] disavow any and all imputations of, and desire to obtain, social equality." In Chicago, however, neither white persons nor Negroes had any crusading fervor either to espouse or to prevent social relations or even intermarriage. Although Negroes developed their own family and community life, there was considerable friendly social intercourse between colored and white people, and marriages across the color-line were not unknown.

Within a generation after the Civil War the community of the free was accepted as a normal part of the city's life. The tradition became set that Negroes could compete for power and prestige in the economic and political spheres. Yet the badge of color marked them as socially different. Also, the fact that no Negroes rose to the highest positions in the commercial and public life of early Chicago suggests that in a vague but nevertheless decisive sense they were thought of as having a subordinate place.

Before the Civil War the Negro was the protagonist of the abolitionist drama. After Emancipation he was no longer a hero around whom stirring battles were fought in the city streets and the courts. He and his people became just one more poverty-stricken group competing in a city where economic and political issues were being fought out behind the façade of racial, national, and religious alignments. It was a city which for the next thirty years was riven by class conflicts and seared by two disastrous fires—but which was steadily laying the foundations for industrial and commercial supremacy in the Middle West.

THEODORE DREISER
The Magnet Attracting:
A Waif Amid Forces

When Caroline Meeber boarded the afternoon train for Chicago, her total outfit consisted of a small trunk, a cheap imitation alligator-skin satchel, a small lunch in a paper box, and a yellow leather snap purse, containing her ticket, a scrap of paper with her sister's address in Van Buren Street, and four dollars in money. It was in August, 1889. She was eighteen years of age, bright, timid, and full of the illusions of ignorance and youth. Whatever touch of regret at parting characterised her thoughts, it was certainly not for advantages now being given up. A gush of tears at her mother's farewell kiss, a touch in her throat when the cars clacked by the flour mill where her father worked by the day, a pathetic sigh as the familiar green environs of the village passed in review, and the threads which bound her so lightly to girlhood and home were irretrievably broken.

To be sure there was always the next station, where one might descend and return. There was the great city, bound more closely by these very trains which came up daily. Columbia City was not so very far away, even once she was in Chicago. What, pray, is a few hours—a few hundred miles? She looked at the little slip bearing her sister's address and wondered. She gazed at the green landscape, now passing in swift review, until her swifter thoughts replaced its impression with vague conjectures of what Chicago might be.

When a girl leaves her home at eighteen, she does one of two things. Either she falls into saving hands and becomes better, or she rapidly assumes the cosmopolitan standard of virtue and becomes worse. Of an intermediate balance, under the circumstances, there is no possibility. The city has its cunning wiles, no less than the infinitely smaller and more human tempter. There are large forces which allure with all the soulfulness of expression possible in the most cultured human. The gleam of a thousand lights is often as effective as the persuasive light in a wooing and fascinating eye. Half the undoing of the unsophisticated and natural mind is accomplished by forces wholly superhuman. A blare of sound, a roar of life, a vast array of human hives, appeal to the astonished senses in equivocal terms. Without a counsellor at hand to whisper cautious interpretations, what falsehoods may not these things breathe into the unguarded ear! Unrecognised for what they are, their beauty, like music, too often relaxes, then weakens, then perverts the simpler human perceptions.

Caroline, or Sister Carrie, as she had been half affectionately termed by the family, was possessed of a mind rudimentary in its power of observation and analysis. Self-interest with her was high, but not strong. It was, nevertheless, her guiding characteristic. Warm with the fancies of youth, pretty with the insipid prettiness of the formative period, possessed of a figure promising eventual shapeliness and an eye alight with certain native intelligence, she was a fair example of the middle American class—two generations removed from the emigrant. Books were beyond her interest—knowledge a sealed book. In the intuitive graces she was still crude. She could scarcely toss her head gracefully. Her hands were almost ineffectual. The feet, though small, were set flatly. And yet she was interested in her charms, quick to understand the keener pleasures of life, ambitious to gain in material things. A half-equipped little knight she was, venturing to reconnoitre the mysterious city and dreaming wild dreams of some vague, far-off supremacy, which should make it prey and subject—the proper penitent, grovelling at a woman's slipper.

"That," said a voice in her ear, "is one of the prettiest little resorts in Wisconsin."

"Is it?" she answered nervously.

The train was just pulling out of Waukesha. For some time she had been conscious of a man behind. She felt him observing her mass of hair. He had been fidgeting, and with natural intuition she felt a certain interest growing in that quarter. Her maidenly reserve, and a certain sense of what was conventional under the circumstances, called her to forestall and deny this familiarity, but the daring and magnetism of the individual, born of past experiences and triumphs, prevailed. She answered.

He leaned forward to put his elbows upon the back of her seat and proceeded to make himself volubly agreeable.

"Yes, that is a great resort for Chicago people. The hotels are swell. You are not familiar with this part of the country, are you?"

"Oh, yes, I am," answered Carrie. "That is, I live at Columbia City. I have never been through here, though."

"And so this is your first visit to Chicago," he observed.

All the time she was conscious of certain features out of the side of her eye. Flush, colourful cheeks, a light moustache, a grey fedora hat. She now turned and looked upon him in full, the instincts of self-protection and coquetry mingling confusedly in her brain.

"I didn't say that," she said.

"Oh," he answered, in a very pleasing way and with an assumed air of mistake, "I thought you did."

Here was a type of the travelling canvasser for a manufacturing house —a class which at that time was first being dubbed by the slang of the day "drummers." He came within the meaning of a still newer term, which had sprung into general use among Americans in 1880, and which concisely expressed the thought of one whose dress or manners are calculated to elicit the admiration of susceptible young women—a "masher." His suit was of a striped and crossed pattern of brown wool, new at that time, but since become familiar as a business suit. The low crotch of the vest revealed a stiff shirt bosom of white and pink stripes. From his coat sleeves protruded a pair of linen cuffs of the same pattern, fastened with large, gold plate buttons, set with the common yellow agates known as "cat's-eyes." His fingers bore several rings—one, the ever-enduring heavy seal—and from his vest dangled a neat gold watch chain, from which was suspended the secret insignia of the Order of Elks. The whole suit was rather tight-fitting, and was finished off with heavy-soled tan shoes, highly polished, and the grey fedora hat. He was, for the order of intellect represented, attractive, and whatever he had to recommend him, you may be sure was not lost upon Carrie, in this, her first glance.

Lest this order of individual should permanently pass, let me put down some of the most striking characteristics of his most successful manner and method. Good clothes, of course, were the first essential, the things without which he was nothing. A strong physical nature, actuated by a keen desire for the feminine, was the next. A mind free of any consideration of the problems or forces of the world and actuated not by greed, but an insatiable love of variable pleasure. His method was always simple. Its principal element was daring, backed, of course, by an intense desire and admiration for the sex. Let him meet with a young woman once and he would approach her with an air of kindly familiarity, not unmixed with pleading, which would result in most cases in a tolerant acceptance. If she showed any tendency to coquetry he would be apt to straighten her tie, or if she "took up" with him at all, to call her by her first name. If he visited a department store it was to lounge familiarly over the counter and ask some leading questions. In more exclusive circles, on the train or in waiting stations, he went slower. If some seemingly vulnerable object appeared he was all attention—to pass the compliments of the day, to lead the way to the parlor car, carrying her grip, or, failing that, to take a seat next her with the hope of being able to court her to her destination. Pillows, books, a footstool, the shade lowered; all these figured in the things which he could do. If, when she reached her destination he did not alight and attend her baggage for her, it was because, in his own estimation, he had signally failed.

A woman should some day write the complete philosophy of clothes. No matter how young, it is one of the things she wholly comprehends. There is an indescribably faint line in the matter of man's apparel which somehow divides for her those who are worth glancing at and those who are not. Once an individual has passed this faint line on the way downward he will get no glance from her. There is another line at which the dress of a man will cause her to study her own. This line the individual at her elbow now marked for Carrie. She became conscious of an inequality. Her own plain blue dress, with its black cotton tape trimmings, now seemed to her shabby. She felt the worn state of her shoes.

"Let's see," he went on, "I know quite a number of people in your town. Morgenroth the clothier and Gibson the dry goods man."

"Oh, do you?" she interrupted, aroused by memories of longings their show windows had cost her.

At last he had a clew to her interest, and followed it deftly. In a few minutes he had come about into her seat. He talked of sales of clothing, his travels, Chicago, and the amusements of that city.

"If you are going there, you will enjoy it immensely. Have you relatives?"

"I am going to visit my sister," she explained.

"You want to see Lincoln Park," he said, "and Michigan Boulevard. They are putting up great buildings there. It's a second New York—great. So much to see—theatres, crowds, fine houses—oh, you'll like that."

There was a little ache in her fancy of all he described. Her insignificance in the presence of so much magnificence faintly affected her. She realised that hers was not to be a round of pleasure, and yet there was something promising in all the material prospect he set forth. There was something satisfactory in the attention of this individual with his good clothes. She could not help smiling as he told her of some popular actress of whom she reminded him. She was not silly, and yet attention of this sort had its weight.

"You will be in Chicago some little time, won't you?" he observed at one turn of the now easy conversation.

"I don't know," said Carrie vaguely—a flash vision of the possibility of her not securing employment rising in her mind.

"Several weeks, anyhow," he said, looking steadily into her eyes.

There was much more passing now than the mere words indicated. He recognised the indescribable thing that made up for fascination and beauty in her. She realised that she was of interest to him from the one standpoint which a woman both delights in and fears. Her manner was simple, though for the very reason that she had not yet learned the many little affectations with which women conceal their true feelings. Some things she did appeared bold. A clever companion—had she ever had one—would have warned her never to look a man in the eyes so steadily.

"Why do you ask?" she said.

"Well, I'm going to be there several weeks. I'm going to study stock at our place and get new samples. I might show you 'round."

"I don't know whether you can or not. I mean I don't know whether I can. I shall be living with my sister, and—"

"Well, if she minds, we'll fix that." He took out his pencil and a little pocket note-book as if it were all settled. "What is your address there?"

She fumbled her purse which contained the address slip.

He reached down in his hip pocket and took out a fat purse. It was filled with slips of paper, some mileage books, a roll of greenbacks. It impressed her deeply. Such a purse had never been carried by any one attentive to her. Indeed, an experienced traveller, a brisk man of the world, had never come within such close range before. The purse, the shiny tan shoes, the smart new suit, and the *air* with which he did things, built up for her a dim world of fortune, of which he was the centre. It disposed her pleasantly toward all he might do.

He took out a neat business card, on which was engraved Bartlett, Caryoe & Company, and down in the left-hand corner, Chas. H. Drouet.

"That's me," he said, putting the card in her hand and touching his name. "It's pronounced Drew-eh. Our family was French, on my father's side."

She looked at it while he put up his purse. Then he got out a letter from a bunch in his coat pocket. "This is the house I travel for," he went on, pointing to a picture on it, "corner of State and Lake." There was pride in his voice. He felt that it was something to be connected with such a place, and he made her feel that way.

"What is your address?" he began again, fixing his pencil to write.

She looked at his hand.

"Carrie Meeber," she said slowly. "Three hundred and fifty-four West Van Buren Street, care S. C. Hanson."

He wrote it carefully down and got out the purse again. "You'll be at home if I come around Monday night?" he said.

"I think so," she answered.

How true it is that words are but the vague shadows of the volumes we mean. Little audible links, they are, chaining together great inaudible feelings and purposes. Here were these two, bandying little phrases, drawing purses, looking at cards, and both unconscious of how inarticulate all their real feelings were. Neither was wise enough to be sure of the working of the mind of the other. He could not tell how his luring succeeded. She could not realise that she was drifting, until he secured her address. Now she felt that she had yielded something—he, that he had gained a victory. Already they felt that they were somehow associated. Already he took control in directing the conversation. His words were easy. Her manner was relaxed.

They were nearing Chicago. Signs were everywhere numerous. Trains flashed by them. Across wide stretches of flat, open prairie they could see lines of telegraph poles stalking across the fields toward the great city. Far away were indications of suburban towns, some big smoke-stacks towering high in the air.

Frequently there were two-story frame houses standing out in the open fields, without fence or trees, lone outposts of the approaching army of homes.

To the child, the genius with imagination, or the wholly untravelled, the approach to a great city for the first time is a wonderful thing. Particularly if it be evening—that mystic period between the glare and gloom of the world when life is changing from one sphere or condition to another. Ah, the promise of the night. What does it not hold for the weary! What old illusion of hope is not here forever repeated! Says the soul of the toiler to itself, "I shall soon be free. I shall be in the ways and the hosts of the merry. The streets, the lamps, the lighted chamber set for dining, are for me. The theatre, the halls, the parties, the ways of rest and the paths of song—these are mine in the night." Though all humanity be still enclosed in the shops, the thrill runs abroad. It is in the air. The dullest feel something which they may not always express or describe. It is the lifting of the burden of toil.

Sister Carrie gazed out of the window. Her companion, affected by her wonder, so contagious are all things, felt anew some interest in the city and pointed out its marvels.

"This is Northwest Chicago," said Drouet. "This is the Chicago River," and he pointed to a little muddy creek, crowded with the huge masted wanderers from far-off waters nosing the black-posted banks. With a puff, a clang, and a clatter of rails it was gone. "Chicago is getting to be a great town," he went on. "It's a wonder. You'll find lots to see here."

She did not hear this very well. Her heart was troubled by a kind of terror. The fact that she was alone, away from home, rushing into a great sea of life and endeavour, began to tell. She could not help but feel a little choked for breath—a little sick as her heart beat so fast. She half closed her eyes and tried to think it was nothing, that Columbia City was only a little way off.

"Chicago! Chicago!" called the brakeman, slamming open the door. They were rushing into a more crowded yard, alive with the clatter and clang of life. She began to gather up her poor little grip and closed her hand firmly upon her purse. Drouet arose, kicked his legs to straighten his trousers, and seized his clean yellow grip.

"I suppose your people will be here to meet you?" he said. "Let me carry your grip."

"Oh, no," she said. "I'd rather you wouldn't. I'd rather you wouldn't be with me when I meet my sister."

"All right," he said in all kindness. "I'll be near, though, in case she isn't here, and take you out there safely."

"You're so kind," said Carrie, feeling the goodness of such attention in her strange situation.

"Chicago!" called the brakeman, drawing the word out long. They were under a great shadowy train shed, where the lamps were already beginning to shine out, with passenger cars all about and the train moving at a snail's pace. The people in the car were all up and crowding about the door.

"Well, here we are," said Drouet, leading the way to the door. "Goodbye, till I see you Monday."

"Good-bye," she answered, taking his proffered hand.

"Remember, I'll be looking till you find your sister."

She smiled into his eyes.

They filed out, and he affected to take no notice of her. A lean-faced, rather commonplace woman recognised Carrie on the platform and hurried forward.

"Why, Sister Carrie!" she began, and there was a perfunctory embrace of welcome.

Carrie realised the change of affectional atmosphere at once. Amid all the maze, uproar, and novelty she felt cold reality taking her by the hand. No world of light and merriment. No round of amusement. Her sister carried with her most of the grimness of shift and toil.

"Why, how are all the folks at home?" she began; "how is father, and mother?"

Carrie answered, but was looking away. Down the aisle, toward the gate leading into the waiting-room and the street, stood Drouet. He was looking back. When he saw that she saw him and was safe with her sister he turned to go, sending back the shadow of a smile. Only Carrie saw it. She felt something lost to her when he moved away. When he disappeared she felt his absence thoroughly. With her sister she was much alone, a lone figure in a tossing, thoughtless sea.

MARY ANTIN
The Promised Land

Having made such good time across the ocean, I ought to be able to proceed no less rapidly on *terra firma,* where, after all, I am more at home. And yet here is where I falter. Not that I hesitated, even for the space of a breath, in my first steps in America. There was no time to hesitate. The most ignorant immigrant, on landing, proceeds to give and receive greetings, to eat, sleep, and rise, after the manner of his own country; wherein he is corrected, admonished, and laughed at, whether by interested friends or the most indifferent strangers; and his American experience is thus begun. The process is spontaneous on all sides, like the education of the child by the family circle. But while the most stupid nursery maid is able to contribute her part toward the result, we do not expect an analysis of the process to be furnished by any member of the family, least of all by the engaging infant. The philosophical maiden aunt alone, or some other witness equally psychological and aloof, is able to trace the myriad efforts by which the little Johnnie or Nellie acquires a secure hold on the disjointed parts of the huge plaything, life.

Now I was not exactly an infant when I was set down, on a May day some fifteen years ago, in this pleasant nursery of America. I had long since acquired the use of my faculties, and had collected some bits of experience, practical and emotional, and had even learned to give an account of them. Still, I had very little perspective, and my observations and comparisons were superficial. I was too much carried away to analyze the forces that were moving me. My Polotzk I knew well before I began to judge it and experiment with it. America was bewildering strange, unimaginably complex, delightfully unexplored. I rushed impetuously out of the cage of my provincialism and looked eagerly about the brilliant universe. My question was, What have we here?—not, What does this mean? That query came much later. When I now become retrospectively introspective, I fall into the predicament of the centipede in the rhyme, who got along very smoothly until he was asked which leg came after which, whereupon he became so rattled that he couldn't take a step. I know I have come on a thousand feet, on wings, winds, and American machines,—I have leaped and run and climbed and crawled,—but to tell which step came after which I find a puzzling matter. Plenty of maiden aunts were present during my second infancy, in the guise of immigrant officials, school-teachers, settlement workers, and sundry other unprejudiced and critical observers. Their statistics I might properly borrow to fill the gaps in my recollections, but I am prevented by my sense of harmony. The individual, we know, is a creature unknown to the statistician, whereas I undertook to give the personal view of everything. So I am bound to unravel, as well as I can, the tangle of events, outer and inner, which made up the first breathless years of my American life.

During his three years of probation, my father had made a number of false starts in business. His history for that period is the history of thousands who come to America, like him, with pockets empty, hands untrained to the use of tools, minds cramped by centuries of repression in their native land. Dozens of these men pass under your eyes every day, my American friend, too absorbed in their honest affairs to notice the looks of suspicion which you cast at them, the repugnance with which you shrink from their touch. You see them shuffle from door to door with a basket of spools and buttons, or bending over the sizzling irons in a basement tailor shop, or rummaging in your ash can, or moving a push-cart from curb to curb, at the command of the burly policeman. "The Jew peddler!" you say, and dismiss him from your premises and from your thoughts, never dreaming that the sordid drama of his days may have a moral that concerns you. What if the creature with the untidy beard carries in his bosom his citizenship papers? What if the cross-legged tailor is supporting a boy in college who is one day going to mend your state constitution for you? What if the ragpicker's daughters are hastening over the ocean to teach your children in the public schools? Think, every time you pass the greasy alien on the street, that he was born thousands of years before the oldest native American; and he may have something to communicate to you, when you two shall have learned a common language. Remember that his very physiognomy is a cipher the key to which it behooves you to search for most diligently.

By the time we joined my father, he had surveyed many avenues of approach toward the coveted citadel of fortune. One of these, heretofore untried, he now proposed to essay, armed with new courage, and cheered on by the presence of his family. In partnership with an energetic little man who had an English chapter in his history, he prepared to set up a refreshment booth on Crescent Beach. But while he was completing arrangements at the beach we remained in town, where we enjoyed the educational advantages of a thickly populated neighborhood; namely, Wall Street, in the West End of Boston.

Anybody who knows Boston knows that the West and North Ends are the wrong ends of that city. They form the tenement district, or, in the newer phrase, the slums of Boston. Anybody who is acquainted with the slums of any American metropolis knows that that is the quarter where poor immigrants foregather, to live, for the most part, as unkempt, half-washed, toiling, unaspiring foreigners; pitiful in the eyes of social missionaries, the despair of boards of health, the hope of ward politicians, the touchstone of American democracy. The well-versed metropolitan knows the slums as a sort of house of detention for poor aliens, where they live on probation till they can show a certificate of good citizenship.

He may know all this and yet not guess how Wall Street, in the West End, appears in the eyes of a little immigrant from Polotzk. What would the sophisticated sight-seer say about Union Place, off Wall Street, where my new home waited for me? He would say that it is no place at all, but a short box of an alley. Two rows of three-story tenements are its sides, a stingy strip of sky is its lid, a littered pavement is the floor, and a narrow mouth its exit.

But I saw a very different picture on my introduction to Union Place. I saw two imposing rows of brick buildings, loftier than any dwelling I had ever lived in. Brick was even on the ground for me to tread on, instead of common earth or boards. Many friendly windows stood open, filled with uncovered heads of women and children. I thought the people were interested in us, which was very neighborly. I looked up to the topmost row of windows, and my eyes were filled with the May blue of an American sky!

In our days of affluence in Russia we had been accustomed to upholstered parlors, embroidered linen, silver spoons and candlesticks, goblets of gold, kitchen shelves shining with copper and brass. We had featherbeds heaped halfway to the ceiling; we had clothes presses dusky with velvet and silk and fine woollen. The three small rooms into which my father now ushered us, up one flight of stairs, contained only the necessary beds, with lean mattresses; a few wooden chairs; a table or two; a mysterious iron structure, which later turned out to be a stove; a couple of unornamental kerosene lamps; and a scanty array of cooking-utensils and crockery. And yet we were all impressed with our new home and its furniture. It was not only because we had just passed through our seven lean years, cooking in earthen vessels, eating black bread on holidays and wearing cotton; it was chiefly because these wooden chairs and tin pans were American chairs and pans that they shone glorious in our eyes. And if there was anything lacking for comfort or decoration we expected it to be presently supplied—at least, we children did. Perhaps my mother alone, of us newcomers, appreciated the shabbiness of the little apartment, and realized that for her there was as yet no laying down of the burden of poverty.

Our initiation into American ways began with the first step on the new soil. My father found occasion to instruct or correct us even on the way from the pier to Wall Street, which journey we made crowded together in a rickety cab. He told us not to lean out of the windows, not to point, and explained the word "greenhorn." We did not want to be "greenhorns," and gave the strictest attention to my father's instructions. I do not know when my parents found opportunity to review together the history of Polotzk in the three years past, for we children had no patience with the subject; my mother's narrative was constantly interrupted by irrelevant questions, interjections, and explanations.

The first meal was an object lesson of much variety. My father produced several kinds of food, ready to eat, without any cooking, from little tin cans that had printing all over them. He attempted to introduce us to a queer, slippery kind of fruit, which he called "banana," but had to give it up for the time being. After the meal, he had better luck with a curious piece of furniture on runners, which he called "rocking-chair." There were five of us newcomers, and we found five different ways of getting into the American machine of perpetual motion, and as many ways of getting out of it. One born and bred to the use of a rocking-chair cannot imagine how ludicrous people can make themselves when attempting to use it for the first time. We laughed immoderately over our various experiments with the novelty, which was a wholesome way of letting off steam after the unusual excitement of the day.

In our flat we did not think of such a thing as storing the coal in the bathtub. There was no bathtub. So in the evening of the first day my father conducted us to the public baths. As we moved along in a little procession, I was delighted with the illumination of the streets. So many lamps, and they burned until morning, my father said, and so people did not need to carry lanterns. In America, then, everything was free, as we had heard in Russia. Light was free; the streets were as bright as a synagogue on a holy day. Music was free; we had been serenaded, to our gaping delight, by a brass band of many pieces, soon after our installation on Union Place.

Education was free. That subject my father had written about repeatedly, as comprising his chief hope for us children, the essence of American opportunity, the treasure that no thief could touch, not even misfortune or poverty. It was the one thing that he was able to promise us when he sent for us; surer, safer than bread or shelter. On our second day I was thrilled with the realization of what this freedom of education meant. A little girl from across the alley came and offered to conduct us to school. My father was out, but we five between us had a few words of English by this time. We knew the word school. We understood. This child, who had never seen us till yesterday, who could not pronounce our names, who was not much better dressed than we, was able to offer us the freedom of the schools of Boston! No application made, no questions asked, no examinations, rulings, exclusions; no machinations, no fees. The doors stood open for every one of us. The smallest child could show us the way.

This incident impressed me more than anything I had heard in advance of the freedom of education in America. It was a concrete proof—almost the thing itself. One had to experience it to understand it.

It was a great disappointment to be told by my father that we were not to enter upon our school career at once. It was too near the end of the term, he said, and we were going to move to Crescent Beach in a week or so. We had to wait until the opening of the schools in September. What a loss of precious time—from May till September!

Not that the time was really lost. Even the interval on Union Place was crowded with lessons and experiences. We had to visit the stores and be dressed from head to foot in American clothing; we had to learn the mysteries of the iron stove, the washboard, and the speaking-tube; we had to learn to trade with the fruit peddler through the window, and not to be afraid of the policeman; and, above all, we had to learn English.

The kind people who assisted us in these important matters form a group by themselves in the gallery of my friends. If I had never seen them from those early days till now, I should still have remembered them with gratitude. When I enumerate the long list of my American teachers, I must begin with those who came to us on Wall Street and taught us our first steps. To my mother, in her perplexity over the cookstove, the woman who showed her how to make the fire was an angel of deliverance. A fairy godmother to us children was she who led us to a wonderful country called "uptown," where, in a dazzlingly beautiful palace called a "department store," we exchanged our hateful homemade European costumes, which pointed us out as "greenhorns" to the children on the street, for real American machine-made garments, and issued forth glorified in each other's eyes.

With our despised immigrant clothing we shed also our impossible Hebrew names. A committee of our friends, several years ahead of us in American experience, put their heads together and concocted American names for us all. Those of our real names that had no pleasing American equivalents they ruthlessly discarded, content if they retained the initials. My mother, possessing a name that was not easily translatable, was punished with the undignified nickname of Annie. Fetchke, Joseph, and Deborah issued as Frieda, Joseph, and Dora, respectively. As for poor me, I was simply cheated. The name they gave me was hardly new. My Hebrew name being Maryashe in full, Mashke for short, Russianized into Marya (*Mar-ya*), my friends said that it would hold good in English as *Mary;* which was very disappointing, as I longed to possess a strange-sounding American name like the others.

I am forgetting the consolation I had, in this matter of names, from the use of my surname, which I have had no occasion to mention until now. I found on my arrival that my father was "Mr. Antin" on the slightest provocation, and not, as in Polotzk, on state occasions alone. And so I was "Mary Antin," and I felt very important to answer to such a dignified title. It was just like America that even plain people should wear their surnames on week days.

As a family we were so diligent under instruction, so adaptable, and so clever in hiding our deficiencies, that when we made the journey to Crescent Beach, in the wake of our small wagon-load of household goods, my father had very little occasion to admonish us on the way, and I am sure he was not ashamed of us. So much we had achieved toward our Americanization during the two weeks since our landing.

Crescent Beach is a name that is printed in very small type on the maps of the environs of Boston, but a life-size strip of sand curves from Winthrop to Lynn; and that is historic ground in the annals of my family. The place is now a popular resort for holiday crowds, and is famous under the name of Revere Beach. When the reunited Antins made their stand there, however, there were no boulevards, no stately bath-houses, no hotels, no gaudy amusement places, no illuminations, no showmen, no tawdry rabble. There was only the bright clean sweep of sand, the summer sea, and the summer sky. At high tide the whole Atlantic rushed in, tossing the seaweeds in his mane; at low tide he rushed out, growling and gnashing his granite teeth. Between tides a baby might play on the beach, digging with pebbles and shells, till it lay asleep on the sand. The whole sun shone by day, troops of stars by night, and the great moon in its season.

Into this grand cycle of the seaside day I came to live and learn and play. A few people came with me, as I have already intimated; but the main thing was that *I* came to live on the edge of the sea—I, who had spent my life inland, believing that the great waters of the world were spread out before me in the Dvina. My idea of the human world had grown enormously during the long journey; my idea of the earth had expanded with every day at sea; my idea of the world outside the earth now budded and swelled during my prolonged experience of the wide and unobstructed heavens.

Not that I got any inkling of the conception of a multiple world. I had had no lessons in cosmogony, and I had no spontaneous revelation of the true position of the earth in the universe. For me, as for my fathers, the sun set and rose, and I did not feel the earth rushing through space. But I lay stretched out in the sun, my eyes level with the sea, till I seemed to be absorbed bodily by the very materials of the world around me; till I could not feel my hand as separate from the warm sand in which it was buried. Or I crouched on the beach at full moon, wondering, wondering, between the two splendors of the sky and the sea. Or I ran out to meet the incoming storm, my face full in the wind, my being a-tingle with an awesome delight to the tips of my fog-matted locks flying behind; and stood clinging to some stake or upturned boat, shaken by the roar and rumble of the waves. So clinging, I pretended that I was in danger, and was deliciously frightened; I held on with both hands, and shook my head, exulting in the tumult around me, equally ready to laugh or sob. Or else I sat, on the stillest days, with my back to the sea, not looking at all, but just listening to the rustle of the waves on the sand; not thinking at all, but just breathing with the sea.

Thus courting the influence of sea and sky and variable weather, I was bound to have dreams, hints, imaginings. It was no more than this per- haps: that the world as I knew it was not large enough to contain all that I saw and felt; that the thoughts that flashed through my mind, not half understood, unrelated to my utterable thoughts, concerned something for which I had as yet no name. Every imaginative growing child has these flashes of intuition, especially one that becomes intimate with some one aspect of nature. With me it was the growing time, that idle summer by the sea, and I grew all the faster because I had been so cramped before. My mind, too, had so recently been worked upon by the impressive expe- rience of a change of country that I was more than commonly alive to im- pressions, which are the seeds of ideas.

Let no one suppose that I spent my time entirely, or even chiefly, in in- spired solitude. By far the best part of my day was spent in play—frank, hearty, boisterous play, such as comes natural to American children. In Polotzk I had already begun to be considered too old for play, excepting set games or organized frolics. Here I found myself included with chil- dren who still played, and I willingly returned to childhood. There were plenty of playfellows. My father's energetic little partner had a little wife and a large family. He kept them in the little cottage next to ours; and that the shanty survived the tumultuous presence of that brood is a won- der to me to-day. The young Wilners included an assortment of boys, girls, and twins, of every possible variety of age, size, disposition, and sex. They swarmed in and out of the cottage all day long, wearing the door-sill hollow, and trampling the ground to powder. They swung out of windows like monkeys, slid up the roof like flies, and shot out of trees like fowls. Even a small person like me couldn't go anywhere without being run over by a Wilner; and I could never tell which Wilner it was be- cause none of them ever stood still long enough to be identified; and also because I suspected that they were in the habit of interchanging conspic- uous articles of clothing, which was very confusing.

You would suppose that the little mother must have been utterly lost, bewildered, trodden down in this horde of urchins; but you are mistaken. Mrs. Wilner was a positively majestic little person. She ruled her brood with the utmost coolness and strictness. She had even the biggest boy under her thumb, frequently under her palm. If they enjoyed the wildest freedom outdoors, indoors the young Wilners lived by the clock. And so at five o'clock in the evening, on seven days in the week, my father's partner's children could be seen in two long rows around the supper table. You could tell them apart on this occasion, because they all had their faces washed. And this is the time to count them: there are twelve little Wilners at table.

I managed to retain my identity in this multitude somehow, and while I was very much impressed with their numbers, I even dared to pick and choose my friends among the Wilners. One or two of the smaller boys I liked best of all, for a game of hide-and-seek or a frolic on the beach. We played in the water like ducks, never taking the trouble to get dry. One day I waded out with one of the boys, to see which of us dared go farthest. The tide was extremely low, and we had not wet our knees when we began to look back to see if familiar objects were still in sight. I thought we had been wading for hours, and still the water was so shallow and quiet. My companion was marching straight ahead, so I did the same. Suddenly a swell lifted us almost off our feet, and we clutched at each other simultaneously. There was a lesser swell, and little waves began to run, and a sigh went up from the sea. The tide was turning—perhaps a storm was on the way—and we were miles, dreadful miles from dry land.

Boy and girl turned without a word, four determined bare legs ploughing through the water, four scared eyes straining toward the land. Through an eternity of toil and fear they kept dumbly on, death at their heels, pride still in their hearts. At last they reached high-water mark—six hours before full tide.

Each has seen the other afraid, and each rejoices in the knowledge. But only the boy is sure of his tongue.

"You was scared, warn't you?" he taunts.

The girl understands so much, and is able to reply:—

"You can schwimmen, I not."

"Betcher life I can schwimmen," the other mocks.

And the girl walks off, angry and hurt.

"An' I can walk on my hands," the tormentor calls after her. "Say, you greenhorn, why don'tcher look?"

The girl keeps straight on, vowing that she would never walk with that rude boy again, neither by land nor sea, not even though the waters should part at his bidding.

I am forgetting the more serious business which had brought us to Crescent Beach. While we children disported ourselves like mermaids and mermen in the surf, our respective fathers dispensed cold lemonade, hot peanuts, and pink popcorn, and piled up our respective fortunes, nickel by nickel, penny by penny. I was very proud of my connection with the public life of the beach. I admired greatly our shining soda fountain, the rows of sparkling glasses, the pyramids of oranges, the sausage chains, the neat white counter, and the bright array of tin spoons. It seemed to me that none of the other refreshment stands on the beach— there were a few—were half so attractive as ours. I thought my father looked very well in a long white apron and shirt sleeves. He dished out ice cream with enthusiasm, so I supposed he was getting rich. It never occurred to me to compare his present occupation with the position for which he had been originally destined; or if I thought about it, I was just as well content, for by this time I had by heart my father's saying, "America is not Polotzk." All occupations were respectable, all men were equal, in America.

F. SCOTT FITZGERALD
My Lost City

July, 1932

There was first the ferry boat moving softly from the Jersey shore at dawn—the moment crystalized into my first symbol of New York. Five years later when I was fifteen I went into the city from school to see Ina Claire in *The Quaker Girl* and Gertrude Bryan in *Little Boy Blue.* Confused by my hopeless and melancholy love for them both, I was unable to choose between them—so they blurred into one lovely entity, the girl. She was my second symbol of New York. The ferry boat stood for triumph, the girl for romance. In time I was to achieve some of both, but there was a third symbol that I have lost somewhere, and lost forever.

I found it on a dark April afternoon after five more years.

"Oh, Bunny," I yelled. *"Bunny!"*

He did not hear me—my taxi lost him, picked him up again half a block down the street. There were black spots of rain on the sidewalk and I saw him walking briskly through the crowd wearing a tan raincoat over his inevitable brown get-up; I noted with a shock that he was carrying a light cane.

"Bunny!" I called again, and stopped. I was still an undergraduate at Princeton while he had become a New Yorker. This was his afternoon walk, this hurry along with his stick through the gathering rain, and as I was not to meet him for an hour it seemed an intrusion to happen upon him engrossed in his private life. But the taxi kept pace with him and as I continued to watch I was impressed: he was no longer the shy little scholar of Holder Court—he walked with confidence, wrapped in his thoughts and looking straight ahead, and it was obvious that his new background was entirely sufficient to him. I knew that he had an apartment where he lived with three other men, released now from all undergraduate taboos, but there was something else that was nourishing him and I got my first impression of that new thing—the Metropolitan spirit.

Up to this time I had seen only the New York that offered itself for inspection—I was Dick Whittington up from the country gaping at the trained bears, or a youth of the Midi dazzled by the boulevards of Paris. I had come only to stare at the show, though the designers of the Woolworth Building and the Chariot Race Sign, the producers of musical comedies and problem plays, could ask for no more appreciative spectator, for I took the style and glitter of New York even above its own valuation. But I had never accepted any of the practically anonymous invitations to debutante balls that turned up in an undergraduate's mail, perhaps because I felt that no actuality could live up to my conception of New York's splendor. Moreover, she to whom I fatuously referred as "my girl" was a Middle Westerner, a fact which kept the warm center of the world out there, so I thought of New York as essentially cynical and heartless —save for one night when she made luminous the Ritz Roof on a brief passage through.

Lately, however, I had definitely lost her and I wanted a man's world, and this sight of Bunny made me see New York as just that. A week before, Monsignor Fay had taken me to the Lafayette where there was spread before us a brilliant flag of food, called an *hors d'oeuvre,* and with it we drank claret that was as brave as Bunny's confident cane—but after all it was a restaurant and afterwards we would drive back over a bridge into the hinterland. The New York of undergraduate dissipation, of Bustanoby's, Shanley's, Jack's, had become a horror and though I returned to it, alas, through many an alcoholic mist, I felt each time a betrayal of a persistent idealism. My participance was prurient rather than licentious and scarcely one pleasant memory of it remains from those days; as Ernest Hemingway once remarked, the sole purpose of the cabaret is for unattached men to find complaisant women. All the rest is a wasting of time in bad air.

But that night, in Bunny's apartment, life was mellow and safe, a finer distillation of all that I had come to love at Princeton. The gentle playing of an oboe mingled with city noises from the street outside, which penetrated into the room with difficulty through great barricades of books; only the crisp tearing open of invitations by one man was a discordant note. I had found a third symbol of New York and I began wondering about the rent of such apartments and casting about for the appropriate friends to share one with me.

Fat chance—for the next two years I had as much control over my own destiny as a convict over the cut of his clothes. When I got back to New York in 1919 I was so entangled in life that a period of mellow monasticism in Washington Square was not to be dreamed of. The thing was to make enough money in the advertising business to rent a stuffy apartment for two in the Bronx. The girl concerned had never seen New York but she was wise enough to be rather reluctant. And in a haze of anxiety and unhappiness I passed the four most impressionable months of my life.

New York had all the iridescence of the beginning of the world. The returning troops marched up Fifth Avenue and girls were instinctively drawn East and North toward them—this was the greatest nation and there was gala in the air. As I hovered ghost-like in the Plaza Red Room of a Saturday afternoon, or went to lush and liquid garden parties in the East Sixties or tippled with Princetonians in the Biltmore Bar I was haunted always by my other life—my drab room in the Bronx, my square foot of the subway, my fixation upon the day's letter from Alabama—would it come and what would it say?—my shabby suits, my poverty, and love. While my friends were launching decently into life I had muscled my inadequate bark into midstream. The gilded youth circling around young Constance Bennett in the Club de Vingt, the classmates in the Yale-Princeton Club whooping up our first after-the-war reunion, the atmosphere of the millionaires' houses that I sometimes frequented—these things were empty for me, though I recognized them as impressive scenery and regretted that I was committed to other romance. The most hilarious luncheon table or the most moony cabaret—it was all the same; from them I returned eagerly to my home on Claremont Avenue—home because there might be a letter waiting outside the door. One by one my great dreams of New York became tainted. The remembered charm of Bunny's apartment faded with the rest when I interviewed a blowsy landlady in Greenwich Village. She told me I could bring girls to the room, and the idea filled me with dismay—why should I want to bring girls to my room?—I had a girl. I wandered through the town of 127th Street, resenting its vibrant life; or else I bought cheap theatre seats at Gray's drugstore and tried to lose myself for a few hours in my old passion for Broadway. I was a failure—mediocre at advertising work and unable to get started as a writer. Hating the city, I got roaring, weeping drunk on my last penny and went home. . . .

. . . Incalculable city. What ensued was only one of a thousand success stories of those gaudy days, but it plays a part in my own movie of New York. When I returned six months later the offices of editors and publishers were open to me, impresarios begged plays, the movies panted for screen material. To my bewilderment, I was adopted, not as a Middle Westerner, not even as a detached observer, but as the arch type of what New York wanted. This statement requires some account of the metropolis in 1920.

There was already the tall white city of today, already the feverish activity of the boom, but there was a general inarticulateness. As much as anyone the columnist F. P. A. guessed the pulse of the individual and the crowd, but shyly, as one watching from a window. Society and the native arts had not mingled—Ellen Mackay was not yet married to Irving Berlin. Many of Peter Arno's people would have been meaningless to the citizen of 1920, and save for F. P. A.'s column there was no forum for metropolitan urbanity.

Then, for just a moment, the "younger generation" idea became a fusion of many elements in New York life. People of fifty might pretend there was still a four hundred or Maxwell Bodenheim might pretend there was a Bohemia worth its paint and pencils—but the blending of the bright, gay, vigorous elements began then and for the first time there appeared a society a little livelier than the solid mahogany dinner parties of Emily Price Post. If this society produced the cocktail party, it also evolved Park Avenue wit and for the first time an educated European could envisage a trip to New York as something more amusing than a gold-trek into a formalized Australian Bush.

For just a moment, before it was demonstrated that I was unable to play the role, I, who knew less of New York than any reporter of six months standing and less of its society than any hall-room boy in a Ritz stag line, was pushed into the position not only of spokesman for the time but of the typical product of that same moment. I, or rather it was "we" now, did not know exactly what New York expected of us and found it rather confusing. Within a few months after our embarkation on the Metropolitan venture we scarcely knew any more who we were and we hadn't a notion what we were. A dive into a civic fountain, a casual brush with the law, was enough to get us into the gossip columns, and we were quoted on a variety of subjects we knew nothing about. Actually our "contacts" included half a dozen unmarried college friends and a few new literary acquaintances—I remember a lonesome Christmas when we had not one friend in the city, nor one house we could go to. Finding no nucleus to which we could cling, we became a small nucleus ourselves and gradually we fitted our disruptive personalities into the contemporary scene of New York. Or rather New York forgot us and let us stay.

This is not an account of the city's changes but of the changes in this writer's feeling for the city. From the confusion of the year 1920 I remember riding on top of a taxicab along deserted Fifth Avenue on a hot Sunday night, and a luncheon in the cool Japanese gardens at the Ritz with the wistful Kay Laurel and George Jean Nathan, and writing all night again and again, and paying too much for minute apartments, and buying magnificent but broken-down cars. The first speakeasies had arrived, the toddle was *passé,* the Montmartre was the smart place to dance and Lillian Tashman's fair hair weaved around the floor among the enliquored college boys. The plays were *Declassée* and *Sacred and Profane Love,* and at the Midnight Frolic you danced elbow to elbow with Marion Davies and perhaps picked out the vivacious Mary Hay in the pony chorus. We thought we were apart from all that; perhaps everyone thinks they are apart from their milieu. We felt like small children in a great bright unexplored barn. Summoned out to Griffith's studio on Long Island, we trembled in the presence of the familiar faces of the *Birth of a Nation;* later I realized that behind much of the entertainment that the city poured forth into the nation there were only a lot of rather lost and lonely people. The world of the picture actors was like our own in that it was in New York and not of it. It had little sense of itself and no center: when I first met Dorothy Gish I had the feeling that we were both standing on the North Pole and it was snowing. Since then they have found a home but it was not destined to be New York.

When bored we took our city with a Huysmans-like perversity. An afternoon alone in our "apartment" eating olive sandwiches and drinking a quart of Bushmill's whiskey presented by Zoë Atkins, then out into the freshly bewitched city, through strange doors into strange apartments with intermittent swings along in taxis through the soft nights. At last we were one with New York, pulling it after us through every portal. Even now I go into many flats with the sense that I have been there before or in the one above or below—was it the night I tried to disrobe in the *Scandals,* or the night when (as I read with astonishment in the paper next morning) "Fitzgerald Knocks Officer This Side of Paradise?" Successful scrapping not being among my accomplishments, I tried in vain to reconstruct the sequence of events which led up to this dénouement in Webster Hall. And lastly from that period I remember riding in a taxi one afternoon between very tall buildings under a mauve and rosy sky; I began to bawl because I had everything I wanted and knew I would never be so happy again.

It was typical of our precarious position in New York that when our child was to be born we played safe and went home to St. Paul—it seemed inappropriate to bring a baby into all that glamor and loneliness. But in a year we were back and we began doing the same things over again and not liking them so much. We had run through a lot, though we had retained an almost theatrical innocence by preferring the role of the observed to that of the observer. But innocence is no end in itself and as our minds unwillingly matured we began to see New York whole and try to save some of it for the selves we would inevitably become.

It was too late—or too soon. For us the city was inevitably linked up with Bacchic diversions, mild or fantastic. We could organize ourselves only on our return to Long Island and not always there. We had no incentive to meet the city half way. My first symbol was now a memory, for I knew that triumph is in oneself; my second one had grown commonplace —two of the actresses whom I had worshipped from afar in 1913 had dined in our house. But it filled me with a certain fear that even the third symbol had grown dim—the tranquillity of Bunny's apartment was not to be found in the ever-quickening city. Bunny himself was married, and about to become a father, other friends had gone to Europe, and the bachelors had become cadets of houses larger and more social than ours. By this time we "knew everybody"—which is to say most of those whom Ralph Barton would draw as in the orchestra on an opening night.

But we were no longer important. The flapper, upon whose activities the popularity of my first books was based, had become *passé* by 1923— anyhow in the East. I decided to crash Broadway with a play, but Broadway sent its scouts to Atlantic City and quashed the idea in advance, so I felt that, for the moment, the city and I had little to offer each other. I would take the Long Island atmosphere that I had familiarly breathed and materialize it beneath unfamiliar skies.

It was three years before we saw New York again. As the ship glided up the river, the city burst thunderously upon us in the early dusk—the white glacier of lower New York swooping down like a strand of a bridge to rise into uptown New York, a miracle of foamy light suspended by the stars. A band started to play on deck, but the majesty of the city made the march trivial and tinkling. From that moment I knew that New York, however often I might leave it, was home.

The tempo of the city had changed sharply. The uncertainties of 1920 were drowned in a steady golden roar and many of our friends had grown wealthy. But the restlessness of New York in 1927 approached hysteria. The parties were bigger—those of Condé Nast, for example, rivaled in their way the fabled balls of the nineties; the pace was faster—the catering to dissipation set an example to Paris; the shows were broader, the buildings were higher, the morals were looser and the liquor was cheaper; but all these benefits did not really minister to much delight. Young people wore out early—they were hard and languid at twenty-one and save for Peter Arno none of them contributed anything new; perhaps Peter Arno and his collaborators said everything there was to say about the boom days in New York that couldn't be said by a jazz band. Many people who were not alcoholics were lit up four days out of seven, and frayed nerves were strewn everywhere; groups were held together by a generic nervousness and the hangover became a part of the day as well allowed-for as the Spanish siesta. Most of my friends drank too much— the more they were in tune to the times the more they drank. And as effort *per se* had no dignity against the mere bounty of those days in New York, a depreciatory word was found for it: a successful programme became a racket—I was in the literary racket.

We settled a few hours from New York and I found that every time I came to the city I was caught up into a complication of events that deposited me a few days later in a somewhat exhausted state on the train for Delaware. Whole sections of the city had grown rather poisonous, but invariably I found a moment of utter peace in riding south through Central Park at dark toward where the façade of 59th Street thrusts its lights through the trees. There again was my lost city, wrapped cool in its mystery and promise. But that detachment never lasted long—as the toiler must live in the city's belly, so I was compelled to live in its disordered mind.

Instead there were the speakeasies—the moving from luxurious bars, which advertised in the campus publications of Yale and Princeton, to the beer gardens where the snarling face of the underworld peered through the German good nature of the entertainment, then on to strange and even more sinister localities where one was eyed by granite-faced boys and there was nothing left of joviality but only a brutishness that corrupted the new day into which one presently went out. Back in 1920 I shocked a rising young business man by suggesting a cocktail before lunch. In 1929 there was liquor in half the downtown offices, and a speakeasy in half the large buildings.

One was increasingly conscious of the speakeasy and of Park Avenue. In the past decade Greenwich Village, Washington Square, Murray Hill, the châteaux of Fifth Avenue had somehow disappeared, or become unexpressive of anything. The city was bloated, glutted, stupid with cake and circuses, and a new expression "Oh yeah?" summed up all the enthusiasm evoked by the announcement of the last super-skyscrapers. My barber retired on a half million bet in the market and I was conscious that the head waiters who bowed me, or failed to bow me, to my table were far, far wealthier than I. This was no fun—once again I had enough of New York and it was good to be safe on shipboard where the ceaseless revelry remained in the bar in transport to the fleecing rooms of France.

"What news from New York?"

"Stocks go up. A baby murdered a gangster."

"Nothing more?"

"Nothing. Radios blare in the street."

I once thought that there were no second acts in American lives, but there was certainly to be a second act to New York's boom days. We were somewhere in North Africa when we heard a dull distant crash which echoed to the farthest wastes of the desert.

"What was that?"

"Did you hear it?"

"It was nothing."

"Do you think we ought to go home and see?"

"No—it was nothing."

In the dark autumn of two years later we saw New York again. We passed through curiously polite customs agents, and then with bowed head and hat in hand I walked reverently through the echoing tomb. Among the ruins a few childish wraiths still played to keep up the pretense that they were alive, betraying by their feverish voices and hectic cheeks the thinness of the masquerade. Cocktail parties, a last hollow survival from the days of carnival, echoed to the plaints of the wounded: "Shoot me, for the love of God, someone shoot me!", and the groans and wails of the dying: "Did you see that United States Steel is down three more points?" My barber was back at work in his shop; again the head waiters bowed people to their tables, if there were people to be bowed. From the ruins, lonely and inexplicable as the sphinx, rose the Empire State Building and, just as it had been a tradition of mine to climb to the Plaza Roof to take leave of the beautiful city, extending as far as eyes could reach, so now I went to the roof of the last and most magnificent of towers. Then I understood—everything was explained: I had discovered the crowning error of the city, its Pandora's box. Full of vaunting pride the New Yorker had climbed here and seen with dismay what he had never suspected, that the city was not the endless succession of canyons that he had supposed but that *it had limits*—from the tallest structure he saw for the first time that it faded out into the country on all sides, into an expanse of green and blue that alone was limitless. And with the awful realization that New York was a city after all and not a universe, the whole shining edifice that he had reared in his imagination came crashing to the ground. That was the rash gift of Alfred E. Smith to the citizens of New York.

Thus I take leave of my lost city. Seen from the ferry boat in the early morning, it no longer whispers of fantastic success and eternal youth. The whoopee mamas who prance before its empty parquets do not suggest to me the ineffable beauty of my dream girls of 1914. And Bunny, swinging along confidently with his cane toward his cloister in a carnival, has gone over to Communism and frets about the wrongs of southern mill workers and western farmers whose voices, fifteen years ago, would not have penetrated his study walls.

All is lost save memory, yet sometimes I imagine myself reading, with curious interest, a *Daily News* of the issue of 1945:

> MAN OF FIFTY RUNS AMUCK IN NEW YORK
> *Fitzgerald Feathered Many Love Nests Cutie Avers*
> *Bumped Off By Outraged Gunman*

So perhaps I am destined to return some day and find in the city new experiences that so far I have only read about. For the moment I can only cry out that I have lost my splendid mirage. Come back, come back, O glittering and white!

MALCOLM X
Homeboy

I looked like Li'l Abner. Mason, Michigan, was written all over me. My kinky, reddish hair was cut hick style, and I didn't even use grease in it. My green suit's coat sleeves stopped above my wrists, the pants legs showed three inches of socks. Just a shade lighter green than the suit was my narrow-collared, three-quarter length Lansing department store topcoat. My appearance was too much for even Ella. But she told me later she had seen countrified members of the Little family come up from Georgia in even worse shape than I was.

Ella had fixed up a nice little upstairs room for me. And she was truly a Georgia Negro woman when she got into the kitchen with her pots and pans. She was the kind of cook who would heap up your plate with such as ham hock, greens, black-eyed peas, fried fish, cabbage, sweet potatoes, grits and gravy, and cornbread. And the more you put away, the better she felt. I worked out at Ella's kitchen table like there was no tomorrow.

Ella still seemed to be as big, black, outspoken and impressive a woman as she had been in Mason and Lansing. Only about two weeks before I arrived, she had split up with her second husband—the soldier, Frank, whom I had met there the previous summer; but she was taking it right in stride. I could see, though I didn't say, how any average man would find it almost impossible to live for very long with a woman whose every instinct was to run everything and everybody she had anything to do with—including me. About my second day there in Roxbury, Ella told me that she didn't want me to start hunting for a job right away, like most newcomer Negroes did. She said that she had told all those she'd brought North to take their time, to walk around, to travel the buses and the subway, and get the feel of Boston, before they tied themselves down working somewhere, because they would never again have the time to really see and get to know anything about the city they were living in. Ella said she'd help me find a job when it was time for me to go to work.

So I went gawking around the neighborhood—the Waumbeck and

Humboldt Avenue Hill section of Roxbury, which is something like Harlem's Sugar Hill, where I'd later live. I saw those Roxbury Negroes acting and living differently from any black people I'd ever dreamed of in my life. This was the snooty-black neighborhood; they called themselves the "Four Hundred," and looked down their noses at the Negroes of the black ghetto, or so-called "town" section where Mary, my other half-sister, lived.

What I thought I was seeing there in Roxbury were high-class, educated, important Negroes, living well, working in big jobs and positions. Their quiet homes sat back in their mowed yards. These Negroes walked along the sidewalks looking haughty and dignified, on their way to work, to shop, to visit, to church. I know now, of course, that what I was really seeing was only a big-city version of those "successful" Negro bootblacks and janitors back in Lansing. The only difference was that the ones in Boston had been brainwashed even more thoroughly. They prided themselves on being incomparably more "cultured," "cultivated," "dignified," and better off than their black brethren down in the ghetto, which was no further away than you could throw a rock. Under the pitiful misapprehension that it would make them "better," these Hill Negroes were breaking their backs trying to imitate white people.

Any black family that had been around Boston long enough to own the home they lived in was considered among the Hill elite. It didn't make any difference that they had to rent out rooms to make ends meet. Then the native-born New Englanders among them looked down upon recently migrated Southern home-owners who lived next door, like Ella. And a big percentage of the Hill dwellers were in Ella's category—Southern strivers and scramblers, and West Indian Negroes, whom both the New Englanders and the Southerners called "Black Jews." Usually it was the Southerners and the West Indians who not only managed to own the places where they lived, but also at least one other house which they rented as income property. The snooty New Englanders usually owned less than they.

In those days on the Hill, any who could claim "professional" status— teachers, preachers, practical nurses—also considered themselves superior. Foreign diplomats could have modeled their conduct on the way the Negro postmen, Pullman porters, and dining car waiters of Roxbury acted, striding around as if they were wearing top hats and cutaways.

I'd guess that eight out of ten of the Hill Negroes of Roxbury, despite the impressive-sounding job titles they affected, actually worked as menials and servants. "He's in banking," or "He's in securities." It sounded as though they were discussing a Rockefeller or a Mellon—and not some gray-headed, dignity-posturing bank janitor, or bond-house messenger. "I'm with an old family" was the euphemism used to dignify the professions of white folks' cooks and maids who talked so affectedly among their own kind in Roxbury that you couldn't even understand them. I don't know how many forty- and fifty-year-old errand boys went down the Hill dressed like ambassadors in black suits and white collars, to downtown jobs "in government," "in finance," or "in law." It has never ceased to amaze me how so many Negroes, then and now, could stand the indignity of that kind of self-delusion.

Soon I ranged out of Roxbury and began to explore Boston proper. Historic buildings everywhere I turned, and plaques and markers and statues for famous events and men. One statue in the Boston Commons astonished me: a Negro named Crispus Attucks, who had been the first man to fall in the Boston Massacre. I had never known anything like that.

I roamed everywhere. In one direction, I walked as far as Boston University. Another day, I took my first subway ride. When most of the people got off, I followed. It was Cambridge, and I circled all around in the Harvard University campus. Somewhere, I had already heard of Harvard—though I didn't know much more about it. Nobody that day could have told me I would give an address before the Harvard Law School Forum some twenty years later.

I also did a lot of exploring downtown. Why a city would have *two* big railroad stations—North Station and South Station—I couldn't understand. At both of the stations, I stood around and watched people arrive and leave. And I did the same thing at the bus station where Ella had met me. My wanderings even led me down along the piers and docks where I read plaques telling about the old sailing ships that used to put into port there.

In a letter to Wilfred, Hilda, Philbert, and Reginald back in Lansing, I told them about all this, and about the winding, narrow, cobblestoned streets, and the houses that jammed up against each other. Downtown Boston, I wrote them, had the biggest stores I'd ever seen, and white people's restaurants and hotels. I made up my mind that I was going to see every movie that came to the fine, air-conditioned theaters.

On Massachusetts Avenue, next door to one of them, the Loew's State Theater, was the huge, exciting Roseland State Ballroom. Big posters out in front advertised the nationally famous bands, white and Negro, that had played there. "COMING NEXT WEEK," when I went by that first time, was Glenn Miller. I remember thinking how nearly the whole evening's music at Mason High School dances had been Glenn Miller's records. What wouldn't that crowd have given, I wondered, to be standing where Glenn Miller's band was actually going to play? I didn't know how familiar with Roseland I was going to become.

Ella began to grow concerned, because even when I had finally had enough sight-seeing, I didn't stick around very much on the Hill. She kept dropping hints that I ought to mingle with the "nice young people my age" who were to be seen in the Townsend Drugstore two blocks from her house, and a couple of other places. But even before I came to Boston, I had always felt and acted toward anyone my age as if they were in the "kid" class, like my younger brother Reginald. They had always looked up to me as if I were considerably older. On weekends back in Lansing where I'd go to get away from the white people in Mason, I'd hung around in the Negro part of town with Wilfred's and Philbert's set. Though all of them were several years older than me, I was bigger, and I actually looked older than most of them.

I didn't want to disappoint or upset Ella, but despite her advice, I began going down into the town ghetto section. That world of grocery stores, walk-up flats, cheap restaurants, poolrooms, bars, storefront churches, and pawnshops seemed to hold a natural lure for me.

Not only was this part of Roxbury much more exciting, but I felt more relaxed among Negroes who were being their natural selves and not putting on airs. Even though I did live on the Hill, my instincts were never—and still aren't—to feel myself any better than any other Negro.

I spent my first month in town with my mouth hanging open. The sharp-dressed young "cats" who hung on the corners and in the poolrooms, bars and restaurants, and who obviously didn't work anywhere, completely entranced me. I couldn't get over marveling at how their hair was straight and shiny like white men's hair; Ella told me this was called a "conk." I had never tasted a sip of liquor, never even smoked a cigarette, and here I saw little black children, ten and twelve years old, shooting craps, playing cards, fighting, getting grown-ups to put a penny or a nickel on their number for them, things like that. And these children threw around swear words I'd never heard before, even, and slang expressions that were just as new to me, such as "stud" and "cat" and "chick" and "cool" and "hip." Every night as I lay in bed I turned these new words over in my mind. It was shocking to me that in town, especially after dark, you'd occasionally see a white girl and a Negro man strolling arm in arm along the sidewalk, and mixed couples drinking in the neon-lighted bars—not slipping off to some dark corner, as in Lansing. I wrote Wilfred and Philbert about that, too.

I wanted to find a job myself, to surprise Ella. One afternoon, something told me to go inside a poolroom whose window I was looking through. I had looked through that window many times. I wasn't yearning to play pool; in fact, I had never held a cue stick. But I was drawn by the sight of the cool-looking "cats" standing around inside, bending over the big, green, felt-topped tables, making bets and shooting the bright-colored balls into the holes. As I stared through the window this particular afternoon, something made me decide to venture inside and talk to a dark, stubby, conk-headed fellow who racked up balls for the pool-players, whom I'd heard called "Shorty." One day he had come outside and seen me standing there and said "Hi, Red," so that made me figure he was friendly.

As inconspicuously as I could, I slipped inside the door and around the side of the poolroom, avoiding people, and on to the back, where Shorty was filling an aluminum can with the powder that pool players dust on their hands. He looked up at me. Later on, Shorty would enjoy teasing me about how with that first glance he knew my whole story. "Man, that cat still *smelled* country!" he'd say, laughing. "Cat's legs was so long and his pants so short his knees showed—an' his head looked like a briar patch!"

But that afternoon Shorty didn't let it show in his face how "country" I appeared when I told him I'd appreciate it if he'd tell me how could somebody go about getting a job like his.

"If you mean racking up balls," said Shorty, "I don't know of no pool joints around here needing anybody. You mean you just want any slave you can find?" A "slave" meant work, a job.

He asked what kind of work I had done. I told him that I'd washed restaurant dishes in Mason, Michigan. He nearly dropped the powder can. "My homeboy! Man, gimme some skin! I'm from Lansing!"

I never told Shorty—and he never suspected—that he was about ten years older than I. He took us to be about the same age. At first I would have been embarrassed to tell him, later I just never bothered. Shorty had dropped out of first-year high school in Lansing, lived a while with an uncle and aunt in Detroit, and had spent the last six years living with his cousin in Roxbury. But when I mentioned the names of Lansing people and places, he remembered many, and pretty soon we sounded as if we had been raised in the same block. I could sense Shorty's genuine gladness, and I don't have to say how lucky I felt to find a friend as hip as he obviously was.

"Man, this is a swinging town if you dig it," Shorty said. "You're my homeboy—I'm going to school you to the happenings." I stood there and grinned like a fool. "You got to go anywhere now? Well, stick around until I get off."

One thing I liked immediately about Shorty was his frankness. When I told him where I lived, he said what I already knew—that nobody in town could stand the Hill Negroes. But he thought a sister who gave me a "pad," not charging me rent, not even running me out to find "some slave," couldn't be all bad. Shorty's slave in the poolroom, he said, was just to keep ends together while he learned his horn. A couple of years before, he'd hit the numbers and bought a saxophone. "Got it right in there in the closet now, for my lesson tonight." Shorty was taking lessons "with some other studs," and he intended one day to organize his own small band. "There's a lot of bread to be made gigging right around here in Roxbury," Shorty explained to me. "I don't dig joining some big band, one-nighting all over just to say I played with Count or Duke or somebody." I thought that was smart. I wished I had studied a horn; but I never had been exposed to one.

All afternoon, between trips up front to rack balls, Shorty talked to me out of the corner of his mouth: which hustlers—standing around, or playing at this or that table—sold "reefers," or had just come out of prison, or were "second-story men." Shorty told me that he played at least a dollar a day on the numbers. He said as soon as he hit a number, he would use the winnings to organize his band.

I was ashamed to have to admit that I had never played the numbers. "Well, you ain't never had nothing to play with," he said, excusing me, "but you start when you get a slave, and if you hit, you got a stake for something."

He pointed out some gamblers and some pimps. Some of them had white whores, he whispered. "I ain't going to lie—I dig them two-dollar white chicks," Shorty said. "There's a lot of that action around here, nights: you'll see it." I said I already had seen some. "You ever had one?" he asked.

My embarrassment at my inexperience showed. "Hell, man," he said, "don't be ashamed. I had a few before I left Lansing—them Polack chicks that used to come over the bridge. Here, they're mostly Italians and Irish. But it don't matter what kind, they're something else! Ain't no different nowhere—there's nothing they love better than a black stud."

Through the afternoon, Shorty introduced me to players and loungers. "My homeboy," he'd say, "he's looking for a slave if you hear anything." They all said they'd look out.

At seven o'clock, when the night ball-racker came on, Shorty told me he had to hurry to his saxophone lesson. But before he left, he held out to me the six or seven dollars he had collected that day in nickel and dime tips. "You got enough bread, homeboy?"

I was okay, I told him—I had two dollars. But Shorty made me take three more. "Little fattening for your pocket," he said. Before we went out, he opened his saxophone case and showed me the horn. It was gleaming brass against the green velvet, an alto sax. He said, "Keep cool, homeboy, and come back tomorrow. Some of the cats will turn you up a slave."

When I got home, Ella said there had been a telephone call from somebody named Shorty. He had left a message that over at the Roseland State Ballroom, the shoeshine boy was quitting that night, and Shorty had told him to hold the job for me.

"Malcolm, you haven't had any experience shining shoes," Ella said. Her expression and tone of voice told me she wasn't happy about my taking that job. I didn't particularly care, because I was already speechless thinking about being somewhere close to the greatest bands in the world. I didn't even wait to eat any dinner.

The ballroom was all lighted when I got there. A man at the front door was letting in members of Benny Goodman's band. I told him I wanted to see the shoeshine boy, Freddie.

"You're going to be the new one?" he asked. I said I thought I was, and he laughed, "Well, maybe you'll hit the numbers and get a Cadillac, too." He told me that I'd find Freddie upstairs in the men's room on the second floor.

But downstairs before I went up, I stepped over and snatched a glimpse inside the ballroom. I just couldn't believe the size of that waxed floor! At the far end, under the soft, rose-colored lights, was the bandstand with the Benny Goodman musicians moving around, laughing and talking, arranging their horns and stands.

A wiry, brown-skinned, conked fellow upstairs in the men's room greeted me. "You Shorty's homeboy?" I said I was, and he said he was Freddie. "Good old boy," he said. "He called me, he just heard I hit the big number, and he figured right I'd be quitting." I told Freddie what the man at the front door had said about a Cadillac. He laughed and said, "Burns them white cats up when you get yourself something. Yeah, I told them I was going to get me one—just to bug them."

Freddie then said for me to pay close attention, that he was going to be busy and for me to watch but not get in the way, and he'd try to get me ready to take over at the next dance, a couple of nights later.

As Freddie busied himself setting up the shoeshine stand, he told me, "Get here early . . . your shoeshine rags and brushes by this footstand . . . your polish bottles, paste wax, suede brushes over here . . . everything in place, you get rushed, you never need to waste motion. . . ."

While you shined shoes, I learned, you also kept watch on customers inside, leaving the urinals. You darted over and offered a small white hand towel. "A lot of cats who ain't planning to wash their hands, sometimes you can run up with a towel and shame them. Your towels are really your best hustle in here. Cost you a penny apiece to launder—you always get at least a nickel tip."

The shoeshine customers, and any from the inside rest room who took a towel, you whiskbroomed a couple of licks. "A nickel or a dime tip, just give 'em that," Freddie said. "But for two bits, Uncle Tom a little—white cats especially like that. I've had them to come back two, three times a dance."

From down below, the sound of the music had begun floating up. I guess I stood transfixed. "You never seen a big dance?" asked Freddie. "Run on awhile, and watch."

There were a few couples already dancing under the rose-colored lights. But even more exciting to me was the crowd thronging in. The most glamorous-looking white women I'd ever seen—young ones, old ones, white cats buying tickets at the window, sticking big wads of green bills back into their pockets, checking the women's coats, and taking their arms and squiring them inside.

Freddie had some early customers when I got back upstairs. Between the shoeshine stand and thrusting towels to me just as they approached the wash basin, Freddie seemed to be doing four things at once. "Here, you can take over the whiskbroom," he said, "just two or three licks—but let 'em feel it."

When things slowed a little, he said, "You ain't seen nothing tonight. You wait until you see a spooks' dance! Man, our own people carry *on!*" Whenever he had a moment, he kept schooling me. "Shoelaces, this drawer here. You just starting out, I'm going to make these to you as a present. Buy them for a nickel a pair, tell cats they need laces if they do, and charge two bits."

Every Benny Goodman record I'd ever heard in my life, it seemed, was filtering faintly into where we were. During another customer lull, Freddie let me slip back outside again to listen. Peggy Lee was at the mike singing. Beautiful! She had just joined the band and she was from North Dakota and had been singing with a group in Chicago when Mrs. Benny Goodman discovered her, we had heard some customers say. She finished the song and the crowd burst into applause. She was a big hit.

"It knocked me out, too, when I first broke in here," Freddie said, grinning, when I went back in there. "But, look, you ever shined any shoes?" He laughed when I said I hadn't, excepting my own. "Well, let's get to work. I never had neither." Freddie got on the stand and went to work on his own shoes. Brush, liquid polish, brush, paste wax, shine rag, lacquer sole dressing . . . step by step, Freddie showed me what to do.

"But you got to get a whole lot faster. You can't waste time!" Freddie showed me how fast on my own shoes. Then, because business was tapering off, he had time to give me a demonstration of how to make the shine rag pop like a firecracker. "Dig the action?" he asked. He did it in slow motion. I got down and tried it on his shoes. I had the principle of it. "Just got to do it faster," Freddie said. "It's a jive noise, that's all. Cats tip better, they figure you're knocking yourself out!"

By the end of the dance, Freddie had let me shine the shoes of three or four stray drunks he talked into having shines, and I had practiced picking up my speed on Freddie's shoes until they looked like mirrors. After we had helped the janitors to clean up the ballroom after the dance, throwing out all the paper and cigarette butts and empty liquor bottles, Freddie was nice enough to drive me all the way home to Ella's on the Hill in the second-hand maroon Buick he said he was going to trade in on his Cadillac. He talked to me all the way. "I guess it's all right if I tell you, pick up a couple of dozen packs of rubbers, two-bits apiece. You notice some of those cats that came up to me around the end of the dance? Well, when some have new chicks going right, they'll come asking you for rubbers. Charge a dollar, generally you'll get an extra tip."

He looked across at me. "Some hustles you're too new for. Cats will ask you for liquor, some will want reefers. But you don't need to have nothing except rubbers—until you can dig who's a cop.

"You can make ten, twelve dollars a dance for yourself if you work everything right," Freddie said, before I got out of the car in front of Ella's. "The main thing you got to remember is that everything in the world is a hustle. So long, Red."

The next time I ran into Freddie I was downtown one night a few weeks later. He was parked in his pearl gray Cadillac, sharp as a tack, "cooling it."

"Man, you sure schooled me!" I said, and he laughed; he knew what I meant. It hadn't taken me long on the job to find out that Freddie had done less shoeshining and towel-hustling than selling liquor and reefers, and putting white "Johns" in touch with Negro whores. I also learned that white girls always flocked to the Negro dances—some of them whores whose pimps brought them to mix business and pleasure, others who came with their black boy friends, and some who came in alone, for a little freelance lusting among a plentiful availability of enthusiastic Negro men.

At the white dances, of course, nothing black was allowed, and that's where the black whores' pimps soon showed a new shoeshine boy what he could pick up on the side by slipping a phone number or address to the white Johns who came around the end of the dance looking for "black chicks."

Most of Roseland's dances were for whites only, and they had white bands only. But the only white band ever to play there at a Negro dance to my recollection, was Charlie Barnet's. The fact is that very few white bands could have satisfied the Negro dancers. But I know that Charlie Barnet's "Cherokee" and his "Redskin Rhumba" drove those Negroes wild. They'd jampack that ballroom, the black girls in way-out silk and satin dresses and shoes, their hair done in all kinds of styles, the men sharp in their zoot suits and crazy conks, and everybody grinning and greased and gassed.

Some of the bandsmen would come up to the men's room at about eight o'clock and get shoeshines before they went to work. Duke Ellington, Count Basie, Lionel Hampton, Cootie Williams, Jimmie Lunceford were just a few of those who sat in my chair. I would really make my shine rag sound like someone had set off Chinese firecrackers. Duke's great alto saxman, Johnny Hodges—he was Shorty's idol—still owes me for a shoeshine I gave him. He was in the chair one night, having a friendly argument with the drummer, Sonny Greer, who was standing there, when I tapped the bottom of his shoes to signal that I was finished. Hodges stepped down, reaching his hand in his pocket to pay me, but then snatched his hand out to gesture, and just forgot me, and walked away. I wouldn't have dared to bother the man who could do what he did with "Daydream" by asking him for fifteen cents.

I remember that I struck up a little shoeshine-stand conversation with Count Basie's great blues singer, Jimmie Rushing. (He's the one famous for "Sent For You Yesterday, Here You Come Today" and things like that.) Rushing's feet, I remember, were big and funny-shaped—not long like most big feet, but they were round and roly-poly like Rushing. Anyhow, he even introduced me to some of the other Basie cats, like Lester Young, Harry Edison, Buddy Tate, Don Byas, Dickie Wells, and Buck Clayton. They'd walk in the rest room later, by themselves. "Hi, Red." They'd be up there in my chair, and my shine rag was popping to the beat of all their records, spinning in my head. Musicians never have had, anywhere, a greater shoeshine-boy fan than I was. I would write to Wilfred and Hilda and Philbert and Reginald back in Lansing, trying to describe it.

I never got any decent tips until the middle of the Negro dances, which is when the dancers started feeling good and getting generous. After the white dances, when I helped to clean out the ballroom, we would throw out perhaps a dozen empty liquor bottles. But after the Negro dances, we would have to throw out cartons full of empty fifth bottles—not rotgut, either, but the best brands, and especially Scotch.

During lulls up there in the men's room, sometimes I'd get in five minutes of watching the dancing. The white people danced as though somebody had trained them—left, one, two; right, three, four—the same steps and patterns over and over, as though somebody had wound them up. But those Negroes—nobody in the world could have choreographed the way they did whatever they felt—just grabbing partners, even the white chicks who came to the Negro dances. And my black brethren today may hate me for saying it, but a lot of black girls nearly got run over by some of those Negro males scrambling to get at those white women; you would have thought God had lowered some of his angels. Times have sure changed; if it happened today, those same black girls would go after those Negro men—and the white women, too.

Anyway, some couples were so abandoned—flinging high and wide, improvising steps and movements—that you couldn't believe it. I could feel the beat in my bones, even though I had never danced.

"*Showtime!*" people would start hollering about the last hour of the dance. Then a couple of dozen really wild couples would stay on the floor, the girls changing to low white sneakers. The band now would really be blasting, and all the other dancers would form a clapping, shouting circle to watch that wild competition as it began, covering only a quarter or so of the ballroom floor. The band, the spectators and the dancers, would be making the Roseland Ballroom feel like a big rocking ship. The spotlight would be turning, pink, yellow, green, and blue, picking up the couples lindy-hopping as if they had gone mad. *"Wail, man, wail!"* people would be shouting at the band; and it *would* be wailing, until first one and then another couple just ran out of strength and stumbled off toward the crowd, exhausted and soaked with sweat. Sometimes I would be down there standing inside the door jumping up and down in my gray jacket with the whiskbroom in the pocket, and the manager would have to come and shout at me that I had customers upstairs.

The first liquor I drank, my first cigarettes, even my first reefers, I can't specifically remember. But I know they were all mixed together with my first shooting craps, playing cards, and betting my dollar a day on the numbers, as I started hanging out at night with Shorty and his friends. Shorty's jokes about how country I had been made us all laugh. I still was country, I know now, but it all felt so great because I was accepted. All of us would be in somebody's place, usually one of the girls', and we'd be turning on, the reefers making everybody's head light, or the whisky aglow in our middles. Everybody understood that my head had to stay kinky a while longer, to grow long enough for Shorty to conk it for me. One of these nights, I remarked that I had saved about half enough to get a zoot.

"Save?" Shorty couldn't believe it. "Homeboy, you never heard of credit?" He told me he'd call a neighborhood clothing store the first thing in the morning, and that I should be there early.

A salesman, a young Jew, met me when I came in. "You're Shorty's friend?" I said I was; it amazed me—all of Shorty's contacts. The salesman wrote my name on a form, and the Roseland as where I worked, and Ella's address as where I lived. Shorty's name was put down as recommending me. The salesman said, "Shorty's one of our best customers."

I was measured, and the young salesman picked off a rack a zoot suit that was just wild: sky-blue pants thirty inches in the knee and angle-narrowed down to twelve inches at the bottom, and a long coat that pinched my waist and flared out below my knees.

As a gift, the salesman said, the store would give me a narrow leather belt with my initial "L" on it. Then he said I ought to also buy a hat, and I did—blue, with a feather in the four-inch brim. Then the store gave me another present: a long, thick-lined, gold-plated chain that swung down lower than my coat hem. I was sold forever on credit.

When I modeled the zoot for Ella, she took a long look and said, "Well, I guess it had to happen." I took three of those twenty-five-cent sepia-toned, while-you-wait pictures of myself, posed the way "hipsters" wearing their zoots would "cool it"—hat dangled, knees drawn close together, feet wide apart, both index fingers jabbed toward the floor. The long coat and swinging chain and the Punjab pants were much more dramatic if you stood that way. One picture, I autographed and airmailed to my brothers and sisters in Lansing, to let them see how well I was doing. I gave another one to Ella, and the third to Shorty, who was really moved: I could tell by the way he said, "Thanks, homeboy." It was part of our "hip" code not to show that kind of affection.

Shorty soon decided that my hair was finally long enough to be conked. He had promised to school me in how to beat the barbershops' three- and four-dollar price by making up congolene, and then conking ourselves.

I took the little list of ingredients he had printed out for me, and went to a grocery store, where I got a can of Red Devil lye, two eggs, and two medium-sized white potatoes. Then at a drugstore near the poolroom, I asked for a large jar of vaseline, a large bar of soap, a large-toothed comb and a fine-toothed comb, one of those rubber hoses with a metal spray-head, a rubber apron and a pair of gloves.

"Going to lay on that first conk?" the drugstore man asked me. I proudly told him, grinning, "Right!"

Shorty paid six dollars a week for a room in his cousin's shabby apartment. His cousin wasn't at home. "It's like the pad's mine, he spends so much time with his woman," Shorty said. "Now, you watch me—"

He peeled the potatoes and thin-sliced them into a quart-sized Mason fruit jar, then started stirring them with a wooden spoon as he gradually poured in a little over half the can of lye. "Never use a metal spoon; the lye will turn it black," he told me.

A jelly-like, starchy-looking glop resulted from the lye and potatoes, and Shorty broke in the two eggs, stirring real fast—his own conk and dark face bent down close. The congolene turned pale-yellowish. "Feel the jar," Shorty said. I cupped my hand against the outside, and snatched it away. "Damn right, it's hot, that's the lye," he said. "So you know it's going to burn when I comb it in—it burns *bad.* But the longer you can stand it, the straighter the hair."

He made me sit down, and he tied the string of the new rubber apron tightly around my neck, and combed up my bush of hair. Then, from the big vaseline jar, he took a handful and massaged it hard all through my hair and into the scalp. He also thickly vaselined my neck, ears and forehead. "When I get to washing out your head, be sure to tell me anywhere you feel any little stinging," Shorty warned me, washing his hands, then pulling on the rubber gloves, and tying on his own rubber apron. "You always got to remember that any congolene left in burns a sore into your head."

The congolene just felt warm when Shorty started combing it in. But then my head caught fire.

I gritted my teeth and tried to pull the sides of the kitchen table together. The comb felt as if it was raking my skin off.

My eyes watered, my nose was running. I couldn't stand it any longer; I bolted to the washbasin. I was cursing Shorty with every name I could think of when he got the spray going and started soap-lathering my head.

He lathered and spray-rinsed, lathered and spray-rinsed, maybe ten or twelve times, each time gradually closing the hot-water faucet, until the rinse was cold, and that helped some.

"You feel any stinging spots?"

"No," I managed to say. My knees were trembling.

"Sit back down, then. I think we got it all out okay."

The flame came back as Shorty, with a thick towel, started drying my head, rubbing hard. *"Easy, man, easy!"* I kept shouting.

"The first time's always worst. You get used to it better before long. You took it real good, homeboy. You got a good conk."

When Shorty let me stand up and see in the mirror, my hair hung down in limp, damp strings. My scalp still flamed, but not as badly; I could bear it. He draped the towel around my shoulders, over my rubber apron, and began again vaselining my hair.

I could feel him combing, straight back, first the big comb, then the fine-tooth one.

Then, he was using a razor, very delicately, on the back of my neck. Then, finally, shaping the sideburns.

My first view in the mirror blotted out the hurting. I'd seen some pretty conks, but when it's the first time, on your *own* head, the transformation, after the lifetime of kinks, is staggering.

The mirror reflected Shorty behind me. We both were grinning and sweating. And on top of my head was this thick, smooth sheen of shining red hair—real red—as straight as any white man's.

How ridiculous I was! Stupid enough to stand there simply lost in admiration of my hair now looking "white," reflected in the mirror in Shorty's room. I vowed that I'd never again be without a conk, and I never was for many years.

This was my first really big step toward self-degradation: when I endured all of that pain, literally burning my flesh to have it look like a white man's hair. I had joined that multitude of Negro men and women in America who are brainwashed into believing that the black people are "inferior"—and white people "superior"—that they will even violate and mutilate their God-created bodies to try to look "pretty" by white standards.

Look around today, in every small town and big city, from two-bit catfish and soda-pop joints into the "integrated" lobby of the Waldorf-Astoria, and you'll see conks on black men. And you'll see black women wearing these green and pink and purple and red and platinum-blonde wigs. They're all more ridiculous than a slapstick comedy. It makes you wonder if the Negro has completely lost his sense of identity, lost touch with himself.

You'll see the conk worn by many, many so-called "upper class" Negroes, and, as much as I hate to say it about them, on all too many Negro entertainers. One of the reasons that I've especially admired some of them, like Lionel Hampton and Sidney Poitier, among others, is that they have kept their natural hair and fought to the top. I admire any Negro man who has never had himself conked, or who has had the sense to get rid of it—as I finally did.

I don't know which kind of self-defacing conk is the greater shame—the one you'll see on the heads of the black so-called "middle class" and "upper class," who ought to know better, or the one you'll see on the heads of the poorest, most downtrodden, ignorant black men. I mean the legal-minimum-wage ghetto-dwelling kind of Negro, as I was when I got my first one. It's generally among these poor fools that you'll see a black kerchief over the man's head, like Aunt Jemima; he's trying to make his conk last longer, between trips to the barbershop. Only for special occasions is this kerchief-protected conk exposed—to show off how "sharp" and "hip" its owner is. The ironic thing is that I have never heard any woman, white or black, express any admiration for a conk. Of course, any white woman with a black man isn't thinking about his hair. But I don't see how on earth a black woman with any race pride could walk down the street with any black man wearing a conk—the emblem of his shame that he is black.

To my own shame, when I say all of this I'm talking first of all about myself—because you can't show me any Negro who ever conked more faithfully than I did. I'm speaking from personal experience when I say of any black man who conks today, or any white-wigged black woman, that if they gave the brains in their heads just half as much attention as they do their hair, they would be a thousand times better off.

FLANNERY O'CONNOR
The Artificial Nigger

Mr. Head awakened to discover that the room was full of moonlight. He sat up and stared at the floor boards—the color of silver—and then at the ticking on his pillow, which might have been brocade, and after a second, he saw half of the moon five feet away in his shaving mirror, paused as if it were waiting for his permission to enter. It rolled forward and cast a dignifying light on everything. The straight chair against the wall looked stiff and attentive as if it were awaiting an order and Mr. Head's trousers, hanging to the back of it, had an almost noble air, like the garment some great man had just flung to his servant; but the face on the moon was a grave one. It gazed across the room and out the window where it floated over the horse stall and appeared to contemplate itself with the look of a young man who sees his old age before him.

Mr. Head could have said to it that age was a choice blessing and that only with years does a man enter into that calm understanding of life that makes him a suitable guide for the young. This, at least, had been his own experience.

He sat up and grasped the iron posts at the foot of his bed and raised himself until he could see the face on the alarm clock which sat on an overturned bucket beside the chair. The hour was two in the morning. The alarm on the clock did not work but he was not dependent on any mechanical means to awaken him. Sixty years had not dulled his responses; his physical reactions, like his moral ones, were guided by his will and strong character, and these could be seen plainly in his features. He had a long tube-like face with a long rounded open jaw and a long depressed nose. His eyes were alert but quiet, and in the miraculous moonlight they had a look of composure and of ancient wisdom as if they belonged to one of the great guides of men. He might have been Vergil summoned in the middle of the night to go to Dante, or better, Raphael, awakened by a blast of God's light to fly to the side of Tobias. The only dark spot in the room was Nelson's pallet, underneath the shadow of the window.

Nelson was hunched over on his side, his knees under his chin and his heels under his bottom. His new suit and hat were in the boxes that they had been sent in and these were on the floor at the foot of the pallet where he could get his hands on them as soon as he woke up. The slop jar, out of the shadow and made snow-white in the moonlight, appeared to stand guard over him like a small personal angel. Mr. Head lay back down, feeling entirely confident that he could carry out the moral mission of the coming day. He meant to be up before Nelson and to have the breakfast cooking by the time he awakened. The boy was always irked when Mr. Head was the first up. They would have to leave the house at four to get to the railroad junction by five-thirty. The train was to stop for them at five forty-five and they had to be there on time for this train was stopping merely to accommodate them.

This would be the boy's first trip to the city though he claimed it would be his second because he had been born there. Mr. Head had tried to point out to him that when he was born he didn't have the intelligence to determine his whereabouts but this had made no impression on the child at all and he continued to insist that this was to be his second trip. It would be Mr. Head's third trip. Nelson had said, "I will've already been there twict and I ain't but ten."

Mr. Head had contradicted him.

"If you ain't been there in fifteen years, how you know you'll be able to find your way about?" Nelson had asked. "How you know it hasn't changed some?"

"Have you ever," Mr. Head had asked, "seen me lost?"

Nelson certainly had not but he was a child who was never satisfied until he had given an impudent answer and he replied, "It's nowhere around here to get lost at."

"The day is going to come," Mr. Head prophesied, "when you'll find you ain't as smart as you think you are." He had been thinking about this trip for several months but it was for the most part in moral terms that he conceived it. It was to be a lesson that the boy would never forget. He was to find out from it that he had no cause for pride merely because he had been born in a city. He was to find out that the city is not a great place. Mr. Head meant him to see everything there is to see in a city so that he would be content to stay at home for the rest of his life. He fell asleep thinking how the boy would at last find out that he was not as smart as he thought he was.

He was awakened at three-thirty by the smell of fatback frying and he leaped off his cot. The pallet was empty and the clothes boxes had been thrown open. He put on his trousers and ran into the other room. The boy had a corn pone on cooking and had fried the meat. He was sitting in the half-dark at the table, drinking cold coffee out of a can. He had on his new suit and his new gray hat pulled low over his eyes. It was too big for him but they had ordered it a size large because they expected his head to grow. He didn't say anything but his entire figure suggested satisfaction at having arisen before Mr. Head.

Mr. Head went to the stove and brought the meat to the table in the skillet. "It's no hurry," he said. "You'll get there soon enough and it's no guarantee you'll like it when you do neither," and he sat down across from the boy whose hat teetered back slowly to reveal a fiercely expressionless face, very much the same shape as the old man's. They were grandfather and grandson but they looked enough alike to be brothers and brothers not too far apart in age, for Mr. Head had a youthful expression by daylight, while the boy's look was ancient, as if he knew everything already and would be pleased to forget it.

Mr. Head had once had a wife and daughter and when the wife died, the daughter ran away and returned after an interval with Nelson. Then one morning, without getting out of bed, she died and left Mr. Head with sole care of the year-old child. He had made the mistake of telling Nelson that he had been born in Atlanta. If he hadn't told him that, Nelson couldn't have insisted that this was going to be his second trip.

"You may not like it a bit," Mr. Head continued. "It'll be full of niggers."

The boy made a face as if he could handle a nigger.

"All right," Mr. Head said. "You ain't ever seen a nigger."

"You wasn't up very early," Nelson said.

"You ain't ever seen a nigger," Mr. Head repeated. "There hasn't been a nigger in this county since we run that one out twelve years ago and that was before you were born." He looked at the boy as if he were daring him to say he had ever seen a Negro.

"How you know I never saw a nigger when I lived there before?" Nelson asked. "I probably saw a lot of niggers."

"If you seen one you didn't know what he was," Mr. Head said, completely exasperated. "A six-month-old child don't know a nigger from anybody else."

"I reckon I'll know a nigger if I see one," the boy said and got up and straightened his slick sharply creased gray hat and went outside to the privy.

They reached the junction some time before the train was due to arrive and stood about two feet from the first set of tracks. Mr. Head carried a paper sack with some biscuits and a can of sardines in it for their lunch. A coarse-looking orange-colored sun coming up behind the east range of mountains was making the sky a dull red behind them, but in front of them it was still gray and they faced a gray transparent moon, hardly stronger than a thumbprint and completely without light. A small tin switch box and a black fuel tank were all there was to mark the place as a junction; the tracks were double and did not converge again until they were hidden behind the bends at either end of the clearing. Trains passing appeared to emerge from a tunnel of trees and, hit for a second by the cold sky, vanish terrified into the woods again. Mr. Head had had to make special arrangements with the ticket agent to have this train stop and he was secretly afraid it would not, in which case, he knew Nelson would say, "I never thought no train was going to stop for you." Under the useless morning moon the tracks looked white and fragile. Both the old man and the child stared ahead as if they were awaiting an apparition.

Then suddenly, before Mr. Head could make up his mind to turn back, there was a deep warning bleat and the train appeared, gliding very slowly, almost silently around the bend of trees about two hundred yards down the track, with one yellow front light shining. Mr. Head was still not certain it would stop and he felt it would make an even bigger idiot of him if it went by slowly. Both he and Nelson, however, were prepared to ignore the train if it passed them.

The engine charged by, filling their noses with the smell of hot metal and then the second coach came to a stop exactly where they were standing. A conductor with the face of an ancient bloated bulldog was on the step as if he expected them, though he did not look as if it mattered one way or the other to him if they got on or not. "To the right," he said.

Their entry took only a fraction of a second and the train was already speeding on as they entered the quiet car. Most of the travelers were still sleeping, some with their heads hanging off the chair arms, some stretched across two seats, and some sprawled out with their feet in the aisle. Mr. Head saw two unoccupied seats and pushed Nelson toward them. "Get in there by the winder," he said in his normal voice which was very loud at this hour of the morning. "Nobody cares if you sit there because it's nobody in it. Sit right there."

"I heard you," the boy muttered. "It's no use in you yelling," and he sat down and turned his head to the glass. There he saw a pale ghost-like face scowling at him beneath the brim of a pale ghost-like hat. His grandfather, looking quickly too, saw a different ghost, pale but grinning, under a black hat.

Mr. Head sat down and settled himself and took out his ticket and started reading aloud everything that was printed on it. People began to stir. Several woke up and stared at him. "Take off your hat," he said to Nelson and took off his own and put it on his knee. He had a small amount of white hair that had turned tobacco-colored over the years and this lay flat across the back of his head. The front of his head was bald and creased. Nelson took off his hat and put it on his knee and they waited for the conductor to come ask for their tickets.

The man across the aisle from them was spread out over two seats, his feet propped on the window and his head jutting into the aisle. He had on a light blue suit and a yellow shirt unbuttoned at the neck. His eyes had just opened and Mr. Head was ready to introduce himself when the conductor came up from behind and growled, "Tickets."

When the conductor had gone, Mr. Head gave Nelson the return half of his ticket and said, "Now put that in your pocket and don't lose it or you'll have to stay in the city."

"Maybe I will," Nelson said as if this were a reasonable suggestion.

Mr. Head ignored him. "First time this boy has ever been on a train," he explained to the man across the aisle, who was sitting up now on the edge of his seat with both feet on the floor.

Nelson jerked his hat on again and turned angrily to the window.

"He's never seen anything before," Mr. Head continued. "Ignorant as the day he was born, but I mean for him to get his fill once and for all."

The boy leaned forward, across his grandfather and toward the stranger. "I was born in the city," he said. "I was born there. This is my second trip." He said it in a high positive voice but the man across the aisle didn't look as if he understood. There were heavy purple circles under his eyes.

Mr. Head reached across the aisle and tapped him on the arm. "The thing to do with a boy," he said sagely, "is to show him all it is to show. Don't hold nothing back."

"Yeah," the man said. He gazed down at his swollen feet and lifted the left one about ten inches from the floor. After a minute he put it down and lifted the other. All through the car people began to get up and move about and yawn and stretch. Separate voices could be heard here and there and then a general hum. Suddenly Mr. Head's serene expression changed. His mouth almost closed and a light, fierce and cautious both, came into his eyes. He was looking down the length of the car. Without turning, he caught Nelson by the arm and pulled him forward. "Look," he said.

A huge coffee-colored man was coming slowly forward. He had on a light suit and a yellow satin tie with a ruby pin in it. One of his hands rested on his stomach which rode majestically under his buttoned coat, and in the other he held the head of a black walking stick that he picked up and set down with a deliberate outward motion each time he took a step. He was proceeding very slowly, his large brown eyes gazing over the heads of the passengers. He had a small white mustache and white crinkly hair. Behind him there were two young women, both coffee-colored, one in a yellow dress and one in a green. Their progress was kept at the rate of his and they chatted in low throaty voices as they followed him.

Mr. Head's grip was tightening insistently on Nelson's arm. As the procession passed them, the light from a sapphire ring on the brown hand that picked up the cane reflected in Mr. Head's eye, but he did not look up nor did the tremendous man look at him. The group proceeded up the rest of the aisle and out of the car. Mr. Head's grip on Nelson's arm loosened. "What was that?" he asked.

"A man," the boy said and gave him an indignant look as if he were tired of having his intelligence insulted.

"What kind of a man?" Mr. Head persisted, his voice expressionless.

"A fat man," Nelson said. He was beginning to feel that he had better be cautious.

"You don't know what kind?" Mr. Head said in a final tone.

"An old man," the boy said and had a sudden foreboding that he was not going to enjoy the day.

"That was a nigger," Mr. Head said and sat back.

Nelson jumped up on the seat and stood looking backward to the end of the car but the Negro had gone.

"I'd of thought you'd know a nigger since you seen so many when you was in the city on your first visit," Mr. Head continued. "That's his first nigger," he said to the man across the aisle.

The boy slid down into the seat. "You said they were black," he said in an angry voice. "You never said they were tan. How do you expect me to know anything when you don't tell me right?"

"You're just ignorant is all," Mr. Head said and he got up and moved over in the vacant seat by the man across the aisle.

Nelson turned backward again and looked where the Negro had disappeared. He felt that the Negro had deliberately walked down the aisle in order to make a fool of him and he hated him with a fierce raw fresh hate; and also, he understood now why his grandfather disliked them. He looked toward the window and the face there seemed to suggest that he might be inadequate to the day's exactions. He wondered if he would even recognize the city when they came to it.

After he had told several stories, Mr. Head realized that the man he was talking to was asleep and he got up and suggested to Nelson that they walk over the train and see the parts of it. He particularly wanted the boy to see the toilet so they went first to the men's room and examined the plumbing. Mr. Head demonstrated the ice-water cooler as if he had invented it and showed Nelson the bowl with the single spigot where the travelers brushed their teeth. They went through several cars and came to the diner.

This was the most elegant car in the train. It was painted a rich egg-yellow and had a wine-colored carpet on the floor. There were wide windows over the tables and great spaces of the rolling view were caught in miniature in the sides of the coffee pots and in the glasses. Three very black Negroes in white suits and aprons were running up and down the aisle, swinging trays and bowing and bending over the travelers eating breakfast. One of them rushed up to Mr. Head and Nelson and said, holding up two fingers, "Space for two!" but Mr. Head replied in a loud voice, "We eaten before we left!"

The waiter wore large brown spectacles that increased the size of his eye whites. "Stan' aside then please," he said with an airy wave of the arm as if he were brushing aside flies.

Neither Nelson nor Mr. Head moved a fraction of an inch. "Look," Mr. Head said.

The near corner of the diner, containing two tables, was set off from the rest by a saffron-colored curtain. One table was set but empty but at the other, facing them, his back to the drape, sat the tremendous Negro. He was speaking in a soft voice to the two women while he buttered a muffin. He had a heavy sad face and his neck bulged over his white collar on either side. "They rope them off," Mr. Head explained. Then he said, "Let's go see the kitchen," and they walked the length of the diner but the black waiter was coming fast behind them.

"Passengers are not allowed in the kitchen!" he said in a haughty voice. "Passengers are NOT allowed in the kitchen!"

Mr. Head stopped where he was and turned. "And there's good reason for that," he shouted into the Negro's chest, "because the cockroaches would run the passengers out!"

All the travelers laughed and Mr. Head and Nelson walked out, grinning. Mr. Head was known at home for his quick wit and Nelson felt a sudden keen pride in him. He realized the old man would be his only support in the strange place they were approaching. He would be entirely alone in the world if he were ever lost from his grandfather. A terrible excitement shook him and he wanted to take hold of Mr. Head's coat and hold on like a child.

As they went back to their seats they could see through the passing windows that the countryside was becoming speckled with small houses and shacks and that a highway ran alongside the train. Cars sped by on it, very small and fast. Nelson felt that there was less breath in the air than there had been thirty minutes ago. The man across the aisle had left and there was no one near for Mr. Head to hold a conversation with so he looked out the window, through his own reflection, and read aloud the names of the buildings they were passing. "The Dixie Chemical Corp!" he announced. "Southern Maid Flour! Dixie Doors! Southern Belle Cotton Products! Patty's Peanut Butter! Southern Mammy Cane Syrup!"

"Hush up!" Nelson hissed.

All over the car people were beginning to get up and take their luggage off the overhead racks. Women were putting on their coats and hats. The conductor stuck his head in the car and snarled, "Firstopppppmry," and Nelson lunged out of his sitting position, trembling. Mr. Head pushed him down by the shoulder.

"Keep your seat," he said in dignified tones. "The first stop is on the edge of town. The second stop is at the main railroad station." He had come by this knowledge on his first trip when he had got off at the first stop and had had to pay a man fifteen cents to take him into the heart of town. Nelson sat back down, very pale. For the first time in his life, he understood that his grandfather was indispensable to him.

The train stopped and let off a few passengers and glided on as if it had never ceased moving. Outside, behind rows of brown rickety houses, a line of blue buildings stood up, and beyond them a pale rose-gray sky faded away to nothing. The train moved into the railroad yard. Looking down, Nelson saw lines and lines of silver tracks multiplying and criss-crossing. Then before he could start counting them, the face in the window started out at him, gray but distinct, and he looked the other way. The train was in the station. Both he and Mr. Head jumped up and ran to the door. Neither noticed that they had left the paper sack with the lunch in it on the seat.

They walked stiffly through the small station and came out of a heavy door into the squall of traffic. Crowds were hurrying to work. Nelson didn't know where to look. Mr. Head leaned against the side of the building and glared in front of him.

Finally Nelson said, "Well, how do you see what all it is to see?"

Mr. Head didn't answer. Then as if the sight of people passing had given him the clue, he said, "You walk," and started off down the street. Nelson followed, steadying his hat. So many sights and sounds were flooding in on him that for the first block he hardly knew what he was seeing. At the second corner, Mr. Head turned and looked behind him at the station they had left, a putty-colored terminal with a concrete dome on top. He thought that if he could keep the dome always in sight, he would be able to get back in the afternoon to catch the train again.

As they walked along, Nelson began to distinguish details and take note of the store windows, jammed with every kind of equipment— hardware, drygoods, chicken feed, liquor. They passed one that Mr. Head called his particular attention to where you walked in and sat on a chair with your feet upon two rests and let a Negro polish your shoes. They walked slowly and stopped and stood at the entrances so he could see what went on in each place but they did not go into any of them. Mr. Head was determined not to go into any city store because on his first trip here, he had got lost in a large one and had found his way out only after many people had insulted him.

They came in the middle of the next block to a store that had a weigh-ing machine in front of it and they both in turn stepped up on it and put in a penny and received a ticket. Mr. Head's ticket said, "You weigh 120 pounds. You are upright and brave and all your friends admire you." He put the ticket in his pocket, surprised that the machine should have got his character correct but his weight wrong, for he had weighed on a grain scale not long before and knew he weighed 110. Nelson's ticket said, "You weigh 98 pounds. You have a great destiny ahead of you but beware of dark women." Nelson did not know any women and he weighed only 68 pounds but Mr. Head pointed out that the machine had probably printed the number upside down, meaning the 9 for a 6.

They walked on and at the end of five blocks the dome of the terminal sank out of sight and Mr. Head turned to the left. Nelson could have stood in front of every store window for an hour if there had not been another more interesting one next to it. Suddenly he said, "I was born here!" Mr. Head turned and looked at him with horror. There was a sweaty brightness about his face. "This is where I come from!" he said.

Mr. Head was appalled. He saw the moment had come for drastic action. "Lemme show you one thing you ain't seen yet," he said and took him to the corner where there was a sewer entrance. "Squat down," he said, "and stick you head in there," and he held the back of the boy's coat while he got down and put his head in the sewer. He drew it back quickly, hearing a gurgling in the depths under the sidewalk. Then Mr. Head explained the sewer system, how the entire city was underlined with it, how it contained all the drainage and was full of rats and how a man could slide into it and be sucked along down endless pitchblack tunnels. At any minute any man in the city might be sucked into the sewer and never heard from again. He described it so well that Nelson was for some seconds shaken. He connected the sewer passages with the entrance to hell and understood for the first time how the world was put together in its lower parts. He drew away from the curb.

Then he said, "Yes, but you can stay away from the holes," and his face took on that stubborn look that was so exasperating to his grandfather. "This is where I come from!" he said.

Mr. Head was dismayed but he only muttered, "You'll get your fill," and they walked on. At the end of two more blocks he turned to the left, feeling that he was circling the dome; and he was correct for in a half-hour they passed in front of the railroad station again. At first Nelson did not notice that he was seeing the same stores twice but when they passed the one where you put your feet on the rests while the Negro polished your shoes, he perceived that they were walking in a circle.

"We done been here!" he shouted. "I don't believe you know where you're at!"

"The direction just slipped my mind for a minute," Mr. Head said and they turned down a different street. He still did not intend to let the dome get too far away and after two blocks in their new direction, he turned to the left. This street contained two and three-story wooden dwellings. Anyone passing on the sidewalk could see into the rooms and Mr. Head, glancing through one window, saw a woman lying on an iron bed, looking out, with a sheet pulled over her. Her knowing expression shook him. A fierce-looking boy on a bicycle came driving down out of nowhere and he had to jump to the side to keep from being hit. "It's nothing to them if they knock you down," he said. "You better keep closer to me."

They walked on for some time on streets like this before he remembered to turn again. The houses they were passing now were all unpainted and the wood in them looked rotten; the street between was narrower. Nelson saw a colored man. Then another. Then another. "Niggers live in these houses," he observed.

"Well come on and we'll go somewheres else," Mr. Head said. "We didn't come to look at niggers," and they turned down another street but they continued to see Negroes everywhere. Nelson's skin began to prickle and they stepped along at a faster pace in order to leave the neighborhood as soon as possible. There were colored men in their undershirts standing in the doors and colored women rocking on the sagging porches. Colored children played in the gutters and stopped what they were doing to look at them. Before long they began to pass rows of stores with colored customers in them but they didn't pause at the entrances of these. Black eyes in black faces were watching them from every direction. "Yes," Mr. Head said, "this is where you were born—right here with all these niggers."

Nelson scowled. "I think you done got us lost," he said.

Mr. Head swung around sharply and looked for the dome. It was nowhere in sight. "I ain't got us lost either," he said. "You're just tired of walking."

"I ain't tired, I'm hungry," Nelson said. "Give me a biscuit."

They discovered then that they had lost the lunch.

"You were the one holding the sack," Nelson said. "I would have kepaholt of it."

"If you want to direct this trip, I'll go on by myself and leave you right here," Mr. Head said and was pleased to see the boy turn white. However, he realized they were lost and drifting farther every minute from the station. He was hungry himself and beginning to be thirsty and since they had been in the colored neighborhood, they had both begun to sweat. Nelson had on his shoes and he was unaccustomed to them. The concrete sidewalks were very hard. They both wanted to find a place to sit down but this was impossible and they kept on walking, the boy muttering under his breath, "First you lost the sack and then you lost the way," and Mr. Head growling from time to time, "Anybody wants to be from this nigger heaven can be from it!"

By now the sun was well forward in the sky. The odor of dinners cooking drifted out to them. The Negroes were all at their doors to see them pass. "Whyn't you ast one of these niggers the way?" Nelson said. "You got us lost."

"This is where you were born," Mr. Head said. "You can ast one yourself if you want to."

Nelson was afraid of the colored men and he didn't want to be laughed at by the colored children. Up ahead he saw a large colored woman lean-ing in a doorway that opened onto the sidewalk. Her hair stood straight out from her head for about four inches all around and she was resting on bare brown feet that turned pink at the sides. She had on a pink dress that showed her exact shape. As they came abreast of her, she lazily lifted one hand to her head and her fingers disappeared into her hair.

Nelson stopped. He felt his breath drawn up by the woman's dark eyes. "How do you get back to town?" he said in a voice that did not sound like his own.

After a minute she said, "You in town now," in a rich low tone that made Nelson feel as if a cool spray had been turned on him.

"How do you get back to the train?" he said in the same reed-like voice.

"You can catch you a car," she said.

He understood she was making fun of him but he was too paralyzed even to scowl. He stood drinking in every detail of her. His eyes traveled up from her great knees to her forehead and then made a triangular path from the glistening sweat on her neck down and across her tremendous bosom and over her bare arm back to where her fingers lay hidden in her hair. He suddenly wanted her to reach down and pick him up and draw him against her and then he wanted to feel her breath on his face. He wanted to look down and down into her eyes while she held him tighter and tighter. He had never had such a feeling before. He felt as if he were reeling down through a pitchblack tunnel.

"You can go a block down yonder and catch you a car take you to the railroad station, Sugarpie," she said.

Nelson would have collapsed at her feet if Mr. Head had not pulled him roughly away. "You act like you don't have any sense!" the old man growled.

They hurried down the street and Nelson did not look back at the woman. He pushed his hat sharply forward over his face which was al-ready burning with shame. The sneering ghost he had seen in the train window and all the foreboding feelings he had on the way returned to him and he remembered that his ticket from the scale had said to beware of dark women and that his grandfather's had said he was upright and brave. He took hold of the old man's hand, a sign of dependence that he seldom showed.

They headed down the street toward the car tracks where a long yel-low rattling trolley was coming. Mr. Head had never boarded a streetcar and he let that one pass. Nelson was silent. From time to time his mouth trembled slightly but his grandfather, occupied with his own problems, paid him no attention. They stood on the corner and neither looked at the Negroes who were passing, going about their business just as if they had been white, except that most of them stopped and eyed Mr. Head and

Nelson. It occurred to Mr. Head that since the streetcar ran on tracks, they could simply follow the tracks. He gave Nelson a slight push and explained that they would follow the tracks on into the railroad station, walking, and they set off.

Presently to their great relief they began to see white people again and Nelson sat down on the sidewalk against the wall of a building. "I got to rest myself some," he said. "You lost the sack and the direction. You can just wait on me to rest myself."

"There's the tracks in front of us," Mr. Head said. "All we got to do is keep them in sight and you could have remembered the sack as good as me. This is where you were born. This is your old home town. This is your second trip. You ought to know how to do," and he squatted down and continued in this vein but the boy, easing his burning feet out of his shoes, did not answer.

"And standing their grinning like a chim-pan-zee while a nigger woman gives you direction. Great Gawd!" Mr. Head said.

"I never said I was nothing but born here," the boy said in a shaky voice. "I never said I would or wouldn't like it. I never said I wanted to come. I only said I was born here and I never had nothing to do with that. I want to go home. I never wanted to come in the first place. It was all your big idea. How you know you ain't following the tracks in the wrong direction?"

This last had occurred to Mr. Head too. "All these people are white," he said.

"We ain't passed here before," Nelson said. This was a neighborhood of brick buildings that might have been lived in or might not. A few empty automobiles were parked along the curb and there was an occasional passerby. The heat of the pavement came up through Nelson's thin suit. His eyelids began to droop, and after a few minutes his head tilted forward. His shoulders twitched once or twice and then he fell over on his side and lay sprawled in an exhausted fit of sleep.

Mr. Head watched him silently. He was very tired himself but they could not both sleep at the same time and he could not have slept anyway because he did not know where he was. In a few minutes Nelson would wake up, refreshed by his sleep and very cocky, and would begin complaining that he had lost the sack and the way. You'd have a mighty sorry time if I wasn't here, Mr. Head thought; and then another idea occurred to him. He looked at the sprawled figure for several minutes; presently he stood up. He justified what he was going to do on the grounds that it is sometimes necessary to teach a child a lesson he won't forget, particularly when the child is always reasserting his position with some new impudence. He walked without a sound to the corner about twenty feet away and sat down on a covered garbage can in the alley where he could look out and watch Nelson wake up alone.

The boy was dozing fitfully, half conscious of vague noises and black forms moving up from some dark part of him into the light. His face worked in his sleep and he had pulled his knees up under his chin. The sun shed a dull dry light on the narrow street; everything looked like exactly what it was. After a while Mr. Head, hunched like an old monkey on the garbage can lid, decided that if Nelson didn't wake up soon, he would make a loud noise by bamming his foot against the can. He looked at his watch and discovered that it was two o'clock. Their train left at six and the possibility of missing it was too awful for him to think of. He kicked his foot backwards on the can and a hollow boom reverberated in the alley.

Nelson shot up onto his feet with a shout. He looked where his grandfather should have been and stared. He seemed to whirl several times and then, picking up his feet and throwing his head back, he dashed down the street like a wild maddened pony. Mr. Head jumped off the can and galloped after but the child was almost out of sight. He saw a streak of gray disappearing diagonally a block ahead. He ran as fast as he could, looking both ways down every intersection, but without sight of him again. Then as he passed the third intersection, completely winded, he saw about half a block down the street a scene that stopped him altogether. He crouched behind a trash box to watch and get his bearings.

Nelson was sitting with both legs spread out and by his side lay an elderly woman, screaming. Groceries were scattered about the sidewalk. A crowd of women had already gathered to see justice done and Mr. Head distinctly heard the old woman on the pavement shout, "You've broken my ankle and your daddy'll pay for it! Every nickel! Police! Police!" Several of the women were plucking at Nelson's shoulder but the boy seemed too dazed to get up.

Something forced Mr. Head from behind the trash box and forward, but only at a creeping pace. He had never in his life been accosted by a policeman. The women were milling around Nelson as if they might suddenly all dive on him at once and tear him to pieces, and the old woman continued to scream that her ankle was broken and to call for an officer. Mr. Head came on so slowly that he could have been taking a backward step after each forward one, but when he was about ten feet away, Nelson saw him and sprang. The child caught him around the hips and clung panting against him.

The women all turned on Mr. Head. The injured one sat up and shouted, "You sir! You'll pay every penny of my doctor's bill that your boy has caused. He's a juve-nile delinquent! Where is an officer? Somebody take this man's name and address!"

Mr. Head was trying to detach Nelson's fingers from the flesh in the back of his legs. The old man's head had lowered itself into his collar like a turtle's; his eyes were glazed with fear and caution.

"Your boy has broken my ankle!" the old woman shouted. "Police!"

Mr. Head sensed the approach of the policeman from behind. He stared straight ahead at the women who were massed in their fury like a solid wall to block his escape. "This is not my boy," he said. "I never seen him before."

He felt Nelson's fingers fall out of his flesh.

The women dropped back, staring at him with horror, as if they were so repulsed by a man who would deny his own image and likeness that they could not bear to lay hands on him. Mr. Head walked on, through a space they silently cleared, and left Nelson behind. Ahead of him he saw nothing but a hollow tunnel that had once been the street.

The boy remained standing where he was, his neck craned forward and his hands hanging by his sides. His hat was jammed on his head so that there were no longer any creases in it. The injured woman got up and shook her fist at him and the others gave him pitying looks, but he didn't notice any of them. There was no policeman in sight.

In a minute he began to move mechanically, making no effort to catch up with his grandfather but merely following at about twenty paces. They walked on for five blocks in this way. Mr. Head's shoulders were sagging and his neck hung forward at such an angle that it was not visible from behind. He was afraid to turn his head. Finally he cut a short hopeful glance over his shoulder. Twenty feet behind him, he saw two small eyes piercing into his back like pitchfork prongs.

The boy was not of a forgiving nature but this was the first time he had ever had anything to forgive. Mr. Head had never disgraced himself before. After two more blocks, he turned and called over his shoulder in a high desperately gay voice, "Let's us go get us a Co' Cola somewheres!"

Nelson, with a dignity he had never shown before, turned and stood with his back to his grandfather.

Mr. Head began to feel the depth of his denial. His face as they walked on became all hollows and bare ridges. He saw nothing they were passing but he perceived that they had lost the car tracks. There was no dome to be seen anywhere and the afternoon was advancing. He knew that if dark overtook them in the city, they would be beaten and robbed. The speed of God's justice was only what he expected for himself, but he could not stand to think that his sins would be visited upon Nelson and that even now, he was leading the boy to his doom.

They continued to walk on block after block through an endless section of small brick houses until Mr. Head almost fell over a water spigot sticking up about six inches off the edge of a grass plot. He had not had a drink of water since early morning but he felt he did not deserve it now. Then he thought that Nelson would be thirsty and they would both drink and be brought together. He squatted down and put his mouth to the nozzle and turned a cold stream of water into his throat. Then he called out in the high desperate voice, "Come on and getcher some water!"

This time the child stared through him for nearly sixty seconds. Mr.

Head got up and walked on as if he had drunk poison. Nelson, though he had not had water since some he had drunk out of a paper cup on the train, passed by the spigot, disdaining to drink where his grandfather had. When Mr. Head realized this, he lost all hope. His face in the waning afternoon light looked ravaged and abandoned. He could feel the boy's steady hate, traveling at an even pace behind him and he knew that (if by some miracle they escaped being murdered in the city) it would continue just that way for the rest of his life. He knew that now he was wandering into a black strange place where nothing was like it had ever been before, a long old age without respect and an end that would be welcome because it would be the end.

As for Nelson, his mind had frozen around his grandfather's treachery as if he were trying to preserve it intact to present at the final judgment. He walked without looking to one side or the other, but every now and then his mouth would twitch and this was when he felt, from some remote place inside himself, a black mysterious form reach up as if it would melt his frozen vision in one hot grasp.

The sun dropped down behind a row of houses and hardly noticing, they passed into an elegant suburban section where mansions were set back from the road by lawns with birdbaths on them. Here everything was entirely deserted. For blocks they didn't pass even a dog. The big white houses were like partially submerged icebergs in the distance. There were no sidewalks, only drives, and these wound around and around in endless ridiculous circles. Nelson made no move to come nearer to Mr. Head. The old man felt that if he saw a sewer entrance he would drop down into it and let himself be carried away; and he could imagine the boy standing by, watching with only a slight interest, while he disappeared.

A loud bark jarred him to attention and he looked up to see a fat man approaching with two bulldogs. He waved both arms like someone shipwrecked on a desert island. "I'm lost!" he called. "I'm lost and can't find my way and me and this boy have got to catch this train and I can't find the station. Oh Gawd I'm lost! Oh hep me Gawd I'm lost!"

The man, who was bald-headed and had on golf knickers, asked him what train he was trying to catch and Mr. Head began to get out his tickets, trembling so violently he could hardly hold them. Nelson had come up to within fifteen feet and stood watching.

"Well," the fat man said, giving him back the tickets, "you won't have time to get back to town to make this but you can catch it at the suburb stop. That's three blocks from here," and he began explaining how to get there.

Mr. Head stared as if he were slowly returning from the dead and when the man had finished and gone off with the dogs jumping at his heels, he turned to Nelson and said breathlessly, "We're going to get home!"

The child was standing about ten feet away, his face bloodless under the gray hat. His eyes were triumphantly cold. There was no light in them, no feeling, no interest. He was merely there, a small figure, waiting. Home was nothing to him.

Mr. Head turned slowly. He felt he knew now what time would be like without seasons and what heat would be like without light and what man would be like without salvation. He didn't care if he never made the train and if it had not been for what suddenly caught his attention, like a cry out of the gathering dusk, he might have forgotten there was a station to go to.

He had not walked five hundred yards down the road when he saw, within reach of him, the plaster figure of a Negro sitting bent over on a low yellow brick fence that curved around a wide lawn. The Negro was about Nelson's size and he was pitched forward at an unsteady angle because the putty that held him to the wall had cracked. One of his eyes was entirely white and he held a piece of brown watermelon.

Mr. Head stood looking at him silently until Nelson stopped at a little distance. Then as the two of them stood there, Mr. Head breathed, "An artificial nigger!"

It was not possible to tell if the artificial Negro were meant to be young or old; he looked too miserable to be either. He was meant to look happy because his mouth was stretched up at the corners but the chipped eye and the angle he was cocked at gave him a wild look of misery instead.

"An artificial nigger!" Nelson repeated in Mr. Head's exact tone.

The two of them stood there with their necks forward at almost the same angle and their shoulders curved in almost exactly the same way and their hands trembling identically in their pockets. Mr. Head looked like an ancient child and Nelson like a miniature old man. They stood gazing at the artificial Negro as if they were faced with some great mystery, some monument to another's victory that brought them together in their common defeat. They could both feel it dissolving their differences like an action of mercy. Mr. Head had never known before what mercy felt like because he had been too good to deserve any, but he felt he knew now. He looked at Nelson and understood that he must say something to the child to show that he was still wise and in the look the boy returned he saw a hungry need for that assurance. Nelson's eyes seemed to implore him to explain once and for all the mystery of existence.

Mr. Head opened his lips to make a lofty statement and heard himself say, "They ain't got enough real ones here. They got to have an artificial one."

After a second, the boy nodded with a strange shivering about his mouth, and said, "Let's go home before we get ourselves lost again."

Their train glided into the suburb stop just as they reached the station and they boarded it together, and ten minutes before it was due to arrive at the junction, they went to the door and stood ready to jump off if it did not stop; but it did, just as the moon, restored to its full splendor, sprang from a cloud and flooded the clearing with light. As they stepped off, the sage grass was shivering gently in shades of silver and the clinkers under their feet glittered with a fresh black light. The treetops, fencing the junction like the protecting walls of a garden, were darker than the sky which was hung with gigantic white clouds illuminated like lanterns.

Mr. Head stood very still and felt the action of mercy touch him again but this time he knew that there were no words in the world that could name it. He understood that it grew out of agony, which is not denied to any man and which is given in strange ways to children. He understood it was all a man could carry into death to give his Maker and he suddenly burned with shame that he had so little of it to take with him. He stood appalled, judging himself with the thoroughness of God, while the action of mercy covered his pride like a flame and consumed it. He had never thought himself a great sinner before but he saw now that his true depravity had been hidden from him lest it cause him despair. He realized that he was forgiven for sins from the beginning of time, when he had conceived in his own heart the sin of Adam, until the present, when he had denied poor Nelson. He saw that no sin was too monstrous for him to claim as his own, and since God loved in proportion as He forgave, he felt ready at that instant to enter Paradise.

Nelson, composing his expression under the shadow of his hat brim, watched him with a mixture of fatigue and suspicion, but as the train glided past them and disappeared like a frightened serpent into the woods, even his face lightened and he muttered, "I'm glad I've went once, but I'll never go back again!"

ALAN DUGAN
Morning Song

Look, it's morning, and a little water gurgles in the tap.
I wake up waiting, because it's Sunday, and turn twice more
than usual in bed, before I rise to cereal and comic strips.
I have risen to the morning danger and feel proud,
and after shaving off the night's disguises, after searching
close to the bone for blood, and finding only a little,
I shall walk out bravely into the daily accident.

KENNETH GANGEMI
Morning Walk

1

Walking through the morning city

The coffee city

City of popping toasters
City of pretty girls

Whitecollar alarmclocks

New people at every corner
Muscled men and curvy girls

City of lost children

Monday-morning clerks
Full of false hopes

Trucks of cold milk
Trucks of warm bread

Strawberries for the skyscrapers

Black cadillacs and secret taxis
Rising men and sinking men

2

Walking through the morning city
Particle in a puff of smoke

Imagination at the flash point
Ideas bulging in my mind

A set of receptors

The center of the city
Spinning on my neck

All that fine machinery

Reflection in city windows
Shadow on city sidewalks

Student of the city

The fine art of walking
The whirlpool of ideas

The classroom city

ROBERT LOWELL
July in Washington

The stiff spokes of this wheel
touch the sore spots of the earth.

On the Potomac, swan-white
power launches keep breasting the sulphurous wave.

Otters slide and dive and slick back their hair,
raccoons clean their meat in the creek.

On the circles, green statues ride like South American
liberators above the breeding vegetation—

prongs and spearheads of some equatorial
backland that will inherit the globe.

The elect, the elected . . . they come here bright as dimes,
and die dishevelled and soft.

We cannot name their names, or number their dates—
circle on circle, like rings on a tree—

but we wish the river had another shore,
some further range of delectable mountains,

distant hills powdered blue as a girl's eyelid.
It seems the least little shove would land us there,

that only the slightest repugnance of our bodies
we no longer control could drag us back.

LE ROI JONES
One Night Stand

We entered the city at noon! High bells. The radio on.
Some kind of Prokovieff; snaring the violent remains of the day
in sharp webs of dissonance.

We roared through the old gates. Iron doors hanging
all grey, with bricks mossed over and gone into chips
dogs walked through.

The river also roared. And what sun we had
disappeared into the water, or buried itself
in the badly pitched tents of the wounded soldiers.

There, also, at the river, blue steel hats glinted
on the sparse grass, and brown showed through
where the grass was trampled.

We came in, with our incredulousness, from the south.
On steely highways from the marble entrails of noon.
We had olives, and the green buds locked on our lutes.

Twisted albion-horns, rusted in warm rain, peasant carts,
loud black bond-servants dazed and out of their wool heads,
Wild shrubs impecuniously sheltered along the concrete,

Rumble of the wheels over cobblestones, The green knocked out.
The old houses dusty seeming & old men watching us slyly
as we come in: all of us laughing too loud.

We *are* foreign seeming persons. Hats flopped so the sun
can't scald our beards; odd shoes, bags of books & chicken.
We have come a long way, & are uncertain which of the masks

is cool.

JOSEPHINE MILES
Moonrise in City Park

Here you have sky high one wall
And one at its shoulder to the sixth floor,
Here you have the two story house with the colonial door;
And says the sign, Beauty Culture,
Beauty Culture, says the sign.

Here you have the stack of dentist offices,
Here shoulder high the Philharmonic wall:
The nice culture of the mouth and music. Over all
The sign glows beauty,
Beauty, glows the sign.

Here rises from the blank and black the moon,
The blond beauty at the colonial door,
The bright blond face ascending from the sixth floor,
With the sign suggesting culture,
Culture, suggesting the sign.

From this park bench look up and say divine,
To the dark levels speak and say divine,
To the moon whisper also and say divine,
And the sign will join you, saying Beauty
Culture, saying the sign.

J. B. JACKSON
The Stranger's Path

As one who is by way of being a professional tourist with a certain painfully acquired knowledge of how to appraise strange cities, I often find
myself brought up short by citizens remarking that I can't really hope to
know a town until I have seen the inside of one of its homes. I usually
agree expecting that there will then ensue an invitation to their house
and a chance to admire one of these shrines of local culture, these epito-
mes of whatever it is the town or city has to offer. All that follows is an
urgent suggestion that I investigate on my own the residential quarter before I presume to form a final opinion. "Ours is a city of homes," they
add; "The downtown section is like that anywhere else but our Country
Club Heights" (or Snob Hill or West End or European Section or Villa
Quarter, depending on where I am) "is considered unique."

   I have accordingly set out to explore that part of the city and many are
the hours I have spent wandering through carefully labyrinthine suburbs,
seeking to discover the *essential* city, as distinguished from that of the
tourist or transient. In retrospect these districts all seem indistinguishable: tree- and garden-lined avenues and lanes, curving about a
landscape of hills with pretty views over other hills; the traffic becomes
sparser, the houses retreat further behind tall trees and expensive flowers; every prospect is green, most prosperous and beautiful. The latest
model cars wait on the carefully raked driveway or at the immaculate
curb, and there comes the sound of tennis being played. When evening
falls, the softest, most domestic lights shine from upstairs windows; the
only reminder of the nearby city is that dusty pink glow in the sky which
in any case the trees all but conceal.

   Yet why have I always been glad to leave? Was it a painful realization
that I was excluded from these rows and rows of (presumably) happy and
comfortable homes that has always ended by making me beat a retreat to
the city proper? Or was it a conviction that I had actually seen this, experienced it, relished it after a fashion countless times and could no longer
derive the slightest spark of inspiration from it? Ascribe it if you like to a

kind of sour grapes, but in the course of years of travel I have come to believe that the home, the domestic establishment, far from being a unique symbol of the local way of life, is essentially the same wherever you go. The lovely higher income residential zone of Spokane is, I suspect, hardly to be distinguished (except for a few interesting but not very significant architectural variations) from the corresponding zone of Oslo or Naples or Rio de Janeiro. Granted the sanctity of the home, its social, cultural, biological importance, is it necessarily the truest index of a society? Offhand I would say the stranger could derive just as revealing an insight into a foreign way of life by listening to a country sermon or reading the classified ads in a popular newspaper or watching the behavior of a crowd during a street altercation—or for that matter by deciphering the graffiti on public walls.

At all events the home is not everything. The residential quarter, despite its undeniable charms, is not the entire city, and if we poor lonely travelers are ignorant of the joys of existence on Monte Vista Terrace and Queen Alexandra Lane we are on the other hand apt to know much more about some other aspects of the city than the life-long resident does. I am thinking in particular of that part of the city devoted to the outsider, the transient, devoted to receiving him and satisfying his immediate needs. I am possibly prone to overemphasize this function of the city, for it is naturally the one I see most of; but who is it, I'd like to know, who keeps the city going, who makes it important to the outside world: the permanent resident with his predictable tastes and habits, or the stranger who brings money and business and new ideas? Both groups, of course, are vital to the community; their efforts are complementary; but there is a peculiar tendency among us to think of the city as a self-contained and even a sort of defensive unit, forever struggling to keep its individuality intact. "Town" in English comes from a Teutonic word meaning hedge or enclosure; strange that this concept, obsolete a thousand years and more, should somehow have managed to stow away and cross the Atlantic, so that even in America we are reluctant to think of our cities as places where strangers come; with us the resident is always given preference. I gather it was quite the opposite in Ancient Egypt; there the suffix corresponding to "town" or "ton" meant "The place one arrives at"—a notion I much prefer.

Anyhow, regardless of our hesitation to think of our cities as "places one arrives at" in pursuit of business or pleasure or new ideas, that is actually what most of them are. Every sizeable community exists partly to satisfy the outsider who visits it. Not only that; there always evolves a special part of town devoted to this purpose. What name to give this zone of transients is something of a problem, for unlike the other subdivisions of the city this one, I think, must be thought of in terms of movement along a pretty well defined axis. For the stranger progresses up a reasonably predictable route from his point of arrival to his final destination— and then, of course, he is likely to retrace his steps. Call it a path, in the sense that it is a way not deliberately constructed or planned for that purpose. Actually the Strangers' Path is, in most cities, easily recognizable, once a few of its landmarks are known, and particularly (so I have found) in American cities of between say twenty and fifty thousand. Larger cities naturally possess a Strangers' Path of their own, but often it is so extensive and complex that it is exceedingly hard to define. As for towns of less than twenty thousand the Path here is rarely fully developed, so that it is equally difficult to trace. Thus the Path I am most familiar with is the one in the smaller American city.

Where it begins is easy enough to establish, for it is the place where the stranger first disembarks. You may object that this can be almost anywhere, but the average stranger still arrives by bus or train or truck, and even if he arrives in his own car he is likely to try and park somewhere outside the more congested downtown area. Arrival therefore signifies a change in the means of transportation: from train or truck or bus or car to something else, and this transfer is likely to take place either at the station or the bus depot. Near these establishments (and for a variety of obvious reasons) you will also find the truck centers, the larger parking lots, and even a taxi stand or two.

So the beginning of the Path is marked by the abandoned means of transportation and the area near the railroad tracks. We are welcomed to the city by a smiling landscape of parking lots, warehouses, pot-holed and weed-grown streets where isolated filling stations and quick-lunch counters are scattered among cinders like survivals of a bombing raid. But where does the Path lead from here? Directly to the center of town? To the hotels or the civic center or the main street? Not necessarily, and I believe we can only begin to follow the strangers' progress into the city when we have found out who these strangers are and what they are after. There are cities, to be sure, where most transients are well-heeled tourists and pleasure seekers; Las Vegas, Nevada, is one, and Monte Carlo is another; so are countless other resort towns all over the globe. The Path in such places usually leads directly to a hotel. But stranger does not always mean tourist, and by and large the strangers who come to town for a day or two belong to a more modest class: not very prosperous, often with no money at all. They are men looking for a job or on their way to a job; men come to buy or sell one item in their line of business, men on a brief holiday. In terms of cash outlay in the local stores no very brilliant public; in terms of labor and potential skills, in terms of experience of other ways of doing things, of other ways of thinking, a very valuable influx indeed. Besides, is it not one of the chief functions of the city to exchange as well as to receive? Furthermore, the greater part of these strangers would seem to be unattached men from some smaller town or from the country. These characteristics are worth bearing in mind, for they make the Path in the average small city what it now is: loud, tawdry, down-at-the-heel, full of dives and small catch-penny businesses, and (in the eyes of the uptown residential white-collar element) more than a little shady and dangerous.

Some urban geographer will be able to explain why the Strangers' Path becomes more respectable the further it gets from its point of origin; why the flophouses and brothels and the poorest among the second-hand shops (now euphemistically called loan establishments—the three golden balls are a thing of the past) the dirtiest and steamiest of Greasy Spoons tend to cluster around those first raffish streets near the depot and bus and truck terminals, and why the city's finest hotel, its most luxurious night club, its largest restaurant with a French name and illustrated menus are all at the other end. But so it is; one terminus of the Path is Skid Row, the other is the local Great White Way, and remote though they seem from each other they are still organically and geographically linked. The moral is clear: the Path caters to every pocketbook, every taste, and what gives it its unifying quality and sets it off from the rest of the city is its eagerness to satisfy the unattached man from out of town, here either for a brief bout of pleasure or on some business errand.

Still, it would be foolish to maintain that the Path is everywhere identical; somewhere between its extremes, one of squalor, the other of opulence, it achieves its most characteristic and vigorous aspect, and it is in this middle region of the Path that the town seems to display all that it has to offer the outsider, though in a crude form. The City as Place of Exchange: such a definition in the residential section, even in the section devoted to public institutions, would seem incongruous, but here you learn its validity. Nearby on a converging street or in a square you find the local produce market. It is not so handsome and prosperous as it once was, for except in the more varied farming regions of the United States it has dwindled to a weekly display of potted plants and fryers and a few seasonal vegetables; Lancaster, Pennsylvania, has a noteworthy exception. But still the market, even in its reduced state, survives in most of the small cities I have visited, and it continues to serve as a center for a group of feed and grain stores, hardware stores and an occasional tractor and implement agency. Here in fact is another one of those transshipment points; the streets surrounding the market are crowded with farm trucks, and with farmers setting out to explore the Path. Exchange is taking place everywhere you look: exchange of goods for cash, exchange of labor for cash (or the promise of cash) in the employment agencies with their opportunities scrawled in chalk on blackboards; exchange of talk and drink and opinion in a dozen bars and beer parlors and lunch counters; exchange of mandolins and foreign pistols and diamond rings against cash—to be exchanged in turn against an hour or so with a girl. The Path bursts into a luxuriance of colored and lighted signs: Chiliburgers. Red Hots. Unborn Calf Oxfords: They're new! They're smart! They're Ivy! Double Feature: Bride of the Gorilla—Monster From Outer Space. Gospel Evangelical Mission. Checks Cashed. Snooker Parlor. The Best Shine in Town! Dr. Logan and His Amazing Europathic Method. Coney Islands. Fortunes Told; Madame LaFay. And Army surplus stores, tattoo parlors, barbershops, poolrooms lined with pinball and slot machines, gift shops with Chinese embroidered coats and tea sets. Along one Path after another—in Paducah and Vicksburg and Poplar Bluff and Quincy—I have run across, to my amazement, strange little establishments (wedged in perhaps between a hotel with only a dark flight of steps on the street and a luggage store going out of business) where they sell joke books and party favors and comic masks—worthy reminders that the Path, for all its stench of beer and burning grease, its bleary eyes and uncertain clutching of doorjams, its bedlam of jukeboxes and radios and barkers, is still dedicated to good times. And in fact the Path is at its gayest and noisiest and most popular from Saturday noon until midnight.

You may call this part of town what you like: Skid Row, the Jungle, the Tenderloin, Hell's Kitchen, or (in the loftier parlance of sociology) a depressed or obsolescent area; but you cannot accurately call it a slum. It is, as I have said, primarily a district for unattached men from out of town. This implies a minority of unattached women, but it does not imply that any families live here. No children are brought up here, no home has to struggle against the atmosphere of anarchy. That is why you find no grocery or household furniture or women's and children's clothing stores, though stores with gifts for women are numerous enough. Not being an urban morphologist, I have no inkling of *why* there are no slum dwellings here, nor, for that matter, of where in the city makeup slums are likely to occur; but I have yet to find anywhere even the remotest connection between an extensive slum area and the Strangers' Path.

But then there is much in the whole matter that mystifies me. I cannot understand why loan establishments always exist cheek by jowl with the large and pretentious small city bank buildings; why the Path merges almost without transition into the financial section of the city. Yet I have observed this too often to be entirely mistaken. Scollay Square in Boston is not far from State Street, the Bowery is not far (in metropolitan terms) from Wall Street, and Chicago's Skid Row, the classic of them all, is only a few blocks from the center of the financial district; and nowhere is there a slum between the two extremes. I imagine the connection here is one easily explained in terms of the XIX Century American city and its exchange function; perhaps the Path was originally a link between warehouse and counting house, between depot and Main Street. And there are other traits I find equally hard to fathom: why the Path rarely if ever touches on the fashionable retail district or the culturally conscious civic center with its monument and museum and library and welfare organizations housed in remodelled old mansions. These two parts of town are of course the favorite haunts of the residents of the city; is that why the Path avoids all contact with them?

When the Path has reached the region of banks and hotels—usually grouped around one or two intersections in the average small city—it has lost much of its loud proletarian quality, and about all that is left is a newsstand with out-of-town papers, a travel agency, and an airline office on the ground floor of the dressy hotel. Here at one of the busiest corners it seems to pause and hesitate: Main Street leads to the substantial older residential district and eventually (if you're persistent and ambitious enough) to beautiful restricted Country Club Heights. Broadway is the beginning of the retail shopping district. The Path finally makes its way to City Hall; and here it is, among the surrounding decrepit brick office buildings dating from the last century that it touches upon another and final aspect of the city: the politico-legal. Lawyers, the legal aid society, bonding companies, insurance agents, a new (but no less rapacious) breed of finance establishments proliferate among dark wainscotted corridors and behind transoms in high-ceilinged rooms. With a kind of artistic appropriateness, the intitial hangdog atmosphere of the depot and flophouse reasserts itself around the last landmark on the Path, the City Hall. Groups of hastily sobered-up faces gather forlornly outside the traffic court and the police court, or on the steps of the City Hall itself, while grimy documents are passed about. From across the street the YMCA, the Salvation Army, the Guild of Temperance Women look on benevolently, wanting to make friends but never quite succeeding. The Red Cross, on the other hand, dwells in proud seclusion in the basement of the Federal Building, several blocks away.

Is it in this manner that the Strangers' Path comes to an end? If so, how sad, and how pointed the moral: start your career in brothels and saloons and you wind up, hat in hand, before the police magistrate. But this is not invariably the case, and for all I have been able to discover the Path (or some portion of it) may go on to other, happier goals. Yet it is here that it ceases to be a distinct feature of the urban landscape; from now on it is dispersed among all the other currents of city life. And the simile which inevitably comes to mind is that of a river, a stream; a powerful, muddy, untidy but immensely fertile stream which, after being joined by its tributaries, briefly cuts its own characteristic channel in the gaudy middle section of its course, then, arrived at the center of town, fans out to deposit its waters and their burden, and vanishes.

There are two reasons for my trying to describe this part of the average American city that I have called the Strangers' Path; First, I wanted to show the people of that city that while they may know the residential section and be immensely proud of it, there is probably something about the downtown section (something very valuable in its way) that they have never recognized. My second reason is that I have derived much pleasure from exploring the Path and learning a few of its landmarks; hours in unknown cities that might otherwise have been dull thereby became enjoyable. And indeed *every* city has such a section; there are remains of it among the ruins of Pompeii; it was an integral part of every medieval town, and I have run across it in its clearest form in Mexico and in the Balkans.

But what many people will ask is, how important is the Strangers' Path to the modern city? What sort of a future does it have? To such questions I can give no educated answer. When I likened it to a river I was using no very original simile, yet a simile having the virtue of aptness and of suggesting two characteristics. The Path, as I see it, has the prime function of introducing new life to the city, of bringing the city into touch with the outside world. (That it also has the no less valuable function of bringing the villager, the lonely field worker or traveling salesman or trucker or the inhabitant of a dehumanized commercial farming landscape into touch with urban culture goes without saying.) Granted that these contacts are not always on a very exalted or even worthwhile scale, and that they are increasingly confined to the lowest class of citizen; nevertheless they are what keep an infinite number of small businesses and arts and crafts alive, and they represent what is after all one of the chief purposes of the city: the serving as a place of general exchange. For my part I cannot conceive of any large community surviving without this ceaseless influx of new wants, new ideas, new manners, new strength, and so I cannot conceive of a city without some section corresponding to the Path.

The simile was further that of a stream which empties into no basin or lake, merely evaporating into the city or perhaps rising to the surface once more outside of town along some highway strip; and it is this lack of a final, well-defined objective that prevents the Path from serving an even more important role in the community and that tends to make it a poor man's district. For when the stranger, the transient, has finished his business, something in the layout of the city should invite him to linger and become part of the town, should impel him to pay his respects, as it were. In other words the Path should open into the center of civic leisure, into a square or plaza where citizens gather.

"Well," says the city planner, "we have given that matter some thought. We have decided to demolish the depressed area of the city (including your so-called Path where the financial return is low, the sanitation bad and the traffic hopeless) and erect a wonderful series of apartment houses for moderate income white-collar workers, who are the backbone of our country. We will landscape the development with wading pools, flagstone walks, groves of Chinese elms, and we are also putting in a series of neighborhood shopping centers. And that is not all," he continues enthusiastically; "the City Hall is being removed, a handsome park will take its place with parking facilities for five hundred cars underneath, and *more* shops, as high-class as possible, will be built around the square." He then goes on to talk about the pedestrian traffic-free center, with frequent references to the Piazza San Marco in Venice.

All well and good; freedom from traffic is what we want and no one can object to a pretty square where man existed before. But I am growing a little weary of the Piazza San Marco. I yield to no one in my admiration of its beauty and social utility, but it seems to me that those who hold it up as the prototype of all civic (traffic-free) centers are not always aware of what makes it what it is. The Piazza is not an area carved out of a residential district; its animation comes not from the art monuments which surround it; on the contrary, it is enclosed on three sides by a maze of streets and alleys whose function is almost exactly that of the Path; moreover the Piazza San Marco has a landing-place where farmers, fishermen, sailors, merchants and travelers all first disembark—or used to disembark—in the city. These prosaic characteristics are what give life to it. And then, how about the universal absence of wheeled traffic in Venice? The Mediterranean plaza is a charming and healthy institution, which American cities would be wise to adopt, but the plaza is organically connected with the workaday life of the city. It has never served, it was never intended to serve, as a place of business. It is the center of group leisure; it is the civic parlor and it therefore adjoins the civic workroom or place of exchange. The notion of a pedestrian plaza in the center of every small American city is a good one, but if it is merely to serve as a focal point for smart shops and "culture" then I still do not see in it any substitute for the Path.

There are others who try to persuade us that the suburban or residential shopping center is the civic center of the future. Mr. Victor Gruen, who is justifiably happy over his enormous (and enormously successful) shopping centers in Detroit and Minneapolis, tells us that these establishments (or rather their handsomely landscaped surroundings) are already serving more and more as the scene of holiday festivities, art shows, pageants, as well as of general sociability and of supervised play for children. I have no doubt of it; but the shopping center, no matter how big, how modern, how beautiful, is the *exact* opposite of the Path. Its public is almost exclusively composed of housewives and children, it imposes a uniformity of taste and income and interests, and its strenuous efforts to be self-contained mean that it automatically rejects anything from outside. And compared to any traditional civic center—market place, bazaar, agora—what bloodless places these shopping centers are! I cannot see a roustabout fresh from the oil fields, or (at the other extreme) a student of manners willingly passing an hour in one of them; though both could spend a day and a night in the Path with pleasure and a certain amount of profit. Art shows indeed! It strikes me that some of our planners need to acquire a more robust idea of city life. Perhaps I do them an injustice, but I often have the feeling that their emphasis on convenience, cleanliness, and safety, their distrust of everything vulgar and small and poor is symptomatic of a very lopsided view of urban culture.

Possibly this is the price we have to pay for planning becoming respectable, but it would be well if a wider and more humane understanding of the city and its problems soon evolved in this country. There is much to be done, and planners are the only ones who can do it. No one, I suppose, would wish to see the Strangers' Path remain as it is: garish and dirty and decaying, forced to expend its vitality in mean and neglected streets, cheated of a final merger with the broader life of the city. Yet even in its present sad state it has the power to suggest the avenue it might become, given imaginative treatment. Among the famous and best loved streets of the world how many of them are simply glorifications of the Strangers' Path! The Rambla in Barcelona, more than a mile of tree-lined boulevard with more trees and a promenade down the center, is such a one, and the Cannebière in Marseilles is another. They both link the harbor (the point of arrival) with the uptown area; neither of them is a show street in terms of architecture, and they are not bordered by expensive or fashionable shops. The public which frequents them at every hour of the day and night is not a "class" public; it is composed of a large cross section of the population of the city, men, women, and children, rich and poor, strangers and natives. It happens that the residential section of both of these cities contain architectural wonders which must be visited: Gaudi's church in Barcelona, and Le Corbusier's Cité Radieuse in Marseilles, and here (as in so many other places) I have done my duty, only to return as fast as possible to the center of town and those marvelous avenues.

There are few greater delights than to walk up and down them in the evening along with thousands of other people; up and down, relishing the lights coming through the trees or shining from the façades, listening to the sounds of music and foreign voices and traffic, enjoying the smell of flowers and good food and the air from the nearby sea. The sidewalks are lined with small shops, bars, stalls, dance halls, movies, booths lighted by acetylene lamps, and everywhere are strange faces, strange costumes, strange and delightful impressions. To walk up such a street into the quieter, more formal part of town, is to be part of a procession, part of a ceaseless ceremony of being initiated into the city and of rededicating the city itself. And that is how our first progress through even the smallest city and town should be: a succession of gay and beautiful streets and squares, all of them extending a universal welcome.

Unlike so many visions of the city of the future this one has a firm basis in reality. The Strangers' Path exists in one form or another in every large community, either (as in most American cities) ignored, or as in the case of Marseilles and Barcelona and many other cities in the Old World, preserved and cherished. Everywhere it is the direct product of our economic and social evolution. If we seek to dam or bury this ancient river, we will live to regret it.

JEAN-PAUL SARTRE
American Cities

For the first few days I was lost. My eyes were not accustomed to the skyscrapers and they did not surprise me; they did not seem like man-made, man-inhabited constructions, but rather like rocks and hills, dead parts of the urban landscape one finds in cities built on a turbulent soil and which you pass without even noticing. At the same time, I was continually and vainly looking for something to catch my attention for a moment—a detail, a square, perhaps, or a public building. I did not yet know that these houses and streets should be seen in the mass.

In order to learn to live in these cities and to like them as Americans do, I had to fly over the immense deserts of the west and south. Our European cities, submerged in human countrysides that have been worked over mile by mile, are continuous. And then we are vaguely aware that far away, across the sea, there is the desert, a myth. For the American, this myth is an everyday reality. We flew for hours between New Orleans and San Francisco, over an earth that was dry and red, clotted with verdigris bushes. Suddenly, a city, a little checkerboard flush with the ground, arose and then, again, the red earth, the Savannah, the twisted rocks of the Grand Canyon, and the snows of the Rocky Mountains.

After a few days of this diet, I came to understand that the American city was, originally, a camp in the desert. People from far away, attracted by a mine, a petroleum field or fertile land, arrived one fine day and settled as quickly as possible in a clearing, near a river. They built the vital parts of the town, the bank, the town hall, the church, and then hundreds of one-storey frame houses. The road, if there was one, served as a kind of spinal column to the town, and then streets were marked out like vertebrae, perpendicular to the road. It would be hard to count the American cities that have that kind of parting in the middle.

Nothing has changed since the time of the covered wagons; every year towns are founded in the United States, and they are founded according to the same methods.

Take Fontana, Tennessee, which is situated near one of the great

T.V.A. dams. Twelve years ago there were pine-trees growing in the mountain's red soil. As soon as the construction of the dam began, the pines were felled and three towns—two white ones of 3000 and 5000 inhabitants each, and one Negro town—sprang from the soil. The workers live there with their families; four or five years ago, when work was in full swing, one birth was recorded each day. Half of the village looks like a pile-dwellers' community: the houses are of wood, with green roofs, and have been built on piles to avoid dampness. The other half is made of collapsible dwellings, "prefabricated houses." They too are of wood; they are constructed about 500 miles away and loaded onto trucks: a single team of men can set one up within four hours after its arrival. The smallest costs the employer two thousand dollars, and he rents them to his workers for nineteen dollars a month (thirty-one dollars if they are furnished). The interiors, with their mass-produced furniture, central heating, electric lamps, and refrigerators, remind one of ship cabins. Every square inch of these antiseptic little rooms has been utilized; the walls have clothes-presses and under the beds there are chests of drawers.

One leaves with a slightly depressed feeling, with the feeling of having seen the careful, small-scale reconstitution of a 1944 flat in the year 3000. The moment one steps outside one sees hundreds of houses, all alike, piled up, squashed against the earth, but retaining in their very form some sort of nomadic look. It looks like a caravan graveyard. The pile-dweller community and the caravan cemetery face one another. Between them a wide road climbs toward the pines. There you have a city, or rather the nucleus of an American city, with all its essential parts. Below is the Woolworth's, higher up the hospital, and at the top, a "mixed" church in which what might be called a minimum service—that is, one valid for all creeds—is conducted.

The striking thing is the lightness, the fragility of these buildings. The village has no weight, it seems barely to rest on the soil; it has not managed to leave a human imprint on the reddish earth and the dark forest; it is a temporary thing. And besides, it will soon take to the road; in two years the dam will be finished, the workers will leave, and the prefabricated houses will be taken down and sent to a Texas oil well or a Georgia cotton plantation, to reconstitute another Fontana, under other skies, with new inhabitants.

This roving village is no exception; in the United States, communities are born as they die—in a day. The Americans have no complaint to make; the main thing is to be able to carry their homes with them. These homes are the collections of objects, furnishings, photographs, and souvenirs belonging to them, that reflect their own image and constitute the inner, living landscape of their dwellings. These are their penates. Like Aeneas, they haul them about everywhere.

The "house" is the shell; it is abandoned on the slightest pretext.

We have workers' communities in France. But they are sedentary, and then they never become real cities; on the contrary, they are the artificial product of neighbouring cities. In America, just as any citizen can theoretically become President, so each Fontana can become Detroit or Minneapolis; all that is needed is a bit of luck. And conversely, Detroit and Minneapolis are Fontanas which have had luck. To take only one example: in 1905 Detroit had a population of 300,000. Its population is now 1,000,000.

The inhabitants of this city are perfectly aware of this luck; they like to recall in their books and films the time when their community was only an outpost. And that is why they pass so easily from city to outpost; they make no distinction between the two. Detroit and Minneapolis, Knoxville and Memphis were *born temporary* and have stayed that way. They will never, of course, take to the road again on the back of a truck. But they remain at the meeting point; they have never reached an internal temperature of solidification.

Things that would not constitute a change of situation for us are, for the American, occasions for real breaks with his past. There are many who, on going off to war, have sold their apartments and everything else, including their suits. What is the point of keeping something that will be outmoded upon their return? Soldiers' wives often reduce their scale of living and go to live more modestly in other neighbourhoods. Thus, sadness and faithfulness to the absent are marked by a removal.

The removals also indicate fluctuations in American fortunes.

It is customary, in the United States, for the fashionable neighbourhoods to slide from the centre to the outskirts of the city; after five years the centre of town is "polluted." If you walk about there, you come upon tumble-down houses that retain a pretentious look beneath their filth; you find a complicated kind of architecture, one-storey frame houses with entrances formed by peristyles supported by columns, gothic chalets, "Colonial houses," etc. These were formerly aristocratic homes, now inhabited by the poor. Chicago's lurid Negro section contain some of these Greco-Roman temples; from the outside they still look well. But inside, twelve rat- and louse-plagued Negro families are crowded together in five or six rooms.

At the same time, changes are continually made within the same place. An apartment house is bought to be demolished, and a larger apartment house is built on the same plot. After five years, the new house is sold to a contractor who tears it down to build a third one. The result is that in the States a city is a moving landscape for its inhabitants, whereas our cities are our shells.

In France, one hears only from very old people what a forty-year-old American said to me in Chicago. "When I was young, this whole neighbourhood was taken up by a lake. But this part of the lake was filled in and built over." And a thirty-five-year-old lawyer who was showing me the Negro section said: "I was born here. Then it was a white section and, apart from servants, you would not have seen a Negro in the streets. Now the white people have left and 250,000 Negroes are crowded into their houses."

M. Verdier, the owner of the "City of Paris" department store in San Francisco, witnessed the earthquake and fire that destroyed three quarters of the city. At that time he was a young man; he remembers the disaster perfectly. He watched the reconstruction of the city which still had an Asiatic look around 1913, and then its rapid Americanization. Thus, he has superimposed memories of three San Franciscos.

We Europeans change within changeless cities, and our houses and neighbourhoods outlive us; American cities change faster than their inhabitants do, and it is the inhabitants who outlive the cities.

I am really visiting the United States in wartime; the vast life of the American city has suddenly become petrified; people hardly change their residences any more. But this stagnation is entirely temporary; the cities have been immobilized like the dancer on the film-screen who stays with his foot suspended in air when the film is stopped; one feels all about one the rising of the sap which will burst open the cities as soon as the war is ended.

First, there are immediate problems; Chicago's Negro section will have to be rebuilt, for instance. The government had begun this before Pearl Harbor. But the government-built apartment houses barely managed to shelter 7000 people. Now, there are 250,000 to be housed. Then the industrialists want to enlarge and transform their factories; the famous abattoirs of Chicago are going to be completely modernized.

Finally, the average American is obsessed by the image of the "modern house" which is considerably publicized and which will be, so we are told, a hundred times more comfortable than the present dwellings and whose construction in huge quantities certainly has its place in the plans for "industrial conversion" which are now springing up almost everywhere.

When the war is over, America will certainly be seized with a real construction fever. Today the American sees his city objectively; he does not dream of finding it ugly, but thinks it really old. If it were even older, like ours, he could find a social past, a tradition in it. We generally live in our grandfathers' houses. Our streets reflect the customs and ways of past centuries; they tend to filter the present; none of what goes on in the Rue Montorgueil or the Rue Pot-de-Fer is completely of the present. But the thirty-year-old American lives in a house that was built when he was twenty.

These houses that are too young to seem *old* seem merely outdated to them; they lag behind the other tools, the car that can be traded in every two years, the refrigerator or the wireless set. That is why they see their cities without vain sentimentality. They have grown slightly attached to them, as one becomes attached to one's car, but they consider them as instruments, rather than anything else, instruments to be exchanged for more convenient ones.

For us a city is, above all, a past; for them it is mainly a future; what they like in the city is everything it has not yet become and everything it can be.

What are the impressions of a European who arrives in an American city? First, he thinks he has been taken in. He has heard only about skyscrapers; New York and Chicago have been described to him as "upright cities." Now his first feeling is, on the contrary, that the average height of an American city is noticeably smaller than that of a French one. The immense majority of houses have only two storeys. Even in the very large cities, the five-storey apartment house is an exception.

Then he is struck by the lightness of the materials used. In the United States stone is less frequently used than in Europe. The skyscraper consists of a coating of concrete applied to a metal framework, and the other buildings are made of brick or wood. Even in the richest cities and the smartest sections, one often finds frame houses. New Orleans' lovely colonial houses are of wood; many of the pretty chalets belonging to the Hollywood stars and film-directors are made of wood; so are the "California style" cottages in San Francisco. Everywhere you find groups of frame houses crushed between two twenty-storeyed buildings.

The brick houses are the colour of dried blood, or, on the contrary, daubed and smeared with bright yellow, green or raw white.[1] In most of the cities, they are rootless cubes or rectangular parallelepipeds, with severely flat façades. All these houses, hastily constructed and made expressly to be hastily demolished, obviously bear a strange resemblance to Fontana's "prefabricated houses."

The lightness of these jerry-built houses, their loud colours alternating with the sombre red of the bricks, the extraordinary variety of their decorations which does not manage to conceal the uniformity of their patterns, all give one the feeling, when in the middle of the city, of walking through the suburbs of a watering town, like Trouville or Cabourg or La Baule. Only those ephemeral seaside chalets with their pretentious architectural style and their fragility can convey to those of my French readers who have never seen the States an idea of the American apartment house.

To complete the impression, I should also like to add that sometimes

1. Kisling and Masson have often complained of the fact that the urban landscape of the United States is not very stimulating to painting. I believe this is partly due to the fact that the cities have already been painted. They do not have the hesitant colours of our own cities. What is one to do with these tones which already are art, or artifice at least? All one can do is leave them alone.

one also thinks of an exposition-city, but an obsolescent, dirty one, like those that ten years later, in some park, survive the celebration that occasioned them. For these shanties quickly grow dirty, particularly in industrial sections.

Chicago, blackened by its smoke, clouded by the Lake Michigan fog, is a dark and gloomy red. Pittsburgh is more gloomy still. And there is nothing more immediately striking than the contrast between the formidable power, the inexhaustible abundance of what is called the "American Colossus" and the puny insignificance of those little houses that line the widest roads in the world. But on second thought, there is no clearer indication that America is not finished, that her ideas and plans, her social structure and her cities have only a strictly temporary reality.

These perfectly straight cities bear no trace of organization. Many of them have the rudimentary structure of a polypary. Los Angeles, in particular, is rather like a big earthworm that might be chopped into twenty pieces without being killed. If you go through this enormous urban cluster, probably the largest in the world, you come upon twenty juxtaposed cities, strictly identical, each with its poor section, its business streets, night-clubs and smart suburb, and you get the impression that a medium-sized urban centre has schizogenetically reproduced itself twenty times.[2]

In America, where the neighbourhoods are added on to each other as the region's prosperity attracts new immigrants, this juxtaposition is the rule. You pass without any transition from a poor street into an aristocratic avenue; a promenade lined with skyscrapers, museums and public monuments and adorned with lawns and trees, suddenly stops short above a smoky station; one frequently discovers at the feet of the largest buildings, along an aristocratic avenue, a "zone" of miserable little kitchen-gardens.

This is due to the fact that these cities that move at a rapid rate are not constructed in order to grow old, but move forward like modern armies, encircling the islands of resistance they are unable to destroy; the past does not manifest itself in them as it does in Europe, through public monuments, but through survivals. The wooden bridge in Chicago which spans a canal two steps away from the world's highest skyscrapers is a survival. The elevated railways, rolling noisily through the central streets of New York and Chicago, supported by great iron pillars and cross-girders, nearly touching the façades of houses on either side, are survivals. They are there simply because no one has taken the time to tear them down, and as a kind of indication of work to be done.

You find this disorder in each individual vista. Nowhere have I seen so many empty lots. Of course they do have a definite function; they are

2. To convey an idea of this city to the reader, I suggest that he try to imagine, not one Côte d'Azur city, but the entire region between Cannes and Menton.

used as car parks. But they break the alignment of the street nonetheless sharply for all that. Suddenly it seems as if a bomb had fallen on three or four houses, reducing them to powder, and as if they had just been swept out: this is a "parking space," two hundred square metres of bare earth with its sole ornament, perhaps, a poster on a big boarding. Suddenly the city seems unfinished, badly assembled; suddenly you rediscover the desert and the big empty site: noticeable at Fontana. I remember this Los Angeles landscape in the middle of the city, two modern apartment houses, two white cubes framing an empty lot with the ground torn up—a parking space. A few abandoned-looking cars were parked there. A palm tree grew like a weed between the cars. Down at the bottom there was a steep grassy hill, rather like the fortification mounds we use for garbage disposal. On top of the mound was a frame house, and a little below this a string stretched between two little trees, with multi-coloured washing hanging out to dry. When one turned around the block of houses, the hill disappeared; its other side had been built up, covered with asphalt, streaked with tar roads, and pierced with a magnificent tunnel.

The most striking aspect of the American city is the vertical disorder. These brick shanties are of varying heights; I noted at random during a walk in Detroit the following successive proportions: one storey, two storeys, one storey, one storey, three storeys. You find the same proportions in Albuquerque or San Antonio, at the other end of the country. In depth, above this irregular crenellation, you see apartment houses of all shapes and dimensions, long cases, thick thirty-storeyed boxes with forty windows to a storey. As soon as there is a bit of fog the colours fade away, and only volumes remain—every variety of polyhedron. Between them, you have enormous empty spaces, empty lots cut out in the sky.

In New York, and even in Chicago, the skyscraper is on home ground, and imposes a new order upon the city. But everywhere else it is out of place; the eye is unable to establish any unity between these tall, gawky things and the little houses that run close to the ground; in spite of itself it looks for that line so familiar in European cities, the sky-line, and cannot find it. That is why the European feels at first as though he were travelling through a rocky chaos that resembles a city—something like Montpellier-le-Vieux—rather than a city.

But the European makes a mistake in visiting American cities as one does Paris or Venice; they are not meant to be seen that way. The streets here do not have the same meaning as our streets. In Europe, a street is half-way between the path of communication and the sheltered "public place." It is on a footing with the cafés, as proved by the use of the "terrasses" that spring up on the sidewalks of the cafés in fine weather. Thus it changes its aspect more than a hundred times a day, for the crowd that throngs the European street changes, and men are its primary element. The American street is a piece of highway. It sometimes stretches over many miles. It does not stimulate one to walk. Ours are oblique and twisting, full of bends and secrets. The American street is a straight line that gives itself away immediately. It contains no mystery. You see the street straight through, from one end to the other no matter what your location in it. And the distances in American cities are too great to permit moving about on foot; in most of them one gets about almost exclusively in cars, on buses and by underground. Sometimes, while going from one appointment to another, I have been carried like a parcel from underground to escalator, from escalator to elevator, from elevator to taxi, from taxi to bus and, again, by metro and elevator, without walking a step.

In certain cities I noticed a real atrophy of the sidewalk. In Los Angeles, for example, on La Cienega, which is lined with bars, theatres, restaurants, antique dealers and private residences, the sidewalks are scarcely more than side-streets that lead customers and guests from the roadway into the house. Lawns have been planted from the façades to the roadway of this luxurious avenue. I followed a narrow path between the lawns for a long time without meeting a living soul, while to my right, cars streaked by on the road; all animation in the street had taken refuge on the high road.

New York and Chicago do not have neighbourhoods, but they do have a neighbourhood life; the American is not familiar with his city; once he is ten "blocks" away from his home, he is lost. This does not mean that there are no crowds in the business streets, but they are crowds that do not linger; people shop or emerge from the Underground to go to their offices.

I rarely saw an occasional Negro day-dreaming before a shop.

Yet one quickly begins to like American cities. Of course they all look alike. And when you arrive at Wichita, Saint Louis or Albuquerque, it is disappointing to realize that, hidden behind these magnificent and promising names, is the same standard checkerboard city with the same red and green traffic lights and the same provincial look. But one gradually learns to tell them apart. Chicago, the noble, lurid city, red as the blood that trickles through its abattoirs, with its canals, the grey water of Lake Michigan and its streets crushed between clumsy and powerful buildings, in no way resembles San Francisco, city of air, salt and sea, built in the shape of an amphitheatre.

And then one finally comes to like their common element, that temporary look. Our beautiful closed cities, full as eggs, are a bit stifling. Our slanting, winding streets run head on against walls and houses; once you are inside the city, you can no longer see beyond it. In America, these long, straight unobstructed streets carry one's glance, like canals, outside the city. You always see mountains or fields or the sea at the end of them, no matter where you may be.

Frail and temporary, formless and unfinished, they are haunted by the presence of the immense geographical space surrounding them. And precisely because their boulevards are highways, they always seem to be stopping places on the roads. They are not oppressive, they do not close you in; nothing in them is definitive, nothing is arrested. You feel, from your first glance, that your contact with these places is a temporary one; either you will leave them or they will change around you.

Let us beware of exaggerating; I have spent Sundays in the American provinces that were more depressing than Sundays anywhere else; I have seen those suburban "colonial style" inns where, at two dollars a head, middle-class families go to eat shrimp cocktails and turkey with cranberry sauce in silence while listening to the electric organ. One must not forget the heavy boredom that weighs over America.

But these slight cities, still so similar to Fontana and the outposts of the Far West, reveal the other side of the United States: their freedom. Here everyone is free—not to criticize or to reform their customs—but to flee them, to leave for the desert or another city. The cities are open, open to the world, and to the future. This is what gives them their adventurous look and, even in their ugliness and disorder, a touching beauty.

3
Place and style

To be at all critically, or as we have been fond of calling it, analytically, minded —over and beyond an inherent love of the general many-coloured picture of things—is to be subject to the superstition that objects and places, coherently grouped, disposed for human use and addressed to it, must have a sense of their own, a mystic meaning proper to themselves to give out, that is, to the participant at once so interested and so detached as to be moved to a report of the matter.

Henry James
The American Scene

Edward Weston

Bruce Davidson

Harry Callahan

Joel Meyerowitz

Joel Meyerowitz

Steve Salmieri

Helen Levitt

Diane Arbus

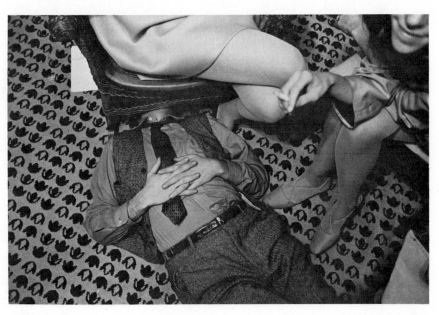

Lee Friedlander

Brett Weston

Walker Evans

Elaine Mayes

Tod Papageorge

ROBERT E. PARK
The City: Suggestions for the Investigation of Human Behavior in the Urban Environment

The city, from the point of view of this paper, is something more than a congeries of individual men and of social conveniences—streets, buildings, electric lights, tramways, and telephones, etc.; something more, also, than a mere constellation of institutions and administrative devices —courts, hospitals, schools, police, and civil functionaries of various sorts. The city is, rather, a state of mind, a body of customs and traditions, and of the organized attitudes and sentiments that inhere in these customs and are transmitted with this tradition. The city is not, in other words, merely a physical mechanism and an artificial construction. It is involved in the vital processes of the people who compose it; it is a product of nature, and particularly of human nature.

The city has, as Oswald Spengler has recently pointed out, its own culture: "What his house is to the peasant, the city is to civilized man. As the house has its household gods, so has the city its protecting Deity, its local saint. The city also, like the peasant's hut, has its roots in the soil." [1]

The city has been studied, in recent times, from the point of view of its geography, and still more recently from the point of view of its ecology. There are forces at work within the limits of the urban community— within the limits of any natural area of human habitation, in fact—which tend to bring about an orderly and typical grouping of its population and institutions. The science which seeks to isolate these factors and to describe the typical constellations of persons and institutions which the cooperation of these forces produce, is what we call human, as distinguished from plant and animal, ecology.

Transportation and communication, tramways and telephones, news-

---

1. Oswald Spengler, *Der Untergang des Abendlandes,* IV (München, 1922), 105.

papers and advertising, steel construction and elevators—all things, in fact, which tend to bring about at once a greater mobility and a greater concentration of the urban populations—are primarily factors in the ecological organization of the city.

The city is not, however, merely a geographical and ecological unit; it is at the same time an economic unit. The economic organization of the city is based on the division of labor. The multiplication of occupations and professions within the limits of the urban population is one of the most striking and least understood aspects of modern city life. From this point of view, we may, if we choose, think of the city, that is to say, the place and the people, with all the machinery and administrative devices that go with them, as organically related; a kind of psychophysical mechanism in and through which private and political interests find not merely a collective but a corporate expression.

Much of what we ordinarily regard as the city—its charters, formal organization, buildings, street railways, and so forth—is, or seems to be, mere artifact. But these things in themselves are utilities, adventitious devices which become part of the living city only when, and in so far as, through use and wont they connect themselves, like a tool in the hand of man, with the vital forces resident in individuals and in the community.

The city is, finally, the natural habitat of civilized man. It is for that reason a cultural area characterized by its own peculiar cultural type:

"It is a quite certain, but never fully recognized, fact," says Spengler, "that all great cultures are city-born. The outstanding man of the second generation is a city-building animal. This is the actual criterion of world-history, as distinguished from the history of mankind: world-history is the history of city men. Nations, governments, politics, and religions—all rest on the basic phenomenon of human existence, the city." [2]

Anthropology, the science of man, has been mainly concerned up to the present with the study of primitive peoples. But civilized man is quite as interesting an object of investigation, and the same time his life is more open to observation and study. Urban life and culture are more varied, subtle, and complicated, but the fundamental motives are in both instances the same. The same patient methods of observation which anthropologists like Boas and Lowie have expended on the study of the life and manners of the North American Indian might be even more fruitfully employed in the investigation of the customs, beliefs, social practices, and general conceptions of life prevalent in Little Italy on the lower North Side in Chicago, or in recording the more sophisticated folkways of the inhabitants of Greenwich Village and the neighborhood of Washington Square, New York.

We are mainly indebted to writers of fiction for our more intimate

2. Oswald Spengler, *Untergang des Abendlandes,* IV, 106.

knowledge of contemporary urban life. But the life of our cities demands a more searching and disinterested study than even Émile Zola has given us in his "experimental" novels and the annals of the Rougon-Macquart family.

We need such studies, if for no other reason than to enable us to read the newspapers intelligently. The reason that the daily chronicle of the newspaper is so shocking, and at the same time so fascinating, to the average reader is because the average reader knows so little about the life of which the newspaper is the record.

The observations which follow are intended to define a point of view and to indicate a program for the study of urban life: its physical organization, its occupations, and its culture.

The city plan and local organization

The city, particularly the modern American city, strikes one at first blush as so little a product of the artless processes of nature and growth, that it is difficult to recognize it as a living entity. The ground plan of most American cities, for example, is a checkerboard. The unit of distance is the block. This geometrical form suggests that the city is a purely artificial construction which might conceivably be taken apart and put together again, like a house of blocks.

The fact is, however, that the city is rooted in the habits and customs of the people who inhabit it. The consequence is that the city possesses a moral as well as a physical organization, and these two mutually interact in characteristic ways to mold and modify one another. It is the structure of the city which first impresses us by its visible vastness and complexity. But this structure has its basis, nevertheless, in human nature, of which it is an expression. On the other hand, this vast organization which has arisen in response to the needs of its inhabitants, once formed, imposes itself upon them as a crude external fact, and forms them, in turn, in accordance with the design and interests which it incorporates. Structure and tradition are but different aspects of a single cultural complex which determines what is characteristic and peculiar to city, as distinguished from village, life and the life of the open fields.

The city plan.—It is because the city has a life quite its own that there is a limit to the arbitrary modifications which it is possible to make (1) in its physical structure and (2) in its moral order.

The city plan, for example, establishes metes and bounds, fixes in a general way the location and character of the city's constructions, and imposes an orderly arrangement, within the city area, upon the buildings which are erected by private initiative as well as by public authority. Within the limitations prescribed, however, the inevitable processes of human nature proceed to give these regions and these buildings a character which it is less easy to control. Under our system of individual ownership, for instance, it is not possible to determine in advance the extent of concentration of population which is likely to occur in any given area. The city cannot fix land values, and we leave to private enterprise, for the most part, the task of determining the city's limits and the location of its residential and industrial districts. Personal tastes and convenience, vocational and economic interests, infallibly tend to segregate and thus to classify the populations of great cities. In this way the city acquires an organization and distribution of population which is neither designed nor controlled.

The Bell Telephone Company is now making, particularly in New York and Chicago, elaborate investigations, the purpose of which is to determine, in advance of its actual changes, the probable growth and distribution of the urban population within the metropolitan areas. The Sage Foundation, in the course of its city-planning studies, sought to find mathematical formulae that would enable them to predict future expansion and limits of population in New York City. The recent development of chain stores has made the problem of location a matter of concern to different chain-store corporations. The result has been the rise of a new profession.

There is now a class of experts whose sole occupation is to discover and locate, with something like scientific accuracy, taking account of the changes which present tendencies seem likely to bring about, restaurants, cigar stores, drug-stores, and other smaller retail business units whose success depends largely on location. Real-estate men are not infrequently willing to finance a local business of this sort in locations which they believe will be profitable, accepting as their rent a percentage of the profits.

Physical geography, natural advantages and disadvantages, including means of transportation, determine in advance the general outlines of the urban plan. As the city increases in population, the subtler influences of sympathy, rivalry, and economic necessity tend to control the distribution of population. Business and industry seek advantageous locations and draw around them certain portions of the population. There spring up fashionable residence quarters from which the poorer classes are excluded because of the increased value of the land. Then there grow up slums which are inhabited by great numbers of the poorer classes who are unable to defend themselves from association with the derelict and vicious.

In the course of time every section and quarter of the city takes on something of the character and qualities of its inhabitants. Each separate part of the city is inevitably stained with the peculiar sentiments of its population. The effect of this is to convert what was at first a mere geographical expression into a neighborhood, that is to say, a locality with sentiments, traditions, and a history of its own. Within this neighborhood the continuity of the historical processes is somehow maintained. The past imposes itself upon the present, and the life of every locality moves on with a certain momentum of its own, more or less independent of the larger circle of life and interests about it.

The organization of the city, the character of the urban environment and of the discipline which it imposes is finally determined by the size of the population, its concentration and distribution within the city area. For this reason it is important to study the growth of cities, to compare the idiosyncrasies in the distribution of city populations. Some of the first things we want to know about the city, therefore are:

What are the sources of the city's population?

What part of its population growth is normal, i.e., due to excess of births over deaths?

What part is due to migration (a) of native stocks? (b) foreign stocks?

What are the outstanding "natural" areas, i.e., areas of population segregation?

How is distribution of population within the city area affected by (a) economic interest, i.e., land values? (b) by sentimental interest, race? vocation, etc.?

Where within the city is the population declining? Where is it expanding?

Where are population growth and the size of families within the different natural areas of the city correlated with births and deaths, with marriages and divorces, with house rents and standards of living?

The neighborhood.—Proximity and neighborly contact are the basis for the simplest and most elementary form of association with which we have to do in the organization of city life. Local interests and associations breed local sentiment, and, under a system which makes residence the basis for participation in the government, the neighborhood becomes the basis of political control. In the social and political organization of the city it is the smallest local unit.

It is surely one of the most remarkable of all social facts that, coming down from untold ages, there should be this instinctive understanding that the man who establishes his home beside yours begins to have a claim upon your sense of comradeship. . . . The neighborhood is a social unit which, by its clear definition of outline, its inner organic completeness, its hair-trigger reactions, may be fairly considered as functioning like a social mind. . . . The local boss, however autocratic he may be in the larger sphere of the city with the power he gets from the neighborhood, must always be in and of the people; and he is very careful not to try to deceive the local people so far as their local interests are concerned. It is hard to fool a neighborhood about its own affairs.[3]

The neighborhood exists without formal organization. The local improvement society is a structure erected on the basis of the spontaneous neighborhood organization and exists for the purpose of giving expression to the local sentiment in regard to matters of local interest.

Under the complex influences of the city life, what may be called the normal neighborhood sentiment has undergone many curious and interesting changes, and produced many unusual types of local communities. More than that, there are nascent neighborhoods and neighborhoods in process of dissolution. Consider, for example, Fifth Avenue, New York, which probably never had an improvement association, and compare with it 135th Street in the Bronx (where the Negro population is probably more concentrated than in any other single spot in the world), which is rapidly becoming a very intimate and highly organized community.

In the history of New York the significance of the name Harlem has changed from Dutch to Irish to Jewish to Negro. Of these changes the last has come most swiftly. Throughout colored America, from Massachusetts to Mississippi and across the continent to Los Angeles and Seattle, its name, which as late as fifteen years ago has scarcely been heard, now stands for the Negro metropolis. Harlem is, indeed, the great Mecca for the sight-seer, the pleasure-seeker, the curious, the adventurous, the enterprising, the ambitious, and the talented of the Negro world; for the lure of it has reached down to every island of the Carib Sea and has penetrated even into Africa.[4]

It is important to know what are the forces which tend to break up the tensions, interests, and sentiments which give neighborhoods their individual character. In general these may be said to be anything and everything that tends to render the population unstable, to divide and concentrate attentions upon widely separated objects of interest.

What part of the population is floating?
Of what elements, i.e., races, classes, etc., is this population composed?
How many people live in hotels, apartments, and tenements?
How many people own their own homes?
What proportion of the population consists of nomads, hobos, gypsies?

On the other hand, certain urban neighborhoods suffer from isolation. Efforts have been made at different times to reconstruct and quicken the

3. Robert A. Woods, "The Neighborhood in Social Reconstruction," *Papers and Proceedings of the Eighth Annual Meeting of the American Sociological Society, 1913.*
4. James Welden Johnson, "The Making of Harlem," *Survey Graphic,* March 1, 1925.

life of city neighborhoods and to bring them in touch with the larger interests of the community. Such is, in part, the purpose of the social settlements. These organizations and others which are attempting to reconstruct city life have developed certain methods and a technique for stimulating and controlling local communities. We should study, in connection with the investigation of these agencies, these methods and this technique, since it is just the method by which objects are practically controlled that reveals their essential nature, that is to say, their predictable character (*Gesetzmässigkeit*).

In many of the European cities, and to some extent in this country, reconstruction of city life has gone to the length of building garden suburbs, or replacing unhealthful and run-down tenements with model buildings owned and controlled by the municipality.

In American cities the attempt has been made to renovate evil neighborhoods by the construction of playgrounds and the introduction of supervised sports of various kinds, including municipal dances in municipal dance halls. These and other devices which are intended primarily to elevate the moral tone of the segregated populations of great cities should be studied in connection with the investigation of the neighborhood in general. They should be studied, in short, not merely for their own sake, but for what they can reveal to us of human behavior and human nature generally.

Colonies and segregated areas.—In the city environment the neighborhood tends to lose much of the significance which it possessed in simpler and more primitive forms of society. The easy means of communication and of transportation, which enable individuals to distribute their attention and to live at the same time in several different worlds, tend to destroy the permanency and intimacy of the neighborhood. On the other hand, the isolation of the immigrant and racial colonies of the so-called ghettos and areas of population segregation tend to preserve and, where there is racial prejudice, to intensify the intimacies and solidarity of the local and neighborhood groups. Where individuals of the same race or of the same vocation live together in segregated groups, neighborhood sentiment tends to fuse together with racial antagonisms and class interests.

Physical and sentimental distances reinforce each other, and the influences of local distribution of the population participate with the influences of class and race in the evolution of the social organization. Every great city has its racial colonies, like the Chinatowns of San Francisco and New York, the Little Sicily of Chicago, and various other less pronounced types. In addition to these, most cities have their segregated vice districts, like that which until recently existed in Chicago, their rendezvous for criminals of various sorts. Every large city has its occupational suburbs, like the Stockyards in Chicago, and its residential enclaves, like Brookline in Boston, the so-called "Gold Coast" in Chicago,

Greenwich Village in New York, each of which has the size and the character of a complete separate town, village, or city, except that its population is a selected one. Undoubtedly the most remarkable of these cities within cities, of which the most interesting characteristic is that they are composed of persons of the same race, or of persons of different races but of the same social class, is East London, with a population of 2,000,000 laborers.

The people of the original East London have now overflowed and crossed the Lea, and spread themselves over the marshes and meadows beyond. This population has created new towns which were formerly rural villages, West Ham, with a population of nearly 300,000; East Ham, with 90,000; Stratford, with its "daughters," 150,000; and other "hamlets" similarly overgrown. Including these new populations, we have an aggregate of nearly two millions of people. The population is greater than that of Berlin or Vienna, or St. Petersburg, or Philadelphia.

It is a city full of churches and places of worship, yet there are no cathedrals, either Anglican or Roman; it has a sufficient supply of elementary schools, but it has no public or high school, and it has no colleges for the higher education and no university; the people all read newspapers, yet there is no East London paper except of the smaller and local kind. . . . In the streets there are never seen any private carriages; there is no fashionable quarter . . . one meets no ladies in the principal thoroughfares. People, shops, houses, conveyances—all together are stamped with the unmistakable seal of the working class.

Perhaps the strangest thing of all is this: in a city of two millions of people there are no hotels! That means, of course, that there are no visitors.[5]

In the older cities of Europe, where the processes of segregation have gone farther, neighborhood distinctions are likely to be more marked than they are in America. East London is a city of a single class, but within the limits of that city the population is segregated again and again by racial, cultural, and vocational interests. Neighborhood sentiment, deeply rooted in local tradition and in local custom, exercises a decisive selective influence upon the populations of the older European cities and shows itself ultimately in a marked way in the characteristics of the inhabitants.

What we want to know of these neighborhoods, racial communities, and segregated city areas, existing within or on the outer rims of great cities, is what we want to know of all other social groups:

What are the elements of which they are composed?
To what extent are they the product of a selective process?

5. Walter Besant, *East London*, pp. 7–9.

How do people get in and out of the group thus formed?

What are the relative permanence and stability of their populations?

What about the age, sex, and social condition of the people?

What about the children? How many of them are born, and how many of them remain?

What is the history of the neighborhood? What is there in the subconsciousness—in the forgotten or dimly remembered experiences—of this neighborhood which determines its sentiments and attitudes?

What is there in clear consciousness, i.e., what are its avowed sentiments, doctrines, etc.?

What does it regard as matter of fact? What is news? What is the general run of attention? What models does it imitate and are these within or without the group?

What is the social ritual, i.e., what things must one do in the neighborhood in order to escape being regarded with suspicion or looked upon as peculiar?

Who are the leaders? What interests of the neighborhood do they incorporate in themselves and what is the technique by which they exercise control?

. . .

Temperament and the Urban Environment

Great cities have always been the melting-pots of races and of cultures. Out of the vivid and subtle interactions of which they have been the centers, there have come the newer breeds and the newer social types. The great cities of the United States, for example, have drawn from the isolation of their native villages great masses of the rural populations of Europe and America. Under the shock of the new contacts the latent energies of these primitive peoples have been released, and the subtler processes of interaction have brought into existence not merely vocational but temperamental, types.

Mobilization of the individual man.—Transportation and communication have effected, among many other silent but far-reaching changes, what I have called the "mobilization of the individual man." They have multiplied the opportunities of the individual man for contact and for association with his fellows, but they have made these contacts and associations more transitory and less stable. A very large part of the populations of great cities, including those who make their homes in tenements and apartment houses, live much as people do in some great hotel, meeting but not knowing one another. The effect of this is to substitute fortuitous and casual relationship for the more intimate and permanent associations of the smaller community.

Under these circumstances the individual's status is determined to a considerable degree by conventional signs—by fashion and "front"—and the art of life is largely reduced to skating on thin surfaces and a scrupulous study of style and manners.

Not only transportation and communication, but the segregation of the urban population tends to facilitate the mobility of the individual man. The processes of segregation establish moral distances which make the city a mosaic of little worlds which touch but do not interpenetrate. This makes it possible for individuals to pass quickly and easily from one moral milieu to another, and encourages the fascinating but dangerous experiment of living at the same time in several different contiguous, but otherwise widely separated, worlds. All this tends to give to city life a superficial and adventitious character; it tends to complicate social relationships and to produce new and divergent individual types. It introduces, at the same time, an element of chance and adventure which adds to the stimulus of city life and gives it, for young and fresh nerves, a peculiar attractiveness. The lure of great cities is perhaps a consequence of stimulations which act directly upon the reflexes. As a type of human behavior it may be explained, like the attraction of the flame for the moth, as a sort of tropism.

The attraction of the metropolis is due in part, however, to the fact that in the long run every individual finds somewhere among the varied manifestations of city life the sort of environment in which he expands and feels at ease; finds, in short, the moral climate in which his peculiar nature obtains the stimulations that bring his innate dispositions to full and free expression. It is, I suspect, motives of this kind which have their basis, not in interest nor even in sentiment, but in something more fundamental and primitive which draw many, if not most, of the young men and young women from the security of their homes in the country into the big, booming confusion and excitement of city life. In a small community it is the normal man, the man without eccentricity or genius, who seems most likely to succeed. The small community often tolerates eccentricity. The city, on the contrary, rewards it. Neither the criminal, the defective, nor the genius has the same opportunity to develop his innate disposition in a small town that he invariably finds in a great city.

Fifty years ago every village had one or two eccentric characters who were treated ordinarily with a benevolent toleration, but who were regarded meanwhile as impracticable and queer. These exceptional individuals lived an isolated existence, cut off by their very eccentricities, whether of genius or of defect, from genuinely intimate intercourse with their fellows. If they had the making of criminals, the restraints and inhibitions of the small community rendered them harmless. If they had the stuff of genius in them, they remained sterile for lack of appreciation or opportunity. Mark Twain's story of *Pudd'n Head Wilson* is a description of one such obscure and unappreciated genius. It is not so true as it was that

Full many a flower is born to blush unseen
And waste its fragrance on the desert air.

Gray wrote the "Elegy in a Country Churchyard" before the rise of the modern metropolis.

In the city many of these divergent types now find a milieu in which, for good or for ill, their dispositions and talents parturiate and bear fruit.

In the investigation of those exceptional and temperamental types which the city has produced we should seek to distinguish, as far as possible, between those abstract mental qualities upon which technical excellence is based and those more fundamental native characteristics which find expression in temperament. We may therefore ask:

To what extent are the moral qualities of individuals based on native character? To what extent are they conventionalized habits imposed upon by them or taken over by them from the group?

What are the native qualities and characteristics upon which the moral or immoral character accepted and conventionalized by the group are based?

What connection or what divorce appears to exist between mental and moral qualities in the groups and in the individuals composing them?

Are criminals as a rule of a lower order of intelligence than non-criminals? If so, what types of intelligence are associated with different types of crime? For example, do professional burglars and professional confidence men represent different mental types?

What are the effects upon these different types of isolation and of mobility, of stimulus and of repression?

To what extent can playgrounds and other forms of recreation supply the stimulation which is otherwise sought for in vicious pleasures?

To what extent can vocational guidance assist individuals in finding vocations in which they will be able to obtain a free expression of their temperamental qualities?

The moral region.—It is inevitable that individuals who seek the same forms of excitement, whether that excitement be furnished by a horse race or by grand opera, should find themselves from time to time in the same places. The result of this is that in the organization which city life spontaneously assumes the population tends to segregate itself, not merely in accordance with its interests, but in accordance with its tastes or its temperaments. The resulting distribution of the population is likely to be quite different from that brought about by occupational interests or economic conditions.

Every neighborhood, under the influences which tend to distribute and segregate city populations, may assume the character of a "moral region." Such, for example, are the vice districts, which are found in most cities. A moral region is not necessarily a place of abode. It may be a mere rendezvous, a place of resort.

In order to understand the forces which in every large city tend to develop these detached milieus in which vagrant and suppressed impulses, passions, and ideals emancipate themselves from the dominant moral order, it is necessary to refer to the fact or theory of latent impulses of men.

The fact seems to be that men are brought into the world with all the passions, instincts, and appetites, uncontrolled and undisciplined. Civilization, in the interests of the common welfare, demands the suppression sometimes, and the control always, of these wild, natural dispositions. In the process of imposing its discipline upon the individual, in making over the individual in accordance with the accepted community model, much is suppressed altogether, and much more finds a vicarious expression in forms that are socially valuable, or at least innocuous. It is at this point that sport, play, and art function. They permit the individual to purge himself by means of symbolic expression of these wild and suppressed impulses. This is the catharsis of which Aristotle wrote in his *Poetic,* and which has been given new and more positive significance by the investigations of Sigmund Freud and the psychoanalysts.

No doubt many other social phenomena such as strikes, wars, popular elections, and religious revivals perform a similar function in releasing the subconscious tensions. But within smaller communities, where social relations are more intimate and inhibitions more imperative, there are many exceptional individuals who find within the limits of the communal activity no normal and healthful expression of their individual aptitudes and temperaments.

The causes which give rise to what are here described as "moral regions" are due in part to the restrictions which urban life imposes; in part to the license which these same conditions offer. We have, until very recently, given much consideration to the temptations of city life, but we have not given the same consideration to the effects of inhibitions and suppressions of natural impulses and instincts under the changed conditions of metropolitan life. For one thing, children, which in the country are counted as an asset, become in the city a liability. Aside from this fact it is very much more difficult to rear a family in the city than on the farm. Marriage takes place later in the city, and sometimes it doesn't take place at all. These facts have consequences the significance of which we are as yet wholly unable to estimate.

Investigation of the problems involved might well begin by a study and comparison of the characteristic types of social organization which exist in the regions referred to.

What are the external facts in regard to the life in Bohemia, the half-world, the red-light district, and other "moral regions" less pronounced in character?

What is the nature of the vocations which connect themselves with the ordinary life of these regions? What are the characteristic mental types which are attracted by the freedom which they offer?

How do individuals find their way into these regions? How do they escape from them?

To what extent are the regions referred to the product of the license; to what extent are they due to the restrictions imposed by city life on the natural man?

Temperament and social contagion.—What lends special importance to the segregation of the poor, the vicious, the criminal, and exceptional persons generally, which is so characteristic a feature of city life, is the fact that social contagion tends to stimulate in divergent types the common temperamental differences, and to suppress characters which unite them with the normal types about them. Association with others of their own ilk provides also not merely a stimulus, but a moral support for the traits they have in common which they would not find in a less select society. In the great city the poor, the vicious, and the delinquent, crushed together in an unhealthful and contagious intimacy, breed in and in, soul and body, so that it has often occurred to me that those long genealogies of the Jukes and the tribes of Ishmael would not show such a persistent and distressing uniformity of vice, crime, and poverty unless they were peculiarly fit for the environment in which they are condemned to exist.

We must then accept these "moral regions" and the more or less eccentric and exceptional people who inhabit them, in a sense, at least, as part of the natural, if not the normal, life of a city.

It is not necessary to understand by the expression "moral region" a place or a society that is either necessarily criminal or abnormal. It is intended rather to apply to regions in which a divergent moral code prevails, because it is a region in which the people who inhabit it are dominated; as people are ordinarily not dominated, by a taste or by a passion or by some interest which has its roots directly in the original nature of the individual. It may be an art, like music, or a sport, like horse-racing. Such a region would differ from other social groups by the fact that its interests are more immediate and more fundamental. For this reason its differences are likely to be due to moral, rather than intellectual, isolation.

Because of the opportunity it offers, particularly to the exceptional and abnormal types of man, a great city tends to spread out and lay bare to the public view in a massive manner all the human characters and traits which are ordinarily obscured and suppressed in smaller communities.

The city, in short, shows the good and evil in human nature in excess. It is this fact, perhaps, more than any other, which justifies the view that would make of the city a laboratory or clinic in which human nature and social processes may be conveniently and profitably studied.

JAMES MERRILL
An Urban Convalescence

Out for a walk, after a week in bed,
I find them tearing up part of my block
And, chilled through, dazed and lonely, join the dozen
In meek attitudes, watching a huge crane
Fumble luxuriously in the filth of years.
Her jaws dribble rubble. An old man
Laughs and curses in her brain,
Bringing to mind the close of *The White Goddess.*

As usual in New York, everything is torn down
Before you have had time to care for it.
Head bowed, at the shrine of noise, let me try to recall
What building stood here. Was there a buildng at all?
I have lived on this same street for a decade.

Wait. Yes. Vaguely a presence rises
Some five floors high, of shabby stone
—Or am I confusing it with another one
In another part of town, or of the world?—
And over its lintel into focus vaguely
Misted with blood (my eyes are shut)
A single garland sways, stone fruit, stone leaves,
Which years of grit had etched until it thrust
Roots down, even into the poor soil of my seeing.
When did the garland become part of me?
I ask myself, amused almost,
Then shiver once from head to toe,

Transfixed by a particular cheap engraving of garlands
Bought for a few francs long ago,
All calligraphic tendril and cross-hatched rondure,

Ten years ago, and crumpled up to stanch
Boughs dripping, whose white gestures filled a cab,
And thought of neither then nor since.
Also, to clasp them, the small, red-nailed hand
Of no one I can place. Wait. No. Her name, her features
Lie toppled underneath that year's fashions.
The words she must have spoken, setting her face
To fluttering like a veil, I cannot hear now,
Let alone understand.

So that I am already on the stair,
As it were, of where I lived,
When the whole structure shudders at my tread
And soundlessly collapses, filling
The air with motes of stone.
Onto the still erect building next door
Are pressed levels and hues—
Pocked rose, streaked greens, brown whites.
Who drained the pousse-café?
Wires and pipes, snapped off at the roots, quiver.

Well, that is what life does. I stare
A moment longer, so. And presently
The massive volume of the world
Closes again.

Upon that book I swear
To abide by what it teaches:
Gospels of ugliness and waste,
Of towering voids, of soiled gusts,
Of a shrieking to be faced
Full into, eyes astream with cold—

With cold?
All right then. With self-knowledge.

Indoors at last, the pages of *Time* are apt
To open, and the illustrated mayor of New York,
Given a glimpse of how and where I work,
To note yet one more house that can be scrapped.

Unwillingly I picture
My walls weathering in the general view.

It is not even as though the new
Buildings did very much for architecture.

Suppose they did. The sickness of our time requires
That these as well be blasted in their prime.
You would think the simple fact of having lasted
Threatened our cities like mysterious fires.

There are certain phrases which to use in a poem
Is like rubbing silver with quicksilver. Bright
But facile, the glamour deadens overnight.
For instance, how 'the sickness of our time'

Enhances, then debases, what I feel.
At my desk I swallow in a glass of water
No longer cordial, scarcely wet, a pill
They had told me not to take until much later.

With the result that back into my imagination
The city glides, like cities seen from the air,
Mere smoke and sparkle to the passenger
Having in mind another destination

Which now is not that honey-slow descent
Of the Champs-Elysées, her hand in his,
But the dull need to make some kind of house
Out of the life lived, out of the love spent.

HENRY MILLER
The Fourteenth Ward

I am a patriot—of the Fourteenth Ward, Brooklyn, where I was raised. The rest of the United States doesn't exist for me, except as idea, or history, or literature. At ten years of age I was uprooted from my native soil and removed to a cemetery, a *Lutheran* cemetery, where the tombstones were always in order and the wreaths never faded.

But I was born in the street and raised in the street. "The post-mechanical open street where the most beautiful and hallucinating iron vegetation," etc. . . . Born under the sign of Aries which gives a fiery, active, energetic and somewhat restless body. *With Mars in the ninth house!*

To be born in the street means to wander all your life, to be free. It means accident and incident, drama, movement. It means above all dream. A harmony of irrelevant facts which gives to your wandering a metaphysical certitude. In the street you learn what human beings really are; otherwise, or afterwards, you invent them. What is not in the open street is false, derived, that is to say, *literature.* Nothing of what is called "adventure" ever approaches the flavor of the street. It doesn't matter whether you fly to the Pole, whether you sit on the floor of the ocean with a pad in your hand, whether you pull up nine cities one after the other, or whether, like Kurtz, you sail up the river and go mad. No matter how exciting, how intolerable the situation, there are always exits, always ameliorations, comforts, compensations, newspapers, religions. But once there was none of this. Once you were free, wild, murderous. . . .

The boys you worshiped when you first came down into the street remain with you all your life. They are the only real heroes. Napoleon, Lenin, Capone—all fiction. Napoleon is nothing to me in comparison with Eddie Carney, who gave me my first black eye. No man I have ever met seems as princely, as regal, as noble, as Lester Reardon who, by the mere act of walking down the street, inspired fear and admiration. Jules Verne never led me to the places that Stanley Borowski had up his sleeve when it came dark. Robinson Crusoe lacked imagination in comparison with Johnny Paul. All these boys of the Fourteenth Ward have a flavor about them still. They were not invented or imagined: they were real. Their names ring out like gold coins—Tom Fowler, Jim Buckley, Matt Owen, Rob Ramsay, Harry Martin, Johnny Dunne, to say nothing of Eddie Carney or the great Lester Reardon. Why, even now when I say Johnny Paul the names of the saints leave a bad taste in my mouth. Johnny Paul was the living Odyssey of the Fourteenth Ward; that he later became a truck driver is an irrelevant fact.

Before the great change no one seemed to notice that the streets were ugly or dirty. If the sewer mains were opened you held your nose. If you blew your nose you found snot in your handkerchief and not your nose. There was more of inward peace and contentment. There was the saloon, the race track, bicycles, fast women and trot horses. Life was still moving along leisurely. In the Fourteenth Ward, at least. Sunday mornings no one was dressed. If Mrs. Gorman came down in her wrapper with dirt in her eyes to bow to the priest—"Good morning, Father!" "Good morning, Mrs. Gorman!"—the street was purged of all sin. Pat McCarren carried his handkerchief in the tailflap of his frock coat; it was nice and handy there, like the shamrock in his buttonhole. The foam was on the lager and people stopped to chat with one another.

In my dreams I come back to the Fourteenth Ward as a paranoiac returns to his obsessions. When I think of those steel-gray battleships in the Navy Yard I see them lying there in some astrologic dimension in which I am the gunnersmith, the chemist, the dealer in high explosives, the undertaker, the coroner, the cuckold, the sadist, the lawyer and contender, the scholar, the restless one, the jolt-head, and the brazen-faced.

Where others remember of their youth a beautiful garden, a fond mother, a sojourn at the seashore, I remember, with a vividness as if it were etched in acid, the grim soot-covered walls and chimneys of the tin factory opposite us and the bright, circular pieces of tin that were strewn in the street, some bright and gleaming, others rusted, dull, copperish, leaving a stain on the fingers; I remember the ironworks where the red furnace glowed and men walked toward the glowing pit with huge shovels in their hands, while outside were the shallow wooden forms like coffins with rods through them on which you scraped your shins or broke your neck. I remember the black hands of the ironmolders, the grit that had sunk so deep into the skin that nothing could remove it, not soap, nor elbow grease, nor money, nor love, nor death. Like a black mark on them! Walking into the furnace like devils with black hands—and later, with flowers over them, cool and rigid in their Sunday suits, not even the rain can wash away the grit. All these beautiful gorillas going up to God with swollen muscles and lumbago and black hands. . . .

For me the whole world was embraced in the confines of the Fourteenth Ward. If anything happened outside it either didn't happen or it was unimportant. If my father went outside that world to fish it was of no interest to me. I remember only his boozy breath when he came home in the evening and opening the big green basket spilled the squirming, goggle-eyed monsters on the floor. If a man went off to the war I remember only that he came back of a Sunday afternoon and standing in front of the minister's house puked up his guts and then wiped it up with his vest. Such was Rob Ramsay, the minister's son. I remember that everybody liked Rob Ramsey—he was the black sheep of the family. They liked him because he was a good-for-nothing and he made no bones about it. Sundays or Wednesdays made no difference to him: you could see him coming down the street under the drooping awnings with his coat over his arm and the sweat rolling down his face; his legs wobbly, with that long, steady roll of a sailor coming ashore after a long cruise; the tobacco juice dribbling from his lips, together with warm, silent curses and some loud and foul ones too. The utter indolence, the insouciance of the man, the obscenities, the sacrilege. Not a man of God, like his father. No, a man who inspired love! His frailties were human frailties and he wore them jauntily, tauntingly, flauntingly, like banderillas. He would come down the warm open street with the gas mains bursting and the air full of sun and shit and oaths and maybe his fly would be open and his suspenders undone, or maybe his vest bright with vomit. Sometimes he came charging down the street, like a bull skidding on all fours, and then the street cleared magically, as if the manholes had opened up and swallowed their offal. Crazy Willy Maine would be standing on the shed over the paint shop, with his pants down, jerking away for dear life. There they stood in the dry electrical crackle of the open street with the gas mains bursting. A tandem that broke the minister's heart.

That was how he was then, Rob Ramsay. A man on a perpetual spree. He came back from the war with medals, and with fire in his guts. He puked up in front of his own door and he wiped up his puke with his own vest. He could clear the street quicker than a machine gun. *Faugh a balla!* That was his way. And a little later, in his warmheartedness, in that fine, careless way he had, he walked off the end of a pier and drowned himself.

I remember him so well and the house he lived in. Because it was on the doorstep of Rob Ramsay's house that we used to congregate in the warm summer evenings and watch the goings-on over the saloon across the street. A coming and going all night long and nobody bothered to pull down the shades. Just a stone's throw away from the little burlesque house called The Bum. All around The Bum were the saloons, and Saturday nights there was a long line outside, milling and pushing and squirming to get at the ticket window. Saturday nights, when the Girl in Blue was in her glory, some wild tar from the Navy Yard would be sure to jump out of his seat and grab off one of Millie deLeon's garters. And a little later that night they'd be sure to come strolling down the street and turn in at the family entrance. And soon they'd be standing in the bed-room over the saloon, pulling off their tight pants and the women yanking off their corsets and scratching themselves like monkeys, while down below they were scuttling the suds and biting each other's ears off, and such a wild, shrill laughter all bottled up inside there, like dynamite evap-orating. All this from Rob Ramsay's doorstep, the old man upstairs saying his prayers over a kerosene lamp, praying like an obscene nanny goat for an end to come, or when he got tired of praying coming down in his nightshirt, like an old leprechaun, and belaying us with a broomstick.

From Saturday afternoon on until Monday morning it was a period with-out end, one thing melting into another. Saturday morning already—how it happened God only knows—you could *feel* the war vessels lying at an-chor in the big basin. Saturday mornings my heart was in my mouth. I could see the decks being scrubbed down and the guns polished and the weight of those big sea monsters resting on the dirty glass lake of the basin was a luxurious weight on me. I was already dreaming of running away, of going to far places. But I got only as far as the other side of the river, about as far north as Second Avenue and Twenty-eighth Street, via the Belt Line. There I played the Orange Blossom Waltz and in the entr'actes I washed my eyes at the iron sink. The piano stood in the rear of the saloon. The keys were very yellow and my feet wouldn't reach to the pedals. I wore a velvet suit because velvet was the order of the day.

Everything that passed on the other side of the river was sheer lunacy: the sanded floor, the argand lamps, the mica pictures in which the snow never melted, the crazy Dutchmen with steins in their hands, the iron sink that had grown such a mossy coat of slime, the woman from Hamburg whose ass always hung over the back of the chair, the courtyard choked with sauerkraut. . . . Everything in three-quarter time that goes on for-ever. I walk between my parents, with one hand in my mother's muff and the other in my father's sleeve. My eyes are shut tight, tight as clams which draw back their lids only to weep.

All the changing tides and weather that passed over the river are in my blood. I can still feel the slipperiness of the big handrail which I leaned against in fog and rain, which sent through my cool forehead the shrill blasts of the ferryboat as she slid out of the slip. I can still see the mossy planks of the ferry slip buckling as the big round prow grazed her sides and the green, juicy water sloshed through the heaving, groaning planks of the slip. And overhead the sea gulls wheeling and diving, making a dirty noise with their dirty beaks, a hoarse, preying sound of inhuman feasting, of mouths fastened down on refuse, of scabby legs skimming the green-churned water.

One passes imperceptibly from one scene, one age, one life to another. Suddenly, walking down a street, be it real or be it a dream, one realizes for the first time that the years have flown, that all this has passed forever and will live on only in memory; and then the memory turns inward with a strange, clutching brilliance and one goes over these scenes and incidents perpetually, in dream and reverie, while walking a street, while lying with a woman, while reading a book, while talking to a stranger . . . suddenly, but always with terrific insistence and always with terrific accuracy, these memories intrude, rise up like ghosts and permeate every fiber of one's being. Henceforward everything moves on shifting levels— our thoughts, our dreams, our actions, our whole life. A parallelogram in which we drop from one platform of our scaffold to another. Henceforward we walk split into myriad fragments, like an insect with a hundred feet, a centipede with soft-stirring feet that drinks in the atmosphere; we walk with sensitive filaments that drink avidly of past and future, and all things melt into music and sorrow; we walk against a united world, asserting our dividedness. All things, as we walk, splitting with us into a myriad iridescent fragments. The great fragmentation of maturity. The great change. In youth we were whole and the terror and pain of the world penetrated us through and through. There was no sharp separation between joy and sorrow: they fused into one, as our waking life fuses with dream and sleep. We rose one being in the morning and at night we went down into an ocean, drowned out completely, clutching the stars and the fever of the day.

And then comes a time when suddenly all seems to be reversed. We live in the mind, in ideas, in fragments. We no longer drink in the wild outer music of the streets—we *remember* only. Like a monomaniac we relive the drama of youth. Like a spider that picks up the thread over and over and spews it out according to some obsessive, logarithmic pattern. If we are stirred by a fat bust it is the fat bust of a whore who bent over on a rainy night and showed us for the first time the wonder of the great milky globes; if we are stirred by the reflections on a wet pavement it is because at the age of seven we were suddenly speared by a premonition of the life to come as we stared unthinkingly into that bright, liquid mirror of the street. If the sight of a swinging door intrigues us it is the memory of a summer's evening when all the doors were swinging softly and where the light bent down to caress the shadow there were golden calves and lace and glittering parasols and through the chinks in the swinging door, like fine sand sifting through a bed of rubies, there drifted the music and the incense of gorgeous unknown bodies. Perhaps when that door parted to give us a choking glimpse of the world, perhaps then we had the first intimation of the great impact of sin, the first intimation that here over little round tables spinning in the light, our feet idly scraping the sawdust, our hands touching the cold stem of a glass, that here over these little round tables which later we are to look at with such yearning and reverence, that here, I say, we are to feel in the years to come the first iron of love, the first stains of rust, the first black, clawing hands of the pit, the bright circular pieces of tin in the streets, the gaunt sootcolored chimneys, the bare elm tree that lashes out in the summer's lightning and screams and shrieks as the rain beats down, while out of the hot earth the snails scoot away miraculously and all the air turns blue and sulphurous. Here over these tables, at the first call, the first touch of a hand, there is to come the bitter, gnawing pain that gripes at the bowels; the wine turns sour in our bellies and a pain rises from the soles of the feet and the round tabletops whirl with the anguish and the fever in our bones at the soft, burning touch of a hand. Here there is buried legend after legend of youth and melancholy, of savage nights and mysterious bosoms dancing on the wet mirror of the pavement, of women chuckling softly as they scratch themselves, of wild sailors' shouts, of long queues standing in front of the lobby, of boats brushing each other in the fog and tugs snorting furiously against the rush of tide while up on the Brooklyn Bridge a man is standing in agony, waiting to jump, or waiting to write a poem, or waiting for the blood to leave his vessels because if he advances another foot the pain of his love will kill him.

The plasm of the dream is the pain of separation. The dream lives on after the body is buried. We walk the streets with a thousand legs and eyes, with furry antennae picking up the slightest clue and memory of the past. In the aimless to and fro we pause now and then, like long, sticky plants, and we swallow whole the live morsels of the past. We open up soft and yielding to drink in the night and the oceans of blood which drowned the sleep of our youth. We drink and drink with an insatiable thirst. We are never whole again, but living in fragments, and all our parts separated by thinnest membrane. Thus when the fleet maneuvers in the Pacific it is the whole saga of youth flashing before your eyes, the dream of the open street and the sound of gulls wheeling and diving with garbage in their beaks; or it's the sound of the trumpet and flags flying and all the unknown parts of the earth sailing before your eyes without dates or meaning, wheeling like the tabletop in an iridescent sheen of power and glory. Day comes when you stand on the Brooklyn Bridge looking down into black funnels belching smoke and the gun barrels gleam and the buttons gleam and the water divides miraculously under the sharp, cutting prow, and like ice and lace, like a breaking and a smoking, the water churns green and blue with a cold incandescence, with the chill of champagne and burnt gills. And the prow cleaves the waters in an unending metaphor: the heavy body of the vessel moves on, with the prow ever dividing, and the weight of her is the unweighable weight of the world, the sinking down into unknown barometric pressures, into unknown geologic fissures and caverns where the waters roll melodiously and the stars turn over and die and hands reach up and grasp and clutch and never seize nor close but clutch and grasp while the stars die out one by one, myriads of them, myriads and myriads of worlds sinking down into cold incandescence, into fuliginous night of green and blue with broken ice and the burn of champagne and the hoarse cry of gulls, their beaks swollen with barnacles, their foul garbaged mouths stuffed forever under the silent keel of the ship.

One looks down from the Brooklyn Bridge on a spot of foam or a little lake of gasoline or a broken splinter or an empty scow; the world goes by upside down with pain and light devouring the innards, the sides of flesh bursting, the spears pressing in against the cartilage, the very armature of the body floating off into nothingness. Passes through you crazy words from the ancient world, signs and portents, the writing on the wall, the chinks of the saloon door, the cardplayers with their clay pipes, the gaunt tree against the tin factory, the black hands stained even in death. One walks the street at night with the bridge against the sky like a harp and the festered eyes of sleep burn into the shanties, deflower the walls; the stairs collapse in a smudge and the rats scamper across the ceiling; a voice is nailed against the door and long creepy things with furry antennae and thousand legs drop from the pipes like beads of sweat. Glad, murderous ghosts with the shriek of night-wind and the curses of warm-legged men; low, shallow coffins with rods through the body; grief-spit drooling down into the cold, waxen flesh, searing the dead eyes, the hard, chipped lids of dead clams. One walks around in a circular cage on shifting levels, stars and clouds under the escalator, and the walls of the cage revolve and there are no men and women without tails or claws, while over all things are written the letters of the alphabet in iron and permanganate. One walks round and round in a circular cage to the roll of drum-fire; the theater burns and the actors go on mouthing their lines; the bladder bursts, the teeth fall out, but the wailing of the clown is like the noise of dandruff falling. One walks around on moonless nights in the valley of craters, valley of dead fires and whitened skulls, of birds without wings. Round and round one walks, seeking the hub and nodality, but the fires are burned to ash and the sex of things is hidden in the finger of a glove.

And then one day, as if suddenly the flesh came undone and the blood beneath the flesh had coalesced with the air, suddenly the whole world roars again and the very skeleton of the body melts like wax. Such a day it may be when first you encounter Dostoevski. You remember the smell of the tablecloth on which the book rests; you look at the clock and it is only five minutes from eternity; you count the objects on the mantelpiece because the sound of numbers is a totally new sound in your mouth, because everything new and old, or touched and forgotten, is a fire and a mesmerism. Now every door of the cage is open and whichever way you walk is a straight line toward infinity, a straight, mad line over which the breakers roar and great rocs of marble and indigo swoop to lower their fevered eggs. Out of the waves beating phosphorescent step proud and prancing the enameled horses that marched with Alexander, their tight-proud bellies glowing with calcium, their nostrils dipped in laudanum. Now it is all snow and lice, with the great band of Orion slung around the ocean's crotch.

It was exactly five minutes past seven, at the corner of Broadway and Kosciusko Street, when Dostoevski first flashed across my horizon. Two men and a woman were dressing a shop window. From the middle of the upper legs down the mannikins were all wire. Empty shoe boxes lay banked against the window like last year's snow. . . .

That is how Dostoevski's name came in. Unostentatiously. Like an old shoe box. The Jew who pronounced his name for me had thick lips; he could not say Vladivostok, for instance, nor Carpathians—but he could say Dostoevski divinely. Even now, when I say Dostoevski, I see again his big, blubbery lips and the thin thread of spittle stretching like a rubber band as he pronounced the word. Between his two front teeth there was a more than usual space; it was exactly in the middle of this cavity that the word Dostoevski quivered and stretched, a thin, iridescent film of sputum in which all the gold of twilight had collected—for the sun was just going down over Kosciusko Street and the traffic overhead was breaking into a spring thaw, a chewing and grinding noise as if the mannikins in their wire legs were chewing each other alive. A little later, when I came to the land of the Houyhnhnms, I heard the same chewing and grinding overhead and again the spittle in a man's mouth quivered and stretched and shone iridescent in a dying sun. This time it is at the Dragon's Gorge: a man standing over me with a rattan stick and banging away with a wild Arabian smile. Again, as if my brain were a uterus, the walls of the world gave way. The name Swift was like a clear, hard pissing against the tin-plate lid of the world. Overhead the green fire-eater, his delicate intestines wrapped in tarpaulin; two enormous milk-white teeth champing down over a belt of black-greased cogs connecting with the shooting gallery and the Turkish bath; the belt of cogs slipping over a frame of bleached bones. The green dragon of Swift moves over the cogs with an endless pissing sound, grinding down fine and foreshortened the human-sized midgets that are sucked in like macaroni. In and out of the esophagus, up and down and around the scapular bones and the mastoid delta, falling through the bottomless pit of the viscera, gurgitating and exgurgitating, the crotch spreading and slipping, the cogs moving on relentlessly, chewing alive all the fine, foreshortened macaroni hanging by the whiskers from the dragon's red gulch. I look into the milk-white smile of the barker, that fanatical Arabian smile which came out of the Dreamland fire, and then I step quietly into the open belly of the dragon. Between the crazy slats of the skeleton that holds the revolving cogs the land of the Houyhnhnms spreads out before me; that hissing, pissing noise in my ears as if the language of men were made of seltzer water.

Up and down over the greasy black belt, over the Turkish baths, through the house of the winds, over the sky-blue waters, between the clay pipes and the silver balls dancing on liquid jets: the infra-human world of fedoras and banjos, of bandannas and black cigars; butterscotch stretching from peg to Winnipeg, beer bottles bursting, spun-glass molasses and hot tamales, surf-roar and griddle sizzle, foam and eucalyptus, dirt, chalk, confetti, a woman's white thigh, a broken oar; the razzle-dazzle of wooden slats, the meccano puzzle, the smile that never comes off, the wild Arabian smile with spits of fire, the red gulch and the green intestines. . . .

O world, strangled and collapsed, where are the strong white teeth? O world, sinking with the silver balls and the corks and the life-preservers, where are the rosy scalps? O glab and glairy, O glabrous world now chewed to a frazzle, under what dead moon do you lie cold and gleaming?

ELIEZER GREENBERG
Visiting Second Avenue

I seldom come to see you, these days,
And except for a used-up old building
They have managed to leave alone—
Like some old souvenir—
I'd never recognize this neighborhood;
You have changed so much, Second Avenue!
But even these trinkets abandoned by the past
Remind me of the treasure here that was ours!

O closest of all these neighboring streets!
I said good-by to you long ago
And try to keep out of your way
—It's painful, now, to come across you,
For when I tread your ground
It's as though I were walking
On my nearest ones' graves.

But must we talk of loss,
Plunging hearts into mourning?
Whoever forgets these things
Has never remembered,
Nor ever shared our joy,
Nor sips of our sorrow now!

But if the woes of sacrifice are vast
They command neither memory nor imagination:
A true treasure can never be wasted!
There is a Great, One-Shot Festival
That burns all the weekdays in eternal flames.

Translated by John Hollander

More than just that one time
Its awakening breath
Can make dry bones live,
Raising them from the valley of death,
Giving them life, winged with faith, and hope.

ALFRED KAZIN
The Block and Beyond

The old drugstore on our corner has been replaced by a second-hand furniture store; the old candy store has been replaced by a second-hand furniture store, the old bakery, the old hardware shop, the old "coffee pot" that was once reached over a dirt road. I was there the day they put a pavement in. That "coffee pot" was the first restaurant I ever sat in, trembling—they served ham and bacon there—over a swiss cheese on rye and coffee in a thick mug without a saucer as I watched the truck drivers kidding the heavily lipsticked girl behind the counter. The whole block is now thick with secondhand furniture stores. The fluttering red canvas signs BARGAINS BARGAINS reach up to the first-floor windows. At every step I have to fight maple love seats bulging out of the doors. It looks as if our old life has been turned out into the street, suddenly reminds me of the nude shamed look furniture on the street always had those terrible first winters of the depression, when we stood around each newly evicted family to give them comfort and the young Communists raged up and down the street calling for volunteers to put the furniture back and crying aloud with their fists lifted to the sky. But on the Chester Street side of the house I make out the letters we carefully pasted there in tar sometime in the fall of either 1924 or 1925:

> DAZZY VANCE
> WORLDS GREATEST PICHER
> 262 STRIKEOUTS
> BROOKLYN NATIONAL LEAG
> GIANTS STINK ON ICE
> DAZZY DAZZY DAZZY

The old barbershop is still there. Once it was owned by two brothers, the younger one fat and greasy and with a waxed stiffly pointed mustache of which he was so proud that he put a photograph of himself in the window with the inscription: "MEN! LOOK AT OUR MUSTACHE AND LOOK AT YOURS!" The older one was dry and sad, the "conscientious" partner. The fat brother had an old fiddle he let me play in the shop when business was bad; he would sprawl in the first barber chair languidly admiring himself in the great mirrors, clicking his teeth over the nudes in the *Police Gazette,* and kept time for me by waving his razor. I never liked him very much; he was what we reproachfully called a "sport," a loud and boastful man; he always smelled of hair lotion. You could see each hair as it ran off the crown of his head so sticky and twisted in lotion that it reflected the light from the bulbs in the ceiling. We were all a little afraid of him. One day he bought a motorcycle on credit, and as he started it from the curb, flew into the window of the delicatessen store. I remember the shiver of the glass as it instantaneously fell out all around him, and as he picked himself up, his face and hands streaming with blood, the sly little smile with which he pointed to the sausages and pickle pots in the street: "Hey you little bastard! Free treat!"

I see the barbershop through the steam from the hot towel fount. The vapor glistened on the unbelievable breasts of the calendar nudes pasted above the mirrors and on the fat bandaged chin of Peaches Browning every day in the *News* and on the great colored drawing all over the front page of the *Graphic* one morning showing Mrs. Ruth Snyder strapped and burning in the electric chair. The smell of hair tonic could never disguise the steaming exhalation of raw female flesh. Everything in that barbershop promised me a first look. On the table, along with the *News* and the *Graphic, College Humor* and the *Police Gazette,* lay several volumes of a pictorial history of the World War. I played the barber's violin for him only because I could then get to sit over those volumes by the hour, lost in the gray photographs and drawings of men going into battle, ruined towns in Serbia, Belgium, and France where one chimney still rose from a house destroyed by shell fire, pictures of the victorious French in 1919 dipping their battle standards in the Rhine. There were two photographs I remember particularly: it was really for them that I went back and back to that barbershop. One showed a group of German officers in full uniform, with all their medals, standing outside a brothel in France with the ladies of the house, who were naked to the waist and wore crosses between their enormous breasts. The officers had their arms comfortably draped over the girls' shoulders, and grinned into the camera. GERMAN KULTUR, ran the caption. HOW THE ENEMY AMUSES ITSELF BEHIND THE LINES. The other photograph showed Kaiser Wilhelm with his retinue, inspecting troops. The Kaiser and the generals were walking on wooden planks; the caption noted that the planks had been laid there to keep the distinguished company from walking in the blood that ran over the field.

The shoemaker is still there; the old laundry is now a printing shop. Next to it is the twin of our old house, connected with ours below the intervening stores by a long common cellar. As I look at the iron grillwork over the glass door, I think of the dark-faced girl who used to stand on that stoop night after night watching for her Italian boy friend. Her widowed mother, dressed always in black, a fat meek woman with a clubfoot, was so horrified by the affair that she went to the neighbors for help. The quarrels of mother and daughter could be heard all over the street. "How can you go around with an Italian? How can you think of it? You're unnatural! You're draining the blood straight from my heart!" Night after night she would sit at her window, watching the girl go off with her *Italyéner*—ominous word that contained all her fear of the Gentiles—and weep. The Italian boy was devoted to the daughter and wanted them to marry. Again and again he tried to persuade the mother, but she would lock the door on him and cry out from behind it in Yiddish: "I have harmed you and your family? I interfere with *your* customs? Go away and leave us be! Leave us be! A Jewish girl is not for you, Mister! Go away!" In desperation, he offered "to become a Jew." No one had ever heard of such a thing, and the mother was so astonished that she gave her consent to the marriage. The boy was overjoyed—but waited until the last possible moment before the wedding to undergo circumcision, and as he walked tremblingly to the canopy, the blood dripping down his trouser legs, fainted dead away. The block never stopped talking about it.

Where now is my beautiful Mrs. Baruch, the "chicken lady," who sat smack in the middle of her store on a bloody kitchen chair plucking and plucking the feathers off her chickens with such a raw hearty laugh that you could hear her a block away? I would stop in her doorway on my way back from school just to watch her work, for as she plucked, plucked the feathers off her chickens with one grimly impatient pull along her right elbow, she seemed instantaneously to draw out of their bellies a great coiling mass of intestines and blood vessels, and—never for a moment letting up in her unending hoarse cackle—scolded and gossiped with the women standing around her. Whenever she looked up and saw me standing in the doorway, she would hold up her hands in mock dismay, feathers sticking to each finger, and her hairy chin trembling with laughter, would call out—"Hey, studént! My Alfred! Come give me a big kiss! Is all right! Your mother left here an hour ago!"

And where is Blumka, our local madwoman, who every Friday afternoon just before the Sabbath began, icy pale under her sleek black pompadour, made the rounds of the block dragging a child's cart behind her and wearing a long satin dress? She often sat on the stoop of our house with her head resting against the glass in the door, gossiping with the neighbors or talking to herself, and never budged until the cart was heaped with charcoal, chicory, the long white Sabbath *khalleh,* and fruit. It was on our steps particularly that she liked to take her rest. Perhaps she enjoyed embarrassing us; perhaps, I used to think, she stopped there because she knew how much I loved watching her, for she would smile and smile at me with a fixed and shameless grin. Shameless was our word for her—a Jewish woman to beg in the streets! She had a brutal directness in the way she did everything—flopped around the streets all Friday long with her cart ignoring everyone with a dreamy contempt unless she wanted to talk; openly demanded her living of us; sat herself down on a stoop whenever she liked, mumbling to herself or jeering at the children; and when she liked, lay flat on the steps singing old Yiddish ditties to herself. Always in the same long black satin dress that came down to her high button shoes, always dragging that battered children's cart behind her, she would sometimes lie there against the glass, her tightly coiled mass of dead-looking hair splitting the light where she lay, her long straight nose and fierce jaw jutting into the air with a kind of insolent defiance. She seemed always to be jeering, but it was hard to find out what she meant by it, for she said everything that came into her mind in the same gruff oddly disdainful tone of voice, her icy pale cheeks moving tensely up and down as she chewed at a piece of bread.

The block: *my* block. It was on the Chester Street side of our house, between the grocery and the back wall of the old drugstore, that I was hammered into the shape of the streets. Everything beginning at Blake Avenue would always wear for me some delightful strangeness and mildness, simply because it was not of my block, *the* block, where the clang of your head sounded against the pavement when you fell in a fist fight, and the rows of storelights on each side were pitiless, watching you. Anything away from the block was good: even a school you never went to, two blocks away: there were vegetable gardens in the park across the street. Returning from "New York," I would take the longest routes home from the subway, get off a station ahead of our own, only for the unexpectedness of walking through Betsy Head Park and hearing the gravel crunch under my feet as I went beyond the vegetable gardens, smelling the sweaty sweet dampness from the pool in summer and the dust on the leaves as I passed under the ailanthus trees. On the block itself everything rose up only to test me.

We worked every inch of it, from the cellars and the backyards to the sickening space between the roofs. Any wall, any stoop, any curving metal edge on a billboard sign made a place against which to knock a ball; any bottom rung of a fire escape ladder a goal in basketball; any sewer cover a base; any crack in the pavement a "net" for the tense sharp tennis that we played by beating a soft ball back and forth with our hands between the squares. Betsy Head Park two blocks away would always feel slightly foreign, for it belonged to the Amboys and the Bristols and the Hopkinsons as much as it did to us. *Our* life every day was fought out on the pavement and in the gutter, up against the walls of the houses and the glass fronts of the drugstore and the grocery, in and out of the fresh steaming piles of horse manure, the wheels of passing carts and automobiles, along the iron spikes of the stairway to the cellar, the jagged edge of the open garbage cans, the crumbly steps of the old farmhouses still left on one side of the street.

As I go back to the block now, and for a moment fold my body up again in its narrow arena—there, just there, between the black of the asphalt and the old women in their kerchiefs and flowered housedresses sitting on the tawny kitchen chairs—the back wall of the drugstore still rises up to test me. Every day we smashed a small black viciously hard regulation handball against it with fanatical cuts and drives and slams, beating and slashing at it almost in hatred for the blind strength of the wall itself. I was never good enough at handball, was always practicing some trick shot that might earn me esteem, and when I was weary of trying, would often bat a ball down Chester Street just to get myself to Blake Avenue. I have this memory of playing one-o'-cat by myself in the sleepy twilight, at a moment when everyone else had left the block. The sparrows floated down from the telephone wires to peck at every fresh pile of horse manure, and there was a smell of brine from the delicatessen store, of egg crates and of the milk scum left in the great metal cans outside the grocery, of the thick white paste oozing out from behind the fresh Hecker's Flour ad on the metal signboard. I would throw the ball in the air, hit it with my bat, then with perfect satisfaction drop the bat to the ground and run to the next sewer cover. Over and over I did this, from sewer cover to sewer cover, until I had worked my way to Blake Avenue and could see the park.

With each clean triumphant ring of my bat against the gutter leading me on, I did the whole length of our block up and down, and never knew how happy I was just watching the asphalt rise and fall, the curve of the steps up to an old farmhouse. The farmhouses themselves were streaked red on one side, brown on the other, but the steps themselves were always gray. There was a tremor of pleasure at one place; I held my breath in nausea at another. As I ran after my ball with the bat heavy in my hand, the odd successiveness of things in myself almost choked me, the world was so full as I ran—past the cobblestoned yards into the old farmhouses, where stray chickens still waddled along the stones; past the little candy store where we went only if the big one on our side of the block was out of Eskimo Pies; past the three neighboring tenements where the last of the old women sat on their kitchen chairs yawning before they went up to make supper. Then came Mrs. Rosenwasser's house, the place on the block I first identified with what was farthest from home, and strangest, because it was a "private" house; then the fences around the monument works, where black cranes rose up above the yard and you could see the smooth gray slabs that would be cut and carved into tombstones, some of them already engraved with the names and dates and family virtues of the dead.

Beyond Blake Avenue was the pool parlor outside which we waited all through the tense September afternoons of the World's Series to hear the latest scores called off the ticker tape—and where as we waited, banging a ball against the bottom of the wall and drinking water out of empty coke bottles, I breathed the chalk off the cues and listened to the clocks ringing in the fire station across the street. There was an old warehouse next to the pool parlor; the oil on the barrels and the iron staves had the same rusty smell. A block away was the park, thick with the dusty gravel I liked to hear my shoes crunch in as I ran round and round the track; then a great open pavilion, the inside mysteriously dark, chill even in summer; there I would wait in the sweaty coolness before pushing on to the wading ring where they put up a shower on the hottest days.

Beyond the park the "fields" began, all those still unused lots where we could still play hard ball in perfect peace—first shooting away the goats and then tearing up goldenrod before laying our bases. The smell and touch of those "fields," with their wild compost under the billboards of weeds, goldenrod, bricks, goat droppings, rusty cans, empty beer bottles, fresh new lumber, and damp cement, lives in my mind as Brownsville's great open door, the wastes that took us through to the west. I used to go round them in summer with my cousins selling near-beer to the carpenters, but always in a daze, would stare so long at the fibrous stalks of the goldenrod as I felt their harshness in my hand that I would forget to make a sale, and usually go off sick on the beer I drank up myself. Beyond! Beyond! Only to see something new, to get away from each day's narrow battleground between the grocery and the back wall of the drugstore! Even the other end of our block, when you got to Mrs. Rosenwasser's house and the monuments works, was dear to me for the contrast. On summer nights, when we played Indian trail, running away from each other on prearranged signals, the greatest moment came when I could plunge into the darkness down the block for myself and hide behind the slabs in the monument works. I remember the air whistling around me as I ran, the panicky thud of my bones in my sneakers, and then the slabs rising in the light from the street lamps as I sped past the little candy store and crept under the fence.

In the darkness you could never see where the crane began. We liked to trap the enemy between the slabs and sometimes jumped them from great mounds of rock just in from the quarry. A boy once fell to his death that way, and they put a watchman there to keep us out. This made the slabs all the more impressive to me, and I always aimed first for that yard whenever we played follow-the-leader. Day after day the monument works became oppressively more mysterious and remote, though it was only just down the block; I stood in front of it every afternoon on my way back from school, filling it with my fears. It was not death I felt there—the slabs were usually faceless. It was the darkness itself, and the wind howling around me whenever I stood poised on the edge of a high slab waiting to jump. Then I would take in, along with the fear, some amazement of joy that I had found my way out that far.

Beyond! Beyond! *Beyond* was "the city," connected only by interminable subway lines and some old Brooklyn-Manhattan trolley car rattling across Manhattan Bridge. At night, as the trolley ground its way home in the rain through miles of unknown streets from some meeting in the Jewish Daily *Forward* building on the East Side to which my father had taken me, I saw the flickering light bulbs in the car, the hard yellow benches on which we sat half asleep, the motorman's figure bulging the green curtain he had drawn against the lights in the car, as a rickety cart stumbling through infinite space—the driver taking us where? *Beyond* was the wheeze of an accordion on the Staten Island ferry boat—the music rocking in such unison with the vibration of the engines as the old man walked in and out of the cars on the lower deck squeezing the tunes out of the pleats that never after would I be able to take a ferry from South Ferry, from Christopher Street, from 23rd, from Dyckman, from 125th, without expecting that same man to come round with his silver-backed accordion and his hat in his hand as he jangled a few coins in a metal plate. *Beyond* was the long shivering blast of the ferry starting out from the Battery in sight of the big Colgate ad across the river in Jersey; the depth of peace as the sun warmed the panels of the doors sliding out to the observation deck; the old Italian shoeshine men walking round and round with their boxes between all those suddenly relaxed New Yorkers comfortably staring at each other in the high wind on the top deck; a garbage scow burning in the upper bay just under Liberty's right arm; the minarets on Ellis Island; the old prison walls under the trees of Governor's Island; then, floating back in the cold dusk toward the diamond-lighted wall of Manhattan skyscrapers, the way we huddled in the great wooden varnish-smelling cabin inside as if we were all getting under the same quilt on a cold night.

Beyond was the canvas awnings over an El station in summer. Inside, the florid red windows had curlicues running up and down their borders. I had never seen anything like them in all the gritty I.R.T. stations below. Those windows were richer than all my present. The long march of snails up and down and around the borders of those windows, the cursive scrolls in the middle patch forever turning back on themselves, promised to lead me straight into the old New York of gaslight and police stations I always looked for in the lower city. And of a winter afternoon—the time for which I most lovingly remember the El, for the color of the winter dusk as it fell through those painted windows, and the beauty of the snow on the black cars and iron rails and tar roofs we saw somewhere off Brooklyn Bridge—when the country stove next to the change booth blazed and blazed as some crusty old woman with a pince-nez gave out change, and the heavy turnstiles crashed with a roar inside the wooden shed—then, among the darkly huddled crowds waiting to go out to the train, looking out on Brooklyn Bridge all dark sweeping cable lines under drifts of snow, I pretended those were gaslights I saw in the streets below, that all old New Yorkers were my fathers, and that the train we waited for could finally take me back—back and back to that old New York of wood and brownstones and iron, where Theodore Roosevelt as Police Commissioner had walked every night.

Beyond was anything old and American—the name *Fraunces Tavern* repeated to us on a school excursion; the eighteenth-century muskets and glazed oil paintings on the wall; the very streets, the deeper you got into Brooklyn, named after generals of the Revolutionary War—Putnam, Gates, Kosciusko, DeKalb, Lafayette, Pulaski. *Beyond* was the sound of *Desbrosses* Street that steaming July morning we crossed back on a Jersey ferry, and the smell of the salt air in the rotting planks floating on the green scummy waters of the Hudson. *Beyond* was the watery floor of the Aquarium that smelled of the eternally wet skins of the seals in the great tank; the curve of lower Broadway around Bowling Green Park when you went up to Wall Street; the yellow wicker seats facing each other in the middle of the El car; the dome of the Manhattan Savings Bank over Chinatown at the entrance to Manhattan Bridge, and then in Brooklyn again, after we had traveled from light into dark, dark into light, along the shuddering shadowy criss-cross of the bridge's pillars, the miles and miles of Gentile cemeteries where crosses toppled up and down endless slopes. *Beyond* was that autumn morning in New Haven when I walked up and down two *red* broken paving stones, smelled the leaves burning in the yard, and played with black battered poker chips near the country stove in an aunt's kitchen; it was the speckles on the bananas hanging in the window of the grocery store another aunt owned in the Negro streets just behind Union Station in Washington; the outrageously warm taste of milk fresh from a cow that summer my mother cooked with a dozen others in the same Catskill boarding house; it was the open trolley cars going to Coney Island, the conductor swinging from bar to bar as he came around the ledge collecting fares; it was the *Robert Fulton* going up the Hudson to Indian Point, the ventilators on the upper deck smelling of soup.

Beyond, even in Brownsville, was the summer sound of *flax* when my mother talked of *der heym.* It was the Negroes singing as they passed under our windows late at night on their way back to Livonia Avenue. It was the Children's Library on Stone Avenue, because they had an awning over the front door; in the long peaceful reading room there were story-book tiles over the fireplace and covered deep wooden benches on each side of it where I read my way year after year from every story of King Alfred the Great to *Twenty Thousand Leagues Under the Sea. Beyond* was the burly Jewish truckers from the wholesale fruit markets on Osborne Street sitting in their dark smoky "Odessa" and "Roumanian" tea-rooms, where each table had its own teapot, and where the men sat over mounds of saucers smoking Turkish cigarettes and beating time to the balalaîka. *Beyond* was the way to the other end of Sutter Avenue, past a store I often went into to buy buttons and thread for my mother, and where the light simmered on the thin upturned curves of the pearl buttons in the window. *Beyond* was the roar in the Pennsylvania freight yards on the way to East New York; even the snow houses we built in the backyard of a cousin's house on Herzl Street waiting to ambush those thieves from Bristol Street. It was the knife grinder's horse and wagon when he stopped on our block, and an "American" voice called up to every window, *Sharpen knives! Sharpen knives!*—that man had obviously come from a long way off.

Beyond! Beyond! It was the clean, general store smell of packaged white bread in the A&P that Passover week I could not eat matzoh, and going home, hid the soft squunchy loaf of Ward's bread under my coat so that the neighbors would not see. It was the way past the car barns at the end of Rockaway Avenue, that week my father was painting in New Lots, and I took that route for the first time, bringing him his lunch one summer afternoon. I could not wait to get out on the other side of the dark subway station. I had never seen another part of Brownsville where the going was so strange, where streets looked so empty, where the sun felt so hot. It was as if there were not enough houses there to stand in its way. When the sun fell across the great white pile of the new Telephone Company building, you could smell the stucco burning as you passed; then some liquid sweetness that came to me from deep in the rings of freshly cut lumber stacked in the yards, and the fresh plaster and paint on the brand-new storefronts. Rawness, sunshiny rawness down the end streets of the city, as I thought of them then—the hot ash-laden stink of the refuse dumps in my nostrils and the only sound at noon the resonant metal plunk of a tin can I kicked ahead of me as I went my way. Then two blocks more, and the car barns I loved. The light falling down the hollows in the corrugated tin roof seemed to say *Go over! Go over!,* marked the place from which the stacked trolley cars began all over again their long weary march into the city. I liked to see them stacked against each other, a thin trail of track leading out of the sheds, then another track, then another, until everywhere you could see, the streets were wild with car tracks pointing the way back to the city.

Beyond was that day they took us first to the Botanic Garden next to the Brooklyn Museum, and after we went through the bamboo gate into the Japanese Garden, crossed over a curved wooden bridge past the stone figure of a heron dreaming in the water, I lay in the grass waiting to eat my lunch out of the shoe box and wondered why water lilies floated half-submerged in the pond and did not sink. They led us into the museum that day, up the big stone steps they had then, through vast empty halls that stung my nose with the prickly smell of new varnish and were lined with the effigies of medieval Japanese warriors—the black stringy hairs on their wigs oppressively unreal, the faces mock-terrible as they glared down at us through their stiffly raised swords, everything in that museum wearisome and empty and smelling of floor polish until they pushed us through a circular room upstairs violently ablaze with John Singer Sargent's watercolors of the Caribbean and into a long room lined with oily dim farmscapes of America in the nineteenth century, and I knew I would come back, that I would have to come back.

Museums and parks were related, both oases to stop in "beyond." But in some way museums and parks were painful, each an explosion of unbearable fullness in my brain. I could never go home from the Brooklyn Museum, a walk around the reservoir in Central Park, or sit in a rowboat Sunday afternoons in Prospect Park—where your voice hallooed against the stone walls of the footbridge as you waited in that sudden cold darkness below, boat against boat, to be pushed on to the boathouse and so end the afternoon—without feeling the same sadness that came after the movies. The day they took us to the Children's Museum—rain was dripping on the porch of that old wooden house, the halls were lined with Audubon prints and were hazel in the thin antique light—I was left with the distinct impression that I had been stirring between my fingers dried earth and fallen leaves that I had found in between the red broken paving stones of some small American town. I seemed to see neighborhood rocks and minerals in the dusty light of the late afternoon slowiy stirring behind glass at the back of the village museum. But that same day they took us to Forest Park in Queens, and I saw a clearing filled with stone picnic tables—*nothing* had ever cried out such a welcome as those stone tables in the clearing—saw the trees in their dim green recede in one long moving tide back into dusk, and gasped in pain when the evening rushed upon us before I had a chance to walk that woodland through.

There was never enough time. The morning they led us through the Natural History Museum, under the skeletons of great whales floating dreamlike on wires from the ceiling, I had to wait afterward against the meteor in the entrance yard for my dizziness to pass. Those whales! those whales! But that same morning they took us across Central Park to the Metropolitan, and entering through the back door in from the park, I was flung spinning in a bewilderment of delight from the Greek discus-throwers to the Egyptians to the long rows of medieval knights to the breasts of Venus glistening in my eyes as she sat—some curtain drawn before her hiding the worst of her nakedness—smiling with Mars and surrounded by their children.

The bewilderment eased, a little, when we went up many white steps directly to the American paintings. There was a long, narrow, corridor-looking room lined with the portraits of seventeenth-century merchants and divines—nothing for me there as they coldly stared at me, their faces uninterruptedly rosy in time. But far in the back, in an alcove near the freight elevator, hung so low and the figures so dim in the faint light that I crouched to take them in, were pictures of New York some time after the Civil War—skaters in Central Park, a red muffler flying in the wind; a gay crowd moving round and round Union Square Park; horse cars charging between the brownstones of lower Fifth Avenue at dusk. I could not believe my eyes. Room on room they had painted my city, my country—Winslow Homer's dark oblong of Union soldiers making camp in the rain, tenting tonight, tenting on the old camp ground as I had never thought I *would* get to see them when we sang that song in school; Thomas Eakins's solitary sculler on the Schuylkill, resting to have his picture taken in the yellow light bright with patches of some raw spring in Pennsylvania showing on the other side of him; and most wonderful to me then, John Sloan's picture of a young girl standing in the wind on the deck of a New York ferryboat—surely to Staten Island, and just about the year of my birth?—looking out to water.

GALWAY KINNELL
The Avenue Bearing the Initial
of Christ into the New World

*Was diese kleine Gasse doch für ein Reich an
sich war . . .*

for Gail

1

pcheek pcheek pcheek pcheek pcheek
They cry. The motherbirds thieve the air
To appease them. A tug on the East River
Blasts the bass-note of its passage, lifted
From the infra-bass of the sea. A broom
Swishes over the sidewalk like feet through leaves.
Valerio's puschcart Ice Coal Kerosene
Moves   clack
               clack
                  clack
On a broken wheelrim. Ringing in its chains
The New Star Laundry horse comes down the street
Like a roofleak whucking in a pail.
At the redlight, where a horn blares,
The Golden Harvest Bakery brakes on its gears,
Squeaks, and seethes in place. A propane-
gassed bus makes its way with big, airy sighs.

Across the street a woman throws open
Her window,
She sets, terribly softly,

Two potted plants on the windowledge
       tic   tic
And bangs shut her window.

A man leaves a doorway tic toc tic toc tic toc tic hurrah
      toc splat on Avenue C tic etc and turns the corner.

Banking the same corner
A pigeon coasts 5th Street in shadows,
Looks for altitude, surmounts the rims of buildings,
And turns white.

The babybirds pipe down. It is day.

   2

In sunlight on the Avenue
The Jew rocks along in a black fur shtraimel,
Black robe, black knickers, black knee-stockings,
Black shoes. His beard like a sod-bottom
Hides the place where he wears no tie.
A dozen children troop after him, barbels flying,
In skullcaps. They are Reuben, Simeon, Levi, Judah, Issachar,
      Zebulun, Benjamin, Dan, Naphtali, Gad, Asher.
With the help of the Lord they will one day become
Courtiers, thugs, rulers, rabbis, asses, adders, wrestlers,
      bakers, poets, cartpushers, infantrymen.

The old man is sad-faced. He is near burial
And one son is missing. The women who bore him sons
And are past bearing, mourn for the son
And for the father, wondering if the man will go down
Into the grave of a son mourning, or if at the last
The son will put his hands on the eyes of his father.

The old man wades towards his last hour.
On 5th Street, between Avenues A and B,
In sunshine, in his private cloud, Bunko Certified Embalmer,
Cigar in his mouth, nose to the wind, leans
At the doorway of Bunko's Funeral Home & Parlour,
Glancing west towards the Ukrainians, eastward idly
Where the Jew rocks towards his last hour.
Sons, grandsons at his heel, the old man
Confronts the sun. He does not feel its rays

Through his beard, he does not understand
Fruits and vegetables live by the sun.
Like his children he is sallow-faced, he sees
A blinding signal in the sky, he smiles.

Bury me not Bunko damned Catholic I pray you in Egypt.

   3

From the Station House
Under demolishment on Houston
To the Power Station on 14th,
Jews, Negroes, Puerto Ricans
Walk in the spring sunlight.

The Downtown Talmud Torah
Blosztein's Cutrate Bakery
Areceba Panataria Hispano
Peanuts Dried Fruit Nuts & Canned Goods
Productos Tropicales
Appetizing Herring Candies Nuts
Nathan Kugler Chicken Store Fresh Killed Daily
Little Rose Restaurant
Rubinstein the Hatter Mens Boys Hats Caps Furnishings
J. Herrmann Dealer in All Kinds of Bottles
Natural Bloom Cigars
Blony Bubblegum
Mueren las Cucarachas Super Potente Garantizada de Matar las
      Cucarachas mas Resistentes
Wenig מצבות
G. Schnee Stairbuilder
Everyouth la Original Loción Eterna Juventud Satisfacción Dinero
      Devuelto
Happy Days Bar & Grill

Through dust-stained windows over storefronts
Curtains drawn aside, onto the Avenue
Thronged with Puerto Ricans, Negroes, Jews,
Baby carriages stuffed with groceries and babies,
The old women peer, blessed damozels
Sitting up there young forever in the cockroached rooms,
Eating fresh-killed chicken, productos tropicales,
Appetizing herring, canned goods, nuts;
They puff out smoke from Natural Bloom cigars

And one day they puff like Blony Bubblegum.
Across the square skies with faces in them
Pigeons skid, crashing into the brick.
From a rooftop a boy fishes at the sky,
Around him a flock of pigeons fountains,
Blown down and swirling up again, seeking the sky.
From a skyview of the city they must seem
A whirlwind on the desert seeking itself;
Here they break from the rims of the buildings
Without rank in the blue military cemetery sky.
A red kite wriggles like a tadpole
Into the sky beyond them, crosses
The sun, lays bare its own crossed skeleton.

To fly from this place—to roll
On some bubbly blacktop in the summer,
To run under the rain of pigeon plumes, to be
Tarred, and feathered with birdshit, Icarus,

In Kugler's glass headdown dangling by yellow legs.

    4

First Sun Day of the year. Tonight,
When the sun will have turned from the earth,
She will appear outside Hy's Luncheonette,
The crone who sells the *News* and the *Mirror,*
The oldest living thing on Avenue C,
Outdating much of its brick and mortar.
If you ask for the *News* she gives you the *Mirror*
And squints long at the nickel in her hand
Despising it, perhaps, for being a nickel,
And stuffs it in her apron pocket
And sucks her lips. Rain or stars, every night
She is there, squatting on the orange crate,
Issuing out only in darkness, like the cucarachas
And strange nightmares in the chambers overhead.
She can't tell one newspaper from another,
She has forgotten how Nain her dead husband looked,
She has forgotten her children's whereabouts
Or how many there were, or what the *News*
And *Mirror* tell about that we buy them with nickels.
She is sure only of the look of a nickel
And that there is a Lord in the sky overhead.

She dwells in a flesh that is of the Lord
And drifts out, therefore, only in darkness
Like the streetlamp outside the Luncheonette
Or the lights in the secret chamber
In the firmament, where Yahweh himself dwells.
Like Magdelene in the Battistero of Saint John
On the carved-up continent, in the land of sun,
She lives shadowed, under a feeble bulb
That lights her face, her crab's hands, her small bulk on the crate.

She is Pulchería mother of murderers and madmen,
She is also Alyona whose neck was a chicken leg.

Mother was it the insufferable wind?
She sucks her lips a little further into the mousehole.
She stares among the stars, and among the streetlamps.

The mystery is hers.

        5

That violent song of the twilight!
Now, in the silence, will the motherbirds
Be dead, and the infantbirds
That were in the dawn merely transparent
Unfinished things, nothing but bellies,
Will they have been shoved out
And in the course of a morning, casually,
On scrawny wings, have taken up the life?

        6

In the pushcart market, on Sunday,
A crate of lemons discharges light like a battery.
Icicle-shaped carrots that through black soil
Wove away lie like flames in the sun.
Onions with their shirts ripped seek sunlight
On green skins. The sun beats
On beets dirty as boulders in cowfields,
On turnips pinched and gibbous
From budging rocks, on embery sweets,
Peanut-shaped Idahos, shore-pebble Long Islands and Maines,
On horseradishes still growing weeds on the flat ends,
Cabbages lying about like sea-green brains

The skulls have been shucked from,
On tomatoes, undented plum-tomatoes, alligator-skinned
Cucumbers, that float pickled
In the wooden tubs of green skim milk—

Sky-flowers, dirt-flowers, underdirt-flowers,
Those that climbed for the sun in their lives
And those that wormed away—equally uprooted,
Maimed, lopped, shucked, and misaimed.

In the market in Damascus a goat
Came to a stall where twelve goatheads
Were lined up for sale. It sniffed them
One by one. Finally thirteen goats started
Smiling in their faintly sardonic way.

A crone buys a pickle from a crone,
It is wrapped in the *Mirror,*
At home she will open the wrapping, stained,
And stare and stare and stare at it.
And the cucumbers, and the melons,
And the leeks, and the onions, and the garlic.

    7

Already the Avenue troughs the light of day.
Southwards, towards Houston and Pitt,
Where Avenue C begins, the eastern ranges
Of the wiped-out lives—punks, lushes,
Panhandlers, pushers, rumsoaks, everyone
Who took it easy when he should have been out failing at some-
    thing—
The pots-and-pans man pushes his cart,
Through the intersection of the light, at 3rd,
Where sunset smashes on the aluminum of it,
On the bottoms, curves, handles, metal panes,
Mirrors: of the bead-curtained cave under the falls
In Freedom, Seekonk Woods leafing the light out,
Halfway to Kingston where a road branched out suddenly,
Between Pamplonne and Les Salins two meeting paths
Over a sea the green of churchsteeple copper.
Of all places on earth inhabited by men
Why is it we find ourselves on this Avenue
Where the dusk gets worse,

And the mirrorman pushing his heaped mirrors
Into the shadows between 3rd and 2nd,
Pushes away a mess of old pots and pans?

The ancient Negro sits as usual
Outside the Happy Days Bar & Grill. He wears
Dark glasses. Every once in a while, abruptly,
He starts to sing, chanting in a hoarse, nearly breaking
Voice—

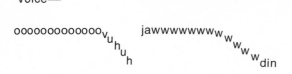

And becomes silent
   Stares into the polaroid Wilderness
Gross-Rosen, Maidanek, Flössenberg, Ravensbruck, Stutthof, Riga,
Bergen-Belsen, Mauthausen, Birkenau, Treblinka, Natzweiler,
Dachau, Buchenwald, Auschwitz—
                        Villages,
Pasture-bordered hamlets on the far side of the river.

    8

The promise was broken too freely
To them and to their fathers, for them to care.
They survive like cedars on a cliff, roots
Hooked in any crevice they can find.
They walk Avenue C in shadows
Neither conciliating its Baalim
Nor whoring after landscapes of the senses,
Tarig bab el Amoud being in the blood
Fumigated by Puerto Rican cooking.

Among women girthed like cedar trees
Other, slenderer ones appear:
One yellow haired, in August,
Under shooting stars on the lake, who
Believed in promises which broke by themselves—
In a German flower garden in the Bronx
The wedding of a child and a child, one flesh
Divided in the Adirondack spring—
One who found in the desert city of the West
The first happiness, and fled therefore—

And by a southern sea, in the pines, one loved
Until the mist rose blue in the trees
Around the spiderwebs that kept on shining,
Each day of the shortening summer.

And as rubbish burns
And the pushcarts are loaded
With fruit and vegetables and empty crates
And clank away on iron wheels over cobblestones,
And merchants infold their stores
And the carp ride motionlessly sleeplessly
In the dark tank in the fishmarket,
The figures withdraw into chambers overhead—
In the city of the mind, chambers built
Of care and necessity, where, hands lifted to the blinds,
They glimpse in mirrors backed with the blackness of the world
Awkward, cherished rooms containing the familiar selves.

9

Children set fires in ashbarrels,
Cats prowl the fires, scraps of fishes burn.

A child lay in the flames.
It was not the plan. Abraham
Stood in terror at the duplicity.
Isaac whom he loved lay in the flames.
The Lord turned away washing
His hands without soap and water
Like a common housefly.

The children laugh.
Isaac means *he laughs.*
Maybe the last instant,
The dying itself, *is* easier,
Easier anyway than the hike
From Pitt the blind gut
To the East River of Fishes,
Maybe it is as the poet said,
And the soul turns to thee
O vast and well-veiled Death
And the body gratefully nestles close to thee—

I think of Isaac reading Whitman in Chicago,
The week before he died, coming across
Such a passage and muttering, Oi!
What shit! And smiling, but not for you—I mean,

For *thee,* Sane and Sacred Death!

10

It was Gold's junkhouse, the one the clacking
Carts that little men pad after in harnesses
Picking up bedbugged mattresses, springs
The stubbornness has been loved out of,
Chairs felled by fat, lampshades lights have burned through,
Linoleum the geometry has been scuffed from,
Carriages a single woman's work has brought to wreck,
Would come to in the dusk and unload before,
That the whole neighborhood came out to see
Burning in the night, flames opening out like
Eyelashes from the windows, men firing the tears in,
Searchlights coming on like streams of water, smashing
On the brick, the water blooming up the wall
Like pale trees, reaching into the darkness beyond.

Nobody mourned, nobody stood around in pajamas
And a borrowed coat steaming his nose in coffee.
It was only Gold's junkhouse.
                                        But this evening
The neighborhood comes out again, everything
That may abide the fire was made to go through the fire
And it was made clean: a few twisted springs,
Charred mattresses (crawling still, naturally),
Perambulator skeletons, bicycles tied in knots—
In a great black pile at the junkhouse door,
Smelling of burnt rubber and hair. Rustwater
Hangs in icicles over the windows and door,
Like frozen piss aimed at trespassers,
Combed by wind, set overnight. Carriages we were babies in,
Springs that used to resist love, that gave in
And were thrown out like whores—the black
Irreducible heap, mausoleum of what we were—
It is cold suddenly, we feel chilled,
Nobody knows for sure what is left of him.

11

The fishmarket closed, the fishes gone into flesh.
The smelts draped on each other, fat with roe,
The marble cod hacked into chunks on the counter,
Butterfishes mouths still open, still trying to eat,
Porgies with receding jaws hinged apart
In a grimace of dejection, as if like cows
They had died under the sledgehammer, perches
In grass-green armor, spotted squeteagues
In the melting ice meek-faced and croaking no more,
Except in the plip plop plip plip in the bucket,
Mud-eating mullets buried in crushed ice,
Tilefishes with scales like chickenfat,
Spanish mackerels, buttercups on the flanks,
Pot-bellied pikes, two-tone flounders
After the long contortion of pushing both eyes
To the brown side that they might look up,
Brown side down, like a mass laying-on of hands,
Or the oath-taking of an army.

The only things alive are the carp
That drift in the black tank in the rear,
Kept living for the usual reason, that they have not died,
And perhaps because the last meal was garbage and they might
     begin stinking
On dying, before the customer was halfway home.
They nudge each other, to be netted,
The sweet flesh to be lifted thrashing in the air,
To be slugged, and then to keep on living
While they are opened on the counter.

Fishes do not die exactly, it is more
That they go out of themselves, the visible part
Remains the same, there is little pallor,
Only the cataracted eyes which have not shut ever
Must look through the mist which crazed Homer.

These are the vegetables of the deep,
The Sheol-flowers of darkness, swimmers
Of denser darknesses where the sun's rays bend for the last time
And in the sky there burns this shifty jellyfish
That degenerates and flashes and re-forms.

271   **The Avenue Bearing the Initial of Christ**

Motes in the eye land is the lid of,
They are plucked out of the green skim milk of the eye.

Fishes are nailed on the wood,
The big Jew stands like Christ, nailing them to the wood,
He scrapes the knife up the grain, the scales fly,
He unnails them, reverses them, nails them again,
Scrapes and the scales fly. He lops off the heads,
Shakes out the guts as if they did not belong in the first place,
And they are flesh for the first time in their lives.

Dear Frau ———— :
    Your husband, ———— , died in the Camp Hospital on ————. May
I express my sincere sympathy on your bereavement. ———— was admitted to the Hospital on ———— with severe symptoms of exhaustion,
complaining of difficulties in breathing and pains in the chest. Despite
competent medication and devoted medical attention, it proved impossible, unfortunately, to keep the patient alive. The deceased voiced no final
requests.

                                        Camp Commandant, ————

On 5th Street Bunko Certified Embalmer Catholic
Leans in his doorway drawing on a Natural Bloom Cigar.
He looks up the street. Even the Puerto Ricans are Jews
And the Chinese Laundry closes on Saturday.

        12

Next door, outside the pink-fronted Bodega Hispano—

(A crying: you imagine
Some baby in its crib, wailing
As if it could foresee everything.
The crying subsides: you imagine
A mother or father clasping
The damned creature in their arms.
It breaks out again,
This time in a hair-raising shriek—ah,
The alleycat, in a pleasant guise,
In the darkness outside, in the alley,
Wauling, shrieking slowly in its blood.

Another, loftier shrieking
Drowns it out. It begins always

On the high note, over a clang of bells:
Hook & Ladder 11 with an explosion of mufflers
Crab-walking out of 5th Street,
Accelerating up the Avenue, siren
Sliding on the rounded distances
Returning fainter and fainter,
Like a bee looping away from where you lie in the grass.

The searchlights catch him at the topfloor window,
Trying to move, nailed in place by the shine.
The bells of Saint Brigid's
On Tompkins Square
Toll for someone who has died—
J'oïs la cloche de Serbonne,
Qui toujours à neuf heures sonne
Le Salut que l'Ange prédit . . .

Expecting the visitation
You lie back on your bed,
The sounds outside
Must be outside. Here
Are only the dead spirituals
Turning back into prayers—
You rise on an elbow
To make sure they come from outside,
You hear nothing, you lay down
Your head on the pillow
Like a pick-up arm—
          swing low
                    swing low
                              sweet
     lowsweet—)

—Carols of the Caribbean, plinkings of guitars.

     13

The garbage disposal truck
Like a huge hunched animal
That sucks in garbage in the place
Where other animals evacuate it
Whines, as the cylinder in the rear
Threshes up the trash and garbage,
Where two men in rubber suits

(It must be raining outside)
Heap it in. The groaning motor
Rises in a whine as it grinds in
The garbage, and between-times
Groans. It whines and groans again.
All about it as it moves down
5th Street is the clatter of trashcans,
The crashes of them as the sanitary engineers
Bounce them on the sidewalk.

If it is raining outside
You can only tell by looking
In puddles, under the lifted streetlamps.

It would be the spring rain.

14

Behind the Power Station on 14th, the held breath
Of light, as God is a held breath, withheld,
Spreads the East River, into which fishes leak:
The brown sink or dissolve,
The white float out in shoals and armadas,
Even the gulls pass them up, pale
Bloated socks of riverwater and rotted seed,
That swirl on the tide, punched back
To the Hell Gate narrows, and on the ebb
Steam seaward, seeding the sea.

On the Avenue, through air tinted crimson
By neon over the bars, the rain is falling.
You stood once on Houston, among panhandlers and winos
Who weave the eastern ranges, learning to be free,
To not care, to be knocked flat and to get up clear-headed
Spitting the curses out. "Now be nice,"
The proprietor threatens; "Be nice," he cajoles.
"Fuck you," the bum shouts as he is hoisted again,
"God fuck your mother." (In the empty doorway,
Hunched on the empty crate, the crone gives no sign.)

That night a wildcat cab whined crosstown on 7th.
You knew even the traffic lights were made by God,
The red splashes growing dimmer the farther away
You looked, and away up at 14th, a few green stars;

And without sequence, and nearly all at once,
The red lights blinked into green,
And just before there was one complete Avenue of green,
The little green stars in the distance blinked.

It is night, and raining. You look down
Towards Houston in the rain, the living streets,
Where instants of transcendence
Drift in oceans of loathing and fear, like lanternfishes,
Or phosphorus flashings in the sea, or the feverish light
Skin is said to give off when the swimmer drowns at night.

From the blind gut Pitt to the East River of Fishes
The Avenue cobbles a swath through the discolored air,
A roadway of refuse from the teeming shores and ghettos
And the Caribbean Paradise, into the new ghetto and new paradise,
This God-forsaken Avenue bearing the initial of Christ
Through the haste and carelessness of the ages,
The sea standing in heaps, which keeps on collapsing,
Where the drowned suffer a C-change,
And remain the common poor.

Since Providence, for the realization of some unknown purpose, has
seen fit to leave this dangerous people on the face of the earth, and
did not destroy it . . .

Listen! the swish of the blood,
The sirens down the bloodpaths of the night,
Bone tapping on the bone, nerve-nets
Singing under the breath of sleep—
We scattered over the lonely seaways,
Over the lonely deserts did we run,
In dark lanes and alleys we did hide ourselves . . .

The heat beats without windows in its night,
The lungs put out the light of the world as they
Heave and collapse, the brain turns and rattles
In its own black axlegrease—

                    In the nighttime
Of the blood they are laughing and saying,
Our little lane, what a kingdom it was!

                    oi weih, oi weih

FRED POWLEDGE
Going Home to Raleigh

Along about Maryland the accents started. Before that, there had been only the usual bored grunts and one unexpected "Thank you" from the people who take your money on the Verrazano and the Goethals, the Jersey Turnpike, the Delaware Memorial. But now, in Maryland, we needed gasoline, and we were confronted again with people other than ourslves who were something more than machines.

The two men in the gas station leveled their eyes at me. Their faces were red and their necks were wrinkled like the tongues of old Army boots; there were Wallace stickers all over their faces; their uniforms were oil-company green, and they probably wore them catfishing on weekends too. There was meanness in their eyes, hating me for having a beard and tan British boots and a New York license plate. *Niggerloverbeatnikradical,* their eyes said, "Faller-rup? *Pream*-yum aw *ragler?*"

There was nothing else to do but put on my own accent a little. It is a facility, I think, that most Southern white expatriates have and that they enjoy using from time to time, especially when talking to Negroes in the North and rednecks in the South. "Yeah, faller-rup with *pream*-yum, annl sure preciatet if you'd check th *bat*rywater too."

The men in the Maryland gas station were surprised, which is what I meant them to be, and in their momentary defensiveness and my momentary assertiveness, we reached a tentative compromise. What I was saying was *I'll buy your gasoline if you're decent and courteous to me. Otherwise, I'll do something violent like ram your gas pumps on the way out or turn in my credit card with a three-page letter explaining why, because I am from the South, too, from the same violence you are, so please don't let the beard and the license plates fool you.*

Then it's okay. They have been civilized just enough by television, by the Interstate Highway System, by the Civil Rights Act of 1964, by being beholden to a large impersonal corporation owned by millionaires that does not like to receive torn-up credit cards, and by the intense personal desire to make money. They pumped the gas and checked the battery water and their eyes said nothing more. I continued on my way home to North Carolina.

I am going home out of obligation and love. There is an obligation to let the grandfather see the grandchild and to observe, a little earlier each trip, that they, too, are growing apart. They do not avoid each other; they simply spend less time together now.

When Polly was four or five we would go home and he would take her by the hand and walk around the block, showing her off to all the neighbors. "Yes, this is my little granddaughter from New York," he would say. Now they meet after the long drive and it is apparent that they have less in common than before. She is eleven years old now, and full of half-conscious fragments of thoughts about propriety and about male and female, and she has long periods of completely un-childlike unselfishness, of almost adult tact. She is polite to him, respectful of him, as never before. But she also turns her head ever so slightly to the side when they kiss. And he walks not so well now, being close to eighty; the days of going around the block are gone forever.

I am also going home to look for things, things I never bothered with before. I know now that something I always knew—the fact that I was adopted—is far more important to me than I had ever before admitted. If you do not know who they are, and most important if you do not know why they gave you away, and you have no reason to believe that you ever will know, then a lot of questions are raised and never answered and a lot of time is wasted. All I know is that I was born in Nash County, North Carolina. I have often toyed with the idea of going to Nashville, the county seat, and asking for the book that shows who was born on February 23, 1935, and seeing if I could recognize myself.

There was a cold, dirty rain falling in New York and the air along the turnpike was even grayer and more foul than usual, and it was difficult to tell when the rain had ended. We started late in the day and drove through the night. There was a piece of filler in the *Times* once that said spring was moving through Siberia at the rate of 35 miles a day. I wondered if the rate was the same for the Eastern United States. It is all expressway and toll road from near our house, in Brooklyn, to Petersburg, Virginia, and from there to Raleigh it is mostly old U.S. 1. We passed through Henderson, North Carolina, as the sun was coming up, and I woke them and told them to look out the window. The rain had stopped for good, and we had passed into spring. Everything down to the edge of the asphalt road was green and wet with dew, not rain, and the flowers and bushes were in bloom. In the fields there were tall and lean black men who had waked hours before, out there in their shirtsleeves, coaxing mules and already well into their first sweat.

I have lived in the city for seven years now, and seven years is a long time to be locked in combat with society. If you live in New York for that length of time, and you are neither very rich nor so poor that you have completely given up hope, the chances are that you are in combat with it a good deal of the time and that you are pretty fed up with it all.

It was, always before, the *logical* place. There was, of course, a variety of logical places for my generation, the Silent one. For many of us, there was a fascination for politics that Northerners, after the Longs, Orval Faubus, Strom Thurmond, and George Wallace, still cannot understand. Some of those who left Chapel Hill when I did, in 1957, returned home to Winston-Salem or Statesville or Rocky Mount to wait patiently and respectfully and then, at the proper time, to take over their fathers' automobile dealerships or feed-and-seed empires or law practices. They kept their eyes on the state legislature, and some of them have made it there already, and some of them are keeping their eyes on the governor's mansion now, and undoubtedly at least one of them will make that, too.

Some of those in my generation went to Washington under the spell of John Kennedy, and they stayed to learn some lessons in practical politics from Lyndon Johnson. When Johnson learned *his* lessons in practical politics, they went to work for foundations and universities, and certainly they will surface again some day. But the rest of us, those of us who were not tied to politics, had to go to New York.

We went there because it was the only place to go. We wanted to act, or to "communicate," or to write. We had been reared in a state that considered itself, rightly, I think, the best of the South. We had gone to a school that had good reason to believe it was the best, too—of its region. So when we left, we put in quick apprenticeships elsewhere and then we headed straight for the city, because that was the only place to go if you wanted to be—had to be—the best of them all, and not just the best of a region.

Now, as we all know, New York has become irredeemably, irretrievably rotten. The nation is finding out how difficult it is to live in the cities, and the inmates of New York, being in the most difficult of all cities, are finding out quicker and more. And so, for the past year or so, I have been half-seriously entertaining the thought of giving up the struggle, selling the beautiful old house in Brooklyn, and moving to a place where the air has a few more years to go; where one can see farther than a block; where there might be something worth seeing, farther than a block; where they pick up the garbage, and where a heavy snowfall might be considered a work of art and not a catastrophe of such magnitude that its perpetrator has to be sought out and publicly condemned. And maybe I could become a Southern Writer; that should not be too difficult.

Often at dinnertime we would talk about this thought, but we never came to any firm conclusions, except to agree that it might be nice but that it also had its drawbacks. Every time we went to Raleigh, we recalled, we had a built-in baby-sitter and almost unlimited time and energy and enough money to have a little fun, but when we scanned the ads we found that there was nothing at the theaters but Elvis Presley movies and after the show there was no place to go.

Not only, however, is it absurd to pretend that by remaining in New York you are really executing a conscious decision to stay and fight; there is nothing, literally nothing, that an individual citizen can do that would make New York more livable for more than an instant. Not even if he is the mayor. You soon learn to question your own motives for staying: are you *really* demonstrating your belief in cities, your faith that large groups of people can live together in peace, or are you some kind of masochist? It just might be that the courageous thing to do would be not to stay and fight, but to recognize and admit that the battle has got too corrupt; that courage could be demonstrated only by leaving, retreating, fleeing. And it just might be that such a town as Raleigh, North Carolina, my home, whose advantages and limitations I know well, should be the place to flee to.

Sitting on the ground in the backyard, feeling spring all around, doing nothing more complicated than picking up tiny pine twigs and thumping them into the air: it was early morning, and all around there was a steady buzz, like June bugs on a string. A neighbor was mowing his yard. The noise stopped, and I realized that it was absolutely quiet. Maybe that's why I woke up as early as I did; no noise has come to mean that something is wrong, what getting a telegram used to mean. A jet passed over, 30,000 or so feet above, and I could hear it distinctly. As my ears adjusted to the new sounds, and to the absence of old ones, I realized that the neighbor had started up his lawnmower again.

Here, I thought, a man can spend an entire day, several days, a week, doing nothing more profound than working on his yard and he can feel as if he has done something useful. There is a little road next to the house that until a couple of years ago was dirt; it is of no use to anyone except those eight or ten families who live on it. Twice, in maybe a minute, cars passed up it. My sister said, "It's just like Grand Central Station out here today."

I got up off the springy ground. I had places to go; graveyards and shopping centers to visit; people to see or look for again. One of the people, a relative, asked me if I had ever met Robert Ruark, the writer. I had, once, when he came to Chapel Hill in a fancy car and impressed everyone. He was said to have gone to his old fraternity house for a drink (real saloons being illegal in North Carolina, then and now), to have expressed dismay at the condition of the wooden bar, and to have written a check for a new one on the spot.

Yes, I said, I had met Robert Ruark the Writer once. "Well," said the relative, "I'm from Southport, and you know Robert Ruark the Writer was from around there, and let me tell you, there are some people there who don't think highly of him *at all* after what he did to them. You know, he wrote a *book* about all that, and some of the people in it, if you were from there, you didn't have any trouble figuring out who was who."

I changed the subject, and I wondered if this lady knew that I was in Raleigh to write about it; and if, after I did it, anybody there would be able to understand that I did it out of love, or perhaps out of a feeling of obligation, or because I was looking for something.

Raleigh is a city, now, of more than a hundred thousand people, and I suppose the people at the Chamber of Commerce think of it as "bustling." Raleigh is the state capital, a city of white-collar workers, and it always has looked down on Durham, 26 miles away, because they had industry in Durham, and the people there were generally considered by Raleigh people to be dirtier, meaner, and dumber. When we were looking for some violent action on weekends, we would go to Durham in convoy, in our fathers' cars, and pick fights with the boys from Durham High. They were always stronger, which is a quality that seems to go with being dirtier, meaner, and dumber, and they always won. The most profound insult any of us could imagine would be the knowledge, or even the suspicion, that one of our girls who was widely thought to be saving it for marriage had given it to a Durham High boy.

In addition to the legislature and the state offices, which Raleigh was and is about as proud of as a city can be of its politicians, they had State College, which then was the school to go to to learn agriculture and animal husbandry and engineering, and which was just getting started as a center of architectural design; they had a nondescript baseball team; two well-thought-of whorehouses; several Negro colleges (one of the reasons I am proud of Raleigh, when I am proud of it, is that Shaw University is there, and Shaw played a part in the origins of the sit-in movement); and a number of satellite country towns, places like Cary and Knightdale, Apex and Fuquay Springs.

Those towns have their own satellites, tiny places like Rolesville and Neuse, New Hope and Bunn and Pearces. Every Saturday the people from all these towns, black and white, would pour into Raleigh on the blue-black roads that Governor Kerr Scott had built for them, and they would all go to Montgomery Ward's and Briggs' Hardware to spend their money quickly and then, while the women were looking at dresses in Hudson-Belk's, the men would lounge around in the public squares, the whites in their square and the blacks in theirs, all of them very unselfconscious in their faded blue overalls. There was some drinking, whiskey in the white square and Catawba grape in the black one, and, by eight or nine o'clock on Saturday night the emergency rooms would be full of the victims of stabbing and shooting wounds.

I worked weekends as a police reporter on the *News and Observer,* while I was going to Chapel Hill, and I quickly learned the subtle differences among the various forms of Saturday-night violence. What was called, then, in newspaper and police shorthand (and probably still is) a "nigger cutting" meant a slashing, usually with a razor blade held rigidly between the stiffened fist and second fingers, just below the fingernails. You wiped it across your victim's face and chest. Wounds inflicted by such weapons produced enormous amounts of blood and gave the doctors untold trouble when they had to sew them up, but they left the victim relatively unharmed and ready, after at most a transfusion, to leave the hospital and return to the battle. He was scarred for life, however. I never learned what the whites did when they wanted to temporarily maim a victim, but their favorite weapon for serious arguments seemed to be a shotgun aimed directly at one's head. The women of both races, when they were really angry, preferred to throw a pot of lye, the hotter the better, into an aggressor's face or upon her breasts. The nice, white, middle-class, white-collar people of Raleigh looked upon these Saturday night blood-lettings, and upon the people who participated in them, as something that did not directly involve them, except when they got too close to a sweaty, unbathed farmer in Hudson-Belk's basement and had to move quickly away in disgust. Not complete disgust, however; for the white-collar people, the bustlers, were not so far removed from Cary and Knightdale themselves.

Now the farmers still come in on Saturday, some of them, but they are more difficult to spot, because they no longer wear overalls. They wear permanent-press pants and white shirts and they drive Mustangs and Camaros because they watch television, too, and they do not all congregate in the public squares downtown because downtown is pretty much dead. Most people go to the shopping centers now, and some of the shopping centers are being built far from downtown, even in Cary and Knightdale. Raleigh itself, as a whole, has slipped a notch or two. The Interstate Highway System just seems to have bypassed Raleigh in favor of the hated Durham, and when they were deciding on the big regional airports, Raleigh didn't get one—it had to be content with the one it had that was hyphenated with Durham. There is not much in the way of television. There are some nice, clean, comfortable theaters (people do not urinate in the aisles and masturbate on the seats, as in New York), but they tend toward inferior and certainly uncontroversial movies. Fayetteville Street is in bad shape. Montgomery Ward's is no longer there; Woolworth's and Briggs' Hardware are, and so is the little newsstand operated by a blind lady and which sells eighteen to twenty *New York Times*es a day, but a lot of the street is loan companies and empty department stores with

"For Rent" signs in the windows, and from the amount of dust on the signs, it looks as if they have been vacant a long time.

Inside Briggs' Hardware, there was Mr. Briggs, looking no different than he looked twenty years ago, and he remembered me. "I would have recognized you sooner," he said, "if it hadn't been for the beard. You live in New York now?" (Others have said things like that and meant them as devastating put-downs, but he did not say it in meanness.) "You know, I get up there fairly often, and I think Lindsay's doing a pretty good job. It's too bad all the abuse they're putting on him." Mr. Briggs said he heard, from time to time, about our generation and what we were doing. "You know," he said, "a lot of you kids did okay. O-*kay*. I'm proud of you." Back in the rear of the store, the sacks of rabbit food he used to sell were no longer there. Mr. Briggs said he couldn't remember if they ever *had* been there.

I had remembered the Capitol square as a green and shady place, cool in the heat of the summertime, funky and damp with tall old trees and statues. The soil was the sort that, if you could dig into it, you could collect in ten minutes enough worms to last a weekend. Nothing had changed. Clouds of pigeons departed every few seconds from one corner of the square for another, occasionally changing direction in mid-flight and heading for, and some landing on, the man who sells peanuts. Across from him, at the main entrance to the square, was the man who sells jonquils wrapped neatly in wet newsprint with a rubber band around each bunch, exactly as before. There was a coin-operated newspaper rack beside him; the *Raleigh Times* was saying that day:

SCORES OF THE FAITHFUL MAKE
PILGRIMAGE FOR CHRIST

It was the Friday before Easter. And there was another headline:

FIRST ANNIVERSARY:
THOUSANDS LAUD KING

It was, also, the anniversary of the death of the Rev. Dr. Martin Luther King, Jr.

Not far away there was my favorite statue, "To the North Carolina Women of the Confederacy." It was a woman and her young son. She sits, holding an open book, and he stands by her side, holding a sword, too young to fight but about to anyway, and on his face that look (you see it often anywhere in the South and on the faces of soldiers in airports) that he thought he knew what he was going off to fight for, but he really didn't.

She looks, not at him, but into the distance, which is occupied by an unmemorable state office building. She has the face that so many of those women from Cary and Knightdale have, and that can be seen, too, even beneath the beehive hairdos and behind the makeup of the women of white-collar Raleigh. It is a face full of past pain and suffering, and anticipating the inevitability of more, but full of wisdom and kindness, too. She is the Southern white woman, the woman they all wanted so badly to put on an unshakable pedestal; the woman they wanted to keep forever chaste, and that they consented to make love on (not to) only because there was a necessity for heirs, and even then guiltily and only in the dark. She puts up with whatever happens, accepts it, accounts for it by saying it was fate or God's will and believing that, she stares off into the distance as the son goes off to die at an early age. And perhaps, at some much later date, she even finds some satisfaction in all the suffering.

When you live in the East, you are shocked, sometimes, by what you see and hear when you venture out into the United States of America, even though you are from there and really should not be shocked at all.

The people look strange. I used to be almost apologetic about the way I looked when I went home. There was something shameful about my appearance, in turtleneck shirts and with my beard and my tight pants and pointy Italian boots.

This time, it was *they* who looked strange to *me*. One becomes accustomed to seeing short skirts and long, flowing hair, and sexy false eyelashes and naturally rounded and bouncy breasts, and it is shocking to go to a place and see that practically no impression has been made by all the expensive pages of cosmetic advertising in *Life* and all the microskirts and magnificent cleavages on the Carson show. The skirts are at the knee, looking obscenely odd there, and it is obvious that they still wear girdles and falsies, and the hair is still teased up at the top of the head and held there by great doses of hair spray and it looks, except for the color (and sometimes that, too) like wands of petrified cotton candy. The white women are made up like dead people, as if they do not want to look pretty.

Perhaps they are afraid to look pretty, or maybe it is just that the competition is nonexistent, or insufficient. In New York, there is plenty of competition, and a woman who might be plain or fat finds it necessary to do something about it. Here, in Raleigh, and in a thousand places like Raleigh, if a woman looks competitively pretty, if she looks as if she *enjoys* seducing and being seduced, she might find herself labeled "too forward," or taken for a whore.

The men wear baggy pants and nondescript shirts and unexciting plaid sports coats, and they look as if they, too, are afraid to stand up straight, as if they are afraid that there is nothing behind their zippers, as if they feel themselves incapable of growing their hair long for fear that someone will make an invidious comparison between them and their wives, the girls they went to high school with. The only ones who look *natural* are the Negroes.

The Negroes in Raleigh look much the way they look in New York and Atlanta and San Francisco, which is to say they carry and dress themselves according to the way they want to carry and dress themselves. For the young, it means bright and exciting clothing; the girls wear shorter dresses than whites their age, and they tended, at Easter time, toward neat, tightly belted trench coats. For the not-so-young, there is some of that three-button tweedy business one sees on *the* black teller in a bank up North, but for what seemed to be all of them, there is an obvious lack of fear, an obvious willingness to dress the way that makes them feel good. They do not wear masks. Even the Negro maids standing on the street corners in the neatly mowed white sections in the afternoon, waiting for the bus that will take them to Fayetteville Street so they can transfer to the bus that takes them to their side of town—they look wise and majestic, not with their heads down (the whites have *their* heads down much more), but with their heads up high, looking unbeaten, never *going* to be beaten.

We went out to dinner at the K & W Cafeteria at five o'clock in the afternoon because my father does not like to stand in lines. Across from us, in another booth, sat a man with his wife. They did not speak more than a dozen words during the entire meal. She was thin, almost gaunt, perhaps forty years old but looking five years older; there was evidence of pain, suffering, anguish on her face, and there was evidence there, too, of the farm, of Garner and Cary. He must have been the same age, but he looked younger, with a brown plaid jacket, a black tie, a brush haircut.

Four times during the course of the meal he got up and walked over to a little table that held the coffeepots and he walked back to the booth and refilled their cups and then returned the pot. He walked slowly, surveying the people around him, perhaps to see if they were looking at him. He almost minced. There is so much about the Southern white male that runs dangerously close to effeminacy. It is in the shy way they hold themselves, the way they sometimes walk, and, often most convincingly, in the way they talk. The couple in the booth were obviously terribly angry, angry at each other, but it was also obvious that this was not a temporary anger. It was a very long-term anger, one that started a long time ago, in Garner or Cary or Knightdale.

I looked around the room, and suddenly I realized that I had been living for the past few days in a geriatric community. The median age of everybody I had seen was far higher than back in New York. All around us were old couples, and widows and widowers, and groups of old women in flowery hats. There were young people here, too, but even they looked like part of the geriatric community in the way they talked and walked and dressed. I wondered if I were exaggerating all this; if I was purposely searching out, and confining myself to, the old people of Raleigh. Did Faulkner purposely confine himself to the white trash community of Mississippi?

"There's a lot going on here," said my friend, who had moved to Raleigh a few months before. "Things aren't as dead as you might think." And his wife told my wife that it might be wrong to judge the ladies by the length of the skirts they wore in Cameron Village, the big shopping center. They were much shorter in the North Hills shopping center, she said.

(There is a Raleigh there that I have not even mentioned, of course, a new Raleigh that swings and does not hide its liquor in brown paper bags and that has a jazz joint named The Frog and the Nightgown. The Raleigh I talk about may be hopelessly outdated, moribund, perhaps already dead and gone. There are people whose company just transferred them to Raleigh and who were born and raised in, say, St. Louis, and who never saw, never see, and never will see the things and people and places I am trying to describe.)

There is a scandal at one of the churches. Members of the congregation are said to have been consulting mediums. The scandal in Raleigh is always so minor, or pathetic, or both.

A woman is quoted as saying, every time one sees her, how much responsibility she has and how her husband is just plain lazy. "And let me tell you: *she* sure runs *that* family."

A man was an alcoholic, became reformed, and is now slipping again. "He never *was* anything."

A young man's recent transgressions are described at length, but not in detail because there are ladies present. He seems to have had difficulties with his appetites for drink and women. "Yes," was the sympathetic reply, "but he went to Chapel Hill."

There is talk about a family picnic on Easter afternoon, with all the aunts and uncles and cousins and their already grown babies. One of the cousins warns me, good-naturedly but with the utmost sincerity: "You folks can go back to New York, but *I* have to *live* here. So please don't bring beer to the picnic."

The Sanitary Barber Shop, which is below the sidewalk, and which I remember as being a Saturday-morning place where you went only to get a crew cut, and where the air was heavy with talk of niggers and poontang, with both subjects being discussed mostly in violent terms, has a sign up now which says that it does razor styling.

When I was a child in Raleigh, there were three main ways to leave. One of them was the Union Bus Station, one of them was U.S. 1, and the third was the train station. The bus station is almost completely black now, except for the drivers and the others who make their living by the uncomfortable transportation of people of moderate means. There were only two or three whites when I walked in, and they were soldiers. Otherwise the station had changed not at all. Outside, there were Trailways and Greyhound buses labeled "Miami" and "New York City" and "St. Petersburg Express" and "Asheville." I asked a driver how many of the people who got on the bus marked "New York" went all the way to New York. "Right many of them get off at Petersburg and Richmond," he said, "and a lot of the rest get off at Washington."

U.S. 1 used to be wonderful and unattainable for me. We were told that it stretched from Maine to Florida, and Raleigh was in the middle of it. Standing beside U.S. 1 and watching the traffic going up and down on it was, for me, almost as exciting as going down to the train station. The people I saw there had been in New York *earlier that day,* or they had left Miami two days before. They had style, the mystery of foreigners. Our eyes met briefly as they passed through with their foreign license plates, the trucks belching and snorting and whining up and down through the gears, dozen of gears, and you knew that they would be driving all night, and when the sun came up tomorrow they would be in another place.

Now U.S. 1 is difficult to find, for there are other and better highways passing through and around Raleigh that are a good deal busier, and much of the traffic from New York to Florida bypasses the city entirely. On the way down, in Maryland, we had left the toll roads briefly to look for a place to eat and I had driven, instinctively, to U.S. 1, certain there would be at least a Howard Johnson's there. There was nothing. It was dead, decrepit, full of automobile junkyards and specialists in the reconstruction of transmissions. And there were Negro motels. Empty, for-sale Negro motels. "Hotel—Colored," said the signs. Next to that, they said, "For Sale."

When the Silver Meteor leaves New York City, I suppose, it is just another train, different from the commuter trains only in that its cars are silver rather than dirty brown. But when it came through Raleigh in my youth, that was something else. We used to go down to the station just to see the Meteor, which went from New York to Miami, come through, or to see its sister trains, the Comet and the Star. I remember the air of the people who were riding those trains—urbane, sophisticated, looking down on Raleigh as if it were a hick town.

The only Negroes who did not shuffle and lower their eyes in the presence of whites back then were the cooks on the Meteor, the Star, and the Comet. They leaned out the Dutch doors of the diners, a full five feet higher than those of us who stood on the platform, looking down on us yokels, looking so infinitely more sophisticated and superior, and we, even the most ardent white supremists among us, dared not say a word.

Now, the Meteor bound for Miami comes through at 12:20 in the early morning, and the northbound Meteor comes through five minutes later. The Comet passes through Raleigh at 9:20 in the evening, and the Star comes at 7:40 P.M. I went down to see the Comet one night. It was raining, and the railroad station looked HO gauge, where in my memory it had been a huge place, full of busy people and gray mail sacks and carts with long-spoked wheels, and green Railway Express trucks. But now it was not only smaller; there were practically no people there. The waiting rooms were empty; there were two or three men at Railway Express. The chalked arrival and departure times on the big blackboard—what few remained—were done in old men's spidery handwriting.

The Comet came in, its head lamp swiveling wildly as before, but it was a tiny train, no longer than the BMT subway—two Diesels to pull it, two mail and express cars, two coaches, and one Pullman. It used to have a diner and as many as eighteen cars, cars with fancy exotic names on their sides, but now the cars have numbers. Almost all of the passengers were Negroes this time. Those who weren't were elderly whites, apparently too scared to fly, who were being put on or taken off the train by their middle-aged children. And since the middle-aged children had children of their own who were grown or off at school, there were no real children at the station that night to see the Comet come in.

Steam poured out of the undersides of the silver cars. Somebody ignored the notice in one of the rest rooms and flushed the toilet in the station, and a brief torrent of water and urine splashed down on the tracks and platform amidst puffs of steam. The Comet used to go from New York to Birmingham, and we used to ride it over part-way and connect with a little steam locomotive that would take us down to Opelika to visit my father's people and their farm. Now the Comet was going from Washington to Atlanta. "They cut it off on both ends," said a conductor, and he seemed happy to be talking with someone who seemed sympathetic. "And they're *about* to cut it between Richmond and Washington. Pretty soon there won't be anything at all. They cut the train and they cut the diner and pretty soon now they're going to cut the train out *all*-together. Right now, nobody but the disagreeable people'll ride it." He inclined his head toward a group of Negroes.

There was more steam, and somebody flushed another toilet, and the train moved unceremoniously out of the station. About all that was left of the memory I had was the wildly-swiveling head lamp on the lead Diesel, and that looked audacious now, sending out such heroic warnings in front of such an inconsequential train.

The cemetery is in the old part of town, and it is covered with hills and tall oaks and elms. There are real gravestones there, unlike the newer cemeteries with their restrictions (my mother is buried in one of those), and there are mausoleums and obelisks rising among the hills and along the tiny stream. It is a good cemetery, a cemetery where people have been allowed to erect the monuments they wanted to erect, and sometimes this policy has produced utter tastelessness and sometimes it has produced monuments of some beauty, but the chief result of the policy is that it somehow makes death as informal as death really is. It reminds the still living that death is not such a big deal.

I drove slowly through the cemetery for a while, trying to remember the locations of three graves that had stuck in my memory ever since I had first seen them, as a child. One was where the Indian princess was buried, one was the grave of the child which had, above its headstone, encased in a glass globe, the child's favorite toys, and one was a stone angel that Thomas Wolfe's father had carved. I spotted a tall man standing amongst the tombstones, looking, except for the color of his green work clothes, like a statue himself. His face and hands were the color and texture of leather, he stood almost six and a half feet tall, and he wore a gray Western hat. I told him what I was looking for, and he got in the car and we drove to the angel. "I'm not sure this is Mr. *Wolfe's* angel," he said, "but this is *the* angel that everybody wants to see. The reason is, her eyes follow you everywhere you go." The angel was magnificently carved, and of perfect size and proportion, and her eyes did, indeed, follow you. I started to say that I thought this was because the sculptor had slightly crossed the eyes, but then I looked closer at the tall man in the Western hat and I saw that his eyes had been sculpted in the same way.

He remembered the child's grave with the glass globe full of toys, but he said it was no longer there. "Some kids broke it all up," he said. Then we went to the Indian princess's grave.

Over the grave there was a sort of pyramid of stone, with the top leveled off, and on the top there was a small Grecian temple with columns. Set just inside the columns, at eye level, there was a sepia engraving of the grave's occupant, who had died in 1897 at the age of twenty-six. Below the picture was the poem:

> *In thy dark eyes' splendor*
> *Where the warm light loves to dwell,*
> *Weary looks, yet tender*
> *Speak their last farewell.*

I looked more closely at the picture. The center of her face had been chipped away—"Some kids done that with a BB gun," said the man—but I could tell that she looked exactly like the pictures of my mother when she was about that age.

Part of the feeling of Raleigh, and of other towns and small cities across the nation, but particularly of places in the South, is the soil. In the South it ranks in importance behind only race, and, of course, the feeling of race is inextricably enmeshed in the feeling of the land. This is not to say that Raleigh is a farm town, with dusty side streets and gas pumps and general stores. It probably never was like that. There are sidewalks and streets and coin-operated car washes and drive-in banks and electronics-research firms and computers and Holiday Inns and quarter-acre "estates" in the new housing developments, as elsewhere. But the feeling is still there, not far beneath the surface, and the migration from Cary and Garner and Knightdale constantly replenishes that feeling. People have written about the soil and the spell it puts on men, especially Southern American men; Hollywood has tried to make movies about it. It is there. It is that feeling, so easy to come by in the South, and so difficult to avoid, of being reliant on, and owing your survival to, the idiosyncracies of that dry red clay. You can be removed from the dirt by a generation, two generations, and still feel yourself bound to it, enslaved by it. The merchants in their jackets and ties, the women shoppers in Cameron Village, even North Hills—they all feel it and show it, even if they do not know it is there.

The young men with red faces, riding around in the Chevy Novas with Confederate battle-flag license plates on the front bumper, wearing their blond hair short in brush cuts, white shirts with starched collars, and no button-downs, and no tie; the ones who run barbershops and used-car lots, looking one step removed from the Klan—they are half a step removed from the soil, and they know it. They also know that the blacks are catching up with them fast, have gone further and faster in terms of dignity and self-esteem since the sit-ins started in 1960 than the white folks of the soil have gone since the Depression. And so they resent and fear the blacks more than anybody else.

They gather on Saturday nights at the roadhouses that feature country music and some modified, toned-down rock, and they buy setups for the liquor they carry in brown-paper bags and they eat ribs and chicken and shrimp and rolls, and they feel up their fatted women in the loose-fitting slacks who, themselves, are only half a step away, and they forget for a spell about the many things they hold in common with the blacks.

Family is another part of the feeling of Raleigh. The big cities do not have this feeling. Even if a daughter lives and is raising her own family in Brooklyn, and her mother and father live only twelve miles away in the

Bronx, it is possible and perfectly reasonable not to visit very often. In Raleigh they "go riding" on Sunday afternoon, first checking on the new housing developments and then the shopping centers and then stopping in at a sister's or a brother's or an aunt's house without warning, which is all right, because the sisters, brothers, and aunts do the same thing. In Raleigh you do not have major family arguments on Sunday afternoon, nor do you lazily kick the Sunday *Times* down to the foot of the bed at two in the afternoon and decide to make love. They visit, and they talk a while, and then they leave. And beneath their talk, sometimes, there is an intense family hatred, distrust, jealousy, spitefulness—a feeling that at times can be as strong as the afflictions and magnetisms of the soil and of race.

It can manifest itself on those simple Sunday afternoon excursions when the disapproval that one member of the family feels for another becomes too urgent; it cannot any longer be suppressed behind gossip about those who are not present: it is now that the truth comes out, the explosions. *You're raising that child perfectly atrociously . . . you are getting fat as a hog . . . you better stop that drinking right now*. But it is at its strongest at forced family gatherings where the strain is great and the opportunity to leave is lacking, gatherings such as funerals.

I remember one: the death was expected, long and drawn out, and when it finally came, the sisters, proud of their Southern aristocratic lineage, descended and looked skeptically at everybody else—at one member of the family who lived in a distant city and who had rented a car at dawn and driven five hundred miles, because he had gotten a *red* car, and a red car was out of place in a funeral procession; at the young woman who recently had joined the family by marriage, because she was from another part of the world and spoke another language and therefore was a "harlot" and a "strumpet" and "probably a thief" and who, when she fought back at these accusations, then became "the most uppity little brown bitch I ever saw"; and, finally, at everybody. Eventually the sisters obtained cardboard boxes from the Colonial Store and loaded their car with the sibling's belongings and left.

In Raleigh, and in the smaller cities and towns of America, you are forever enslaved by your kin. Other people know or knew your mother and father, sisters and brothers, and you are forever judged against that knowledge. If you are worthless and no-count, and your kin aren't, then you are a black sheep. If you try to be successful, and your father was a mundane clerk or an alcoholic or a philanderer, you are putting on airs and it is only a matter of time before the genes for mundaneness, alcoholism, or philandering take over and reduce you to the same shambles.

There is no getting away, if you stay. A few have tried to live their own lives in their hometowns, but they have not been very successful. It is much easier to start another life someplace new, and so they go from Raleigh to Charlotte, and then, some of them, to Atlanta, and, a few, to New York, and their places in Raleigh are filled by those who had to leave Cary and Garner and Knightdale.

In New York, you can go as far as you want. Perhaps they have the right idea in Brooklyn, on the street where we live, where there are many Italian families, whose children have all grown up and moved to Jersey or Lon Gyland, and who come back on weekends to eat Mamma's spaghetti and to show off the new Polara, and who do not stay long, and that is that.

Maybe, though, I am exaggerating all this, and it really is the rain. Easter weekend started out with nice skies and thumping twigs in the back yard, but now it is raining, and it has been raining, and it is affecting our plans and our tempers. You can feel the initial politeness wear off and the edges start to roughen, and occasionally as you enter a room you can hear snatches of their conversations, and you wonder, from the way the subject is abruptly changed, if they are talking about you: how much nicer you'd look if you shaved; how much you've drunk in three days out of that bottle of vodka you brought; whether you're bringing up your child right. And you are there with your wife, in the bedroom at night, talking about them and wishing there were some way to communicate.

So little changes, so little has changed. For every Sanitary Barber Shop that now offers razor styling, there are a dozen vacant lots where I used to play that have not changed at all. In New York City it would have changed a dozen times—and, most of all, the people would have changed. In New York the old people disappear and are never heard of again. Here, in Raleigh, they stay around, and each time you come back you see how they have aged and you wonder if you have passed the same number of years in the same amount of time. A bent, white-haired man, in a neat suit, vest, and starched white shirt and tie, hobbles down the street, one step at the time, taking an eternity to walk from his house to the end of the block, pausing there, turning slowly, taking another eternity to return, and you realize that this was his walk for the day. "That's Dr. Williams. He's pretty bad off," they say.

You remember Dr. Williams, the preacher at one of the more powerful churches, the recipient of a fancy car once from his loving congregation (and the object of much criticism from those who were not so loving), now reduced to hobbling, unable to drive the car, something in his eyes. Fear? Pain? Where is God now?

All these people, with their pain and tragedy and so little humor left, so little time to laugh, watching the Newlywed Game and getting the facts all mixed up, placing bets on who will win and then not paying very good attention and being incorrect about who *did* win, and getting little kicks from the way the wives bitch theatrically at their shrimpy husbands (watching it sadistically, like watching the wrestling or the roller derby or the geek in the carnival), voting for Nixon and thinking they were pretty liberal because they knew a *lot* of people who were voting for Wallace; their hands gnarled and beaten and twisted and sometimes their fingers severed in the course of serving, over a period of several decades, some governor or textile-millowner or fertilizer supplier whom they still refer to with utmost reverence as Mister Bob or Mister Jim or something, and who probably doesn't have the slightest idea who *they* are, or were— sitting there being fair game for all the television commercials that promise to end the pains of arthritis and cold miseries and psoriasis and piles —*promising to end their pain.*

They used to be able to dismiss most everything that bothered them with the quotation from Matthew, the one about setting the sheep on the right hand and the goats on the left. It explained everything; the white folks got the life eternal and the nigras got the everlasting punishment. There it is, right there in the Holy Bible. But lately some smartass preacher with sideburns from Columbia or Yale has been down there talking about missions to the inner city, and they don't go to church as religiously as they used to. They sit and watch television commercials. Where is their God now? Perhaps He is within the picture tube.

The family picnic was held, despite the rain. Within an hour or so, the sky cleared and the men wandered out into the backyard, the women stayed inside and talked, and the children explored the woods. Some of them caught poison oak. I managed to eat three different kinds of deviled eggs and two different kinds of potato salad. For the first time in my memory, since leaving home, nobody talked about niggers or hippies.

The grass was good, and so was the pine straw, and the ground was springy beneath our feet. We inspected the greenhouse my cousin David was building. It was good, when you came in from outside, scraping your shoes on the driveway, then again on the steps, then the rubber mat, then the other mat inside the door, all in an attempt to get the red clay off your shoes. In New York you never do this unless it has been raining or snowing hard or you inadvertently stepped in a mess left by a dog.

On the way back from the picnic Polly burst into tears and said she wanted to live in Raleigh. She said there were five good reasons why we should move there: not so much pollution, not so much hatred, more room, shopping centers, and one other reason I cannot recall. Then she asked me to give her five good reasons why we *couldn't* move. I was unable to answer, either to her satisfaction or mine.

Walt Disney's Wonderful World of Color is on, its volume somewhat louder than necessary, and we sit across the room, talking over it all. It is about a little Indian boy who is expelled from his tribe and who becomes friendly with an eagle. The eagle, of course, saves the little boy's life and everything works out okay. There is some spectacular photography. The conversation continues. There is talk of a young man with glaucoma, of the most recent family tragedy (a relative was burned badly in a fire in her home; her daughter and grandchildren died by fire a few years ago; her husband's first wife burned to death).

"Remember when Pat came through here with that string of stuff, son?" I remembered; my cousin, who was an officer in the Army, had commanded a convoy that had passed through Raleigh right after Pearl Harbor. We had walked up to U.S. 70, a block away, and watched them come through. Pat had stopped and we had all talked for a few minutes, and then he drove away, and it was very much like one of those movies about the glory of war.

My father remembered that it was an all-Negro regiment that Pat was conveying. I did not remember that; I remembered only that they were soldiers.

"Do you remember, Daddy, when Pat left his car in the back yard right after Pearl Harbor and you put it up on blocks and stored the tires in the basement?" He did not remember that.

We remember what we want to remember, I suppose, and we forget what we want to forget, and between the two of us, I doubt that we could put together much of a history book. I already have asked about one thing that is very important to me, the circumstances of my adoption, and he doesn't remember that. We have lived, together, more than one hundred and twelve years, and perhaps it is time to be less serious about searching for things that cannot be found.

On the way back to Brooklyn, we took the coastal route. I told them it was because I was bored with interstate highways and turnpikes and I wanted to see the ocean again. But the coastal route took us down U.S. 64, through Nashville, the seat of Nash County, and that may have been the real reason. I thought, for a moment, as we drove past the court-house, of stopping and going in and opening that book to February 23, 1935. But I decided not to. I was in a hurry, I suppose, to get home.

RALPH ELLISON
Harlem Is Nowhere

One must descend to the basement and move along a confusing mazelike hall to reach it. Twice the passage seems to lead against a blank wall; then at last one enters the brightly lighted auditorium. And here, finally, are the social workers at the reception desks; and there, waiting upon the benches rowed beneath the pipes carrying warmth and water to the floors above, are the patients. One sees white-jacketed psychiatrists carrying charts appear and vanish behind screens that form the improvised interviewing cubicles. All is an atmosphere of hurried efficiency; and the concerned faces of the patients are brightened by the friendly smiles and low-pitched voices of the expert workers. One has entered the Lafargue Psychiatric Clinic.

This clinic (whose staff receives no salary and whose fee is only twenty-five cents—to those who can afford it) is perhaps the most successful attempt in the nation to provide psychotherapy for the underprivileged. Certainly it has become in two years one of Harlem's most important institutions. Not only is it the sole mental clinic in the section, it is the only center in the city where both Negroes and whites may receive extended psychiatric care. Thus its importance transcends even its great value as a center for psychotherapy: it represents an underground extension of democracy.

As one of the few institutions dedicated to recognizing the total implication of Negro life in the United States, the Lafargue Clinic rejects all stereotypes, and may be said to concern itself with any possible variations between the three basic social factors shaping an American Negro's personality: he is viewed as a member of a racial and cultural minority; as an American citizen caught in certain political and economic relationships; and as a modern man living in a revolutionary world. Accordingly, each patient, whether white or black, is approached dynamically as a being possessing a cultural and biological past who seeks to make his way toward the future in a world wherein each discovery about himself must be made in the here and now at the expense of hope, pain and fear

—a being who in responding to the complex forces of America has become confused.

Leaving the Lafargue Clinic for a while, what are some of the forces which generate this confusion? Who is this total Negro whom the clinic seeks to know; what is the psychological character of the scene in which he dwells; how describe the past which he drags into this scene, and what is the future toward which he stumbles and becomes confused? Let us begin with the scene: Harlem.

To live in Harlem is to dwell in the very bowels of the city; it is to pass a labyrinthine existence among streets that explode monotonously skyward with the spires and crosses of churches and clutter under foot with garbage and decay. Harlem is a ruin—many of its ordinary aspects (its crimes, its casual violence, its crumbling buildings with littered area-ways, ill-smelling halls and vermin-invaded rooms) are indistinguishable from the distorted images that appear in dreams, and which, like muggers haunting a lonely hall, quiver in the waking mind with hidden and threatening significance. Yet this is no dream but the reality of well over four hundred thousand Americans; a reality which for many defines and colors the world. Overcrowded and exploited politically and economically, Harlem is the scene and symbol of the Negro's perpetual alienation in the land of his birth.

But much has been written about the social and economic aspects of Harlem; we are here interested in its psychological character—a character that arises from the impact between urban slum conditions and folk sensibilities. Historically, American Negroes are caught in a vast process of change that has swept them from slavery to the condition of industrial man in a space of time so telescoped (a bare eighty-five years) that it is possible literally for them to step from feudalism into the vortex of industrialism simply by moving across the Mason-Dixon line.

This abruptness of change and the resulting clash of cultural factors within Negro personality account for some of the extreme contrasts found in Harlem, for both its negative and its positive characteristics. For if Harlem is the scene of the folk-Negro's death agony, it is also the setting of his transcendence. Here it is possible for talented youths to leap through the development of decades in a brief twenty years, while beside them white-haired adults crawl in the feudal darkness of their childhood. Here a former cotton picker develops the sensitive hands of a surgeon, and men whose grandparents still believe in magic prepare optimistically to become atomic scientists. Here the grandchildren of those who possessed no written literature examine their lives through the eyes of Freud and Marx, Kierkegaard and Kafka, Malraux and Sartre. It explains the nature of a world so fluid and shifting that often within the mind the real and the unreal merge, and the marvelous beckons from behind the same sordid reality that denies its existence.

Hence the most surreal fantasies are acted out upon the streets of Harlem; a man ducks in and out of traffic shouting and throwing imaginary grenades that actually exploded during World War I; a boy participates in the rape-robbery of his mother; a man beating his wife in a park uses boxing "science" and observes Marquess of Queensberry rules (no rabbit punching, no blows beneath the belt); two men hold a third while a lesbian slashes him to death with a razor blade; boy gangsters wielding homemade pistols (which in the South of their origin are but toy symbols of adolescent yearning for manhood) shoot down their young rivals. Life becomes a masquerade, exotic costumes are worn every day. Those who cannot afford to hire a horse wear riding habits; others who could not afford a hunting trip or who seldom attend sporting events carry shooting sticks.

For this is a world in which the major energy of the imagination goes not into creating works of art, but to overcome the frustrations of social discrimination. Not quite citizens and yet Americans, full of the tensions of modern man but regarded as primitives, Negro Americans are in desperate search for an identity. Rejecting the second-class status assigned them, they feel alienated and their whole lives have become a search for answers to the questions: Who am I, What am I, Why am I, and Where? Significantly, in Harlem the reply to the greeting, "How are you?" is very often, "Oh, man, I'm *nowhere*"—a phrase revealing an attitude so common that it has been reduced to a gesture, a seemingly trivial word. Indeed, Negroes are not unaware that the conditions of their lives demand new definitions of terms like *primitive* and *modern, ethical* and *unethical, moral* and *immoral, patriotism* and *treason, tragedy* and *comedy, sanity* and *insanity*.

But for a long time now—despite songs like the "Blow Top Blues" and the eruption of expressions like *frantic, buggy* and *mad* into Harlem's popular speech, doubtless a word-magic against the states they name—calm in face of the unreality of Negro life becomes increasingly difficult. And while some seek relief in strange hysterical forms of religion, in alcohol and drugs, and others learn to analyze the causes for their predicament and join with others to correct them, an increasing number have found their way to the Lafargue Psychiatric Clinic.

In relation to their Southern background, the cultural history of Negroes in the North reads like the legend of some tragic people out of mythology, a people which aspired to escape from its own unhappy homeland to the apparent peace of a distant mountain; but which, in migrating, made some fatal error of judgment and fell into a great chasm of mazelike passages that promise ever to lead to the mountain but end ever against a wall. Not that a Negro is worse off in the North than in the South, but that in the North he surrenders and does not replace certain important supports to his personality. He leaves a relatively static social order in which, having experienced its brutality for hundreds of years—indeed, having been formed within it and by it—he has developed those techniques of survival to which Faulkner refers as "endurance," and an ease of movement within explosive situations which makes Hemingway's definition of courage, "grace under pressure," appear mere swagger. He surrenders the protection of his peasant cynicism—his refusal to hope for the fulfillment of hopeless hopes—and his sense of being "at home in the world" gained from confronting and accepting (for day-to-day living, at least) the obscene absurdity of his predicament. Further, he leaves a still authoritative religion which gives his life a semblance of metaphysical wholeness; a family structure which is relatively stable; and a body of folklore—tested in life-and-death terms against his daily experience with nature and the Southern white man—that serves him as a guide to action.

These are the supports of Southern Negro rationality (and, to an extent, of the internal peace of the United States); humble, but of inestimable psychological value, they allow Southern Negroes to maintain their almost mystical hope for a future of full democracy—a hope accompanied by an irrepressible belief in some Mecca of equality, located in the North and identified by the magic place names New York, Chicago, Detroit. A belief sustained (as all myth is sustained by ritual) by identifying themselves ritually with the successes of Negro celebrities, by reciting their exploits and enumerating their dollars, and by recounting the swiftness with which they spiral from humble birth to headline fame. And doubtless the blasting of this dream is as damaging to Negro personality as the slum scenes of filth, disorder and crumbling masonry in which it flies apart.

When Negroes are barred from participating in the main institutional life of society they lose far more than economic privileges or the satisfaction of saluting the flag with unmixed emotions. They lose one of the bulwarks which men place between themselves and the constant threat of chaos. For whatever the assigned function of social institutions, their psychological function is to protect the citizen against the irrational, incalculable forces that hover about the edges of human life like cosmic destruction lurking within an atomic stockpile.

And it is precisely the denial of this support through segregation and discrimination that leaves the most balanced Negro open to anxiety.

Though caught not only in the tensions arising from his own swift history, but in those conflicts created in modern man by a revolutionary world, he cannot participate fully in the therapy which the white American achieves through patriotic ceremonies and by identifying himself with American wealth and power. Instead, he is thrown back upon his own "slum-shocked" institutions.

But these, like his folk personality, are caught in a process of chaotic change. His family disintegrates, his church splinters; his folk wisdom is discarded in the mistaken notion that it in no way applies to urban living; and his formal education (never really his own) provides him with neither scientific description nor rounded philosophical interpretation of the profound forces that are transforming his total being. Yet even his art is transformed; the lyrical ritual elements of folk jazz—that artistic projection of the only real individuality possible for him in the South, that embodiment of a superior democracy in which each individual cultivated his uniqueness and yet did not clash with his neighbors—have given way to the near-themeless technical virtuosity of bebop, a further triumph of technology over humanism. His speech hardens; his movements are geared to the time clock; his diet changes; his sensibilities quicken and his intelligence expands. But without institutions to give him direction, and lacking a clear explanation of his predicament—the religious ones being inadequate, and those offered by political and labor leaders obviously incomplete and opportunistic—the individual feels that his world and his personality are out of key. The phrase "I'm nowhere" expresses the feeling borne in upon many Negroes that they have no stable, recognized place in society. One's identity drifts in a capricious reality in which even the most commonly held assumptions are questionable. One "is" literally, but one is nowhere; one wanders dazed in a ghetto maze, a "displaced person" of American democracy.

And as though all this were not enough of a strain on a people's sense of the rational, the conditions under which it lives are seized upon as proof of its inferiority. Thus the frustrations of Negro life (many of them the frustrations of *all* life during this historical moment) permeate the atmosphere of Harlem with what Dr. Frederick Wertham, Director of the Lafargue Clinic, terms "free-floating hostility," a hostility that bombards the individual from so many directions that he is often unable to identify it with any specific object. Some feel it the punishment of some racial or personal guilt and pray to God; others (called "evil Negroes" in Harlem) become enraged with the world. Sometimes it provokes dramatic mass responses, and the results are the spontaneous outbreaks called the "Harlem riots" of 1935 and 1943.

And why have these explosive matters—which are now a problem of our foreign policy—been ignored? Because there is an argument in progress between black men and white men as to the true nature of American reality. Following their own interests, white impose interpretations upon Negro experience that are not only false but, in effect, a denial of Negro humanity (witness the shock when A. Philip Randolph questions, on the basis of Negro experience, the meaning of *treason*). Too weak to shout down these interpretations, Negroes live nevertheless as they have to live, and the concrete conditions of their lives are more real than white men's arguments.

And it is here exactly that lies the importance of the Lafargue Psychiatric Clinic—both as a scientific laboratory and as an expression of forthright democratic action in its scientific willingness to dispense with preconceived notions and accept the realities of Negro, i.e., *American* life. It recognizes that the personality damage that brought it into being represents not the disintegration of a people's fiber, but the failure of a way of life. For not only is it an antidote to this failure, it represents a victory over another of its aspects.

For ten years, while heading various psychiatric institutions, Dr. Wertham had fought for a psychiatric center in which Negroes could receive treatment. But whether he approached politicians, city agencies or philanthropists, all gave excuses for not acting. The agencies were complacent, the politicians accused him of harboring political rather than humanitarian motives; certain liberal middlemen, who stand between Negroes and philanthropic dollars, accused him of trying to establish a segregated institution. Finally it was decided to establish the clinic without money or official recognition. The results were electric. When his fellow psychiatrists were asked to contribute their services, Dr. Wertham was overwhelmed with offers. These physicians, all of whom hold jobs in institutions which discriminate against Negroes, were eager to overcome this frustration to their science; and like some Southern Negroes who consider that part of themselves best which they hide beneath their servility, they consider their most important work that which is carried out in a Harlem basement.

Here, in the basement, a frustrated science goes to find its true object: the confused of mind who seek reality. Both find the source of their frustrations in the sickness of the social order. As such, and in spite of the very fine work it is doing, a thousand Lafargue clinics could not dispel the sense of unreality that haunts Harlem. Knowing this, Dr. Wertham and his interracial staff seek a modest achievement: to give each bewildered patient an insight into the relation between his problems and his environment, and out of this understanding to reforge the will to endure in a hostile world.

STAN STEINER
The Chicanos

The girl was thirteen when she tried to kill herself. She was "tired of working." But she was too inexperienced with death to die, and she lived through her death. To escape her loneliness she married, at fifteen. Her child was born that year, but her husband was sent to prison. "I got a car. The car broke down. I couldn't pay for it. They wanted to sue me. So I forged a check." In the barrios of Denver to be left with a baby, without a husband, at fifteen, was to be lonelier than death. She became a prostitute.

"I worked the town. They call it hustling. I wouldn't go for less than thirty dollars. Because I needed the money. I got it too. All you have to do is be nice," the young girl said. "But to go out and hustle I had to be under the influence of narcotics."

Diana Perea told her own life story to the National Conference on Poverty in the Southwest, held in January, 1965, to launch the War on Poverty. In the winter sun of Tucson, Arizona, the nearly two hundred delegates who had gathered under the auspices of the Choate Foundation, to hear Vice President Hubert Humphrey, were as overwhelmed by the frail and frightened girl as she was by the presidential emissary. "Go back and tell them [your people] that the war against unemployment, discrimination, disease, and ignorance has begun. Tell them to get out and fight!" the Vice President said. "The wonderful thing about the War on Poverty is that we have the means to win it. We cannot fail." He reminded his listeners, "Fifteen minutes from where we sit tonight there is abject poverty."

In the audience was Diana Perea. A few weeks later she succeeded in killing herself.

Her death was due to an overdose of narcotics, the autopsy report declared. There were some nonmedical causes. On the frontispiece of the Summary Report of the National Conference on Poverty in the Southwest there was a black border of mourning around these simple words:

DIANA PEREA
1946–1965
VICTIM OF POVERTY

Death is an ordinary thing. No one would have heard of the young girl from the streets of Denver's barrio if she had not happened to share a microphone with the Vice President of the United States.

In the streets misery is said to be so common no one notices. Life in the barrios is cruel—to outsiders, for the sons and daughters of the poor, it is said, are too hardened and brutalized to be able to do anything but fight to survive.

A young girl cries of a brown child dying of hunger in the barrios of San Antonio:

In the land of the free
    and the home of the brave,
He is dying of hunger,
    he cannot be saved;
Come brothers and sisters
    and weep by his grave.
This is our child—

The ordeal of these youths is bemoaned by sympathetic writers. Not by the youth. Diana Perea did not weep. The Chicana was matter of fact: this is the way it is. Life in the barrio streets is just a way of life—happy, unhappy, ordinary, exciting, boring, deadly. The streets are not dangerous, they are only treacherous. It doesn't frighten youth. Seldom do they curse the barrio. They curse themselves for their inability to survive. It is not the barrio that the Chicano fears, but the lonely and hostile world outside.

Loneliness, the coldness of urban life, is what depresses the Chicano. In his family there is a warmth and gregarious love voiced with passion, uninhibited honesty, and gusto. The city frustrates and mutes this love. Faced with a society that he feels is hostile, the barrio youth becomes lost. He tries to defend himself by forming a gang, not just to fight for his manhood, his *macho,* but for his right to be a Chicano.

"The most brutal method of birth control is the one we practice on ourselves," a young man writes in *La Raza.*

To *La Raza Chicana,* a young girl writes a bitter note: "I wish to compliment brother Perfecto Vallego and his friends for doing with Caterino B. Heredia. Keep up the good work, Baby, you and the cops [can] get together on the Chicano Annual School. Your game is as bad as the racist cop who goes after Chicano's who fail to halt. You dudes don't have to kill your brothers; Uncle Sam is doing that for you in Viet Nam. You are shooting the wrong guy. *No sean tan pendejos.* If you have enough *huevos* [testicles] to shoot your brother you should be able to take on a racist cop."

The street gangs of the barrios are different from those in most ghettos. In a sense they are born not solely of poverty, but also of cultural pride. Like street-corner chambers of commerce the gangs of barrio youth defend the spirit of La Raza with bravado and youthful boisterousness.

Of the many barrio gangs the oldest and best known is that of the legendary Pachucos, who have become a heroic myth. They were born in blood that was real enough, and they not only are remembered but are imitated with awe. They began on a day in August, 1942. In the tensions of World War II, the racial hatreds of Los Angeles were about to erupt in what was to be known as the "Zoot Suit Riots." Two groups of Chicanos had a boyish fight over a pretty girl and hurt pride, in a gravel pit on the outskirts of the city. In the morning the body of young José Díaz was found on a dirt road nearby, dead. Bored newspapermen, seeking local color, dubbed the gravel pit the "Sleepy Lagoon" (it had a mud puddle in it), and an orgy of sensational headlines celebrated the boy's death.

Not one but twenty-four Mexican boys were arrested; nine were convicted of second-degree murder. All were freed later, two years later, when the Court of Appeals reversed the sentences unanimously for "lack of evidence."

The "Sleepy Lagoon" case is still remembered bitterly in the barrios, much as the Dreyfus case in France, or that of the Scottsboro Boys in the Deep South.

Amid headlines of hysteria—"Zoot Suit Hoodlums" and "Pachuco Gangsters"—the Los Angeles police raided the barrios, blockaded the main streets, searched every passing car and passer-by. Six hundred Chicanos were taken into custody in a two-day sweep that Police Captain Joseph Reed called "a drive on Mexican gangs." The Los Angeles sheriff's "Bureau of *Foreign* Relations" justified the dragnet by officially philosophizing that the Chicanos' "desire to kill, or at least let blood" was an "inborn characteristic."

The next summer the tensions exploded. When a fist fight broke out on a downtown street between a gang of Chicano boys and U.S. Navy men in June, 1943, fourteen off-duty policemen led by a lieutenant of the Detective Squad set up an impromptu group of vigilantes they named the "Vengeance Squad" and set out "to clean up" the Mexicans.

Night after night hundreds of restless and beached sailors of the U.S. Navy, bored and frustrated by their inaction in the war against Japan, seized upon the nearest available dark-skinned enemies—the young Chicanos—and beat them up. The white rioters toured the barrios in convoys of taxi cabs, attacking every brown boy they found on the streets, in bars and restaurants and movie houses, by the dozens, by the hundreds, while the Los Angeles police looked the other way. No sailor was arrested. Inspired by the inflammatory news stories about "zoot suit roughnecks," the white rioters sought out these most of all—zoot suits were an early Humphrey Bogart style Mexicanized by Chicano boys and lately revived in its classic form by *Bonnie and Clyde.*

It was a long, hot summer week. When the white rioters exhausted their racial fervor, the riots—known not as the "U.S. Navy Riots" but oddly as the "Zoot Suit Riots"—had left hundreds of injured and a residue of race hatred in Los Angeles.

The zoot-suit boys were Pachucos. Where the name came from is vague, but it may have been taken from the city of Pachuco in Mexico, known for its brilliantly hued costumes. In the riots, these gangs of Pachucos were not the aggressors but the defenders of the barrios. They were an early self-defense group. Youths who never knew the Pachucos remember them not as victims but as resistance fighters of the streets, the Minutemen of *machismo,* who fought to defend the reputation of La Raza. Wherever the barrio youth organize, the spirit of the Pachucos is evoked and revived.

"I hope you tell the story of the Pachucos," a Brown Beret says to me. "We have to learn about our heroes."

One of many Pachuco-type gangs is the Vatos. It is a fictitious name of a small gang in the San Fernando Valley of Los Angeles whose "territory" ranges from Laurel Canyon Boulevard to O'Melveny Street. The Vatos hang out mostly in the dark alleys near Acala Avenue, a poorly lit thoroughfare.

A member of the Vatos talks of his gang:

"This is the story of life in a Mexican barrio. The barrio is called 'San Fer.' The kids, so-called Pachucos, run this barrio. Life in this barrio is rough, harsh. The boys learned early to carry can openers and knives. As soon as they got a little older they graduated to switchblades, lengths of chain, and guns, if they could get hold of them.

"Boys joined together to form street gangs, and some of them sported the Pachuco brand between the thumb and forefinger of their left hand," the Vato says. "This gang is the stuff of life, as the Pachuco knows it."

The gang member has to prove his manhood and his ability to survive.

"He will undertake the most fantastic stunts to prove a great deal. He will risk his life and his freedom to maintain his growing reputation as a tough fighter, a rugged guy." These rituals are not merely rites of initiation, or idle bravado. The gang youth has to demonstrate not only that he can fight in the streets, but that he has the strength to withstand the hostility of society, to stand up to the *placa,* the police, and if he is courageous enough, to become visible to the outsider, by wearing a Brown Beret. "That is real *macho,*" a Los Angeles community leader says.

It is a new kind of political and urban *pachuquismo.* The society outside the barrio is defied by the gang. Consciously the rituals of brotherhood enforce the laws and culture of the barrio. Inside the gang the Chicano is insulated from his own conflicts. The Chicanos "find conflicts so perplexing and so full of both cultures—that of their parents and that of America—that [they] create their own world of *pachuquismo,*" says the Vato.

The Vato goes on: "The Vatos have created their own language, Pachucano, their own style of dress, their own folklore, and their own behavior patterns. The Vatos have developed a barrio group spirit. The Vatos in this area are better organized and a little tighter, due to the fact that it is a smaller group; and therefore all the Vatos participate in the activities planned by them.

"They formed a closely knit group that regarded the Anglos as their natural enemies."

In every barrio the social clubs and folk religious societies have always existed in semisecrecy, with their own rules and symbols, hidden from the world outside. Chicano gangs are the progeny of that invisible heritage—to outsiders—by which the barrio has protected itself. They re-create in their own youthful way, the society and culture of their forefathers; yet they are urban.

Eliezer Risco, the editor of *La Raza,* describes these methods of barrio organizations as "our own survival techniques. It is difficult for the culture of a minority to survive in the larger society. If we can utilize them for social action, now that we are stronger, we will surprise the country," he says. "The country won't know where our strength is coming from or how we organize."

In the dark alleyways and gregarious streets, the Brown Berets began. They have developed a political *pachuquismo.* A generation ago they would have been a street gang, nothing more. Less obvious are the barrio origins of the youthful leaders of the La Raza movements that have gained national prominence and importance. Cesar Chavez, Rodolfo "Corky" Gonzales, Reies Tijerina: these men learned their organizing techniques on the back streets of the barrio.

"They say the La Raza movements come from the universities. I disagree," says "José," the "Field Marshal" of the Brown Berets. "I say they come from the streets."

So few youths in the barrios graduated from high school in the past, or entered college, that those who achieved that miraculous feat feared to look down from their pinnacle of anxiety. If they did, the barrios beneath them seemed a bottomless arroyo. And yet, in the wholly anglicized realms of higher education they were also strangers.

"You see a Chicano [university] student is alienated from his language; he is de-culturized and finally dehumanized so as to be able to function in a white, middle-class, protestant bag," the *Chicano Student News* reports. "It is damn obvious to the Chicano in college that education means one of two things: either accept the system—study, receive a diploma, accept the cubicle and the IBM machine in some lousy bank or factory, and move out of the barrio—or reject the system. . . ."

Youths who made it to the university clung to their privileged and precarious achievements: non-Mexican name and anglicized accent, an Ivy League suit, a blond wife, and a disdain for the "dumb Mexicans" left behind. "THE PURPLE TIO TOMAS" (Uncle Tom), *El Gallo* has dubbed these high achievers. "This is the middle class Tomás. He isn't a Tomás because he lives on the other side of town, but because the Purple Tomás believes he is better than other Chicanos. Purple is the Royal Color!" The would-be intellectual *patróns*—"the new conservatives," Corky Gonzales calls them.

Now the university students have begun to climb down from their lonely success to the streets of the barrios and the fields of the campesinos. They come as on a pilgrimage, seeking an identity. Los Angeles community leader Eduardo Pérez says, "I find that many Mexicans-turned-Spanish are coming back into the fold and are being identified for what they are: Mexicans." They have a "pride in being Mexican."

In the vineyards of Delano, when the striking grape pickers gathered their banners and walked north on the highway in their 250-mile pilgrimage to Sacramento to see the Governor, the university Chicanos who walked with the *huelguistas* were wide-eyed with wonder. Not only were these young people from the universities, but they were the children of the barrios who had at last escaped, had "made it." Some even had blond hair.

Here were "farm workers with dark faces, aged prematurely by the California sun, marching side by side with students with youthful faces," wrote Daniel de los Reyes in the union newspaper *El Malcriado*, the "farm workers with black hair and a determined look, by the side of blond and red-haired students with brilliant, sparkling eyes." It was "a spectacle to see, these thousands and thousands of young people" who had come "because the Farm Workers Organizing Committee had agreed to join side by side with their brothers, the students." There was a tone of wonder in the union newspaper story. It seemed unbelievable, this "brotherhood against ignorance and poverty." These were "the same students we have seen so many times on the picketlines at the vineyards of DiGiorgio, the same youth working so tirelessly on the boycotts," declared *El Malcriado.*

Still it was not to be believed. The university students respected, listened to, and obeyed the campesinos of the fields; that was what was so strange. It was as though they who were illiterate were the teachers of the university students.

The experience of the *huelga* was a strange and exhilarating one for the students as well, for it profoundly affected the lives of many who had come. Luis Valdez, who went on to found El Centro Cultural Campesino, and Eliezer Risco, who became editor of *La Raza,* were but two of dozens of student leaders whose lives were changed by their pilgrimage to the vineyards of Delano.

"I was writing my thesis," Risco recalls. "I came thinking, well, it's a way of doing my research. But it was my Graduate School."

Venustiano Olguin was a brilliant student in a graduate school of the University of California at Los Angeles and was studying for his Ph.D. The son of a bracero who had grown up in the migrant barrios of the Coachella Valley, he had worked his way to first place in his high school class and graduated with honors from the University of Redlands.

"I'd been very successful with the system." But he had begun to have the uneasy feeling he was becoming a "Tío Tomás," an Uncle Tom. "At UCLA I knew that somewhere along the line I had been betraying something." He did not know what.

One summer the young man and some of his fellow students in the United Mexican American Students (UMAS) had a meeting with Cesar Chavez. Olguin went to Delano—not to stay, just to look around and help the farm workers if he could. He decided to join *La Huelga.* He has abandoned the honors of higher education that he says were anglicizing him, indoctrinating him with materialistic values, and forcing him to reject his Mexican heritage. He lives on $5 a week strike pay. "Some people think I am crazy. But I think my life is very rich." In the campesinos he feels he has found "a special kind of courage," of manhood. "I've learned more than in all the time I was in graduate school."

University communities of Chicanos were affected as strongly. In San Antonio, Texas, a leader of the Mexican American Youth Organization recalls how the campesinos of the Rio Grande Valley became godfathers of his group. "The strike of the farm workers got everyone excited. St. Mary's University students got together to see what they could do," says William Vazquez. "And that is how we began."

Luis Valdez, whose life was changed by Delano, feels it is a necessary school for students. "In advance of their people, the Chicano leader in the cities and universities must go through the whole bourgeois scene, find it distasteful, and then strike out in new directions. This is what happened with Corky Gonzales and Cesar Chavez. Divorcing themselves from the petty aims of success, they see the middle class for what it is. Then they can see the lower class plain.

"In short, they discover there is a world out there," Valdez says.

Out of the upheaval have come dozens of new barrio and university clubs. In the last few years there has been more youth organizing than in the entire history of the Chicanos. University students have been especially outspoken and active. The United Mexican American Students (UMAS) in California and the National Organization of Mexican American Students (NOMAS, literally "No More") in Texas are but two of more than thirty groups on the campuses alone.

The university and barrio youth are talking and walking together. David Sanchez, the prime minister of the Brown Berets, talks to students at UCLA, while the students of UMAS walk not only on the picket lines of the campesinos of Delano but also beside the Brown Berets protesting school conditions in East Los Angeles. The *Chicano Student News* reports: "UMAS is an organization of Chicano college students which is bringing the business of education back into the Chicano community"; and the headline says, "UMAS COMES HOME!"

"Old hatreds and quarrels are being put aside," *La Raza* writes, for *"Todos son Chicanos"*—"We are all Chicanos."

Several dozen Chicanos gathered at a dude ranch near Santa Barbara on the California seacost for one of the many conferences of students and barrio youths. Eduardo Pérez, who helped run the conference, describes the occasion:

"Nowadays the young lions and lionesses have their own cars, buy their own clothes, work their way through college, and are very much on their own. Their whole thinking and outlook on life is as different from ours as night is from day.

"These Mexican American 'world leaders of tomorrow' are an exceptional breed. They can put on a *charro* [the real cowboy Mexican] costume and be proud of it. They can even put on American clothes and feel at ease. They can eat enchiladas and hamburgers on the same plate, tacos and pizza in one sitting, and possibly drink tequila with beer as a chaser and feel right at home. They have become anglicized, but only to the point that there is no excuse for them not being accepted. They take pride in being of Mexican ancestry and do not deny being what they are. These kids don't change their names just to become Spanish or European heirs. . . ."

In spite of the ease with which they seemed to go from one culture to another, the young Chicanos suffered an inner paralysis. They doubted not their emotions or their thoughts, but to create one culture out of two so different. Pérez had written of another youth conference, "The Mexican Americans attending (most of them) did not really understand themselves . . . and how they happened to be in the mess they're in."

The university and barrio youth had this in common too.

"I stand naked in the world, lost in angry solitude," the Chicano poet Benjamin Luna writes in *La Raza*. The loneliness of the urban society— impersonal, cold, efficient, foreign to his heart—evokes the feeling of a hostile world. The futility the Chicano feels is not fatalism, but a rage of frustration.

> *Soy Indio con alma hambrienta,*
> *traigo en la sangre coraje,*
> *rojo coraje en la sangre.*
>
> I am Indian with a hungry soul,
> tragic in the passionate blood,
> red passion in the blood.
>
> I stand naked in the world,
> hungry
> homeless
> despised. . . .

In the barrios, brotherhood is in the blood, the blood of La Raza. "One boy will bring beer, while others will bring *rifa;* still others bring money for the use of activities, or gas in a member's car. This is a thing that goes on every night with something different every night that can be called a 'dead kick.' " At best, their inner brotherhood is limited by the outer world of their "natural enemy," and at worst is defined by it.

A Brown Beret laments, "We are not what we were when we started out. All those TV cameras and news reporters took over our image and changed us into their image of us."

"Who am I?" asks a young woman in a suburban church of Los Angeles. "I have been afraid to speak up for my rights. Rights? What rights do we have? So many of our youth plead guilty in court when they know they are not guilty of anything. Anything but being a Mexican."

. . .

"Soul searching," Dr. Ernesto Galarza calls it. The scholar, a sparse man of wiry thoughts and whitening hair, who talks with hard, dry words, is recognized by many of the Chicano youth leaders as the dean of the La Raza movement; perhaps the dean emeritus. "There is an incredible amount of soul searching going on among this generation. Of questioning. Of seeking," he says one midnight over coffee in a motel in Santa Barbara, where he has gone to teach a youth workshop.

"Many of these youth have been propelled into crises of considerable tension. There have been tragic losses, where some of them have been torn asunder by the conflicts, internal and external, within themselves. There has been a loss of much potential. The youth are resilient, however.

"I believe there are few phoneys in this generation. Anyone who believes this is a time for the promotion of Uncle Toms, of acquiescence, among the younger generation of Mexicans, is mistaken. Unquestionably this generation is confronted with some crippling problems. But *that* is not one of them," says the scholar.

Dr. Galarza's weary eyes light up when he talks of these youths. "I am delighted by the happenstance of the last ten years. There has been the growth of quite a small army of young men, a phalanx of potential leaders who are searching for a breakthrough. The younger generation holds much promise.

"It is too early to foresee where these movements will lead. There is little unity of thought. There is precious little cohesion. Every movement is its own little stirring of activity. In five or ten years, there may be a reckoning; a culmination.

"We will wait," the scholar says, "and we will see."

Of course, the youth will not wait. They want action now, ideology later. Having had a small glimpse of their cultural identity, they want the rest; and having had a foretaste of Chicano power, they yearn for more: "Mañana is here!" says Maclovio Barraza, leader of the Arizona miners.

"Who the hell are we? What are we? Where do we belong? Study it! Announce it to the world!" Joe Benitos, a Chicano leader in Arizona, exclaims impatiently. "Let's end this hangup about identity. We know who we are. In order to survive we have learned survival skills. Sure, but let's not confuse our survival skills in Anglo society with our culture. We have a parallel culture. We have to keep it. I say we can do it. We don't have to be one of *them!*"

His impatience with the talk of the "identity crisis" is typical of the young Chicano. Benitos feels the problem of identity is perpetuated by university study projects, "so that they will have something to study"; he has worked with several of these projects. "I've been there," he says. "And that's not where it's at.

"Yes, having two cultures creates problems. Why emphasize the problems? Why not emphasize the opportunities it gives the Chicano in the new world scene?

"There is a Chicano wave coming in," says Benitos. "I see it as part of the world-wide scene. As the world shrinks everyone will have to learn more than one language, one culture. Everyone will have to be bilingual and trilingual. It will put us in a fantastic position, if we can keep our languages and cultures.

"Our experience will be a lesson for the whole world," he says.

"Chicano" is a new word, not yet in the dictionary. La Raza writers cannot yet define it except by what it is not; the Chicano is not, they say, half-Mexican, half-American, who blends two cultures in his being. He is not just one more second- and third-generation city-bred descendant of a rural villager who has learned to drive a car like a wild horse and pay for it on the installment plan. La Raza is a new people with a new culture and the Chicano is its youngest offspring. He has inherited many things from Mexico and the United States, but he imitates neither. The Chicano is a new man.

In the La Raza newspapers there appears a "Definition of the Word Chicano" by Benito Rodríguez. He is a member of MANO (Hand), a group of Chicano ex-convicts in San Antonio, Texas. Rodríguez's words, even more than his ideas, the way he writes, the style, the language he uses, give some of the feeling of being a Chicano in the barrio of a modern city. Even in the pale English translation the strong flavor of that life comes through, although it is stronger in the Spanish. He writes:

"Many designations have been used to refer to us, the descendants of Mexicans. Every ten or fifteen years, or so, we feel like searching for a new image of ourselves. First, in the time of the 'Wild West' we were 'Mexican bandits,' then 'greasers,' then 'Mescins,' and now we are 'Spanish Americans,' 'Mexican Americans,' 'Americans,' etc.

"The migrant Mexicans, workers in the field, call themselves Chicapatas (short legs), or Raza (race, as in Raza del Sol, People of the Sun). City workers use the term Chicano a little more. The phrase Mexican-American is really used by the middle-class Mexicans. What is truly Mexican is covered by a layer, Chicano, to satisfy all the conditions in which we find ourselves. How shall we describe ourselves tomorrow, or the day after?

"Now they want to make us half Mexicans and half Americans, as if they were talking about geography. Well, we already know who we are. Why do we come on like a chicken with its head cut off? Why do we let them make fakes, if we are Chicanos down to the phlegm in our mouths? If you don't like the taste you'll swallow it anyway.

"Just because we've seen their marvelous technology doesn't mean we believe that those who exploit us are gods."

Benito Rodríguez concludes with a curse that is pure Chicano: "A poor man who thinks he lives in heaven is gonna get fucked, coming and going."

N. SCOTT MOMADAY
The Night Chanter

Los Angeles, 1952   *February 20*

He left today. It was raining, and I gave him my coat. You know, I hated to give it up; it was the only one I had. We stood outside on the platform. He was looking down, and I was trying to think of something to say. The tracks were all wet—you know how the rails shine in the rain—and there were people all around, saying goodbye to each other. He had a sack and a suitcase—you know, one of those little tin boxes with three stripes painted on it. We had walked all the way in the rain, and the shoulders of that coat—his coat—were all wet and stained. He tried to keep the sack inside of his coat, but part of it got wet. He took it out and tried to dry it when we got to the station, but it was already getting soft. I guess it fell apart afterward. He looked pretty bad. His hands were still bandaged, and he couldn't use them very well. It took us a long time to get there. He couldn't walk very fast. It was a good coat, gray gabardine, but it was old and it hadn't been cleaned in a long time. I don't remember where I got it. I got it secondhand, and there was a big hole in the right pocket. You don't really need a coat like that around here, except when it rains.

It was getting dark when I came back, and it stopped raining for a while. I got downtown and the streets were wet and all the lights were going on. You know, it's dark down there all the time, even at noon, and the lights are always on. But at night when it rains the lights are everywhere. They shine on the pavement and the cars. They are all different colors; they go on and off and move all around. The stores are all lighted up inside, and the windows are full of shiny things. Everything is clean and bright and new-looking.

You have to watch where you're going. There's always a big crowd of people down there, especially after it rains, and a lot of noise. You hear the cars on the wet streets, starting and stopping. You hear a lot of whistles and horns, and there's a lot of loud music all around. Those old men who stand around on the corners and sell papers, they're always yelling at you, but you can't understand them. I can't, anyway.

I walked right along because it was going to rain again, and I was getting cold. I didn't want to be down there anyway. I kept thinking about him being sick like that on the train. He looked pretty bad, like he might need some help. There was still a lot of blue and swelling around his eyes, and you could see that his nose was broken. His hands were all bandaged up. Now you know you're not going to help a man who's all beat up like that, not if you don't know him. You're going to be afraid of him. I kept thinking about that, how nobody was going to help him, and I got to feeling bad; I got lonesome, too, I guess. It started to rain again, and it was kind of lonesome down there in the streets, everybody going someplace, going home.

I came out of the tunnel on 3rd Street and turned around toward Bunker Hill Avenue. It was raining pretty hard again, and my shirt was all wet and sticky—you know how wool smells when it gets all wet—and I went into The Silver Dollar, Henry's place. It was warm in there. It's a pretty good place; there's a juke box, and there's always some Indians, drinking and fooling around. You can get drunk in there, and as long as you don't get sick or start a fight or something, nobody says anything. Martinez comes in there sometimes, and then everybody gets real quiet. You know, they call him *culebra*. He's a cop, and a bad one. He's always looking for trouble, and if he's got it in for you—if you make him mad—you better look out. But Henry always gives him a bottle—and money, too, I guess. He's good to him, you know? And if you behave yourself in there, he lets you alone.

It was pretty crowded on account of the rain. I wanted a drink, but I didn't have any money, so I asked Manygoats if he could pay me back. He was with some girl I didn't know—she's new around here, from Oklahoma, I think—and he's owed me some money for a long time. He gets paid by the week, and he gets some lease money from home, too. He was acting pretty big, because of that girl, I guess, and he gave me three dollars. She was good-looking, that girl—you know, great big breasts—and I kind of wanted to meet her. I could have talked to her, I guess; she seemed real nice and friendly, but I could tell that Manygoats wanted me to leave. He was making out all right; he had some plans, I guess. So I told him I had to meet somebody outside, and he sure was glad. If he hadn't paid me back, I could have had some fun with him. Right away I was sorry I said that—about meeting somebody, I mean—because then I had to leave. There were some other guys I knew, Howard and Tosamah and Cruz and those guys, but they were all having a big time together. They had some plans, I guess. I guess I didn't care much, either. I didn't feel like going anyplace, so I bought a bottle of wine and came on home.

You could see the rain around the streetlights. They made funny yellow circles against the clouds and the buildings, and the rain was steady and fine. It was dark out there, except for the streetlights, and there was nobody around, just a car now and then. And it would go along pretty slow and sound like it does in the rain, and when it passed you could see the tail-lights, how they make those wavy red lines in the street.

There's no light downstairs; it blew out a long time ago. There was nobody around. I couldn't hear anybody, and the stairs were dark. I forgot to get some matches at Henry's place, and I had to feel my way up the stairs. When I came in here, the window was open. That's the first thing I saw, that the window was open and the rain was coming in and the sill was dripping inside. I felt bad about that, forgetting to close the window, because the floor leaks and that old woman Carlozini downstairs, she gets pretty mad. It leaks on her bed, I guess, and one time she told the landlord about it. I turned on the light and, sure enough, there was a big wet spot on the floor. I tried to wipe it up, but it was pretty well soaked in. She's out someplace again, and I hope she really ties one on. She's going to tell the landlord as sure as anything. Well, it's the only window in here, you know, and it gets pretty stale if you don't keep it open. You have to open the door, too, so there's a draft. I remember how I was sitting there this afternoon with my feet up on the sill. It was just beginning to sprinkle a little, and he had that little suitcase out on the bed, and I could hear him moving around behind me. There was a big pigeon flying around out there in the street, and I was trying to get it to come up on the sill. You know, you can do that sometimes if you put some crumbs around. But that one—it was a great big one, with a lot of blue and purple on its neck—it couldn't seem to make up its mind. It just sailed around for a while, and finally it flew up on the roof across the street. There were some others over there, a lot of them. We just forgot about that window, that's all.

It was pretty cold in here when I came in, and I took off that wet shirt and turned the radiator on. I was afraid the furnace wasn't on, but pretty soon the pipes began knocking and there was a little heat coming out. I put my shirt over the radiator, and pretty soon you could really smell the wool. It got almost dry, and I was afraid it was going to get burned, so I put it on again. It was all warm, and it really felt good. I thought about eating something. Milly brought some groceries up here yesterday; she's always doing that, and it comes out of her own pocket, too. We put some cheese and crackers and a couple of candy bars in that sack he had. There's quite a bit left, I guess, some bread and some cans of chili and stuff. But I wasn't very hungry, and I had that bottle of wine. Now that he's gone, I don't know if Milly's going to come around anymore. I guess she will. It got pretty hot in here after a while, and I had to turn the heat off. It's funny how those pipes make all that noise. You can hear them all over the building, especially when there's nobody around.

I kept thinking about him. I wish Milly was here. She liked him a whole lot, and she's always talking to me about him. She thought he was going to be O.K. around here, I guess. She wouldn't get drunk with us or any-thing like that, but she would always come around with some groceries and we would eat together, the three of us. She was always asking him about the reservation and the army and prison and all at first, but he didn't like to talk about it much, and she caught on after a while. And then she talked about other things. We kidded her a lot, and she liked it, and pretty soon she didn't bring all those papers around anymore. She was new on the job, and at first she used to bring a lot of questionnaires and read them to us, a lot of silly questions about education and health and the kind of work we were doing and all, and she would write down a lot of that stuff. I didn't care, but he got mad about it and said it wasn't any of her business. She took it all right, and that's when she stopped bringing all those forms and things around. He started to like her after that, and I was glad. We got along pretty well together. She was sorry to see him go. She wouldn't let on, but I could tell that she felt pretty bad. She had to work today, or I guess she would have gone down to the sta-tion with us. Maybe she'll come around tomorrow. Maybe not.

I kept thinking about last night, too. We went up there on the hill, him and me, with Tosamah and Cruz. There were a lot of Indians up there, and we really got going after a while. We were all pretty drunk by that time, and there were a couple of drums, and some guy had a flute. There was a lot of liquor up there, and everybody was feeling pretty good. We started singing some of those real old-time songs, and it was still and cool up there. Somebody built a fire, and we heated the drums until they were good and tight and you could really hear them. And pretty soon they started to dance. Mercedes Tenorio had some turtle shells and she started a stomp dance. You know, she was going all around with those shells in the firelight and calling out just like an old-timer, "Ee he! Oh ho! Ah ha!" And everybody started to answer in the same way, and they all got behind her and she was leading them all around. I kind of wanted to get in there, too, but he didn't care much about it, and he couldn't dance anyway on account of being all banged up like that, so we just stood back and watched.

You can forget about everything up there. We could see all the lights down below, a million lights, I guess, and all the cars moving around, so small and slow and far away. We could see one whole side of the city, all the way to the water, but we couldn't hear anything down there. All we could hear was the drums and the singing. There were some stars, and it was like we were way out in the desert someplace and there was a squaw dance or a sing going on, and everybody was getting good and drunk and happy.

He wanted to tell me something, and we went off a little way by our-selves. We were both pretty drunk, and we just stood around out there in the dark, listening. I guess we were thinking the same thing. I don't know what he wanted to say. I guess he wanted *me* to say something first, so I started to talk about the way it was going to be. We had some plans about that. We were going to meet someplace, maybe in a year or two, maybe more. He was going home, and he was going to be all right again. And someday I was going home, too, and we were going to meet someplace out there on the reservation and get drunk together. It was going to be the last time, and it was something we had to do. We were going out into the hills on horses and alone. It was going to be early in the morning, and we were going to see the sun coming up. It was going to be good again, you know? We were going to get drunk for the last time, and we were going to sing the old songs. We were going to sing about the way it used to be, how there was nothing all around but the hills and the sunrise and the clouds. We were going to be drunk and, you know, peaceful—beautiful. We had to do it a certain way, just right, because it was going to be the last time.

I told him about that. It was a plan we had. You know, I made all of that up when he was in the hospital, and it was just talk at first. But he believed in it, I guess, and the next day he asked me about it. I had to remember what it was, and then I guess I started to believe in it, too. It was a plan we had, just the two of us, and we weren't ever going to tell anybody about it.

"House made of dawn." I used to tell him about those old ways, the stories and the sings, Beautyway and Night Chant. I sang some of those things, and I told him what they meant, what I thought they were about. We would get drunk, both of us, and then he would want me to sing like that. Well, we were up there on the hill last night, and we could hear the drums and the flute away off, and it was dark and cool and peaceful. I told him about the plan we had, and we were getting pretty drunk, and I started to sing all by myself. The others were singing, too, but it was the wrong kind of thing, and I wanted to pray. I didn't want them to hear me, because they were having a good time, and I was ashamed, I guess. I kept it down because I didn't want anybody but him to hear.

> *Tségihi.*
> House made of dawn,
> House made of evening light,
> House made of dark cloud,
> House made of male rain,
> House made of dark mist,
> House made of female rain,
> House made of pollen,
> House made of grasshoppers,
> Dark cloud is at the door.
> The trail out of it is dark cloud.
> The zigzag lightning stands high upon it.
> Male deity!

Your offering I make.
I have prepared a smoke for you.
Restore my feet for me,
Restore my legs for me,
Restore my body for me,
Restore my mind for me,
Restore my voice for me.
This very day take out your spell for me.
Your spell remove for me.
You have taken it away for me;
Far off it has gone.
Happily I recover.
Happily my interior becomes cool.
Happily I go forth.
My interior feeling cool, may I walk.
No longer sore, may I walk.
Impervious to pain, may I walk.
With lively feelings, may I walk.
As it used to be long ago, may I walk.
Happily may I walk.
Happily, with abundant dark clouds, may I walk.
Happily, with abundant showers, may I walk.
Happily, with abundant plants, may I walk.
Happily, on a trail of pollen, may I walk.
Happily may I walk.
Being as it used to be long ago, may I walk.
May it be beautiful before me,
May it be beautiful behind me,
May it be beautiful below me,
May it be beautiful above me,
May it be beautiful all around me.
In beauty it is finished.

He was unlucky. You could see that right away. You could see that he wasn't going to get along around here. Milly thought he was going to be all right, I guess, but she didn't understand how it was with him. He was a longhair, like Tosamah said. You know, you have to change. That's the only way you can live in a place like this. You have to forget about the way it was, how you grew up and all. Sometimes it's hard, but you have to do it. Well, he didn't want to change, I guess, or he didn't know how. He came here from prison, too, and that was bad. He was on parole, and he had to do everything right the first time. That made it a lot harder for him; he wasn't as lucky as the rest of us. He was going to get us all in trouble, Tosamah said. Tosamah sized him up right away, and he warned me about him. But, you know, Tosamah doesn't understand either. He talks pretty big all the time, and he's educated, but he doesn't understand.

One night I was up here by myself—he was out someplace—and Tosamah came in. I didn't much want to talk to him, you know, because he's always showing off and making fun of things. He was feeling pretty good, I guess, and he started right in the way he does. "You take that poor cat," he said. "They gave him every advantage. They gave him a pair of shoes and told him to go to school. They deloused him and gave him a lot of free haircuts and let him fight on their side. But was he grateful? Hell, no, man. He was too damn dumb to be civilized. So what happened? They let him alone at last. They thought he was harmless. They thought he was going to plant some beans, man, and live off the fat of the land. Oh, he was going to make his way, all right. He would get some fat little squaw all knocked up, and they would lie around all day and get drunk and raise a lot of little government wards. They would make some pottery, man, and boost the economy. But it didn't turn out that way. He turned out to be a real primitive sonuvabitch, and the first time he got hold of a knife he killed a man. That must have embarrassed the hell out of them.

"And do you know what he said? I mean, do you have any *idea* what that cat said? A *snake,* he said. He killed a goddam *snake! The corpus delicti,* see, *he threatened to turn himself into a snake,* for crissake, and rattle around a little bit. Now ain't that something, though? Can you *imagine* what went on at that trial? There was this longhair, see, cold sober, of sound mind, and the goddam judge looking on, and the prosecutor trying to talk sense to that poor degenerate Indian: 'Tell us about it, man. Give it to us straight.' 'Well, you honors, it was this way, see? I cut me up a little snake meat out there in the sand.' Christ, man, that must have been our finest hour, better than Little Bighorn. That little no-count cat must have had the whole Jesus scheme right in the palm of his hand. Think of it! *What's-His-Name v. United States.* I mean, where's the legal precedent man? When you stop to think about it, due process is a hell of a remedy for snakebite.

"They put that cat away, man. They *had* to. It's part of the Jesus scheme. *They,* man. They put all of us renegades, us diehards, away sooner or later. They've got the right idea. They put us away before we're born. They're an almighty wise and cautious bunch, those cats, full of discretion. You've got to admire them, man; they know the score. I mean they see through us. They know what we're waiting for. We don't fool them for a minute. Listen here, Benally, one of these nights there's going to be a full red moon, a hunter's moon, and we're going to find us a wagon train full of women and children. Now you won't believe this, but I drink to that now and then."

He's always going on like that, Tosamah, talking crazy and showing off, but he doesn't understand. I got to thinking about it, though, anyway. About *him;* about him being afraid of that man out there, so afraid he didn't know what to do. That, you know, being so scared of something like that—that's what Tosamah doesn't understand. He's educated, and he doesn't believe in being scared like that. But he doesn't come from the reservation. He doesn't know how it is when you grow up out there someplace. You grow up out there, you know, someplace like Kayenta or Lukachukai. You grow up in the night, and there are a lot of funny things going on, things you don't know how to talk about. A baby dies, or a good horse. You get sick, or the corn dries up for no good reason. Then you remember something that happened the week before, something that wasn't right. You heard an owl, maybe, or you saw a funny kind of whirlwind; somebody looked at you sideways and a moment too long. And then you *know*. You just know. Maybe your aunt or your grandmother was a witch. Maybe you knew she was, because she was always going around at night, around the corrals; maybe you saw her sometimes, like she was talking to the dogs or the sheep, and when you looked again she wasn't there. You just know, and you can't help being scared. It was like that with him, I guess. It might have been like that.

We got along all night; we had some pretty good times. I remember the first time he came around. It was pretty early. I had been there about an hour, I guess, and the foreman called me. I thought he was going to bawl me out because I had punched in late, but I guess he didn't know about that. I went into the office, and there *he* was, with the foreman and some other guy, a Relocation officer. We shook hands and the foreman said he was going to start him out on my line, and would I show him around? I was glad, because DeBenedictus had been laid off the week before, and there was nobody across from me on the line and I didn't have anybody to talk to. I needed a stapler pretty bad, too, because I was having to do two jobs and a lot of orders were piling up. Well, I showed him how to punch in and took him around to meet some of the guys. I could tell he was kind of shy and scared—you know how it is when you start to work in a new place—and then I took him over to my line and showed him how to staple. He was good with his hands, and he caught on all right. He was just learning, you know, and it was kind of slow at first. He made some mistakes, too, but I played like I didn't notice, and after a while we were turning those things out pretty good.

He was looking right down at his work all the time, like I wasn't even there. I knew how he felt, so I didn't try to talk to him, and every time it slowed up we just stood there looking up the line for the next piece, like we were really busy thinking about it, you know, and it was part of the job. It was getting on toward noon, and I noticed that he hadn't brought a lunch bag. I was trying to think what I ought to do about that. I didn't know if he had any money. It's funny, but I hadn't thought about that before, and I got to worrying about it. I didn't want to embarrass him or anything, and I guess he was thinking about it, too, because when the whistle blew he acted like he didn't know what it was and went right on working. Anyway, it turned out all right. We punched out, and I took him over to the Coke machine. He had some Relocation money, I guess. He had some change, anyway, and I was glad. We got a couple of Cokes and went on out into the yard. Everybody was sitting around out there eating lunch. They were being pretty friendly, too, but I didn't want to get in with them because I knew he would have been embarrassed. They kid around a lot down there, those guys. They're always calling you chief and talking about firewater and everything. I don't mind, but I didn't know how he would take it. I was afraid it might hurt his feelings or something. He was used to it, though, because he had been in the army, and in prison, too, but I didn't know that then. Right away we went off by ourselves. I had a sandwich, and I asked him if he wanted to split it with me, but he said he wasn't hungry. I ate about half of it and acted like I didn't want any more. I put the rest of it down on the plank between us and kept hoping he would change his mind and take it, but he didn't. Finally I had to throw it away.

He didn't have anyplace to stay. The Relocation people were looking around, I guess, but they hadn't found a place, and he was going to spend the night at the Indian Center. There's a storeroom down there in the alley, where they keep the food and clothing that people have donated, you know. You can stay there sometimes if you don't have anyplace else to go. It's just an old frame building, and you can see through the cracks in the walls, but you can make a pretty good bed out of those old coats and things, and you can keep warm. But there's no toilet and no lights, and somebody's always bringing a girl in there to fool around. A lot of guys get sick in there, too, and it always smells kind of sour and bad. I told him about that and said he could move in with me if he wanted to. He didn't say anything, but after work he went down and talked to the Relocation people, and that night he came with that little suitcase up to my room.

It was a long time before he would talk to anyone. Oh, after a while we talked a whole lot, him and me, but it was about things that happened around here. You know, Milly and those other social workers would come around sometimes, and we kidded around about them afterward. We got in with some of the other guys and got drunk and fooled around. But it was a long time before he would talk about himself—and then he never said much. I guess it's that way with most of us. If you come from the reservation, you don't talk about it much; I don't know why. I guess you figure that it won't do you much good, so you just forget about it. You think about it sometimes; you can't help it, but then you just try to put it out of your mind. There's a whole lot more to think about, and it mixes you up sometimes if you don't just go along with it. I guess if we all came from the same place it would be different; we could talk about it, you know, and we could understand.

We were kind of alike, though, him and me. After a while he told me where he was from, and right away I knew we were going to be friends. We're related somehow, I think. The Navajos have a clan they call by the name of that place. I was there once, too. That was eight or ten years ago, I guess, and I was going to the Santa Fe Indian School, and some of us went over there for the big dance they have in November. It was cold that winter, and there was a lot of snow all around. It's a pretty good place; there are mountains and canyons around there, and there's a lot of red in the rocks. Except for the mountains, it's like the land south of Wide Ruins, where I come from, full of gullies and brush and red rocks. And he didn't have any family, either, just his grandfather. He said his grandfather used to have a bunch of sheep. I herded sheep from the time I could walk.

It didn't snow much out there, but when it did the whole land as far as you could see was covered with it. It went on sometimes all night, and you could see it outside through the smoke hole, swirling around in the black sky. And sometimes the flakes came in and melted on the floor around the fire, and you were glad there was a fire. You could hear the wind, and you were little and you could get way down under the blankets and see the firelight moving around on the logs of the roof and the walls, and the floor was yellow and warm and you could put your hand in the dust and feel how warm it was. And you knew that your grandfather was there, looking out for you. You woke up sometimes, and he was there stirring the fire to keep it going, and you knew that everything was all right. And the next morning you got up and went out and it was cold and there was snow all around. Maybe the sun was out and the snow was so bright it hurt your eyes. It drifted up against the hogan and covered the top of it, and the hogan looked like a little hill all covered with snow and you could see the smoke coming out of it and smell the coffee and the mutton. You put your hands in the snow and rubbed your face with it and it made you come alive and feel good and your hands were red and wet with the cold snow. You were little and you looked all around at the snow; it was piled up on the brush and you could see the dark branches under it, and the sheep were bleating in the corral and the poles of the fence were heaped high with snow, and underneath you could see the wood, how it was almost black with water. There was a gully a little way off, and inside of it, where the snow had fallen off, the earth was a deep red and there were bits of brush growing out of it and covered with snow. They looked like handfuls of cotton or wool. Everything was changed. It was bright and beautiful all around, and you felt like yelling and running and jumping up and down. You went in and put your hands to the fire. Your grandfather scolded you and smiled, because you were little and he knew how you felt. He cut off a piece of mutton and put it down for you.

You could smell the coffee and hear it boiling in the pot, even after he took it off the fire and poured it into the cups. You could see it, how black and hot it was, and there was a lot of smoke coming out of the cups. You had to let it set a while because the cups were made of enamelware and they could burn your hands. It was hard to wait, because you were cold and you knew how good it was going to taste. But the meat cooled right away and you could pick it up and it made your fingers warm. The fat was full of juice and smoke, and sometimes there was a little burned crust on it, hard black flakes that you could feel on your teeth, and the meat was tough and good to chew. And after a while you could pick up the cup and hold it in your hands. It was good just to hold it. You could see the dull shine of it, where the grease from your fingers was, and the black smoking coffee inside. And when you drank it, it was better than the meat. You could feel it all good and hot and strong inside of you, and the good hard grounds on your teeth and tongue. You hurried, because you were little and the snow was outside and there was a lot to do. You took the sheep out in the bright morning and had to look for grass under the snow. It was hard to find and you had to brush the snow off of it and your hands were wet and ached with cold. But you were happy anyway, because you were out with the sheep and could talk and sing to yourself and the snow was new and deep and beautiful. You thought of going to the trading post for water. Your grandfather went once a week, and sometimes twice, in the wagon; and if he didn't need the water right away, he waited for you to bring the sheep in, and you went with him. He didn't like to leave the sheep alone, but it was only for a little while, and he knew how much you wanted to go. The water was low in the barrel; you had looked inside the night before and there was only enough for the morning. You thought about the road, the hillsides and the way through the flats, and you hoped the snow wouldn't melt too soon into mud. It would be all right; it wasn't like the long hard rains. It would be all right if you didn't stay out too long with the sheep. You hurried and looked hard for the grass. And afterward, when you brought the sheep back, your grandfather had filled the barrel with snow and there was plenty of water again. But he took you to the trading post anyway, because you were little and had looked forward to it. There were people inside, a lot of them, because there was a big snow on the ground and they needed things and they wanted to stand around and smoke and talk about the weather. You were little and there was a lot to see, and all of it was new and beautiful: bright new buckets and tubs, saddles and ropes, hats and shirts and boots, a big glass case all filled with candy. Frazer was the trader's name. He gave you a piece of hard red candy and laughed because you couldn't make up your mind to take it at first, and you wanted it so much you didn't know what to do. And he gave your grandfather some tobacco and brown paper. And when he had smoked, your grandfather talked to the trader for a long time and you didn't know what they were saying and you just looked around at all the new and beautiful things. And after a while the trader put some things out on the counter, sacks of flour and sugar, a slab of salt pork, some canned goods, and a little bag full of the hard red candy. And your grandfather took off one of his rings and gave it to the trader. It was a small green stone, set carelessly in thin silver. It was new and it wasn't worth very much, not all the trader gave for it anyway. And the trader opened one of the cans, a big can of whole tomatoes, and your grandfather sprinkled sugar on the tomatoes and the two of you ate them right there and drank bottles of sweet red soda pop. And it was getting late and you rode home in the sunset and the whole land was cold and white. And that night your grandfather hammered the strips of silver and told you stories in the fire-light. And you were little and right there in the center of everything, the sacred mountains, the snow-covered mountains and the hills, the gullies and the flats, the sundown and the night, everything—where you were lit-tle, where you were and had to be.

It was kind of hard for him, you know, getting used to everything. We had to get down there pretty early and put in a day's work. And then at night we would go down to Henry's place and fool around. We would get drunk and have a good time. There were always some girls down there, and on paydays we acted pretty big.

But he was unlucky. Everything went along all right for about two months, I guess. And it would have gone all right after that, too, if they had just let him alone. Maybe . . . you never know about a guy like that; but they wouldn't let him alone. The parole officer, and welfare, and the Relocation people kept coming around, you know, and they were always after him about something. They wanted to know how he was doing, had he been staying out of trouble, and all. I guess that got on his nerves after a while, especially the business about drinking and running around. They were always *warning* him, you know? Telling him how he had to stay out of trouble, or else he was going to wind up in prison again. I guess he had to think about that all the time, because they wouldn't let him forget it. Sometimes they talked to me about him, too, and I said he was getting along all right. But he wasn't. And I could see why, but I didn't know how to tell them about it. They wouldn't have understood any-way. You have to get *used* to everything, you know; it's like starting out someplace where you've never been before, and you don't know where you're going or why or when you have to get there, and everybody's look-ing at you, waiting for you, wondering why you don't hurry up. And they can't help you because you don't know how to talk to them. They have a lot of *words,* and you know they mean something, but you don't know what, and your own words are no good because they're not the same;

they're different, and they're the only words you've got. Everything is different, and you don't know how to get used to it. You see the way it is, how everything is going on without you, and you start to worry about it. You wonder how you can get yourself into the swing of it, you know? And you don't know how, but you've got to do it because there's nothing else. And you *want* to do it, because you can see how good it is. It's better than anything you've ever had; it's money and clothes and having plans and going someplace fast. You can see what it's like, but you don't know how to get into it; there's too much of it and it's all around you and you can't get hold of it because it's going on too fast. You have to get used to it first, and it's hard. You've got to be left alone. You've got to put a lot of things out of your mind, or you're going to get all mixed up. You've got to take it easy and get drunk once in a while and just forget about who you are. It's hard, and you want to give up. You think about getting out and going home. You want to think that you belong someplace, I guess. You go up there on the hill and you hear the singing and the talk and you think about going home. But the next day you know it's no use; you know that if you went home there would be nothing there, just the empty land and a lot of old people, going noplace and dying off. And you've got to forget about that, too. Well, they were always coming around and warning him. They wouldn't let him alone, and pretty soon I could see that he was getting all mixed up.

There was some trouble down at the plant. We were shorthanded for a while, and we had to put in a lot of overtime. Daniels—he's the foreman —was getting pretty nervous, I guess, because a lot of orders were coming in, and we were running pretty far behind. He's a hard man to work for anyway—he's all business, you know, and he won't stand for any fooling around on the job—but he was *really* worried about that time, and he was watching us pretty close and getting on us pretty bad.

One night after we had worked a twelve-hour day, we went over to Tosamah's place and got up a poker game. There were five or six of us, I guess, and we were all drinking a lot and having fun. We had to get up early the next day, and after a while I started to worry about the time. It was getting late, and I was dead tired. He was tired, too, and the liquor was getting to him. He didn't know Tosamah very well, and Tosamah was feeling pretty good, going on about everything, you know, and talking big. Well, I could tell that he didn't like it much; it was getting on his nerves. I kept telling him that we ought to go on back home and get some sleep, but he wouldn't listen to me. He just kept on sitting there, listening to Tosamah go on about everything and getting more and more drunk. I guess Tosamah knew what he was thinking, too, because pretty soon he started in on him; not directly, you know, but he started talking about *longhairs* and the reservation and all. I kept wishing he would shut up, and I guess the others did, too—all except Cruz; he was just grinning like a fool—

because right away they got quiet and just started looking down at their hands, you know, like they were trying to decide what to do. I knew that something bad was going to happen.

You know, some people smile when they get mad, and the madder they get the more they smile. He was like that. He just sat there and smiled, and that was a bad sign, but I guess nobody knew it but me. I knew there was going to be some trouble, and I was getting scared. And, sure enough, pretty soon he just flew off the handle. It was like everything just exploded inside of him, and he jumped up from the table and started for Tosamah. But he was crazy drunk, and he couldn't stay on his feet. He stumbled backward and fell against the sink. He was looking for Tosamah, and it was a bad, scary look, but he couldn't get his eyes to hold still, you know, and he couldn't move. He just leaned there, trying to get hold of himself, and shaking all over like he was having a kind of coughing fit or something. It all happened real quick, and Cruz started to laugh, and then the others did, too; and that seemed to take all the fight out of him. It was like he had to give up when they laughed; it was like all of a sudden he didn't care about anything anymore. You know, at the time I was glad it ended up like that, because if there had been a fight they would have blamed it on him. But I got to thinking afterward that he was hurt by what had happened; he was hurt inside somehow, and pretty bad.

He didn't go to work the next day, or the next. I couldn't get him to go, and he wouldn't even talk to me. He was ashamed, I guess, or maybe he thought I was mad at him. Right away Daniels wanted to know where he was, and I said he was sick. He didn't say anything, Daniels, but just swore a couple of times and left me alone. I'm pretty sure he didn't believe me. The orders kept coming in and we weren't catching up at all.

He was passed out when I got home. He stayed drunk for two days. He didn't go anywhere; he just stayed up here in the room, I guess, and drank himself sick. I guess I knew then that he was going to lose that job, and I felt pretty bad, because he needed it. It was a good job, and he could handle it all right. But, sure enough, when he went back Daniels was looking out for him. He came over to the line and just stood there, looking over his shoulder, you know, inspecting everything he did. Now you know it's hard to work like that, with somebody important watching you all the time, and I could see that he was starting to sweat. He made a couple of mistakes, and Daniels got on him right away. They weren't anything to get excited about, just some loose or crooked staples, but Daniels acted like it was a big thing, and he was talking loud and calling attention to it. Well, that was more than he could take, I guess; Daniels had been riding him all morning, and pretty soon he just got enough of it. Finally he just dropped everything and looked at Daniels hard, like maybe he was going to hit him or something, and walked out. I guess that took

Daniels by surprise, because he just stood there for a minute with his mouth open. And then he was really burned up, you know, and he went running all around like he didn't know what to do and yelling about "these damned no-good greasers" and all. But I think he felt kind of foolish, too. We were shorthanded, and it takes time to find and train a good man like that. Well, he had no right to stand over him that way and call attention to his mistakes. We were doing all right; we were getting the job done.

He went downhill pretty fast after that. Sometimes he was here when I came in from work, and sometimes he wasn't. He was drunk about half the time, and I couldn't keep up with him. I tried to get him to slow down, you know, but he just got mad whenever I said anything about it, and it made him worse. Right away his money ran out, and he started hitting me up for a loan every night, almost. Pretty soon I wouldn't give him any more, but you know what he did? He started asking Milly for money. He would tell her he needed some new clothes, or bus fare to look for a job or something, and she would give him two or three dollars, sometimes five, every time. And he would just blow it in on liquor right away. I told her what he was doing, but she said she knew it; she just felt sorry for him. The Relocation people got him a job with the schools, taking care of the grounds and all, but he showed up drunk a couple of times and they fired him after the first week and a half. Milly got him a job, too; it was a night job at some bakery, and she said the pay was pretty good. But he didn't even bother to show up for it. You know, if he could just have held on the first time, to that first job down there on my line, he might have been all right. We liked each other, and we worked pretty well together. I could kind of keep an eye on him down there, you know, look out for him, and that was good. I guess he needed somebody to look out for him. Nobody but Milly and me gave a damn what happened to him.

We had some good times—a few, even after that. Sometimes Milly would come around in the morning on Sundays, and she would bring a basket with maybe some sandwiches and Kool-Aid and apples and cookies inside. And we would get on the bus, the three of us, and go all the way out to Santa Monica. We would find us some place out there on the beach where there weren't too many people, you know, and we would just sit around down there in the sun and talk and kid each other and look at the swimmers and the birds and the ocean. Milly had a little white swimsuit, and she always brought it along, and sometimes she would go out in the water and we would watch her. I felt kind of funny when she was dressed like that, and, you know, he would make jokes and say things about her sometimes, and I laughed all right, but I didn't like it much, because I thought a lot of her and she was good to us. I never said anything when he talked like that. It would have been worse if I had, because he would have made fun of me, you know, and said I had some plans with her and all. It wasn't like that. She liked him better than me, I think, and I was always afraid that he might hurt her somehow. She was easy-going and friendly to everybody. She *trusted* everybody, I guess; some people are just like that. And she had had a hard time all her life. It would have been pretty easy to hurt her.

Sometimes when we went out like that, the three of us, she would tell us about her family and all, how it was when she was little. She was raised on a farm someplace, and I guess her people had it pretty hard. She talked about her dad a lot. He had worked himself to death on that farm, she said, trying to get things to grow. The ground was no good, and nothing much ever came out of it. He had to work a long time just to get enough money so she could go to school. She said she always meant to pay him back, but he died before she could do it.

She fell in love with some guy and they were married for a while. She only talked about that once, and all she said was that everything was all right for a little while, better than it had ever been. Then right away she started talking about something else. It was like she was going to cry, you know; you could tell that something bad had happened. But she talked about good things, too. She was always remembering something funny, and she laughed a lot. I never knew anybody who was always ready to laugh like that. And she was always getting us to laugh, too. You could see how easy it would be to hurt her.

No, wait a minute. There was someone who laughed, who was ready to laugh, whose eyes were laughing. Yes, one summer there was a girl at Cornfields, yes.

And pretty soon she would get us talking, too. We felt kind of free and easy with her, you know, and we told her things we wouldn't tell to just anybody. We didn't mean to, exactly; it just happened that way, because she was always laughing and kind of open, you know, and you could see that she wasn't making fun of you. We used to tell her about the reservation, and it was all right, you know, because we made a kind of joke out of it; we talked about the funny things that had happened to us. One day it was like that, and we were just sitting around down there in the sand and looking out at the water. It had been kind of cold and foggy all that week, but that day was clear and warm, and we were feeling good and kind of lazy out there. Milly had been in the water, and she came over and sat down between us. Her hair was wet and she was laughing and there were beads of water all over her face and arms and legs. She looked real pretty that way, you know, all clean and cool and fresh-look-ing. Her skin was white and clean, and she put her feet down under the sand and wiggled her toes. He had been trying for a couple of days to straighten himself out, talking about getting a job and all. Milly believed him, and I guess I did, too. Anyway, we were having a good time, the three of us, laughing and kidding around and talking about all kinds of things.

Somehow we got to talking about horses. He was telling us about a horse he used to have. It was a good one, small and fast, you know, but it hadn't been broken all the way. It acted kind of wild sometimes, and it had a mean streak in it, like a mule. That horse liked the water, he said. It always wanted to go, to take out for the river. It would get away sometimes, and he would have to go looking for it. And he always found it in the same place, just standing there in the river, looking around like everything was just the way it ought to be. Well, one day he was riding that horse back from the fields, and he came across some old man. That old man was important, somehow; he was a governor or a medicine man or something. He was real *dignified,* you know, and he never smiled. Well, he wanted a ride. He said O.K., and he took that old man up on the horse behind him. They started out all right, but they had to cross the river. And when they got right in the middle of the river, that crazy horse just decided to lie down and that old man fell off in the river. He was old, and I guess he thought that was the damnedest horse he had ever seen. He got up, you know, and he was looking kind of bad, like a wet hen. He didn't say a word; he just shook his head and walked off. And his shoes were all full of water, and you could hear him squeak along for quite a while.

When Milly heard that, the way he told it, she got so tickled she didn't know what to do. She couldn't stop laughing, and pretty soon we had to laugh, too. And then she got the hiccups, and that just made it worse. We almost laughed ourselves sick. We were just sitting there shaking and the tears were coming out of our eyes and we were acting like a bunch of damn fools, I guess, and we didn't care. She was pretty when she laughed.

There was a girl at Cornfields one summer.

Milly believed him, you know, because she wanted to believe everybody; she was like that, and she made us believe it, too, that everything was going to be all right, and we were happy and making some plans about how it was going to be.

Pony, they called her, and she laughed, and her skin was light and she had long little hands and she wore a dark blue velveteen blouse and a corn-blossom necklace with an old najahe like the moon and one perfect powder-blue stone. . . .

I guess he believed it. But it wasn't going to be like that. It wasn't going to turn out right, because it was too late; everything had gone too far with him, you know, and he was already sick inside. Maybe he was sick a long time, always, and nobody knew it, and it was just coming out for the first time and you could see it. It might have been like that.

*There was a girl at Cornfields one summer, and she laughed, and you
never saw her again. You had been away at school, and it was the first
time you were homesick and it was good to be out there again. It looked
just the same, like the land was going on forever and nothing had
changed. You got off the bus at Chambers and walked all the way to the
trading post at Wide Ruins, and you weren't used to walking way out like
that and it took a long time and it was hot and you were tired. You went
in there to get a cold drink, and old man Frazer acted like he was glad to
see you. And you were feeling pretty big, because you had been away
and you figured you had seen what there was to see. It was hot, and it
was getting on toward late afternoon, and you didn't feel much like walking the rest of the way home. You were kind of hoping that your grandfather might be coming for water, but Frazer said that he had been there
the day before. You were glad just to be inside where it was cool, and
Frazer acted like he was glad to see you, and the two of you stood
around talking about everything. He said there was going to be a squaw
dance near Cornfields the next night. And you hadn't been to a squaw
dance in a long time. It sounded good to you, and right away you wanted
to go. You were feeling pretty big, and you started trading with Frazer
just like an old-timer, kind of slow and easy, like you didn't care much
about it. And after a while you asked him if he had any good horses for
sale. He had a good black, he said, but it was worth a lot of money and
he didn't figure to sell it right away. You just nodded and let it go for a
while, but then you told him you had an uncle over there west of Cornfields who had a fine old* ketoh *that he was going to give you. He had had
it for a long time, you said, and it was good work; there was a great spider web in the center and a circle of little matching ones all around, and
the silver was heavy and thick. But it was old, you said, the kind you
didn't see around much anymore. And you acted like that was too bad, it
being so old and out of style, and right away you could see that he was
thinking about it hard. He asked you when you were going to get it, and
you acted like you hadn't thought much about it and said maybe if you
went to that squaw dance you would talk to your uncle about it. And then
he asked you what you were going to do with it when you got it. Well,
you said, you didn't know for sure, you didn't see things like that anymore. You guessed you would hold on to it for a while and see what happened. And that's when he said, "Come on, let me show you that horse;
it's a good one." It was, too. It was a pretty little black, all sleek and
round and long-legged. It looked like it could run. It looked kind of slow,
you said, and lazy, like maybe it wasn't getting enough exercise. Maybe
you would buy that horse, you said, but first you would have to try it out
for a couple of days. If he wanted, you said, you would ride that horse
out to Cornfields and try to get the* ketoh. *He said no at first, but you*

329   **The Night Chanter**

went on about your uncle, how the trader at Ganado had seen that ketoh and wanted to buy it, and finally he got a bridle and led the horse out and put the reins in your hand.

The black horse felt good under you, and you let it lope all the way out to your grandfather's place. The sun was going down and the land was red and a little wind was getting up and it was cool and you were home again.

It's going to rain all night, I guess. It's cold and rainy up there on the hill, and nobody's there. It's dark and quiet and muddy up there. It will be muddy for a long time. He wanted me to tell him how it was going to be, you know. It's funny how it can be so clear like that one night and rain the next, and go on raining like it wasn't ever going to stop. Maybe he's out of it, you know? He's way out there someplace by now, and maybe it isn't raining and he's awake and he can see the stars and the moonlight on the land. The train will slow down and begin to climb the mountains around Williams and Flagstaff and the moonlight will be all over the trees and you can see the black trees against the sky. Maybe he's awake and all right.

And then the train will head south and east and down on the land, and the sun will come up out there and you can see a long way out across the land. You can see the sun coming up on the Painted Desert and the dark gullies and the red and purple earth in the early morning, all beautiful and still, and the land reaching out toward Wide Ruins and Klagetoh and Cornfields.

You felt good out there, like everything was all right and still and cool inside you, and that black horse loping along like the wind. Your grandfather was another year older and he cried; he cried because your mother and father were dead and he had raised you and you had gone away and you were coming home. You were coming home like a man, on a black and beautiful horse. He sang about it. It was all right, everything, and there was nothing to say.

You were tired then, and you went to sleep thinking of the morning. And at first light you went out and knew where you were. And it was the same, the way you remembered it, the way you knew it had to be; and nothing had changed. The first light, you thought, that little while before sunup; it would always be the same out there. That was the way it was, that's all. It was that way on the day you were born, and it would be that way on the day you died. It was cold, and you could feel the cold on your face and hands. The clouds were the same, smoky and small and far away, and the land was dark and still and it went all around to the sky. Nothing could fill it but the sun that was coming up, and then it would be bright, brighter than water, and the brightness would be made of a hundred colors and the land would almost hurt your eyes. But at first light it was soft and gray and very still. There was no sound, nothing. The sky was waiting all around, and the east was white, like a shell. At first light the land was alone and very still. And you were there where you wanted to be, and alone. You didn't want to see anyone, or hear anyone speak. There was nothing to say.

The sun came up behind you and you rode the black horse out on the way to Cornfields. It was a good horse, all right, better than most. It was deep and wide in the chest, and long-winded. It could go on loping and loping like that all the way if you wanted to hurry. But it was early enough, and you didn't have far to go, half a day's ride and a little more. You could see the earth going away under you, and you could feel and hear the hoofs. It was early enough, and the heat was holding off; and the black horse carried you just hard enough into the slow morning air. It was good going out like that, and it made you want to pray.

> I am the Turquoise Woman's son.
> On top of Belted Mountain,
> Beautiful horse—slim like a weasel.
> My horse has a hoof like striped agate;
> His fetlock is like a fine eagle plume;
> His legs are like quick lightning.
> My horse's body is like an eagle-plumed arrow;
> My horse has a tail like a trailing black cloud.
> I put flexible goods on my horse's back;
> The Little Holy Wind blows through his hair.
> His mane is made of short rainbows.
> My horse's ears are made of round corn.
> My horse's eyes are made of big stars.
> My horse's head is made of mixed waters—
> From the holy waters—he never knows thirst.
> My horse's teeth are made of white shell.
> The long rainbow is in his mouth for a bridle,
>   and with it I guide him.
> When my horse neighs, different-colored horses
>   follow.
> When my horse neighs, different-colored sheep
>   follow.
>   I am wealthy, because of him.
>   Before me peaceful,
>   Behind me peaceful,
>   Under me peaceful,
>   Over me peaceful,
>   All around me peaceful—
>   Peaceful voice when he neighs.
> I am Everlasting and Peaceful.
> I stand for my horse.

You went up by Klagetoh, to the trading post there, and spent the early afternoon inside, talking and laughing, boasting of the black horse, until the sun was low and it was cool again. You rode on to Sam Charley's place, and he went the rest of the way with you. And the two of you laughed and made jokes about the girls at school—the Nambé girls and Apaches—and Sam Charley's horse was old and used to work. It was a poor thing beside the black, and the black horse danced around and threw its head and wanted to run. There was no ketoh, but the black horse was yours for a while and you were riding it out to Cornfields and that was all that mattered.

And there, afterward, a little way west of Cornfields, the sun was going down and the sunset was deep and purple on the sky and the night fell with cold. And there were wagons and fires, and you could hear the talk and smell the smoke and the coffee and the fried bread. And there was a spotted moon coming up in the east, like a concho hammered out thin and deep in the center. And the drums. You heard the drums, and you wished you were still on the way and alone, miles away, where you could hear the drums and see only the moonlight on the land and then at last the fires a long way off. You can hear the drums a long way on the land at night and you don't know where they are until you see the fires, because the drums are all around on the land, going on and on for miles, and then you come over a hill and suddenly there they are, the fires and the drums, and still they sound far away.

They began the dance and you stood away and watched. There was a girl on the other side, and she was laughing and beautiful, and it was good to look at her. The firelight moved on her skin and she was laughing. The firelight shone on the blue velveteen of her blouse and on the pale new moon najahe of the corn blossom. And after a while you watched her all the time when she wasn't looking, because you saw slowly how beautiful she was. She was slender and small; she moved a little to the drums, standing in place, and her long skirt swayed at her feet and there were dimes on her moccasins.

"Hey, hosteen." Sam Charley's hand was on your shoulder. "She has her eye on you. She's thinking it over."

"That is a fine necklace," you said. "Who is she?"

"Ei yei! It's a fine necklace! Maybe you want to give her something for it, huh? They call her Pony. She lives over yonder by Naslini, I think."

And after a while there were many couples dancing around the fires. They passed slowly in front of you, under their blankets, holding hands, stepping out lightly to the drums, the shapes of their bodies close together and dark against the fires. And you lost sight of her. You looked all around, but she was gone. Sam Charley said something, but you couldn't hear what it was; you could hear only the drums, going on like the beat of your heart. And then she was holding on to your arm, laughing, and she said, "Come on, or give me something that is worth a lot of money." Her laughter was a certain thing; it made you careless and sure *of yourself, and you wanted always to hear it. She gave you her blanket and led you out in the open by the fires. And you let the blanket fall over your back and you held it open to her and she stepped inside of it. She was small and close beside you, laughing, and you held her for a long time in the dance. You went slowly together, slowly in time around the fires, and she was laughing beside you and the moon was high and the drums were going on far out into the night and the black horse was teth-ered close by in the camps and the moon and the fires shone upon the dark blue velvet of its rump and flanks and your hand lay upon dark blue velvet and looking down you saw the little footsteps of the girl licking out upon the firelit sand, the small white angles of the soles and the deep red sheaths and the shining silver dimes. And you never saw her again.*

We were coming home one night from Henry's place. We had been standing around outside with a lot of other guys, and we were talking pretty loud and having a big time, you know, but after a while it broke up, and it was late and we decided to come on home. We were just walking along kind of slow and talking pretty loud, I guess, and the street was dark and empty. There's an alley down there. It's a dead end and empty, except for a pile of used lumber and some garbage cans. It's always dark in there at night because the nearest streetlight is down at the end of the block. There are a lot of pigeons in there in the daytime, because people are always throwing things away in there; there's always a lot of cans and broken glass and stuff lying around, and it smells pretty bad. Well, we were going by that alley, and Martinez stepped out in front of us. He just stood there at first, tapping that stick in his hand and looking at us. He made us jump, coming out of that dark alley like that, and right away we shut up, you know, and I was scared. Then he told us to go into the alley, and he followed us. I was sober right away; it was dark in there and he was close and I could barely see him. I didn't know what he was going to do, and I was scared and shaking.

"Hello, Benally," he said, real soft and easy like. I couldn't see his face, but I knew he was smiling the way he does when he knows you're scared. We were just going home, I said, and I asked him what he wanted. He just stood there, smiling and watching us sweat, I guess, and all the time tapping that stick in his hand. "Let's see your hands, Benally." He was close to us, and we had our backs to the wall. I raised my hands up and held them out. I was almost touching him. He had a flashlight, you know, and he turned it on. "Your hands, Benally, they're shaking," he said, like he wondered why and was worried about it. He made me keep my hands there for a long time in the bright light, and they were shaking bad and I couldn't hold them still. Then he asked me how much money I had. He knew I had been paid, I guess, and I gave him all I had left. He looked at the money for a long time, like maybe it wasn't enough, and I was scared and shaking. Pretty soon, "Hello," he said. "Who's your friend, Benally?" And he stepped in front of him and held the light up to his face. I told him his name and said he was out of work; he was looking for a job and didn't have any money. Martinez told him to hold out his hands, and he did, slowly, like maybe he wasn't going to at first, with the palms up. I could see his hands in the light and they were open and almost steady. "Turn them over," Martinez said, and he was looking at them and they were almost steady. Then suddenly the light jumped and he brought the stick down hard and fast. I couldn't see it, but I heard it crack on the bones of the hands, and it made me sick. He didn't cry out or make a sound, but I could see him there against the wall, doubled up with pain and holding his hands. And the light went out and Martinez went by me in the dark, and I could hear him breathe, short and quick, like he was laughing, you know. We got out of there and went on home. His hands weren't broken, but they were swollen up pretty bad and the next day he could barely move his fingers and there were big ugly marks above his knuckles, all yellow and purple. We told Milly that we had been working on that radiator, you know, and it fell over on his hands.

He couldn't forget about it. It was like that time at Tosamah's place, you know? He didn't say anything—and even when it happened he didn't say anything; he just doubled over down there against the wall and held his hands—but he couldn't forget about it. He would sit around, looking down all the time at his hands. Sometimes I would say something, and it was like he didn't hear me, like he had something bad on his mind and he had to do something but he didn't know what it was. Then he would look up after a while and ask me what I had said. It was getting harder and harder to talk to him. Milly would say something funny, you know, and she and I would laugh and look at him, and he would smile, but you could tell that he was thinking about something else and hadn't heard. And even when he got drunk it was different somehow. He used to get drunk and happy, and we would laugh and kid around a lot, but after that night it was different.

One day I came by for him and we went out to Westwood. Sometimes, when I'm pretty well caught up on the line, Daniels lets me take the truck out on a delivery. It's a nice break, you know, because you get a chance to see everything and get some fresh air. When there wasn't a big hurry and I had to go way out someplace like that, I would take him along. Daniels never found out, or I guess I would have been fired. Well, it was a nice day, and he was just sitting around up here, like he didn't know what to do, so I told him to come on and he seemed pretty glad to go. We went out on Wilshire, and it was a nice day and it was getting on toward noon. I didn't have to be back until one, and it was only going to take a few minutes to unload. I figured when I was through we would have time to get a hamburger and drive down by the beach. I always liked Westwood, and it was a nice day and there were a lot of people walking around on the streets. I backed the truck into the alley and pulled up to the dock. The cab was out a little way on the sidewalk, and the people had to go around. He waited in the cab while I unloaded. It wasn't a big order, and I was through pretty quick. I got back in the truck and started to pull out, but he told me to wait. "Let's go," I said. We just had time to beat the noon-hour traffic on Wilshire and get on down to the beach. But he made me wait, and we were just sitting there, you know, and I didn't know what was going on and I was getting kind of mad. Pretty soon a woman came out of one of the shops, and he nodded and wanted me to look at her. She was all dressed up and just walking along kind of slow and looking in the windows. She passed right in front of us, you know, and he leaned back a little like he didn't want her to see him. I didn't know what was going on. She was good-looking, all right, but she wasn't young or big anywhere and I couldn't see anything to get excited about. She was rich-looking and kind of slim; you could tell that she had been out in the sun and her skin was kind of golden, you know, and she had on a plain white dress and little white shoes and gloves. She was good-looking, all right. She had on sunglasses, and her mouth was small and pretty with some kind of pale color on her lips, and her hair wasn't long but it was neat and shiny and clean-looking; there was one streak of silver in it, clean and wide, and all around it the dark, shining hair, almost copper-colored in the sun. We watched her out of sight.

He said he knew her. He used to work for her, I guess, and she liked him. She was going to help him, he said. She liked him a lot, and, you know, they fooled around and everything, and she was going to help him get a job and go away from the reservation, but then he got himself in trouble. He kept saying that: that she liked him and was going to help him some way, but he got himself in trouble. I didn't believe him at first, and I was kind of mad because he was going on like that, bragging and joking about some white woman. But I found out later that he was telling the truth. When he got hurt, you know, he talked about her and said her name, and he was hurt bad and out of his mind, and you could tell that he wasn't making it up. It's funny, but even at first, when I thought he was kidding around, he acted somehow like he knew all about her and she was special and good and she liked him a lot. I saw her again at the hospital. She was good-looking, all right, like those women you see in the magazines.

He didn't look for a job anymore.

I wish we had remembered to close that window. Rain. I wish it would stop raining. This place is always cold and kind of empty when it rains. We were going to tear out some pictures of horses and cars and boats and put them up on the walls. Milly brought some curtains over one time, but we never did get around to putting them up. Maybe I'll put them up tomorrow. She'd get a kick out of that. We used to kid him about that little suitcase. It was over there in the corner, and there was one little spider that always wanted to make a web across it. Milly would come in and brush it away, but that little spider got right to work and made another web in the same place. It never gave up, and finally we told her to leave it alone. That spider was our roommate, we said, and she didn't have any right to come around all the time, trying to evict it. Then she was always talking about how nobody, even a spider, ought to live in a suitcase and she was going to bring some tin shears and make a doll house out of it; that spider ought to have a little rocking chair, she said. It gets cold in here when it rains. It's a good place; you could fix it up real nice. There are a lot of good places around here. I could find some place with a private bathroom if I wanted to, easy. A man with a good job can do just about anything he wants.

Old Carlozini ought to be getting home pretty soon. She's old, and she ought not to be out in the rain like that. One of these days she's going to just fall down and die in the street, or they're going to find her all alone in that little room of hers. She has a few little things, you know, some dishes and spoons, and every morning about five-thirty you can hear her moving around down there. She always wears that old black hat when she goes out. It looks funny on her because it's big and the brim droops down all around her head and there's an old beat-up flower that hangs down over one eye and bounces around when she walks. She never says hello or anything, but she's always watching you, like maybe she thinks you're going to sneak up on her or steal something from her. She can hear you on the stairs, you know, and she always opens her door a little, just a crack, and watches you go by. That's about all she has to do, I guess.

One time we were going out, and old Carlozini was sitting down there on the stairs, all bent over and still, like she was going to sleep. The door of her room was wide open, and she was just sitting out there on the stairs, and it was the first time we had ever seen the inside of her room. It was real dark and dirty-looking, and even out there on the stairs we could smell it. I guess it was the first time that door had ever been left open like that. She never takes a bath, and you know how old people smell and how they like to shut themselves up in the dark. It was pretty bad, that smell. Well, we started to go around her and she said something. We turned and she was looking up at us and her eyes were all wet. "Vincenzo is not well," she said. "It is very bad this time." She had a little cardboard box in her hands and she held it out to us. We didn't know what she was talking about, but we looked inside that box and there was a little dead animal of some kind, a guinea pig, I guess; it had black and white fur and it was kind of curled up on its side and there was a dirty white cloth under it. "Oh, it is very bad this time," she said, and she was shaking her head. We didn't know what to say, and she was crying and looking at us like maybe we could make it all right if we wanted to. It was like she was being real friendly and nice to us, you know, so we would make it all right. "His name is Vincenzo," she said. "He's very smart, you know; he can stand up straight, just like you gentlemen, and clap his little hands." And her eyes lit up and she had to smile, thinking about it. She went on like that, like that little thing was still alive and maybe it was going to stand up and clap its hands like a baby. It made me real sad to see her, so old and lonely and carrying on like that, and she kept saying "you gentlemen" and everything. We didn't know what to do, and we just listened to her and looked down at that little furry animal. And then after a while he said he thought it was dead. At first I thought he shouldn't have said that; it seemed kind of mean somehow, you know? But I guess she had to be told. I think maybe she knew it was dead all the time, and she was just waiting for someone to say it, because she didn't know how to say it herself. All at once she jerked that little box away and looked at him real hard for a minute, like she was hurt and couldn't understand how it was, why on earth he should say a thing like that. But then she just nodded and slumped over a little bit. She didn't say any more, and she wasn't crying; it was like she was real tired, you know, and didn't have any strength left. I asked her if she wanted us to take Vincenzo out to the alley, but she just sat there and didn't say anything. She was just sitting there on the stairs, holding that little dead animal real close to her, and she looked awful small and alone and the night was coming on and it was getting dark down there. It's funny, you know; that little animal was her friend, I guess, and she kept it down there in her room, always, maybe, and we didn't even know about it. And afterward it was just the same. She never said anything to us again.

There's always a lot of rain this time of the year. It isn't bad; it lets up after a while, and then everything is bright and clean. It's a good place to live. There's always a lot going on, a lot of things to do and see once you find your way around. Once you find your way around and get used to everything, you wonder how you ever got along out there where you came from. There's nothing there, you know, just the land, and the land is empty and dead. Everything is here, everything you could ever want. You never have to be alone. You go downtown and there are a lot of people all around, and they're having a good time. You see how it is with them, how they get along and have money and nice things, radios and cars and clothes and big houses. And you want those things; you'd be crazy not to want them. And you can have them, too; they're so *easy* to have. You go down to those stores, and they're full of bright new things and you can buy just about anything you want. The people are real friendly most of the time and they're always ready to help you out. They don't even know you, but they're friendly anyway; they go out of their way to be nice. They shake your hand and pay attention to you; and sometimes you don't know how to act, you know, but they try to make it easy for you. It's like they *want* you to get along, like they're looking out for you. The Relocation people are all right, too. It's not like Tosamah says. They know how it is when you first come, how scared you are and all, and they look out for you. They pay your way; they get you a job and a place to stay; I guess they even take care of you if you get sick. You don't have to worry about a thing.

"No, sirree, Benally, you don't have to worry about a thing." That's what Tosamah says. He's always going on about Relocation and Welfare and Termination and all, and that little fat Cruz is always right behind him, smiling and nodding like he knew what it was all about. I used to listen to Tosamah. He's a clown, and you have to laugh at some of the things he says. But you have to know how to take it, too. He likes to get under your skin; he'll make a fool out of you if you let him.

Let's see . . . let's see; Manygoats gave me three dollars, and I bought a bottle of wine. I wonder who that great big girl was. I have two dollars and eleven cents. I wish I had some more of that wine. I wish I had another bottle of wine . . . and a dollar bill . . . and two dimes . . . and two pennies.

Ei yei! with a name like that, and she had dimes . . . dimes on her shoes.

She's from Oklahoma, I think.

Henry, you keep that dollar bill and those two pennies. Give me twelve shiny dimes. For old time's sake, Henry, give me twelve shiny dimes. Time's dimes, shine wine.

Maybe the rain will let up for a while.

He didn't look for a job anymore. It's funny, you know? Everything happened real fast. We had a fight. I couldn't talk to him. He was always drunk. We used to get drunk together, and it was all right because it made us loose and happy and we could kid around and forget about things. But after a while, after that night when Martinez . . . or maybe it was before that; I don't know. Maybe it was Tosamah, too, and that white woman, everything. But it wasn't fun anymore. The liquor didn't seem to make any difference; he was just the same, sitting around and looking down like he hated everything, like he hated himself and hated being drunk and hated Milly and me, and I couldn't talk to him. Every time I tried to say anything, he just got mad. It had to stop, you know? I could see that something real bad was going to happen if it didn't stop, but I couldn't do anything. He wouldn't let anybody help him, and I guess I got mad, too, and one day we had a fight. He was crazy drunk and ugly. He had thrown up all over himself, and he couldn't do anything about it, I guess, and he was just sitting there and saying the worst thing he could think of, over and over. I didn't like to hear that kind of talk, you know; it made me kind of scared, and I told him to cut it out. I guess I was more scared than mad; anyway, I had had about all I could take. I was tired of worrying about him all the time, and he was getting worse and something bad was going to happen and I didn't want any part of it. He just went on and it was worse and he was mad and snarling those things at me, and I was sick of it and I told him to get out. Pretty soon he got up and staggered around and he was all red and sweaty and shaking, and he was looking wild, you know, and I didn't care because I was mad. O.K., he said, that was it, and I could go to hell and he was leaving. He was going out to look for *culebra*, he said; he was going to get even with *culebra*, and I told him to go ahead, I didn't give a damn. He went out and slammed the door, and I was glad, and I could hear him on the stairs, like he was crazy and was going to fall and hurt himself, and I didn't care.

I cooled off, and right away I was sorry and I started to worry about him. But I figured it didn't do any good. It had to stop, you know; something had to happen. He didn't come back, and I was worried. I waited up for a long time, and it was getting late. I had a hard time going to sleep. I kept listening for him, but he didn't come back. I kept telling myself that maybe it was a good thing, him going out by himself like that. He was drunk and sick, you know, and he couldn't get very far. I figured maybe he had been picked up and thrown in jail; maybe they could see that he was sick and they would get a doctor to take care of him. He didn't come back that night, and the next day I had to go to work and I was glad to be busy. I worked hard on the line, and it was like everything was all right. He would be there when I got home, and we would straighten everything out.

He didn't come back for three days. I went right home from work every day and he wasn't there. I kept going down to Henry's place and all around, back and forth, and nobody had seen him. He wasn't in jail. I didn't know what to do. Then, three nights later, I woke up and heard something down there on the stairs. I went out and turned on the light in the hall, and I could see him down there in the dark at the foot of the stairs, like he was dead. Old Carlozini's door was open just a crack, and she was looking out at him. The light from her room made a line across him, and he was all twisted up and still. It was him, all right, and he was almost dead. I thought he was dead, and I didn't know what to do. I ran down there and I couldn't think and I forgot about that light not working and I tried to turn it on. I yelled at that old woman to open her door, but she just stood there, and I had to push her out of the way; I pushed hard, and maybe she fell—I don't know but I got that door open. He was lying there on his stomach and I turned him over and I wanted to get sick and cry. He was all broken and torn and covered with blood. Most of the blood was dry; it had dried up on his clothes and in his hair. He had lost an awful lot of blood, and his skin was pale yellow in the light. His eyes were swollen shut and his nose was broken and his mouth was raw and bleeding. And his hands were broken; they were broken all over. That was all I could see, his head and his hands, and I didn't want to open his clothing. I had to look away. It was the worst beating I had ever seen. I wanted to bring him up here, you know, but he couldn't get up and I was afraid to move him. I got a blanket and covered him, and then I went out and called an ambulance. Pretty soon it came, and they put him on a stretcher. He couldn't talk to them, and they told me I had to come along.

The rest of the night I waited around down there at the hospital. There were lots of doctors and nurses hurrying all around, and they wouldn't tell me anything, and I thought maybe he was dead or going to die, and I was just sitting there waiting, not knowing where he was or what was happening to him. After a while it got light outside, and one of the nurses came up to me and started asking me a lot of questions. They were silly questions, all about his family and his medical record and insurance and everything like that. I didn't know how to answer most of them, and I kept trying to get her to tell me how he was. She just went on, like those questions were the most important thing of all and acting like maybe I wasn't telling her the truth. She said they were going to have to file a police report, and she wanted to know exactly what had happened, and did he have any relatives who could come right away. And finally she said he was unconscious, and the doctor didn't know yet if he was going to be all right. She said it would be quite a long time before I could see him, and I told her I would wait. I guess she could see that I was pretty worried, and after a while she brought me a cup of coffee. Later, I remembered about going to work, and I called in and told Daniels that I was sick. He said O.K.

I waited all day. Late that afternoon they took me up to his room. It was dark in there and he was lying on his back asleep. They had cleaned him up pretty well and his head and arms and chest were all bandaged. They said I could sit in there by the bed if I wanted to. They had done about all they could, I guess, and everything seemed to be all right for the time being. Every once in a while a nurse would come in and look at him. He didn't wake up, and finally they told me I had to go home.

That night I called that white woman; I don't know why, but I figured I ought to do it. I didn't want Milly to know what had happened, and I couldn't think of anybody else to call. I guess I got all mixed up on the phone. She didn't know what I was talking about at first, and she kept asking me who I was and why I was calling her. I said I hoped she didn't mind me bothering her like that, but he was hurt pretty bad and I didn't know what else to do. She got real quiet for a minute, like she was think-ing about it, you know, and then she thanked me and hung up. And two days later she came to the hospital.

I had been there for a while. He was awake and he could open one of his eyes, but his face was partly bandaged and it was hard for him to talk. I was going on about everything, you know, like it was going to be all right; that's when I made up those plans. Pretty soon she came into the room, and I knew right away who she was. She was all dressed up and good-looking and you could smell the perfume she had on. I was kind of embarrassed and I didn't know what to do and I got up to leave. But she said it was all right and please don't go, and she came over and shook my hand and thanked me again. My being there didn't seem to bother her at all, and right away she started talking to him. She said she was sorry he was sick, and she was sure he would be well again soon. She went on talking kind of fast, like she knew just what she wanted to say. I felt funny being there, but she didn't seem to mind, and she started telling him about her son, Peter. Peter was growing up, she said, and she had wanted to bring him along, but Peter was busy with his friends and couldn't come. She said that she had thought about *him* a lot and won-dered how he was and what he was doing, you know, and she always thought kindly of him and he would always be her friend. Peter always asked her about the Indians, she said, and she used to tell him a story about a young Indian brave. He was born of a bear and a maiden, she said, and he was noble and wise. He had many adventures, and he be-came a great leader and saved his people. It was the story Peter liked best of all, and she always thought of *him*, Abel, when she told it. It was real nice the way she said it, like she thought a whole lot of him, and I could tell that story was kind of secret and important to her, you know, and it made me kind of ashamed to be there listening. She said she was awfully glad that I had called her, because she wouldn't have missed seeing him again for the world. I was glad that she had come, and I guess he was, too, but he didn't ever say anything about it afterward. I couldn't tell what he was thinking. He had turned his head away, like maybe the pain was coming back, you know.

Ei yei! A bear! A bear and a maiden. And she was a white woman and she thought it up, you know, made it up out of her own mind, and it was like that old grandfather talking to me, telling me about *Esdzá shash nadle,* or *Dzil quigi,* yes, just like that. How was it? I remember, yes; you drink a little wine and you remember. A long time ago it was dark, and you looked in the fire and listened, and he was going on with his work and talking, going on about all he knew, and he knew everything and there was no end to the stories and the songs.

And after those things happened, the people came down from the mesas. And they were afraid of *Esdzá shash nadle*. They buried the Calendar Stone and wrapped blankets made of feathers around their dead; they ran away, leaving their possessions. And there on the rock where they lived, they left the likeness of a bear.

Grandson, it was here, here at Kin tqel that they killed two of the cave people. There were twelve brothers and two sisters. It was time for the sisters to marry. And there were two old men, the Bear and the Snake. They went to the top of a mountain and bathed themselves. They put on fine clothes and were changed into men; they became young men, strong and good-looking. They smoked pipes, and the smoke was sweet, and it rolled down the mountain. The sisters came upon the trail of sweet smoke and were enchanted, and they climbed after it to the source. "Where do you come from?" the elder sister asked. "I came from the mountain," said the Bear. "And I came from the plain," said the Snake. The sisters drew smoke from the pipes and fell asleep. And when they awoke they knew that they had lain with a bear and a snake, and they were afraid. They ran away, the elder sister to the summit and the younger to the plain. The elder sister came at last to the great kiva of the Yeí bichai. Four holy men and four holy women came out to greet her. The women bathed and anointed her; they touched her with corn meal and pollen, and she was beautiful. She bore a female child. There were tufts of hair in back of its ears and down on its arms and legs. And then the Yei told the people to sing the Mountain Chant, and from that time on the elder sister was called the Bear Maiden.

Afterward a male child was born, and the Bear Maiden left it alone. The child cried, and an owl heard it and carried it away. The child grew and became strong. He was going to be a hunter, and the owl was afraid and meant to kill him. But the wind spoke to the child and told him to run away; he must follow the Río Mancos to the east.

He came of age and married the elder daughter of a great chief, and he was then a medicine man. But the younger daughter was beautiful, and he thought about her. He lay with her and she did not know who he was. But then she knew. She was going to bear a child and was ashamed. And when the child was born she hid it among the leaves. The child was found by the Bear.

> With beauty before me,
> With beauty behind me,
> With beauty above me,
> With beauty below me,
> With beauty all around me . . .

It's dark and rainy up there on the hill, and last night it was cool and clear. We went off by ourselves, you know, and we could hear the singing and see the stars. It's funny, but we didn't want to turn around. We knew the lights were there, all the rows and squares of light far below, and it was beautiful. I guess we knew without looking that it was great and beautiful, that everything was there, and beyond there was nothing but the black water and the sky. But we didn't want to turn around. We could hear the singing and see the stars. There was a faint yellow glare like smoke on the sky, but the sky was too much for it, and at the center we could see the stars, how small and still they were. And he was going home.

I prayed. He was going home, and I wanted to pray. Look out for me, I said; look out each day and listen for me. And we were going together on horses to the hills. We were going to ride out in the first light to the hills. We were going to see how it was, and always was, how the sun came up with a little wind and the light ran out upon the land. We were going to get drunk, I said. We were going to be all alone, and we were going to get drunk and sing. We were going to sing about the way it always was. And it was going to be right and beautiful. It was going to be the last time. And he was going home.

JACK McMANIS
Remembering the Third Avenue El

When Don Quixote God
came to New York City
(before I was a believer)
and rode gay
as a rodeo cowboy
down Third Avenue
on that iron Rosinante
with hooves flaking light
from bygone times,
every fireplug was exalted
and geysered forth fountains
to the immense joy
of East Side children
who cavorted
like celebrating dolphins
in the fresh rivergutters.
When Our Lord got ready
to go back to heaven
He chose to take off
from Chatham Square
Bowery el station
(though mightily displeased
at all the drunk angels),
and the spavined old nag,
ribs clackety-clack
like a marimba band
on amateur night,
after delivering
Him safely
to His launch pad
for the stars

and points beyond,
lay down and died
and was sold,
though the angels
left behind
didn't share
in the transaction;
they drank wine
and wept remembering
the warm wind-shadow
and the cantering
of the rheumatic
iron horse.

WILLIAM CARLOS WILLIAMS
Overture to a Dance of Locomotives

1

Men with picked voices chant the names
of cities in a huge gallery: promises
that pull through descending stairways
to a deep rumbling.

     The rubbing feet
of those coming to be carried quicken a
grey pavement into soft light that rocks
to and fro, under the domed ceiling,
across and across from pale
earthcolored walls of bare limestone.

Covertly the hands of a great clock
go round and round! Were they to
move quickly and at once the whole
secret would be out and the shuffling
of all ants be done forever.

A leaning pyramid of sunlight, narrowing
out at a high window, moves by the clock;
discordant hands straining out from
a center: inevitable postures infinitely
repeated—

two—twofour—twoeight!

Porters in red hats run on narrow platforms.

This way ma'am!
                    —important not to take
the wrong train!

             Lights from the concrete
ceiling hang crooked but—
                   Poised horizontal
on glittering parallels the dingy cylinders
packed with a warm glow—inviting entry—
pull against the hour. But brakes can
hold a fixed posture till—
                   The whistle!

Not twoeight. Not twofour. Two!

Gliding windows. Colored cooks sweating
in a small kitchen. Taillights—
In time: twofour!
In time: twoeight!

—rivers are tunneled: trestles
cross oozy swampland: wheels repeating
the same gesture remain relatively
stationary: rails forever parallel
return on themselves infinitely.
                  The dance is sure.

ALLEN GINSBERG
A Supermarket in California

What thoughts I have of you tonight, Walt Whitman, for I walked down the sidestreets under the trees with a headache self-conscious looking at the full moon.

In my hungry fatigue, and shopping for images, I went into the neon fruit supermarket, dreaming of your enumerations!

What peaches and what penumbras! Whole families shopping at night! Aisles full of husbands! Wives in the avocados, babies in the tomatoes!— and you, Garcia Lorca, what were you doing down by the watermelons?

I saw you, Walt Whitman, childless, lonely old grubber, poking among the meats in the refrigerator and eyeing the grocery boys.

I heard you asking questions of each: Who killed the pork chops? What price bananas? Are you my Angel?

I wandered in and out of the brilliant stacks of cans following you, and followed in my imagination by the store detective.

We strode down the open corridors together in our solitary fancy tasting artichokes, possessing every frozen delicacy, and never passing the cashier.

Where are we going, Walt Whitman? The doors close in an hour. Which way does your beard point tonight?

(I touch your book and dream of our odyssey in the supermarket and feel absurd.)

Will we walk all night through solitary streets? The trees add shade to shade, lights out in the houses, we'll both be lonely.

Will we stroll dreaming of the lost America of love past blue automobiles in driveways, home to our silent cottage?

Ah, dear father, graybeard, lonely old courage-teacher, what America did you have when Charon quit poling his ferry and you got out on a smoking bank and stood watching the boat disappear on the black waters of Lethe?

Interactions

A Confession

If someone was walking across
your lawn last night, it was me.
While you dreamt of prowlers, I was
prowling down empty lanes, to breathe
the conifer coolness of just
before dawn. Your flowers were closed,
your windows black and withdrawn.

Sometimes I see a square of
yellow light shining through the trees,
and I cross the grass and look in.
Your great body on the bed
is nude and white, and though I'm starved
for love like everyone, the sight
of your black sex leaves me cold.

What would I say to a squad car
if it came on its noiseless tires
and picked me out with its lights, like
a cat or a rabbit? That I
only wanted to see how people
live, not knowing how? That I
haven't had a woman in months?

Therefore I stay out of sight
and do not speak. Or if I speak,
I make small animal sounds
to myself, so as not to wake you.
They were tears full of seed. What
I wanted to do was enter
and bend and touch you on the cheek.

Robert Mezey

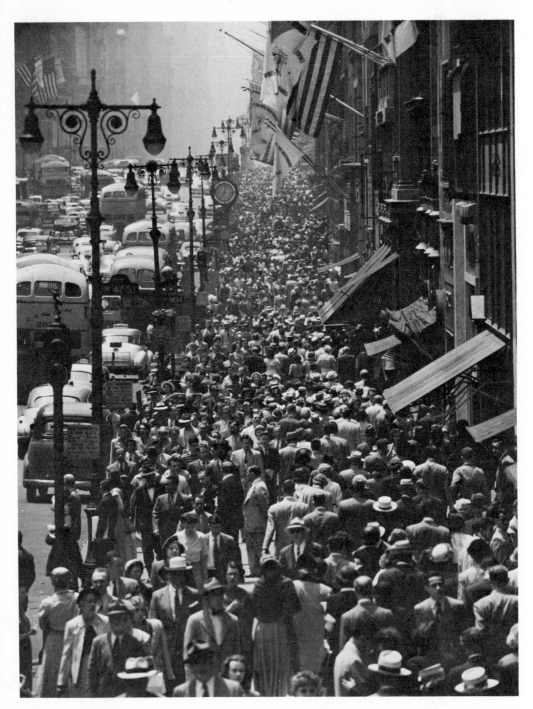

Andreas Feininger

Weegee

Lewis W. Hine

Helen Levitt

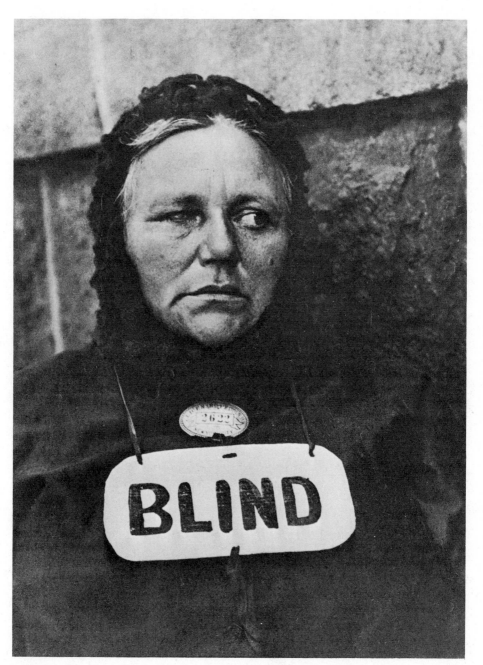

Paul Strand

Ray K. Metzker

Donald Blumberg

Yasuhiro Ishimoto

Steven Foster

Neal Boenzi

Norman Snyder

Norman Snyder

Duane Michals

W. Eugene Smith

Garry Winogrand

FRED DAVIS
The Cabdriver and His Fare:
Facets of a Fleeting Relationship[1]

Even in an urban and highly secularized society such as ours, most service relationships, be they between a professional and his client or a
menial and his patron, are characterized by certain constraints on too
crass a rendering and consuming of the service.[2] That is to say, in the
transaction, numerous interests besides that of simply effecting an economic exchange are customarily attended to and dealt with. The moral
reputation of the parties,[3] their respective social standing, and the skill
and art with which the service is performed [4] are but a few of the non-in-
strumental values which are usually incorporated into the whole act.

Tenuous though such constraints may become at times, particularly in
large cities where anonymous roles only, segmentally related, occur in
great profusion, it is at once evident that for them to exist at all something approximating a community must be present. Practitioners and
clients must be sufficiently in communication for any untoward behavior
to stand a reasonable chance of becoming known, remarked upon, remembered, and, in extreme cases, made public. And, whereas the exercise of sanctions does not necessarily depend on a community network [5]
that is closely integrated (or one in which there is a total identity of values and interests), it does depend on there being some continuity and
stability in the relationships that make up the network, so that, at mini-

1.   This article is based largely on notes and observations made by me over a six-month
period in 1948 when I worked as a cabdriver for one of the larger taxicab firms in Chicago. I am greatly indebted to Erving Goffman, Everett C. Hughes, and Howard S. Becker
for their comments and criticisms.
2.   Talcott Parsons, *The Social System* (Glencoe, Ill.: Free Press, 1951), pp. 48–56.
3.   Erving Goffman, *The Presentation of Self in Everyday Life* (Edinburgh: University of
Edinburgh Social Science Research Centre, 1956), pp. 160–62.
4.   Everett C. Hughes, *Men and Their Work* (Glencoe, Ill.: Free Press, 1958), pp. 88–101.
5.   Because it better delineates the boundaries and linkages of informal sanctioning
groups found in large cities, the term "network" is used here to qualify the more global
concept of "community." See Elizabeth Bott, *Family and Social Network* (London: Tavi-
stock, 1957), pp. 58–61.

mum, participants may in the natural course of events be able to identify actions and actors to one another.[6]

It is mainly, though not wholly, from this vantage point that big-city cabdriving as an occupation is here discussed, particularly the relationship between cabdriver and fare and its consequences for the occupational culture.[7] Approximating in certain respects a provincial's caricature of the broad arc of social relations in the metropolis, this relationship affords an extreme instance of the weakening and attenuation of many of the constraints customary in other client-and-patron-oriented services in our society. As such, its analysis can perhaps point up by implication certain of the rarely considered preconditions for practitioner-client relations found in other, more firmly structured, services and professions.

In a large city like Chicago the hiring of a cab by a passenger may be conceived of in much the same way as the random collision of particles in an atomic field. True, there are some sectors of the field in which particles come into more frequent collision than others, for example, downtown, at railroad depots, and at the larger neighborhood shopping centers. But this kind of differential activity within the field as a whole provides little basis for predicting the coupling of any two specific particles.

To a much more pronounced degree than is the case in other client-and-patron-oriented services, the occupation of cabdriver provides its practitioners with few, if any, regularities by which to come upon, build up, and maintain a steady clientele. The doctor has his patients, the schoolteacher her pupils, the janitor his tenants, the waitress her regular diners; and in each case server and served remain generally in some continuing or renewable relationship. By contrast, the cabdriver's day consists of a long series of brief contacts with unrelated persons of whom he has no foreknowledge, just as they have none of him, and whom he is not likely to encounter again.

Furthermore, by virtue of the differential spatial, social, and organizational arrangements of the community, it is also likely that the clients of these other practitioners will, in some manner at least, know one another and be related to one another in ways that often transcend the simple circumstance of sharing the same services: they may also be friends, kin, neighbors, or colleagues. For this reason the clientele of most practitioners is something more than an aggregate of discrete individuals; it is, as well, a rudimentary social universe and forum to which the practitioner must address himself in other than purely individual terms.[8]

6. Robert K. Merton, "The Role Set: Problems in Sociological Theory," *British Journal of Sociology*, VIII, No. 2 (June, 1957), 114.
7. Parallel studies of this aspect of occupational culture are: Hughes, *op. cit.*, pp. 42–55; Howard S. Becker, "The Professional Dance Musician and his Audience," *American Journal of Sociology*, LVII (September, 1951), 136–44; Ray Gold, "Janitors versus Tenants: A Status-Income Dilemma," *American Journal of Sociology*, LVII (March, 1952), 486–93.
8. Merton, *op. cit.*, pp. 110–12.

The cabdriver, by comparison, has no such clientele. He has no fixed business address, and his contacts with passengers are highly random and singular. To a striking degree he is a practitioner without reputation because those who ride in his cab do not comprise, except perhaps in the most abstract sense, anything approximating a social group. They neither know nor come into contact with one another in other walks of life, and, even if by chance some do, they are unaware of their ever having shared the services of the same anonymous cabdriver. Even were the driver deliberately to set out to build up a small nucleus of steady and favored passengers, the time-space logistics of his job would quickly bring such a scheme to nought. Unable to plot his location in advance or to distribute time according to a schedule, he depends on remaining open to all comers wherever he finds himself. Much more so than other classes of service personnel, cabdrivers are both the fortuitous victims and the beneficiaries of random and highly impersonal market contingencies.

This set of circumstances—fleeting, onetime contact with a heterogeneous aggregate of clients, unknown to one another—exerts an interesting influence on the role of cabdriver.

Unable, either directly through choice or indirectly through location, to select clients, the cabdriver is deprived of even minimal controls. His trade therefore exposes him to a variety of hazards and exigencies which few others, excepting policemen, encounter as frequently; for example: stick-ups, belligerent drunks, women in labor, psychopaths, counterfeiters, and fare-jumpers. Unlike the policeman's, however, his control over them is more fragile.

Nor, incidentally, is the cabdriver's social status or level of occupational skill of much help in inducing constraint in fares. Patently, his status is low, in large part precisely because, unlike the professional and other practitioners commanding prestige, he can hardly be distinguished from his clients in task-relevant competence. Not only is the operation of a motor car a widely possessed skill, but a large proportion of fares have, for example, a very good idea of the best routes to their destination, the rules and practices of the road, and the charges for a trip. Though they are rarely as adept or sophisticated in these matters as the cabdriver, the discrepancy is so small than many think they know the driver's job as well as he does. Periodically, a cabdriver will boldly challenge a difficult and critical passenger to take over the wheel himself. Others, wishing to impress on the fare that theirs is a real service requiring special talent and skill, will resort to darting nimbly in and out of traffic, making neatly executed U-turns and leaping smartly ahead of other cars when the traffic light changes.

Goffman [9] speaks of a category of persons who in some social encoun-

9. Goffman, *op. cit.*, p. 95.

ters are treated as if they were not present, whereas in fact they may be indispensable for sustaining the performance. He terms these "non-persons" and gives as an example a servant at a social gathering. Although cabdrivers are not consistently approached in this way by fares, it happens often enough for it to become a significant theme of their work. Examples are legion. Maresca [10] tells of the chorus girl who made a complete change from street clothing into stage costume as he drove her to her theater. More prosaic instances include the man and wife who, managing to suppress their anger while on the street, launch into a bitter quarrel the moment they are inside the cab; or the well-groomed young couple who after a few minutes roll over on the back seat to begin petting; or the businessman who loudly discusses details of a questionable business deal. Here the driver is expected to, and usually does, act as if he were merely an extension of the automobile he operates. In actuality, of course, he is acutely aware of what goes on in his cab, and, although his being treated as a non-person implies a degraded status, it also affords him a splendid vantage point from which to witness a rich variety of human schemes and entanglements.

The fleeting nature of the cabdriver's contact with the passenger at the same time also makes for his being approached as someone to whom intimacies can be revealed and opinions forthrightly expressed with little fear of rebuttal, retaliation, or disparagement. And though this status as an accessible person is the product of little more than the turning inside-out of his non-person status—which situation implies neither equality nor respect for his opinion—it nevertheless does afford him glimpses of the private lives of individuals which few in our society, apart from psychiatrists and clergy, are privileged to note as often or in such great variety. It is probably not a mistaken everyday generalization that big-city cabdrivers, on their part, feel less compunction about discussing their own private lives, asking probing questions, and "sounding off" on a great many topics and issues than do others who regularly meet the public, but less fleetingly.[11]

In cabdriving, therefore, propriety, deference, and "face" are, in the nature of the case, weaker than is the case in most other service relationships. This absence contributes to a heightened preoccupation with and focusing on the purely instrumental aspect of the relationship which for the driver is the payment he receives for his services. This perhaps would be less blatantly the case were it not for the gratuity or tip. For the non-cab-owning company driver, the sum collected in tips amounts

10. James V. Maresca, *My Flag Is Down* (New York: E. P. Dutton & Co., 1945). Essentially the same incident is related by an unidentified cabdriver on the documentary recording of Tony Schwartz, *The New York Taxi Driver* (Columbia Records, ML5309, 1959).
11. Cf. Schwartz, *op. cit.* In fact, these characteristic qualities, with a work-adapted, bitter-sweet admixture of cynicism and sentimentality, comprise the core of the personality widely imputed to cabdrivers by the riding public. Cf. Hughes, *op. cit.*, pp. 23–41.

roughly to 40 per cent of his earnings. Considering, for example, that in Chicago in the late forties a hard-working cabdriver, who worked for ten hours a day, six days a week, would on the average take home approximately seventy-five dollars a week including tips, the importance of tipping can readily be appreciated. For the family man who drives, tips usually represent the difference between a subsistence and a living wage. Also, tips are, apart from taxes, money "in the clear," in that the driver does not have to divide them with the company as he does his metered collections.[12] Sum for sum, therefore, tips represent greater gain for him than do metered charges.

It would probably be incorrect to hold that pecuniary considerations are the sole ones involved in the cabdriver's attitude toward the tip. Yet in such tip-sensitive occupations as cabdriving, waitering, and bellhopping to suggest [13] that the tip's primary significance is its symbolic value as a token of affection or appreciation for a service well performed would be even wider of the mark. Vindictive caricatures abound among cabdrivers, as they do among waiters, waitresses, and bellhops, of the "polite gentleman" or "kind lady" who with profuse thanks and flawless grace departs from the scene having "stiffed" (failed to tip) them. In occupations where the tip constitutes so large a fraction of the person's earnings, the cash nexus, while admittedly not the only basis upon which patrons are judged, is so important as to relegate other considerations to a secondary place. Will the fare tip or will he "stiff"? How much will he tip? The answers remain in nearly every instance problematic to the end. Not only is there no sure way of predicting the outcome, but in a culture where the practice of tipping is neither as widespread nor as standardized as in many Continental countries, for example, the driver cannot in many cases even make a guess.

No regular scheme of work can easily tolerate so high a degree of ambiguity and uncertainty in a key contingency. Invariably, attempts are made to fashion ways and means of greater predictability and control; or, failing that, of devising formulas and imagery to bring order and reason in otherwise inscrutable and capricious events. In the course of a long history a rich body of stereotypes, beliefs, and practices [14] has grown up whose function is that of reducing uncertainty, increasing calculability, and providing coherent explanations.

A basic dichotomy running through the cabdriver's concept of his client world is of regular cab users and of non-cab users, the latter referred to

12. In Chicago in 1948 the company driver's share of the metered sum was 42½ per cent. Since that time the proportion has been increased slightly.
13. Cf. William F. Whyte, *Human Relations in the Restaurant Industry* (New York: McGraw-Hill Book Co., 1948), p. 100.
14. Cf. here and in the section to follow the pertinent remarks of Hughes on "guilty knowledge" developed by those in a service occupation with reference to their clientele. Hughes, *op. cit.*, pp. 81–82.

as "jerks," "slobs," "yokels," "public transportation types," and a host of other derogatory terms. The former class, though viewed as quite heterogeneous within itself, includes all who customarily choose cabs in preference to other forms of local transportation, are conversant with the cab-passenger role, and, most of all, accept, if only begrudgingly, the practice of tipping. By comparison, the class of non-cab users includes that vast aggregate of persons who resort to cabs only in emergencies or on special occasions, and are prone too often to view the hiring of a cab as simply a more expensive mode of transportation.

Take, for example, the familiar street scene following a sudden downpour or unexpected breakdown in bus service, when a group of individuals cluster about a bus stop, several of whom dart from the curb now and then in hope of hailing a cab. Such persons are almost by definition non-cab users or they would not be found at a bus stop in the rain; nor would they be keeping an eye out for a possible bus. A potential fare in this predicament is to the cabdriver a foul-weather friend, and drivers are on occasion known to hurdle by in spiteful glee, leaving the supplicant standing.

He who hires a cab only on special occasions, frequently to impress others or, perhaps, himself alone, is another familiar kind of non-cab user. Writing of his experiences as a London cabdriver, Hodge relates a by no means uncommon encounter:

> But tonight is different. Perhaps the Pools have come up for once. Anyhow, he's got money. He signals me with exaggerated casualness from the cinema entrance. . . . She steps in daintily, the perfect lady, particularly where she puts her feet. As soon as she's safely inside, he whispers the address . . . and adds, as one man of the world to another, "No hurry, driver." Then he dives in with such utter *savoire faire, comme il faut,* and what not, that he trips over the mat and lands face first on the back seat.[15]

Perhaps the most obvious kind of non-user is the person who, after hailing a cab, will ask the driver some such question as, "How much will it cost to take me to 500 Elm Street?" By this simple inquiry this person stands revealed as one who takes a narrow view of cab travel and from whom not much, if anything, can be expected by way of tip. On the other hand, regular cab users demonstrate in a variety of ways that for them this is a customary and familiar mode of travel. The manner in which they hail a cab, when and how they announce their destination, the ease with which they enter and exit, how they sit—these, and more, though difficult to describe in precise detail, comprise the Gestalt.

There exists among drivers an extensive typology of cab users, the at-

---

15.   Herbert Hodge, "I Drive a Taxi," *Fact,* No. 22 (January, 1939), pp. 28–29.

tributes imputed to each type having a certain predictive value, particularly as regards tipping. Some of the more common and sharply delineated types are:

The Sport.—The cabdriver's image of this type combines in one person those attributes of character which he views as ideal. While the Sport's vocation may be any one of many, his status derives more from his extra-vocational activities, e.g., at the race track, prize fights, ball games, popular restaurants, and bars. He is the perennial "young man on the town." Gentlemanly without being aloof, interested without becoming familiar, he also is, of course, never petty. Most of all, his tips are generous, and even on very short rides he will seldom tip less than a quarter. A favorite success story among cabdrivers describes at length and in fine detail the handsome treatment accorded the driver on an all-night tour with a Sport.[16]

The Blowhard.—The Blowhard is a false Sport. While often wearing the outer mantle of the Sport, he lacks the real Sport's casualness, assured manners, and comfortable style. Given to loquaciousness, he boasts and indiscriminately fabricates tales of track winnings, sexual exploits, and the important people he knows. Often holding out the promise of much by way of tip, he seldom lives up to his words.

The Businessman.—These are the staple of the cab trade, particularly for drivers who work by day. Not only are they the most frequently encountered; their habits and preferences are more uniform than those of any other type: the brisk efficiency with which they engage a cab, their purposefulness and disinclination to partake of small talk. Though not often big tippers, they are thought fair. Thus they serve as something of a standard by which the generosity or stinginess of others is judged.

The Lady Shopper.—Although almost as numerous as businessmen, Lady Shoppers are not nearly as well thought of by cabdrivers. The stereotype is a middle-aged woman, fashionably though unattractively dressed, sitting somewhat stiffly at the edge of her seat and wearing a fixed glare which bespeaks her conviction that she is being "taken for a ride." Her major delinquency, however, is undertipping; her preferred coin is a dime, no more or less, regardless of how long or arduous the trip. A forever repeated story is of the annoyed driver, who, after a grueling trip with a Lady Shopper, hands the coin back, telling her, "Lady, keep your lousy dime. You need it more than I do." [17]

16. As in the past, the Sport still serves as something of a hero figure in our culture, particularly among the working classes. A type midway between the Playboy and the Bohemian, his unique appeal rests perhaps on the ease and assurance with which he is pictured as moving between and among social strata, untainted by upper-class snobbishness, middle-class conventionality and lower-class vulgarity. In *The Great Gatsby,* Fitzgerald gives us a penetrative exposition of the myth of the Sport and its undoing at the hands of the class system.
17. The stereotype of women as poor tippers is widely shared by other tip-sensitive occupations. Cf. Frances Donovan, *The Woman Who Waits* (Boston: Badger, 1920).

Live Ones.[18]—Live Ones are a special category of fare usually encountered by the cabdriver who works by night. They are, as a rule, out-of-town conventioneers or other revelers who tour about in small groups in search of licentious forms of entertainment: cabarets, burlesques, strip-tease bars, pick-up joints, etc. As often as not, they have already had a good deal to drink when the cabdriver meets them, and, being out-of-towners they frequently turn to him for recommendations on where to go. In the late forties an arrangement existed in Chicago whereby some of the more popular Near North Side and West Madison Street "clip joints" rewarded cabdrivers for "steering" Live Ones to their establishments. Some places paid fifty cents "a head"; others a dollar "for the load." As do the many others who regularly cater to Live Ones—e.g., waitresses, bartenders, female bar companions (B-girls), night-club hosts and hostesses, entertainers, prostitutes—cabdrivers often view them as fair game. And while their opportunities for pecuniary exploitation are fewer and more limited than those open, for example, to B-girls and night-club proprietors, many drivers feel less inhibited about padding charges and finagling extras from Live Ones than they do from other fares. Often extravagant in their tips because of high spirits and drink, Live Ones are also frequently careless and forget to tip altogether. Knowing that Lives Ones are out to "blow their money" anyway, many drivers believe they are justified in seeing to it that they are not deprived of a small portion.

Although the cab culture's typology of fares stems in a large part from the attempt to order experience, reduce uncertainty, and further calculability of the tip, it is questionable of course as to how accurate or efficient it is. For, as has often been remarked, stereotypes and typologies have a way of imparting a symmetry and regularity to behavior which are, at best, only crudely approximated in reality. Too often it happens, for example, that a fare tabbed as a Sport turns out to be a Stiff (non-tipper), that a Blowhard matches his words with a generous tip, or that a Lady Shopper will give fifteen or even twenty cents. The persistence of the typology therefore has perhaps as much to do with the cabdriver's a posteriori reconstructions and rationalizations of fare behavior as it does with the typology's predictive efficiency.

To protect and insure themselves against an unfavorable outcome of tipping, many drivers will, depending upon circumstances, employ diverse tactics and stratagems (some more premeditated than others) to increase the amount of tip or to compensate for its loss should it not be forthcoming. Certain of these are listed below. It should be understood however, that in the ordinary instance the driver makes no attempt to manipulate

18. The term "Live Ones" is employed in a variety of pursuits as apparently diverse as retail selling, night-club entertainment, traveling fairs, and panhandling. Generally, it designates persons who are "easy touches," eager to succumb to the oftentimes semifraudulent proposals of the operator. Cf. W. Jack Peterson and Milton A. Maxwell, "The Skid Row Wino," *Social Problems,* V (Spring, 1958), 312.

the fare, believing resignedly that in the long run such means bear too little fruit for the effort and risk.

Making change.—Depending on the tariff and the amount handed him, the driver can fumble about in his pockets for change, or make change in such denominations as often to embarrass a fare into giving a larger tip than he had intended. The efficacy of this tactic depends naturally on the determination and staying power of the fare, qualities which many fares are averse to demonstrate, particularly when it comes to small change.

The hard-luck story.—This is usually reserved for young persons and others who, for whatever reason, evidence an insecure posture vis-à-vis the driver. Typically, the hard-luck story consists of a catalogue of economic woes, e.g., long and hard hours of work, poor pay, insulting and unappreciative passengers, etc. In "confiding" these to the fare, the driver pretends to esteem him as an exceptionally sympathetic and intelligent person who, unlike "the others," can appreciate his circumstances and act accordingly. Most drivers, however, view the hard-luck story as an unsavory form of extortion, beneath their dignity. Furthermore, while it may work in some cases, its potential for alienating tips is probably as great as its success at extracting them.

Fictitious charges.—The resort to fictitious and fraudulent charges occurs most commonly in those cases in which the driver feels that he has good reason to believe that the fare will, either through malice or ignorance, not tip and when the fare impresses him as being enough of a non-cab user as not to know when improper charges are being levied. Once, when I complained to a veteran cabdriver about having been "stiffed" by a young couple, newly arrived in Chicago, to whom I had extended such extra services as carrying luggage and opening doors, I was told: "Wise up kid! When you pick up one of these yokels at the Dearborn Station carrying a lot of cheap straw luggage on him, you can bet ninety-nine times out of a hundred that he isn't going to tip you. Not that he's a mean guy or anything, but where he comes from, they never heard of tipping. What I do with a yokel like that is to take him to where he's going, show him what the fare is on the meter, and tell him that it costs fifteen cents extra for each piece of luggage. Now, he doesn't know that there's no charge for hand luggage, but that way I'm sure of getting my tip out of him."

The "psychological" approach.—Possibly attributing more art to their trade than is the case, some drivers are of the opinion that a cab ride can be tailored to fit a passenger in much the same way as can a suit of clothes. One cabdriver, boasting of his success at getting tips, explained: "In this business you've got to use psychology. You've got to make the ride fit the person. Now, take a businessman. He's in a hurry to get someplace and he doesn't want a lot of bullshit and crapping around. With him you've got to keep moving. Do some fancy cutting in and out, give the cab a bit of a jerk when you take off from a light. Not reckless, mind you, but plenty of zip. He likes that.[19] With old people, it's just the opposite. They're more afraid than anyone of getting hurt or killed in a cab. Take it easy with them. Creep along, open doors for them, help them in and out, be real folksy. Call them 'Sir' and 'Ma'am' and they'll soon be calling you 'young man.' They're suckers for this stuff, and they'll loosen up their pocketbooks a little bit."

In the last analysis, neither the driver's typology of fares nor his stratagems further to any marked degree his control of the tip. Paradoxically, were these routinely successful in achieving predictability and control, they would at the same time divest the act of tipping of its most distinguishing characteristics—of its uncertainty, variability, and of the element of revelation in its consummation. It is these—essentially the problematic in human intercourse [20]—which distinguish the tip from the fixed service charge. And though another form of remuneration might in the end provide the cabdriver with a better wage and a more secure livelihood, the abrogation of tipping would also lessen the intellectual play which uncertainty stimulates and without which cabdriving would be for many nothing more than unrelieved drudgery.

That the practice of tipping, however, expressively befits only certain kinds of service relationships and may under slightly altered circumstances easily degenerate into corruption or extortion is demonstrated, ironically enough, by the predicament of some cabdrivers themselves. To give an example: In the garage out of which I worked, nearly everyone connected with maintenance and assignment of cabs expected tips from drivers for performing many of the routine tasks associated with their jobs, such as filling a tank with gas, changing a tire, or adjusting a carburetor. Although they resented it, drivers had little recourse but to tip. Otherwise, they would acquire reputations as "stiffs" and "cheapskates," be kept waiting interminably for repairs, and find that faulty and careless work had been done on their vehicles. Particularly with the dispatcher did the perversion of the tipping system reach extortionate proportions. His power derived from the assignment of cabs; to protect themselves from being assigned "pots" (cabs that would break down in the middle of the day), drivers tipped him fifty cents at the beginning of every week. Since nearly every driver tipped the dispatcher and since there were more drivers than good cabs, a certain number of drivers would still be assigned "pots." Some, wishing to insure doubly against this would then raise the bribe to a dollar and a half a week, causing the others to follow suit in a

19. Cf. Hodge, *op. cit.*, p. 17.
20. Cf. Donovan, *op. cit.*, p. 262.

vicious spiral. If little else, this shows how the tip—as distinguished from the gift, honorarium, inducement, or bribe—depends for its expressive validity on there not being a too close, long sustained, or consequential relationship between the parties to a service transaction.

Among service relationships in our society, that between the big city cabdriver and his fare is, due to the way in which they come into contact with each other, especially subject to structural weakness. The relationship is random, fleeting, unrenewable, and largely devoid of socially integrative features which in other client and patron oriented services help sustain a wider range of constraints and controls between the parties to the transaction. (Much the same might be said of such service occupations as waitress, bellhop and hotel doorman, the chief difference being, however, that these operate from a spatially fixed establishment, which in itself permits of greater identifiability, renewability, and hence constraint in one's relationship to them.) As a result, the tendency of the relationship is to gravitate sharply and in relatively overt fashion toward those few issues having to do with the basic instrumental terms of the exchange. The very fact of tipping, its economic centrality and the cab culture's preoccupation with mastering its many vagaries reflect in large part the regulative imbalance inherent in the relationship.

By inference, this analysis raises anew questions of how to account for the many more formidable and apparently more binding practitioner-client constraints found in other personal service fields, in particular the professions. To such matters as career socialization, colleague groups, socially legitimated skill monopolies, and professional secrecy there might be added a certain safe modicum of continuity, stability, and homogeneity of clientele.[21] For, given too great and random a circulation of clients among practitioners, as might occur for example under certain bureaucratic schemes for providing universal and comprehensive medical service, the danger is that informal social control networks would not come into being in the community, and, as in big-city cabdriving, relations between servers and served would become reputationless, anonymous, and narrowly calculative.

21. William J. Goode, "Community within a Community: The Professions," *American Sociological Review*, XXII, No. 2 (April, 1957), 198–200, and Eliot Freidson, "Varieties of Professional Practice," draft version of unpublished paper, 1959.

SAUL BELLOW
Looking for Mr. Green

Whatsoever thy hand findeth to do, do it with
thy might. . . .

Hard work? No, it wasn't really so hard. He wasn't used to walking and stair-climbing, but the physical difficulty of his new job was not what George Grebe felt most. He was delivering relief checks in the Negro district, and although he was a native Chicagoan this was not a part of the city he knew much about—it needed a depression to introduce him to it. No, it wasn't literally hard work, not as reckoned in foot-pounds, but yet he was beginning to feel the strain of it, to grow aware of its peculiar difficulty. He could find the streets and numbers, but the clients were not where they were supposed to be, and he felt like a hunter inexperienced in the camouflage of his game. It was an unfavorable day, too—fall, and cold, dark weather, windy. But, anyway, instead of shells in his deep trenchcoat pocket he had the cardboard of checks, punctured for the spindles of the file, the holes reminding him of the holes in player-piano paper. And he didn't look much like a hunter, either; his was a city figure entirely, belted up in this Irish conspirator's coat. He was slender without being tall, stiff in the back, his legs looking shabby in a pair of old tweed pants gone through and fringy at the cuffs. With this stiffness, he kept his head forward, so that his face was red from the sharpness of the weather; and it was an indoors sort of face with gray eyes that persisted in some kind of thought and yet seemed to avoid definiteness of conclusion. He wore sideburns that surprised you somewhat by the tough curl of the blond hair and the effect of assertion in their length. He was not so mild as he looked, nor so youthful; and nevertheless there was no effort on his part to seem what he was not. He was an educated man; he was a bachelor; he was in some ways simple; without lushing, he liked a drink; his luck had not been good. Nothing was deliberately hidden.

He felt that his luck was better than usual today. When he had reported for work that morning he had expected to be shut up in the relief office at a clerk's job, for he had been hired downtown as a clerk, and he was glad to have, instead, the freedom of the streets and welcomed, at least at first, the vigor of the cold and even the blowing of the hard wind. But on the other hand he was not getting on with the distribution of the checks. It was true that it was a city job; nobody expected you to push too hard at a city job. His supervisor, that young Mr. Raynor, had practically told him that. Still, he wanted to do well at it. For one thing, when he knew how quickly he could deliver a batch of checks, he would know also how much time he could expect to clip for himself. And then, too, the clients would be waiting for their money. That was not the most important consideration, though it certainly mattered to him. No, but he wanted to do well, simply for doing-well's sake, to acquit himself decently of a job because he so rarely had a job to do that required just this sort of energy. Of this peculiar energy he now had a superabundance; once it had started to flow, it flowed all too heavily. And, for the time being anyway, he was balked. He could not find Mr. Green.

So he stood in his big-skirted trenchcoat with a large envelope in his hand and papers showing from his pocket, wondering why people should be so hard to locate who were too feeble or sick to come to the station to collect their own checks. But Raynor had told him that tracking them down was not easy at first and had offered him some advice on how to proceed. "If you can see the postman, he's your first man to ask, and your best bet. If you can't connect with him, try the stores and tradespeople around. Then the janitor and the neighbors. But you'll find the closer you come to your man the less people will tell you. They don't want to tell you anything."

"Because I'm a stranger."

"Because you're white. We ought to have a Negro doing this, but we don't at the moment, and of course you've got to eat, too, and this is public employment. Jobs have to be made. Oh, that holds for me too. Mind you, I'm not letting myself out. I've got three years of seniority on you, that's all. And a law degree. Otherwise, you might be back of the desk and I might be going out into the field this cold day. The same dough pays us both and for the same, exact, identical reason. What's my law degree got to do with it? But you have to pass out these checks, Mr. Grebe, and it'll help if you're stubborn, so I hope you are."

"Yes, I'm fairly stubborn."

Raynor sketched hard with an eraser in the old dirt of his desk, left-handed, and said, "Sure, what else can you answer to such a question. Anyhow, the trouble you're going to have is that they don't like to give information about anybody. They think you're a plain-clothes dick or an installment collector, or summons-server or something like that. Till you've been seen around the neighborhood for a few months and people know you're only from the relief."

It was dark, ground-freezing, pre-Thanksgiving weather; the wind played hob with the smoke, rushing it down, and Grebe missed his gloves, which he had left in Raynor's office. And no one would admit knowing Green. It was past three o'clock and the postman had made his last delivery. The nearest grocer, himself a Negro, had never heard the name Tulliver Green, or said he hadn't. Grebe was inclined to think that it was true, that he had in the end convinced the man that he wanted only to deliver a check. But he wasn't sure. He needed experience in interpreting looks and signs and, even more, the will not to be put off or denied and even the force to bully if need be. If the grocer did know, he had got rid of him easily. But since most of his trade was with reliefers, why should he prevent the delivery of a check? Maybe Green, or Mrs. Green, if there was a Mrs. Green, patronized another grocer. And was there a Mrs. Green? It was one of Grebe's great handicaps that he hadn't looked at any of the case records. Raynor should have let him read files for a few hours. But he apparently saw no need for that, probably considering the job unimportant. Why prepare systematically to deliver a few checks?

But now it was time to look for the janitor. Grebe took in the building in the wind and gloom of the late November day—trampled, frost-hardened lots on one side; on the other, an automobile junk yard and then the infinite work of Elevated frames, weak-looking, gaping with rubbish fires; two sets of leaning brick porches three stories high and a flight of cement stairs to the cellar. Descending, he entered the underground passage, where he tried the doors until one opened and he found himself in the furnace room. There someone rose toward him and approached, scraping on the coal grit and bending under the canvas-jacketed pipes.

"Are you the janitor?"

"What do you want?"

"I'm looking for a man who's supposed to be living here. Green."

"What Green?"

"Oh, you maybe have more than one Green?" said Grebe with new, pleasant hope. "This is Tulliver Green."

"I don't think I c'n help you, mister. I don't know any."

"A crippled man."

The janitor stood bent before him. Could it be that he was crippled? Oh, God! what if he was. Grebe's gray eyes sought with excited difficulty to see. But no, he was only very short and stooped. A head awakened from meditation, a strong-haired beard, low, wide shoulders. A staleness of sweat and coal rose from his black shirt and the burlap sack he wore as an apron.

"Crippled how?"

Grebe thought and then answered with the light voice of unmixed candor, "I don't know. I've never seen him." This was damaging, but his only other choice was to make a lying guess, and he was not up to it. "I'm delivering checks for the relief to shut-in cases. If he weren't crippled he'd come to collect himself. That's why I said crippled. Bedridden, chairridden—is there anybody like that?"

This sort of frankness was one of Grebe's oldest talents, going back to childhood. But it gained him nothing here.

"No suh. I've got four buildin's same as this that I take care of. I don' know all the tenants, leave alone the tenants' tenants. The rooms turn over so fast, people movin' in and out every day. I can't tell you."

The janitor opened his grimy lips but Grebe did not hear him in the piping of the valves and the consuming pull of air to flame in the body of the furnace. He knew, however, what he had said.

"Well, all the same, thanks. Sorry I bothered you. I'll prowl around upstairs again and see if I can turn up someone who knows him."

Once more in the cold air and early darkness he made the short circle from the cellarway to the entrance crowded between the brickwork pillars and began to climb to the third floor. Pieces of plaster ground under his feet; strips of brass tape from which the carpeting had been torn away marked old boundaries at the sides. In the passage, the cold reached him worse than in the street; it touched him to the bone. The hall toilets ran like springs. He thought grimly as he heard the wind burning around the building with a sound like that of the furnace, that this was a great piece of constructed shelter. Then he struck a match in the gloom and searched for names and numbers among the writings and scribbles on the walls. He saw *Whoody-doody go to Jesus,* and zigzags, caricatures, sexual scrawls, and curses. So the sealed rooms of pyramids were also decorated, and the caves of human dawn.

The information on his card was, *Tulliver Green—Apt 3D.* There were no names, however, and no numbers. His shoulders drawn up, tears of cold in his eyes, breathing vapor, he went the length of the corridor and told himself that if he had been lucky enough to have the temperament for it he would bang on one of the doors and bawl out "Tulliver Green!" until he got results. But it wasn't in him to make an uproar and he continued to burn matches, passing the light over the walls. At the rear, in a corner off the hall, he discovered a door he had not seen before and he thought it best to investigate. It sounded empty when he knocked, but a young Negress answered, hardly more than a girl. She opened only a bit, to guard the warmth of the room.

"Yes suh?"

"I'm from the district relief station on Prairie Avenue. I'm looking for a man named Tulliver Green to give him his check. Do you know him?"

No, she didn't; but he thought she had not understood anything of what he had said. She had a dream-bound, dream-blind face, very soft and black, shut off. She wore a man's jacket and pulled the ends together at her throat. Her hair was parted in three directions, at the sides and transversely, standing up at the front in a dull puff.

"Is there somebody around here who might know?"

"I jus' taken this room las' week."

He observed that she shivered, but even her shiver was somnambulistic and there was no sharp consciousness of cold in the big smooth eyes of her handsome face.

"All right, miss, thank you. Thanks," he said, and went to try another place.

Here he was admitted. He was grateful, for the room was warm. It was full of people, and they were silent as he entered—ten people, or a dozen, perhaps more, sitting on benches like a parliament. There was no light, properly speaking, but a tempered darkness that the window gave, and everyone seemed to him enormous, the men padded out in heavy work clothes and winter coats, and the women huge, too, in their sweaters, hats, and old furs. And, besides, bed and bedding, a black cooking range, a piano piled towering to the ceiling with papers, a diningroom table of the old style of prosperous Chicago. Among these people Grebe, with his cold-heightened fresh color and his smaller stature, entered like a schoolboy. Even though he was met with smiles and good will, he knew, before a single word was spoken, that all the currents ran against him and that he would make no headway. Nevertheless he began. "Does anybody here know how I can deliver a check to Mr. Tulliver Green?"

"Green?" It was the man that had let him in who answered. He was in short sleeves, in a checkered shirt, and had a queer, high head, profusely overgrown and long as a shako; the veins entered it strongly from his forehead. "I never heard mention of him. Is this where he live?"

"This is the address they gave me at the station. He's a sick man, and he'll need his check. Can't anybody tell me where to find him?"

He stood his ground and waited for a reply, his crimson wool scarf wound about his neck and drooping outside his trenchcoat, pockets weighted with the block of checks and official forms. They must have realized that he was not a college boy employed afternoons by a bill collector, trying foxily to pass for a relief clerk, recognized that he was an older man who knew himself what need was, who had had more than an average seasoning in hardship. It was evident enough if you looked at the marks under his eyes and at the sides of his mouth.

"Anybody know this sick man?"

"No suh." On all sides he saw heads shaken and smiles of denial. No one knew. And maybe it was true, he considered, standing silent in the earthen, musky human gloom of the place as the rumble continued. But he could never really be sure.

"What's the matter with this man?" said shako-head.

"I've never seen him. All I can tell you is that he can't come in person for his money. It's my first day in this district."

"Maybe they given you the wrong number?"

"I don't believe so. But where else can I ask about him?" He felt that this persistence amused them deeply, and in a way he shared their amusement that he should stand up so tenaciously to them. Though smaller, though slight, he was his own man, he retracted nothing about himself, and he looked back at them, gray-eyed, with amusement and also with a sort of courage. On the bench some man spoke in his throat, the words impossible to catch, and a woman answered with a wild, shrieking laugh, which was quickly cut off.

"Well, so nobody will tell me?"

"Ain't nobody who knows."

"At least, if he lives here, he pays rent to someone. Who manages the building?"

"Greatham Company. That's on Thirty-ninth Street."

Grebe wrote it in his pad. But, in the street again, a sheet of wind-driven paper clinging to his leg while he deliberated what direction to take next, it seemed a feeble lead to follow. Probably this Green didn't rent a flat, but a room. Sometimes there were as many as twenty people in an apartment; the real-estate agent would know only the lessee. And not even the agent could tell you who the renters were. In some places the beds were even used in shifts, watchmen or jitney drivers or short-order cooks in night joints turning out after a day's sleep and surrendering their beds to a sister, a nephew, or perhaps a stranger, just off the bus. There were large numbers of newcomers in this terrific, blight-bitten portion of the city between Cottage Grove and Ashland, wandering from house to house and room to room. When you saw them, how could you know them? They didn't carry bundles on their backs or look picturesque. You only saw a man, a Negro, walking in the street or riding in the car, like everyone else, with his thumb closed on a transfer. And therefore how were you supposed to tell? Grebe thought the Greatham agent would only laugh at his question.

But how much it would have simplified the job to be able to say that Green was old, or blind, or consumptive. An hour in the files, taking a few notes, and he needn't have been at such a disadvantage. When Raynor gave him the block of checks he asked, "How much should I know about these people?" Then Raynor had looked as though he were preparing to accuse him of trying to make the job more important than it was. He smiled, because by then they were on fine terms, but nevertheless he had been getting ready to say something like that when the confusion began in the station over Staika and her children.

Grebe had waited a long time for this job. It came to him through the pull of an old schoolmate in the Corporation Counsel's office, never a close friend, but suddenly sympathetic and interested—pleased to show, moreover, how well he had done, how strongly he was coming on even in these miserable times. Well, he was coming through strongly, along with the Democratic administration itself. Grebe had gone to see him in City Hall, and they had had a counter lunch or beers at least once a month for a year, and finally it had been possible to swing the job. He didn't mind being assigned the lowest clerical grade, nor even being a messenger, though Raynor thought he did.

This Raynor was an original sort of guy and Grebe had taken to him immediately. As was proper on the first day, Grebe had come early, but he waited long, for Raynor was late. At last he darted into his cubicle of an office as though he had just jumped from one of those hurtling huge red Indian Avenue cars. His thin, rough face was wind-stung and he was grinning and saying something breathlessly to himself. In his hat, a small fedora, and his coat, the velvet collar a neat fit about his neck, and his silk muffler that set off the nervous twist of his chin, he swayed and turned himself in his swivel chair, feet leaving the ground; so that he pranced a little as he sat. Meanwhile he took Grebe's measure out of his eyes, eyes of an unusual vertical length and slightly sardonic. So the two men sat for a while, saying nothing, while the supervisor raised his hat from his miscombed hair and put it in his lap. His cold-darkened hands were not clean. A steel beam passed through the little makeshift room, from which machine belts once had hung. The building was an old factory.

"I'm younger than you; I hope you won't find it hard taking orders from me," said Raynor. "But I don't make them up, either. You're how old, about?"

"Thirty-five."

"And you thought you'd be inside doing paper work. But it so happens I have to send you out."

"I don't mind."

"And it's mostly a Negro load we have in this district."

"So I thought it would be."

"Fine. You'll get along. *C'est un bon boulot.* Do you know French?"

"Some."

"I thought you'd be a university man."

"Have you been in France?" said Grebe.

"No, that's the French of the Berlitz School. I've been at it for more than a year, just as I'm sure people have been, all over the world, office boys in China and braves in Tanganyika. In fact, I damn well know it. Such is the attractive power of civilization. It's overrated, but what do you want? *Que voulez-vous?* I get *Le Rire* and all the spicy papers, just like in Tanganyika. It must be mystifying, out there. But my reason is that I'm aiming at the diplomatic service. I have a cousin who's a courier, and the way he describes it is awfully attractive. He rides in the *wagon-lits* and reads books. While we—What did you do before?"

"I sold."

"Where?"

"Canned meat at Stop and Shop. In the basement."

"And before that?"

"Window shades, at Goldblatt's."

"Steady work?"

"No, Thursdays and Saturdays. I also sold shoes."

"You've been a shoe-dog too. Well. And prior to that? Here it is in your folder." He opened the record. "Saint Olaf's College, instructor in classical languages. Fellow, University of Chicago, 1926–27. I've had Latin, too. Let's trade quotations—*'Dum spiro spero.'* "

" *'Da dextram misero.'* "

" *'Alea jacta est.'* "

" *'Excelsior.'* "

Raynor shouted with laughter, and other workers came to look at him over the partition. Grebe also laughed, feeling pleased and easy. The luxury of fun on a nervous morning.

When they were done and no one was watching or listening, Raynor said rather seriously, "What made you study Latin in the first place? Was it for the priesthood?"

"No."

"Just for the hell of it? For the culture? Oh, the things people think they can pull!" He made his cry hilarious and tragic. "I ran my pants off so I could study for the bar, and I've passed the bar, so I get twelve dollars a week more than you as a bonus for having seen life straight and whole. I'll tell you, as a man of culture, that even though nothing looks to be real, and everything stands for something else, and that thing for another thing, and that thing for a still further one—there ain't any comparison between twenty-five and thirty-seven dollars a week, regardless of the last reality. Don't you think that was clear to your Greeks? They were a thoughtful people, but they didn't part with their slaves."

This was a great deal more than Grebe had looked for in his first interview with his supervisor. He was too shy to show all the astonishment he felt. He laughed a little, aroused, and brushed at the sunbeam that covered his head with its dust. "Do you think my mistake was so terrible?"

"Damn right it was terrible, and you know it now that you've had the whip of hard times laid on your back. You should have been preparing yourself for trouble. Your people must have been well off to send you to the university. Stop me, if I'm stepping on your toes. Did your mother pamper you? Did your father give in to you? Were you brought up tenderly, with permission to go and find out what were the last things that everything else stands for while everybody else labored in the fallen world of appearances?"

"Well, no, it wasn't exactly like that." Grebe smiled. *The fallen world of appearances!* no less. But now it was his turn to deliver a surprise. "We weren't rich. My father was the last genuine English butler in Chicago—"

"Are you kidding?"

"Why should I be?"

"In a livery?"

"In livery. Up on the Gold Coast."

"And he wanted you to be educated like a gentleman?"

"He did not. He sent me to the Armour Institute to study chemical engineering. But when he died I changed schools."

He stopped himself, and considered how quickly Raynor had reached him. In no time he had your valise on the table and all your stuff unpacked. And afterward, in the streets, he was still reviewing how far he might have gone, and how much he might have been led to tell if they had not been interrupted by Mrs. Staika's great noise.

But just then a young woman, one of Raynor's workers, ran into the cubicle exclaiming. "Haven't you heard all the fuss?"

"We haven't heard anything."

"It's Staika, giving out with all her might. The reporters are coming. She said she phoned the papers, and you know she did."

"But what is she up to?" said Raynor.

"She brought her wash and she's ironing it here, with our current, because the relief won't pay her electric bill. She has her ironing board set up by the admitting desk, and her kids are with her, all six. They never are in school more than once a week. She's always dragging them around with her because of her reputation."

"I don't want to miss any of this," said Raynor, jumping up. Grebe, as he followed with the secretary, said, "Who is this Staika?"

"They call her the 'Blood Mother of Federal Street.' She's a professional donor at the hospitals. I think they pay ten dollars a pint. Of course it's no joke, but she makes a very big thing out of it and she and the kids are in the papers all the time."

A small crowd, staff and clients divided by a plywood barrier, stood in the narrow space of the entrance, and Staika was shouting in a gruff, mannish voice, plunging the iron on the board and slamming it on the metal rest.

"My father and mother came in a steerage, and I was born in our house, Robey by Huron. I'm no dirty immigrant. I'm a U.S. citizen. My husband is a gassed veteran from France with lungs weaker'n paper, that hardly can he go to the toilet by himself. These six children of mine, I have to buy the shoes for their feet with my own blood. Even a lousy little white Communion necktie, that's a couple of drops of blood; a little piece of mosquito veil for my Vadja so she won't be ashamed in church for the other girls, they take my blood for it by Goldblatt. That's how I keep goin'. A fine thing if I had to depend on the relief. And there's plenty of people on the rolls—fakes! There's nothin' *they* can't get, that can go and wrap bacon at Swift and Armour any time. They're lookin' for them by the Yards. They never have to be out of work. Only they rather lay in their lousy beds and eat the public's money." She was not afraid, in a predominantly Negro station, to shout this way about Negroes.

Grebe and Raynor worked themselves forward to get a closer view of the woman. She was flaming with anger and with pleasure at herself, broad and huge, a golden-headed woman who wore a cotton cap laced with pink ribbon. She was barelegged and had on black gym shoes, her Hoover apron was open and her great breasts, not much restrained by a man's undershirt, hampered her arms as she worked at the kid's dress on the ironing board. And the children, silent and white, with a kind of locked obstinacy, in sheepskins and lumberjackets, stood behind her. She had captured the station, and the pleasure this gave her was enormous. Yet her grievances were true grievances. She was telling the truth. But she behaved like a liar. The look of her small eyes was hidden, and while she raged she also seemed to be spinning and planning.

"They send me out college case workers in silk pants to talk me out of what I got comin'. Are they better'n me? Who told them? Fire them. Let 'em go and get married, and then you won't have to cut electric from people's budget."

The chief supervisor, Mr. Ewing, couldn't silence her and he stood with folded arms at the head of his staff, bald, bald-headed, saying to his subordinates like the ex-school principal he was, "Pretty soon she'll be tired and go."

"No she won't," said Raynor to Grebe. "She'll get what she wants. She knows more about the relief even than Ewing. She's been on the rolls for years, and she always gets what she wants because she puts on a noisy show. Ewing knows it. He'll give in soon. He's only saving face. If he gets bad publicity, the Commissioner'll have him on the carpet, downtown. She's got him submerged; she'll submerge everybody in time, and that includes nations and governments."

Grebe replied with his characteristic smile, disagreeing completely. Who would take Staika's orders, and what changes could her yelling ever bring about?

No, what Grebe saw in her, the power that made people listen, was that her cry expressed the war of flesh and blood, perhaps turned a little crazy and certainly ugly, on this place and this condition. And at first, when he went out, the spirit of Staika somehow presided over the whole district for him, and it took color from her; he saw her color, in the spotty curb fires, and the fires under the El, the straight alley of flamy gloom.

Later, too, when he went into a tavern for a shot of rye, the sweat of beer, association with West Side Polish streets, made him think of her again.

He wiped the corners of his mouth with his muffler, his handkerchief being inconvenient to reach for, and went out again to get on with the delivery of his checks. The air bit cold and hard and a few flakes of snow formed near him. A train struck by and left a quiver in the frames and a bristling icy hiss over the rails.

Crossing the street, he descended a flight of board steps into a basement grocery, setting off a little bell. It was a dark, long store and it caught you with its stinks of smoked meat, soap, dried peaches, and fish. There was a fire wrinkling and flapping in the little stove, and the proprietor was waiting, an Italian with a long, hollow face and stubborn bristles. He kept his hands warm under his apron.

No, he didn't know Green. You knew people but not names. The same man might not have the same name twice. The police didn't know, either, and mostly didn't care. When somebody was shot or knifed they took the body away and didn't look for the murderer. In the first place, nobody would tell them anything. So they made up a name for the coroner and called it quits. And in the second place, they didn't give a goddamn anyhow. But they couldn't get to the bottom of a thing even if they wanted to. Nobody would get to know even a tenth of what went on among these people. They stabbed and stole, they did every crime and abomination you ever heard of, men and men, women and women, parents and children, worse than the animals. They carried on their own way, and the horrors passed off like a smoke. There was never anything like it in the history of the whole world.

It was a long speech, deepening with every word in its fantasy and passion and becoming increasingly senseless and terrible: a swarm amassed by suggestion and invention, a huge, hugging, despairing knot, a human wheel of heads, legs, bellies, arms, rolling through his shop.

Grebe felt that he must interrupt him. He said sharply, "What are you talking about! All I asked was whether you knew this man."

"That isn't even the half of it. I been here six years. You probably don't want to believe this. But suppose it's true?"

"All the same," said Grebe, "there must be a way to find a person."

The Italian's close-spaced eyes had been queerly concentrated, as were his muscles, while he leaned across the counter trying to convince Grebe. Now he gave up the effort and sat down on his stool. "Oh—I suppose. Once in a while. But I been telling you, even the cops don't get anywhere."

"They're always after somebody. It's not the same thing."

"Well, keep trying if you want. I can't help you."

But he didn't keep trying. He had no more time to spend on Green. He slipped Green's check to the back of the block. The next name on the list was *Field, Winston.*

He found the back-yard bungalow without the least trouble; it shared a lot with another house, a few feet of yard between. Grebe knew these two-shack arrangements. They had been built in vast numbers in the days before the swamps were filled and the streets raised, and they were all the same—a boardwalk along the fence, well under street level, three or four ball-headed posts for clotheslines, greening wood, dead shingles, and a long, long flight of stairs to the rear door.

A twelve-year-old boy let him into the kitchen, and there the old man was, sitting by the table in a wheel chair.

"Oh, it's d' Government man," he said to the boy when Grebe drew out his checks. "Go bring me my box of papers." He cleared a space on the table.

"Oh, you don't have to go to all that trouble," said Grebe. But Field laid out his papers: Social Security card, relief certification, letters from the state hospital in Manteno, and a naval discharge dated San Diego, 1920.

"That's plenty," Grebe said. "Just sign."

"You got to know who I am," the old man said. "You're from the Government. It's not your check, it's a Government check and you got no business to hand it over till everything is proved."

He loved the ceremony of it, and Grebe made no more objections. Field emptied his box and finished out the circle of cards and letters.

"There's everything I done and been. Just the death certificate and they can close book on me." He said this with a certain happy pride and magnificence. Still he did not sign; he merely held the little pen upright on the golden-green corduroy of his thigh. Grebe did not hurry him. He felt the old man's hunger for conversation.

"I got to get better coal," he said. "I send my little gran'son to the yard with my order and they fill his wagon with screening. The stove ain't made for it. It fall through the grate. The order says Franklin County egg-size coal."

"I'll report it and see what can be done."

"Nothing can be done, I expect. You know and I know. There ain't no little ways to make things better, and the only big thing is money. That's the only sunbeams, money. Nothing is black where it shines, and the only place you see black is where it ain't shining. What we colored have to have is our own rich. There ain't no other way."

Grebe sat, his reddened forehead bridged levelly by his close-cut hair and his cheeks lowered in the wings of his collar—the caked fire shone hard within the isinglass-and-iron frames but the room was not comfortable—sat and listened while the old man unfolded his scheme. This was to create one Negro millionaire a month by subscription. One clever, good-hearted young fellow elected every month would sign a contract to use the money to start a business employing Negroes. This would be advertised by chain letters and word of mouth, and every Negro wage earner would contribute a dollar a month. Within five years there would be sixty millionaires.

"That'll fetch respect," he said with a throat-stopped sound that came out like a foreign syllable. "You got to take and organize all the money that gets thrown away on the policy wheel and horse race. As long as they can take it away from you, they got no respect for you. Money, that's d' sun of human kind!" Field was a Negro of mixed blood, perhaps Cherokee, or Natchez; his skin was reddish. And he sounded, speaking about a golden sun in this dark room, and looked, shaggy and slab-headed, with the mingled blood of his face and broad lips, the little pen still upright in his hand, like one of the underground kings of mythology, old judge Minos himself.

And now he accepted the check and signed. Not to soil the slip, he held it down with his knuckles. The table budged and creaked, the center of the gloomy, heathen midden of the kitchen covered with bread, meat, and cans, and the scramble of papers.

"Don't you think my scheme'd work?"

"It's worth thinking about. Something ought to be done, I agree."

"It'll work if people will do it. That's all. That's the only thing, any time. When they understand it in the same way, all of them."

"That's true," said Grebe, rising. His glance met the old man's.

"I know you got to go," he said. "Well, God bless you, boy, you ain't been sly with me. I can tell it in a minute."

He went back through the buried yard. Someone nursed a candle in a shed, where a man unloaded kindling wood from a sprawl-wheeled baby buggy and two voices carried on a high conversation. As he came up the sheltered passage he heard the hard boost of the wind in the branches and against the house fronts, and then, reaching the sidewalk, he saw the needle-eye red of cable towers in the open icy height hundreds of feet above the river and the factories—those keen points. From here, his view was obstructed all the way to the South Branch and its timber banks, and the cranes beside the water. Rebuilt after the Great Fire, this part of the city was, not fifty years later, in ruins again, factories boarded up, buildings deserted or fallen, gaps of prairie between. But it wasn't desolation that this made you feel, but rather a faltering of organization that set free a huge energy, an escaped, unattached, unregulated power from the giant raw place. Not only must people feel it but, it seemed to Grebe, they were compelled to match it. In their very bodies. He no less than others, he realized. Say that his parents had been servants in their time, whereas he was not supposed to be one. He thought that they had never done any service like this, which no one visible asked for, and probably flesh and blood could not even perform. Nor could anyone show why it should be performed; or see where the performance would lead. That did not mean that he wanted to be released from it, he realized with a grimly pensive face. On the contrary. He had something to do. To be compelled to feel this energy and yet have no task to do—that was horrible; that was suffering; he knew what that was. It was now quitting time. Six o'clock. He could go home if he liked, to his room, that is, to wash in hot water, to pour a drink, lie down on his quilt, read the paper, eat some liver paste on crackers before going out to dinner. But to think of this actually made him feel a little sick, as though he had swallowed hard air. He had six checks left, and he was determined to deliver at least one of these: Mr. Green's check.

So he started again. He had four or five dark blocks to go, past open lots, condemned houses, old foundations, closed schools, black churches, mounds, and he reflected that there must be many people alive who had once seen the neighborhood rebuilt and new. Now there was a second layer of ruins; centuries of history accomplished through human massing. Numbers had given the place forced growth; enormous numbers had also broken it down. Objects once so new, so concrete that it could have occurred to anyone they stood for other things, had crumbled. Therefore, reflected Grebe, the secret of them was out. It was that they stood for themselves by agreement, and were natural and not unnatural by agreement, and when the things themselves collapsed the agreement became visible. What was it, otherwise, that kept cities from looking peculiar? Rome, that was almost permanent, did not give rise to thoughts like these. And was it abidingly real? But in Chicago, where the cycles were so fast and the familiar died out, and again rose changed, and died again in thirty years, you saw the common agreement or convenant, and you were forced to think about appearances and realities. (He remembered Raynor and he smiled. Raynor was a clever boy.) Once you had grasped this, a great many things became intelligible. For instance, why Mr. Field should conceive such a scheme. Of course, if people were to agree to create a millionaire, a real millionaire would come into existence. And if you wanted to know how Mr. Field was inspired to think of this, why, he had within sight of his kitchen window the chart, the very bones of a successful scheme—the El with its blue and green confetti of signals. People consented to pay dimes and ride the crash-box cars, and so it was a success. Yet how absurd it looked; how little reality there was to start with. And yet Yerkes, the great financier who built it, had known that he could get people to agree to do it. Viewed as itself, what a scheme of a scheme it seemed, how close to an appearance. Then why wonder at Mr. Field's idea? He had grasped a principle. And then Grebe remembered, too, that Mr. Yerkes had established the Yerkes Observatory and endowed it with millions. Now how did the notion come to him in his New

York museum of a palace or his Aegean-bound yacht to give money to astronomers? Was he awed by the success of his bizarre enterprise and therefore ready to spend money to find out where in the universe being and seeming were identical? Yes, he wanted to know what abides; and whether flesh is Bible grass; and he offered money to be burned in the fire of suns. Okay, then, Grebe thought further, these things exist because people consent to exist with them—we have got so far—and also there is a reality which doesn't depend on consent but within which consent is a game. But what about need, the need that keeps so many vast thousands in position? You tell me that, you *private* little gentleman and *decent* soul—he used these words against himself scornfully. Why is the consent given to misery? And why so painfully ugly? Because there is *something* that is dismal and permanently ugly? Here he sighed and gave it up, and thought it was enough for the present moment that he had a real check in his pocket for a Mr. Green who must be real beyond question. If only his neighbors didn't think they had to conceal him.

This time he stopped at the second floor. He struck a match and found a door. Presently a man answered his knock and Grebe had the check ready and showed it even before he began. "Does Tulliver Green live here? I'm from the relief."

The man narrowed the opening and spoke to someone at his back.

"Does he live here?"

"Uh-uh. No."

"Or anywhere in this building? He's a sick man and he can't come for his dough." He exhibited the check in the light, which was smoky—the air smelled of charred lard—and the man held off the brim of his cap to study it.

"Uh-uh. Never seen the name."

"There's nobody around here that uses crutches?"

He seemed to think, but it was Grebe's impression that he was simply waiting for a decent interval to pass.

"No, suh. Nobody I ever see."

"I've been looking for this man all afternoon"—Grebe spoke out with sudden force—"and I'm going to have to carry this check back to the station. It seems strange not to be able to find a person to *give* him something when you're looking for him for a good reason. I suppose if I had bad news for him I'd find him quick enough."

There was a responsive motion in the other man's face. "That's right, I reckon."

"It almost doesn't do any good to have a name if you can't be found by it. It doesn't stand for anything. He might as well not have any," he went on, smiling. It was as much of a concession as he could make to his desire to laugh.

"Well, now, there's a little old knot-back man I see once in a while. He might be the one you lookin' for. Downstairs."

"Where? Right side or left? Which door?"

"I don't know which. Thin-face little knot-back with a stick."

But no one answered at any of the doors on the first floor. He went to the end of the corridor, searching by matchlight, and found only a stairless exit to the yard, a drop of about six feet. But there was a bungalow near the alley, an old house like Mr. Field's. To jump was unsafe. He ran from the front door, through the underground passage and into the yard. The place was occupied. There was a light through the curtains, upstairs. The name on the ticket under the broken, scoop-shaped mailbox was Green! He exultantly rang the bell and pressed against the locked door. Then the lock clicked faintly and a long staircase opened before him. Someone was slowly coming down—a woman. He had the impression in the weak light that she was shaping her hair as she came, making herself presentable, for he saw her arms raised. But it was for support that they were raised; she was feeling her way downward, down the wall, stumbling. Next he wondered about the pressure of her feet on the treads; she did not seem to be wearing shoes. And it was a freezing stairway. His ring had got her out of bed, perhaps, and she had forgotten to put them on. And then he saw that she was not only shoeless but naked; she was entirely naked, climbing down while she talked to herself, a heavy woman, naked and drunk. She blundered into him. The contact of her breasts, though they touched only his coat, made him go back against the door with a blind shock. See what he had tracked down, in his hunting game!

The woman was saying to herself, furious with insult, "So I cain't——k, huh? I'll show that son-of-a-bitch kin I, cain't I."

What should he do now? Grebe asked himself. Why, he should go. He should turn away and go. He couldn't talk to this woman. He couldn't keep her standing naked in the cold. But when he tried he found himself unable to turn away.

He said, "Is this where Mr. Green lives?"

But she was still talking to herself and did not hear him.

"Is this Mr. Green's house?"

At last she turned her furious drunken glance on him. "What do you want?"

Again her eyes wandered from him; there was a dot of blood in their enraged brilliance. He wondered why she didn't feel the cold.

"I'm from the relief."

"Awright, what?"

"I've got a check for Tulliver Green."

This time she heard him and put out her hand.

"No, no, for *Mr.* Green. He's got to sign," he said. How was he going to get Green's signature tonight!

"I'll take it. He cain't."

He desperately shook his head, thinking of Mr. Field's precautions about identification. "I can't let you have it. It's for him. Are you Mrs. Green?"

"Maybe I is, and maybe I ain't. Who want to know?"

"Is he upstairs?"

"Awright. Take it up yourself, you goddamn fool."

Sure, he was a goddamn fool. Of course he could not go up because Green would probably be drunk and naked, too. And perhaps he would appear on the landing soon. He looked eagerly upward. Under the light was a high narrow brown wall. Empty! It remained empty!

"Hell with you, then!" he heard her cry. To deliver a check for coal and clothes, he was keeping her in the cold. She did not feel it, but his face was burning with frost and self-ridicule. He backed away from her.

"I'll come tomorrow, tell him."

"Ah, hell with you. Don' never come. What you doin' here in the night-time? Don' come back." She yelled so that he saw the breadth of her tongue. She stood astride in the long cold box of the hall and held on to the banister and the wall. The bungalow itself was shaped something like a box, a clumsy, high box pointing into the freezing air with its sharp, wintry lights.

"If you are Mrs. Green, I'll give you the check," he said, changing his mind.

"Give here, then." She took it, took the pen offered with it in her left hand, and tried to sign the receipt on the wall. He looked around, almost as though to see whether his madness was being observed, and came near believing that someone was standing on a mountain of used tires in the auto-junking shop next door.

"But are you Mrs. Green?" he now thought to ask. But she was already climbing the stairs with the check, and it was too late, if he had made an error, if he was now in trouble, to undo the thing. But he wasn't going to worry about it. Though she might not be Mrs. Green, he was convinced that Mr. Green was upstairs. Whoever she was, the woman stood for Green, whom he was not to see this time. Well, you silly bastard, he said to himself, so you think you found him. So what? Maybe you really did find him—what of it? But it was important that there was a real Mr. Green whom they could not keep him from reaching because he seemed to come as an emissary from hostile appearances. And though the self-ridicule was slow to diminish, and his face still blazed with it, he had, nevertheless, a feeling of elation, too. "For after all," he said, "he *could* be found!"

JOHN HOLLANDER
Helicon

Allen said, *I am searching for the true cadence.* Gray
Stony light had flashed over Morningside Drive since noon,
Mixing high in the east with a gray smoky darkness,
Blackened steel trusses of Hell-Gate faintly etched into it,
Gray visionary gleam, revealing the clarity of
Harlem's grid, like a glimpse of a future city below:
When the fat of the land shall have fallen into the dripping pan,
The grill will still be stuck with brown crusts, clinging to
Its bars, and neither in the fire nor out of it.
So is it coming about. But in my unguessing days
Allen said, *They still give you five dollars a pint at St. Luke's,
No kickback to the interne, either,* and I leaned out
Over the parapet and dug my heel in the hard,
Unyielding concrete below, and kicked again, and missed
The feeling of turf with water oozing its way to the top
Or of hard sand, making way for life. And was afraid,
Not for the opening of vessels designed to keep
Their rich dark cargo from the air, but for the kind
Of life that led from this oldest of initiations
Ending in homelessness, despondency and madness,
And for the moment itself when I should enter through
Those dirty-gray stone portals into the hospital
Named for the Greek doctor, abandoning all hope
Of home or of self-help. The heights of Morningside
Sloped downward, to the north, under the iron line
The subway holds to above it, refusing to descend
Under the crashing street. St. John the Divine's gray bulk
Posed, in its parody of history, just in the south.
Dry in the mouth and tired after a night of love
I followed my wild-eyed guide into the darkening door.

Inquiries and directions. Many dim rooms, and the shades
Of patient ghosts in the wards, caught in the privileged
Glimpses that the hurrying visitor always gets;
Turnings; errors; wanderings; while Allen chattered on:
*I mean someday to cry out against the cities, but first
I must find the true cadence.* We finally emerged
Into a dismal chamber, bare and dusty, where, suddenly,
Sunlight broke over a brown prospect of whirling clouds
And deepening smoke to plummet down, down to the depths
Of the darknesses, where, recessed in a tiny glory of light
A barely-visible man made his way in a boat
Along an amber chasm closing in smoke above him—
Two huge paintings by Thomas Cole opened, like airshaft
Windows, on darkening hearts, there by the blood bank.
We waited then and the dead hospital-white of the cots
Blinded my eyes for a while, and filled my ears with the silence
Of blanketing rushes of blood. Papers and signatures. Waiting;
And then being led by the hand into a corner across
The narrow room from Allen. We both lay down in the whiteness.
The needle struck. There was no pain, and as Allen waved,
I turned to the bubbling fountain, welling down redly beside me
And vanishing into the plasma bottle. My life drained of richness
As the light outside seemed to darken.

                                          Darker and milder the stream
Of blood was than the flashing, foaming spray I remembered
Just then, when, the summer before, with some simple souls who
     knew
Not Allen, I'd helped to fill Columbia's public fountains
With some powdered detergent and concentrated essence of grape,
Having discovered the circulation of water between them
To be a closed system. The sun of an August morning fired
Resplendently overhead; maiden teachers of English
From schools in the south were moving whitely from class to class
When the new, bubbling wine burst from the fountain's summits
Cascading down to the basins. The air was full of grapes
And little birds from afar clustered about their rims,
Not daring to drink, finally, and all was light and wine.
I forgot what we'd felt or said. My trickle of blood had died,
As the light outside seemed to brighten.

                                     Then rest; then five dollars. Then
     Allen
Urged us out onto the street. The wind sang around the corner,
Blowing in from the sound and a siren screeched away
Up Amsterdam Avenue. *Now you have a chocolate malted*

And then you're fine, he said, and the wind blew his hair like feathers,
And we both dissolved into nineteen forty-eight, to be whirled
Away into the wildwood of time, I to leave the city
For the disorganized plain, spectre of the long drink
Taken of me that afternoon. *Turning a guy*
On, said Allen last year to the hip pyschiatrists
Down in Atlantic City, *that's the most intimate thing*
You can ever do to him. Perhaps. I have bled since
To many cadences, if not to the constant tune
Of the heart's yielding and now I know how hard it is
To turn the drops that leaky faucets make in unquiet
Nights, the discrete tugs of love in its final scene,
Into a stream, whether thicker or thinner than blood, and I know
That opening up at all is harder than meeting a measure:
With night coming on like a death, a ruby of blood is a treasure.

NORMAN MAILER
The Man Who Studied Yoga

1

I would introduce myself if it were not useless. The name I had last night
will not be the same as the name I have tonight. For the moment, then,
let me say that I am thinking of Sam Slovoda. Obligatorily, I study him,
Sam Slovoda who is neither ordinary nor extraordinary, who is not young
nor yet old, not tall nor short. He is sleeping, and it is fit to describe him
now, for like most humans he prefers sleeping to not sleeping. He is a
mild pleasant-looking man who has just turned forty. If the crown of his
head reveals a little bald spot, he has nourished in compensation the
vanity of a mustache. He has generally when he is awake an aggreeable
manner, at least with strangers; he appears friendly, tolerant, and genial.
The fact is that like most of us, he is full of envy, full of spite, a gossip, a
man who is pleased to find others are as unhappy as he, and yet—this is
the worst to be said—he is a decent man. He is better than most. He
would prefer to see a more equitable world, he scorns prejudice and privilege, he tries to hurt no one, he wishes to be liked. I will go even further.
He has one serious virtue—he is not fond of himself, he wishes he was
better. He would like to free himself of envy, of the annoying necessity to
talk about his friends, he would like to love people more; specifically, he
would like to love his wife more, and to love his two daughters without
the tormenting if nonetheless irremediable vexation that they closet his
life in the dusty web of domestic responsibilities and drudging for money.

How often he tells himself with contempt that he has the cruelty of a
kind weak man.

May I state that I do not dislike Sam Slovoda; it is just that I am disappointed in him. He has tried too many things and never with a whole
heart. He has wanted to be a serious novelist and now merely indulges
the ambition; he wished to be of consequence in the world, and has
ended, temporarily perhaps, as an overworked writer of continuity for
comic magazines; when he was young he tried to be a bohemian and in-

stead acquired a wife and family. Of his appetite for a variety of new experience I may say that it is matched only by his fear of new people and novel situations.

I will give an instance. Yesterday, Sam was walking along the street and a bum approached him for money. Sam did not see the man until too late; lost in some inconsequential thought, he looked up only in time to see a huge wretch of a fellow with a red twisted face and an outstretched hand. Sam is like so many; each time a derelict asks for a dime, he feels a coward if he pays the money, and is ashamed of himself if he doesn't. This once, Sam happened to think, I will not be bullied, and hurried past. But the bum was not to be lost so easily. "Have a heart, Jack," he called after in a whisky voice, "I need a drink bad." Sam stopped, Sam began to laugh. "Just so it isn't for coffee, here's a quarter," he said; and he laughed, and the bum laughed. "You're a man's man," the bum said. Sam went away pleased with himself, thinking about such things as the community which existed between all people. It was cheap of Sam. He should know better. He should know he was merely relieved the situation had turned out so well. Although he thinks he is sorry for bums, Sam really hates them. Who knows what violence they can offer?

At this time, there is a powerful interest in Sam's life, but many would ridicule it. He is in the process of being psychoanalyzed. Myself, I do not jeer. It has created the most unusual situation between Sam and me. I could go into details but they are perhaps premature. It would be better to watch Sam awaken.

His wife, Eleanor, has been up for an hour, and she has shut the window and neglected to turn off the radiator. The room is stifling. Sam groans in a stupor which is neither sleep nor refreshment, opens one eye, yawns, groans again, and lies twisted, strangled and trussed in pajamas which are too large for him. How painful it is for him to rise. Last night there was a party, and this morning, Sunday morning, he is awakening with a hangover. Invariably, he is depressed in the morning, and it is no different today. He finds himself in the flat and familiar dispirit of nearly all days.

It is snowing outside. Sam finally lurches to the window, and opens it for air. With the oxygen of a winter morning clearing his brain, he looks down six stories into the giant quadrangle of the Queens housing development in which he lives, staring morosely at the inch of slush which covers the monotonous artificial park that separates his apartment building from an identical structure not two hundred feet away. The walks are black where the snow has melted, and in the children's playground, all but deserted, one swing oscillates back and forth, pushed by an irritable little boy who plays by himself among the empty benches, swaddled in galoshes, muffler, and overcoat. The snow falls sluggishly, a wet snow which probably will turn to rain. The little boy in the playground gives one last disgusted shove to the swing and trudges away gloomily, his over-shoes leaving a small animal track behind him. Back of Sam, in the four-room apartment he knows like a blind man, there is only the sound of Eleanor making breakfast.

Well, thinks Sam, depression in the morning is a stage of his analysis, Dr. Sergius has said.

This is the way Sam often phrases his thoughts. It is not altogether his fault. Most of the people he knows think that way and talk that way, and Sam is not the strongest of men. His language is doomed to the fashion of the moment. I have heard him remark mildly, almost apologetically, about his daughters: "My relation with them still suffers because I haven't worked through all my feminine identifications." The saddest thing is that the sentence has meaning to Sam even if it will not have meaning to you. A great many ruminations, discoveries, and memories contribute their connotation to Sam. It has the significance of a cherished line of po-etry to him.

Although Eleanor is not being analyzed, she talks in a similar way. I have heard her remark in company, "Oh, you know Sam, he not only thinks I'm his mother, he blames me for being born." Like most women, Eleanor can be depended upon to employ the idiom of her husband.

What amuses me is that Sam is critical of the way others speak. At the party last night he was talking to a Hollywood writer, a young man with a great deal of energy and enthusiasm. The young man spoke something like this: "You see, boychick, I can spike any script with yaks, but the thing I can't do is heartbreak. My wife says she's gonna give me heart-break. The trouble is I've had a real solid-type life. I mean I've had my ups and downs like all of humanity, but there's never been a shriek in my life. I don't know how to write shrieks."

On the trip home, Sam had said to Eleanor, "It was disgraceful. A writer should have some respect for language."

Eleanor answered with a burlesque of Sam's indignation. "Listen, I'm a real artist-type. Culture is for comic-strip writers."

Generally, I find Eleanor attractive. In the ten years they have been married she has grown plump, and her dark hair which once was long is now cropped in a mannish cut of the prevailing mode. But, this is quib-bling. She still possesses her best quality, a healthy exuberance which glows in her dark eyes and beams in her smile. She has beautiful teeth. She seems aware of her body and pleased with it. Sam tells himself he would do well to realize how much he needs her. Since he has been in analysis he has come to discover that he remains with Eleanor for more essential reasons than mere responsibility. Even if there were no chil-dren, he would probably cleave to her.

Unhappily, it is more complicated than that. She is always—to use their phrase—competing with him. At those times when I do not like

Eleanor, I am irritated by her lack of honesty. She is too sharp-tongued, and she does not often give Sam what he needs most, a steady flow of uncritical encouragement to counteract the harshness with which he views himself. Like so many who are articulate on the subject, Eleanor will tell you that she resents being a woman. As Sam is disappointed in life, so is Eleanor. She feels Sam has cheated her from a proper development of her potentialities and talent, even as Sam feels cheated. I call her dishonest because she is not so ready as Sam to put the blame on herself.

Sam, of course, can say all this himself. It is just that he experiences it in a somewhat different way. Like most men who have been married for ten years, Eleanor is not quite real to him. Last night at the party, there were perhaps half a dozen people whom he met for the first time, and he talked animatedly with them, sensing their reactions, feeling their responses, aware of the life in them, as they were aware of the life in him. Eleanor, however, exists in his nerves. She is a rather vague embodiment, he thinks of her as "she" most of the time, someone to conceal things from. Invariably, he feels uneasy with her. It is too bad. No matter how inevitable, I am always sorry when love melts into that pomade of affection, resentment, boredom and occasional compassion which is the best we may expect of a man and woman who have lived together a long time. So often, it is worse, so often no more than hatred.

They are eating breakfast now, and Eleanor is chatting about the party. She is pretending to be jealous about a young girl in a strapless evening gown, and, indeed, she does not have to pretend altogether. Sam, with liquor inside him, had been leaning over the girl; obviously he had coveted her. Yet, this morning, when Eleanor begins to talk about her, Sam tries to be puzzled.

"Which girl was it now?" he asks a second time.

"Oh, you know, the hysteric," Eleanor says, "the one who was parading her bazooms in your face." Eleanor has ways of impressing certain notions upon Sam. "She's Charlie's new girl."

"I didn't know that," Sam mutters. "He didn't seem to be near her all evening."

Eleanor spreads marmalade over her toast and takes a bite with evident enjoyment. "Apparently, they're all involved. Charles was funny about it. He said he's come to the conclusion that the great affairs of history are between hysterical women and detached men."

"Charles hates women," Sam says smugly. "If you notice, almost everything he says about them is a discharge of aggression." Sam has the best of reasons for not liking Charles. It takes more than ordinary character for a middle-aged husband to approve of a friend who moves easily from woman to woman.

"At least Charles discharges his aggression," Eleanor remarks.

"He's almost a classic example of the Don Juan complex. You notice how masochistic his women are?"

"I know a man or two who's just as masochistic."

Sam sips his coffee. "What made you say the girl was an hysteric?"

Eleanor shrugs. "She's an actress. And I could see she was a tease."

"You can't jump to conclusions," Sam lectures. "I had the impression she was a compulsive. Don't forget you've got to distinguish between the outer defenses, and the more deeply rooted conflicts."

I must confess that this conversation bores me. As a sample it is representative of the way Sam and Eleanor talk to each other. In Sam's defense I can say nothing; he has always been too partial to jargon.

I am often struck by how eager we are to reveal all sorts of supposedly ugly secrets about ourselves. We can explain the hatred we feel for our parents, we are rather pleased with the perversions to which we are prone. We seem determinedly proud to be superior to ourselves. No motive is too terrible for our inspection. Let someone hint, however, that we have bad table manners and we fly into a rage. Sam will agree to anything you may say about him, provided it is sufficiently serious—he will be the first to agree he has fantasies of murdering his wife. But tell him that he is afraid of waiters, or imply to Eleanor that she is a nag, and they will be quite annoyed.

Sam has noticed this himself. There are times when he can hear the jargon in his voice, and it offends him. Yet, he seems powerless to change his habits.

An example: He is sitting in an armchair now, brooding upon his breakfast, while Eleanor does the dishes. The two daughters are not home; they have gone to visit their grandmother for the week-end. Sam had encouraged the visit. He had looked forward to the liberty Eleanor and himself would enjoy. For the past few weeks the children had seemed to make the most impossible demands upon his attention. Yet now they are gone and he misses them, he even misses their noise. Sam, however, cannot accept the notion that many people are dissatisfied with the present, and either dream of the past or anticipate the future. Sam must call this "ambivalence over possessions." Once he even felt obliged to ask his analyst, Dr. Sergius, if ambivalence over possessions did not characterize him almost perfectly, and Sergius whom I always picture with the flat precision of a coin's head—bald skull and horn-rimmed glasses—answered in his German accent, "But, my dear Mr. Slovoda, as I have told you, it would make me happiest if you did not include in your reading, these psychoanalytical text-works."

At such rebukes, Sam can only wince. It is so right, he tells himself, he is exactly the sort of ambitious fool who uses big words when small ones would do.

2

While Sam sits in the armchair, gray winter light is entering the windows, snow falls outside. He sits alone in a modern seat, staring at the gray, green, and beige décor of their living room. Eleanor was a painter before they were married, and she has arranged this room. It is very pleasant, but like many husbands, Sam resents it, resents the reproductions of modern painters upon the wall, the slender coffee table, a freeform poised like a spider on wire legs, its feet set onto a straw rug. In the corner, most odious of all, is the playmate of his children, a hippopotamus of a television-radio-and-phonograph cabinet with the blind monstrous snout of the video tube.

Eleanor has set the Sunday paper near his hand. Soon, Sam intends to go to work. For a year, he has been giving a day once or twice a month to a bit of thought and a little writing on a novel he hopes to begin sometime. Last night, he told himself he would work today. But he has little enthusiasm now. He is tired, he is too depressed. Writing for the comic strips seems to exhaust his imagination.

Sam reads the paper as if he were peeling an enormous banana. Flap after flap of newsprint is stripped away and cast upon the straw rug until only the Magazine Section is left. Sam glances through it with restless irritability. A biography of a political figure runs its flatulent prose into the giant crossword puzzle at the back. An account of a picturesque corner of the city becomes lost in statistics and exhortations on juvenile delinquency, finally to emerge with photographs about the new style of living which desert architecture provides. Sam looks at a wall of windows in rotogravure with a yucca tree framing the pool.

There is an article about a workingman. His wife and his family are described, his apartment, his salary and his budget. Sam reads a description of what the worker has every evening for dinner, and how he spends each night of the week. The essay makes its point; the typical American workingman must watch his pennies, but he is nonetheless secure and serene. He would not exchange his life for another.

Sam is indignant. A year ago he had written a similar article in an attempt to earn some extra money. Subtly, or so he thought, he had suggested that the average workingman was raddled with insecurity. Naturally, the article had been rejected.

Sam throws the Magazine Section away. Moments of such anger torment him frequently. Despite himself, Sam is enraged at editorial dishonesty, at the smooth strifeless world which such articles present. How angry he is—how angry and how helpless. "It is the actions of men and not their sentiments which make history," he thinks to himself, and smiles wryly. In his living room he would go out to tilt the windmills of a vast, powerful, and hypocritical society; in his week of work he labors in an editorial cubicle to create spaceships, violent death, women with golden tresses and wanton breasts, men who act with their fists and speak with patriotic slogans.

I know what Sam feels. As he sits in the armchair, the Sunday papers are strewn around him, carrying their war news, their murders, their parleys, their entertainments, mummery of a real world which no one can grasp. It is terribly frustrating. One does not know where to begin.

Today, Sam considers himself half a fool for having been a radical. There is no longer much consolation in the thought that the majority of men who succeed in a corrupt and acquisitive society are themselves obligatorily corrupt, and one's failure is therefore the price of one's idealism. Sam cannot recapture the pleasurable bitterness which resides in the notion that one has suffered for one's principles. Sergius is too hard on him for that.

They have done a lot of work on the subject. Sergius feels that Sam's concern with world affairs has always been spurious. For example, they have uncovered in analysis that Sam wrote his article about the worker in such a way as to make certain it would be refused. Sam, after all, hates editors; to have such a piece accepted would mean he is no better than they, that he is a mediocrity. So long as he fails he is not obliged to measure himself. Sam, therefore, is being unrealistic. He rejects the world with his intellect, and this enables him not to face the more direct realities of his present life.

Sam will argue with Sergius but it is very difficult. He will say, "Perhaps you sneer at radicals because it is more comfortable to ignore such ideas. Once you became interested it might introduce certain unpleasant changes in your life."

"Why," says Sergius, "do you feel it so necessary to assume that I am a bourgeois interested only in my comfort?"

"How can I discuss these things," says Sam, "if you insist that my opinions are the expression of neurotic needs, and your opinions are merely dispassionate medical advice?"

"You are so anxious to defeat me in an argument," Sergius will reply. "Would you admit it is painful to relinquish the sense of importance which intellectual discussion provides you?"

I believe Sergius has his effect. Sam often has thoughts these days which would have been repellent to him years ago. For instance, at the moment, Sam is thinking it might be better to live the life of a worker, a simple life, to be completely absorbed with such necessities as food and money. Then one could believe that to be happy it was necessary only to have more money, more goods, less worries. It would be nice, Sam thinks wistfully, to believe that the source of one's unhappiness comes not from oneself, but from the fault of the boss, or the world, or bad luck.

Sam has these casual daydreams frequently. He likes to think about other lives he might have led, and he envies the most astonishing variety of occupations. It is easy enough to see why he should wish for the life of an executive with the power and sense of command it may offer, but virtually from the same impulse Sam will wish himself a bohemian living in an unheated loft, his life a catch-as-catch-can from day to day. Once, after reading an article, Sam even wished himself a priest. For about ten minutes it seemed beautiful to him to surrender his life to God. Such fancies are common, I know. It is just that I, far better than Sam, know how serious he really is, how fanciful, how elaborate, his imagination can be.

The phone is ringing. Sam can hear Eleanor shouting at him to answer. He picks up the receiver with a start. It is Marvin Rossman who is an old friend, and Marvin has an unusual request. They talk for several minutes, and Sam squirms a little in his seat. As he is about to hang up, he laughs. "Why, no, Marvin, it gives me a sense of adventure," he says.

Eleanor has come into the room toward the end of this conversation. "What is it all about?" she asks.

Sam is obviously a bit agitated. Whenever he attempts to be most casual, Eleanor can well suspect him. "It seems," he says slowly, "that Marvin has acquired a pornographic movie."

"From whom?" Eleanor asks.

"He said something about an old boy friend of Louise's."

Eleanor laughs. "I can't imagine Louise having an old boy friend with a dirty movie."

"Well, people are full of surprises," Sam says mildly.

"Look, here," says Eleanor suddenly. "Why did he call us?"

"It was about our projector."

"They want to use it?" Eleanor asks.

"That's right." Sam hesitates. "I invited them over."

"Did it ever occur to you I might want to spend my Sunday some other way?" Eleanor asks crossly.

"We're not doing anything," Sam mumbles. Like most men, he feels obliged to act quite nonchalantly about pornography. "I'll tell you, I am sort of curious about the film. I've never seen one, you know."

"Try anything once, is that it?"

"Something of the sort." Sam is trying to conceal his excitement. The truth is that in common with most of us, he is fascinated by pornography. It is a minor preoccupation, but more from lack of opportunity than anything else. Once or twice, Sam has bought the sets of nude photographs which are sold in marginal bookstores, and with guilty excitement has hidden them in the apartment.

"Oh, this is silly," Eleanor says. "You were going to work today."

"I'm just not in the mood."

"I'll have to feed them," Eleanor complains. "Do we have enough liquor?"

"We can get beer." Sam pauses. "Alan Sperber and his wife are coming too."

"Sam, you're a child."

"Look, Eleanor," says Sam, controlling his voice, "if it's too much trouble, I can take the projector over there."

"I ought to make you do that."

"Am I such an idiot that I must consult you before I invite friends to the house?"

Eleanor has the intuition that Sam, if he allowed himself, could well drown in pornography. She is quite annoyed at him, but she would never dream of allowing Sam to take the projector over to Marvin Rossman's where he could view the movie without her—that seems indefinably dangerous. Besides she would like to see it, too. The mother in Eleanor is certain it cannot hurt her.

"All right, Sam," she says, "but you are a child."

More exactly, an adolescent, Sam decides. Ever since Marvin phoned, Sam has felt the nervous glee of an adolescent locking himself in the bathroom. Anal fixation, Sam thinks automatically.

While Eleanor goes down to buy beer and cold cuts in a delicatessen, Sam gets out the projector and begins to clean it. He is far from methodical in this. He knows the machine is all right, he has shown movies of Eleanor and his daughters only a few weeks ago, but from the moment Eleanor left the apartment, Sam has been consumed by an anxiety that the projection bulb is burned out. Once he has examined it, he begins to fret about the motor. He wonders if it needs oiling, he blunders through a drawer of household tools looking for an oilcan. It is ridiculous. Sam knows that what he is trying to keep out of his mind are the reactions Sergius will have. Sergius will want to "work through" all of Sam's reasons for seeing the movie. Well, Sam tells himself, he knows in advance what will be discovered: detachment, not wanting to accept Eleanor as a sexual partner, evasion of responsibility, etc. etc. The devil with Sergius. Sam has never seen a dirty movie, and he certainly wants to.

He feels obliged to laugh at himself. He could not be more nervous, he knows, if he were about to make love to a woman he had never touched before. It is really disgraceful.

When Eleanor comes back, Sam hovers about her. He is uncomfortable with her silence. "I suppose they'll be here soon," Sam says.

"Probably."

Sam does not know if he is angry at Eleanor or apprehensive that she is angry at him. Much to his surprise he catches her by the waist and hears himself saying, "You know, maybe tonight when they're gone . . . I mean, we do have the apartment, to ourselves." Eleanor moves neither toward him nor away from him. "Darling, it's not because of the movie," Sam goes on, "I swear. Don't you think maybe we could . . ."

"Maybe," says Eleanor.

3

The company has arrived, and it may be well to say a word or two about them. Marvin Rossman who has brought the film is a dentist, although it might be more accurate to describe him as a frustrated doctor. Rossman is full of statistics and items of odd information about the malpractice of physicians, and he will tell these things in his habitually gloomy voice, a voice so slow, so sad, that it almost conceals the humor of his remarks. Or, perhaps, that is what creates his humor. In his spare time, he is a sculptor, and if Eleanor may be trusted, he is not without talent. I often picture him working in the studio loft he has rented, his tall bony frame the image of dejection. He will pat a piece of clay to the armature, he will rub it sadly with his thumb, he will shrug, he does not believe that anything of merit could come from him. When he talked to Sam over the phone, he was pessimistic about the film they were to see. "It can't be any good," he said in his melancholy voice. "I know it'll be a disappointment." Like Sam, he has a mustache, but Rossman's will droop at the corners.

Alan Sperber who has come with Rossman is the subject of some curiosity for the Slovodas. He is not precisely womanish; in fact, he is a large plump man, but his voice is too soft, his manners too precise. He is genial, yet he is finicky; waspish, yet bland; he is fond of telling long rather affected stories, he is always prepared with a new one, but to general conversation he contributes little. As a lawyer, he seems miscast. One cannot image him inspiring a client to confidence. He is the sort of heavy florid man who seems boyish at forty, and the bow ties and gray flannel suits he wears do not make him appear more mature.

Roslyn Sperber, his wife, used to be a schoolteacher, and she is a quiet nervous woman who talks a great deal when she is drunk. She is normally quite pleasant, and has only one habit which is annoying to any degree. It is a little flaw, but social life is not unlike marriage in that habit determines far more than vice or virtue. This mannerism which has become so offensive to the friends of the Sperbers is Roslyn's social pretension. Perhaps I should say intellectual pretension. She entertains people as if she were conducting a salon, and in her birdlike voice is forever forcing her guests to accept still another intellectual canapé. "You must hear Sam's view of the world market," she will say, or "Has Louise told you her statistics on divorce?" It is quite pathetic for she is so eager to please. I have seen her eyes fill with tears at a sharp word from Alan.

Marvin Rossman's wife, Louise, is a touch grim and definite in her opinions. She is a social welfare worker, and will declare herself with force whenever conversation impinges on those matters where she is expert. She is quite opposed to psychoanalysis, and will say without quarter, "It's all very well for people in the upper-middle area"—she is referring to the upper middle class—"but, it takes more than a couch to solve the problems of . . ." and she will list narcotics, juvenile delinquency, psychosis, relief distribution, slum housing, and other descriptions of our period. She recites these categories with an odd anticipation. One would guess she was ordering a meal.

Sam is fond of Marvin but he cannot abide Louise. "You'd think she discovered poverty," he will complain to Eleanor.

The Slovodas do feel superior to the Rossmans and the Sperbers. If pressed, they could not offer the most convincing explanation why. I suppose what it comes down to is that Sam and Eleanor do not think of themselves as really belonging to a class, and they feel that the Sperbers and Rossmans are petit-bourgeois. I find it hard to explain their attitude. Their company feels as much discomfort and will apologize as often as the Slovodas for the money they have, and the money they hope to earn. They are all of them equally concerned with progressive education and the methods of raising children to be well adjusted—indeed, they are discussing that now—they consider themselves relatively free of sexual taboo, or put more properly, Sam and Eleanor are no less possessive than the others. The Slovodas' culture is not more profound; I should be hard put to say that Sam is more widely read, more seriously informed, than Marvin or Alan, or for that matter, Louise. Probably, it comes to this: Sam, in his heart, thinks himself a rebel, and there are few rebels who do not claim an original mind. Eleanor has been a bohemian and considers herself more sophisticated than her friends who merely went to college and got married. Louise Rossman could express it most soundly. "Artists, writers, and people of the creative layer have in their occupational ideology the belief that they are classless."

One thing I might remark about the company. They are all being the most unconscionable hypocrites. They have rushed across half the city of New York to see a pornographic film, and they are not at all interested in each other at the moment. The women are giggling like tickled children at remarks which cannot possibly be so funny. Yet, they are all determined to talk for a respectable period of time. No less, it must be serious talk. Roslyn has said once, "I feel so funny at the thought of seeing such a movie," and the others have passed her statement by.

At the moment, Sam is talking about value. I might note that Sam loves conversation and thrives when he can expound an idea.

"What are our values today?" he asks. "It's really fantastic when you stop to think of it. Take any bright talented kid who's getting out of college now."

"My kid brother, for example." Marvin interposes morosely. He passes his bony hand over his sad mustache, and somehow the remark has become amusing, much as if Marvin had said, "Oh, yes, you have reminded me of the trials, the worries, and the cares which my fabulous yonger brother heaps upon me."

"All right, take him," Sam says. "What does he want to be?"

"He doesn't want to be anything." says Marvin.

"That's my point," Sam says excitedly. "Rather than work at certain occupations, the best of these kids would rather do nothing at all."

"Alan has a cousin," Roslyn says, "who swears he'll wash dishes before he becomes a businessman."

"I wish that were true," Eleanor interrupts. "It seems to me everybody is conforming more and more these days."

They argue about this. Sam and Eleanor claim the country is suffering from hysteria; Alan Sperber disagrees and says it's merely a reflection of the headlines; Louise says no adequate criteria exist to measure hysteria; Marvin says he doesn't know anything at all.

"More solid liberal gains are being made in this period," says Alan, "than you would believe. Consider the Negro—"

"Is the Negro any less maladjusted?" Eleanor shouts with passion.

Sam maneuvers the conversation back to his thesis. "The values of the young today, and by the young I mean the cream of the kids, the ones with ideas, are a reaction of indifference to the culture crisis. It really is despair. All they know is what they don't want to do."

"That is easier," Alan says genially.

"It's not altogether unhealthy," Sam says. "It's a corrective for smugness and a false value of the past, but it has created new false value." He thinks it worth emphasizing. "False value seems always to beget further false value."

"Define your terms," says Louise, the scientist.

"No, look," Sam says, "there's no revolt, there's no acceptance. Kids today don't want to get married, and—"

Eleanor interrupts. "Why should a girl rush to get married? She loses all chance for developing herself."

Sam shrugs. They are all talking at once. "Kids don't want to get married," he repeats, "and they don't want not to get married. They merely drift."

"It's a problem we'll all have to face with our own kids in ten years," Alan says, "although I think you make too much of it, Sam."

"My daughter," Marvin states. "She's embarrassed I'm a dentist. Even more embarrassed than I am." They laugh.

Sam tells a story about his youngest, Carol Ann. It seems he had a fight with her, and she went to her room. Sam followed, he called through the door.

"No answer," Sam says. "I called her again, 'Carol Ann.' I was a little worried you understand, because she seemed so upset, so I said to her, 'Carol Ann, you know I love you.' What do you think she answered?"

"What?" asks Roslyn.

"She said, 'Daddie, why are you so anxious?' "

They all laugh again. There are murmurs about what a clever thing it was to say. In the silence which follows, Roslyn leans forward and says quickly in her high voice, "You must get Alan to tell you his wonderful story about the man who studied yogi."

"Yoga," Alan corrects. "It's too long to tell."

The company prevails on him.

"Well," says Alan, in his genial courtroom voice, "it concerns a friend of mine named Cassius O'Shaugnessy."

"You don't mean Jerry O'Shaugnessy, do you?" asks Sam.

Alan does not know Jerry O'Shaugnessy. "No, no, this is Cassius O'Shaugnessy," he says. "He's really quite an extraordinary fellow." Alan sits plumply in his chair, fingering his bow tie. They are all used to his stories, which are told in a formal style and exhibit the attempt to recapture a certain note of urbanity, wit, and *élan* which Alan has probably copied from someone else. Sam and Eleanor respect his ability to tell these stories, but they resent the fact that he talks *at* them.

"You'd think we were a jury of his inferiors," Eleanor has said. "I hate being talked down to." What she resents is Alan's quiet implication that his antecedents, his social position, in total his life outside the room is superior to the life within. Eleanor now takes the promise from Alan's story by remarking, "Yes, and let's see the movie when Alan has finished."

"Ssh," Roslyn says.

"Cassius was at college a good while before me," says Alan, "but I knew him while I was an undergraduate. He would drop in and visit from time to time. An absolutely extraordinary fellow. The most amazing career. You see, he's done about everything."

"I love the way Alan tells it," Roslyn pipes nervously.

"Cassius was in France with Dos Passos and Cummings, he was even arrested with e.e. After the war, he was one of the founders of the Dadaist school, and for a while I understand he was Fitzgerald's guide to the gold of the Côte d'Azur. He knew everybody, he did everything. Do you realize that before the twenties had ended, Cassius had managed his father's business and then entered a monastery? It is said he influenced T. S. Eliot."

"Today, we'd call Cassius a psychopath," Marvin observes.

"Cassius called himself a great dilettante," Alan answers, "although perhaps the nineteenth-century Russian conception of the great sinner would be more appropriate. What do you say if I tell you this was only the beginning of his career?"

"What's the point?" Louise asks.

"Not yet," says Alan, holding up a hand. His manner seems to say that if his audience cannot appreciate the story, he does not feel obliged to continue. "Cassius studied Marx in the monastery. He broke his vows, quit the Church, and became a Communist. All through the thirties he was a figure in the Party, going to Moscow, involved in all the Party struggles. He left only during the Moscow trials."

Alan's manner while he relates such stories is somewhat effeminate. He talks with little caresses of his hand, he mentions names and places with a lingering ease as if to suggest that his audience and he are aware, above all, of nuance. The story as Alan tells it is drawn overlong. Suffice it that the man about whom he is talking, Cassius O'Shaugnessy, becomes a Trotskyist, becomes an anarchist, is a pacifist during the second World War, and suffers it from a prison cell.

"I may say," Alan goes on, "that I worked for his defense, and was successful in getting him acquitted. Imagine my dolor when I learned that he had turned his back on his anarchist friends and was living with gangsters."

"This is weird," Eleanor says.

"Weird, it is," Alan agrees. "Cassius got into some scrape, and disappeared. What could you do with him? I learned only recently that he had gone to India and was studying yoga. In fact, I learned it from Cassius himself. I asked him of his experiences at Brahna-puth-thar, and he told me the following story."

Now Alan's voice alters, he assumes the part of Cassius and speaks in a tone weary of experience, wise and sad in its knowledge. " 'I was sitting on my haunches contemplating my naval,' Cassius said to me, 'when of a sudden I discovered my navel under a different aspect. It seemed to me that if I were to give a counter-clockwise twist, my navel would unscrew.' "

Alan looks up, he surveys his audience which is now rapt and uneasy, not certain as yet whether a joke is to come. Alan's thumb and forefinger pluck at the middle of his ample belly, his feet are crossed upon the carpet in symbolic suggestion of Cassius upon his haunches.

" 'Taking a deep breath, I turned, and the abysses of Vishtarni loomed beneath. My navel had begun to unscrew. I knew I was about to accept the reward of three years of contemplation. So,' said Cassius, 'I turned and I turned,' " Alan's fingers now revolving upon his belly, " 'and after a period I knew that with one more turn my navel would unscrew itself forever. At the edge of revelation, I took one sweet breath, and turned my navel free.' "

Alan looks up at his audience.

" 'Damn,' said Cassius, 'if my ass didn't fall off.' "

4

The story has left the audience in an exasperated mood. It has been a most untypical story for Alan to tell, a little out of place, not offensive exactly, but irritating and inconsequential. Sam is the only one to laugh with more than bewildered courtesy, and his mirth seems excessive to everyone but Alan, and of course, Roslyn, who feels as if she has been the producer. I suppose what it reduces to, is a lack of taste. Perhaps that is why Alan is not the lawyer one would expect. He does not have that appreciation—as necessary in his trade as for an actor—of what is desired at any moment, of that which will encourage as opposed to that which does not encourage a stimulating but smooth progression of logic and sentiment. Only a fool would tell so long a story when everyone is awaiting the movie.

Now, they are preparing. The men shift armchairs to correspond with the couch, the projector is set up, the screen is unfolded. Sam attempts to talk while he is threading the film, but no one listens. They seem to realize suddenly that a frightful demand has been placed upon them. One does not study pornography in a living room with a beer glass in one's hand, and friends at the elbow. It is the most unsatisfactory of compromises; one can draw neither the benefits of solitary contemplation nor of social exchange. There is, at bottom, the same exasperated fright which one experiences in turning the shower tap and receiving cold water when the flesh has been prepared for heat. Perhaps that is why they are laughing so much now that the movie is begun.

A title, *The Evil Act,* twitches on the screen, shot with scars, holes, and the dust lines of age. A man and woman are sitting on a couch, they are having coffee. They chat. What they say is conveyed by printed words upon an ornately flowered card, interjected between glimpses of their casual gestures, a cup to the mouth, a smile, a cigarette being lit. The man's name, it seems, is Frankie Idell; he is talking to his wife, Magnolia. Frankie is dark, he is sinister, he confides in Magnolia, his dark counterpart, with a grimace of his brows, black from make-up pencil.

This is what the titles read:

Frankie: She will be here soon.
Magnolia: This time the little vixen will not escape.
Frankie: No, my dear, this time we are prepared. (*He looks at his watch.*)
Frankie: Listen, she knocks!

There is a shot of a tall blond woman knocking on the door. She is probably over thirty, but by her short dress and ribboned hat it is suggested that she is a girl of fifteen.

Frankie: Come in, Eleanor.

As may be expected, the audience laughs hysterically at this. It is so wonderful a coincidence. "How I remember Frankie," says Eleanor Slovoda, and Roslyn Sperber is the only one not amused. In the midst of the others' laughter, she says in a worried tone, obviously adrift upon her own concerns, "Do you think we'll have to stop the film in the middle to let the bulb cool off?" The others hoot, they giggle, they are weak from the combination of their own remarks and the action of the plot.

Frankie and Magnolia have sat down on either side of the heroine, Eleanor. A moment passes. Suddenly, stiffly, they attack. Magnolia from her side kisses Eleanor, and Frankie commits an indecent caress.

Eleanor: How dare you? Stop!
Magnolia: Scream, my little one. It will do you no good. The walls are soundproofed.
Frankie: We've fixed a way to make you come across.
Eleanor: This is hideous. I am hitherto undefiled. Do not touch me!

The captions fade away. A new title takes their place. It says, *But There Is No Escape From The Determined Pair.* On the fade-in, we discover Eleanor in the most distressing situation. Her hands are tied to loops running from the ceiling, and she can only writhe in helpless perturbation before the deliberate and progressive advances of Frankie and Magnolia. Slowly they humiliate her, with relish they probe her.

The audience laughs no longer. A hush has come upon them. Eyes unblinking they devour the images upon Sam Slovoda's screen.

Eleanor is without clothing. As the last piece is pulled away, Frankie and Magnolia circle about her in a grotesque of pantomime, a leering of lips, limbs in a distortion of desire. Eleanor faints. Adroitly, Magnolia cuts her bonds. We see Frankie carrying her inert body.

Now, Eleanor is trussed to a bed, and the husband and wife are tormenting her with feathers. Bodies curl upon the bed in postures so complicated, in combinations so advanced, that the audience leans forward, Sperbers, Rossmans, and Slovodas, as if tempted to embrace the moving images. The hands trace abstract circles upon the screen, passes and recoveries upon a white background so illuminated that hollows and swells, limb to belly and mouth to undescribables, tip of a nipple, orb of a navel, swim in giant magnification, flow and slide in a lurching yawing fall, blotting out the camera eye.

A little murmur, all unconscious, passes from their lips. The audience sways each now finally lost in himself, communing hungrily with shadows, violated or violating, fantasy triumphant.

At picture's end, Eleanor the virgin whore is released from the bed. She kisses Frankie, she kisses Magnolia. "You dears," she says, "let's do it again." The projector lamp burns empty light, the machine keeps turning, the tag of film goes *slap-tap, slap-tap, slap-tap, slap-tap, slap-tap, slap-tap.*

"Sam, turn it off," says Eleanor.

But when the room lights are on, they cannot look at one another. "Can we see it again?" someone mutters. So, again, Eleanor knocks on the door, is tied, defiled, ravished, and made rapturous. They watch it soberly now, the room hot with the heat of their bodies, the darkness a balm for orgiastic vision. To the Deer Park, Sam is thinking, to the Deer Park of Louis XV were brought the most beautiful maidens of France, and there they stayed, dressed in fabulous silks, perfumed and wigged, the mole drawn upon their cheek, ladies of pleasure awaiting the pleasure of the king. So Louis had stripped an empire, bankrupt a treasury, prepared a deluge, while in his garden on summer evenings the maidens performed their pageants, eighteenth-century tableaux of the evil act, beauteous instruments of one man's desire, lewd translation of a king's power. That century men sought wealth so they might use its fruits; this epoch men lusted for power in order to amass more power, a compounding of power into pyramids of abstraction whose yield are cannon and wire enclosure, pillars of statistics to the men who are the kinds of this century and do no more in power's leisure time than go to church, claim to love their wives, and eat vegetables.

Is it possible, Sam wonders, that each of them here, two Rossmans, two Sperbers, two Slovodas, will cast off their clothes when the movie is done and perform the orgy which tickles at the heart of their desire? They will not, he knows, they will make jokes when the projector is put away, they will gorge the plate of delicatessen Eleanor provides, and swallow more beer, he among them. He will be the first to make jokes.

Sam is right. The movie has made him extraordinarily alive to the limits of them all. While they sit with red faces, eyes bugged, glutting sandwiches of ham, salami, and tongue, he begins the teasing.

"Roslyn," he calls out, "is the bulb cooled off yet?"

She cannot answer him. She chokes on beer, her face glazes, she is helpless with self-protecting laughter.

"Why are you so anxious, Daddie?" Eleanor says quickly.

They begin to discuss the film. As intelligent people they must dominate it. Someone wonders about the actors in the piece, and discussion begins afresh. "I fail to see," says Louise, "why they should be hard to classify. Pornography is a job to the criminal and prostitute element."

"No, you won't find an ordinary prostitute doing this," Sam insists. "It requires a particular kind of personality."

"They have to be exhibitionists," says Eleanor.

"It's all economic," Louise maintains.

"I wonder what those girls felt?" Roslyn asks. "I feel sorry for them."

"I'd like to be the cameraman," says Alan.

"I'd like to be Frankie," says Marvin sadly.

There is a limit to how long such a conversation may continue. The jokes lapse into silence. They are all busy eating. When they begin to talk again, it is of other things. Each dollop of food sops the agitation which the movie has spilled. They gossip about the party the night before, they discuss which single men were interested in which women, who got drunk, who got sick, who said the wrong thing, who went home with someone else's date. When this is exhausted, one of them mentions a play the others have not seen. Soon they are talking about books, a concert, a one-man show by an artist who is a friend. Dependably, conversation will voyage its orbit. While the men talk of politics, the women are discussing fashions, progressive schools, and recipes they have attempted. Sam is uncomfortable with the division; he knows Eleanor will resent it, he knows she will complain later of the insularity of men and the basic contempt they feel for women's intelligence.

"But you collaborated," Sam will argue. "No one forced you to be with the women."

"Was I to leave them alone?" Eleanor will answer.

"Well, why do the women always have to go off by themselves?"

"Because the men aren't interested in what we have to say."

Sam sighs. He has been talking with interest, but really he is bored. These are nice pleasant people, he thinks, but they are ordinary people, exactly the sort he has spent so many years with, making little jokes, little gossip, living little everyday events, a close circle where everyone mothers the other by his presence. The womb of middle-class life, Sam decides heavily. He is in a bad mood indeed. Everything is laden with dissatisfaction.

Alan has joined the women. He delights in preparing odd dishes when friends visit the Sperbers, and he is describing to Eleanor how he makes blueberry pancakes. Marvin draws closer to Sam.

"I wanted to tell you," he says, "Alan's story reminded me. I saw Jerry O'Shaugnessy the other day."

"Where was he?"

Marvin is hesitant. "It was a shock, Sam. He's on the Bowery. I guess he's become a wino."

"He always drank a lot," says Sam.

"Yeah." Marvin cracks his bony knuckles. "What a stinking time this is, Sam."

"It's probably like the years after 1905 in Russia," Sam says.

"No revolutionary party will come out of this."

"No," Sam says, "nothing will come."

He is thinking of Jerry O'Shaugnessy. What did he look like? what did he say? Sam asks Marvin, and clucks his tongue at the dispiriting answer. It is a shock to him. He draws closer to Marvin, he feels a bond. They have, after all, been through some years together. In the thirties they have been in the Communist Party, they have quit together, they are both weary of politics today, still radicals out of habit, but without enthusiasm and without a cause. "Jerry was a hero to me," Sam says.

"To all of us," says Marvin.

The fabulous Jerry O'Shaugnessy, thinks Sam. In the old days, in the Party, they had made a legend of him. All of them with their middle-class origins and their desire to know a worker-hero.

I may say that I was never as fond of Jerry O'Shaugnessy as was Sam. I thought him a showman and too pleased with himself. Sam, however, with his timidity, his desire to travel, to have adventure and know many women, was obliged to adore O'Shaugnessy. At least he was enraptured with his career.

Poor Jerry who ends as a bum. He has been everything else. He has been a trapper in Alaska, a chauffeur for gangsters, an officer in the Foreign Legion, a labor organizer. His nose was broken, there were scars on his chin. When he would talk about his years at sea or his experiences in Spain, the stenographers and garment workers, the radio writers and unemployed actors would listen to his speeches as if he were the prophet of new romance, and their blood would be charged with the magic of revolutionary vision. A man with tremendous charm. In those days it had been easy to confuse his love for himself with his love for all underprivileged workingmen.

"I thought he was still in the Party," Sam says.

"No," says Marvin, "I remember they kicked him out a couple of years ago. He was supposed to have piddled some funds, that's what they say."

"I wish he'd taken the treasury," Sam remarks bitterly. "The Party used him for years."

Marvin shrugs. "They used each other." His mustache droops. "Let me tell you about Sonderson. You know he's still in the Party.The most progressive dentist in New York." They laugh.

While Marvin tells the story, Sam is thinking of other things. Since he has quit Party work, he has studied a great deal. He can tell you about prison camps and the secret police, political murders, the Moscow trials, the exploitation of Soviet labor, the privileges of the bureaucracy; it is all painful to him. He is straddled between the loss of a country he has never seen, and his repudiation of the country in which he lives. "Doesn't the Party seem a horror now?" he bursts out.

Marvin nods. They are trying to comprehend the distance between

Party members they have known, people by turn pathetic, likable, or annoying—people not unlike themselves—and in contrast the immensity of historic logic which deploys along statistics of the dead.

"It's all schizoid," Sam says. "Modern life is schizoid."

Marvin agrees. They have agreed on this many times, bored with the petulance of their small voices, yet needing the comfort of such complaints. Marvin asks Sam if he has given up his novel, and Sam says, "Temporarily." He cannot find a form, he explains. He does not want to write a realistic novel, because reality is no longer realistic. "I don't know what it is," says Sam. "To tell you the truth, I think I'm kidding myself. I'll never finish this book. I just like to entertain the idea I'll do something good some day." They sit there in friendly depression. Conversation has cooled. Alan and the women are no longer talking.

"Marvin," asks Louise, "what time is it?"

They are ready to go. Sam must say directly what he had hoped to approach by suggestion. "I was wondering," he whispers to Rossman, "would you mind if I held onto the film for a day or two?"

Marvin looks at him. "Oh, why of course, Sam," he says in his morose voice. "I know how it is." He pats Sam on the shoulder as if, symbolically, to convey the exchange of ownership. They are fellow conspirators.

"If you ever want to borrow the projector," Sam suggests.

"Nah," says Marvin, "I don't know that it would make much difference."

It has been, when all is said, a most annoying day. As Sam and Eleanor tidy the apartment, emptying ash trays and washing the few dishes, they are fond neither of themselves nor each other. "What a waste today has been," Eleanor remarks, and Sam can only agree. He has done no writing, he has not been outdoors, and still it is late in the evening, and he has talked too much, eaten too much, is nervous from the movie they have seen. He knows that he will watch it again with Eleanor before they go to sleep; she has given her assent to that. But as is so often the case with Sam these days, he cannot await their embrace with any sure anticipation. Eleanor may be in the mood or Eleanor may not; there is no way he can control the issue. It is depressing; Sam knows that he circles about Eleanor at such times with the guilty maneuvers of a sad hound. Resent her as he must, be furious with himself as he will, there is not very much he can do about it. Often, after they have made love, they will lie beside each other in silence, each offended, each certain the other is to blame. At such times, memory tickles them with a cruel feather. Not always has it been like this. When they were first married, and indeed for the six months they lived together before marriage, everything was quite different. Their affair was very exciting to them; each told the other with some hyperbole but no real mistruth that no one in the past had ever been comparable as lover.

I suppose I am a romantic. I always feel that this is the best time in people's lives. There is, after all, so little we accomplish, and that short period when we are beloved and triumph as lovers is sweet with power. Rarely are we concerned then with our lack of importance; we are too important. In Sam's case, disillusion means even more. Like so many young men, he entertained the secret conceit that he was an extraordinary lover. One cannot really believe this without supporting at the same time the equally secret conviction that one is fundamentally inept. It is— no matter what Sergius would say—a more dramatic and therefore more attractive view of oneself than the sober notion which Sam now accepts with grudging wisdom, that the man as lover is dependent upon the bounty of the woman. As I say, he accepts the notion, it is one of the lineaments of maturity, but there is a part of him which, no matter how harried by analysis, cannot relinquish the antagonism he feels that Eleanor has respected his private talent so poorly, and has not allowed him to confer its benefits upon more women. I mock Sam, but he would mock himself on this. It hardly matters; mockery cannot accomplish everything, and Sam seethes with that most private and tender pain: even worse than being unattractive to the world is to be unattractive to one's mate; or, what is the same and describes Sam's case more accurately, never to know in advance when he shall be undesirable to Eleanor.

I make perhaps too much of the subject, but that is only because it is so important to Sam. Relations between Eleanor and him are not really that bad—I know other couples who have much less or nothing at all. But comparisons are poor comfort to Sam; his standards are so high. So are Eleanor's. I am convinced the most unfortunate people are those who would make an art of love. It sours other effort. Of all artists, they are certainly the most wretched.

Shall I furnish a model? Sam and Eleanor are on the couch and the projector, adjusted to its slowest speed, is retracing the elaborate pantomime of the three principals. If one could allow these shadows a life . . . but indeed such life has been given them. Sam and Eleanor are no more than an itch, a smart, a threshold of satisfaction; the important share of themselves has steeped itself in Frankie-, Magnolia-, and Eleanor-of-the-film. Indeed the variations are beyond telling. It is the most outrageous orgy performed by five ghosts.

Self-critical Sam! He makes love in front of a movie, and one cannot say that it is unsatisfactory any more than one can say it is pleasant. It is dirty, downright porno dirty, it is a lewd slop-brush slapped through the middle of domestic exasperations and breakfast eggs. It is so dirty that only half of Sam—he is quite divisible into fractions—can be exercised at all. The part that is his brain worries along like a cuckolded burgher. He is taking the pulse of his anxiety. Will he last long enough to satisfy Eleanor? Will the children come back tonight? He cannot help it. In the midst of the circus, he is suddenly convinced the children will walk through the door. "Why are you so anxious, Daddie?"

So it goes. Sam the lover is conscious of exertion. One moment he is Frankie Idell, destroyer of virgins—take that! you whore!—the next, body moving, hands caressing, he is no more than some lines from a psychoanalytical text. He is thinking about the sensitivity of his scrotum. He has read that this is a portent of femininity in a male. How strong is his latent homosexuality worries Sam, thrusting stiffly, warm sweat running cold. Does he identify with Eleanor-of-the-film?

Technically, the climax is satisfactory. They lie together in the dark, the film ended, the projector humming its lonely revolutions in the quiet room. Sam gets up to turn it off; he comes back and kisses Eleanor upon the mouth. Apparently, she has enjoyed herself more than he; she is tender and fondles the tip of his nose.

"You know, Sam," she says from her space beside him, "I think I saw this picture before."

"When?"

"Oh, you know when. That time."

Sam thinks dully that women are always most loving when they can reminisce about infidelity.

"That time!" he repeats.

"I think so."

Racing forward from memory like the approaching star which begins as a point on the mind and swells to explode the eyeball with its odious image, Sam remembers, and is weak in the dark. It is ten years, eleven perhaps, before they were married, yet after they were lovers. Eleanor has told him, but she has always been vague about details. There had been two men it seemed, and another girl, and all had been drunk. They had seen movie after movie. With reluctant fascination, Sam can conceive the rest. How it had pained him, how excited him. It is years now since he has remembered, but he remembers. In the darkness he wonders at the unreasonableness of jealous pain. That night was impossible to imagine any longer—therefore it is more real; Eleanor his plump wife who presses a pigeon's shape against her housecoat, forgotten heroine of black orgies. It had been meaningless, Eleanor claimed; it was Sam she loved, and the other had been no more than a fancy of which she wished to rid herself. Would it be the same today, thinks Sam, or had Eleanor been loved by Frankie, by Frankie of the other movies, by Frankie of the two men she never saw again on that night so long ago?

The pleasure I get from this pain, Sam thinks furiously.

It is not altogether perverse. If Eleanor causes him pain, it means after all that she is alive for him. I have often observed that the reality of a person depends upon his ability to hurt us; Eleanor as the vague accusing embodiment of the wife is different, altogether different, from Eleanor who lies warmly in Sam's bed, an attractive Eleanor who may wound his flesh. Thus, brother to the pleasure of pain, is the sweeter pleasure which follows pain. Sam, tired, lies in Eleanor's arms, and they talk with the cozy trade words of old professionals, agreeing that they will not make love again before a movie, that it was exciting but also not without detachment, that all in all it has been good but not quite right, that she had loved this action he had done, and was uncertain about another. It is their old familiar critique, a sign that they are intimate and well disposed. They do not talk about the act when it has failed to fire; then they go silently to sleep. But now, Eleanor's enjoyment having mollified Sam's sense of no enjoyment, they talk with the apologetics and encomiums of familiar mates. Eleanor falls asleep, and Sam falls almost asleep, curling next to her warm body, his hand over her round belly with the satisfaction of a sculptor. He is drowsy, and he thinks drowsily that these few moments of creature-pleasure, this brief compassion he can feel for the body that trusts itself to sleep beside him, his comfort in its warmth, is perhaps all the meaning he may ask for his life. That out of disappointment, frustration, and the passage of dreary years come these few moments when he is close to her, and their years together possess a connotation more rewarding than the sum of all which has gone into them.

But then he thinks of the novel he wants to write, and he is wide-awake again. Like the sleeping pill which fails to work and leaves one warped in an exaggeration of the ills which sought the drug, Sam passes through the promise of sex-emptied sleep, and is left with nervous loins, swollen jealousy of an act ten years dead, and sweating irritable resentment of the woman's body which hinders his limbs. He has wasted the day, he tells himself, he has wasted the day as he has wasted so many days of his life, and tomorrow in the office he will be no more than his ten fingers typing plot and words for Bramba the Venusian and Lee-Lee Deeds, Hollywood Star, while that huge work with which he has cheated himself, holding it before him as a covenant of his worth, that enormous novel which would lift him at a bound from the impasse in which he stifles, whose dozens of characters would develop a vision of life in bountiful complexity, lies foundered, rotting on a beach of purposeless effort. Notes here, pages there, it sprawls through a formless wreck of incidental ideas and half-episodes, utterly without shape. He has not even a hero for it.

One could not have a hero today, Sam thinks, a man of action and contemplation, capable of sin, large enough for good, a man immense. There is only a modern hero damned by no more than the ugliness of wishes whose satisfaction he will never know. One needs a man who could walk the stage, someone who—no matter who, not himself. Someone, Sam thinks, who reasonably could not exist.

The novelist, thinks Sam, perspiring beneath blankets, must live in paranoia and seek to be one with the world; he must be terrified of experience and hungry for it; he must think himself nothing and believe he is superior to all. The feminine in his nature cries for proof he is a man; he dreams of power and is without capacity to gain it; he loves himself above all and therefore despises all that he is.

He is that, thinks Sam, he is part of the perfect prescription, and yet he is not a novelist. He lacks energy and belief. It is left for him to write an article some day about the temperament of the ideal novelist.

In the darkness, memories rise, yeast-swells of apprehension. Out of bohemian days so long ago, comes the friend of Eleanor, a girl who had been sick and was committed to an institution. They visited her, Sam and Eleanor, they took the suburban train and sat on the lawn of the asylum grounds while patients circled about intoning a private litany, or shuddering in boob-blundering fright from an insect that crossed their skin. The friend had been silent. She had smiled, she had answered their questions with the fewest words, and had returned again to her study of sunlight and blue sky. As they were about to leave, the girl had taken Sam aside. "They violate me," she said in a whisper. "Every night when the doors are locked, they come to my room and they make the movie. I am the heroine and am subjected to all variety of sexual viciousness. Tell them to leave me alone so I may enter the convent." And while she talked, in a horror of her body, one arm scrubbed the other. Poor tortured friend. They had seen her again, and she babbled, her face had coarsened into an idiot leer.

Sam sweats. There is so little he knows, and so much to know. Youth of the depression with its economic terms, what can he know of madness or religion? They are both so alien to him. He is the mongrel, Sam thinks, brought up without religion from a mother half Protestant and half Catholic, and a father half Catholic and half Jew. He is the quarter-Jew, and yet he is a Jew, or so he feels himself, knowing nothing of Gospel, tabernacle, or Mass, the Jew through accident, through state of mind. What . . . whatever did he know of penance? self-sacrifice? mortification of the flesh? the love of his fellow man? Am I concerned with my relation to God? ponders Sam, and smiles sourly in the darkness. No, that has never concerned him, he thinks, not for better nor for worse. "They are making the movie," says the girl into the ear of memory, "and so I cannot enter the convent."

How hideous was the mental hospital. A concentration camp, decides Sam. Perhaps it would be the world some day, or was that only his projection of feelings of hopelessness? "Do not try to solve the problems of the world," he hears from Sergius, and pounds a lumpy pillow.

However could he organize his novel? What form to give it? It is so complex. Too loose, thinks Sam, too scattered. Will he ever fall asleep? Wearily, limbs tense, his stomach too keen, he plays again the game of putting himself to sleep. "I do not feel my toes," Sam says to himself, "my toes are dead, my calves are asleep, my calves are sleeping . . ."

In the middle from wakefulness to slumber, in the torpor which floats beneath blankets, I give an idea to Sam. "Destroy time, and chaos may be ordered," I say to him.

"Destroy time, and chaos may be ordered," he repeats after me, and in desperation to seek his coma, mutters back, "I do not feel my nose, my nose is numb, my eyes are heavy, my eyes are heavy."

So Sam enters the universe of sleep, a man who seeks to live in such a way as to avoid pain, and succeeds merely in avoiding pleasure. What a dreary compromise is life!

MURIEL RUKEYSER
Nuns in the Wind

As I came out of the New York Public Library
you said your influence on my style would be noticed
and from now on there would be happy poems.
                        It was at that moment
the street was assaulted by a covey of nuns
going directly toward the physics textbooks.
Tragic fiascos shadowed that whole spring.
The children sang streetfuls, and I thought:
O to be the King in the carol
kissed and at peace; but recalling Costa Brava
the little blossoms in the mimosa tree
and later, the orange cliff, after they sent me out,
I knew there was no peace.
                        You smiled, saying   :   Take it easy.

That was the year of the five-day fall of cities.
        First day, no writers. Second, no telephones. Third,
        no venereal diseases. Fourth, no income tax. And on
        the fifth, at noon.
The nuns blocked the intersections, reading.
I used to go walking in the triangle of park,
seeing that locked face, the coarse enemy skin,
the eyes with all the virtues of a good child,
but no child was there, even when I thought, Child!
the 4 a.m. cop could never understand.
You said, not smiling, You are the future for me,
but you were the present and immediate moment
and I am empty-armed without, until to me is given
two lights to carry   :   my life and the light of my death.

If the wind would rise, those black throbbing umbrellas
fly downstreet, the flapping robes unfolding,

my dream would be over, poisons cannot linger
when the wind rises. . . .

All that year, the classical declaration of war was lacking.
There was a lot of lechery and disorder.
And I am queen on that island.

Well, I said suddenly in the tall and abstract room,
time to wake up.
Now make believe you can help yourself alone.
And there it was, the busy crosstown noontime
crossing, peopled with nuns.
                    Now, bragging now,
the flatfoot slambang victory,
                    thanks to a trick of wind
will you see faces blow, and though their bodies
by God's grace will never blow,
cities shake in the wind, the year's over,
calendars tear, and their clothes blow. O yes!

JAMES ALAN McPHERSON
Gold Coast

That spring, when I had a great deal of potential and no money at all, I took a job as a janitor. That was when I was still very young and spent money very freely, and when, almost every night, I drifted off to sleep lulled by sweet anticipation of that time when my potential would suddenly be realized and there would be capsule biographies of my life on dust jackets of many books, all proclaiming: ". . . He knew life on many levels. From shoeshine boy, free-lance waiter, 3rd cook, janitor, he rose to . . ." I had never been a janitor before and I did not really have to be one and that is why I did it. But now, much later, I think it might have been because it is possible to be a janitor without really becoming one, and at parties or at mixers when asked what it was I did for a living, it was pretty good to hook my thumbs in my vest pockets and say comfortably: "Why, I am an apprentice janitor." The hippies would think it degenerate and really dig me and it made me feel good that people in Philosophy and Law and Business would feel uncomfortable trying to make me feel better about my station while wondering how the hell I had managed to crash the party.

"What's an apprentice janitor?" they would ask.

"I haven't got my card yet," I would reply. "Right now I'm just taking lessons. There's lots of complicated stuff you have to learn before you get your card and your own building."

"What kind of stuff?"

"Human nature, for one thing. *Race* nature, for another."

"Why race?"

"Because," I would say in a low voice looking around lest someone else should overhear, "you have to be able to spot Jews and Negroes who are passing."

"That's terrible," would surely be said then with a hint of indignation.

"It's an art," I would add masterfully.

After a good pause I would invariably be asked: "But you're a Negro yourself, how can you keep your own people out?"

At which point I would look terribly disappointed and say: "*I don't keep them out. But if they get in it's my job to make their stay just as miserable as possible. Things are changing.*"

Now the speaker would just look at me in disbelief.

"It's Janitorial Objectivity," I would say to finish the thing as the speaker began to edge away. "Don't hate me," I would call after him to his considerable embarrassment. "Somebody has to do it."

It was an old building near Harvard Square. Conrad Aiken had once lived there and in the days of the Gold Coast, before Harvard built its great Houses, it had been a very fine haven for the rich; but that was a world ago and this building was one of the few monuments of that era which had survived. The lobby had a high ceiling with thick redwood beams and it was replete with marble floor, fancy ironwork, and an old-fashioned house telephone that no longer worked. Each apartment had a small fireplace, and even the large bathtubs and chain toilets, when I was having my touch of nature, made me wonder what prominent personage of the past had worn away all the newness. And, being there, I felt a certain affinity toward the rich.

It was a funny building; because the people who lived there made it old. Conveniently placed as it was between the Houses and Harvard Yard, I expected to find it occupied by a company of hippies, hopeful working girls, and assorted graduate students. Instead, there were a majority of old maids, dowagers, asexual middle-aged men, homosexual young men, a few married couples and a teacher. No one was shacking up there, and walking through the quiet halls in the early evening, I sometimes had the urge to knock on a door and expose myself just to hear someone breathe hard for once.

It was a Cambridge spring: down by the Charles happy students were making love while sad-eyed middle-aged men watched them from the bridge. It was a time of activity: Law students were busy sublimating, Business School people were making records of the money they would make, the Harvard Houses were clearing out, and in the Square bearded pot-pushers were setting up their restaurant tables in anticipation of the Summer School faithfuls. There was a change of season in the air, and to comply with its urgings, James Sullivan, the old superintendent, passed his three beaten garbage cans on to me with the charge that I should take up his daily rounds of the six floors, and with unflinching humility, gather whatever scraps the old-maid tenants had refused to husband.

I then became very rich, with my own apartment, a sensitive girl, a stereo, two speakers, one tattered chair, one fork, a job, and the urge to acquire. Having all this and youth besides made me pity Sullivan: he had been in that building thirty years and had its whole history recorded in the little folds of his mind, as his own life was recorded in the wrinkles of his face. All he had to show for his time there was a berserk dog, a wife almost as mad as the dog, three cats, bursitis, acute myopia, and a drinking problem. He was well over seventy and could hardly walk, and his weekly check of twenty-two dollars from the company that managed the building would not support anything. So, out of compromise, he was retired to superintendent of my labor.

My first day as a janitor, while I skillfully lugged my three overflowing cans of garbage out of the building, he sat on his bench in the lobby, faded and old and smoking in patched, loose blue pants. He watched me. He was a chain smoker and I noticed right away that he very carefully dropped all of the ashes and butts on the floor and crushed them under his feet until there was a yellow and gray smear. Then he laboriously pushed the mess under the bench with his shoe, all the while eyeing me like a cat in silence as I hauled the many cans of muck out to the big disposal unit next to the building. When I had finished, he gave me two old plates to help stock my kitchen and his first piece of advice.

"Sit down, for Chrissake, and take a load off your feet," he told me.

I sat on the red bench next to him and accepted the wilted cigarette he offered me from the crushed package he kept in his sweater pocket.

"Now I'll tell you something to help you get along in the building," he said.

I listened attentively.

"If any of these sons-of-bitches ever ask you to do something extra, be sure to charge them for it."

I assured him that I absolutely would.

"If they can afford to live here, they can afford to pay. The bastards."

"Undoubtedly," I assured him again.

"And another thing," he added. "Don't let any of these girls shove any cat shit under your nose. That ain't your job. You tell them to put it in a bag and take it out themselves."

I reminded him that I knew very well my station in life, and that I was not about to haul cat shit or anything of that nature. He looked at me through his thick-lensed glasses. He looked like a cat himself. "That's right," he said at last. "And if they still try to sneak it in the trash be sure to make the bastards pay. They can afford it." He crushed his seventh butt on the floor and scattered the mess some more while he lit up another. "I never hauled out no cat shit in the thirty years I been here and you don't do it either."

"I'm going to wash my hands," I said.

"Remember," he called after me, "don't take no shit from any of them."

I protested once more that, upon my life, I would never, never do it, not even for the prettiest girl in the building. Going up in the elevator, I felt comfortably resolved that I would never do it. There were no pretty girls in the building.

I never found out what he had done before he came there, but I do know that being a janitor in that building was as high as he ever got in life. He had watched two generations of the rich pass the building on their way to the Yard, and he had seen many governors ride white horses thirty times into that same Yard to send sons and daughters of the rich out into life to produce, to acquire, to procreate and to send back sons and daughters so that the cycle would continue. He had watched the cycle from when he had been able to haul the cans out for himself, and now he could not, and he was bitter.

He was Irish, of course, and he took pride in Irish accomplishments when he could have none of his own. He had known Frank O'Connor when that writer had been at Harvard. He told me on many occasions how O'Connor had stopped to talk every day on his way to the Yard. He had also known James Michael Curley, and his most colorful memory of the man was a long ago day when he and James Curley sat in a Boston bar and one of Curley's runners had come in and said: "Hey Jim, Sol Bernstein the Jew wants to see you." And Curley, in his deep, memorial voice had said to James Sullivan: "Let us go forth and meet this Israelite Prince." These were his memories, and I would obediently put aside my garbage cans and laugh with him over the hundred or so colorful, insignificant little details which made up a whole lifetime of living in the basement of Harvard. And although they were of little value to me then, I knew that they were the reflections of a lifetime and the happiest moments he would ever have, being sold to me cheap, as youthful time is cheap, for as little time and interest as I wanted to spend. It was a buyer's market.

In those days I believed myself gifted with a boundless perception and attached my daily garbage route with a gusto superenforced by the happy knowledge that behind each of the fifty or so doors in our building lived a story which could, if I chose to grace it with the magic of my pen, become immortal. I watched my tenants fanatically, noting their perversions, their visitors, and their eating habits. So intense was my search for material that I had to restrain myself from going through their refuse scrap by scrap; but at the topmost layers of muck, without too much hand-soiling in the process, I set my perceptions to work. By late June, however, I had discovered only enough to put together a skimpy, rather naïve Henry Miller novel. The most colorful discoveries being:

1. The lady in #24 was an alumna of Paducah College.
2. The couple in #55 made love at least five hundred times a week and the wife had not yet discovered the pill.
3. The old lady in #36 was still having monthly inconvenience.
4. The two fatsos in #56 consumed nightly an extraordinary amount of chili.

5. The fat man in #54 had two dogs that were married to each other, but he was not married to anyone at all.

6. The middle-aged single man in #63 threw out an awful lot of flowers.

Disturbed by the snail's progress I was making, I confessed my futility to James one day as he sat on his bench chain-smoking and smearing butts on my newly waxed lobby floor. "So you want to know about the tenants?" he said, his cat's eyes flickering over me.

I nodded.

"Well the first thing to notice is how many Jews there are."

"I haven't noticed many Jews," I said.

He eyed me in amazement.

"Well, a few," I said quickly to prevent my treasured perception from being dulled any further.

"A few, hell," he said. "There's more Jews here than anybody."

"How can you tell?"

He gave me that undecided look again. "Where do you think all that garbage comes from?" He nooded feebly toward my bulging cans. I looked just in time to prevent a stray noodle from slipping over the brim. "That's right," he continued. "Jews are the biggest eaters in the world. They eat the best too."

I confessed then that I was of the chicken-soup generation and believed that Jews ate only enough to muster strength for their daily trips to the bank.

"Not so!" he replied emphatically. "You never heard the expression: 'Let's get to the restaurant before the Jews get there'?"

I shook my head sadly.

"You don't know that in certain restaurants they take the free onions and pickles off the tables when they see Jews coming?"

I held my head down in shame over the bounteous heap.

He trudged over to my can and began to turn back the leaves of noodles and crumpled tissues from #47 with his hand. After a few seconds of digging he unmucked an empty paté can. "Look at that," he said triumphantly. "Gourmet stuff, no less."

"That's from #44," I said.

"What else?" he said all-knowingly. "In 1946 a Swedish girl moved in up there and took a Jewish girl for her roommate. Then the Swedish girl moved out and there's been a Jewish Dynasty up there ever since."

I recalled that #44 was occupied by a couple that threw out a good number of S. S. Pierce cans, Chivas Regal bottles, assorted broken records, and back issues of *Evergreen* and the *Realist*.

"You're right," I said.

"Of course," he replied as if there was never any doubt. "I can spot them anywhere, even when they think they're passing." He leaned closer and said in a you-and-me voice: "But don't ever say anything bad about them in public, the Anti-Defamation League will get you."

Just then his wife screamed for him from the second floor, and the dog joined her and beat against the door. He got into the elevator painfully and said: "Don't ever talk about them in public. You don't know who they are and that Defamation League will take everything you got."

Sullivan did not really hate Jews. He was just bitter toward anyone better off than himself. He liked me because I seemed to like hauling garbage and because I listened to him and seemed to respect what he said and seemed to imply, by lingering on even when he repeated himself, that I was eager to take what wisdom he had for no other reason than that I needed it in order to get along.

He lived with his wife on the second floor and his apartment was very dirty because both of them were sick and old, and neither could move very well. His wife swept dirt out into the hall, and two hours, after I had mopped and waxed their section of the floor, there was sure to be a layer of dirt, grease, and crushed-scattered tobacco from their door to the end of the hall. There was a smell of dogs and cats and age and death about their door, and I did not ever want to have to go in there for any reason because I feared something about it I cannot name.

Mrs. Sullivan, I found out, was from South Africa. She loved animals much more than people and there was a great deal of pain in her face. She kept little pans of meat posted at strategic points about the building, and I often came across her in the early morning or late at night throwing scraps out of the second-floor window to stray cats. Once, when James was about to throttle a stray mouse in their apartment, she had screamed at him to give the mouse a sporting chance. Whenever she attempted to walk she had to balance herself against a wall or a rail, and she hated the building because it confined her. She also hated James and most of the tenants. On the other hand, she loved the *Johnny Carson Show,* she loved to sit outside on the front steps (because she could get no further unassisted), and she loved to talk to anyone who would stop to listen. She never spoke coherently except when she was cursing James, and then she had a vocabulary like a sailor. She had great, shrill lungs, and her screams, accompanied by the rabid barks of the dog, could be heard all over the building. She was never really clean, her teeth were bad, and the first most pathetic thing in the world was to see her sitting on the steps in the morning watching the world pass, in a stained smock and a fresh summer blue hat she kept just to wear downstairs, with no place in the world to go. James told me, on the many occasions of her screaming, that she was mentally disturbed and could not control herself. The admirable thing about him was the he never lost his temper with her, no matter how rough her curses became and no matter who heard them. And the second most pathetic thing in the world was to see them slowly making their way in Harvard Square, he supporting her, through the hurrying crowds of miniskirted summer girls, J-Pressed Ivy Leaguers, beatniks, and bused Japanese tourists, decked in cameras, who would take pictures of every inch of Harvard Square except them. Once, he told me, a hippie had brushed past them and called back over his shoulder: "Don't break any track records, Mr. and Mrs. Speedy Molasses."

Also on the second floor lived Miss O'Hara, a spinster who hated Sullivan as only an old maid can hate an old man. Across from her lived a very nice, gentle, celibate named Murphy who had once served with Montgomery in North Africa and who was now spending the rest of his life cleaning his little apartment and gossiping with Miss O'Hara. It was an Irish floor.

I never found out just why Miss O'Hara hated the Sullivans with such a passion. Perhaps it was because they were so unkempt and she was so superciliously clean. Perhaps it was because Miss O'Hara had a great deal of Irish pride and they were stereotyped Irish. Perhaps it was because she merely had no reason to like them. She was a fanatic about cleanliness and put out her little bit of garbage wrapped very neatly in yesterday's *Christian Science Monitor* and tied in a bow with a fresh piece of string. Collecting all those little neat packages, I would wonder where she got the string and imagined her at night picking meat-market locks with a hairpin and hobbling off with yards and yards of white cord concealed under the gray sweater she always wore. I could even imagine her back in her little apartment chuckling and rolling the cord into a great white ball by candlelight. Then she would stash it away in her breadbox. Miss O'Hara kept her door slightly open until late at night, and I suspected that she heard everything that went on in the building. I had the feeling that I should never dare to make love with gusto for fear that she would overhear and write down all my happy-time phrases, to be maliciously recounted to me if she were ever provoked.

She had been in the building longer than Sullivan, and I suppose that her greatest ambition in life was to outlive him and then attend his wake with a knitting ball and needles. She had been trying to get him fired for twenty-five years or so and did not know when to quit. On summer nights when I painfully mopped the second floor, she would offer me root beer, apples, or cupcakes while trying to pump me for evidence against him.

"He's just a filthy old man, Robert," she would declare in a little-old-lady whisper. "And don't think you have to clean up those dirty old butts of his. Just report him to the Company."

"Oh, I don't mind," I would tell her, gulping the root beer as fast as possible.

"Well, they're both a couple of lushes, if you ask me. They haven't been sober a day in twenty-five years."

"Well, she's sick too, you know."

"Ha!" She would throw up her hands in disgust. "She's only sick when he doesn't give her the booze."

I fought to keep down a burp. "How long have *you* been here?"

She motioned for me to step out of the hall and into her dark apartment. "Don't tell him,"—she nodded towards Sullivan's door—"but I've been here for thirty-four years." She waited for me to be taken aback. The she added: "And it was a better building before those two lushes came."

She then offered me an apple, asked five times if the dog's barking bothered me, forced me to take a fudge brownie, said that the cats had wet the floor again last night, got me to dust the top of a large chest too high for her to reach, had me pick up the minute specks of dust which fell from my dustcloth, pressed another root beer on me, and then showed me her family album. As an afterthought, she had me take down a big old picture of her great-grandfather, also too high for her to reach, so that I could dust that too. Then together we picked up the dust from it which might have fallen to the floor. "He's really a filthy old man, Robert," she said in closing, "and don't be afraid to report him to the property manager any time you want."

I assured her that I would do it at the slightest provocation from Sullivan, finally accepted an apple but refused the money she offered, and escaped back to my mopping. Even then she watched me, smiling, from her half-opened door.

"Why does Miss O'Hara hate you?" I asked James once.

He lifted his cigaretted hand and let the long ash fall elegantly to the floor. "That old bitch has been an albatross around my neck ever since I got here," he said. "Don't trust her, Robert. It was her kind that sat around singing hymns and watching them burn saints in this state."

There was never an adequate answer to my question. And even though the dog was noisy and would surely kill someone if it ever got loose, no one could really dislike the old man because of it. The dog was all they had. In his garbage each night, for every wine bottle, there would be an equally empty can of dog food. Some nights he took the brute out for a long walk, when he could barely walk himself, and both of them had to be led back to the building.

In those days I had forgotten that I was first of all a black and I had a very lovely girl who was not first of all a black. We were both young and optimistic then, and she believed with me in my potential and liked me partly because of it; and I was happy because she belonged to me and not to the race, which made her special. It made me special too because I did not have to wear a beard or hate or be especially hip or ultra-Ivy Leaguish. I did not have to smoke pot or supply her with it, or be for any other cause at all except myself. I only had to be myself, which pleased me; and I only had to produce, which pleased both of us. Like many of the artistically inclined rich, she wanted to own in someone else what she could not own in herself. But this I did not mind, and I forgave her for it because she forgave me moods and the constant smell of garbage and a great deal of latent hostility. She only minded James Sullivan and all the valuable time I was wasting listening to him rattle on and on. His conversations, she thought, were useless, repetitious, and promised nothing of value to me. She was accustomed to the old-rich whose conversations meandered around a leitmotiv of how well off they were and how much they would leave behind very soon. She was not at all cold, but she had been taught how to tolerate the old-poor and perhaps toss them a greeting in passing. But nothing more.

Sullivan did not like her when I first introduced them because he saw that she was not a hippie and could not be dismissed. It is in the nature of things that liberal people will tolerate two interracial hippies more than they will an intelligent, serious-minded mixed couple. The former liaison is easy to dismiss as the dregs of both races, deserving of each other and the contempt of both races; but the latter poses a threat because there is no immediacy or overpowering sensuality or "you-pick-my-fleas-I'll-pick-yours" apparent on the surface of things, and people, even the most publicly liberal, cannot dismiss it so easily.

"That girl is Irish, isn't she?" he had asked one day in my apartment soon after I had introduced them.

"No," I said definitely.

"What's her name again?"

"Judy Smith," I said, which was not her name at all.

"Well, I can spot it," he said. "She's got Irish blood, all right."

"Everybody's got a little Irish blood," I told him.

He looked at me cattily and craftily from behind his thick lenses. "Well, she's from a good family, I suppose."

"I suppose," I said.

He paused to let some ashes fall to the rug. "They say the Colonel's Lady and Nelly O'Grady are sisters under the skin." Then he added: "Rudyard Kipling."

"That's true," I said with equal innuendo, "that's why you have to maintain a distinction by marrying the Colonel's Lady."

An understanding passed between us then, and we never spoke more on the subject.

Almost every night the cats wet the second floor while Meg Sullivan watched the *Johnny Carson Show* and the dog howled and clawed the door. During commercials Meg would curse James to get out and stop dropping ashes on the floor or to take the dog out or something else, totally unintelligible to those of us on the fourth, fifth and sixth floors. Even after the *Carson Show* she would still curse him to get out, until finally he would go down to the basement and put away a bottle or two of wine. There was a steady stench of cat functions in the basement, and with all the grease and dirt, discarded trunks, beer bottles, chairs, old tools and the filthy sofa on which he sometimes slept, seeing him there made me want to cry. He drank the cheapest sherry, the wino kind, straight from the bottle; and on many nights that summer at 2:00 A.M. my phone would ring me out of bed.

"Rob? Jimmy Sullivan here. What are you doing?"

There was nothing suitable to say.

"Come on down to the basement for a drink."

"I have to be at work at eight-thirty," I would protest.

"Can't you have just one drink?" he would say pathetically.

I would carry down my own glass so that I would not have to drink out of the bottle. Looking at him on the sofa, I could not be mad because now I had many records for my stereo, a story that was going well, a girl who believed in me and belonged to me and not to the race, a new set of dishes, and a tomorrow morning with younger people.

"I don't want to burden you unduly," he would always preface.

I would force myself not to look at my watch and say: "Of course not."

"My Meg is not in the best health, you know," he would say, handing the bottle to me.

"She's just old."

"The doctors say she should be in an institution."

"That's no place to be."

"I'm a sick man myself, Rob. I can't take much more. She's crazy."

"Anybody who loves animals can't be crazy."

He took another long draw from the bottle. "I won't live another year. I'll be dead in a year."

"You don't know that."

He looked at me closely, without his glasses, so that I could see the desperation in his eyes. "I just hope Meg goes before I do. I don't want them to put her in an institution after I'm gone."

At 2:00 A.M. with the cat stench in my nose and a glass of bad sherry standing still in my hand because I refused in my mind to touch it, and when all my dreams of greatness were above him and the basement and the building itself, I did not know what to say. The only way I could keep from hating myself was to talk about the AMA or the Medicare program or hippies. He was pure hell on all three. To him, the medical profession was "morally bankrupt," Medicare was a great farce which deprived oldsters like himself of their "rainy-day dollars," and hippies were "dropouts from the human race." He could rage on and on in perfect phrases about all three of his major dislikes, and I had the feeling that because the sentences were so well constructed and well turned, he might have memorized them from something he had read. But then he was extremely well read and it did not matter if he had borrowed a phrase or two from someone else. The ideas were still his own.

It would be 3:00 A.M. before I knew it, and then 3:30, and still he would go on. He hated politicians in general and liked to recount, at these times, his private catalogue of political observations. By the time he got around to Civil Rights it would be 4:00 A.M., and I could not feel sorry or responsible for him at that hour. I would begin to yawn and at first he would just ignore it. Then I would start to edge toward the door, and he would see that he could hold me no longer, not even by declaring that he wanted to be an honorary Negro because he loved the race so much.

"I hope I haven't burdened you unduly," he would say again.

"Of course not," I would say, because it was over then and I could leave him and the smell of the cats there and sometimes I would go out in the cool night and walk around the Yard and be thankful that I was only an assistant janitor, and a transient one at that. Walking in the early dawn and seeing the Summer School fellows sneak out of the girls' dormitories in the Yard gave me a good feeling, and I thought that tomorrow night it would be good to make love myself so that I could be busy when he called.

"Why don't you tell that old man your job doesn't include baby-sitting with him?" Jean told me many times when she came over to visit during the day and found me sleeping.

I would look at her and think to myself about social forces and the pressures massing and poised, waiting to attack us. It was still July then. It was hot and I was working good. "He's just an old man," I said. "Who else would listen to him?"

"You're too soft. As long as you do your work you don't have to be bothered with him."

"He could be a story if I listened long enough."

"There are too many stories about old people."

"No," I said, thinking about us again, "there are just too many people who have no stories."

Sometimes he would come up and she would be there, but I would let him come in anyway, and he would stand in the room looking dirty and uncomfortable, offering some invented reason for having intruded. At these times something silent would pass between them, something I cannot name, which would reduce him to exactly what he was: an old man, come out of his basement to intrude where he was not wanted. But all the time this was being communicated, there would be a surface, friendly conversation between them. And after five minutes or so of being unwelcome, he would apologize for having come, drop a few ashes on the rug and back out the door. Downstairs we could hear his wife screaming.

We endured and aged and August was almost over. Inside the building the cats were still wetting, Meg was still screaming, the dog was getting madder, and Sullivan began to drink during the day. Outside it was hot and lush and green, and the summer girls were wearing shorter miniskirts and no panties and the middle-aged men down by the Charles were going wild on their bridge. Everyone was restless for change, for August is the month when undone summer things must be finished or regretted all through the winter.

Being imaginative people, Jean and I played a number of original games. One of them we called "Social Forces," the object of which was to see which side could break us first. We played it with the unknown nightriders who screamed obscenities from passing cars. And because that was her side I would look at her expectantly, but she would laugh and say: "No." We played it at parties with unaware blacks who attempted to enchant her with skillful dances and hip vocabulary, believing her to be community property. She would be polite and aloof, and much later, it then being my turn, she would look at me expectantly. And I would force a smile and say: "No." The last round was played while taking her home in a subway car, on a hot August night, when one side of the car was black and tense and hating and the other side was white and of the same mind. There was not enough room on either side for the two of us to sit and we would not separate; and so we stood, holding on to a steel post through all the stops, feeling all the eyes, between the two sides of the car and the two sides of the world. We aged. And, getting off finally at the stop which was no longer ours, we looked at each other, again expectantly, and there was nothing left to say.

I began to avoid the old man, would not answer the door when I knew it was he who was knocking, and waited until very late at night, when he could not possibly be awake, to haul the trash down. I hated the building then; and I was really a janitor for the first time. I slept a lot and wrote very little. And I did not give a damn about Medicare, the AMA, the building, Meg or the crazy dog. I began to consider moving out.

In that same month, Miss O'Hara finally succeeded in badgering Murphy, the celibate Irishman, and a few other tenants into signing a complaint about the dog. No doubt Murphy signed because he was a nice fellow and women like Miss O'Hara had always dominated him. He did not really mind the dog: he did not really mind anything. She called him "Frank Dear," and I had the feeling that when he came to that place, fresh from Montgomery's Campaign, he must have had a will of his own; but she had drained it all away, year by year, so that now he would do anything just to be agreeable.

One day soon after the complaint, the Property Manager came around to tell Sullivan that the dog had to be taken away. Miss O'Hara told me the good news later, when she finally got around to my door.

"Well, that crazy dog is gone now, Robert. Those two are enough."

"Where is the dog?" I asked.

"I don't know, but Albert Rustin made them get him out. You should have seen the old drunk's face," she said. "That dirty useless old man."

"You should be at peace now," I said.

"Almost," was her reply. "The best thing would be to get rid of those two old boozers along with the dog."

I congratulated Miss O'Hara again and then went out. I knew that the old man would be drinking and would want to talk. I did not want to talk. But very late that evening he called on the telephone and caught me in.

"Rob?" he said. "James Sullivan here. Would you come down to my apartment like a good fellow? I want to ask you something important."

I had never been in his apartment before and did not want to go then. But I went down anyway.

They had three rooms, all grimy from corner to corner. There was a peculiar odor in that place I did not want to ever smell again, and his wife was dragging herself around the room talking in mumbles. When she saw me come in the door, she said: "I can't clean it up. I just can't. Look at that window. I can't reach it. I can't keep it clean." She threw up both her hands and held her head down and to the side. "The whole place is dirty and I can't clean it up."

"What do you want?" I said to Sullivan.

"Sit down." He motioned me to a kitchen chair. "Have you changed that bulb on the fifth floor?"

"It's done."

He was silent for a while, drinking from a bottle of sherry, and he offered me some and a dirty glass. "You're the first person who's been here in years," he said. "We couldn't have company because of the dog."

Somewhere in my mind was a note that I should never go into his apartment. But the dog had not been the reason. "Well, he's gone now," I said, fingering the dirty glass of sherry.

He began to cry. "They took my dog away," he said. "It was all I had. How can they take a man's dog away from him?"

There was nothing I could say.

"I couldn't do nothing," he continued. After a while he added: "But I know who it was. It was that old bitch O'Hara. Don't ever trust her, Rob. She smiles in your face but it was her kind that laughed when they burned Joan of Arc in this state."

Seeing him there, crying and making me feel unmanly because I wanted to touch him or say something warm, also made me eager to be far away and running hard. "Everybody's got problems," I said. "I don't have a girl now."

He brightened immediately, and for a while he looked almost happy in his old cat's eyes. Then he staggered over to my chair and held out his hand. I did not touch it, and he finally pulled it back. "I know how you feel," he said. "I know just how you feel."

"Sure," I said.

"But you're a young man, you have a future. But not me. I'll be dead inside of a year."

Just then his wife dragged in to offer me a cigar. They were being hospitable and I forced myself to drink a little of the sherry.

"They took my dog away today," she mumbled. "That's all I had in the world, my dog."

I looked at the old man. He was drinking from the bottle.

During the first week of September one of the middle-aged men down by the Charles got tired of looking and tried to take a necking girl away from her boyfriend. The police hauled him off to jail, and the girl pulled down her dress tearfully. A few days later another man exposed himself near the same spot. And the same week a dead body was found on the banks of the Charles.

The miniskirted brigade had moved out of the Yard and it was quiet and green and peaceful there. In our building another Jewish couple moved into #44. They did not eat gourmet stuff and, on occasion, threw out pork-and-beans cans. But I had lost interest in perception. I now had many records for my stereo, loads of S. S. Pierce stuff, and a small bottle of Chivas Regal which I never opened. I was working good again and did not miss other things as much; or at least I told myself that.

The old man was coming up steadily now, at least three times a day, and I had resigned myself to it. If I refused to let him in he would always come back later with a missing bulb on the fifth floor. We had taken to buying cases of beer together, and when he had finished his half, which was very frequently, he would come up to polish off mine. I began to enjoy talking about politics, the AMA, Medicare, and hippies, and listening to him recite from books he had read. I discovered that he was very well read in history, philosophy, literature and law. He was extraordinarily fond of saying: "I am really a cut above being a building superintendent. Circumstances made me what I am." And even though he was drunk and dirty and it was very late at night, I believed him and liked him anyway because having him there was much better than being alone. After he had gone I could sleep and I was not lonely in sleep; and it did not really matter how late I was at work the next morning, because when I really thought about it all, I discovered that nothing really matters except not being old and being alive and having potential to dream about, and not being alone.

Whenever I passed his wife on the steps she would say: "That no-good bastard let them take my dog away." And whenever her husband complained that he was sick she said: "That's good for him. He took my dog away."

Sullivan slept in the basement on the sofa almost every night because his wife would think about the dog after the *Carson Show* and blame him for letting it be taken away. He told her, and then me, that the dog was on a farm in New Hampshire; but that was unlikely because the dog had been near mad, and it did not appease her. It was nearing autumn and she was getting violent. Her screams could be heard for hours through the halls and I knew that beyond her quiet door Miss O'Hara was plotting again. Sullivan now had little cuts and bruises on his face and hands, and one day he said: "Meg is like an albatross around my neck. I wish she was dead. I'm sick myself and I can't take much more. She blamed me for the dog and I couldn't help it."

"Why don't you take her out to see the dog?" I said.

"I couldn't help it Rob," he went on. "I'm old and I couldn't help it."

"You ought to just get her out of here for a while."

He looked at me, drunk as usual. "Where would we go? We can't even get past the Square."

There was nothing left to say.

"Honest to God, I couldn't help it," he said. He was not saying it to me.

That night I wrote a letter from a mythical New Hampshire farmer telling them that the dog was very fine and missed them a great deal because he kept trying to run off. I said that the children and all the other dogs liked him and that he was not vicious any more. I wrote that the open air was doing him a lot of good and added that they should feel absolutely free to come up to visit the dog at any time. That same night I gave him the letter.

One evening, some days later, I asked him about it.

"I tried to mail it, I really tried," he said.

"What happened?"

"I went down to the Square and looked for cars with New Hampshire license plates. But I never found anybody."

"That wasn't even necessary, was it?"

"It had to have a New Hampshire postmark. You don't know my Meg."

"Listen," I said. "I have a friend who goes up there. Give me the letter and I'll have him mail it."

He held his head down. "I'll tell you the truth. I carried that letter in my pocket so much it got ragged and dirty and I got tired of carrying it. I finally just tore it up."

Neither one of us said anything for a while.

"If I could have sent it off it would have helped some," he said at last. "I know it would have helped."

"Sure," I said.

"I wouldn't have to ask anybody if I had my strength."

"I know."

"If I had my strength I would have mailed it myself."

"I know," I said.

That night we both drank from his bottle of sherry and it did not matter at all that I did not provide my own glass.

In late September the Cambridge police finally picked up the bearded pot-pusher in the Square. He had been in a restaurant all summer, at the same table, with the same customers flocking around him; but now that summer was over, they picked him up. The leaves were changing. In the early evening students passed the building and Meg, blue-hatted and waiting on the steps, carrying sofas and chairs and coffee tables to their suites in the Houses. Down by the Charles the middle-aged men were catching the last phases of summer sensuality before the grass grew cold and damp, and before the young would be forced indoors to play. I wondered what those hungry, spying men did in the winter or at night when it was too dark to see. Perhaps, I thought, they just stood there and listened.

In our building Miss O'Hara was still listening. She had never stopped. When Meg was outside on the steps it was very quiet and I felt good that Miss O'Hara had to wait a long, long time before she heard anything. The company gave the halls and ceilings a new coat of paint, but it was still old in the building. James Sullivan got his yearly two-week vacation and they went to the Boston Common for six hours: two hours going, two hours sitting on the benches, and two hours coming back. Then they both sat on the steps, watching, and waiting.

At first I wanted to be kind because he was old and dying in a special way and I was young and ambitious. But at night, in my apartment, when I heard his dragging feet in the hall outside and knew that he would be drunk and repetitious and imposing on my privacy, I did not want to be kind any more. There were girls outside and I knew that I could have one now because that desperate look had finally gone somewhere deep inside. I was young and now I did not want to be bothered.

"Did you read about the lousy twelve per cent Social Security increase those bastards in Washington gave us?"

"No."

He would force himself past me, trying to block the door with my body, and into the room. "When those old pricks tell me to count my blessings, I tell them, 'You're not one of them.' " He would seat himself at the table without meeting my eyes. "The cost of living's gone up more than twelve per cent in the last six months."

"I know."

"What unmitigated bastards."

I would try to be busy with something on my desk.

"But the Texas Oil Barons got another depletion allowance."

"They can afford to bribe politicians," I would mumble.

"They tax away our rainy-day dollars and give us a lousy twelve per cent."

"It's tough."

He would know that I did not want to hear any more and he would know that he was making a burden of himself. It made me feel bad that it was so obvious to him, but I could not help myself. It made me feel bad that I disliked him more every time I heard a girl laugh on the street far below my window. So I would nod occasionally and say half-phrases and smile slightly at something witty he was saying for the third time. If I did not offer him a drink he would go sooner and so I gave him Coke when he hinted at how dry he was. Then, when he had finally gone, saying, "I hope I haven't burdened you unduly," I went to bed and hated myself.

If I am a janitor it is either because I have to be a janitor or because I want to be a janitor. And if I do not have to do it, and if I no longer want to do it, the easiest thing in the world, for a young man, is to step up to something else. Any move away from it is a step up because there is no job more demeaning than that of a janitor. One day I made myself suddenly realize that the three dirty cans would never contain anything of value to me, unless, of course, I decided to gather material for Harold Robbins or freelance for the *Realist*. Neither alternative appealed to me.

Toward dawn one day, during the first part of October, I rented a U-Haul truck and took away two loads of things I had accumulated. The records I packed very carefully, and the stereo I placed on the front seat of the truck beside me. I slipped the Chivas Regal and a picture of Jean under some clothes in a trunk I will not open for a long time. And I left the rug on the floor because it was dirty and too large for my new apartment. I also left the two plates given to me by James Sullivan, for no reason at all. Sometimes I want to go back to get them, but I do not know how to ask for them or explain why I left them in the first place. But sometimes at night, when there is a sleeping girl beside me, I think that I cannot have them again because I am still young and do not want to go back into that building.

I saw him once in the Square walking along very slowly with two shopping bags, and they seemed very heavy. As I came up behind him I saw him put them down and exercise his arms while the crowd moved in two streams around him. I had an instant impulse to offer help and I was close enough to touch him before I stopped. I will never know why I stopped. And after a few seconds of standing behind him and knowing that he was not aware of anything at all except the two heavy bags waiting to be lifted after his arms were sufficiently rested, I moved back into the stream of people which passed on the left of him. I never looked back.

ANN PETRY
In Darkness and Confusion

William Jones took a sip of coffee and then put his cup down on the kitchen table. It didn't taste right and he was annoyed because he always looked forward to eating breakfast. He usually got out of bed as soon as he woke up and hurried into the kitchen. Then he would take a long time heating the corn bread left over from dinner the night before, letting the coffee brew until it was strong and clear, frying bacon and scrambling eggs. He would eat very slowly—savoring the early-morning quiet and the just-rightness of the food he'd fixed.

There was no question about early morning being the best part of the day, he thought. But this Saturday morning in July it was too hot in the apartment. There were too many nagging worries that kept drifting through his mind. In the heat he couldn't think clearly—so that all of them pressed in against him, weighed him down.

He pushed his plate away from him. The eggs had cooked too long; much as he liked corn bread it tasted like sand this morning—grainy and coarse inside his throat. He couldn't help wondering if it scratched the in-side of his stomach in the same way.

Pink was moving around in the bedroom. He cocked his head on one side, listening to her. He could tell exactly what she was doing, as though he were in there with her. The soft heavy sound of her stock-inged feet as she walked over to the dresser. The dresser drawer being pulled out. That meant she was getting a clean slip. Then the thud of her two hundred pounds landing in the rocker by the window. She was sitting down to comb her hair. Untwisting the small braids she'd made the night before. She would unwind them one by one, putting the hairpins in her mouth as she went along. Now she was brushing it, for he could hear the creak of the rocker; she was rocking back and forth, humming under her breath as she brushed.

He decided that as soon as she came into the kitchen he would go back to the bedroom, get dressed, and go to work. For his mind was al-ready on the mailbox. He didn't feel like talking to Pink. There simply had to be a letter from Sam today. There had to be.

He was thinking about it so hard that he didn't hear Pink walk toward the kitchen.

When he looked up she was standing in the doorway. She was a short, enormously fat woman. The only garment she had on was a bright pink slip that magnified the size of her body. The skin on her arms and shoulders and chest was startlingly black against the pink material. In spite of the brisk brushing she had given her hair, it stood up stiffly all over her head in short wiry lengths, as though she wore a turban of some rough dark-gray material.

He got up from the table quickly when he saw her. "Hot, ain't it?" he said, and patted her arm as he went past her toward the bedroom.

She looked at the food on his plate. "You didn't want no breakfast?" she asked.

"Too hot," he said over his shoulder.

He closed the bedroom door behind him gently. If she saw the door was shut, she'd know that he was kind of low in his mind this morning and that he didn't feel like talking. At first he moved about with energy— getting a clean work shirt, giving his shoes a hasty brushing, hunting for a pair of clean socks. Then he stood still in the middle of the room, holding his dark work pants in his hand while he listened to the rush and roar of water running in the bathtub.

Annie May was up and taking a bath. And he wondered if that meant she was going to work. Days when she went to work she used a hot comb on her hair before she ate her breakfast, so that before he left the house in the morning it was filled with the smell of hot irons sizzling against hair grease.

He frowned. Something had to be done about Annie May. Here she was only eighteen years old and staying out practically all night long. He hadn't said anything to Pink about it, but Annie May crept into the house at three and four and five in the morning. He would hear her key go in the latch and then the telltale click as the lock drew back. She would shut the door very softly and turn the bolt. She'd stand there awhile, waiting to see if they woke up. Then she'd take her shoes off and pad down the hall in her stockinged feet.

When she turned the light on in the bathroom, he could see the clock on the dresser. This morning it was four-thirty when she came in. Pink, lying beside him, went on peacefully snoring. He was glad that she didn't wake up easy. It would only worry her to know that Annie May was carrying on like that.

Annie May put her hands on her hips and threw her head back and laughed whenever he tried to tell her she had to come home earlier. The smoky smell of the hot irons started seeping into the bedroom and he finished dressing quickly.

He stopped in the kitchen on his way out. "Got to get to the store early today," he explained. He was sure Pink knew he was hurrying downstairs to look in the mailbox. But she nodded and held her face up for his kiss. When he brushed his lips against her forehead he saw that her face was wet with perspiration. He thought with all that weight she must feel the heat something awful.

Annie May nodded at him without speaking. She was hastily swallowing a cup of coffee. Her dark thin hands made a pattern against the thick white cup she was holding. She had pulled her hair out so straight with the hot combs that, he thought, it was like a shiny skullcap fitted tight to her head. He was surprised to see that her lips were heavily coated with lipstick. When she was going to work she didn't use any, and he wondered why she was up so early if she wasn't working. He could see the red outline of her mouth on the cup.

He hadn't intended to say anything. It was the sight of the lipstick on the cup that forced the words out. "You ain't workin' today?"

"No," she said lazily. "Think I'll go shopping." She winked at Pink, and it infuriated him.

"How you expect to keep a job when you don't show up half the time?" he asked.

"I can always get another one." She lifted the coffee cup to her mouth with both hands and her eyes laughed at him over the rim of the cup.

"What time did you come home last night?" he asked abruptly.

She stared out of the window at the blank brick wall that faced the kitchen. "I dunno," she said finally. "It wasn't late."

He didn't know what to say. Probably she was out dancing somewhere. Or maybe she wasn't. He was fairly certain that she wasn't. Yet he couldn't let Pink know what he was thinking. He shifted his feet uneasily and watched Annie May swallow the coffee. She was drinking it fast.

"You know you ain't too big to get your butt whipped," he said finally.

She looked at him out of the corner of her eyes. And he saw a deep smoldering sullenness in her face that startled him. He was conscious that Pink was watching both of them with a growing apprehension.

Then Annie May giggled. "You and who else?" she said lightly. Pink roared with laughter. And Annie May laughed with her.

He banged the kitchen door hard as he went out. Striding down the outside hall, he could still hear them laughing. And even though he knew Pink's laughter was due to relief because nothing unpleasant had happened, he was angry. Lately every time Annie May looked at him there was open, jeering laughter in her eyes, as though she dared him to say anything to her. Almost as though she thought he was a fool for working so hard.

She had been a nice little girl when she first came to live with them six years ago. He groped in his mind for words to describe what he thought Annie May had become. A Jezebel, he decided grimly. That was it.

And he didn't want Pink to know what Annie May was really like. Because Annie May's mother, Lottie, had been Pink's sister. And when Lottie died, Pink took Annie May. Right away she started finding excuses for anything she did that was wrong. If he scolded Annie May he had to listen to a sharp lecture from Pink. It always started off the same way: "Don't care what she done, William. You ain't goin' to lay a finger on her. She ain't got no father and mother except us. . . ."

The quick spurt of anger and irritation at Annie May had sent him hurrying down the first flight of stairs. But he slowed his pace on the next flight because the hallways were so dark that he knew if he wasn't careful he'd walk over a step. As he trudged down the long flights of stairs he began to think about Pink. And the hot irritation in him disappeared as it usually did when he thought about her. She was so fat she couldn't keep on climbing all these steep stairs. They would have to find another place to live—on a first floor where it would be easier for her. They'd lived on this top floor for years, and all the time Pink kept getting heavier and heavier. Every time she went to the clinic the doctor said the stairs were bad for her. So they'd start looking for another apartment and then because the top floors cost less, why, they stayed where they were. And—

Then he stopped thinking about Pink because he had reached the first floor. He walked over to the mailboxes and took a deep breath. Today there'd be a letter. He knew it. There had to be. It had been too long a time since they had had a letter from Sam. The last ones that came he'd said the same thing. Over and over. Like a refrain. "Ma, I can't stand this much longer." And then the letters just stopped.

As he stood there, looking at the mailbox, half afraid to open it for fear there would be no letter, he thought back to the night Sam graduated from high school. It was a warm June night. He and Pink got all dressed up in their best clothes. And he kept thinking me and Pink have got as far as we can go. But Sam—he made up his mind Sam wasn't going to earn his living with a mop and a broom. He was going to earn it wearing a starched white collar, and a shine on his shoes and a crease in his pants.

After he finished high school Sam got a job redcapping at Grand Central. He started saving his money because he was going to go to Lincoln —a college in Pennsylvania. It looked like it was no time at all before he was twenty-one. And in the army. Pink cried when he left. Her huge body shook with her sobbing. He remembered that he had only felt queer and lost. There was this war and all the young men were being drafted. But why Sam—why did he have to go?

It was always in the back of his mind. Next thing Sam was in a camp in Georgia. He and Pink never talked about his being in Georgia. The closest they ever came to it was one night when she said, "I hope he gets used to it quick down there. Bein' born right here in New York there's lots he won't understand."

Then Sam's letters stopped coming. He'd come home from work and say to Pink casually, "Sam write today?" She'd shake her head without saying anything.

The days crawled past. And finally she burst out. "What you keep askin' for? You think I wouldn't tell you?" And she started crying.

He put his arm around her and patted her shoulder. She leaned hard against him. "Oh, Lord," she said. "He's my baby. What they done to him?"

Her crying like that tore him in little pieces. His mind kept going around in circles. Around and around. He couldn't think what to do. Finally one night after work he sat down at the kitchen table and wrote Sam a letter. He had written very few letters in his life because Pink had always done it for him. And now standing in front of the mailbox he could even remember the feel of the pencil in his hand; how the paper looked —blank and challenging—lying there in front of him; that the kitchen clock was ticking and it kept getting louder and louder. It was hot that night, too, and he held the pencil so tight that the inside of his hand was covered with sweat.

He had sat and thought a long time. Then he wrote: "Is you all right? Your Pa." It was the best he could do. He licked the envelope and addressed it with the feeling that Sam would understand.

He fumbled for his key ring, found the mailbox key, and opened the box quickly. It was empty. Even though he could see it was empty he felt around inside it. Then he closed the box and walked toward the street door.

The brilliant sunlight outside made him blink after the darkness of the hall. Even now, so early in the morning, it was hot in the street. And he thought it was going to be a hard day to get through, what with the heat and its being Saturday and all. Lately he couldn't seem to think about anything but Sam. Even at the drugstore where he worked as a porter, he would catch himself leaning on the broom or pausing in his mopping to wonder what had happened to him.

The man who owned the store would say to him sharply, "Boy, what the hell's the matter with you? Can't you keep your mind on what you're doing?" And he would go on washing windows, or mopping the floor, or sweeping the sidewalk. But his thoughts, somehow, no matter what he was doing, drifted back to Sam.

As he walked toward the drugstore he looked at the houses on both sides of the street. He knew this street as he knew the creases in the old felt hat he wore the year round. No matter how you looked at it, it wasn't a good street to live on. It was a long cross-town street. Almost half of it on one side consisted of the backs of the three theaters on One Hundred Twenty-fifth Street—a long blank wall of gray brick. There were few trees on the street. Even these were a source of danger, for at night shadowy, vague shapes emerged from the street's darkness, lurking near the trees, dodging behind them. He had never been accosted by any of those dissembodied figures, but the very stealth of their movements revealed a dishonest intent that frightened him. So when he came home at night he walked an extra block or more in order to go through One Hundred Twenty-fifth Street and enter the street from Eighth Avenue.

Early in the morning like this, the street slept. Window shades were drawn down tight against the morning sun. The few people he passed were walking briskly on their way to work. But in those houses where the people still slept, the window shades would go up about noon, and radios would blast music all up and down the street. The bold-eyed women who lived in these houses would lounge in the open windows and call to each other back and forth across the street.

Sometimes when he was on his way home to lunch they would call out to him as he went past, "Come on in, Poppa!" And he would stare straight ahead and start walking faster.

When Sam turned sixteen it seemed to him the street was unbearable. After lunch he and Sam went through this block together—Sam to school and he on his way back to the drugstore. He'd seen Sam stare at the lounging women in the windows. His face was expressionless, but his eyes were curious.

"I catch you goin' near one of them women and I'll beat you up and down the block," he'd said grimly.

Sam didn't answer him. Instead he looked down at him with a strangely adult look, for even at sixteen Sam had been a good five inches taller than he. After that when they passed through the block, Sam looked straight ahead. And William got the uncomfortable feeling that he had already explored the possibilities that the block offered. Yet he couldn't be sure. And he couldn't bring himself to ask him. Instead he walked along beside him, thinking desperately, We gotta move. I'll talk to Pink. We gotta move this time for sure.

That Sunday after Pink came home from church they looked for a new place. They went in and out of apartment houses along Seventh Avenue and Eighth Avenue, One Hundred Thirty-fifth Street, One Hundred Forty-fifth Street. Most of the apartments they didn't even look at. They just asked the super how much the rents were.

It was late when they headed for home. He had irritably agreed with Pink that they'd better stay where they were. Twenty-two dollars a month was all they could afford.

"It ain't a fit place to live, though," he said. They were walking down Seventh Avenue. The street looked wide to him, and he thought with distaste of their apartment. The rooms weren't big enough for a man to move around in without bumping into something. Sometimes he thought that was why Annie May spent so much time away from home. Even at thirteen she couldn't stand being cooped up like that in such a small amount of space.

And Pink said, "You want to live on Park Avenue? With a doorman bowin' you in and out. 'Good mornin', Mr. William Jones. Does the weather suit you this mornin'?' " Her voice was sharp, like the crack of a whip.

That was five years ago. And now again they ought to move on account of Pink not being able to stand the stairs any more. He decided that Monday night after work he'd start looking for a place.

It was even hotter in the drugstore than it was in the street. He forced himself to go inside and put on a limp work coat. Then broom in hand he went to stand in the doorway. He waved to the superintendent of the building on the corner. And watched him as he lugged garbage cans out of the areaway and rolled them to the curb. Now, that's the kind of work he didn't want Sam to have to do. He tried to decide why that was. It wasn't just because Sam was his boy and it was hard work. He searched his mind for the reason. It didn't pay enough for a man to live on decently. That was it. He wanted Sam to have a job where he could make enough to have good clothes and a nice home.

Sam's being in the army wasn't so bad, he thought. It was his being in Georgia that was bad. They didn't treat colored people right down there. Everybody knew that. If he could figure out some way to get him farther north Pink wouldn't have to worry about him so much.

The very sound of the word "Georgia" did something to him inside. His mother had been born there. She had talked about it a lot and painted such vivid pictures of it that he felt he knew the place—the heat, the smell of the earth, how cotton looked. And something more. The way her mouth had folded together whenever she had said, "They hate niggers down there. Don't you never none of you children go down there."

That was years ago, yet even now, standing here on Fifth Avenue, remembering the way she said it turned his skin clammy cold in spite of the heat. And of all the places in the world, Sam had to go to Georgia. Sam, who was born right here in New York, who had finished high school here —they had to put him in the army and send him to Georgia.

He tightened his grip on the broom and started sweeping the sidewalk in long, even strokes. Gradually the rhythm of the motion stilled the agitation in him. The regular back-and-forth motion was so pleasant that he kept on sweeping long after the sidewalk was clean. When Mr. Yudkin, who owned the store, arrived at eight-thirty he was still outside with the broom. Even now he didn't feel much like talking, so he only nodded in response to the druggist's brisk, "Good morning! Hot today!"

William followed him into the store and began polishing the big mirror in back of the soda fountain. He watched the man out of the corner of his eye as he washed his hands in the back room and exchanged his suit coat for a crisp white laboratory coat. And he thought maybe when the war is over Sam ought to study to be a druggist instead of a doctor or a lawyer.

As the morning wore along, customers came in in a steady stream. They got Bromo-Seltzers, cigarettes, aspirin, cough medicine, baby bottles. He delivered two prescriptions that cost five dollars. And the cash register rang so often it almost played a tune. Listening to it he said to himself, yes, Sam ought to be a druggist. It's clean work and it pays good.

A little after eleven o'clock three young girls came in. "Cokes," they said, and climbed up on the stools in front of the fountain. William was placing new stock on the shelves and he studied them from the top of the stepladder. As far as he could see, they looked exactly alike. All three of them. And like Annie May. Too thin. Too much lipstick. Their dresses were too short and too tight. Their hair was piled on top of their heads in slicked set curls.

"Aw, I quit that job," one of them said. "I wouldn't get up that early in the morning for nothing in the world."

That was like Annie May, too. She was always changing jobs. Because she could never get to work on time. If she was due at a place at nine she got there at ten. If at ten, then she arrived about eleven. He knew, too, that she didn't earn enough money to pay for all the cheap, bright-colored dresses she was forever buying.

Her girl friends looked just like her and just like these girls. He'd seen her coming out of the movie houses on One Hundred Twenty-fifth Street with two or three of them. They were all chewing gum and they nudged each other and talked too loud and laughed too loud. They stared hard at every man who went past them.

Mr. Yudkin looked up at him sharply, and he shifted his glance away from the girls and began putting big bottles of Father John's medicine neatly on the shelf in front of him. As he stacked the bottles up he wondered if Annie May would have been different if she'd stayed in high school. She had stopped going when she was sixteen. He had spoken to Pink about it. "She oughtn't to stop school. She's too young," he'd said.

And because Annie May was Pink's sister's child all Pink had done had been to shake her head comfortably. "She's tired of going to school. Poor little thing. Leave her alone."

So he hadn't said anything more. Pink always took up for her. And he and Pink didn't fuss at each other like some folks do. He didn't say anything to Pink about it, but he took the afternoon off from work to go to see the principal of the school. He had to wait two hours to see her. And he studied the pictures on the walls in the outer office, and looked down at his shoes while he tried to put into words what he'd say—and how he wanted to say it.

The principal was a large-bosomed white woman. She listened to him long enough to learn that he was Annie May's uncle. "Ah, yes, Mr. Jones," she said. "Now in my opinion——"

And he was buried under a flow of words, a mountain of words, that went on and on. Her voice was high-pitched and loud, and she kept talking until he lost all sense of what she was saying. There was one phrase she kept using that sort of jumped at him out of the mass of words—"a slow learner."

He left her office feeling confused and embarrassed. If he could only have found the words he could have explained that Annie May was bright as a dollar. She wasn't any "slow learner." Before he knew it he was out in the street, conscious only that he'd lost a whole afternoon's pay and he never had got to say what he'd come for. And he was boiling mad with himself. All he'd wanted was to ask the principal to help him persuade Annie May to finish school. But he'd never got the words together.

When he hung up his soiled work coat in the broom closet at eight o'clock that night he felt as though he'd been sweeping floors, dusting fixtures, cleaning fountains, and running errands since the beginning of time itself. He looked at himself in the cracked mirror that hung on the door of the closet. There was no question about it; he'd grown older-looking since Sam went in the army. His hair was turning a frizzled gray at the temples. His jawbones showed up sharper. There was a stoop in his shoulders.

"Guess I'll get a haircut," he said softly. He didn't really need one. But on a Saturday night the barbershop would be crowded. He'd have to wait a long time before Al got around to him. It would be good to listen to the talk that went on—the arguments that would get started and never really end. For a little while all the nagging worry about Sam would be pushed so far back in his mind, he wouldn't be aware of it.

The instant he entered the barbershop he could feel himself begin to relax inside. All the chairs were full. There were a lot of customers waiting. He waved a greeting to the barbers. "Hot, ain't it?" he said and mopped his forehead.

He stood there a minute, listening to the hum of conversation, before he picked out a place to sit. Some of the talk, he knew, would be violent, and he always avoided those discussions because he didn't like violence —even when it was only talk. Scraps of talk drifted past him.

"White folks got us by the balls——"

"Well, I dunno. It ain't just white folks. There's poor white folks gettin' their guts squeezed out, too——"

"Sure. But they're white. They can stand it better."

"Sadie had two dollars on 546 yesterday and it came out and——"

"You're wrong, man. Ain't no two ways about it. This country's set up so that——"

"Only thing to do, if you ask me, is shoot all them crackers and start out new——"

He finally settled himself in one of the chairs in the corner—not too far from the window and right in the middle of a group of regular customers who were arguing hotly about the war. It was a good seat. By looking in the long mirror in front of the barbers he could see the length of the shop.

Almost immediately he joined in the conversation. "Them Japs ain't got a chance——" he started. And he was feeling good. He'd come in at just the right time. He took a deep breath before he went on. Most every time he started talking about the Japs the others listened with deep respect. Because he knew more about them than the other customers. Pink worked for some Navy people and she told him what they said.

He looked along the line of waiting customers, watching their reaction to his words. Pretty soon they'd all be listening to him. And then he stopped talking abruptly. A soldier was sitting in the far corner of the shop, staring down at his shoes. Why, that's Scummy, he thought. He's at the same camp where Sam is. He forgot what he was about to say. He got up and walked over to Scummy. He swallowed all the questions about Sam that trembled on his lips.

"Hiya, son," he said. "Sure is good to see you."

As he shook hands with the boy he looked him over carefully. He's changed, he thought. He was older. There was something about his eyes that was different than before. He didn't seem to want to talk. After that first quick look at William he kept his eyes down, staring at his shoes.

Finally William couldn't hold the question back any longer. It came out fast. "How's Sam?"

Scummy picked up a newspaper from the chair beside him. "He's all right," he mumbled. There was a long silence. Then he raised his head and looked directly at William. "Was the las' time I seen him." He put a curious emphasis on the word "las'."

William was conscious of a trembling that started in his stomach. It went all through his body. He was aware that conversation in the barbershop had stopped. There was a cone of silence in which he could hear the scraping noise of the razors—a harsh sound, loud in the silence. Al was putting thick oil on a customer's hair and he turned and looked with the hair-oil bottle still in his hand, tilted up over the customer's head. The men sitting in the tilted-back barber's chairs twisted their necks around —awkwardly, slowly—so they could look at Scummy.

"What you mean—the las' time?" William asked sharply. The words beat against his ears. He wished the men in the barbershop would start talking again, for he kept hearing his own words. "What you mean— the las' time?" Just as though he were saying them over and over again. Something had gone wrong with his breathing, too. He couldn't seem to get enough air in through his nose.

Scummy got up. There was something about him that William couldn't give a name to. It made the trembling in his stomach worse.

"The las' time I seen him he was O.K." Scummy's voice made a snarling noise in the barbershop.

One part of William's mind said, yes, that's it. It's hate that makes him look different. It's hate in his eyes. You can see it. It's in his voice, and you can hear it. He's filled with it.

"Since I seen him las'," he went on slowly, "he got shot by a white MP. Because he wouldn't go to the nigger end of a bus. He had a bullet put through his guts. He took the MP's gun away from him and shot the bastard in the shoulder." He put the newspaper down and started toward the door; when he reached it he turned around. "They court-martialed him," he said softly. "He got twenty years at hard labor. The notice was posted in the camp the day I left." Then he walked out of the shop. He didn't look back.

There was no sound in the barbershop as William watched him go down the street. Even the razors had stopped. Al was still holding the hair-oil bottle over the head of his customer. The heavy oil was falling on the face of the man sitting in the chair. It was coming down slowly—one drop at a time.

The men in the shop looked at William and then looked away. He thought, I mustn't tell Pink. She mustn't ever get to know. I can go down to the mailbox early in the morning and I can get somebody else to look in it in the afternoon, so if a notice comes I can tear it up.

The barbers started cutting hair again. There was the murmur of conversation in the shop. Customers got up out of the tilted-back chairs. Someone said to him, "You can take my place."

He nodded and walked over to the empty chair. His legs were weak and shaky. He couldn't seem to think at all. His mind kept dodging away from the thought of Sam in prison. Instead the familiar details of Sam's growing up kept creeping into his thoughts. All the time the boy was in grammar school he made good marks. Time went so fast it seemed like it was just overnight and he was in long pants. And then in high school.

He made the basketball team in high school. The whole school was proud of him, for his picture had been in one of the white papers. They got two papers that day. Pink cut the pictures out and stuck one in the mirror of the dresser in their bedroom. She gave him one to carry in his wallet.

While Al cut his hair he stared at himself in the mirror until he felt as though his eyes were crossed. First he thought, maybe it isn't true. Maybe Scummy was joking. But a man who was joking didn't look like Scummy looked. He wondered if Scummy was AWOL. That would be bad. He told himself sternly that he mustn't think about Sam here in the barbershop—wait until he got home.

He was suddenly angry with Annie May. She was just plain no good. Why couldn't something have happened to her? Why did it have to be

Sam? Then he was ashamed. He tried to find an excuse for having wanted harm to come to her. It looked like all his life he'd wanted a little something for himself and Pink and then when Sam came along he forgot about those things. He wanted Sam to have all the things that he and Pink couldn't get. It got to be too late for them to have them. But Sam— again he told himself not to think about him. To wait until he got home and in bed.

Al took the cloth from around his neck, and he got up out of the chair. Then he was out on the street, heading toward home. The heat that came from the pavement seeped through the soles of his shoes. He had forgotten how hot it was. He forced himself to wonder what it would be like to live in the country. Sometimes on hot nights like this, after he got home from work, he went to sit in the park. It was always cooler there. It would probably be cool in the country. But then it might be cold in winter— even colder than the city.

The instant he got in the house he took off his shoes and his shirt. The heat in the apartment was like a blanket—it made his skin itch and crawl in a thousand places. He went into the living room, where he leaned out of the window, trying to cool off. Not yet, he told himself. He mustn't think about it yet.

He leaned farther out of the window, to get away from the innumerable odors that came from the boxlike rooms in back of him. They cut off his breath, and he focused his mind on them. There was the greasy smell of cabbage and collard greens, smell of old wood and soapsuds and disinfectant, a lingering smell of gas from the kitchen stove, and over it all Annie May's perfume.

Then he turned his attention to the street. Up and down as far as he could see, folks were sitting on the stoops. Not talking. Just sitting. Somewhere up the street a baby wailed. A woman's voice rose sharply as she told it to shut up.

Pink wouldn't be home until late. The white folks she worked for were having a dinner party tonight. And no matter how late she got home on Saturday night she always stopped on Eighth Avenue to shop for her Sunday dinner. She never trusted him to do it. It's a good thing, he thought. If she ever took a look at me tonight she'd know there was something wrong.

A key clicked in the lock, and he drew back from the window. He was sitting on the couch when Annie May came in the room.

"You're home early, ain't you?" he asked.

"Oh, I'm going out again," she said.

"You shouldn't stay out so late like you did last night," he said mildly. He hadn't really meant to say it. But what with Sam—

"What you think I'm going to do? Sit here every night and make small talk with you?" Her voice was defiant. Loud.

"No," he said, and then added, "but nice girls ain't runnin' around the streets at four o'clock in the mornin'." Now that he'd started he couldn't seem to stop. "Oh, I know what time you come home. And it ain't right. If you don't stop it you can get some other place to stay."

"It's O.K. with me," she said lightly. She chewed the gum in her mouth so it made a cracking noise. "I don't know what Auntie Pink married a little runt like you for, anyhow. It wouldn't bother me a bit if I never saw you again." She walked toward the hall. "I'm going away for the week end," she added over her shoulder. "And I'll move out on Monday."

"What you mean for the week end?" he asked sharply. "Where you goin'?"

"None of your damn business," she said, and slammed the bathroom door hard.

The sharp sound of the door closing hurt his ears so that he winced, wondering why he had grown so sensitive to sounds in the last few hours. What'd she have to say that for, anyway, he asked himself. Five feet five wasn't so short for a man. He was taller than Pink, anyhow. Yet compared to Sam, he supposed he was a runt, for Sam had just kept on growing until he was six feet tall. At the thought he got up from the chair quickly, undressed, and got in bed. He lay there trying to still the trembling in his stomach; trying even now not to think about Sam, because it would be best to wait until Pink was in bed and sound asleep so that no expression on his face, no least little motion, would betray his agitation.

When he heard Pink come up the stairs just before midnight he closed his eyes. All of him was listening to her. He could hear her panting outside on the landing. There was a long pause before she put her key in the door. It took her all that time to get her breath back. She's getting old, he thought. I mustn't let her know about Sam.

She came into the bedroom, and he pretended to be asleep. He made himself breathe slowly. Evenly. Thinking, I can get through tomorrow all right. I won't get up much before she goes to church. She'll be so busy getting dressed she won't notice me.

She went out of the room and he heard the soft murmur of her voice talking to Annie May. "Don't you pay no attention, honey. He don't mean a word of it. I know menfolks. They's always tired and out of sorts by the time Saturdays come around."

"But I'm not going to stay here any more."

"Yes, you is. You think I'm goin' to let my sister's child be turned out? You goin' to be right here."

They lowered their voices. There was laughter. Pink's deep and rich and slow. Annie May's high-pitched and nervous. Pink said, "You looks lovely, honey. Now, have a good time."

The front door closed. This time Annie May didn't slam it. He turned over on his back, making the springs creak. Instantly Pink came into the bedroom to look at him. He lay still, with his eyes closed, holding his breath for fear she would want to talk to him about what he'd said to Annie May and would wake him up. After she moved away from the door he opened his eyes.

There must be some meaning in back of what had happened to Sam. Maybe it was some kind of judgment from the Lord, he thought. Perhaps he shouldn't have stopped going to church. His only concession to Sunday was to put on his best suit. He wore it just that one day, and Pink pressed the pants late on Saturday night. But in the last few years it got so that every time he went to church he wanted to stand up and yell, "You Goddamn fools! How much more you goin' to take?"

He'd get to thinking about the street they lived on, and the sight of the minister with his clean white collar turned hind side to and the sound of his buttery voice were too much. One Sunday he'd actually gotten on his feet, for the minister was talking about the streets of gold up in heaven; the words were right on the tip of his tongue when Pink reached out and pinched his behind sharply. He yelped and sat down. Someone in back of him giggled. In spite of himself a slow smile had spread over his face. He stayed quiet through the rest of the service, but after that he didn't go to church at all.

This street where he and Pink lived was like the one where his mother had lived. It looked like he and Pink ought to have gotten further than his mother had. She had scrubbed floors, washed, and ironed in the white folks' kitchens. They were doing practically the same thing. That was another reason he stopped going to church. He couldn't figure out why these things had to stay the same, and if the Lord didn't intend it like that, why didn't He change it?

He began thinking about Sam again, so he shifted his attention to the sounds Pink was making in the kitchen. She was getting the rolls ready for tomorrow. Scrubbing the sweet potatoes. Washing the greens. Cutting up the chicken. Then the thump of the iron. Hot as it was, she was pressing his pants. He resisted the impulse to get up and tell her not to do it.

A little later, when she turned the light on in the bathroom, he knew she was getting ready for bed. And he held his eyes tightly shut, made his body rigidly still. As long as he could make her think he was sound asleep she wouldn't take a real good look at him. One real good look and she'd know there was something wrong. The bed sagged under her weight as she knelt down to say her prayers. Then she was lying down beside him. She sighed under her breath as her head hit the pillow.

He must have slept part of the time, but in the morning it seemed to him that he had looked up at the ceiling most of the night. He couldn't remember actually going to sleep.

When he finally got up, Pink was dressed and ready for church. He sat down in a chair in the living room away from the window, so the light wouldn't shine on his face. As he looked at her he wished that he could find relief from the confusion of his thoughts by taking part in the singing and the shouting that would go on in church. But he couldn't. And Pink never said anything about his not going to church. Only sometimes like today, when she was ready to go, she looked at him a little wistfully.

She had on her Sunday dress. It was made of a printed material—big red and black poppies splashed on a cream-colored background. He wouldn't let himself look right into her eyes, and in order that she wouldn't notice the evasiveness of his glance he stared at the dress. It fit snugly over her best corset, and the corset in turn constricted her thighs and tightly encased the rolls of flesh around her waist. She didn't move away, and he couldn't keep on inspecting the dress, so he shifted his gaze up to the wide cream-colored straw hat she was wearing far back on her head. Next he noticed that she was easing her feet by standing on the outer edges of the high-heeled patent-leather pumps she wore.

He reached out and patted her arm. "You look nice," he said, picking up the comic section of the paper.

She stood there looking at him while she pulled a pair of white cotton gloves over her roughened hands. "Is you all right, honey?" she asked.

"Course," he said, holding the paper up in front of his face.

"You shouldn't talk so mean to Annie May," she said gently.

"Yeah, I know," he said, and hoped she understood that he was apologizing. He didn't dare lower the paper while she was standing there looking at him so intently. Why doesn't she go, he thought.

"There's grits and eggs for breakfast."

"O.K." He tried to make his voice sound as though he were so absorbed in what he was reading that he couldn't give her all of his attention. She walked toward the door, and he lowered the paper to watch her, thinking that her legs looked too small for her body under the vastness of the printed dress, that womenfolks sure were funny—she's got that great big pocketbook swinging on her arm and hardly anything in it. Sam used to love to tease her about the size of the handbags she carried.

When she closed the outside door and started down the stairs, the heat in the little room struck him in the face. He almost called her back so that he wouldn't be there by himself—left alone to brood over Sam. He decided that when she came home from church he would make love to her. Even in the heat the softness of her body, the smoothness of her skin, would comfort him.

He pulled his chair up close to the open window. Now he could let himself go. He could begin to figure out something to do about Sam. There's gotta be comething, he thought. But his mind wouldn't stay put. It kept going back to the time Sam graduated from high school. Nineteen seventy-five his dark-blue suit had cost. He and Pink had figured and figured and finally they'd managed it. Sam had looked good in the suit; he was so tall and his shoulders were so broad it looked like a tailor-made suit on him. When he got his diploma everybody went wild—he'd played center on the basketball team, and a lot of folks recognized him.

The trembling in his stomach got worse as he thought about Sam. He was aware that it had never stopped since Scummy had said those words "the las' time." It had gone on all last night until now there was a tautness and a tension in him that left him feeling as though his eardrums were strained wide open, listening for sounds. They must be a foot wide open, he thought. Open and pulsing with the strain of being open. Even his nostrils were stretched open like that. He could feel them. And a weight behind his eyes.

He went to sleep sitting there in the chair. When he woke up his whole body was wet with sweat. It musta got hotter while I slept, he thought. He was conscious of an ache in his jawbones. It's from holding 'em shut so tight. Even his tongue—he'd been holding it so still in his mouth it felt like it was glued there.

Attracted by the sound of voices, he looked out of the window. Across the way a man and a woman were arguing. Their voices rose and fell on the hot, still air. He could look directly into the room where they were standing, and he saw that they were half undressed.

The woman slapped the man across the face. The sound was like a pistol shot, and for an instant William felt his jaw relax. It seemed to him that the whole block grew quiet and waited. He waited with it. The man grabbed his belt and lashed out at the woman. He watched the belt rise and fall against her brown skin. The woman screamed with the regularity of clockwork. The street came alive again. There was the sound of voices, the rattle of dishes. A baby whined. The woman's voice became a murmur of pain in the background.

"I gotta get me some beer," he said aloud. It would cool him off. It would help him to think. He dressed quickly, telling himself that Pink wouldn't be home for hours yet and by that time the beer smell would be gone from his breath.

The street outside was full of kids playing tag. They were all dressed up in their Sunday clothes. Red socks, blue socks, danced in front of him all the way to the corner. The sight of them piled up the quivering in his stomach. Sam used to play in this block on Sunday afternoons. As he walked along, women thrust their heads out of the opened windows, calling to the children. It seemed to him that all the voices were Pink's voice saying, "You, Sammie, stop that runnin' in your good cloes!"

He was so glad to get away from the sight of the children that he ignored the heat inside the barroom of the hotel on the corner and determinedly edged his way past girls in sheer summer dresses and men in loud plaid jackets and tight-legged cream-colored pants until he finally reached the long bar.

There was such a sense of hot excitement in the place that he turned to look around him. Men with slicked, straightened hair were staring through half-closed eyes at the girls lined up at the bar. One man sitting at a table close by kept running his hand up and down the bare arm of the girl leaning against him. Up and down. Down and up. William winced and looked away. The jukebox was going full blast, filling the room with high, raw music that beat about his ears in a queer mixture of violence and love and hate and terror. He stared at the brilliantly colored moving lights on the front of the jukebox as he listened to it, wishing that he had stayed at home, for the music made the room hotter.

"Make it a beer," he said to the bartender.

The beer glass was cold. He held it in his hand, savoring the chill of it, before he raised it to his lips. He drank it down fast. Immediately he felt the air grow cooler. The smell of beer and whisky that hung in the room lifted.

"Fill it up again," he said. He still had that awful trembling in his stomach, but he felt as though he were really beginning to think. Really think. He found he was arguing with himself.

"Sam mighta been like this. Spendin' Sunday afternoons whorin'."

"But he was part of me and part of Pink. He had a chance—"

"Yeah. A chance to live in one of them hell-hole flats. A chance to get himself a woman to beat."

"He woulda finished college and got a good job. Mebbe been a druggist or a doctor or a lawyer—"

"Yeah. Or mebbe got himself a stable of women to rent out on the block—"

He licked the suds from his lips. The man at the table nearby had stopped stroking the girl's arm. He was kissing her—forcing her closer and closer to him.

"Yeah," William jeered at himself. "That coulda been Sam on a hot Sunday afternoon—"

As he stood there arguing with himself he thought it was getting warmer in the bar. The lights were dimmer. I better go home, he thought. I gotta live with this thing some time. Drinking beer in this place ain't going to help any. He looked out toward the lobby of the hotel, attracted by the sound of voices. A white cop was arguing with a frowzy-looking girl who had obviously had too much to drink.

"I got a right in here. I'm mindin' my own business," she said with one eye on the bar.

"Aw, go chase yourself." The cop gave her a push toward the door. She stumbled against a chair.

William watched her in amusement. "Better than a movie," he told himself.

She straightened up and tugged at her girdle. "You white son of a bitch," she said.

The cop's face turned a furious red. He walked toward the woman, waving his nightstick. It was then that William saw the soldier. Tall. Straight. Creases in his khaki pants. An overseas cap cocked over one eye. Looks like Sam looked that one time he was home on furlough, he thought.

The soldier grabbed the cop's arm and twisted the nightstick out of his hand. He threw it half the length of the small lobby. It rattled along the floor and came to a dead stop under a chair.

"Now what'd he want to do that for?" William said softly. He knew that night after night the cop had to come back to this hotel. He's the law, he thought, and he can't let— Then he stopped thinking about him, for the cop raised his arm. The soldier aimed a blow at the cop's chin. The cop ducked and reached for his gun. The soldier turned to run.

It's happening too fast, William thought. It's like one of those horse-race reels they run over fast at the movies. Then he froze inside. The quivering in his stomach got worse. The soldier was heading toward the door. Running. His foot was on the threshold when the cop fired. The soldier dropped. He folded up as neatly as the brown-paper bags Pink brought home from the store, emptied, and then carefully put in the kitchen cupboard.

The noise of the shot stayed in his eardrums. He couldn't get it out. "Jesus Christ!" he said. Then again, "Jesus Christ!" The beer glass was warm. He put it down on the bar with such violence some of the beer slopped over on his shirt. He stared at the wet place, thinking Pink would be mad as hell. Him out drinking in a bar on Sunday. There was a stillness in which he was conscious of the stink of the beer, the heat in the room, and he could still hear the sound of the shot. Somebody dropped a glass, and the tinkle of it hurt his ears.

Then everybody was moving toward the lobby. The doors between the bar and the lobby slammed shut. High, excited talk broke out.

The tall, thin black man standing next to him said, "That ties it. It ain't even safe here where we live. Not no more. I'm goin' to get me a white bastard of a cop and nail his hide to a street sign."

"Is the soldier dead?" someone asked.

"He wasn't movin' none," came the answer.

They pushed hard against the doors leading to the lobby. The doors stayed shut.

He stood still, watching them. The anger that went through him was so great that he had to hold on to the bar to keep from falling. He felt as though he were going to burst wide open. It was like having seen Sam killed before his eyes. Then he heard the whine of an ambulance siren. His eardrums seemed to be waiting to pick it up.

"Come on, what you waitin' for?" he snarled the words at the people milling around the lobby doors. "Come on!" he repeated, running toward the street.

The crowd followed him to the One Hundred Twenty-sixth Street entrance of the hotel. He got there in time to see a stretcher bearing a limp khaki-clad figure disappear inside the ambulance in front of the door. The ambulance pulled away fast, and he stared after it stupidly.

He hadn't known what he was going to do, but he felt cheated. Let down. He noticed that it was beginning to get dark. More and more people were coming into the street. He wondered where they'd come from and how they'd heard about the shooting so quickly. Every time he looked around there were more of them. Curious, eager voices kept asking, "What happened? What happened?" The answer was always the same. Hard. Angry. "A white cop shot a soldier."

Someone said, "Come on to the hospital. Find out what happened to him."

In front of the hotel he had been in the front of the crowd. Now there were so many people in back of him and in front of him that when they started toward the hospital, he moved along with them. He hadn't decided to go—the forward movement picked him up and moved him along without any intention on his part. He got the feeling that he had lost his identity as a person with a free will of his own. It frightened him at first. Then he began to feel powerful. He was surrounded by hundreds of people like himself. They were all together. They could do anything.

As the crowd moved slowly down Eighth Avenue, he saw that there were cops lined up on both sides of the street. Mounted cops kept coming out of the side streets, shouting, "Break it up! Keep moving. Keep moving."

The cops were scared of them. He could tell. Their faces were dead white in the semidarkness. He started saying the words over separately to himself. Dead. White. He laughed. White cops. White MP's. They got us coming and going, he thought. He laughed again. Dead. White. The words were funny said separately like that. He stopped laughing suddenly because a part of his mind repeated: twenty years, twenty years.

He licked his lips. It was hot as all hell tonight. He imagined what it would be like to be drinking swallow after swallow of ice-cold beer. His throat worked and he swallowed audibly.

The big black man walking beside him turned and looked down at him. "You all right, brother?" he asked curiously.

"Yeah," he nodded. "It's them sons of bitches of cops. They're scared of us." He shuddered. The heat was terrible. The tide of hate quivering in his stomach made him hotter. "Wish I had some beer," he said.

The man seemed to understand not only what he had said but all the things he had left unsaid. For he nodded and smiled. And William thought this was an extraordinary night. It was as though, standing so close together, so many of them like this—as though they knew each other's thoughts. It was a wonderful thing.

The crowd carried him along. Smoothly. Easily. He wasn't really walking. Just gliding. He was aware that the shuffling feet of the crowd made a muffled rhythm on the concrete sidewalk. It was slow, inevitable. An ominous sound, like a funeral march. With the regularity of a drumbeat. No. It's more like a pulse beat, he thought. It isn't a loud noise. It just keeps repeating over and over. But not that regular, because it builds up to something. It keeps building up.

The mounted cops rode their horses into the crowd. Trying to break it up into smaller groups. Then the rhythm was broken. Seconds later it started again. Each time the tempo was a little faster. He found he was breathing the same way. Faster and faster. As though he were running. There were more and more cops. All of them white. They had moved the colored cops out.

"They done that before," he muttered.

"What?" said the man next to him.

"They moved the colored cops out," he said.

He heard the man repeat it to someone standing beside him. It became part of the slow shuffling rhythm on the sidewalk. "They moved the colored cops." He heard it go back and back through the crowd until it was only a whisper of hate on the still, hot air. "They moved the colored cops."

As the crowd shuffled back and forth in front of the hospital, he caught snatches of conversation. "The soldier was dead when they put him in the ambulance." "Always tryin' to fool us." "Christ! Just let me get my hands on one of them cops."

He was thinking about the hospital and he didn't take part in any of the conversations. Even now across the long span of years he could remember the helpless, awful rage that had sent him hurrying home from this same hospital. Not saying anything. Getting home by some kind of instinct.

Pink had come to this hospital when she had had her last child. He could hear again the cold contempt in the voice of the nurse as she listened to Pink's loud grieving. "You people have too many children anyway," she said.

It left him speechless. He had his hat in his hand and he remembered how he wished afterward that he'd put it on in front of her to show her what he thought of her. As it was, all the bitter answer that finally surged into his throat seemed choke him. No words would come out. So he stared at her lean, spare body. He let his eyes stay a long time on her flat breasts. White uniform. White shoes. White stockings. White skin.

Then he mumbled, "It's too bad your eyes ain't white, too." And turned on his heel and walked out.

It wasn't any kind of answer. She probably didn't even know what he was talking about. The baby dead, and all he could think of was to tell her her eyes ought to be white. White shoes, white stockings, white uniform, white skin, and blue eyes.

Staring at the hospital, he saw with satisfaction that frightened faces were appearing at the windows. Some of the lights went out. He began to feel that this night was the first time he'd ever really been alive. Tonight everything was going to be changed. There was a growing, swelling sense of power in him. He felt the same thing in the people around him.

The cops were aware of it, too, he thought. They were out in full force. Mounties, patrolmen, emergency squads. Radio cars that looked like oversize bugs crawled through the side streets. Waited near the curbs. Their white tops stood out in the darkness. "White folks riding in white cars." The laughter that followed the words had a rough, raw rhythm. It repeated the pattern of the shuffling feet.

Someone said, "They got him at the station house. He ain't here." And the crowd started moving toward One Hundred Twenty-third Street.

Great God in the morning, William thought, everybody's out here. There were girls in thin summer dresses, boys in long coats and tight-legged pants, old women dragging kids along by the hand. A man on crutches jerked himself past to the rhythm of the shuffling feet. A blind man tapped his way through the center of the crowd, and it divided into two separate streams as it swept by him. At every street corner William noticed someone stopped to help the blind man up over the curb.

The street in front of the police station was so packed with people that he couldn't get near it. As far as he could see they weren't doing anything. They were simply standing there. Waiting for something to happen. He recognized a few of them: the woman with the loose, rolling eyes who sold shopping bags on One Hundred Twenty-fifth Street; the lucky-number peddler—the man with the white parrot on his shoulder; three sisters of the Heavenly Rest for All movement—barefooted women in loose white robes.

Then, for no reason that he could discover, everybody moved toward One Hundred Twenty-fifth Street. The motion of the crowd was slower now because it kept increasing in size as people coming from late church services were drawn into it. It was easy to identify them, he thought. The women wore white gloves. The kids were all slicked up. Despite the more gradual movement he was still being carried along effortlessly, easily. When someone in front of him barred his way, he pushed against the person irritably, frowning in annoyance because the smooth forward flow of his progress had been stopped.

It was Pink who stood in front of him. He stopped frowning when he recognized her. She had a brown-paper bag tucked under her arm, and he knew she had stopped at the corner store to get the big bottle of cream soda she always brought home on Sundays. The sight of it made him envious, for it meant that this Sunday had been going along in an orderly, normal fashion for her while he— She was staring at him so hard he was suddenly horribly conscious of the smell of the beer that had spilled on his shirt. He knew she had smelled it, too, by the tighter grip she took on her pocketbook.

"What you doing out here in this mob? A Sunday evening and you drinking beer," she said grimly.

For a moment he couldn't answer her. All he could think of was Sam. He almost said, "I saw Sam shot this afternoon," and he swallowed hard.

"This afternoon I saw a white cop kill a colored soldier," he said. "In the bar where I was drinking beer. I saw it. That's why I'm here. The glass of beer I was drinking went on my clothes. The cop shot him in the back. That's why I'm here."

He paused for a moment, took a deep breath. This was how it ought to be, he decided. She had to know sometime and this was the right place to tell her. In this semidarkness, in this confusion of noises, with the low, harsh rhythm of the footsteps sounding against the noise of the horses' hoofs.

His voice thickened. "I saw Scummy yesterday," he went on. "He told me Sam's doing time at hard labor. That's why we ain't heard from him. A white MP shot him when he wouldn't go to the nigger end of a bus. Sam shot the MP. They gave him twenty years at hard labor."

He knew he hadn't made it clear how to him the soldier in the bar was Sam; that it was like seeing his own son shot before his very eyes. I don't even know whether the soldier was dead, he thought. What made me tell her about Sam out here in the street like this, anyway? He realized with a sense of shock that he really didn't care that he had told her. He felt strong, powerful, aloof. All the time he'd been talking he wouldn't look right at her. Now, suddenly, he was looking at her as though she were a total stranger. He was coldly wondering what she'd do. He was prepared for anything.

But he wasn't prepared for the wail that came from her throat. The sound hung in the hot air. It made the awful quivering in his stomach worse. It echoed and re-echoed the length of the street. Somewhere in the distance a horse whinnied. A woman standing way back in the crowd groaned as though the sorrow and the anguish in that cry were more than she could bear.

Pink stood there for a moment. Silent. Brooding. Then she lifted the big bottle of soda high in the air. She threw it with all her might. It made a wide arc and landed in the exact center of the plate-glass window of a furniture store. The glass crashed in with a sound like a gunshot.

A sigh went up from the crowd. They surged toward the broken window. Pink followed close behind. When she reached the window, all the glass had been broken in. Reaching far inside, she grabbed a small footstool and then turned to hurl it through the window of the dress shop next door. He kept close behind her, watching her as she seized a new missile from each store window that she broke.

Plate-glass windows were being smashed all up and down One Hundred Twenty-fifth Street—on both sides of the street. The violent, explosive sound fed the sense of power in him. Pink had started this. He was proud of her, for she had shown herself to be a fit mate for a man of his type. He stayed as close to her as he could. So in spite of the crashing, splintering sounds and the swarming, violent activity around him, he knew the exact moment when she lost her big straw hat; when she took off the high-heeled patent-leather shoes and flung them away, striding swiftly along in her stockinged feet. That her dress was hanging crooked on her.

He was right in back of her when she stopped in front of a hat store. She carefully appraised all the hats inside the broken window. Finally she reached out, selected a small hat covered with purple violets, and fastened it securely on her head.

"Woman's got good sense," a man said.

"Man, oh, man! Let me get in there," said a rawboned woman who thrust her way forward through the jam of people to seize two hats from the window.

A roar of approval went up from the crowd. From then on when a window was smashed it was bare of merchandise when the people streamed past it. White folks owned these stores. They'd lose and lose and lose, he thought with satisfaction. The words "twenty years" re-echoed in his mind. I'll be an old man, he thought. Then: I may be dead before Sam gets out of prison.

The feeling of great power and strength left him. He was so confused by its loss that he decided this thing happening in the street wasn't real. It was so dark, there were so many people shouting and running about, that he almost convinced himself he was having a nightmare. He was aware that his hearing had now grown so acute he could pick up the tiniest sounds: the quickened breathing and the soft, gloating laughter of the crowd; even the sound of his own heart beating. He could hear these things under the noise of the breaking glass, under the shouts that were coming from both sides of the street. They forced him to face the fact that this was no dream but a reality from which he couldn't escape. The quivering in his stomach kept increasing as he walked along.

Pink was striding through the crowd just ahead of him. He studied her to see if she, too, was feeling as he did. But the outrage that ran through her had made her younger. She was tireless. Most of the time she was leading the crowd. It was all he could do to keep up with her, and finally he gave up the attempt—it made him too tired.

He stopped to watch a girl who was standing in a store window, clutching a clothes model tightly around the waist. "What's she want that for?" he said aloud. For the model had been stripped of clothing by the passing crowd, and he thought its pinkish torso was faintly obscene in its resemblance to a female figure.

The girl was young and thin. Her back was turned toward him, and there was something so ferocious about the way her dark hands gripped the naked model that he resisted the onward movement of the crowd to stare in fascination. The girl turned around. Her nervous hands were tight around the dummy's waist. It was Annie May.

"Oh, no!" he said, and let his breath come out with a sigh.

Her hands crept around the throat of the model and she sent it hurtling through the air above the heads of the crowd. It landed short of a window across the street. The legs shattered. The head rolled toward the curb. The waist snapped neatly in two. Only the torso remained whole and in one piece.

Annie May stood in the empty window and laughed with the crowd when someone kicked the torso into the street. He stood there, staring at her. He felt that now for the first time he understood her. She had never had anything but badly paying jobs—working for young white women who probably despised her. She was like Sam on that bus in Georgia. She didn't want just the nigger end of things, and here in Harlem there wasn't anything else for her. All along she'd been trying the only way she knew how to squeeze out of life a little something for herself.

He tried to get closer to the window where she was standing. He had to tell her that he understood. And the crowd, tired of the obstruction that he had made by standing still, swept him up and carried him past. He stopped thinking and let himself be carried along on a vast wave of feeling. There was so much plate glass on the sidewalk that it made a grinding noise under the feet of the hurrying crowd. It was a dull, harsh sound that set his teeth on edge and quickened the trembling of his stomach.

Now all the store windows that he passed were broken. The people hurrying by him carried tables, lamps, shoeboxes, clothing. A woman next to him held a wedding cake in her hands—it went up in tiers of white frosting with a small bride and groom mounted at the top. Her hands were bleeding, and he began to look closely at the people nearest him. Most of them, too, had cuts on their hands and legs. Then he saw there was blood on the sidewalk in front of the windows; blood dripping down the jagged edges of the broken windows. And he wanted desperately to go home.

He was conscious that the rhythm of the crowd had changed. It was faster, and it had taken on an ugly note. The cops were using their nightsticks. Police wagons drew up to the curbs. When they pulled away, they were full of men and women who carried loot from the stores in their hands.

The police cars slipping through the streets were joined by other cars with loudspeakers on top. The voices coming through the loudspeakers were harsh. They added to the noise and the confusion. He tried to listen to what the voices were saying. But the words had no meaning for him. He caught one phrase over and over: "Good people of Harlem." It made him feel sick.

He repeated the words "of Harlem." We don't belong anywhere, he thought. There ain't no room for us anywhere. There wasn't no room for Sam in a bus in Georgia. There ain't no room for us here in New York. There ain't no place but top floors. The top-floor black people. And he laughed, and the sound stuck in his throat.

After that he snatched a suit from the window of a men's clothing store. It was a summer suit. The material felt crisp and cool. He walked away with it under his arm. He'd never owned a suit like that. He simply sweated out the summer in the same dark pants he wore in winter. Even while he stroked the material, a part of his mind sneered—you got summer pants; Sam's got twenty years.

He was surprised to find that he was almost at Lenox Avenue, for he hadn't remembered crossing Seventh. At the corner the cops were shoving a group of young boys and girls into a police wagon. He paused to watch. Annie May was in the middle of the group. She had a yellow-fox jacket dangling from one hand.

"Annie May!" he shouted. "Annie May!" The crowd pushed him along faster and faster. She hadn't seen him. He let himself be carried forward by the movement of the crowd. He had to find Pink and tell her that the cops had taken Annie May.

He peered into the dimness of the street ahead of him, looking for her; then he elbowed his way toward the curb so that he could see the other side of the street. He forgot about finding Pink, for directly opposite him was the music store that he passed every night coming home from work. Young boys and girls were always lounging on the sidewalk in front of it. They danced a few steps while they listened to the records being played inside the shop. All the records sounded the same—a terribly magnified woman's voice bleating out a blues song in a voice that sounded to him like that of an animal in heat—an old animal, tired and beaten, but with an insinuating know-how left in her. The white men who went past the store smiled as their eyes lingered on the young girls swaying to the music.

"White folks got us comin' and goin'. Backwards and forwards," he muttered. He fought his way out of the crowd and walked toward a no-parking sign that stood in front of the store. He rolled it up over the curb.

It was heavy, and the effort made him pant. It took all his strength to send it crashing through the glass on the door.

Almost immediately an old woman and a young man slipped inside the narrow shop. He followed them. He watched them smash the records that lined the shelves. He hadn't thought of actually breaking the records, but once he started he found the crisp, snapping noise pleasant. The feeling of power began to return. He didn't like these records, so they had to be destroyed.

When they left the music store there wasn't a whole record left. The old woman came out of the store last. As he hurried off up the street he could have sworn he smelled the sharp, acrid smell of smoke. He turned and looked back. He was right. A thin wisp of smoke was coming through the store door. The old woman had long since disappeared in the crowd.

Farther up the street he looked back again. The fire in the record shop was burning merrily. It was making a glow that lit up that part of the street. There was a new rhythm now. It was faster and faster. Even the voices coming from the loudspeakers had taken on the urgency of speed.

Fire trucks roared up the street. He threw his head back and laughed when he saw them. That's right, he thought. Burn the whole damn place down. It was wonderful. Then he frowned. "Twenty years at hard labor." The words came back to him. He was a fool. Fire wouldn't wipe that out. There wasn't anything that would wipe it out.

He remembered then that he had to find Pink. To tell her about Annie May. He overtook her in the next block. She's got more stuff, he thought. She had a table lamp in one hand, a large enamel kettle in the other. The lightweight summer coat draped across her shoulders was so small it barely covered her enormous arms. She was watching a group of boys assault the steel gates in front of a liquor store. She frowned at them so ferociously he wondered what she was going to do. Hating liquor the way she did, he half expected her to cuff the boys and send them on their way up the street.

She turned and looked at the crowd in back of her. When she saw him she beckoned to him. "Hold these," she said. He took the lamp, the kettle, and the coat she held out to him, and he saw that her face was wet with perspiration. The print dress was darkly stained with it.

She fastened the hat with the purple flowers securely on her head. Then she walked over to the gate. "Git out the way," she said to the boys. Bracing herself in front of the gate, she started tugging at it. The gate resisted. She pulled at it with a sudden access of such furious strength that he was frightened. Watching her, he got the feeling that the resistance of the gate had transformed it in her mind. It was no longer a gate—it had become the world that had taken her son, and she was wreaking vengeance on it.

The gate began to bend and sway under her assault. Then it was down.

She stood there for a moment, staring at her hands—big drops of blood oozed slowly over the palms. The she turned to the crowd that had stopped to watch.

"Come on, you niggers," she said. Her eyes were little and evil and triumphant. "Come on and drink up the white man's liquor." As she strode off up the street, the beflowered hat dangled precariously from the back of her head.

When he caught up with her she was moaning, talking to herself in husky whispers. She stopped when she saw him and put her hand on his arm.

"It's hot, ain't it?" she said, panting.

In the midst of all this violence, the sheer commonplaceness of her question startled him. He looked at her closely. The rage that had been in her was gone, leaving her completely exhausted. She was breathing too fast in uneven gasps that shook her body. Rivulets of sweat streamed down her face. It was as though her triumph over the metal gate had finished her. The gate won anyway, he thought.

"Let's go home, Pink," he said. He had to shout to make his voice carry over the roar of the crowd, the sound of breaking glass.

He realized she didn't have the strength to speak, for she only nodded in reply to his suggestion. Once we get home she'll be all right, he thought. It was suddenly urgent that they get home, where it was quiet, where he could think, where he could take something to still the tremors in his stomach. He tried to get her to walk a little faster, but she kept slowing down until, when they entered their own street, it seemed to him they were barely moving.

In the middle of the block she stood still. "I can't make it," she said. "I'm too tired."

Even as he put his arm around her she started going down. He tried to hold her up, but her great weight was too much for him. She went down slowly, inevitably, like a great ship capsizing. Until all of her huge body was crumpled on the sidewalk.

"Pink," he said. "Pink. You gotta get up," he said it over and over again.

She didn't answer. He leaned over and touched her gently. Almost immediately afterward he straightened up. All his life, moments of despair and frustration had left him speechless—strangled by the words that rose in his throat. This time the words poured out.

He sent his voice raging into the darkness and the awful confusion of noises. "The sons of bitches," he shouted. "The sons of bitches."

ELLIOT LIEBOW
Men and Jobs

A pickup truck drives slowly down the street. The truck stops as it comes abreast of a man sitting on a cast-iron porch and the white driver calls out, asking if the man wants a day's work. The man shakes his head and the truck moves on up the block, stopping again whenever idling men come within calling distance of the driver. At the Carry-out corner, five men debate the question briefly and shake their heads no to the truck. The truck turns the corner and repeats the same performance up the next street. In the distance, one can see one man, then another, climb into the back of the truck and sit down. In starts and stops, the truck finally disappears.

What is it we have witnessed here? A labor scavenger rebuffed by his would-be prey? Lazy, irresponsible men turning down an honest day's pay for an honest day's work? Or a more complex phenomenon marking the intersection of economic forces, social values and individual states of mind and body?

Let us look again at the driver of the truck. He has been able to recruit only two or three men from each twenty or fifty he contacts. To him, it is clear that the others simply do not choose to work. Singly or in groups, belly-empty or belly-full, sullen or gregarious, drunk or sober, they confirm what he has read, heard and knows from his own experience: these men wouldn't take a job if it were handed to them on a platter.[1]

Quite apart from the question of whether or not this is true of some of the men he sees on the street, it is clearly not true of all of them. If it were, he would not have come here in the first place; or having come, he

---

1. By different methods, perhaps, some social scientists have also located the problem in the men themselves, in their unwillingness or lack of desire to work: "To improve the underprivileged worker's performance, one must help him to learn *to want* . . . higher social goals for himself and his children. . . . The problem of changing the work habits and motivation of [lower class] people . . . is a problem of changing the goals, the ambitions, and the level of cultural and occupational aspiration of the underprivileged worker." (Emphasis in original.) Allison Davis, "The Motivation of the Underprivileged Worker," p. 90.

would have left with an empty truck. It is not even true of most of them, for most of the men he sees on the street this weekday morning do, in fact, have jobs. But since, at the moment, they are neither working nor sleeping, and since they hate the depressing room or apartment they live in, or because there is nothing to do there,[2] or because they want to get away from their wives or anyone else living there, they are out on the street, indistinguishable from those who do not have jobs or do not want them. Some, like Boley, a member of a trash-collection crew in a suburban housing development, work Saturdays and are off on this weekday. Some, like Sweets, work nights cleaning up middle-class trash, dirt, dishes and garbage, and mopping the floors of the office buildings, hotels, restaurants, toilets and other public places dirtied during the day. Some men work for retail businesses such as liquor stores which do not begin the day until ten o'clock. Some laborers, like Tally, have already come back from the job because the ground was too wet for pick and shovel or because the weather was too cold for pouring concrete. Other employed men stayed off the job today for personal reasons: Clarence to go to a funeral at eleven this morning and Sea Cat to answer a subpoena as a witness in a criminal proceeding.

Also on the street, unwitting contributors to the impression taken away by the truck driver, are the halt and the lame. The man on the cast-iron steps strokes one gnarled arthritic hand with the other and says he doesn't know whether or not he'll live long enough to be eligible for Social Security. He pauses, then adds matter-of-factly, "Most times, I don't care whether I do or don't." Stoopy's left leg was polio-withered in childhood. Raymond, who looks as if he could tear out a fire hydrant, coughs up blood if he bends or moves suddenly. The quiet man who hangs out in front of the Saratoga apartments has a steel hook strapped onto his left elbow. And had the man in the truck been able to look into the wine-clouded eyes of the man in the green cap, he would have realized that the man did not even understand he was being offered a day's work.

Others, having had jobs and been laid off, are drawing unemployment compensation (up to $44 per week) and have nothing to gain by accepting work which pays little more than this and frequently less.

Still others, like Bumdoodle the numbers man, are working hard at illegal ways of making money, hustlers who are on the street to turn a dollar any way they can: buying and selling sex, liquor, narcotics, stolen goods, or anything else that turns up.

Only a handful remains unaccounted for. There is Tonk, who cannot bring himself to take a job away from the corner, because, according to the other men, he suspects his wife will be unfaithful if given the opportunity. There is Stanton, who has not reported to work for four days now,

2. The comparison of sitting at home along with being in jail is commonplace.

not since Bernice disappeared. He bought a brand new knife against her return. She had done this twice before, he said, but not for so long and not without warning, and he had forgiven her. But this time, "I ain't got it in me to forgive her again." His rage and shame are there for all to see as he paces the Carry-out and the corner, day and night, hoping to catch a glimpse of her.

And finally, there are those like Arthur, able-bodied men who have no visible means of support, legal or illegal, who neither have jobs nor want them. The truck driver, among others, believes the Arthurs to be representative of all the men he sees idling on the street during his own working hours. They are not, but they cannot be dismissed simply because they are a small minority. It is not enough to explain them away as being lazy or irresponsible or both because an able-bodied man with responsibilities who refuses work is, by the truck driver's definition, lazy and irresponsible. Such an answer begs the question. It is descriptive of the facts; it does not explain them.

Moreover, despite their small numbers, the don't-work-and-don't-want-to-work minority is especially significant because they represent the strongest and clearest expression of those values and attitudes associated with making a living which, to varying degrees, are found throughout the streetcorner world. These men differ from the others in degree rather than in kind, the principal difference being that they are carrying out the implications of their values and experiences to their logical, inevitable conclusions. In this sense, the others have yet to come to terms with themselves and the world they live in.

Putting aside, for the moment, what the men say and feel, and looking at what they actually do and the choices they make, getting a job, keeping a job, and doing well at it is clearly of low priority. Arthur will not take a job at all. Leroy is supposed to be on his job at 4:00 P.M. but it is already 4:10 and he still cannot bring himself to leave the free games he has accumulated on the pinball machine in the Carry-out. Tonk started a construction job on Wednesday, worked Thursday and Friday, then didn't go back again. On the same kind of job, Sea Cat quit in the second week. Sweets had been working three months as a busboy in a restaurant, then quit without notice, not sure himself why he did so. A real estate agent, saying he was more interested in getting the job done than in the cost, asked Richard to give him an estimate on repairing and painting the inside of a house, but Richard, after looking over the job, somehow never got around to submitting an estimate. During one period, Tonk would not leave the corner to take a job because his wife might prove unfaithful; Stanton would not take a job because his woman had been unfaithful.

Thus, the man-job relationship is a tenuous one. At any given moment, a job may occupy a relatively low position on the streetcorner scale of real values. Getting a job may be subordinated to relations with women or to other non-job considerations; the commitment to a job one already has is frequently shallow and tentative.

The reasons are many. Some are objective and reside principally in the job; some are subjective and reside principally in the man. The line between them, however, is not a clear one. Behind the man's refusal to take a job or his decision to quit one is not a simple impulse or value choice but a complex combination of assessments of objective reality on the one hand, and values, attitudes and beliefs drawn from different levels of his experience on the other.

Objective economic considerations are frequently a controlling factor in a man's refusal to take a job. How much the job pays is a crucial question but seldom asked. He knows how much it pays. Working as a stock clerk, a delivery boy, or even behind the counter of liquor stores, drug stores and other retail businesses pays one dollar an hour. So, too, do most busboy, car-wash, janitorial and other jobs available to him. Some jobs, such as dishwasher, may dip as low as eighty cents an hour and others, such as elevator operator or work in a junk yard, may offer $1.15 or $1.25. Take-home pay for jobs such as these ranges from $35 to $50 a week, but a take-home pay of $45 for a five-day week is the exception rather than the rule.

One of the principal advantages of these kinds of jobs is that they offer fairly regular work. Most of them involve essential services and are therefore somewhat less responsive to business conditions than are some higher paying, less menial jobs. Most of them are also inside jobs not dependent on the weather, as are construction jobs and other higher-paying outside work.

Another seemingly important advantage of working in hotels, restaurants, office and apartment buildings and retail establishments is that they frequently offer an opportunity for stealing on the job. But stealing can be a two-edged sword. Apart from increasing the cost of the goods or services to the general public, a less obvious result is that the practice usually acts as a depressant on the employee's own wage level. Owners of small retail establishments and other employers frequently anticipate employee stealing and adjust the wage rate accordingly. Tonk's employer explained why he was paying Tonk $35 for a 55-60 hour workweek. These men will all steal, he said. Although he keeps close watch on Tonk, he estimates that Tonk steals from $35 to $40 a week.[3] What he steals, when added to his regular earnings, brings his take-home pay to $70 or $75 per week. The employer said he did not mind this because Tonk is worth that much to the business. But if he were to pay Tonk outright the full value of his labor, Tonk would still be stealing $35-$40 per week and this, he said, the business simply would not support.

3. Exactly the same estimate as the one made by Tonk himself. On the basis of personal knowledge of the stealing routine employed by Tonk, however, I suspect the actual amount is considerably smaller.

This wage arrangement, with stealing built-in, was satisfactory to both parties, with each one independently expressing his satisfaction. Such a wage-theft system, however, is not as balanced and equitable as it appears. Since the wage level rests on the premise that the employee will steal the unpaid value of his labor, the man who does not steal on the job is penalized. And furthermore, even if he does not steal, no one would believe him; the employer and others believe he steals because the system presumes it.

Nor is the man who steals, as he is expected to, as well off as he believes himself to be. The employer may occasionally close his eyes to the worker's stealing but not often and not for long. He is, after all, a businessman and cannot always find it within himself to let a man steal from him, even if the man is stealing his own wages. Moreover, it is only by keeping close watch on the worker that the employer can control how much is stolen and thereby protect himself against the employee's stealing more than he is worth. From this viewpoint, then, the employer is not in wage-theft collusion with the employee. In the case of Tonk, for instance, the employer was not actively abetting the theft. His estimate of how much Tonk was stealing was based on what he thought Tonk was able to steal despite his own best efforts to prevent him from stealing anything at all. Were he to have caught Tonk in the act of stealing, he would, of course, have fired him from the job and perhaps called the police as well. Thus, in an actual if not in a legal sense, all the elements of entrapment are present. The employer knowingly provides the conditions which entice (force) the employee to steal the unpaid value of his labor, but at the same time he punishes him for theft if he catches him doing so.

Other consequences of the wage-theft system are even more damaging to the employee. Let us, for argument's sake, say that Tonk is in no danger of entrapment; that his employer is willing to wink at the stealing and that Tonk, for his part, is perfectly willing to earn a little, steal a little. Let us say, too, that he is paid $35 a week and allowed to steal $35. His money income—as measured by the goods and services he can purchase with it—is, of course, $70. But not all of his income is available to him for all purposes. He cannot draw on what he steals to build his self-respect or to measure his self-worth. For this, he can draw only on his earnings —the amount given him publicly and voluntarily in exchange for his labor. His "respect" and "self-worth" income remains at $35—only half that of the man who also receives $70 but all of it in the form of wages. His earnings publicly measure the worth of his labor to his employer, and they are important to others and to himself in taking the measure of his worth as a man.[4]

With or without stealing, and quite apart from any interior processes

---

4. Some public credit may accrue to the clever thief but not respect.

going on in the man who refuses such a job or quits it casually and without apparent reason, the objective fact is that menial jobs in retailing or in the service trades simply do not pay enough to support a man and his family. This is not to say that the worker is underpaid; this may or may not be true. Whether he is or not, the plain fact is that, in such a job, he cannot make a living. Nor can he take much comfort in the fact that these jobs tend to offer more regular, steadier work. If he cannot live on the $45 or $50 he makes in one week, the longer he works, the longer he cannot live on what he makes.[5]

Construction work, even for unskilled laborers, usually pays better, with the hourly rate ranging from $1.50 to $2.60 an hour.[6] Importantly, too, good references, a good driving record, a tenth grade (or any high school) education, previous experience, the ability to "bring police clearance with you" are not normally required of laborers as they frequently are for some of the jobs in retailing or in the service trades.

Construction work, however, has its own objective disadvantages. It is, first of all, seasonal work for the great bulk of the laborers, beginning early in the spring and tapering off as winter weather sets in.[7] And even during the season the work is frequently irregular. Early or late in the season, snow or temperatures too low for concrete frequently sends the laborers back home, and during late spring or summer, a heavy rain on Tuesday or Wednesday, leaving a lot of water and mud behind it, can

5. It might be profitable to compare, as Howard S. Becker suggests, gross aspects of income and housing costs in this particular area with those reported by Herbert Gans for the low-income working class in Boston's West End. In 1958, Gans reports, median income for the West Enders was just under $70 a week, a level considerably higher than that enjoyed by the people in the Carry-out neighborhood five years later. Gans himself rented a six-room apartment in the West End for $46 a month, about $10 more than the going rate for long-time residents. In the Carry-out neighborhood, rooms that could accommodate more than a cot and a miniature dresser—that is, rooms that qualified for family living—rented for $12 to $22 a week. Ignoring differences that really can't be ignored—the privacy and self-contained efficiency of the multi-room apartment as against the fragmented, public living of the rooming-house "apartment," with a public toilet on a floor always different from the one your room is on (no matter, it probably doesn't work, anyway)—and assuming comparable states of disrepair, the West Enders were paying $6 or $7 a month for a room that cost the Carry-outers at least $50 a month, and frequently more. Looking at housing costs as a percentage of income—and again ignoring what cannot be ignored: that what goes by the name of "housing" in the two areas is not at all the same thing—the median income West Ender could get a six-room apartment for about 12 percent of his income, while his 1963 Carry-out counterpart, with a weekly income of $60 (to choose a figure from the upper end of the income range), often paid 20–33 percent of his income for one room. See Herbert J. Gans, The Urban Villagers, pp. 10–13.
6. The higher amount is 1962 union scale for building laborers. According to the Wage Agreement Contract for Heavy Construction Laborers (Washington, D.C., and vicinity) covering the period from May 1, 1963 to April 30, 1966, minimum hourly wage for heavy construction laborers was to go from $2.75 (May 1963) by annual increments to $2.92, effective November 1, 1965.
7. "Open-sky" work, such as building overpasses, highways, etc., in which the workers and materials are directly exposed to the elements, traditionally begins in March and ends around Thanksgiving. The same is true for much of the street repair work and the laying of sewer, electric, gas, and telephone lines by the city and public utilities, all important employers of laborers. Between Thanksgiving and March, they retain only skeleton crews selected from their best, most reliable men.

mean a two or three day workweek for the pick-and-shovel men and other unskilled laborers.[8]

The elements are not the only hazard. As the project moves from one construction stage to another, laborers—usually without warning—are laid off, sometimes permanently or sometimes for weeks at a time. The more fortunate or the better workers are told periodically to "take a walk for two, three days."

Both getting the construction job and getting to it are also relatively more difficult than is the case for the menial jobs in retailing and the service trades. Job competition is always fierce. In the city, the large construction projects are unionized. One has to have ready cash to get into the union to become eligible to work on these projects and, being eligible, one has to find an opening. Unless one "knows somebody," say a foreman or a laborer who knows the day before that they are going to take on new men in the morning, this can be a difficult and disheartening search.

Many of the nonunion jobs are in suburban Maryland or Virginia. The newspaper ads say, "Report ready to work to the trailer at the intersection of Rte. 11 and Old Bridge Rd., Bunston, Virginia (or Maryland)," but this location may be ten, fifteen, or even twenty-five miles from the Carry-out. Public transportation would require two or more hours to get there, if it services the area at all. Without access to a car or to a car-pool arrangement, it is not worthwhile reading the ad. So the men do not. Jobs such as these are usually filled by word of mouth information, beginning with someone who knows someone or who is himself working there and looking for a paying rider. Furthermore, nonunion jobs in outlying areas tend to be smaller projects of relatively short duration and to pay somewhat less than scale.

Still another objective factor is the work itself. For some men, whether the job be digging, mixing mortar, pushing a wheelbarrow, unloading materials, carrying and placing steel rods for reinforcing concrete, or building or laying concrete forms, the work is simply too hard. Men such as Tally and Wee Tom can make such work look like child's play; some of the older work-hardened men, such as Budder and Stanton, can do it too, although not without showing unmistakable signs of strain and weariness at the end of the workday. But those who lack the robustness of a Tally

8. In a recent year, the crime rate in Washington for the month of August jumped 18 percent over the preceding month. A veteran police officer explained the increase to David L. Bazelon, Chief Judge, U.S. Court of Appeals for the District of Columbia. "It's quite simple. . . . You see, August was a very wet month. . . . These people wait on the street corner each morning around 6:00 or 6:30 for a truck to pick them up and take them to a construction site. If it's raining, that truck doesn't come, and the men are going to be idle that day. If the bad weather keeps up for three days . . . we know we are going to have trouble on our hands—and sure enough, there invariably follows a rash of purse-snatchings, house-breakings and the like. . . . These people have to eat like the rest of us, you know." David L. Bazelon, Address to the Federal Bar Association, p. 3.

or the time-inured immunity of a Budder must either forego jobs such as these or pay a heavy toll to keep them. For Leroy, in his early twenties, almost six feet tall but weighing under 140 pounds, it would be as difficult to push a loaded wheelbarrow, or to unload and stack 96-pound bags of cement all day long, as it would be for Stoopy with his withered leg.

Heavy, backbreaking labor of the kind that used to be regularly associated with bull gangs or concrete gangs is no longer characteristic of laboring jobs, especially those with the larger, well-equipped construction companies. Brute strength is still required from time to time, as on smaller jobs where it is not economical to bring in heavy equipment or where the small, undercapitalized contractor has none to bring in. In many cases, however, the conveyor belt has replaced the wheelbarrow or the Georgia buggy, mechanized forklifts have eliminated heavy, manual lifting, and a variety of digging machines have replaced the pick and shovel. The result is fewer jobs for unskilled laborers and, in many cases, a work speed-up for those who do have jobs. Machines now set the pace formerly set by men. Formerly, a laborer pushed a wheelbarrow of wet cement to a particular spot, dumped it, and returned for another load. Another laborer, in hip boots, pushed the wet concrete around with a shovel or a hoe, getting it roughly level in preparation for the skilled finishers. He had relatively small loads to contend with and had only to keep up with the men pushing the wheelbarrows. Now, the job for the man pushing the wheelbarrow is gone and the wet concrete comes rushing down a chute at the man in the hip boots who must "spread it quick or drown."

Men who have been running an elevator, washing dishes, or "pulling trash" cannot easily move into laboring jobs. They lack the basic skills for "unskilled" construction labor, familiarity with tools and materials, and tricks of the trade without which hard jobs are made harder. Previously unused or untrained muscles rebel in pain against the new and insistent demands made upon them, seriously compromising the man's performance and testing his willingness to see the job through.

A healthy, sturdy, active man of good intelligence requires from two to four weeks to break in on a construction job.[9] Even if he is willing somehow to bull his way through the first few weeks, it frequently happens that his foreman or the craftsman he services with materials and general assistance is not willing to wait that long for him to get into condition or to learn at a glance the difference in size between a rough 2″ x 8″ and a finished 2″ x 10″. The foreman and the craftsman are themselves "under the gun" and cannot "carry" the man when other men, who are

9. Estimate of Mr. Francis Greenfield, President of the International Hod Carriers, Building and Common Laborers' District Council of Washington, D.C., and Vicinity. I am indebted to Mr. Greenfield for several points in these paragraphs dealing with construction laborers.

already used to the work and who know the tools and materials, are lined up to take the job.

Sea Cat was "healthy, sturdy, active and of good intelligence." When a judge gave him six weeks in which to pay his wife $200 in back child-support payments, he left his grocery-store job in order to take a higher-paying job as a laborer, arranged for him by a foreman friend. During the first week the weather was bad and he worked only Wednesday and Friday, cursing the elements all the while for cheating him out of the money he could have made. The second week, the weather was fair but he quit at the end of the fourth day, saying frankly that the work was too hard for him. He went back to his job at the grocery store and took a second job working nights as a dishwasher in a restaurant,[10] earning little if any more at the two jobs than he would have earned as a laborer, and keeping at both of them until he had paid off his debts.

Tonk did not last as long as Sea Cat. No one made any predictions when he got a job in a parking lot, but when the men on the corner learned he was to start on a road construction job, estimates of how long he would last ranged from one to three weeks. Wednesday was his first day. He spent that evening and night at home. He did the same on Thursday. He worked Friday and spent Friday evening and part of Saturday draped over the mailbox on the corner. Sunday afternoon, Tonk decided he was not going to report on the job the next morning. He explained that after working three days, he knew enough about the job to know that it was too hard for him. He knew he wouldn't be able to keep up and he'd just as soon quit now as get fired later.

Logan was a tall, two-hundred-pound man in his late twenties. His back used to hurt him only on the job, he said, but now he can't straighten up for increasingly longer periods of time. He said he had traced this to the awkward walk he was forced to adopt by the loaded wheelbarrows which pull him down into a half-stoop. He's going to quit, he said, as soon as he can find another job. If he can't find one real soon, he guesses he'll quit anyway. It's not worth it, having to walk bent over and leaning to one side.

Sometimes, the strain and effort is greater than the man is willing to admit, even to himself. In the early summer of 1963, Richard was rooming at Nancy's place. His wife and children were "in the country" (his grandmother's home in Carolina), waiting for him to save up enough money so that he could bring them back to Washington and start over again after a disastrous attempt to "make it" in Philadelphia. Richard had gotten a job with a fence company in Virginia. It paid $1.60 an hour. The first few evenings, when he came home from work, he looked ill from exhaustion and

10. Not a sinecure, even by streetcorner standards.

the heat. Stanton said Richard would have to quit, "he's too small [thin] for that kind of work." Richard said he was doing O.K. and would stick with the job.

At Nancy's one night, when Richard had been working about two weeks, Nancy and three or four others were sitting around talking, drinking, and listening to music. Someone asked Nancy when was Richard going to bring his wife and children up from the country. Nancy said she didn't know, but it probably depended on how long it would take him to save up enough money. She said she didn't think he could stay with the fence job much longer. This morning, she said, the man Richard rode to work with knocked on the door and Richard didn't answer. She looked in his room. Richard was still asleep. Nancy tried to shake him awake. "No more digging!" Richard cried out. "No more digging! I can't do no more God-damn digging!" When Nancy finally managed to wake him, he dressed quickly and went to work.

Richard stayed on the job two more weeks, then suddenly quit, ostensibly because his pay check was three dollars less than what he thought it should have been.

In summary of objective job considerations, then, the most important fact is that a man who is able and willing to work cannot earn enough money to support himself, his wife, and one or more children. A man's chances for working regularly are good only if he is willing to work for less than he can live on, and sometimes not even then. On some jobs, the wage rate is deceptively higher than on others, but the higher the wage rate, the more difficult it is to get the job, and the less the job security. Higher-paying construction work tends to be seasonal and, during the season, the amount of work available is highly sensitive to business and weather conditions and to the changing requirements of individual projects.[11] Moreover, high-paying construction jobs are frequently beyond the physical capacity of some of the men, and some of the low-paying jobs are scaled down even lower in accordance with the self-fulfilling assumption that the man will steal part of his wages on the job.[12]

Bernard assesses the objective job situation dispassionately over a cup

11. The overall result is that, in the long run, a Negro laborer's earnings are not substantially greater—and may be less—that those of the busboy, janitor, or stock clerk. Herman P. Miller, for example, reports that in 1960, 40 percent of all jobs held by Negro men were as laborers or in the service trades. The average annual wage for nonwhite nonfarm laborers was $2,400. The average earning of nonwhite, service workers was $2,500 (*Rich Man, Poor Man,* p. 90). Francis Greenfield estimates that in the Washington vicinity, the 1965 earnings of the union laborer who works whenever work is available will be about $3,200. Even this figure is high for the man on the streetcorner. Union men in heavy construction are the aristocrats of the laborers. Casual day labor and jobs with small firms in the building and construction trades, or with firms in other industries, pay considerably less.
12. For an excellent discussion of the self-fulfilling assumption (or prophecy) as a social force, see "The Self-Fulfilling Prophecy," Ch. XI, in Robert K. Merton's *Social Theory and Social Structure.*

of coffee, sometimes poking at the coffee with his spoon, sometimes staring at it as if, like a crystal ball, it holds tomorrow's secrets. He is twenty-seven years old. He and the woman with whom he lives have a baby son, and she has another child by another man. Bernard does odd jobs —mostly painting—but here it is the end of January, and his last job was with the Post Office during the Christmas mail rush. He would like postal work as a steady job, he says. It pays well (about $2.00 an hour) but he has twice failed the Post Office examination (he graduated from a Washington high school) and has given up the idea as an impractical one. He is supposed to see a man tonight about a job as a parking attendant for a large apartment house. The man told him to bring his birth certificate and driver's license, but his license was suspended because of a backlog of unpaid traffic fines. A friend promised to lend him some money this evening. If he gets it, he will pay the fines tomorrow morning and have his license reinstated. He hopes the man with the job will wait till tomorrow night.

A "security job" is what he really wants, he said. He would like to save up money for a taxicab. (But having twice failed the postal examination and having a bad driving record as well, it is highly doubtful that he could meet the qualifications or pass the written test.) That would be "a good life." He can always get a job in a restaurant or as a clerk in a drugstore but they don't pay enough, he said. He needs to take home at least $50 to $55 a week. He thinks he can get that much driving a truck somewhere. . . . Sometimes he wishes he had stayed in the army. . . . A security job, that's what he wants most of all, a real security job. . . .

When we look at what the men bring to the job rather than at what the job offers the men, it is essential to keep in mind that we are not looking at men who come to the job fresh, just out of school perhaps, and newly prepared to undertake the task of making a living, or from another job where they earned a living and are prepared to do the same on this job. Each man comes to the job with a long job history characterized by his not being able to support himself and his family. Each man carries this knowledge, born of his experience, with him. He comes to the job flat and stale, wearied by the sameness of it all, convinced of his own incompetence, terrified of responsibility—of being tested still again and found wanting. Possible exceptions are the younger men not yet, or just, married. They suspect all this but have yet to have it confirmed by repeated personal experience over time. But those who are or have been married know it well. It is the experience of the individual and the group; of their fathers and probably their sons. Convinced of their inadequacies, not only do they not seek out those few better-paying jobs which test their resources, but they actively avoid them, gravitating in a mass to the menial, routine jobs which offer no challenge—and therefore pose no threat—to the already diminished images they have of themselves.

Thus Richard does not follow through on the real estate agent's offer. He is afraid to do on his own—minor plastering, replacing broken windows, other minor repairs and painting—exactly what he had been doing for months on a piecework basis under someone else (and which provided him with a solid base from which to derive a cost estimate).

Richard once offered an important clue to what may have gone on in his mind when the job offer was made. We were in the Carry-out, at a time when he was looking for work. He was talking about the kind of jobs available to him.

I graduated from high school [Baltimore] but I don't know anything. I'm dumb. Most of the time I don't even say I graduated, 'cause then somebody asks me a question and I can't answer it, and they think I was lying about graduating. . . . They graduated me but I didn't know anything. I had lousy grades but I guess they wanted to get rid of me.

I was at Margaret's house the other night and her little sister asked me to help her with her homework. She showed me some fractions and I knew right away I couldn't do them. I was ashamed so I told her I had to go to the bathroom.

And so it must have been, surely, with the real estate agent's offer. Convinced that "I'm dumb . . . I don't know anything," he "knew right away" he couldn't do it, despite the fact that he had been doing just this sort of work all along.

Thus, the man's low self-esteem generates a fear of being tested and prevents him from accepting a job with responsibilities or, once on a job, from staying with it if responsibilities are thrust on him, even if the wages are commensurately higher. Richard refuses such a job, Leroy leaves one, and another man, given more responsibility and more pay, knows he will fail and proceeds to do so, proving he was right about himself all along. The self-fulfilling prophecy is everywhere at work. In a hallway, Stanton, Tonk and Boley are passing a bottle around. Stanton recalls the time he was in the service. Everything was fine until he attained the rank of corporal. He worried about everything he did then. Was he doing the right thing? Was he doing it well? When would they discover their mistake and take his stripes (and extra pay) away? When he finally lost his stripes, everything was all right again.

Lethargy, disinterest and general apathy on the job, so often reported by employers, has its streetcorner counterpart. The men do not ordinarily talk about their jobs or ask one another about them.[13] Although most of the men know who is or is not working at any given time, they may or

13. This stands in dramatic contrast to the leisure-time conversation of stable, working-class men. For the coal miners (of Ashton, England), for example, "the topic [of conversation] which surpasses all others in frequency is work—the difficulties which have been encountered in the day's shift, the way in which a particular task was accomplished, and so on." Josephine Klein, *Samples from English Cultures*, Vol. I, p. 88.

may not know what particular job an individual man has. There is no overt interest in job specifics as they relate to this or that person, in large part perhaps because the specifics are not especially relevant. To know that a man is working is to know approximately how much he makes and to know as much as one needs or wants to know about how he makes it. After all, how much difference does it make to know whether a man is pushing a mop and pulling trash in an apartment house, a restaurant, or an office building, or delivering groceries, drugs, or liquor, or, if he's a laborer, whether he's pushing a wheelbarrow, mixing mortar, or digging a hole. So much does one job look like every other that there is little to choose between them. In large part, the job market consists of a narrow range of nondescript chores calling for nondistinctive, undifferentiated, unskilled labor. "A job is a job."

A crucial factor in the streetcorner man's lack of job commitment is the overall value he places on the job. *For his part, the streetcorner man puts no lower value on the job than does the larger society around him.* He knows the social value of the job by the amount of money the employer is willing to pay him for doing it. In a real sense, every pay day, he counts in dollars and cents the value placed on the job by society at large. He is no more (and frequently less) ready to quit and look for another job than his employer is ready to fire him and look for another man. Neither the streetcorner man who performs these jobs nor the society which requires him to perform them assesses the job as one "worth doing and worth doing well." Both employee and employer are contemptuous of the job. The employee shows his contempt by his reluctance to accept it or keep it, the employer by paying less than is required to support a family.[14] Nor does the low-wage job offer prestige, respect, interesting work, opportunity for learning or advancement, or any other compensation. With few exceptions, jobs filled by the streetcorner men are at the bottom of the employment ladder in every respect, from wage level to prestige. Typically, they are hard, dirty, uninteresting and underpaid. The rest of society (whatever its ideal values regarding the dignity of labor) holds the job of the dishwasher or janitor or unskilled laborer in low esteem if not outright contempt.[15] So does the streetcorner man. He cannot do otherwise. He cannot draw from a job those social values which other people do not put into it.[16]

14. It is important to remember that the employer is not entirely a free agent. Subject to the constraints of the larger society, he acts for the larger society as well as for himself. Child labor laws, safety and sanitation regulations, minimum wage scales in some employment areas, and other constraints, are already on the books; other control mechanisms, such as a guaranteed annual wage, are to be had for the voting.
15. See, for example, the U.S. Bureau of the Census, *Methodology and Scores of Socioeconomic Status.* The assignment of the lowest SES ratings to men who hold such jobs is not peculiar to our own society. A low SES rating for "the shoeshine boy or garbage man . . . seems to be true for all [industrial] countries." Alex Inkeles, "Industrial Man," p. 8.
16. That the streetcorner man downgrades manual labor should occasion no surprise. Merton points out that "the American stigmatization of manual labor . . . *has been found*

Only occasionally does spontaneous conversation touch on these matters directly. Talk about jobs is usually limited to isolated statements of intention, such as "I think I'll get me another gig [job]," "I'm going to look for a construction job when the weather breaks," or "I'm going to quit. I can't take no more of his shit." Job assessments typically consist of nothing more than a noncommittal shrug and "It's O.K." or "It's a job."

One reason for the relative absence of talk about one's job is, as suggested earlier, that the sameness of job experiences does not bear reiteration. Another and more important reason is the emptiness of the job experience itself. The man sees middle-class occupations as a primary source of prestige, pride and self-respect; his own job affords him none of these. To think about his job is to see himself as others see him, to remind him of just where he stands in this society.[17] And because society's criteria for placement are generally the same as his own, to talk about his job can trigger a flush of shame and a deep, almost physical ache to change places with someone, almost anyone, else.[18] The desire to be a person in his own right, to be noticed by the world he lives in, is shared by each of the men on the streetcorner. Whether they articulate this desire (as Tally does below) or not, one can see them position themselves to catch the attention of their fellows in much the same way as plants bend or stretch to catch the sunlight.[19]

Tally and I were in the Carry-out. It was summer, Tally's peak earning season as a cement finisher, a semiskilled job a cut or so above that of the unskilled laborer. His take-home pay during these weeks was well over a hundred dollars—"a lot of bread." But for Tally, who no longer had a family to support, bread was not enough.

"You know that boy came in last night? That Black Moozlem? That's what I ought to be doing. I ought to be in his place."
"What do you mean?"
"Dressed nice, going to [night] school, got a good job."

---

to hold rather uniformly in all social classes" (emphasis in original; *Social Theory and Social Structure*, p. 145). That he finds no satisfaction in such work should also occasion no surprise: "[There is] a clear positive correlation between the over-all status of occupations and the experience of satisfaction in them." Inkeles, "Industrial Man," p. 12.
17. "[In our society] a man's work is one of the things by which he is judged, and certainly one of the more significant things by which he judges himself. . . . A man's work is one of the more important parts of his social identity, of his self; indeed, of his fate in the one life he has to live." Everett C. Hughes, *Men and Their Work*, pp. 42–43.
18. Noting that lower-class persons "are constantly exposed to evidence of their own irrelevance," Lee Rainwater spells out still another way in which the poor are poor: "The identity problems of lower class persons make the soul-searching of middle class adolescents and adults seem rather like a kind of conspicuous consumption of psychic riches" ("Work and Identity in the Lower Class," p. 3).
19. Sea Cat cuts his pants legs off at the calf and puts a fringe on the raggedy edges. Tonk breaks his "shades" and continues to wear the horn-rimmed frames minus the lenses. Richard cultivates a distinctive manner of speech. Lonny gives himself a birthday party. And so on.

"He's no better off than you, Tally. You make more than he does."

"It's not the money. [Pause] It's position, I guess. He's got position. When he finish school he gonna be a supervisor. People respect him. . . . Thinking about people with position and education gives me a feeling right here [pressing his fingers into the pit of his stomach]."

"You're educated, too. You have a skill, a trade. You're a cement finisher. You can make a building, pour a sidewalk."

"That's different. Look, can anybody do what you're doing? Can anybody just come up and do your job? Well, in one week I can teach you cement finishing. You won't be as good as me 'cause you won't have the experience but you'll be a cement finisher. That's what I mean. Anybody can do what I'm doing and that's what gives me this feeling. [Long pause] Suppose I like this girl. I go over to her house and I meet her father. He starts talking about what he done today. He talks about operating on somebody and sewing them up and about surgery. I know he's a doctor 'cause of the way he talks. Then she starts talking about what she did. Maybe she's a boss or a supervisor. Maybe she's a lawyer and her father says to me, 'And what do you do, Mr. Jackson?' [Pause] You remember at the courthouse, Lonny's trial? You and the lawyer was talking in the hall? You remember? I just stood there listening. I didn't say a word. You know why? 'Cause I didn't even know what you was talking about. That's happened to me a lot."

"Hell, you're nothing special. That happens to everybody. Nobody knows everything. One man is a doctor, so he talks about surgery. Another man is a teacher, so he talks about books. But doctors and teachers don't know anything about concrete. You're a cement finisher and that's your specialty."

"Maybe so, but when was the last time you saw anybody standing around talking about concrete?"

The streetcorner man wants to be a person in his own right, to be noticed, to be taken account of, but in this respect, as well as in meeting his money needs, his job fails him. The job and the man are even. The job fails the man and the man fails the job.

Furthermore, the man does not have any reasonable expectation that, however bad it is, his job will lead to better things. Menial jobs are not, by and large, the starting point of a track system which leads to even better jobs for those who are able and willing to do them. The busboy or dishwasher in a restaurant is not on a job track which, if negotiated skillfully, leads to chef or manager of the restaurant. The busboy or dishwasher who works hard becomes, simply, a hard-working busboy or dishwasher. Neither hard work nor perseverance can conceivably carry the janitor to a sit-down job in the office building he cleans up. And it is the apprentice who becomes the journeyman electrician, plumber, steam fitter or bricklayer, not the common unskilled Negro laborer.

Thus, the job is not a stepping stone to something better. It is a dead end. It promises to deliver no more tomorrow, next month or next year than it does today.

Delivering little, and promising no more, the job is "no big thing." The man appears to treat the job in a cavalier fashion, working and not working as the spirit moves him, as if all that matters is the immediate satisfaction of his present appetites, the surrender to present moods, and the indulgence of whims with no thought for the cost, the consequences, the future. To the middle-class observer, this behavior reflects a "present-time orientation"—an "inability to defer gratification." It is this "present-time" orientation—as against the "future orientation" of the middle-class person—that "explains" to the outsider why Leroy chooses to spend the day at the Carry-out rather than report to work; why Richard, who was paid Friday, was drunk Saturday and Sunday and penniless Monday; why Sweets quit his job today because the boss looked at him "funny" yesterday.

But from the inside looking out, what appears as a "present-time" orientation to the outside observer is, to the man experiencing it, as much a future orientation as that of his middle-class counterpart.[20] The difference between the two men lies not so much in their different orientations to time as in their different orientations to future time or, more specifically, to their different futures.[21]

The future orientation of the middle-class person presumes, among other things, a surplus of resources to be invested in the future and a belief that the future will be sufficiently stable both to justify his investment (money in a bank, time and effort in a job, investment of himself in marriage and family, etc.) and to permit the consumption of his investment at a time, place and manner of his own choosing and to his greater satisfaction. But the streetcorner man lives in a sea of want. He does not, as a rule, have a surplus of resources, either economic or psychological. Gratification of hunger and the desire for simple creature comforts cannot be long deferred. Neither can support for one's flagging self-esteem. Living on the edge of both economic and psychological subsistence, the streetcorner man is obliged to expend all his resources on maintaining himself from moment to moment.[22]

20. Taking a somewhat different point of view, S. M. Miller and Frank Riessman suggest that "the entire concept of deferred gratification may be inappropriate to understanding the essence of workers' lives" ("The Working Class Subculture: A New View," p. 87).
21. This sentence is a paraphrase of a statement made by Marvin Cline at a 1965 colloquium at the Mental Health Study Center, National Institute of Mental Health.
22. And if, for the moment, he does sometimes have more money than he chooses to spend or more food than he wants to eat, he is pressed to spend the money and eat the food anyway since his friends, neighbors, kinsmen, or acquaintances will beg or borrow whatever surplus he has or, failing this, they may steal it. In one extreme case, one of the men admitted taking the last of a woman's surplus food allotment after she had explained that, with four children, she could not spare any food. The prospect that consumer soft goods not consumed by oneself will be consumed by someone else may be re-

As for the future, the young streetcorner man has a fairly good picture of it. In Richard or Sea Cat or Arthur he can see himself in his middle twenties; he can look at Tally to see himself at thirty, at Wee Tom to see himself in his middle thirties, and at Budder and Stanton to see himself in his forties. It is a future in which everything is uncertain except the ultimate destruction of his hopes and the eventual realization of his fears. The most he can reasonably look forward to is that these things do not come too soon. Thus, when Richard squanders a week's pay in two days it is not because, like an animal or a child, he is "present-time oriented," unaware of or unconcerned with his future. He does so precisely because he is aware of the future and the hopelessness of it all.

Sometimes this kind of response appears as a conscious, explicit choice. Richard had had a violent argument with his wife. He said he was going to leave her and the children, that he had had enough of everything and could not take any more, and he chased her out of the house. His chest still heaving, he leaned back against the wall in the hallway of his basement apartment.

"I've been scuffling for five years," he said. "I've been scuffling for five years from morning till night. And my kids still don't have anything, my wife don't have anything, and I don't have anything.

"There," he said, gesturing down the hall to a bed, a sofa, a couple of chairs and a television set, all shabby, some broken. "There's everything I have and I'm having trouble holding onto that."

Leroy came in, presumably to petition Richard on behalf of Richard's wife, who was sitting outside on the steps, afraid to come in. Leroy started to say something but Richard cut him short.

"Look, Leroy, don't give me any of that action. You and me are entirely different people. Maybe I look like a boy and maybe I act like a boy sometimes but I got a man's mind. You and me don't want the same things out of life. Maybe some of the same, but you don't care how long you have to wait for yours and *I—want—mine—right—now.*" [23]

---

lated to the way in which portable consumer durable goods, such as watches, radios, television sets or phonographs, are sometimes looked at as a form of savings. When Shirley was on welfare, she regularly took her television set out of pawn when he got her monthly check. Not so much to watch it, she explained, as to have something to fall back on when her money runs out toward the end of the month, For her and others, the television set or the phonograph is her savings, the pawnshop is where she banks her savings, and the pawn ticket is her bankbook.

23. This was no simple rationalization for irresponsibility. Richard had indeed "been scuffling for five years" trying to keep his family going. Until shortly after this episode, Richard was known and respected as one of the hardest-working men on the street. Richard had said, only a couple of months earlier, "I figure you got to get out there and try. You got to try before you can get anything." His wife Shirley confirmed that he had always tried. "If things get tough, with me I'll get all worried. But Richard get worried, he don't want me to see him worried. . . . He *will* get out there. He's shoveled snow, picked

Thus, apparent present-time concerns with consumption and indulgences—material and emotional—reflect a future-time orientation. "I want mine right now" is ultimately a cry of despair, a direct response to the future as he sees it.[24]

In many instances, it is precisely the streetcorner man's orientation to the future—but to a future loaded with "trouble"—which not only leads to a greater emphasis on present concerns ("I want mine right now") but also contributes importantly to the instability of employment, family and friend relationships, and to the general transient quality of daily life.

Let me give some concrete examples. One day, after Tally had gotten paid, he gave me four twenty-dollar bills and asked me to keep them for him. Three days later he asked me for the money. I returned it and asked why he did not put his money in a bank. He said that the banks close at two o'clock. I argued that there were four or more banks within a two-block radius of where he was working at the time and that he could easily get to any one of them on his lunch hour. "No, man," he said, "you don't understand. They close at two o'clock and they closed Saturday and Sunday. Suppose I get into trouble and I got to make it [leave]. Me get out of town, and everything I got in the world layin' up in that bank? No good! No good!"

In another instance, Leroy and his girl friend were discussing "trouble." Leroy was trying to decide how best to go about getting his hands on some "long green" (a lot of money), and his girl friend cautioned him about "trouble." Leroy sneered at this, saying he had had "trouble" all his life and wasn't afraid of a little more. "Anyway," he said, "I'm famous for leaving town." [25]

Thus, the constant awareness of a future loaded with "trouble" results

---

beans, and he's done some of everything. . . . He's not ashamed to get out there and get us something to eat." At the time of the episode reported above, Leroy was just starting marriage and raising a family. He and Richard were not, as Richard thought, "entirely different people." Leroy had just not learned, by personal experience over time, what Richard had learned. But within two years Leroy's marriage had broken up and he was talking and acting like Richard. "He just let go completely," said one of the men on the street.

24. There is no mystically intrinsic connection between "present-time" orientation and lower-class persons. Whenever people of whatever class have been uncertain, skeptical or downright pessimistic about the future, "I want mine right now" has been one of the characteristic responses, although it is usually couched in more delicate terms: e.g., Omar Khayyam's "Take the cash and let the credit go," or Horace's *"Carpe diem."* In wartime, especially, all classes tend to slough off conventional restraints on sexual and other behavior (i.e., become less able or less willing to defer gratification). And when inflation threatens, darkening the fiscal future, persons who formerly husbanded their resources with commendable restraint almost stampede one another rushing to spend their money. Similarly, it seems that future-time orientation tends to collapse toward the present when persons are in pain or under stress. The point here is that, the label notwithstanding (what passes for) present-time orientation appears to be a situation-specific phenomenon rather than a part of the standard psychic equipment of Cognitive Lower Class Man.

25. And proceeded to do just that the following year when "trouble"—in this case, a grand jury indictment, a pile of debts, and a violent separation from his wife and children —appeared again.

in a constant readiness to leave, to "make it," to "get out of town," and discourages the man from sinking roots into the world he lives in.[26] Just as it discourages him from putting money in the bank, so it discourages him from committing himself to a job, especially one whose payoff lies in the promise of future rewards rather than in the present. In the same way, it discourages him from deep and lasting commitments to family and friends or to any other persons, places or things, since such commitments could hold him hostage, limiting his freedom of movement and thereby compromising his security which lies in that freedom.

What lies behind the response to the driver of the pickup truck, then, is a complex combination of attitudes and assessments. The streetcorner man is under continuous assault by his job experiences and job fears. His experiences and fears feed on one another. The kind of job he can get— and frequently only after fighting for it, if then—steadily confirms his fears, depresses his self-confidence and self-esteem until finally, terrified of an opportunity even if one presents itself, he stands defeated by his experiences, his belief in his own self-worth destroyed and his fears a confirmed reality.

26. For a discussion of "trouble" as a focal concern of lower-class culture, see Walter Miller, "Lower Class Culture as a Generating Milieu of Gang Delinquency," pp. 7, 8.

LLOYD ZIMPEL
Ovenmen

Nightly, Prokop watched the mixer, its hum in his head and throb in his bowels. Even when he slept he heard and felt it, the hot sun under the blind his wife never pulled quite down all the way enough like the oven heat to sweat him awake certain he had somehow, impossibly, dozed off on the job. Then children shouting in the sun-struck street told him where he was.

Nightly he walked the high catwalk with the sand mixing in the huge open drum at his feet. Between the mixer and the archway to the now-dark foundry worked his crew in the white light of the coreroom alley and the shadows of the oven; the operators of the half-dozen blowers, their helpers, the rod-men and dippers, the loader, the ovenman. What went into every job, what that job took out of man, Prokop knew. At one time or another in his eight years—except for the oven—he had put in a solid stint in each. Did something go amiss? With a buffaloing nudge of his shoulder he moved the incompetent aside and demonstrated with flourishes how sound cores were blown, stacked and dipped, just so. "Show him how, Prokop!" came the cry then, to needle the fellow who needed showing no more than they needled him, the pushy foreman.

The foundry's contract for five months past with three months to run was for tractor transmission housings. In eight years Prokop couldn't remember an easier job. No tricky spots on the cores to crack, even the housing neck was thick and easy to blow. Piecework rates, set early, remained unchanged; the crew made money and stayed happy.

It was not a bad crew: a half-dozen family men who could be counted on, a dozen others who bore some, but not overly much, watching. The ovenmen though, that was a different story. They came and went so often that Prokop was tired of breaking them in. One after another, a new one every week, stood around awkwardly flexing his fingers in the thick asbestos gloves, gauntlets to the elbow, or cracking his knees on the dolly jack-handle, while the loader, Tony, did the work of showing how. All too often Prokop loaded his own sand, letting Tony bail out the greenhorn who in his first night jammed seven racks in the back of the oven which held six, all needing to be got out at once. Just the same, Prokop preferred throwing his own sand all night to a half-hour's killing oven work. It damn near scared him how the ovenmen took it—even for the short time each hung on. And short it was—he hardly learned the name of last week's ovenman before that suffering fellow, his skin dried and cracking, his scorched hair sprung like steel wool, shuffled up beneath the catwalk perch and called in a voice baked harsh, "This's the last shift I'll roast my ass! Get me my time tonight!"

The mixer stood next to the open-sided shed housing the raw sand. Tony, plying his wheelbarrow between sandpile and mixer hopper, kept the door open. A breeze worked in and into its path the ovenman, whoever he was this week, found his way between cries of "Rack! Rack!" for a moment's cooling. On the catwalk Prokop looked down as the poor son-of-a-bitch swallowed another salt tablet, retied the sopping sweat rag around his forehead and trotted back to the heat.

"How's the new man doing?" It was Prokop's most frequent question to Tony, no matter who the new man was. "So-so." At the lunch break they were sitting with sandwiches and beer in the cool sand under the high roof of the shed. It reminded Prokop of the majestically vaulted ice-houses of his youth—great mounds of brown wet sawdust and tier after tier of sawdust-sprinkled ice in perpetual twilight; the great ceiling high above where pigeons cooed in the rafters and sparrows fluttered. If all the machines in the coreroom were quiet and the oven turned down and not a person spoke, he could hear pigeons move restlessly above on their night perches. Where they fouled the sand the runner on the morning shift would scrape it clean.

"Ever seen one of those old ice-houses?" he asked Tony, who was—what?—twenty-one, half Prokop's age.

"What? Ice-house? I guess not. How about ass-house?"

From the near darkness of the shed Prokop looked back into the coreroom where the crew ate sitting on sand-slicked benches or hunkered against the base of the blowers. Now he heard the ripping of the chain as it raced through the tackle to raise the oven door. An ovenman took his lunch break on the run, between bites hauling out the racks before the cores burned. Even outside on the sand, thirty yards away, Prokop heard the throaty roar of the oven's burners and felt a great hot breath subtly increase the shed's temperature. Then came the quieter ratchet sound of the dolly as the ovenman pumped down another rack to cool for the dippers.

Prokop dug out a dollar and car keys and sent Tony for more beer, then pressed the buzzer to send the crew back to work. He loaded his own sand, replacing all that had crusted in the mixer over the break, tossing in the binder and water and climbed to the catwalk to observe the mix. He ran a handful through his fingers, brought a pinch of it to his nose. No one believed him but he swore that an off mix smelled bad.

"I hadda wait at the store," said Tony, returning a full hour later. The beer went into its cool hideaway in the sand.

"Well, hell," Prokop warned. "You better not take advantage."

Tony winked, saluted, and ambled down the alleyway to offer the apprentice ovenman a word of advice. It was this newcomer's third day. Prokop, preferring to avoid ovenmen until they had stayed long enough to blend with the crew, had hardly noticed him; that was Tony's job.

Now from his vantage Prokop marked the ragged carrying-on of the new man scurrying in the hot gloom before the oven. He was an odd foreign fellow, with an ear-bruising accent the one or two times Prokop had heard him, and hair that bristled out at the sides like a wild man's. His baggy overalls and oversized khaki shirt were not so different from what the others wore, but his short TB-like slightness seemed more properly wrapped in a European suit, thick and ill-fitting, of the kind Prokop remembered from 1946 Berliners trudging to their gray jobs past the entrance to the compound where Pfc. Prokop pulled guard duty every damned third day.

Baum was his name, Tony told him. Usually ovenmen were gone before anyone got past calling them "Buddy."

The shadows before the oven leaped now with a spurt of activity. The ovenman jumped first to the clock, then to temperature gauge, then to tackle, then to dolly. A flurry of racks were due out at the same time and Tony was nowhere in sight. Baum dashed in and out of the oven while great billowing waves of heat shot back to Prokop and beyond. With his gloved hands flapping like wings, the ovenman was all awkwardness. Whatever set procedures Tony had shown him he'd not yet learned. One arm flung before his face to partly ward off the heat, he entered the oven peeking from under the crook of his elbow, as cautious as a man edging into a knife fight, his other hand pushing the dolly by its long handle and apparently hoping for the good luck to get its wheels under a rack. But the dolly jackknifed and he pulled out to make another pass. By now he'd been boiled clear through. He dropped the handle, ran out, cooled for a few moments, and desperately tried again. And failed again.

Prokop knew that with luck a good man with some experience could get into the oven, pump up the rack and have it out, door closed, in ten to twelve seconds. That was all a man could stand. One trip per rack had to be the rule. Baum was taking three. Once Prokop counted four.

He finally found Tony combing his hair in the toilet. "What's wrong with that guy? He takes three or four passes at each rack. The door is up for two, three minutes. We can't have that."

Tony shrugged. "He don't understand too good. That's what you get if you're gonna hire refugees that can't talk English." But he went without complaint to give the greenhorn another hand.

"Look here," he pointed out to Baum the sharp swings up and down on the temp graph. "They should be like this." He made a gentle waving line with his hand. "Door's open too long, see?"

Sweating heavily, his eyes burned red at the rims, the ovenman nodded, nodded, nodded, but said nothing. He kept licking his lips as though they were parched beyond relief.

"You understand?"

"Ya, unnerstan'," said Baum.

Left to himself again he rushed into the oven only to fly out as if struck by an invisible hand that knocked the air out of him. Gloves flailing before his face like a man battling hawks at his eyes, he tried again. Then, suddenly remembering, ran to the temp graph to see how much heat he'd lost for leaving the door up too long.

Watching, Prokop itched all over. From the looks of it, Baum was addled by the heat. He climbed down the ladder, and dug a beer from the sandpile. The usual 3:00 A.M. breeze was up, but it could not counter the warm suffusion that came with each opening of the oven door. Given a few more days the poor bastard might come around, Prokop told himself, not hopefully.

He put off talking to Baum, even the next night when the dippers came up with the first of the complaints about hairline cracks in the cores. The necks came off in their hands. Instead of easing the racks down the last crucial half-inch, Baum was dropping them off the dolly, jarring, cracking, the cores.

"What the hell you teaching these ovenmen anyway?" Prokop asked Tony. "No wonder none of them last, they never learn their job right."

"It ain't my job to do the teaching," Tony grumbled, but he dropped his wheelbarrow and shuffled through the sand-drifted alley back to the oven for a long earnest conversation with the nodding ovenman.

Prokop watched: The runt keeps nodding sure, sure, but he don't understand a word, I bet. He was stung by what Tony had said—it was after all the foreman's job to see that the new men were properly broken in. Yet he'd told Tony more than once, you've worked the ovens, you know more about them than me. Hell, it was a good foreman who knew who to get to do a job. Did he have to do it all himself?

All the same, he vaguely told himself he'd talk to Baum when the chance came up, and in the meantime practiced his criticism on Tony, who dropped his wheelbarrow in the alley and spread his hands to look up at Prokop. "Why you yelling at *me?*" The loader still went for beer, but later found business elsewhere when Prokop pointedly headed for the sandpile at the break; then, casting injured glances at the foreman, slunk about for an hour after.

Far from Baum having gotten handier in his tasks, Prokop glumly judged that two weeks, three weeks on the job had in fact lent him greater clumsiness with the dolly and no more adroitness in getting in and out of the oven. He worked at not much less than a dead run all shift just to meet his minimum and still was a good forty-five minutes catching up after the shift ended, and all strung out and exhausted so that the foreman never expected to see him make it in for the next shift.

But he always did. In four weeks Baum had put in more time than the previous four ovenmen altogether. He was almost permanent. For that alone Prokop owed him something, and on a night when the poor bastard inexplainably had time enough to pause to catch his breath in the breeze from the shed, Prokop guiltily rose out of the darkness of the sandpile and held out a beer. "Have a cool one," he said. "That's sure hot work."

But in a calm gesture with the hand that held his sweat rag, far different from his herky-jerky way with the dolly, the ovenman refused the offer. He fixed Prokop with quick dark eyes, recalling to the foreman the house-to-house gypsy furnace repairman who had talked his way into the basement from which Prokop had all but to throw him out. "It make *sveat* too much!" the ovenman declared.

"Hell, it's healthy to sweat, get all that poison out of you." But Prokop saw that whatever lay behind that thin harrowed face with its three day growth of black beard never varying in length and the eyes which sunk deeper and deeper into the skull with each day in the ovens—that would not compromise for a can of beer.

"Too much *heat*," Baum wagged his finger sternly. "No drink." Then he turned and hastened back to his duties, as if the foreman had taken up his time much too foolishly.

Later Prokop said to Tony, "I didn't realize the guy had lost so much weight. He's all bones."

"That's why they all quit. Remember Randall? Lost seventeen pounds in six days. You sweat it out."

Indeed you did, thought Prokop. What hellishness was this that could reduce a man by three pounds or more per day—in thirty days a man would be a stick—and leave him looking sad as Christ crucified?

Later that week when the superintendent came by on his semi-weekly stroll, Prokop told him, "We ought to take a good look at the oven job. It might be set too tough. We can't keep a man on it any length of time."

The super gingerly plucked his sweat-stuck white shirt from his armpits. "Can't be too bad. We studied it with all the others."

Prokop admitted that was so. "But we keep losing the men."

"Tell you what—I'll have personnel send you some colored boys. See how they take the heat."

"It's not that we need anybody right now. We've got a guy who's trying, but who can say how long he'll last?" He wouldn't take up this subject with the super soon again. The old boy would be lining up whatever un-employables personnel could find, and sending them in for Prokop to fry. He saw himself yelling *next* and pointing each new man on to the oven where the last ragged geezer had just fallen, swollen tongue between cracked lips, after minutes in the heat. He watched the super's fat back retire from the coreroom, and took his problem out to the sandpile.

There Tony, resting in the gloom, turned away Prokop's offer of beer and got at once to what was eating him. "Seems like what I've really got is *two* jobs, don't it?" he said darkly.

"I'll put you in for goddamned doubletime," said Prokop.

"Okay," the loader said in a wounded voice. "Okay." He started back to work. "You know it's not my fault we're all losing money on the bum cores he turns out."

"Nobody said it was."

Tony stopped at the door to the coreroom. "Well, I sure as hell get treated like it was. Hell, I try to tell him but he don't understand English worth a damn. That's what you get for hiring a Jew just off the boat."

"It doesn't take English to shove those racks in and out of the oven," said Prokop, brushing past Tony to climb to the catwalk.

He shunned the loader the rest of the night, then paid for it next shift when Tony failed to show. Without his coach the ovenman dashed about like one demented; somehow he got through the shift. Prokop did all his own loading for the first time in years. His hands, when he squirted soap on them to wash up, were tender from the shovel, all the old calluses had worn away in years of nothing but pushing the mixer button.

The next night Tony was back with no more than a nod for the fore-man. Nursing sore hands, Prokop had little to say to him anyway. Or to anyone. When two of the dippers came up he met them with a scowl.

"Hairlines comin' through worse than ever, Prokop." They were from the batch the ovenman had baked last night on his own.

The foreman waved them away with a grunt. He started the rounds of the operators. "Blow 'em tighter, you guys, we're getting too many hair-line cracks."

They stared in amazement. He knew as well as they where hairlines came from. But he brushed off their questions, leaving them to turn dirty looks back toward the ovens and to bitch about the matter amongst themselves during the break.

When the super came up that evening, he leaned on the rail to the lad-der, plucked at his sweaty shirt and talked about the weather and his kid who was due home from college next week, and somewhere amidst it all warned that *hairline cracks were getting through*. He smoothed over some spilled sand with his polished oxford. "Your piece work rate has been going down steady for three weeks. Hate to see it happen. You know how the men get to feeling."

Prokop raised his hand in a little never-you-fear gesture, as if he and the men were totally at peace over the whole issue in a way a front office man would never understand. But as soon as the super was gone he angrily signalled to Tony.

"We're getting more bad cores than ever—"

"You blamin' *me?*" cried Tony in exasperation. "Well, just shove it all up your rear, Prokop!" And he walked off the job, owing the foreman God knows how much for beer and favors over fifteen months.

For three shifts until personnel sent him Tony's replacement—a man seeing his first foundry coreroom—the foreman not only did his own loading but tried as well to provide advice to the frantic ovenman. All those years he had successfully avoided the ovens and no one the wiser and now look. He lay awake days, like a man knowing his dread time would come: the oven door would open and he'd have to walk in. As Baum did dozens of times a shift, night after night.

"I shouldn't be getting back here in the heat so much," he told the ovenman one night when called to direct the rescue of a rack that had angled and jammed in the oven's deepest corner. "It's a matter of my health."

This drew only a befuddled stare from the ovenman, and Prokop hastened away from the opened door feeling laid waste no more by the heat than by his duty to keep a man in that desolate job.

Hardly had he gained the healthier atmosphere of the catwalk than he heard a cry and turned to see Baum come trotting unevenly toward him, his usual cornered look now twisted with anguish. He held one hand carefully before him, as if balancing an egg in the palm. He had stumbled, caught himself with a good firm grip on a rack not ten seconds out of the back of the oven, the glove on that unfortunate hand off as he went to mop his forehead.

Prokop hated to look. The sweat-moistened hand had cooked. "You *gotta* be careful. No question about it. For God's sake, watch your step!" Outraged, sickened, he fetched the ointment tube from the tin box where the bandaids and the extra salt tablets were stored. Now he had a one-handed overnman. "Come in early tomorrow and have the first-shift nurse take a look at that. I'll get some help for you the rest of the night."

But he couldn't find it. When he had gone down the line with no success and came at last to blower six, even Arnie, usually easy-going, was as hard-nosed as the others. It would screw up his piecework. What would the union say? Prokop was ready to hold aloft Baum's puffed hand and cry, "Help me while this heals! Don't you think of anything but money?"

Swearing, he accompanied Baum back to the oven where the ovenman examined his chart and told Prokop which racks were due. But Baum had to retreat quickly from the area, his bad hand far too sensitive to take the heat.

"Everybody handles their own for the rest of the night!" Prokop yelled. The bitching began. With three hours to go it meant several trips apiece into the fire. Nobody wanted it. "Screw the complaining!" Prokop shouted. "Do what I say or get the hell out!"

He'd made a dozen enemies, piecework was shot to hell, a quarter of the cores were ruined, but he got through the shift without having to brave the oven himself, and he was ready to admit that that alone was worth whatever it cost.

When he came on the next night he found a note stuck into a joint on the catwalk rail. It was written in what looked like a foreign language. At last he puzzled it through: "She sent me to go home two days the nurse. Herschel."

Well, wasn't that damned nice of her to do for old Hersch! He looked furiously out over the coreroom. The crew was coming on; not one of them looked his way, as if afraid of what he might ask if he caught an eye. As soon as he had pushed the buzzer and they were all at work, he walked through the silent, dark foundry to the other the side of the building where the super sat in his office behind his cooling fan, framed pictures of wife and kids on his desk.

There were, the super told him, no extras on tap for tonight; maybe tomorrow a temporary would be available; it wasn't a promise.

"Well, what about that oven? Who's going to run it?"

"You," the super calmly said. "It's no big deal."

Just what he had expected; they'd get him yet. He came back through the silent foundry toward the bright light of the coreroom trying to tell himself there was nothing sinister in the fat old bastard; it was only logical, he was the logical one. On a good night the mixer took hardly ten minutes of work; let him put that spare time to constructive use. It was logical, true enough, but he came down the alleyway as scared as if an ugly unknown torture awaited.

From the hook on the wall by the temp graph he took Baum's old khaki shirt and the big asbestos gloves. Instead of joshing him as he half expected, after last night the operators and helpers seemed not to see him. He had seven hours to go: it seemed to him the sum of his life.

The first racks filled. He set the dolly under one, rolled it before the black oven door, stood back and grabbed the chain tackle, pulled hand over hand. He had never felt the heat this close before; the shock of it took his breath away. In spite of himself, he backed off. The roar of the burners was so loud they must surely be turned up too high; he raced to the gauge: no, they were down as low as the valves would go. He got behind the dolly, quickly lined it up and shoved it at the oven. It had to roll all the way to the back—ten or twelve feet into the oven. He kept close to the rack, as if it would protect him, wrapped one arm around his head and guided the dolly beneath the door, into the depths.

He tried to hold his breath but couldn't and his lungs balooned with pain at the seared air. Even behind the protection of his free arm, his eyes clouded and he could not see how far into the black oven he had yet to go. His toes sought to curl away from the burning soles of his shoes. Only for an instant did his clothing shield his body, then it seemed to take fire, his skin puckering away from it. Panic rose; in another instant he would have dropped the handle and fled, as it had annoyed him to see Baum do so many times. But instead, some lucky reflex let him trip the dolly; the rack settled evenly enough if a bit out of line, and he burst free of the oven, giving the dolly a fierce tug and letting it roll off by itself. He grabbed the chain to keep from stumbling, and with one strong jerk brought the door down to cut off the heat. It was like a return from the grave.

He turned away to wipe his face. Thre was no sweat on it, it had burned away. Out of the gloom, shot with brilliant spears fed into his vision by his scalding eyes, he saw the operators and helpers gladly watching. He turned his back on them. "Rack here!" It was like a vengeful curse meant for him. Then, almost simultaneously, from the other operators came the call, "Rack! Rack here! Rack!" He set himself against an impulse to flee, grabbed the dolly and went to get them, every goddamned one.

Salt tablets corroded his belly, water did not help. His face took fire, and hands went raw inside the asbestos mitts so that he could not grip the dolly's hot handle squarely, but hooked it with the heel of his hand, butted it, made fists and caught it against his knuckles, finally insulated it with a two-inch wrap of gunny-sack.

It all took too much time. Happy to see his fumbling the operators grumbled, called angrily for speed, a little speed, how about it? Even Baum was faster.

Into the oven he dashed and each time fled gasping. In his nostrils the mucous fried; his eyes framed themselves in stiff red rims that pinched when he blinked. Vision blurred. His sweat stopped; from Baum's example he figured it would start again in time. At the water fountain he splashed his face, but water brought no relief. He could not spit, his body refusing to give up that moisture. The operators yelled at his dallying. They had been yelling all along, wasn't he listening?

No sweat, no sweat, he mindlessly told himself, trotting the alley like an obedient dog. The dolly jounced behind him. No sweat.

At the lunch break he went out back to the sand. Normally cool it now burned like all else. Surprised but willing, the new loader went for the beer Prokop desperately ordered. "What's your name, kid?"

"Louie."

"You're doing okay," Prokop said bleakly.

The beer boiled like lye in his throat and he could not finish the first can. In disgust he threw it into the dark and turned to see the super pause at the doorway, his eye thoughtfully following the can's glinting arc into the tall weeds.

"How's it going on the oven?"

Prokop leaped up to tell him. "It's a regular bitch. I never really knew." It seemed like there should be much more to say.

The super nodded, almost smiling. "Do what you can." For the rest of the lunch break he hung around the blowers, pinching the sand, checking the seams of the molds, sneaking a glance into the shed for signs of more beer. Prokop nudged the remaining cans out of sight, downed salt tablets and water, and checked the mix. Before he pressed the buzzer to summon his crew he put in five minutes noisily wrestling racks into place at the blowers. Far from standing by to note his extra work, the super had disappeared. With a groan Prokop impelled himself back to the oven. Still yards off his tender skin wrinkled away from the heat. The clock-watching operators griped at him for a fast buzzer.

Through that night and the next he ran and staggered. His skin dried and flaked, grew dark and leathery, his hair like wire. "What's the matter?" his wife asked uneasily on the second morning, not sure if she should be bothering him. "Why didn't you eat your lunch?" He had brought the black bucket home unopened.

"I'm on the oven!" he cried.

"Why you?" she said. "You're the foreman."

Distractedly he waved her away and stumbled unshaven to his bed, his sleep all nightmarish tossing, and the children with their shouts outside woke him again and again.

On the third night he came to work knowing the ovenman would not be there again. Yet in despairing weariness he tried to forestall that certainty. If he made three stoplights running, then the ovenman would be there. He made four, but in his belly knew it was no use. A fifth would be the clincher. He didn't make it. So then he knew. Tears came to his eyes.

The oven wouldn't wait. He came to it as heavy as if filled with his own wet sand. "Rack!" cried the operators. "Rack! Rack!" deliberately bunching them to keep him scrambling. Enough's enough, he wanted to tell them. But he held no malice; they didn't know how tough the oven was. If they did they wouldn't push him—but he wasn't sure.

On his first trip of the night beyond the door one shoe sole split from the heat. He leaned against the wall to look at it—cracked straight across the middle. The material was artificial, plastic, not leather. They weren't cheap either. To protect his foot he wound a gunny sack around the busted shoe, wet it at the puddle under the fountain for traction. Two steps into the oven and the bulky bandage began steaming; he came out trailing smoke, like something from a swampy wilderness; the hot burlap stink cut like acid fumes into the dried tissues of his nostrils—one thing more to endure. All the hollows in his head were already expanded to their limits, stretched by heat and the smell of scorched sand. His joints creaked like the ratchet of the dolly, as if the moisture that greased the bone hinges had boiled off. How could he last the night? He leaned his weight—how much had he lost the past two shifts?—against the dolly handle to bring out a hot rack and found the burlap had steamed dry and gave no grip. Down he went on the oven floor, struggling instantly to his feet, unburned but with the flesh of one flank now stiff as with a good sunburn and sensitive to heat. He turned that side away from the oven door, and into his pained vision appeared the white shirt of the superintendent, behind whom came Baum.

"Keep this man off the ovens for another week at least," said the super, pointing to the hand.

Sagging, Prokop looked at neither visitor, but fixed his gaze on the wounded hand, bound in a light gauze strip and not the pillow of bandages he had somehow expected. Baum held it limply before his chest as if an invisible sling supported it.

"Put him on dipping," said the super. "Something like that." He gave Prokop a last long look, from the scraggly two-day beard on the tanned face to the bulb of sacking protecting his foot, then turned and with a fat, splay-footed gait strolled out of the foreman's anguished sight.

Baum slowly flexed the fingers of the offending hand. "It is the nurse, she say," he said sadly, as if he personally did not agree with her.

Prokop kept his eyes on the burnt paw. He recognized apology and sympathy in the voice—this was the only other one around who knew the oven. They were brothers in fiery agony. No consolation there, but at least the balm of recognition between men who knew their duty.

Heat-addled and guilty, Prokop flung himself at the chain tackle, and above the racket of the door's ascent and the fearsome roar of the burners croaked out through his dried windpipe, "Go dip!"

ROBERT COOVER
The Elevator

1

Every morning without exception and without so much as reflecting upon it, Martin takes the self-service elevator to the fourteenth floor, where he works. He will do so today. When he first arrives, however, he finds the lobby empty, the old building still possessed of its feinting shadows and silences, desolate though mutely expectant, and he wonders if today it might not turn out differently.

It is 7:30 A.M.: Martin is early and therefore has the elevator entirely to himself. He steps inside: this tight cell! he thinks with a kind of unsettling shock, and confronts the panel of numbered buttons. One to fourteen, plus "B" for basement. Impulsively, he presses the "B"—seven years and yet to visit the basement! He snorts at his timidity.

After a silent moment, the doors rumble shut. All night alert waiting for this moment! The elevator sinks slowly into the earth. The stale gloomy odors of the old building having aroused in him an unreasonable sense of dread and loss, Martin imagines suddenly he is descending into hell. *Tra la perduta gente,* yes! A mild shudder shakes him. Yet, Martin decides firmly, would that it were so. The old carrier halts with a quiver. The automatic doors yawn open. Nothing, only a basement. It is empty and nearly dark. It is silent and meaningless.

Martin smiles inwardly at himself, presses the number "14." "Come on, old Charon," he declaims broadly, "Hell's the other way!"

2

Martin waited miserably for the stench of intestinal gas to reach his nostrils. Always the same. He supposed it was Carruther, but he could never prove it. Not so much as a telltale squeak. But it was Carruther who always led them, and though the other faces changed, Carruther was always among them.

They were seven in the elevator: six men and the young girl who operated it. The girl did not participate. She was surely offended, but she never gave a hint of it. She possessed a surface detachment that not even Carruther's crude proposals could penetrate. Much less did she involve herself in the coarse interplay of men. Yet certainly, Martin supposed, they were a torment to her.

And, yes, he was right—there it was, faint at first, almost sweet, then slowly thickening, sickening, crowding up on him—

"Hey! Who fahred thet shot?" cried Carruther, starting it.

"Mart fahred-it!" came the inexorable reply. And then the crush of loud laughter.

"*What!* Is that Martin fartin' again?" bellowed another, as their toothy thicklipped howling congealed around him.

"Aw *please,* Mart! *don't fart!*" cried yet another. It would go on until they left the elevator. The elevator was small: their laughter packed it, jammed at the walls. "Have a heart, Mart! don't *part* that fart!"

It's not me, *it's not me,* Martin insisted. But only to himself. It was no use. It was fate. Fate and Carruther. (More laughter, more brute jabs.) A couple times he had protested. "Aw, Marty, you're just modest!" Carruther had thundered. Booming voice, big man. Martin hated him.

One by one, the other men filed out of the elevator at different floors, holding their noses. "Old farty Marty!" they would shout to anyone they met on their way out, and it always got a laugh, up and down the floor. The air cleared slightly each time the door opened.

In the end, Martin was always left alone with the girl who operated the elevator. His floor, the fourteenth, was the top one. When it all began, long ago, he had attempted apologetic glances toward the girl on exiting, but she had always turned her shoulder to him. Maybe she thought he was making a play for her. Finally he was forced to adopt the custom of simply ducking out as quickly as possible. She would in any case assume his guilt.

Of course, there was an answer to Carruther. Yes, Martin knew it, had rehearsed it countless times. The only way to meet that man was on his home ground. And he'd do it, too. When the time came.

3

Martin is alone on the elevator with the operator, a young girl. She is neither slender nor plump, but fills charmingly her orchid-colored uniform. Martin greets her in his usual friendly manner and she returns his greeting with a smile. Their eyes meet momentarily. Hers are brown.

When Martin enters the elevator, there are actually several other people crowded in, but as the elevator climbs through the musky old building, the others, singly or in groups, step out. Finally, Martin is left alone with the girl who operates the elevator. She grasps the lever, leans against it, and the cage sighs upward. He speaks to her, makes a light-hearted joke about elevators. She laughs and

Alone on the elevator with the girl, Martin thinks: if this elevator should crash, I would sacrifice my life to save her. Her back is straight and sub-tle. Her orchid uniform skirt is tight, tucks tautly under her blossoming hips, describes a kind of cavity there. Perhaps it is night. Her calves are muscular and strong. She grasps the lever.

The girl and Martin are alone on the elevator, which is rising. He con-centrates on her round hips until she is forced to turn and look at him. His gaze coolly courses her belly, her pinched and belted waist, past her taut breasts, meets her excited stare. She breathes deeply, her lips parted. They embrace. Her breasts plunge softly against him. Her mouth is sweet. Martin has forgotten whether the elevator is climbing or not.

4

Perhaps Martin will meet Death on the elevator. Yes, going out for lunch one afternoon. Or to the drugstore for cigarettes. He will press the button in the hall on the fourteenth floor, the doors will open, a dark smile will beckon. The shaft is deep. It is dark and silent. Martin will rec-ognize Death by His silence. He will not protest.

> He *will* protest! oh God! no matter what the
> the sense of emptiness underneath breath lurching out
> The shaft is long and narrow. The shaft is dark.
> He will not protest.

5

Martin, as always and without so much as reflecting upon it, takes the self-service elevator to the fourteenth floor, where he works. He is early, but only by a few minutes. Five others join him, greetings are exchanged. Though tempted, he is not able to risk the "B," but presses the "14" in-stead. Seven years!

As the automatic doors press together and the elevator begins its slow complaining ascent, Martin muses absently on the categories. This small room, so commonplace and so compressed, he observes with a certain melancholic satisfaction, this elevator contains them all: space, time, cause, motion, magnitude, class. Left to our own devices, we would prob-ably discover them. The other passengers chatter with self-righteous smiles (after all, they are on time) about the weather, the elections, the work that awaits them today. They stand, apparently motionless, yet mov-ing. Motion: perhaps that's all there is to it after all. Motion and the medium. Energy and weighted particles. Force and matter. The image grips him purely. Ascent and the passive reorganization of atoms.

At the seventh floor, the elevator stops and a woman departs it. Only a trace of her perfume remains. Martin alone remarks—to himself, of course—her absence, as the climb begins again. Reduced by one. But the totality of the universe is suffused: each man contains all of it, loss is inconceivable. Yet, if that is so—and a tremor shudders coolly through Martin's body—then the totality is as nothing. Martin gazes around at his four remaining fellow passengers, a flush of compassion washing in behind the tremor. One must always be alert to the possibility of action, he reminds himself. But none apparently need him. If he could do the work for them today, give them the grace of a day's contemplation . . .

The elevator halts, suspended and vibrant, at the tenth floor. Two men leave. Two more intermediate stops, and Martin is alone. He has seen them safely through. Although caged as ever in his inexorable melancholy, Martin nonetheless smiles as he steps out of the self-service elevator on the fourteenth floor. "I am pleased to participate," he announces in full voice. But, as the elevator doors close behind him and he hears the voided descent, he wonders: Wherein now is the elevator's totality?

6

The cable snaps at the thirteenth floor. There is a moment's deadly motionlessness—then a sudden breathless plunge! The girl, terrified, turns to Martin. They are alone. Though inside his heart is bursting its chambers in terror, he remains outwardly composed. "I think it is safer lying on your back," he says. He squats to the floor, but the girl remains transfixed with shock. Her thighs are round and sleek under the orchid skirt, and in the shadowed— "Come," he says. "You may lie on me. My body will absorb part of the impact." Her hair caresses his cheek, her buttocks press like a sponge into his groin. In love, moved by his sacrifice, she weeps. To calm her, he clasps her heaving abdomen, strokes her soothingly. The elevator whistles as it drops.

7

Martin worked late in the office, clearing up the things that needed to be done before the next day, routine matters, yet part of the uninterrupted necessity that governed his daily life. Not a large office, Martin's, though he needed no larger, essentially neat except for the modest clutter on top of his desk. The room was equipped only with that desk and a couple chairs, bookcases lining one wall, calendar posted on another. The overhead lamp was off, the only light in the office being provided by the fluorescent lamp on Martin's desk.

Martin signed one last form, sighed, smiled. He retrieved a cigarette, half-burned but still lit, from the ashtray, drew heavily on it, then, as he exhaled with another prolonged sigh, doubled the butt firmly in the black bowl of the ashtray. Still extinguishing it, twisting it among the heap of crumpled filters in the ashtray, he glanced idly at his watch. He was astonished to discover that the watch said twelve-thirty—and had stopped! Already after midnight!

He jumped up, rolled down his sleeves, buttoned them, whipped his suit jacket off the back of his chair, shoved his arms into it. Bad enough twelve-thirty—but my God! how much *later* was it? The jacket still only three-quarters of the way up his back, tie askew, he hastily stacked the loose papers on his desk and switched off the lamp. He stumbled through the dark room out into the hallway, lit by one dull yellow bulb, pulled his office door to behind him. The thick solid catch knocked hollowly in the vacant corridor.

He buttoned his shirt collar, straightened his tie and the collar of his jacket, which was doubled under on his right shoulder, as he hurried down the passageway past the other closed office doors of the fourteenth floor to the self-service elevator, his heels hammering away the stillness on the marble floor. He trembled, inexplicably. The profound silence of the old building disturbed him. Relax, he urged himself; we'll know what time it is soon enough. He pushed the button for the elevator, but nothing happened. Don't tell me I have to walk down! he muttered bitterly to himself. He poked the button again, harder, and this time he heard below a solemn rumble, a muffled thump, and an indistinct grinding plaint that grieved progressively nearer. It stopped and the doors of the elevator opened to receive him. Entering, Martin felt a sudden need to glance back over his shoulder, but he suppressed it.

Once inside, he punched the number "1" button on the self-service panel. The doors closed, but the elevator, instead of descending, continued to climb. Goddamn this old wreck! Martin swore irritably, and he jiggled the "1" button over and over. Just this night! The elevator stopped, the doors opened, Martin stepped out. Later, he wondered why he had done so. The doors slid shut behind him, he heard the elevator descend, its amused rumble fading distantly. Although here it was utterly dark, shapes seemed to form. Though he could see nothing distinctly, he was fully aware that he was not alone. His hand fumbled on the wall for the elevator button. Cold wind gnawed at his ankles, the back of his neck. Fool! wretched fool! he wept, there *is* no fifteenth floor! Pressed himself against the wall, couldn't find the button, couldn't even find the elevator door, and even the very wall was only

8

Carruther's big voice boomed in the small cage.

"Mart fahred-it!" came the certain reply. The five men laughed. Martin flushed. The girl feigned indifference. The fetor of fart vapours reeked in the tight elevator.

"Martin, damn it, cut the fartin'!"

Martin fixed his cool gaze on them. "Carruther fucks his mother," he said firmly. Carruther hit him full in the face, his glasses splintered and fell, Martin staggered back against the wall. He waited for the second blow, but it didn't come. Someone elbowed him, and he slipped to the floor. He knelt there, weeping softly, searched with his hands for his glasses. Martin tasted the blood from his nose, trickling into his mouth. He couldn't find the glasses, couldn't even see.

"Look out, baby!" Carruther thundered. "Farty Marty's jist tryin' to git a free peek up at your pretty drawers!" Crash of laughter. Martin felt the girl shrink from him.

9

Her soft belly presses like a sponge into his groin. No, safer on your back, love, he thinks, but pushes the thought away. She weeps in terror, presses her hot wet mouth against his. To calm her, he clasps her soft buttocks, strokes them soothingly. So sudden is the plunge, they seem suspended in air. She has removed her skirt. How will it feel? he wonders.

10

Martin, without so much as reflecting on it, automatically takes the self-service elevator to the fourteenth floor, where he works. The systematizing, that's what's wrong, he concludes, that's what cracks them up. He is late, but only by a few minutes. Seven others join him, anxious, sweating. They glance nervously at their watches. None of them presses the "B" button. Civilities are hurriedly interchanged.

Their foolish anxiety seeps out like a bad spirit, enters Martin. He finds himself looking often at his watch, grows impatient with the elevator. Take it easy, he cautions himself. Their blank faces oppress him. Bleak. Haunted. Tyrannized by their own arbitrary regimentation of time. Torture self-imposed, yet in all probability inescapable. The elevator halts jerkily at the third floor, quivering their sallow face-flesh. They frown. No one has pushed the three. A woman enters. They all nod, harumph, make jittery little hand motions to incite the doors to close. They are all more or less aware of the woman (she has delayed them, damn her!), but only Martin truly remarks—to himself—her whole presence, as the elevator resumes its upward struggle. The accretion of tragedy. It goes on, ever giving birth to itself. Up and down, up and down. Where will it end? he wonders. Her perfume floats gloomily in the stale air. These deformed browbeaten mind-animals. Suffering and insufferable. Up and down. He closes his eyes. One by one, they leave him.

He arrives, alone, at the fourteenth floor. He steps out of the old elevator, stares back into its spent emptiness. There, only there, is peace, he concludes warily. The elevator doors press shut.

11

Here on this elevator, my elevator, created by me, moved by me, doomed by me, I, Martin, proclaim my omnipotence! In the end, doom touches all! MY doom! I impose it! TREMBLE!

12

The elevator shrieks insanely as it drops. Their naked bellies slap together, hands grasp, her vaginal mouth closes spongelike on his rigid organ. Their lips lock, tongues knot. The bodies: how will they find them? Inwardly, he laughs. He thrusts up off the plummeting floor. Her eyes are brown and, with tears, love him.

13

But—ah!—the doomed, old man, the DOOMED! What are they to us, to ME? ALL! We, I love! Let their flesh sag and dewlaps tremble, let their odors offend, let their cruelty mutilate, their stupidity enchain —but let them laugh, father! FOREVER! let them cry!

14

but hey! theres this guy see he gets on the goddamn elevator and its famous how hes got him a doodang about five feet long Im not kiddin you none five feet and he gets on the—yeah! can you imagine a bastard like that boardin a friggin pubic I mean public elevator? hoohah! no I dont know his name Mert I think or Mort but the crux is he is possessed of this motherin digit biggern ole Rahab see—do with it? I dont know I think he wraps it around his leg or carries it over his shoulder or somethin jee-*zuss!* what a problem! why I bet hes *killt* more poor bawdies than I ever dipped my poor worm in! once he was even a—listen! Carruther tells this as the goddamn truth I mean he *respects* that bastard—he was even one a them jackoff gods I forget how you call them over there with them Eye-talians after the big war see them dumb types when they seen him furl out this here five foot hose of his one day—he was just tryin to get the goddamn knots out Carruther says—why they thought he musta been a goddamn jackoff god or somethin and wanted to like employ him or whatever you do with a god and well Mort he figgered it to be a not so miserable occupation dont you know better anyhow than oildrillin with it in Arabia or stoppin holes in Dutch dikes like hes been doin so the bastard he stays on there a time and them little quiff there in that Eyetalian place they grease him up with hogfat or olive oil and all workin together like vested virgins they pull him off out there in the fields and spray the crops and well Mort he says *he* says its the closest hes ever got to the real mccoy jeezuss! hes worth a thousand laughs! and they bring him all the old aunts and grannies and he splits them open a kinda stupendous euthanasia for the old ladies and he blesses all their friggin procreations with a swat of his doodang and even does a little welldiggin on the side but he gets in trouble with the Roman churchers on accounta not bein circumcised and they wanta whack it off but Mort says no and they cant get close to him with so prodigious a batterin ram as hes got so they work a few miracles on him and wrinkle up his old pud with holy water and heat up his semen so it burns up the fields and even one day ignites a goddamn volcano and *jeezuss!* he wastes no time throwin that thing over his shoulder and hightailin it *outa* there I can tell you! but now like Im sayin them pastoral days is dead and gone and hes goin up and down in elevators like the rest of us and so here he is boardin the damn cage and theys a bunch of us bastards clownin around with the little piece who operates that deathtrap kinda brushin her swell butt like a occasional accident and sweet jeezus her gettin fidgety and hot and half fightin us off and half pullin us on and playin with that lever *zoom!* wingin up through that scraper and just then ole Carruther jeezuss he really breaks you up sometimes that crazy bastard he hefts up her little purple skirt and whaddaya know! the little quiff aint wearin no skivvies! its somethin *beautiful* man I mean a sweet cleft peach right outa some foreign orchard and poor ole Mort he is kinda part gigglin and part hurtin and for a minute the rest of us dont see the pointa the whole agitation but then that there incredible thing suddenly pops up quivery right under his chin like the friggin eye of god for crissake and then theres this big wild rip and man! it rears up and splits outa there like a goddamn redwood topplin *gawdamighty!* and knocks old Carruther *kapow!* right to the deck! his best buddy and that poor little cunt she takes one glim of that impossible rod wheelin around in there and whammin the walls and she faints dead away and *jeeezusss!* she tumbles right on that elevator lever and man! I thought for a minute we was *all* dead

15

They plunge, their damp bodies fused, pounding furiously, in terror, in joy, the impact is

I, Martin, proclaim against all dooms the inde-
structible seed

Martin does not take the self-service elevator to the fourteenth floor, as is his custom, but, reflecting upon it for once and out of a strange premonition, determines instead to walk the fourteen flights. Halfway up, he hears the elevator hurtle by him and then the splintering crash from below. He hesitates, poised on the stair. Inscrutable is the word he finally settles upon. He pronounces it aloud, smiles faintly, sadly, somewhat wearily, then continues his tedious climb, pausing from time to time to stare back down the stairs behind him.

WALT WHITMAN
Crossing Brooklyn Ferry

1

Flood-tide below me! I see you face to face!
Clouds of the west—sun there half an hour high—I see you also face to
    face.

Crowds of men and women attired in the usual costumes, how curious
    you are to me!
On the ferry-boats the hundreds and hundreds that cross, returning
    home, are more curious to me than you suppose,
And you that shall cross from shore to shore years hence are more to
5   me, and more in my meditations, than you might suppose.

2

The impalpable sustenance of me from all things at all hours of the day,
The simple, compact, well-join'd scheme, myself disintegrated, every one
    disintegrated yet part of the scheme,
The similitudes of the past and those of the future,
The glories strung like beads on my smallest sights and hearings, on the
    walk in the street and the passage over the river,
10 The current rushing so swiftly and swimming with me far away,
The others that are to follow me, the ties between me and them,
The certainty of others, the life, love, sight, hearing of others.

Others will enter the gates of the ferry and cross from shore to shore,
Others will watch the run of the flood-tide,
Others will see the shipping of Manhattan north and west, and the
15 heights of Brooklyn to the south and east,
Others will see the islands large and small;
Fifty years hence, others will see them as they cross, the sun half an hour
    high,

A hundred years hence, or ever so many hundred years hence, others will
    see them,
Will enjoy the sunset, the pouring-in of the flood-tide, the falling-back to
    the sea of the ebb-tide.

3

20   It avails not, time nor place—distance avails not,
I am with you, you men and women of a generation, or ever so many
    generations hence,
Just as you feel when you look on the river and sky, so I felt,
Just as any of you is one of a living crowd, I was one of a crowd,
Just as you are refresh'd by the gladness of the river and the bright flow,
    I was refresh'd,
Just as you stand and lean on the rail, yet hurry with the swift current, I
25   stood yet was hurried,
Just as you look on the numberless masts of ships and the thick-stemm'd
    pipes of steamboats, I look'd.

I too many and many a time cross'd the river of old,
Watched the Twelfth-month sea-gulls, saw them high in the air floating
    with motionless wings, oscillating their bodies,
Saw how the glistening yellow lit up parts of their bodies and left the rest
    in strong shadow,
30   Saw the slow-wheeling circles and the gradual edging toward the south,
Saw the reflection of the summer sky in the water,
Had my eyes dazzled by the shimmering track of beams.
Look'd at the fine centrifugal spokes of light round the shape of my head
    in the sunlit water,
Look'd on the haze on the hills southward and south-westward,
35   Look'd on the vapor as it flew in fleeces tinged with violet,
Look'd toward the lower bay to notice the vessels arriving,
Saw their approach, saw aboard those that were near me,
Saw the white sails of schooners and sloops, saw the ships at anchor,
The sailors at work in the rigging or out astride the spars,
The round masts, the swinging motion of the hulls, the slender serpentine
40   pennants,
The large and small steamers in motion, the pilots in their pilot-houses,
The white wake left by the passage, the quick tremulous whirl of the
    wheels,
The flags of all nations, the falling of them at sunset,
The scallop-edged waves in the twilight, the ladled cups, the frolicsome
    crests and glistening,

The stretch afar growing dimmer and dimmer, the gray walls of the
45   granite storehouses by the docks,
On the river the shadowy group, the big steam-tug closely flank'd on
     each side by the barges, the hay-boat, the belated lighter,
On the neighboring shore the fires from the foundry chimneys burning
     high and glaringly into the night,
Casting their flicker of black contrasted with wild red and yellow light
     over the tops of houses, and down into the clefts of streets.

4

These and all else were to me the same as they are to you,
50   I loved well those cities, loved well the stately and rapid river,
The men and women I saw were all near to me,
Others the same—others who look back on me because I look'd forward
     to them,
(The time will come, though I stop here to-day and to-night.)

5

What is it then between us?
55   What is the count of the scores or hundreds of years between us?

Whatever it is, it avails not—distance avails not, and place avails not,
I too lived, Brooklyn of ample hills was mine,
I too walk'd the streets of Manhattan island, and bathed in the waters
     around it,
I too felt the curious abrupt questionings stir within me,
60   In the day among crowds of people sometimes they came upon me,
In my walks home late at night or as I lay in my bed they came upon me,
I too had been struck from the float forever held in solution,
I too had receiv'd identity by my body,
That I was I knew was of my body, and what I should be I knew I should
     be of my body.

6

65   It is not upon you alone the dark patches fall,
The dark threw its patches down upon me also,
The best I had done seem'd to me blank and suspicious,
My great thoughts as I supposed them, were they not in reality meagre?
Nor is it you alone who know what it is to be evil,
70   I am he who knew what it was to be evil,
I too knitted the old knot of contrariety,

Blabb'd, blush'd, resented, lied, stole, grudg'd,
Had guile, anger, lust, hot wishes I dared not speak,
Was wayward, vain, greedy, shallow, sly, cowardly, malignant,
75 The wolf, the snake, the hog, not wanting in me,
The cheating look, the frivolous word, the adulterous wish, not wanting,
Refusals, hates, postponements, meanness, laziness, none of these wanting,
Was one with the rest, the days and haps of the rest,
Was call'd by my nighest name by clear loud voices of young men as they saw me approaching or passing,
Felt their arms on my neck as I stood, or the negligent leaning of their
80 flesh against me as I sat,
Saw many I loved in the street or ferry-boat or public assembly, yet never told them a word.
Lived the same life with the rest, the same old laughing, gnawing, sleeping,
Play'd the part that still looks back on the actor or actress,
The same old role, the role that is what we make it, as great as we like,
85 Or as small as we like, or both great and small.

7

Closer yet I approach you,
What thought you have of me now, I had as much of you—I laid in my stores in advance,
I consider'd long and seriously of you before you were born.

Who was to know what should come home to me?
90 Who knows but I am enjoying this?
Who knows, for all the distance, but I am as good as looking at you now, for all you cannot see me?

8

Ah, what can ever be more stately and admirable to me than mast-hemm'd Manhattan?
River and sunset and scallop-edg'd waves of flood-tide?
The sea-gulls oscillating their bodies, the hay-boat in the twilight, and the belated lighter?
What gods can exceed these that clasp me by the hand, and with voices I
95 love call me promptly and loudly by my nighest name as I approach?
What is more subtle than this which ties me to the woman or man that looks in my face?
Which fuses me into you now, and pours my meaning into you?

We understand then do we not?

What I promis'd without mentioning it, have you not accepted?

¹⁰⁰ What the study could not teach—what the preaching could not accomplish is accomplish'd, is it not?

9

Flow on, river! flow with the flood-tide, and ebb with the ebb-tide!

Frolic on, crested and scallop-edg'd waves!

Gorgeous clouds of the sunset! drench with your splendor me, or the men and women generations after me!

Cross from shore to shore, countless crowds of passengers!

¹⁰⁵ Stand up, tall masts of Mannahatta! stand up, beautiful hills of Brooklyn!

Throb, baffled and curious brain! throw out questions and answers!

Suspend here and everywhere, eternal float of solution!

Gaze, loving and thirsting eyes, in the house or street or public assembly!

Sound out, voices of young men! loudly and musically call me by my nighest name!

¹¹⁰ Live, old life! play the part that looks back on the actor or actress!

Play the old role, the role that is great or small according as one makes it!

Consider, you who peruse me, whether I may not in unknown ways be looking upon you;

Be firm, rail over the river, to support those who lean idly, yet haste with the hasting current;

Fly on, sea-birds! fly sideways, or wheel in large circles high in the air;

¹¹⁵ Receive the summer sky, you water, and faithfully hold it till all downcast eyes have time to take it from you!

Diverge, fine spokes of light, from the shape of my head, or any one's head, in the sunlit water!

Come on, ships from the lower bay! pass up or down, white-sail'd schooners, sloops, lighters!

Flaunt away, flags of all nations! be duly lower'd at sunset!

Burn high your fires, foundry chimneys! cast black shadows at nightfall! cast red and yellow light over the tops of the houses!

¹²⁰ Appearances, now or henceforth, indicate what you are,

You necessary film, continue to envelop the soul,

About my body for me, and your body for you, be hung out divinest aromas,

Thrive, cities—bring your freight, bring your shows, ample and sufficient rivers,

Expand, being than which none else is perhaps more spiritual,

¹²⁵ Keep your places, objects than which none else is more lasting.

You have waited, you always wait, you dumb, beautiful ministers,
We receive you with free sense at last, and are insatiate henceforward,
Not you any more shall be able to foil us, or withhold yourselves from us,
We use you, and do not cast you aside—we plant you permanently within
    us,
130 We fathom you not—we love you—there is perfection in you also,
You furnish your parts toward eternity,
Great or small, you furnish your parts toward the soul.

5
Visions:
the city and beyond

Acquainted with the Night

I have been one acquainted with the night.
I have walked out in rain—and back in rain.
I have outwalked the furthest city light.

I have looked down the saddest city lane.
I have passed by the watchman on his beat.
And dropped my eyes, unwilling to explain.

I have stood still and stopped the sound of feet
When far away an interrupted cry
Came over houses from another street,

But not to call me back or say good-by;
And further still at an unearthly height
One luminary clock against the sky

Proclaimed the time was neither wrong nor right.
I have been one acquainted with the night.

                                        Robert Frost

Jerry N. Uelsmann

Weegee

Alfred Stieglitz

Robert Frank

Alwyn Scott Turner

William Eggleston

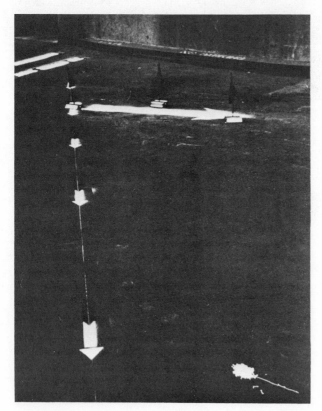

Minor White

Alfred Stieglitz

Ed Ruscha

Robert Adams

Andre Kertész

Stephen Shore

Ken Chara

(on following two pages)

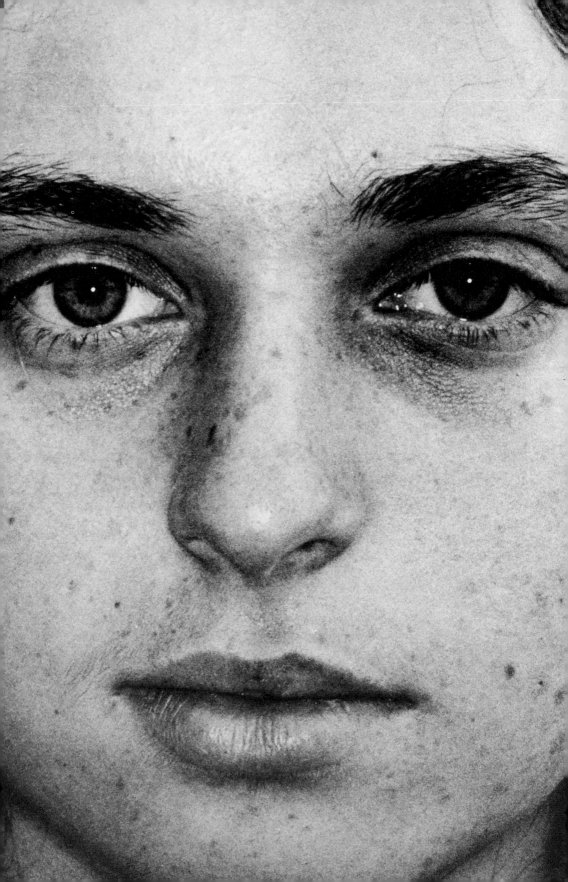

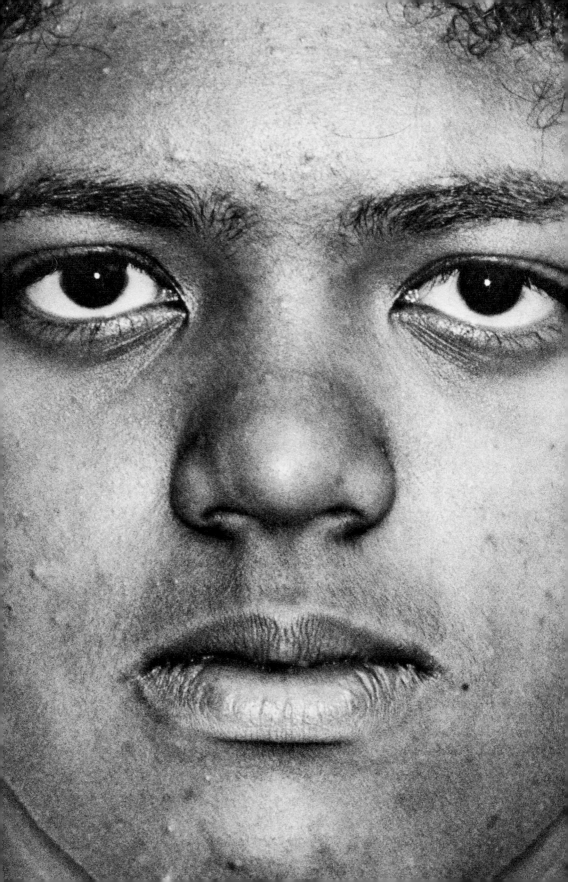

KENNETH E. BOULDING
The Death of the City:
A Frightened Look at Postcivilization

Civilization, it is clear from the Latin meaning of the word, is what goes on in cities—conversely, a city is a peculiar product of the state of man known as civilization. The traditional view of civilization is that it represents a higher state of mankind than the precivilized or savage society which preceded it and that it is indeed a state of mankind which has never been fully realized. When there are elements in modern society of which we sharply disapprove, we are apt to reprove them by calling them "uncivilized." The traditional view of the history of man, therefore, is that of a general spread of cities and of civilization over the world from its origins in Egypt, Sumeria, and the Indus, and a gradual refinement and "urbanity" of life and manners as a result.

Even in civilized man, however, there is a deep ambivalence about the city. The city is not only Zion, the city of God; it is Babylon, the scarlet woman. On the one hand, we have the opposition of urbane splendor and culture with rural cloddishness and savagery; on the other hand, we have the opposition of urban vice, corruption and cruelty, as against rural virtue and purity. The Bible, to take but one instance, furnishes us with innumerable examples of this deep ambivalence towards the city. It is at once the house of God and the house of iniquity. Amos, the herdsman, denounces it; Jeremiah weeps over it; Christ is crucified in it. One of the great threads through the Bible is the destruction and rebuilding of the city—a pattern which is wholly characteristic of the age of civilization.

Before considering the death of the city we must consider its birth. We must ask, that is, what is it in the social system that we call civilization that produces dense agglomerations of mankind rather than the relatively even distribution of population that is characteristic of precivilized societies. The answer seems to be that there are two different types of cities; the political and the economic. Economic cities may be further classified as trade cities, production cities and extraction cities, according to the proportion of these activities which takes place in them.

The political city is probably the earliest of all cities. All civilization is a by-product of agriculture; that is, of the domestication of crops and animals and the resultant food surplus from the food producer. Such a food surplus is a necessary, but not a sufficient condition for the development of civilization and the establishment of cities. There are many examples of primitive peoples which have enjoyed food surpluses for substantial periods of time and which have "wasted" these in elaborate rituals or in the sheer enjoyment of life. The city arises first when political means are devised to channel these food surpluses into the hands of a ruler. The first organization is an army which can extract the food surpluses from the food producer by means of coercion and hence can feed itself. If there is something left over from the consumption of the army, there will be food available to feed priests, kings, and artisans and so the possibility arises of erecting temples and palaces. Because military organizations tend to produce other military organizations as their enemies, the palaces and temples usually have to be surrounded by a wall. So the institution of war which is also highly characteristic of the age of civilization begins.

The agglomeration of the city here serves mainly defensive purposes. If we ask why the products of the food surplus are not distributed fairly evenly over the countryside, the answer is that if they were so distributed, they could not be defended. The characteristic obverse of the defense city, therefore, is a poor and miserable countryside in which the food producers produce more than they can eat themselves but have their surplus taken away from them without being given much in return. With this food surplus, the rulers feed their armies, their priests, their servants and their artisans. They build pyramids and palaces, Parthenons, and cathedrals. These artifacts, however, are concentrated in the cities, partly because it is convenient for a ruler to have a court, that is, an entourage around him and to keep his army where he can oversee it. Partly also, the city arises because the citizens can build a wall around it and keep their possessions temporarily safe. The defense city, however, is unstable—no matter how high the walls they will eventually be breached. I do not believe anyone has ever calculated the expectation of life of a defense city, but it must be fairly small; I would be surprised if it were more than two or three hundred years. The inevitable pattern of a defense city is the pattern of rise and fall. Jerusalem, Nineveh, Babylon, Carthage, and Rome all followed the same grim rhythm.

Trade and manufacture often begin in the political city, for the first traders and artisans gather under the shadow of the fortification. Nevertheless, economics is different from politics; an economic city is different from the political city. The economic city begins when man discovers that under some circumstances it may be cheaper to produce and to trade than to coerce. In the pure defense society, the ruler has to feed the soldiers that coerce the food producers to extract the food surplus. The subsistence of the soldiers may be considered as a cost of the food surplus extracted. Under some circumstances, this may be so large as to eat up almost the whole of the food surplus. It may then be cheaper for the city to produce something and to trade it with the food producers for the food surplus. Instead of feeding soldiers, we now feed artisans and merchants, and with the product of the artisans and the services of the merchants we extract the food surplus from the food producers by offering them something in exchange. Trade and production, we observe, go hand in hand. Without production there would be nothing to trade; without trade there would be no point in production.

It is the combination of production, trade, and defense that produces the great civilizations. Defense must go beyond the cities to establish a reign of law over the whole countryside. This it can only do if the food producers are not hopelessly exploited. That is, it is trade and production that make the establishment of widespread law possible. Only if there are widespread law and security, however, are widespread trade and production possible. These two aspects of the great civilization, therefore, reinforce each other. There seems to be a profound historical tendency, however, for defense to encroach upon the production and trade aspects of society to the point where the society becomes unstable. The costs of defense become cumulatively greater and the society less able to support them until the civilization crumbles.

We still need to ask ourselves why trade and production should produce concentrations of men into cities. The question here is why, in the absence of any necessity for defense, do not the economic activities of trade and production spread themselves evenly over the geographical field? There seem to be two answers to this question. One is to be found in the mere existence of the cost of transport. Lösch [1] has shown in his brilliant work on the location of industry that even if we started off with economic activity uniformly distributed over a homogeneous plain, the existence of costs of transport alone would result in a geographical structuring of the economic activity simply under the impact of the principle of profit maximization. The lines of transport will develop a roughly hexagonal pattern and at the nodes where the lines of transport come together, concentrations of economic activity, that is, cities, will develop.

The second cause of urban concentrations of economic activity is the heterogeneity of what might be called economic space. We see this in its simplest form in the extractive city such as a mining city. This obviously has to be where the mine is. Such a city is usually short-lived and has something of the air of a camp, but if the mine is rich it can afford an opera house and it will temporarily have many of the marks of a classical city. Fishing, we may note, which is a permanent form of sea mining,

1. Lösch, August, *The Economics of Location* (New Haven, 1954).

produces villages rather than cities, because the "mine" is not rich enough to support a large population.

A society where the agricultural surplus is extracted by trade will produce market towns in the middle of farming country. These can become cities of a kind, especially if they are allied with a cathedral which makes it a spiritual, political city. The great trading cities, however, generally have established themselves at points where there was a sharp break in the cost of transport; that is, at the ports. The importance of this factor is reflected in the number of cities of more than one-half-million people in many parts of the world located at a point of discontinuity between water and land transportation. The location of mankind is dominated by two facts about cost of transport. The first is that, by and large, water transportation is cheaper by almost an order of magnitude than land transportation, although this differential has been diminishing in the course of the last two hundred years. The second is that the transshipment from water to land transportation is also extremely costly. I have frequently, and so far without success, urged that the geographers draw a really significant map of the world in which the distances would be in proportion to cost of transport. A general projection of this kind is, of course, impossible, but it would be possible to do this in a polar projection based upon a particular point, such as for instance, New York City. That is, we could draw a map of the world in which the position of each point was determined by its direction from New York and in which its distance from New York was proportionate to the cost of transport from New York. We could do this fairly easily for a particular commodity such as wheat. Such a map would be almost totally unrecognizable and yet it would represent a much truer picture than the usual projections. The oceans would shrink to a little puddle in the middle of the map with small extensions up great rivers. Around this puddle would spread the world port city, and we would see New York, Boston, Philadelphia, Baltimore, London, Hamburg, Calcutta, Bombay, Tokyo, Sydney, and so on, clustered around the puddle of the oceans and forming an almost continuous world city. This would even include St. Louis, Minneapolis, Cleveland, Detroit, Chicago, and Duluth. Away from the world port city would stretch the great land hinterlands, and even the points of transshipment themselves would bulk large. If we impose the Lösch hexagons on a projection of this kind, we get a pretty fair explanation, I suspect, of the distribution of world's population.

We finally come to the production or manufacturing city which is the result of a certain heterogeneity in pure economic space. This takes two forms; the existence of economies of scale in the production of a single commodity, and the existence of what the economist calls external economies; that is, economies in one line of production as a result of the existence of neighboring producing operations. Large automobile plants are generally more efficient than small. This fact alone will lead to the concentration of production of automobiles in a few plants, and therefore in a few places, and the population of automobile workers will be concentrated there as well. The presence of one automobile plant in a city, however, may make it cheaper to put another one there for various subtle reasons. It is not surprising, therefore, to find specialized manufacturing cities like Pittsburgh, Manchester, and Detroit.

So much then for the birth of the city and the reasons that have given rise to it. What gave rise to the city, however, is the same set of causes that gave rise to civilization. The crux of my argument now is that civilization is passing away and that the city will pass away with it.

We are now passing through a period of transition in the state of man quite as large and as far reaching as the transition from precivilized to civilized society. I call this the transition from civilization to postcivilization. This idea is shocking to many people who still think that what is going on in the world today is a simple extension of the movement from precivilized to civilized society. In fact, however, I think we have to recognize that we are moving towards a state of man which is as different from civilization as civilization itself was from the precivilized societies which preceded it. This is what we mean by the innocent term "economic development." There is something ironic in the reflection that just at the moment when civilization has, in effect, extended itself over the whole world and when precivilized societies exist only in rapidly declining pockets, postcivilization is stalking on the heels of civilization itself and is creating the same kind of disruption and disturbance in civilized societies that civilization produces on precivilized societies.

Just as civilization is a product of the food surplus which proceeds from agriculture, which represents a higher level of organization of food production than primitive hunting and food gathering, so postcivilization is a product of science, that is, of a higher level of organization of human knowledge and the organization of this knowledge into know-how. The result of this is an increase in the productivity of human labor, especially in the production of commodities, which is quantitatively so large as to create a qualitatively different kind of society. The food surplus upon which classical civilization rested was extremely meager. In the Roman Empire at its height, for instance, it is doubtful whether more than twenty or twenty-five per cent of the total population were in nonfood-producing occupations. That is, it took about seventy-five per cent of the total population to feed the hundred per cent, and only twenty or twenty-five per cent could be spared to fight wars, to establish states, and to build the great monuments of civilization, both of architecture and of literature.

In the United States at the moment, which is the part of the world furthest advanced toward postcivilization, we can now produce all our food requirements with about ten per cent of the population and still have an embarrassing agricultural surplus. This is a change in an order of magnitude. We can now devote ninety per cent of the population to nonagricultural pursuits. In the production of many other commodities, the increase in the productivity of labor is even more spectacular and with the coming of automation, we may find even another order of magnitude change in this quantity. By contrast there are many occupations, notably the service trades, in which there has been very little technical change over the past few thousand years. In such occupations as hair-cutting, teaching, and personal services generally, the productivity of labor has shown little change. As a result of these differential changes in the productivity of labor, there has been an enormous revolution in the relative price structure. The prices of those commodities in the production of which technical improvement has occurred have fallen drastically relative to those commodities and services the production of which has been technologically stagnant. Furthermore, no end is at present in sight for this process. It is doubtful whether we have even reached the mid-point of this enormous process of change. We devote increasing resources to technological improvement and to the advance of knowledge and up to now there seems to be little in the way of diminishing returns to this activity. I do not believe this to be an infinite process and I have a strong conviction that all processes, even this one, eventually reach something like an equilibrium. The equilibrium level of knowledge and technology which the present process of scientific and technological development implies, however, is still a very long way in the future, and most certainly is beyond the level of our present imaginations. It is by no means impossible to suppose a world at the end of this process in which we can produce our whole food supply with one per cent of the population, in which we can produce all basic commodities such as clothing, housing, and so on with perhaps another two or three per cent or perhaps even at most ten per cent, and in which, therefore, economic life revolves very largely around the organization of personal services. We have not yet begun to think out the details of such an economy. It is clear that many of its institutions and forms of organization will be very different from what is now familiar to us.

In the meantime the rise of postcivilization is presenting an enormous crisis to the institution of civilizations, whether these are the lingering institutions of civilization in the postcivilized countries or whether these are what might be thought of as the civilized, that is, the poor countries. The nature of the present crisis may be dramatically reflected in the observation that Indonesia, which we think of as one of the poorest countries in the world in desperate need of economic development, has in fact about the same population and per capita income as the Roman Empire at its height. Jakarta is a city at least as large as ancient Rome, if perhaps not quite as splendid. In many ways the level of life and civilization in Indonesia goes beyond that of Augustan Rome. Yet, this is a country which is desperately unhappy with its present state and very anxious to rise out of it.

Just as civilization almost always produces a disastrous impact upon the precivilized societies with which it comes into contact—witness for instance the sad history of the American Indians—it also seems all too probable that the impact of postcivilized on civilized societies will be equally disastrous. There are three major aspects of this breakdown of the institutions of civilization. The first is the breakdown of the system of national defense. I have elaborated elsewhere on this phenomenon [2] so that I need not develop the proposition here. The breakdown is the result partly of a dimunition in the cost of transport of violence which, coupled with the increase in the range of the deadly missile, has shattered what might be called the classical system of unconditional national security. These two phenomenon have destroyed what I call "unconditional viability" even for the largest nations, and in particular have rendered the cities of the world pitilessly vulnerable.

The second symptom of the disintegration of civilization is the population explosion in the civilized countries, and even in the incipient postcivilized countries. Classical civilization maintained whatever equilibrium it had because its high birthrates were offset by high death rates. In the ideal type of civilized society, we might suppose a birth and death rate of about forty with an expectation of life at birth of twenty-five. In postcivilized society, the expectation of life at birth rises to seventy. An equilibrium of population under these circumstances requires birth and death rates of about fourteen per thousand. The first impact of postcivilized techniques, however, on civilized society is frequently a dramatic reduction in the death rate. In many tropical countries, for instance, in the last twenty years, death rates have been reduced from twenty-five or thirty per thousand to about ten per thousand simply as a result of the introduction of DDT and relatively primitive measures of public health. The birth rate, however, stays up at forty with the result that these societies are now suffering a three per cent per annum population increase. This puts a burden on them in the current investment in human resources which may be more than they can bear, and it may therefore prevent them from making the transition into postcivilization. Postcivilized society requires as one of its conditions a large investment in human resources, that is, education. A poor, civilized society may prove to be incapable of devoting enough resources to education in the face of the three per cent per annum increase and in the face of its enormous numbers of children. Under these circumstances, it can easily regress towards even lower levels of civilization until the death rate rises once again or until some methods of population control are adopted. There are many parts of the world

2. *Conflict and Defense* (New York, 1961).

today in which we may be repeating the history of Ireland from 1700 to 1846—a gloomy prospect indeed.

It is the third aspect of the disintegration of civilization with which we are mainly concerned here, however. This is the disintegration of what might be called the classical city. The classical city is a well-integrated social organization. It has clearly defined boundaries and limits and it earns its living by a judicious combination of politics (that is, exploitation), production, and trade. It is unsanitary, so that its death rate is high; it almost certainly does not reproduce itself and it continually renews itself by drawing on the excess population as well as on the excess food supply of the country. There is a sharp differentiation between the culture of the city and of the country. The city is also a focus of loyalty and even the national state is frequently only an extension—or a colony—of the capital city.

In postcivilization all the conditions which gave rise to the classical city have gone. The parameters of the great equations of society have changed to the point where the classical city is no longer included as one of the solutions. The things which give rise to the need for concentrations all disappear. The city is now, for instance, utterly defenseless; it is a sitting duck for the H-bomb, and so called civil defense in the cities becomes little more than an obscene attempt to persuade the civilian population that they are thoroughly expendable in a modern war. The diminution in the cost of transport both of commodities and of communications has greatly diminished the value of concentrations of population for the purposes of trade and human intercourse. The classical city is based fundamentally on the necessity for face-to-face communication. For many purposes even today this necessity remains. The telephone, for instance, is not an adequate substitute for a personal conversation simply because it uses so restricted a channel that much of the nuances of communication which are transmitted, for instance, through gesture are lost. The possibility of communication by means of modulated light beams, however, has opened up an enormous number of long-distance channels, and it may well be that in the not-too-distant future we shall each sit in our own studies and conduct long-distance televised conferences with people all over the world. We are very far from having exhausted the implications, both political and economic, of the communications revolution in which we are living. Stock markets and legislative assemblies, for instance, in a physical sense are civilized rather than postcivilized institutions, and one doubts whether they will survive another fifty or one hundred years with the present type of development.

The impact of the automobile on the city is one stage in its disintegration, and this has been well-documented. We are all familiar, I am sure, with the notion of Los Angeles as the first postcivilized urban agglomeration—an agglomeration created by and poisoned by the automobile.

Under no circumstances could Los Angeles be called a city in the classical sense of the word. We must now recognize, indeed, I think, that California has become the first example of what I would call the "state city," that is, an urban agglomeration state-wide in its extent. Even the Shasta Dam has become a weekend playground for people from Los Angeles, and of course, the tentacles of the Los Angeles water system tend to engulf the whole West!

Another symptom of the disintegration of the city is the enormous rise in this country of part-time farming. The number of part-time farms is now close to, if it does not already exceed, the number of full-time farms. This represents in effect a dramatic explosion of the city over the countryside. Many of these part-time farmers commute forty or fifty miles to work in a city factory. The notion of the United States as consisting essentially of three or four loose, sprawling megalopolises separated by small stretches of largely empty countryside is by no means remote.

We can almost say that the city is destroyed by its own success. The paradox here is that by the time ninety per cent of the population are urban, the city has really ceased to have any meaning in itself. The converse of this phenomenon is the disappearance of rural life as a distinctive and peculiar sub-culture within the society. Over large parts of the United States this has already happened. The Iowa farmer has an occupational subculture but he does not have a rural subculture. He is merely an ex-urbanite who happens to be living on a farm, and he earns his living by thoroughly urban methods. He is, furthermore, a professional, usually with a college degree, and he is far more remote, say, from the European peasant than he is from the American factory engineer.

We may very well ask ourselves, therefore, whether we visualize a period in the not very distant future when in postcivilized societies, the city will really have disappeared altogether as an entity. We can even visualize a society in which the population is spread very evenly over the world in almost self-sufficient households, each circulating and processing everlastingly its own water supply through its own algae, each deriving all the power it needs from its own solar batteries, each in communication with anybody it wants to communicate with through its personalized television, each with immediate access to all the cultural resources of the world through channels of communications to libraries and other cultural repositories, each basking in the security of an invisible and cybernetic world state in which each man shall live under his vine and his own fig tree and none shall make him afraid. There may be a few radioactive holes to mark the sites of the older cities and a few interesting ruins that have escaped destruction. This vision is, of course, pure science fiction, but in these days one must not despise science fiction as a way of keeping up with the news.

Some modifications of this rather idyllic picture have to be made even in postcivilization, I suspect. A high level postcivilized stable technology would almost have to be based on the oceans for sources for its basic raw materials, as the mines and the fossil fuels will very soon be gone. There will, therefore, be some manufacturing concentrations around the shores of the world. We may even see a revival of the form of the classical city for pure pleasure where people can enjoy the luxury of walking and of face-to-face communication. Inequality of income in such a society is likely to be reflected in the fact that the poor will drive vehicles and the rich will walk. We are already, I think, beginning to see this movement in the movement of the rich into the city centers and the development of the mall. These cities, however, will be stage sets—they will arise out of the very freedom and luxury of the society rather than out of its necessities.

Just as we are deeply ambivalent toward the classical city and toward civilizations, so we are likely to be equally ambivalent towards postcivilization and we are likely to find a deep nostalgia for the city. Even in the new Jerusalem (the mile-cube city, we may observe perhaps only just around the corner as being the only practical way of having twenty million people living together) there will be nostalgia for the old Jerusalem and for Athens. We may well find a new race of prophets extolling the virtues of civilization—its purity, honesty, and simplicity, its closeness to nature, and its closeness to God by contrast with the even deadlier vices of postcivilized society. The only real hope for the classical city, however, is that nothing ever really passes away! Man has evolved in the great process of evolution but he has not displaced the amoeba; he has had to learn to coexist with, and indeed be symbiotic with, all the previous orders of life, even though many particular species have passed away. Similarly, in social evolution I suspect that higher forms do not necessarily displace the older and presumably "lower" forms. In the great ecosystem of the new society we may find a certain coexistence between postcivilized, civilized, and even precivilized social forms. Every evolutionary development has its price, and there may always be those who do not wish to pay it. My elegy of the city, therefore, may be premature and we may find for a long time to come the new Jerusalem and the old living side by side even on this tiny spaceship of a planet.

EDGAR ALLAN POE
The City in the Sea

Lo! Death has reared himself a throne
In a strange city lying alone
Far down within the dim West,
Where the good and the bad and the worst and the best
5   Have gone to their eternal rest.
There shrines and palaces and towers
(Time-eaten towers that tremble not!)
Resemble nothing that is ours.
Around, by lifting winds forgot,
10   Resignedly beneath the sky
The melancholy waters lie.

No rays from the holy heaven come down
On the long night-time of that town;
But light from out the lurid sea
15   Streams up the turrets silently—
Gleams up the pinnacles far and free—
Up domes—up spires—up kingly halls—
Up fanes—up Babylon-like walls—
Up shadowy long-forgotten bowers
20   Of sculptured ivy and stone flowers—
Up many and many a marvellous shrine
Whose wreathéd friezes intertwine
The viol, the violet, and the vine.

Resignedly beneath the sky
25   The melancholy waters lie.
So blend the turrets and shadows there
That all seem pendulous in air,
While from a proud tower in the town
Death looks gigantically down.

30 There open fanes and gaping graves
Yawn level with the luminous waves;
But not the riches there that lie
In each idol's diamond eye—
Not the gaily-jewelled dead
35 Tempt the waters from their bed;
For no ripples curl, alas!
Along that wilderness of glass—
No swellings tell that winds may be
Upon some far-off happier sea—
40 No heavings hint that winds have been
On seas less hideously serene.

But lo, a stir is in the air!
The wave—there is a movement there!
As if the towers had thrust aside,
45 In slightly sinking, the dull tide—
As if their tops had feebly given
A void within the filmy Heaven.
The waves have now a redder glow—
The hours are breathing faint and low—
50 And when, amid no earthly moans,
Down, down that town shall settle hence,
Hell, rising from a thousand thrones,
Shall do it reverence.

HART CRANE
The Tunnel

Performances, assortments, résumés—
Up Times Square to Columbus Circle lights
Channel the congresses, nightly sessions,
Refractions of the thousand theatres, faces—
Mysterious kitchens. . . . You shall search them all.
Someday by heart you'll learn each famous sight
And watch the curtain lift in hell's despite;
You'll find the garden in the third act dead,
Finger your knees—and wish yourself in bed
With tabloid crime-sheets perched in easy sight.

      Then let you reach your hat
      and go.
      As usual, let you—also
      walking down—exclaim
      to twelve upward leaving
      a subscription praise
      for what time slays.

Or can't you quite make up your mind to ride;
A walk is better underneath the L a brisk
Ten blocks or so before? But you find yourself
Preparing penguin flexions of the arms,—
As usual you will meet the scuttle yawn:
The subway yawns the quickest promise home.

Be minimum, then, to swim the hiving swarms
Out of the Square, the Circle burning bright—

Avoid the glass doors gyring at your right,
Where boxed alone a second, eyes take fright
—Quite unprepared rush naked back to light:
And down beside the turnstile press the coin
Into the slot. The gongs already rattle.

And so
of cities you bespeak
subways, rivered under streets
and rivers. . . . In the car
the overtone of motion
underground, the monotone
of motion is the sound
of other faces, also underground—

"Let's have a pencil Jimmy—living now
at Floral Park
Flatbush—on the fourth of July—
like a pigeon's muddy dream—potatoes
to dig in the field—travlin the town—too—
night after night—the Culver line—the
girls all shaping up—it used to be—"

Our tongues recant like beaten weather vanes.
This answer lives like verdigris, like hair
Beyond extinction, surcease of the bone;
And repetition freezes—"What

"what do you want? getting weak on the links?
fandaddle daddy don't ask for change—IS THIS
FOURTEENTH? it's half past six she said—if
you don't like my gate why did you
swing on it, why *didja*
swing on it
anyhow—"

And somehow anyhow swing—
The phonographs of hades in the brain
Are tunnels that re-wind themselves, and love
A burnt match skating in a urinal—
Somewhere above Fourteenth TAKE THE EXPRESS
To brush some new presentiment of pain—

"But I want service in this office SERVICE
I said—after
the show she cried a little afterwards but—"

Whose head is swinging from the swollen strap?
Whose body smokes along the bitten rails,
Bursts from a smoldering bundle far behind
In back forks of the chasms of the brain,—
Puffs from a riven stump far out behind
In interborough fissures of the mind . . . ?

And why do I often meet your visage here,
Your eyes like agate lanterns—on and on
Below the toothpaste and the dandruff ads?
—And did their riding eyes right through your side,
And did their eyes like unwashed platters ride?
And Death, aloft,—gigantically down
Probing through you—toward me, O evermore!
And when they dragged your retching flesh,
Your trembling hands that night through Baltimore—
That last night on the ballot rounds, did you
Shaking, did you deny the ticket, Poe?

For Gravesend Manor change at Chambers Street.
The platform hurries along to a dead stop.

The intent escalator lifts a serenade
Stilly
Of shoes, umbrellas, each eye attending its shoe, then
Bolting outright somewhere above where streets
Burst suddenly in rain. . . . The gongs recur:
Elbows and levers, guard and hissing door.
Thunder is galvothermic here below. . . . The car
Wheels off. The train rounds, bending to a scream,
Taking the final level for the dive
Under the river—
And somewhat emptier than before,
Demented, for a hitching second, humps; then
Lets go. . . . Toward corners of the floor
Newspapers wing, revolve and wing.
Blank windows gargle signals through the roar.

And does the Dæmon take you home, also,
Wop washerwoman, with the bandaged hair?
After the corridors are swept, the cuspidors—
The gaunt sky-barracks cleanly now, and bare,
O Genoese, do you bring mother eyes and hands
Back home to children and to golden hair?

Dæmon, demurring and eventful yawn!
Whose hideous laughter is a bellows mirth
—Or the muffled slaughter of a day in birth—
O cruelly to inoculate the brinking dawn
With antennæ toward worlds that glow and sink;—
To spoon us out more liquid than the dim
Locution of the eldest star, and pack
The conscience navelled in the plunging wind,
Umbilical to call—and straightway die!

O caught like pennies beneath soot and steam,
Kiss of our agony thou gatherest;
Condensed, thou takest all—shrill ganglia
Impassioned with some song we fail to keep.
And yet, like Lazarus, to feel the slope,
The sod and billow breaking,—lifting ground,
—A sound of waters bending astride the sky
Unceasing with some Word that will not die . . . !

                    *   *   *

A tugboat, wheezing wreaths of steam,
Lunged past, with one galvanic blare stove up the
        River.
I counted the echoes assembling, one after one,
Searching, thumbing the midnight on the piers.
Lights, coasting, left the oily tympanum of waters;
The blackness somewhere gouged glass on a sky.
And this thy harbor, O my City, I have driven under,
Tossed from the coil of ticking towers. . . .
        Tomorrow,
And to be. . . . Here by the River that is East—
Here at the waters' edge the hands drop memory;
Shadowless in that abyss they unaccounting lie.
How far away the star has pooled the sea—
Or shall the hands be drawn away, to die?

Kiss of our agony Thou gatherest,
                O Hand of Fire
                        gatherest—

LOUIS SIMPSON
Lines Written near San Francisco

1

I wake and feel the city trembling.
Yes, there is something unsettled in the air
And the earth is uncertain.

And so it was for the tenor Caruso.
He couldn't sleep—you know how the ovation
Rings in your ears, and you re-sing your part.

And then the ceiling trembled
And the floor moved. He ran into the street.
Never had Naples given him such a reception!

The air was darker than Vesuvius.
"O mamma mia,"
He cried, "I've lost my voice!"

At that moment the hideous voice of Culture,
Hysterical woman, thrashing her arms and legs,
Shrieked from the ruins.

At that moment everyone became a performer.
Otello and Don Giovanni
And Figaro strode on the midmost stage.

In the high window of a burning castle
Lucia raved. Black horses
Plunged through fire, dragging the wild bells.

The curtains were wrapped in smoke. Tin swords
Were melting; masks and ruffs
Burned—and the costumes of the peasants' chorus.

Night fell. The white moon rose
And sank in the Pacific. The tremors
Passed under the waves. And Death rested.

2

Now, as we stand idle,
Watching the silent, bowler-hatted man,
The engineer, who writes in the smoking field;

Now as he hands the paper to a boy,
Who takes it and runs to a group of waiting men,
And they disperse and move toward their wagons,

Mules bray and the wagons move—
Wait! Before you start
(Already the wheels are rattling on the stones)

Say, did your fathers cross the dry Sierras
To build another London?
Do Americans always have to be second-rate?

Wait! For there are spirits
In the earth itself, or in the air, or sea.
Where are the aboriginal American devils?

Cloud shadows, pine shadows
Falling across the bright Pacific bay . . .
(Already they have nailed rough boards together)

Wait only for the wind
That rustles in the eucalyptus tree.
Wait only for the light

That trembles on the petals of a rose.
(The mortar sets—banks are the first to stand)
Wait for a rose, and you may wait forever.

The silent man mops his head and drinks
Cold lemonade. "San Francisco
Is a city second only to Paris."

3

Every night, at the end of America
We taste our wine, looking at the Pacific.
How sad it is, the end of America!

While we were waiting for the land
They'd finished it—with gas drums
On the hilltops, cheap housing in the valleys

Where lives are mean and wretched.
But the banks thrive and the realtors
Rejoice—they have their America.

Still, there is something unsettled in the air.
Out there on the Pacific
There's no America but the Marines.

Whitman was wrong about the People,
But right about himself. The land is within.
At the end of the open road we come to ourselves.

Though mad Columbus follows the sun
Into the sea, we cannot follow.
We must remain, to serve the returning sun,

And to set tables for death.
For we are the colonists of Death—
Not, as some think, of the English.

And we are preparing thrones for him to sit,
Poems to read, and beds
In which it may please him to rest.

This is the land
The pioneers looked for, shading their eyes
Against the sun—a murmur of serious life.

MARSHALL McLUHAN
Roads and Paper Routes

It was not until the advent of the telegraph that messages could travel faster than a messenger. Before this, roads and the written word were closely interrelated. It is only since the telegraph that information has detached itself from such solid commodities as stone and papyrus, much as money had earlier detached itself from hides, bullion, and metals, and has ended as paper. The term "communication" has had an extensive use in connection with roads and bridges, sea routes, rivers, and canals, even before it became transformed into "information movement" in the electric age. Perhaps there is no more suitable way of defining the character of the electric age than by first studying the rise of the idea of transportation as communication, and then the transition of the idea from transport to information by means of electricity. The word "metaphor" is from the Greek *meta* plus *pherein,* to carry across or transport. In this book we are concerned with all forms of transport of goods and information, both as metaphor and exchange. Each form of transport not only carries, but translates and transforms, the sender, the receiver, and the message. The use of any kind of medium or extension of man alters the patterns of interdependence among people, as it alters the ratios among our senses.

It is a persistent theme of this book that all technologies are extensions of our physical and nervous systems to increase power and speed. Again, unless there were such increases of power and speed, new extensions of ourselves would not occur or would be discarded. For an increase of power or speed in any kind of grouping of any components whatever is itself a disruption that causes a change of organization. The alteration of social groupings, and the formation of new communities, occur with the increased speed of information movement by means of paper messages and road transport. Such speed-up means much more control at much greater distances. Historically, it meant the formation of the Roman Empire and the disruption of the previous city-states of the Greek world. Before the use of papyrus and alphabet created the incentives for building fast, hard-surface roads, the walled town and the city-state were natural forms that could endure.

Village and city-state essentially are forms that include all human needs and functions. With greater speed and, therefore, greater military control at a distance, the city-state collapsed. Once inclusive and self-contained, its needs and functions were extended in the specialist activities of an empire. Speed-up tends to separate functions, both commercial and political, and acceleration beyond a point in any system becomes disruption and breakdown. So when Arnold Toynbee turns, in *A Study of History,* to a massive documentation of "the breakdowns of civilizations," he begins by saying: "One of the most conspicuous marks of disintegration, as we have already noticed, is . . . when a disintegrating civilisation purchases a reprieve by submitting to forcible political unification in a universal state." Disintegration and reprieve, alike, are the consequence of ever faster movement of information by couriers on excellent roads.

Speed-up creates what some economists refer to as a *center-margin* structure. When this becomes too extensive for the generating and control center, pieces begin to detach themselves and to set up new center-margin systems of their own. The most familiar example is the story of the American colonies of Great Britain. When the thirteen colonies began to develop a considerable social and economic life of their own, they felt the need to become centers themselves, with their own margins. This is the time when the original center may make a more rigorous effort of centralized control of the margins, as, indeed, Great Britain did. The slowness of sea travel proved altogether inadequate to the maintenance of so extensive an empire on a mere center-margin basis. Land powers can more easily attain a unified center-margin pattern than sea powers. It is the relative slowness of sea travel that inspires sea powers to foster multiple centers by a kind of seeding process. Sea powers thus tend to create centers without margins, and land empires favor the center-margin structure. Electric speeds create centers everywhere. Margins cease to exist on this planet.

Lack of homogeneity in speed of information movement creates diversity of patterns in organization. It is quite predictable, then, that any new means of moving information will alter any power structure whatever. So long as the new means is everywhere available at the same time, there is a possibility that the structure may be changed without breakdown. Where there are great discrepancies in speeds of movement, as between air and road travel or between telephone and typewriter, serious conflicts occur within organizations. The metropolis of our time has become a test case for such discrepancies. If homogeneity of speeds were total, there would be no rebellion and no breakdown. With print, political unity via homogeneity became feasible for the first time. In ancient Rome, however, there was only the light paper manuscript to pierce the opacity, or to reduce the discontinuity, of the tribal villages; and when the paper supplies failed, the roads were vacated, as they were in our own age during gas-rationing. Thus the old city-state returned, and feudalism replaced republicanism.

It seems obvious enough that technical means of speed-up should wipe out the independence of villages and city-states. Whenever speed-up has occurred, the new centralist power always takes action to homogenize as many marginal areas as possible. The process that Rome effected by the phonetic alphabet geared to its paper routes has been occurring in Russia for the last century. Again, from the current example of Africa we can observe how very much visual processing of the human psyche by alphabetic means will be needed before any appreciable degree of homogenized social organization is possible. Much of this visual processing was done in the ancient world by nonliterate technologies, as in Assyria. The phonetic alphabet has no rival, however, as a translator of man out of the closed tribal echo-chamber into the neutral visual world of lineal organization.

The situation of Africa today is complicated by the new electronic technology. Western man is himself being de-Westernized by his own new speed-up, as much as the Africans are being detribalized by our old print and industrial technology. If we understood our own media old and new, these confusions and disruptions could be programmed and synchronized. The very success we enjoy in specializing and separating functions in order to have speed-up, however, is at the same time the cause of inattention and unawareness of the situation. It has ever been thus in the Western world at least. Self-consciousness of the causes and limits of one's own culture seems to threaten the ego structure and is, therefore, avoided. Nietzsche said understanding stops action, and men of action seem to have an intuition of the fact in their shunning the dangers of comprehension.

The point of the matter of speed-up by wheel, road, and paper is the extension of power in an ever more homogeneous and uniform space. Thus the real potential of the Roman technology was not realized until printing had given road and wheel a much greater speed than that of the Roman vortex. Yet the speed-up of the electronic age is as disrupting for literate, lineal, and Western man as the Roman paper routes were for tribal villagers. Our speed-up today is not a slow explosion outward from center to margins but an instant implosion and an interfusion of space and functions. Our specialist and fragmented civilization of center-margin structure is suddenly experiencing an instantaneous reassembling of all its mechanized bits into an organic whole. This is the new world of the global village. The village, as Mumford explains in *The City in History,* had achieved a social and institutional extension of all human faculties. Speed-up and city aggregates only served to separate these from one another in more specialist forms. The electronic age cannot sustain the very low gear of a center-margin structure such as we associate with the past two thousand years of the Western world. Nor is this a question of values. If we understood our older media, such as roads and the written word, and if we valued their human effects sufficiently, we could reduce or even eliminate the electronic factor from our lives. Is there an instance of any culture that understood the technology that sustained its structure and was prepared to keep it that way? If so, that would be an instance of values or reasoned preference. The values or preferences that arise from the mere automatic operation of this or that technology in our social lives are not capable of being perpetuated.

In the chapter on the wheel it will be shown that transport without wheels had played a big role before the wheel, some of which was by sledge, over both snow and bogs. Much of it was by pack animal— woman being the first pack animal. Most wheel-less transport in the past, however, was by river and by sea, a fact that is today as richly expressed as ever in the location and form of the great cities of the world. Some writers have observed that man's oldest beast of burden was woman, because the male had to be free to run interference for the woman, as ball-carrier, as it were. But that phase belonged to the prewheel stage of transport, when there was only the tractless waste of man the hunter and food-gatherer. Today, when the greatest volume of transport consists in the moving of information, the wheel and the road are undergoing recession and obsolescence; but in the first instance, given the pressure for, and from, wheels, there had to be roads to accommodate them. Settlements had created the impulse for exchange and for the increasing movement of raw material and produce from countryside to processing centers, where there was division of labor and specialist craft skills. Improvement of wheel and road more and more brought the town to the country in a reciprocal spongelike action of give-and-take. It is a process we have seen in this century with the motorcar. Great improvements in roads brought the city more and more to the country. The road became a substitute for the country by the time people began to talk about "taking a spin in the country." With superhighways the road became a wall between man and the country. Then came the stage of the highway as city, a city stretching continuously across the continent, dissolving all earlier cities into the sprawling aggregates that desolate their populations today.

With air transport comes a further disruption of the old town-country complex that had occurred with wheel and road. With the plane the cities began to have the same slender relation to human needs that museums do. They became corridors of showcases echoing the departing forms of industrial assembly lines. The road is, then, used less and less for travel, and more and more for recreation. The traveler now turns to the airways, and thereby ceases to experience the act of traveling. As people used to say that an ocean liner might as well be a hotel in a big city, the jet traveler, whether he is over Tokyo or New York, might just as well be in a cocktail lounge so far as travel experience is concerned. He will begin to travel only after he lands.

Meantime, the countryside, as oriented and fashioned by plane, by highway, and by electric information-gathering, tends to become once more the nomadic trackless area that preceded the wheel. The beatniks gather on the sands to meditate *haiku.*

The principal factors in media impact on existing social forms are acceleration and disruption. Today the acceleration tends to be total, and thus ends space as the main factor in social arrangements. Toynbee sees the acceleration factor as translating the physical into moral problems, pointing to the antique road crowded with dog carts, wagons, and rickshaws as full of minor nuisance, but also minor dangers. Further, as the forces impelling traffic mount in power, there is no more problem of hauling and carrying, but the physical problem is translated into a psychological one as the annihilation of space permits easy annihilation of travelers as well. This principle applies to all media study. All means of interchange and of human interassociation tend to improve by acceleration. Speed, in turn, accentuates problems of form and structure. The older arrangements had not been made with a view to such speeds, and people begin to sense a draining-away of life values as they try to make the old physical forms adjust to the new and speedier movement. These problems, however, are not new. Julius Caesar's first act upon assuming power was to restrict the night movement of wheeled vehicles in the city of Rome in order to permit sleep. Improved transport in the Renaissance turned the medieval walled towns into slums.

Prior to the considerable diffusion of power through alphabet and papyrus, even the attempts of kings to extend their rule in spatial terms were opposed at home by the priestly bureaucracies. Their complex and unwieldy media of stone inscription made wide-ranging empires appear very dangerous to such static monopolies. The struggles between those who exercised power over the hearts of men and those who sought to control the physical resources of nations were not of one time and place. In the Old Testament just this kind of struggle is reported in the Book of Samuel (I, viii) when the children of Israel besought Samuel to give them a king. Samuel explained to them the nature of kingly, as opposed to priestly, rule:

> This will be the manner of the King that shall reign over you: he will take your sons, and appoint them unto him for his chariots; and they shall run before his chariots: and he will appoint them unto him for captains of thousands, and captains of fifties; and he will set some to plough his ground, and to reap his harvest, and to make his instruments of war, and the

instruments of his chariots. And he will take your daughters to be confectionaries, and to be cooks and to be bakers. And he will take your fields, and your vineyards, and your oliveyards, even the best of them, and give them to his servants.

Paradoxically, the effect of the wheel and of paper in organizing new power structures was not to decentralize but to centralize. A speed-up in communications always enables a central authority to extend its operations to more distant margins. The introduction of alphabet and papyrus meant that many more people had to be trained as scribes and administrators. However, the resulting extension of homogenization and of uniform training did not come into play in the ancient or medieval world to any great degree. It was not really until the mechanization of writing in the Renaissance that intensely unified and centralized power was possible. Since this process is still occurring, it should be easy for us to see that it was in the armies of Egypt and Rome that a kind of democratization by uniform technological education occurred. Careers were then open to talents for those with literate training. In the chapter on the written word we saw how phonetic writing translated tribal man into a visual world and invited him to undertake the visual organization of space. The priestly groups in the temples had been more concerned with the records of the past and with the control of the inner space of the unseen than with outward military conquest. Hence, there was a clash between the priestly monopolizers of knowledge and those who wished to apply it abroad as new conquest and power. (This same clash now recurs between the university and the business world.) It was this kind of rivalry that inspired Ptolemy II to establish the great library at Alexandria as a center of imperial power. The huge staff of civil servants and scribes assigned to many specialist tasks was an antithetic and countervailing force to the Egyptian priesthood. The library could serve the political organization of empire in a way that did not interest the priesthood at all. A not-dissimilar rivalry is developing today between the atomic scientists and those who are mainly concerned with power.

If we realize that the city as center was in the first instance an aggregate of threatened villagers, it is then easier for us to grasp how such harassed companies of refugees might fan out into an empire. The city-state as a form was not a response to peaceful commercial development, but a huddling for security amidst anarchy and dissolution. Thus the Greek city-state was a tribal form of inclusive and integral community, quite unlike the specialist cities that grew up as extensions of Roman military expansion. The Greek city-states eventually disintegrated by the usual action of specialist trading and the separation of functions that Mumford portrays in *The City in History*. The Roman cities began that way—as specialist operations of the central power. The Greek cities ended that way.

If a city undertakes rural trade, it sets up at once a center-margin relation with the rural area in question. That relation involves taking staples and raw produce from the country in exchange for specialist products of the craftsman. If, on the other hand, the same city attempts to engage in overseas trade, it is more natural to "seed" another city center, as the Greeks did, rather than to deal with the overseas area as a specialized margin or raw material supply.

A brief review of the structural changes in the organization of space as they resulted from wheel, road, and papyrus could go as follows: There was first the village, which lacked all of these group extensions of the private physical body. The village, however, was already a form of community different from that of food-gathering hunters and fishers, for villagers may be sedentary and may begin a division of labor and functions. Their being congregated is, itself, a form of acceleration of human activities which provides momentum for further separation and specialization of action. Such are the conditions for the extension of feet-as-wheel to speed production and exchange. These are, also, the conditions that intensify communal conflicts and ruptures that send men huddling into ever larger aggregates, in order to resist the accelerated activities of other communities. The villages are swept up into the city-state by way of resistance and for the purpose of security and protection.

The village had institutionalized all human functions in forms of low intensity. In this mild form everyone could play many roles. Participation was high, and organization was low. This is the formula for stability in any type of organization. Nevertheless, the enlargement of village forms in the city-state called for greater intensity and the inevitable separation of functions to cope with this intensity and competition. The villagers had all participated in the seasonal rituals that in the city became the specialized Greek drama. Mumford feels that "The village measure prevailed in the development of the Greek cities, down to the fourth century . . ." (*The City in History*). It is this extension and translation of the human organs into the village model without loss of corporal unity that Mumford uses as a criterion of excellence for city forms in any time or locale. This biological approach to the man-made environment is sought today once more in the electric age. How strange that the idea of the "human scale" should have seemed quite without appeal during the mechanical centuries.

The natural tendency of the enlarged community of the city is to increase the intensity and accelerate functions of every sort, whether of speech, or crafts, or currency and exchange. This, in turn, implies an inevitable extension of these actions by subdivision or, what is the same thing, new invention. So that even though the city was formed as a kind of protective hide or shield for man, this protective layer was purchased at the cost of maximized struggle within the walls. War games such as those described by Herodotus began as ritual blood baths between the citizenry. Rostrum, law courts, and marketplace all acquired the intense image of devisive competition that is nowadays called "the rat race." Nevertheless, it was amidst such irritations that man produced his greatest inventions as counter-irritants. These inventions were extensions of himself by means of concentrated toil, by which he hoped to neutralize distress. The Greek word *ponos,* or "toil," was a term used by Hippocrates, the father of medicine, to describe the fight of the body in disease. Today this idea is called *homeostasis,* or equilibrium as a strategy of the staying power of any body. All organizations, but especially biological ones, struggle to remain constant in their inner condition amidst the variations of outer shock and change. The man-made social environment as an extension of man's physical body is no exception. The city, as a form of the body politic, responds to new pressures and irritations by resourceful new extensions—always in the effort to exert staying power, constancy, equilibrium, and *homeostasis.*

The city, having been formed for protection, unexpectedly generated fierce intensities and new hybrid energies from accelerated interplay of functions and knowledge. It burst forth into aggression. The alarm of the village, followed by the resistance of the city, expanded into the exhaustion and inertia of empire. These three stages of the disease and irritation syndrome were felt, by those living through them, as normal physical expressions of counter-irritant recovery from disease.

The third stage of struggle for equilibrium among the forces within the city took the form of empire, or a universal state, that generated the extension of human senses in wheel, road, and alphabet. We can sympathize with those who first saw in these tools a providential means of bringing order to distant areas of turbulence and anarchy. These tools would have seemed a glorious form of "foreign aid," extending the blessings of the center to the barbarian margins. At this moment, for example, we are quite in the dark about the political implications of Telstar. By outering these satellites as extensions of our nervous system, there is an automatic response in all the organs of the body politic of mankind. Such new intensity of proximity imposed by Telstar calls for radical rearrangement of all organs in order to maintain staying power and equilibrium. The teaching and learning process for every child will be affected sooner rather than later. The time factor in every decision of business and finance will acquire new patterns. Among the peoples of the world strange new vortices of power will appear unexpectedly.

The full-blown city coincides with the development of writing— especially of phonetic writing, the specialist form of writing that makes a division between sight and sound. It was with this instrument that Rome was able to reduce the tribal areas to some visual order. The effects of phonetic literacy do not depend upon persuasion or cajolery for their acceptance. This technology for translating the resonating tribal world into Euclidean lineality and visuality is automatic. Roman roads and Roman streets were uniform and repeatable wherever they occurred. There was no adaptation to the contours of local hill or custom. With the decline of papyrus supplies, the wheeled traffic stopped on these roads, too. Deprivation of papyrus, resulting from the Roman loss of Egypt, meant the decline of bureaucracy, and of army organization as well. Thus the medieval world grew up without uniform roads or cities or bureaucracies, and it fought the wheel, as later city forms fought the railways; and as we, today, fight the automobile. For new speed and power are never compatible with existing spatial and social arrangements.

Writing about the new straight avenues of the seventeenth-century cities, Mumford points to a factor that was also present in the Roman city with its wheeled traffic; namely, the need for broad straight avenues to speed military movements, and to express the pomp and circumstance of power. In the Roman world the army was the work force of a mechanized wealth-creating process. By means of soldiers as uniform and replaceable parts, the Roman military machine made and delivered the goods, very much in the manner of industry during the early phases of the industrial revolution. Trade followed the legions. More than that, the legions were the industrial machine, itself; and numerous new cities were like new factories manned by uniformly trained army personnel. With the spread of literacy after printing, the bond between the uniformed soldier and the wealth-making factory hand became less visible. It was obvious enough in Napoleon's armies. Napoleon, with his citizen-armies, was the industrial revolution itself, as it reached areas long protected from it.

The Roman army as a mobile, industrial wealth-making force created in addition a vast consumer public in the Roman towns. Division of labor always creates a separation between producer and consumer, even as it tends to separate the place of work and the living space. Before Roman literate bureaucracy, nothing comparable to the Roman consumer specialists had been seen in the world. This fact was institutionalized in the individual known as "parasite," and in the social institution of the gladiatorial games. (*Panem et circenses*.) The private sponge and the collective sponge, both reaching out for their rations of sensation, achieved a horrible distinctness and clarity that matched the raw power of the predatory army machine.

With the cutting-off of the supplies of papyrus by the Mohammedans, the Mediterranean, long a Roman lake, became a Muslim lake, and the Roman center collapsed. What had been the margins of this center-margin structure became independent centers on a new feudal, structural base. The Roman center collapsed by the fifth century A.D. as wheel, road, and paper dwindled into a ghostly paradigm of former power.

Papyrus never returned. Byzantium, like the medieval centers, relied heavily on parchment, but this was too expensive and scarce a material to speed commerce or even education. It was paper from China, gradually making its way through the Near East to Europe, that accelerated education and commerce steadily from the eleventh century, and provided the basis for "the Renaissance of the twelfth century," popularizing prints and, finally, making printing possible by the fifteenth century.

With the moving of information in printed form, the wheel and the road came into play again after having been in abeyance for a thousand years. In England, pressure from the press brought about hard-surface roads in the eighteenth century, with all the population and industrial rearrangement that entailed. Print, or mechanized writing, introduced a separation and extension of human functions unimaginable even in Roman times. It was only natural, therefore, that greatly increased wheel speeds, both on road and in factory, should be related to the alphabet that had once done a similar job of speed-up and specialization in the ancient world. Speed, at least in its lower reaches of the mechanical order, always operates to separate, to extend, and to amplify functions of the body. Even specialist learning in higher education proceeds by ignoring interrelationships; for such complex awareness slows down the achieving of expertness.

The post roads of England were, for the most part, paid for by the newspapers. The rapid increase of traffic brought in the railway, that accommodated a more specialized form of wheel than the road. The story of modern America that began with the discovery of the white man by the Indians, as a wag has truly said, quickly passed from exploration by canoe to development by railway. For three centuries Europe invested in America for its fish and its furs. The fishing schooner and the canoe preceded the road and the postal route as marks of our North American spatial organization. The European investors in the fur trade naturally did not want the trapping lines overrun by Tom Sawyers and Huck Finns. They fought land surveyors and settlers, like Washington and Jefferson, who simply would not think in terms of mink. Thus the War of Independence was deeply involved in media and staple rivalries. Any new medium, by its acceleration, disrupts the lives and investments of whole communities. It was the railway that raised the art of war to unheard-of intensity, making the American Civil War the first major conflict fought by rail, and causing it to be studied and admired by all European general staffs, who had not yet had an opportunity to use railways for a general blood-letting.

War is never anything less than accelerated technological change. It begins when some notable disequilibrium among existing structures has been brought about by inequality of rates of growth. The very late industrialization and unification of Germany had left her out of the race for staples and colonies for many years. As the Napoleonic wars were technologically a sort of catching-up of France with England, the First World War was itself a major phase of the final industrialization of Germany and

America. As Rome had not shown before, and Russia has shown today, militarism is itself the main route of technological education and acceleration for lagging areas.

Almost unanimous enthusiasm for improved routes of land transportation followed the War of 1812. Furthermore, the British blockade of the Atlantic coast had compelled an unprecedented amount of land carriage, thus emphasizing the unsatisfactory character of the highways. War is certainly a form of emphasis that delivers many a telling touch to lagging social attention. However, in the very Hot Peace since the Second War, it is the highways of the mind that have been found inadequate. Many have felt dissatisfaction with our educational methods since Sputnik, in exactly the same spirit that many complained about the highways during the War of 1812.

Now that man has extended his central nervous system by electric technology, the field of battle has shifted to mental image-making-and-breaking, both in war and in business. Until the electric age, higher education had been a privilege and a luxury for the leisured classes; today it has become a necessity for production and survival. Now, when information itself is the main traffic, the need for advanced knowledge presses on the spirits of the most routine-ridden minds. So sudden an upsurge of academic training into the marketplace has in it the quality of classical peripety or reversal, and the result has been a wild guffaw from the gallery and the campus. The hilarity, however, will die down as the Executive Suites are taken over by the Ph.D.s.

For an insight into the ways in which the acceleration of wheel and road and paper rescramble population and settlement patterns, let us glance at some instances provided by Oscar Handlin in his study *Boston's Immigrants.* In 1790, he tells us, Boston was a compact unit with all workers and traders living in sight of each other, so that there was no tendency to section residential areas on a class basis: "But as the town grew, as the outlying districts became more accessible, the people spread out and at the same time were localized in distinctive areas." That one sentence capsulates the theme of this chapter. The sentence can be generalized to include the art of writing: "As knowledge was spread out visually and as it became more accessible in alphabetic form, it was localized and divided into specialties." Up to the point just short of electrification, increase of speed produces division of function, and of social classes, and of knowledge.

At electric speed, however, all that is reversed. Implosion and contraction then replace mechanical explosion and expansion. If the Handlin formula is extended to power, it becomes: "As power grew, and as outlying areas became accessible to power, it was localized in distinctive delegated jobs and functions." This formula is a principle of acceleration at all levels of human organization. It concerns especially those extensions of our physical bodies that appear in wheel and road and paper messages. Now that we have extended not just our physical organs but the nervous system, itself, in electric technology, the principle of specialism and division as a factor of speed no longer applies. When information moves at the speed of signals in the central nervous system, man is confronted with the obsolescence of all earlier forms of acceleration, such as road and rail. What emerges is a total field of inclusive awareness. The old patterns of psychic and social adjustment become irrelevant.

Until the 1820s, Handlin tells us, Bostonians walked to and fro, or used private conveyances. Horse-drawn buses were introduced in 1826, and these speeded up and extended business a great deal. Meantime the speed-up of industry in England had extended business into the rural areas, dislodging many from the land and increasing the rate of immigration. Sea transport of immigrants became lucrative and encouraged a great speed-up of ocean transport. Then the Cunard Line was subsidized by the British government in order to ensure swift contact with the colonies. The railways soon linked into this Cunard service, to convey mail and immigrants inland.

Although America developed a massive service of inland canals and river steamboats, they were not geared to the speeding wheels of the new industrial production. The railroad was needed to cope with mechanized production, as much as to span the great distances of the continent. The steam railroad as an accelerator proved to be one of the most revolutionary of all extensions of our physical bodies, creating a new political centralism and a new kind of urban shape and size. It is to the railroad that the American city owes its abstract grid layout, and the nonorganic separation of production, consumption, and residence. It is the motorcar that scrambled the abstract shape of the industrial town, mixing up its separated functions to a degree that has frustrated and baffled both planner and citizen. It remained for the airplane to complete the confusion by amplifying the mobility of the citizen to the point where urban space as such was irrelevant. Metropolitan space is equally irrelevant for the telephone, the telegraph, the radio, and television. What the town planners call "the human scale" in discussing ideal urban spaces is equally unrelated to these electric forms. Our electric extensions of ourselves simply by-pass space and time, and create problems of human involvement and organization for which there is no precedent. We may yet yearn for the simple days of the automobile and the superhighway.

WILLIAM S. BURROUGHS
Crab Nebula

They do not have what they call "emotion's oxygen" in the atmosphere. The medium in which animal life breathes is not in that soulless place— Yellow plains under white hot blue sky—Metal cities controlled by The Elders who are heads in bottles—Fastest brains preserved forever—Only form of immortality open to The Insect People of Minraud—An intricate bureaucracy wired to the control brains directs all movement—Even so there is a devious underground operating through telepathic misdirection and camouflage—The partisans make recordings ahead in time and leave the recordings to be picked up by control stations while they are free for a few seconds to organize underground activities—Largely the underground is made up of adventurers who intend to outthink and displace the present heads—There has been one revolution in the history of Minraud—Purges are constant—Fallen heads destroyed in The Ovens and replaced with others faster and sharper to evolve more total weapons—The principal weapon of Minraud is of course heat—In the center of all their cities stand The Ovens where those who disobey the control brains are brought for total disposal—A conical structure of iridescent metal shimmering heat from the molten core of a planet where lead melts at noon—The Brass And Copper Streets surround The Oven —Here the tinkers and smiths work pounding out metal rhythms as prisoners and criminals are led to Disposal—The Oven Guards are red crustacean men with eyes like the white hot sky—Through contact with oven pain and captured enemies they sometimes mutate to breathe in emotions—They often help prisoners to escape and a few have escaped with the prisoners—

(When K9 entered the apartment he felt the suffocation of Minraud crushing his chest stopping his thoughts—He turned on reserve ate dinner and carried conversation—When he left the host walked out with him down the streets of Minraud past the ovens empty and cold now—calm dry mind of the guide beside him came to the corner of 14th and Third—

"I must go back now," said the guide—"Otherwise it will be too far to go alone."

He smiled and held out his hand fading in the alien air—)

K9 was brought to the ovens by red guards in white and gold robe of office through the Brass and Copper Sreet under pounding metal hammers—The oven heat drying up life source as white hot metal lattice closed around him—

"Second exposure—Time three point five," said the guard—

K9 walked out into The Brass And Copper Streets—A slum area of vending booths and smouldering slag heaps crossed by paths worn deep in phosphorescent metal—In a square littered with black bones he encountered a group of five scorpion men—Faces of transparent pink cartilage burning inside—stinger dripping the oven poison—Their eyes flared with electric hate and they slithered forward to surround him but drew back at sight of the guard—

They walked on into an area of tattoo booths and sex parlors—A music like wind through fine metal wires bringing a measure of relief from the terrible dry heat—Black beetle musicians saw this music out of the air swept by continual hot winds from plains that surround the city—The plains are dotted with villages of conical paper-thin metal houses where a patient gentle crab people live unmolested in the hottest regions of the planet—

Controller of the Crab Nebula on a slag heap of smouldering metal under the white hot sky channels all his pain into control thinking—He is protected by heat and crab guards and the brains armed now with The Blazing Photo from Hiroshima and Nagasaki—The brains under his control are encased in a vast structure of steel and crystal spinning thought patterns that control whole galaxies thousand years ahead on the chessboard of virus screens and juxtaposition formulae—

So The Insect People Of Minraud formed an alliance with the Virus Power Of The Vegetable People to occupy planet earth—The gimmick is reverse photosynthesis—The Vegetable People suck up oxygen and all equivalent sustenance of animal life—Always the colorless sheets between you and what you see taste touch smell eat—And these green vegetable junkies slowly using up your oxygen to stay on the nod in carbon dioxide—

When K9 entered the café he felt the colorless smell of the vegetable people closing round him taste and sharpness gone from the food people blurring in slow motion fade out—And there was a whole tank full of vegetable junkies breathing it all in—He clicked some reverse combos through the pinball machine and left the café—In the street citizens were yacking like supersonic dummies—The SOS addicts had sucked up all the silence in the area were now sitting around in blue blocks of heavy metal the earth's crust buckling ominously under their weight—He shrugged: "Who am I to be critical?"

He knew what it meant to kick an SOS habit: White hot agony of thawing metal—And the suffocating panic of carbon dioxide withdrawal—

Virus defined as the three-dimensional coordinate point of a controller —Transparent sheets with virus perforations like punch cards passed through the host on the soft machine feeling for a point of intersection— The virus attack is primarily directed against affective animal life—Virus of rage hate fear ugliness swirling round you waiting for a point of intersection and once in immediately perpetrates in your name some ugly noxious or disgusting act sharply photographed and recorded becomes now part of the virus sheets constantly presented and represented before your mind screen to produce more virus word and image around and around it's all around you the invisible hail of bring down word and image—

What does virus do wherever it can dissolve a hole and find traction? —It starts eating—And what does it do with what it eats?—It makes exact copies of itself that start eating to make more copies that start eating to make more copies that start eating and so forth to the virus power the fear hate virus slowly replaces the host with virus copies—Program empty body—A vast tapeworm of bring down word and image moving through your mind screen always at the same speed on a slow hydraulic-spine axis like the cylinder gimmick in the adding machine—How do you make someone feel stupid?—You present to him all the times he talked and acted and felt stupid again and again any number of times fed into the combo of the soft calculating machine geared to find more and more punch cards and feed in more and more images of stupidity disgust propitiation grief apathy death—The recordings leave electromagnetic patterns—That is any situation that causes rage will magnetize rage patterns and draw around the rage word and image recordings—Or some disgusting sex practice once the connection is made in childhood whenever the patterns are magnetized by sex desire the same word and image will be presented—And so forth—The counter move is very simple—This is machine strategy and the machine can be redirected—Record for ten minutes on a tape recorder—Now run the tape back without playing and cut in other words at random—Where you have cut in and re-recorded words are wiped off the tape and new words in their place—You have turned time back ten minutes and wiped electromagnetic word patterns off the tape and substituted other patterns—You can do the same with mind tape after working with the tape recorder—(This takes some experimentation)—The old mind tapes can be wiped clean—Magnetic word dust falling from old patterns—Word falling—Photo falling—"Last week Robert Kraft of the Mount Wilson and Palomar Observatories reported some answers to the riddle of exploding stars—Invariably he found the exploding star was locked by gravity to a nearby star—The two stars are in a strange symbiotic relationship—One is a small hot blue star—(Mr. Bradly) Its companion is a larger red star—(Mr. Martin)—

Because the stellar twins are so close together the blue star continually pulls fuel in the form of hydrogen gas from the red star—The motion of the system spins the hydrogen into an incandescent figure eight—One circle of the eight encloses one star—The other circle encloses the other—supplied with new fuel the blue star ignites."—Quote, *Newsweek*, Feb. 12, 1962—

The Crab Nebula observed by the Chinese in 1054 A.D. is the result of a supernova or exploding star—Situated approximately three thousand light years from the earth—(Like three thousand years in hot claws at the window—You got it?—)—Before they blow up a star they have a spot picked out as many light years away as possible—Then they start draining all the fuel and charge to the new pitch and siphon themselves there right after and on their way rejoicing—You notice we don't have as much time as people had say a hundred years ago?—Take your clothes to the laundry write a letter pick up your mail at American Express and the day is gone—They are short-timing us as many light years as they can take for the getaway—It seems that there were survivors on The Crab Pitch who are not in all respects reasonable men—And The Nova Law moving in fast—So they start the same old lark sucking all the charge and air and color to a new location and then?—*Sput*—You notice something is sucking all the flavor out of food the pleasure out of sex the color out of everything in sight?—Precisely creating the low pressure area that leads to nova—So they move cross the wounded galaxies always a few light years ahead of the Nova Heat—That is they did—The earth was our set —And they walked right into the antibiotic handcuffs—It will readily be seen that having created one nova they must make other or answer for the first—I mean three thousand years in hot claws at the window like a giant crab in slag heaps of smouldering metal—Also the more novas the less time between they are running out of pitches—So they bribe the natives with a promise of transportation and immortality—

"Yeah, man, flesh and junk and charge stacked up bank vaults full of it —Three thousand years of flesh—So we leave the bloody apes behind and on our way rejoicing right?—It's the only way to live—"

And the smart operators fall for it every fucking time—Talk about marks—One of our best undercover operators is known as The Rube— He perfected The Reverse Con—Comes on honest and straight and the smart operators all think they are conning him—How could they think otherwise until he slips on the antibiotic handcuffs—

"There's a wise guy born every minute," he says.

"Closing time gentlemen—The stenographer will take your depositions—"

"So why did I try to blow up the planet?—Pea under the shell—Now you see it now you don't—Sky shift to cover the last pitch—Take it all out with us and hit the road—I am made of metal and that metal is radioactive—Radioactivity can be absorbed up to a point but radium clock hands tick away—Time to move on—Only one turnstile—Heavy planet—Travel with Minraud technicians to handle the switchboard and Venusians to make flesh and keep the show on the road—Then The Blazing Photo and we travel on—Word *is* flesh and word *is* two that is the human body is compacted of two organisms and where you have two you have word and word is flesh and when they started tampering with the word that was it and the blockade was broken and The Nova Heat moved in—The Venusians sang first naturally they were in the most immediate danger—They live underwater in the body with an air line—And that air line is the word—Then the technicians spilled and who can blame them after the conditions I assigned to keep them technicians—Like three thousand years in hot claws—So I am alone as always—You understand nova is where I am born in such pain no one else survives in one piece —Born again and again cross the wounded galaxies—I am alone but not what you call 'lonely'—Loneliness is a product of dual mammalian structure—'Loneliness,' 'love,' 'friendship,' all the rest of it—I am not two—I am *one*—But to maintain my state of oneness I need twoness in other life forms—Other must talk so that I can remain silent—If another becomes one then I am two—That makes two ones makes two and I am no longer one—Plenty of room in space you say?—But I am not one in space I am one in time—Metal time—Radioactive time—So of course I tried to keep you all out of space—That is the end of time—And those who were allowed out sometimes for special services like creating a useful religious concept went always with a Venusian guard—All the 'mystics' and 'saints'—All except my old enemy Hassan i Sabbah who wised up the marks to space and said they could be one and need no guard no other half no word—

"And now I have something to say to all you angle boys of the cosmos who thought you had an in with The Big Operator—*'Suckers! Cunts! Marks!—I hate you all—And I never intended to cut you in or pay you off with anything but horse shit—And you can thank The Rube if you don't go up with the apes—Is that clear enough or shall I make it even clearer? You are the suckers cunts marks I invented to explode this dead whistle stop and go up with it—'*"

ROBERT DUNCAN
This Place Rumord To
Have Been Sodom

                                        might have been.
Certainly these ashes might have been pleasures.
Pilgrims on their way toward the Holy Places remark
this place. Isn't it plain to all
that these mounds were palaces? This was once
a city among men, a gathering together of spirit?
It was measured by the Lord and found wanting.

It was measured by the Lord and found wanting,
destroyd by the angels that inhabit longing.
Surely this is Great Sodom where such cries
as if men were birds flying up from the swamp
ring in our ears, where such fears that were once
desires walk, almost spectacular,
stalking the desolate circles, red-eyed.

This place rumord to have been a City surely was,
separated from us by the hand of the Lord.
The devout have laid out gardens in the desert,
drawn water from springs where the light was blighted.
How tenderly they must attend these friendships
or all is lost. All *is* lost.
Only the faithful hold this place green.

Only the faithful hold this place green
where the crown of fiery thorns descends.
Men that once lusted grow listless. A spirit
wrappd in a cloud, ashes more than ashes,
fire more than fire, ascends.

Only those new friends gather joyous here,
where the world like Great Sodom lies under fear.

The world like Great Sodom lies under love
and knows not the hand of the Lord that moves.
This the friends teach where such cries
as if men were birds fly up from the crowds
gatherd and howling in the heat of the sun.
In the Lord Whom the friends have named at last Love
the Images and Love of the friends never die.

This place rumord to have been Sodom is blessd
in the Lord's eyes.

PAUL AND PERCIVAL GOODMAN
A New Community:
The Elimination
of the Difference
Between Production and Consumption

**Quarantining the work,
quarantining the homes**

Men like to make things, to handle the materials and see them take shape and come out as desired, and they are proud of the products. And men like to work and be useful, for work has a rhythm and springs from spontaneous feelings just like play, and to be useful makes people feel right. Productive work is a kind of creation, it is an extension of human personality into nature. But it is also true that the private or state capitalist relations of production, and machine industry as it now exists under whatever system, have so far destroyed the instinctive pleasures of work that economic work is what all ordinary men dislike. (Yet unemployment is dreaded, and people who don't like their work don't know what to do with their leisure.) In capitalist or state-socialist economies, efficiency is measured by profits and expansion rather than by handling the means. Mass production, analyzing the acts of labor into small steps and distributing the products far from home, destroys the sense of creating anything. Rhythm, neatness, style belong to the machine rather than to the man.

The division of economy into production and consumption as two opposite poles means that we are far from the conditions in which work could be a way of life. A way of life requires merging the means in the end, and work would have to be thought of as a continuous process of satisfying activity, satisfying in itself and satisfying in its useful end. Such considerations have led many moralist-economists to want to turn back the clock to conditions of handicraft in a limited society, where the relations of guilds and small markets allow the master craftsmen a say and a hand in every phase of production, distribution, and consumption. Can we achieve the same values with modern technology, a national economy, and a democratic society? With this aim, let us reanalyze efficiency and machine production.

Characteristic of American offices and factories is the severe discipline with regard to punctuality. (In some states the law requires time clocks, to protect labor and calculate the insurance.) Now no doubt in many cases where workers cooperate in teams, where business is timed by the mails, where machines use a temporary source of power, being on time and on the same time as everybody else is essential to efficiency. But by and large it would make little difference at what hour each man's work began and ended, so long as the job itself was done. Often the work could be done at home or on the premises indifferently, or part here part there. Yet this laxity is never allowed, except in the typical instances of hack-writing or commercial art—typical because these workers have an uneasy relation to the economy in any case. (There is a lovely story of how William Faulkner asked M-G-M if he could work at home, and when they said, "Of course," he went back to Oxford, Mississippi.)

Punctuality is demanded not primarily for efficiency but for the discipline itself. Discipline is necessary because the work is onerous; perhaps it makes the idea of working even more onerous, but it makes the work itself much more tolerable, for it is a structure, a decision. Discipline establishes the work in an impersonal secondary environment where, once one has gotten out of bed early in the morning, the rest easily follows. Regulation of time, separation from the personal environment: These are signs that work is not a way of life; they are the methods by which, for better or worse, work that cannot be energized directly by personal concern can get done, unconfused by personal concern.

In the Garden City plans, they "quarantined the technology" from the homes; more generally, we quarantine the work from the homes. But it is even truer to say that we quarantine the homes from the work. For instance, it is calamitous for a man's wife or children to visit him at work; this privilege is reserved for the highest bosses.

Reanalyzing production

In planning a region of satisfying industrial work, we therefore take account of four main principles:

1. A closer relation of the personal and productive environments, making punctuality reasonable instead of disciplinary, and introducing phases of home and small-shop production; and vice versa, finding appropriate technical uses for personal relations that have come to be considered unproductive.

2. A role for all workers in all stages of the production of the product; for experienced workers a voice and hand in the design of the product

and the design and operation of the machines; and for all a political voice on the basis of what they know best, their specific industry, in the national economy.

3. A schedule of work designed on psychological and moral as well as technical grounds, to give the most well-rounded employment to each person, in a diversified environment. Even in technology and economics, the men are ends as well as means.

4. Relatively small units with relative self-sufficiency, so that each community can enter into a larger whole with solidarity and independence of viewpoint.

These principles are mutually interdependent.

1. To undo the present separation of work and home environments, we can proceed both ways: (a) Return certain parts of production to home-shops or near home; and (b) Introduce domestic work and certain productive family-relations, which are now not considered part of the economy at all, into the style and relations of the larger economy.

(a) Think of the present proliferation of machine-tools. It could once be said that the sewing machine was the only widely distributed productive machine; but now, especially because of the last war, the idea of thousands of small machine shops, powered by electricity, has became familiar; and small power-tools are a best-selling commodity. In general, the change from coal and steam to electricity and oil has relaxed one of the greatest causes for concentration of machinery around a single driving-shaft.

(b) Borsodi, going back to the economics of Aristotle, has proved, often with hilarious realism, that home production, such as cooking, cleaning, mending, and entertaining has a formidable economic, though not cash, value. The problem is to lighten and enrich home production by the technical means and some of the expert attitudes of public production, but without destroying its individuality.

But the chief part of finding a satisfactory productive life in homes and families consists in the analysis of personal relations and conditions: e.g., the productive cooperation of man and wife as it exists on farms, or the productive capabilities of children and old folk, now economically excluded. This involves sentimental and moral problems of extreme depth and delicacy that could only be solved by the experiments of integrated communities.

2. A chief cause of the absurdity of industrial work is that each machine worker is acquainted with only a few processes, not the whole order of production. And the thousands of products are distributed he knows not how or where. Efficiency is organized from above by expert managers who first analyze production into its simple processes, then synthesize these into combinations built into the machines, then arrange the logistics of supplies, etc., and then assign the jobs.

As against this efficiency organized from above, we must try to give this function to the workers. This is feasible only if the workers have a total grasp of all the operations. There must be a school of industry, academic and not immediately productive, connected with the factory. Now let us distinguish apprentices and graduates. To the apprentices, along with their schooling, is assigned the more monotonous work; to the graduates, the executive and coordinating work, the fine work, the finishing touches. The masterpiece that graduates an apprentice is a new invention, method, or other practical contribution advancing the industry. The masters are teachers, and as part of their job hold free discussions looking to basic changes.

Such a setup detracts greatly from the schedule of continuous production; but it is a question whether it would not prove more efficient in the long run to have the men working for themselves and having a say in the distribution. By this we do not mean merely economic democracy or socialist ownership. These are necessary checks but are not the political meaning of industrialism as such. What is needed is the organization of economic democracy on the basis of the productive units, where each unit, relying on its own expertness and the bargaining power of what it has to offer, cooperates with the whole of society. This is syndicalism, simply an industrial town meeting. To guarantee the independent power of each productive unit, it must have a relative regional self-sufficiency; this is the union of farm and factory.

3. Machine work in its present form is often stultifying, not a "way of life." The remedy is to assign work on psychological and moral as well as technical and economic grounds. The object is to provide a well-rounded employment. Work can be divided as team work and individual work, or physical work and intellectual work. And industries can be combined in a neighborhood to give the right variety. For instance, cast glass, blown glass, and optical instruments; or more generally, industry and agriculture, and factory and domestic work. Probably most important, but difficult to conjure with, is the division in terms of faculties and powers, routine and initiation, obeying and commanding.

The problem is to envisage a well-rounded schedule of jobs for each man, and to arrange the buildings and the farms so that the schedule is feasible.

4. The integration of factory and farm brings us to the idea of regionalism and regional relative autonomy. These are the following main parts:

(a) Diversified farming as the basis of self-subsistence and, therefore, small urban centers (200,000).

(b) A number of mutually dependent industrial centers, so that an important part of the national economy is firmly controlled. (The thought is always to have freedom secured by real power.)

(c) These industries developed around regional resources of field, mine, and power.

Diversified farmers can be independent, and small farms have therefore always been a basis of social stability, though not necessarily of peasant conservatism. On the other hand, for the machines now desirable, the farmer needs cash and links himself with the larger economy of the town.

The political problem of the industrial worker is the reverse, since every industry is completely dependent on the national economy, for both materials and distribution. But by regional interdependence of industries and the close integration of factory and farm work—factory workers taking over in the fields at peak seasons, farmers doing factory work in the winter; town people, especially children, living in the country; farmers domestically making small parts for the factories—the industrial region as a whole can secure for itself independent bargaining power in the national whole.

The general sign of this federal system is the distinction of the local regional market from the national market. In transport, the local market is served by foot, bicycle, cart, and car; the national market by plane and trailer-truck.

(Now all of this—decentralized units, double markets, the selection of industries on political and psychological as well as economic and technical grounds—all this seems a strange and roundabout way of achieving an integrated national economy, when at present this unity already exists with a tightness that leaves nothing to be desired, and an efficiency that is even excessive. But we are aiming at a different standard of efficiency, one in which invention will flourish and the job will be its own incentive; and most important, at the highest and nearest ideals of external life: liberty, responsibility, self-esteem as a workman, and initiative. Compared with these aims the present system has nothing to offer us.)

A piazza in the town

With us at present in America, a man who is fortunate enough to have useful and important work to do that is called for and socially accepted, work that has initiative and exercises his best energies—such a man (he is one in a thousand among us) is likely to work not only very hard but too hard; he finds himself, as if compulsively, always going back to his meaningful job, as if the leisurely pursuits of society were not attractive. But we would hope that where every man has such work, where society is organized only to guarantee that he has, that people will have a more good-humored and easygoing attitude. Not desiring to get away from their work to a leisure that amounts to very little (for where there is no

A Schedule and Its Model

Typical Schedule of Activities for Members of a Commune (*numerals equal months*)

Basic Work	Master Workman	Apprentice Workman	Farmer	Farm Family	Ages 6 to 14	Ages 15 to 18
Factory	8(a)	6				1
Industrial Agriculture		3(d)	2(d)	X		1
Diversified Agriculture			{8	X	X	
Domestic Industry			{8	X(e)		1
Formal and Technical Learning		2(b)				1(b)
Technical Teaching	1(b)		1(b)			
General Education					X	5
Study and Travel						2(f)
Individual Work (c)	2					
Unscheduled (g)	1	1	1	1	X	1

Notes on the Schedule
(a) The factory work of the master workman and workwoman includes executive and fine work.
(b) The time of technical education runs concurrently with the working period.
(c) Graduate work at one's own time and place could be in a traveling trailer or country cottage; could comprise designing, drafting, assemblage of hand-assembled wholes (e.g., radios or clocks), finishing operations (lens-grinding), etc.
(d) Master farmwork in industrial agriculture includes supervision and maintenance and is divided cooperatively to spread over the year. The more mechanical work at peak seasons is done by the factory apprentices.
(e) Farm-family industry includes the making of parts for the factories, cooperation with industrial agriculture (e.g., field kitchens), educational care of boarding city children.
(f) The spread of activity of the youth over many categories, including two months of travel, gives them an acquaintance with the different possibilities.
(g) Activity at one's own fancy or imagination—vocational, avocational, recreational, etc.
(X) Activities engaged in as occasion arises.

man's work there is no man's play), people will be leisurely about their work—it is all, one way or another, making use of the time.

Now, the new community has *closed squares* like those described by Camillo Sitte. Such squares are the *definition* of a city.

Squares are not avenues of motor or pedestrian traffic, but are places where people remain. Place of work and home are close at hand, but in the city square is what is still more interesting—the other people.

The easygoing leisure of piazzas is a long simple interim, just as easy going people nowadays are often happiest on train trips or driving to work, the time in-between. Conscience is clear because a useful task will begin at a set time (not soon). The workers of the new community give themselves long lunchtimes indeed. For, supposing ten men are needed on a machine or a line for four hours' work: they arrange to start sometime in midafternoon, and where should they find each other, to begin, but in the piazza.

On one side of the piazza opens the factory; another entrance is a small library, provided with ashtrays. As in all other squares, there is a clock with bells; it's a reminder, not a tyrant.

The leisure of piazzas is made of repetitive small pleasures like feeding pigeons and watching a fountain. These are ways of being with the other people and striking up conversations. It is essential to have outdoor and indoor tables with drinks and small food.

There is the noise of hammering, and the explosions of tuning a motor, from small shops a little way off. But if it's a quieter square, there may be musicians. Colored linen and silk are blowing on a line—not flags but washing! For everything is mixed up here. At the same time, there is something of the formality of a college campus.

Another face of the piazza is an apartment house, where an urban family is making a meal. They go about this as follows. The ground floor of the building is not only a restaurant but a foodstore; the farmers deliver their produce here. The family cooks upstairs, phones down for their uncooked meat, vegetables, salad, and fixings, and these are delivered by dumbwaiter, cleaned and peeled—the potatoes peeled and spinach washed by machine. They dress and season the roast to taste and send it back with the message: "Medium rare about 1845." The husband observes, unfortunately for the twentieth time, that when he was a student in Paris a baker on the corner used to roast their chickens in his oven. Simpler folk, who live in smaller row houses up the block, consider this procedure a lot of foolishness; they just shop for their food, prepare it themselves, cook it, and eat it. But they don't have factory jobs: they run a lathe in the basement.

The main exit from the square is almost cut off by a monument with an inscription. But we cannot decipher the future inscription. The square seems enclosed.

In the famous piazzas described and measured in all their asymmetry by Camillo Sitte, the principal building, the building that gives its name to the place, as the Piazza San Marco or the Piazza dei Signori, is a church, town hall or guild hall. What are such principal buildings in the squares we are here describing? We don't know.

The windmill and water tower here, that work the fountain and make the pool, were put up gratuitously simply because such an ingenious machine is beautiful.

A farm and its children

Let us rear all the children in the natural environment where they are many and furnish a society for one another. This has an immense pedagogic advantage, for the business of the country environment is plain to the eyes, it is not concealed in accounts and factories. The mechanism of urban production is clear to adult minds; the nature of farm production is not much clearer to the adults than to the children of ten or eleven.

Integrating town and country, we are able to remedy the present injustice whereby the country bears the burden of rearing and educating more than its share of the population, then loses 50% of the investment at maturity. (And then the cities complain that the youth have been educated on rural standards!) If the city children go to the country schools, the city bears its pro rata share of the cost and has the right to a say in the policy.

The parents who work in the city live in small houses on nearby farms: that is home for the children. But when they leave for work, the children are not alone but are still at home on the farm. Some such arrangement is necessary, for it is obvious that we cannot, as the urban home continues to break down, be satisfied with the pathos of crèches, nursery-schools, and kindergartens.

To the farmers, the city families are the most valuable source of money income.

The best society for growing children, past the age of total dependency, is other children, older and younger by easy grades. It is a rough society but characterized at worst by conflict rather than by loving, absolute authority. These children, then, no longer sleep with their parents, but in a dormitory.

From quite early, children are set to work feeding the animals and doing chores that are occasionally too hard for them. Perhaps urban sentiment can here alleviate the condition of farm and city children both.

Everybody praises diversified farming as a way of life. Yet the farm youth migrate to the city when they can. (Just as everybody praises lovely Ireland, but the young Irish leave in droves.) This is inevitable when all the advertised social values, broadcast by radio and cinema, are urban values. It is universally admitted that these values are claptrap; but they are more attractive than nothing. To counteract this propaganda, the farm-sociologists try to establish a social opinion specifically rural, they revive square dances and have 4-H clubs and contests, organized by the farmers' collectives and cooperatives.

But is it necessary for "farm" and "city" to compete? All values are human values.

Regional and national economy

The large number of diversified farms means, on the one hand, that the region is self-subsistent, but on the other that the farmers have little crop to export outside the region. Their cash comes, however, from the city market, from domestic industry, from some industrial agriculture, and from housing the city folk. If farmers have a specialized crop, such as grapes or cotton, it is processed in the town. All this guarantees a tight local economy.

Now, even apart from political freedom, such a tight local economy is essential if there is to be a close relation between production and consumption, for it means that prices and the value of labor will not be so subject to the fluctuations of the vast general market. A man's work, meaningful during production, will somewhat carry through the distribution and what he gets in return. That is, within limits, the nearer a system gets to simple household economy, the more it is an economy of specific things and services that are bartered, rather than an economy of generalized money.

"Economy of things rather than money"—this formula is the essence of regionalism. The persons of a region draw on their local resources and cooperate directly, without the intermediary of national bookkeeping with its millions of clashing motives never resoluble face-to-face. The regional development of the TVA, brought together power and fertilizer for farms, navigation and the prevention of erosion, the control of floods and the processing of foods, national recreation, and in this natural cooperation it produced a host of ingenious inventions. All of this (in its inception) was carried on in relative autonomy, under the loose heading of "general welfare."

The kind of life looked for in this new community depends on the awareness of local distinctness, and this is also the condition of political freedom as a group of industries and farm cooperatives, rather than as a multitude of abstract votes and consumers with cash.

Yet every machine economy *is* a national and international economy. The fraction of necessary goods that can be produced in a planned region is very substantial, but it is still a fraction. And this fact is the salvation of regionalism! For otherwise regionalism succumbs to provincialism —whether we consider art or literature, or the characters of the people, or the fashions in technology. The regional industrialists in their meeting find that, just because their region is strong and productive, they are subject to wide circles of influence, they have to keep up.

Refinement

Let us try to envisage the moral ideal of such a community as we are describing.

In the luxury city of consumers' goods, society was geared to an expanding economy—capital investment and consumption had to expand at all costs, or even especially at all costs. In the third community that we shall describe in this book, "maximum security, minimum regulation," we shall find that, in order to achieve the aim of social security and human liberty, a part of the economy must never be allowed to expand at all.

But in this present, middle-of-the-road, plan there is no reason why the economy either must expand or must not expand. Every issue is particular and comes down to the particular question: "Is it worthwhile to expand along this new line? Is it worth the trouble to continue along that old line!"

This attitude is a delicate one, hard for us Americans to grasp clearly: we always like to do it bigger and better, or we jump to something new, or we cling. But when people are accustomed to knowing what they are lending their hands to, when they know the operations and the returns, when they don't have to prove something competitively, then they are just in the business, so to speak, of judging the relation of means and ends. They are all efficiency experts. And then, curiously, they may soon hit on a new conception of efficiency itself, very unlike that of the engineers of Veblen. When they can say, "It would be more efficient to make it this way," they may go on to say, "And it would be even *more* efficient to forget it altogether."

Efficient for what? For the way of life as a whole. Now in all times honorable people have used this criterion as a negative check: *"We* don't do that kind of thing, even if it's convenient or profitable." But envisage doing it positively and inventively: "Let's do it, it becomes us. Or let's omit it and simplify, it's a lag and a drag."

Suppose that one of the masters, away on his two months of individual

---

Some Elementary Principles for the Moral Selection of Machines

1. Utility
   (Functionalist beauty)

2. Transparency of operation

   A. Repairability by the average well-educated person
      (Freedom)

B. Constructivist beauty

3. Relative independence of machine from non-ubiquitous power

4. Proportion between total effort and utility
   (Neo-Functionalist beauty)

---

work, drafting designs for furniture, should, having studied the furniture of the Japanese, decide to dispense with chairs. Such a problem might create a bitter struggle in the national economy, one thing leading to another.

The economy, like any machine economy, would expand, for it creates a surplus. It would expand into refinement. The Japanese way is a powerful example. They cover the floor with deep washable mats and dispense with chairs and dispense with the floor. It is too much trouble to clutter the room with furniture. It is not too much trouble to lavish many days' work on the minute carving on the inside of a finger pull of a shoji. They dispense with the upholstery but take pains in arranging the flowers. They do not build permanent partitions in a room because the activities of life are always varying.

When production becomes an integral part of life, the workman becomes an artist. It is the definition of an artist that he follows the medium, and finds new possibilities of expression in it. He is not bound by the fact that things have always been made in a certain way, nor even by the fact that it is these things that have been made. Our industrialists—even International Business Machines—are very much concerned these days to get "creative" people, and they make psychological studies on how to foster an "atmosphere of creativity"; but they don't sufficiently conjure with the awful possibility that truly creative people might tell them to shut up shop. They wish to use creativity in just the way that it cannot be used, for it is a process that also generates its own ends.

LE CORBUSIER
The Authorities Are Badly Informed

I had dinner and spent four hours talking to a government official at the home of a mutual friend who is one of the leading architects in America. We had agreed to discuss the problems of contemporary city planning.

I made my own position clear: thus far I have never had anything to do with politics; I am an artisan. I make plans. An inventor's attitude is different from that of a politician. The investigator is absorbed in the search for the reason for things and the search for the relations of men with their milieu. His destiny is to discover, to know and create. To seek and, consequently, to doubt. To make more perfect and, consequently, to change. On his side, the politician keeps himself informed, chooses and executes. He brings different virtues into play. He is part of an equation that is much shorter than that of a discoverer.

I have traveled through most of the world. I have seen the men of the USSR, of Germany, of Italy, of the USA, and of all the other more quiet countries.[1] I realize that the most gigantic enterprise in the world, the USA, has no sound technical plan and no ethical certitude. That verdict came to me through architecture and city planning. It is up to us to study the problem carefully, to arrive at conclusions and, after mature reflection, to suggest *plans* to responsible leaders.

For a long time I have had many opportunities to meet leaders. I am astonished to see—I always judge on the basis of things in my craft—the inconsistency of their information, the uncertainty of their convictions, the tragic deficiency of their decisions. *What is the crucial question for them?* Where is its sounding board? A question is scarcely broached before its various aspects become external facets which are like mirrors of opinion. Decisions are not made on the basis of the objective facts in themselves, in accordance with the line of their movement and development; decisions are made in order "to avoid unfavorable publicity," in order "to square accounts" with X in the opposition group, as a favor to

1. Written in 1935.

one's relatives or friends. But *appropriate measures?* That is, things hacked out of the reality of the materials and circumstances? They aren't taken! *You would lose your job!* Whether you are a mayor, a Representative, a cabinet officer, or an agent of the people, you are looking for an exit—an honorable one—but not an avenue, an artery to break up, to clear, to put in order—a road leading to the new times. The amount of courage is in proportion to the legitimate necessity of avoiding the loss of the job. The USSR created an admirable phrase: "The main line . . ." "It is in the main line of development. . . ." "It is not in the main line of development. . . ." The men were not up to the ideal; in some cases they fell very low. In architecture and city planning, for instance, they allowed themselves to sink and choke in the most treacherous and execrable quicksands. Disaster, treason, a slap in the face of the sympathetic élite of the world. To console ourselves we say: "A slight, youthful fever. It will pass!" Meanwhile, it is a raging fever!

The official eagerly asks me to explain. I talk about my "radiant city" ideas. I make them more graphic and clear with crayons. The basic thesis, studied for years, has a certain purity. My interlocutor is now delighted, now uneasy; he follows the firm line of the reasoning; with me he sees the fans that open out at the crossroads of the idea onto a stream of consequences. He is so sincere, so serious, so full of a sense of responsibility that he reacts in all his being. I am serenely at home in my pure and true system. But his head swarms with orders given, with orders to be issued tomorrow morning, with terrible decisions to be made in a month, in six months; every one of his actions upsets customary procedures, shifts enormous sums of money, enriching some, ruining others. A perilous and inescapable position! I know these leaders! They are all in inextricable positions! He stops me: "Excuse me, but if I did what you suggest, well, tomorrow . . ." etc. . . .

"But, my dear sir, admit that now you are talking politics. Your argument is political. I am talking about the *plan,* the central idea, the trajectory, the direction. You are the artilleryman who fires the gun at the proper moment, but the plan is the objective at which you are shooting. First you have to know what you are shooting at. Then fire."—"True. Our life is confused; we are gasping wildly."—"A page is turning; humanity is abandoning a civilization, is being caught up in machine civilization. It is a revolution and not an evolution; we are moving out immediately and moving in tomorrow. Living from day to day is no longer enough, its incoherence crushes our enterprises. Consider: your American cities are mortally ill. Your social tone is disturbed by the effects of the progressive and finally catastrophic denaturalization of the urban situation. During the euphoria of prosperity (artificial), your industries made all kinds of stupid things. There is a crushing waste in the USA: a mad, sterile tumult. There are tornadoes of dollars, but they no longer go into your pockets—that is,

into people's stomachs, spirits, or hearts. It was necessary to stop everything, that everything stop! With an admirable energy, the Government is
doing everything that it can to drive back the harbingers of death;
throughout the country it has initiated vast public works; to overcome the
slums, it is having new urban quarters built, with four-story units. The
United States needs five million dwelling units. Well, if the cities in the
United States carry out their reconstruction on a four-story basis, they
will be lost! It is a basic, fundamental error. I tell you that as an architect
and city planner. It is recognized that sprawling garden cities were a mistake; it was realized that the skyscrapers of New York and Chicago had
killed circulation. It was decided—rather hastily!—that four-story buildings would solve the problem. I say that with four-story constructions cars
will not be able to circulate and that the coming leisure of machine civilization will find nothing to work with, neither sites nor buildings. And that
building on a four-story scale is discouragingly retrogressive. And that
such a dogma, promulgated by important officials, is emphatically a mistake. At the very moment of modern society's great metamorphosis, badly
informed authorities make decisions which run counter to the very nature
of the circumstances. It is agonizing."

My slight experience with government officials is that they are not well
informed. They do not have the time to keep themselves informed and reflect.

If only one of them had an interest in this matter, a genius for it—if he
were, so to speak, the Colbert of today—that would be enough. A well-in-
formed man, strong in his convictions, passionate, breaks through obstacles. He would enlighten his colleagues, he would carry them along with
him. It is a question of love. That is all there is to it! Loving with all his
being a great constructive idea and having freedom of mind and being
above easy props, knowing how to create, to look ahead, to build the
scaffolding of tomorrow. And may those who look back be turned into
statues of salt, as happened once before at Sodom!

Another of our table conversations on board ship: we were completely
different beings and thoroughly good friends. A precise and daring surgeon (extraordinarily daring, apparently), imbued with a strong and im-
placable morality—a Canadian. Then an important industrialist, all of
whose reactions reveal that he is a bourgeois, but I notice that he is open
to rational and altruistic conceptions. He is French, and a practicing
Catholic. Finally, an architect and city planner who is now crushed, now
suddenly exalted by being called a poet!

We talk about the USSR. My companions have no leanings toward Soviet experiments. We admit that, everything considered, nothing can be
"new," in spite of the dazzling fruits of modern techniques. That there
are only ineluctable consequences. But—and this is where our reflection
makes sense: the first man is shocked by the USSR, the second is not at-

tracted to it in any way, the third, having been there several times, tells what he experienced. The only useful and true conclusion, which sums up the whole thing, and which developed spontaneously and unanimously is this: *Nothing can be new, except this fact (which is everything): a +* *sign controls society in the USSR and not a − sign.*

What our societies need, depressed and putrefied as they are by the effect of money, is the + sign inscribed in the bottom of every heart. That is enough, that is everything. It is hope. Hope is enough to make the days radiant. That is the conquest that remains to be made.

Lunch with the assistant police commissioner of New York, at Police Headquarters on Center Street:

"Well, sir, you carry on your shoulders the heaviest load in New York: policing the city, the insoluble problem of circulation, public health."

"The commissioner presides over receptions at City Hall, while in our offices there is an endless procession of messy jobs caused by the problems of the city."

"A million and a half cars every day in a city designed for horse and buggy traffic. Please pass me the menu." On the back I sketch the only possible solution of the modern city's traffic problem:

If we continue to build housing based on a central stairway serving two (or even four) apartments on each floor, the number of persons accommodated *is too small. There are too many house doors;* and since the purpose of a car is *to take you to the door,* the street will be carried along from door to door, *at the foot of the houses,* ad infinitum. The houses will be on a street flanked by two sidewalks. And the fate of the pedestrian will be bound up with that of the motorcar: cars and pedestrians will be in the same bed: *two miles an hour and sixty miles an hour mixed up together, helter-skelter.* The senseless folly of today.

The lot of the pedestrian must be separated from that of the car. That is the problem.

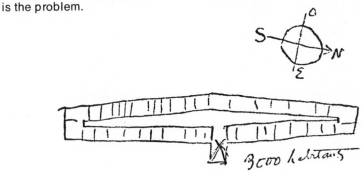

Let's build housing units large enough to accommodate from twenty-five hundred to three thousand people. Elevators and "interior streets." Such a construction represents a "housing unit." There it is possible to organize the "common services," *which are the key of the new domestic economy.*

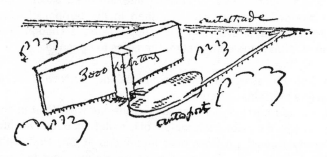

If three thousand persons enter through one door, the next door will be far away. And so on. That is the solution! The autoport, for the arrival, departure, and parking of cars spreads out in front of the door of the housing unit. A branch road connects the autoport with the nearest highway. Autoports and highways are twenty feet above the ground. The housing unit is also twenty feet above the ground, raised up on piles. Nothing encumbers the ground; all of the ground is for pedestrians: 100 per cent of the ground for pedestrians, cars up in the air, separation of pedestrians and cars. The pedestrian, moving two miles an hour, left in peace, cars free to travel at full speed, sixty miles an hour, ninety miles an hour. . . .

One principal remains to be emphasized: the necessity of having a sufficient density in urban agglomerations.

It is our particular folly to meet the problem of concentration which the city—by definition—implies, with village or small town densities: 20, 50 persons per acre. Construction takes up 12 per cent of the ground, 88 per cent is free for parks and fields for sport, one of the keys to the problem of leisure time in the future. . . .

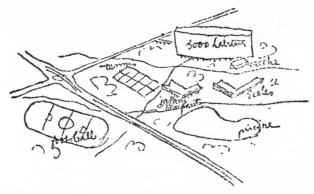

And here is the city reorganized in its normal and harmonious cellular state, *the city in the service of men.* The disappearance of the city of horror . . .

"Then the present cities must be demolished?"

"I'll draw the two transformations which New York has already accomplished and the third which remains to be accomplished for the salvation of the city."

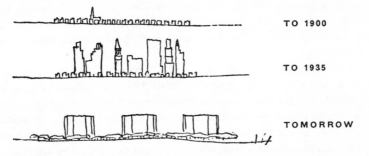

TO 1900

TO 1935

TOMORROW

Up to 1900, the standard city of everywhere and always, before the development of fast machines. Up to 1935, the springing up of modern technique: the conquest of height. The skyscrapers are too small and the tiny houses remain at the foot of the skyscrapers. A modern metabolic change imposed on a pre-machine age cardiac system. That is the agony of today.

The third transformation involves a wise and well-considered program of great public works, on the scale of modern times.

The amiable assistant commissioner of New York looked at me with admiring and slightly quizzical eyes. He is a frank man; we shook hands cordially. He returned to Headquarters to wrestle with the problems of gangsters, tuberculosis, accidents, traffic jams, and the ferocious horde of financial interests. The next day I embarked for the return trip to Paris, the city roofed over by the gay sky, where the malady is the same as it is in New York and where there is perhaps even blacker uncertainty, since most of our administrators are unaware of Manhattan, the fairy catastrophe which is the laboratory of the new times.

DONALD BARTHELME
The Balloon

The balloon, beginning at a point on Fourteenth Street, the exact location of which I cannot reveal, expanded northward all one night, while people were sleeping, until it reached the Park. There, I stopped it; at dawn the northernmost edges lay over the Plaza; the free-hanging motion was frivolous and gentle. But experiencing a faint irritation at stopping, even to protect the trees, and seeing no reason the balloon should not be allowed to expand upward, over the parts of the city it was already covering, into the "air space" to be found there, I asked the engineers to see to it. This expansion took place throughout the morning, soft imperceptible sighing of gas through the valves. The balloon then covered forty-five blocks north-south and an irregular area east-west, as many as six crosstown blocks on either side of the Avenue in some places. That was the situation, then.

But it is wrong to speak of "situations," implying sets of circumstances leading to some resolution, some escape of tension; there were no situations, simply the balloon hanging there—muted heavy grays and browns for the most part, contrasting with walnut and soft yellows. A deliberate lack of finish, enhanced by skillful installation, gave the surface a rough, forgotten quality; sliding weights on the inside, carefully adjusted, anchored the great, vari-shaped mass at a number of points. Now we have had a flood of original ideas in all media, works of singular beauty as well as significant milestones in the history of inflation, but at that moment there was only *this balloon,* concrete particular, hanging there.

There were reactions. Some people found the balloon "interesting." As a response this seemed inadequate to the immensity of the balloon, the suddenness of its appearance over the city; on the other hand, in the absence of hysteria or other societally-induced anxiety, it must be judged a calm, "mature" one. There was a certain amount of initial argumentation about the "meaning" of the balloon; this subsided, because we have learned not to insist on meanings, and they are rarely even looked for now, except in cases involving the simplest, safest phenomena. It was agreed that since the meaning of the balloon could never be known absolutely, extended discussion was pointless, or at least less purposeful than the activities of those who, for example, hung green and blue paper lanterns from the warm gray underside, in certain streets, or seized the oc-

584

casion to write messages on the surface, announcing their availability for the performance of unnatural acts, or the availability of acquaintances.

Daring children jumped, especially at those points where the balloon hovered close to a building, so that the gap between balloon and building was a matter of a few inches, or points where the balloon actually made contact, exerting an ever-so-slight pressure against the side of a building, so that balloon and building seemed a unity. The upper surface was so structured that a "landscape" was presented, small valleys as well as slight knolls, or mounds; once atop the balloon, a stroll was possible, or even a trip, from one place to another. There was pleasure in being able to run down an incline, then up the opposing slope, both gently graded, or in making a leap from one side to the other. Bouncing was possible, because of the pneumaticity of the surface, and even falling, if that was your wish. That all these varied motions, as well as others, were within one's possibilities, in experiencing the "up" side of the balloon, was extremely exciting for children, accustomed to the city's flat, hard skin. But the purpose of the balloon was not to amuse children.

Too, the number of people, children and adults, who took advantage of the opportunities described was not so large as it might have been: a certain timidity, lack of trust in the balloon, was seen. There was, furthermore, some hostility. Because we had hidden the pumps, which fed helium to the interior, and because the surface was so vast that the authorities could not determine the point of entry—that is, the point at which the gas was injected—a degree of frustration was evidenced by those city officers into whose province such manifestations normally fell. The apparent purposelessness of the balloon was vexing (as was the fact that it was "there" at all). Had we painted, in great letters, *"Laboratory Tests Prove"* or *"18% More Effective"* on the sides of the balloon, this difficulty would have been circumvented. But I could not bear to do so. On the whole, these officers were remarkably tolerant, considering the dimensions of the anomaly, this tolerance being the result of, first, secret tests conducted by night that convinced them that little or nothing could be done in the way of removing or destroying the balloon, and, secondly, a public warmth that arose (not uncolored by touches of the aforementioned hostility) toward the balloon, from ordinary citizens.

As a single balloon must stand for a lifetime of thinking about balloons, so each citizen expressed, in the attitude he chose, a complex of attitudes. One man might consider that the balloon had to do with the notion *sullied,* as in the sentence *The big balloon sullied the otherwise clear and radiant Manhattan sky.* That is, the balloon was, in this man's view, an imposture, something inferior to the sky that had formerly been there, something interposed between the people and their "sky." But in fact it was January, the sky was dark and ugly; it was not a sky you could look up into, lying on your back in the street, with pleasure, unless pleasure, for you, proceeded from having been threatened, from having been misused. And the underside of the balloon was a pleasure to look up into, we had seen to that, muted grays and browns for the most part, contrasted with walnut and soft, forgotten yellows. And so, while this man was thinking *sullied,* still there was an admixture of pleasurable cognition in his thinking, struggling with the original perception.

Another man, on the other hand, might view the balloon as if it were part of a system of unanticipated rewards, as when one's employer walks in and says, "Here, Henry, take this package of money I have wrapped for you, because we have been doing so well in the business here, and I admire the way you bruise the tulips, without which bruising your department would not be a success, or at least not the success that it is." For this man the balloon might be a brilliantly heroic "muscle and pluck" experience, even if an experience poorly understood.

Another man might say, "Without the example of——, it is doubtful that——would exist today in its present form," and find many to agree with him, or to argue with him. Ideas of "bloat" and "float" were introduced, as well as concepts of dream and responsibility. Others engaged in remarkably detailed fantasies having to do with a wish either to lose themselves in the balloon, or to engorge it. The private character of these wishes, of their origins, deeply buried and unknown, was such that they were not much spoken of; yet there is evidence that they were widespread. It was also argued that what was important was what you felt when you stood under the balloon; some people claimed that they felt sheltered, warmed, as never before, while enemies of the balloon felt, or reported feeling, constrained, a "heavy" feeling.

Critical opinion was divided:

"monstrous pourings"

                                                                "harp"

XXXXXXX "certain contrasts with darker
  portions"

            "inner joy"

  "large, square corners"

 "conservative eclecticism that has so far governed
  modern balloon design"

        :::::::: "abnormal vigor"

  "warm, soft, lazy passages"

 "Has unity been sacrificed for a sprawling
  quality?"

"Quelle catastrophe!"

"munching"

People began, in a curious way, to locate themselves in relation to aspects of the balloon: "I'll be at that place where it dips down into Forty-seventh Street almost to the sidewalk, near the Alamo Chile House," or, "Why don't we go stand on top, and take the air, and maybe walk about a bit, where it forms a tight, curving line with the façade of the Gallery of Modern Art—" Marginal intersections offered entrances within a given time duration, as well as "warm, soft, lazy passages" in which . . . But it is wrong to speak of "marginal intersections," each intersection was crucial, none could be ignored (as if, walking there, you might not find someone capable of turning your attention, in a flash, from old exercises to new exercises, risks and escalations). Each intersection was crucial, meeting of balloon and building, meeting of balloon and man, meeting of balloon and balloon.

It was suggested that what was admired about the balloon was finally this: that it was not limited, or defined. Sometimes a bulge, blister, or subsection would carry all the way east to the river on its own initiative, in the manner of an army's movements on a map, as seen in a headquarters remote from the fighting. Then that part would be, as it were, thrown back again, or would withdraw into new dispositions; the next morning, that part would have made another sortie, or disappeared altogether. This ability of the balloon to shift its shape, to change, was very pleasing, especially to people whose lives were rather rigidly patterned, persons to whom change, although desired, was not available. The balloon, for the twenty-two days of its existence, offered the possibility, in its randomness, of mislocation of the self, in contradistinction to the grid of precise, rectangular pathways under our feet. The amount of specialized training currently needed, and the consequent desirability of long-term commitments, has been occasioned by the steadily growing importance of complex machinery, in virtually all kinds of operations; as this tendency increases, more and more people will turn, in bewildered inadequacy, to solutions for which the balloon may stand as a prototype, or "rough draft."

I met you under the balloon, on the occasion of your return from Norway; you asked if it was mine; I said it was. The balloon, I said, is a spontaneous autobiographical disclosure, having to do with the unease I felt at your absence, and with sexual deprivation, but now that your visit to Bergen has been terminated, it is no longer necessary or appropriate. Removal of the balloon was easy; trailer trucks carried away the depleted fabric, which is now stored in West Virginia, awaiting some other time of unhappiness, sometime, perhaps, when we are angry with one another.

A. R. AMMONS
The City Limits

When you consider the radiance, that it does not withhold
itself but pours its abundance without selection into every
nook and cranny not overhung or hidden; when you consider

that birds' bones make no awful noise against the light but
lie low in the light as in a high testimony; when you consider
the radiance, that it will look into the guiltiest

swervings of the weaving heart and bear itself upon them,
no flinching into disguise or darkening; when you consider
the abundance of such resource as illuminates the glow-blue

bodies and gold-skeined wings of flies swarming the dumped
guts of a natural slaughter or the coil of shit and in no
way winces from its storms of generosity; when you consider

that air or vacuum, snow or shale, squid or wolf, rose or lichen,
each is accepted into as much light as it will take, then
the heart moves roomier, the man stands and looks about, the

leaf does not increase itself above the grass, and the dark
work of the deepest cells is of a tune with May bushes
and fear lit by the breadth of such calmly turns to praise.

PAOLI SOLERI
Arcology: The City in the Image of Man

Architecture is in the process of becoming the physical definition of a multilevel, human ecology. It will be arc-ology. Arcology, instrumented by science and technology, will be an aesthetocompassionate phenomenon. Its advent will be the implosion of the flat megalopolis of today into an urban solid of superdense and human vitality.

1. Arcology, or ecological architecture
This is the definition of urban structures so "dense" as to host life, work, education, culture, leisure, and health for hundreds of thousands of people per square mile. The weak veneer of life ridden with blight and stillness, which megalopolis and suburbia are, is thus transformed and miniaturized into a metropolitan solid, saturated with flux and liveliness.

2. Arcology and man
Man, a creature of culture, is given such instrumentality as to have his reach greatly incremented. Education, culture, production, service, health, play, and an untouched countryside are at his fingertips. He can walk to them from his home, the place where he is master and the place he can define and construct by himself if he so pleases.

3. Arcology and change
As for the cities we have, we will live with them. We cannot live for them. Thus, while effort will go into improving what we have, great and persistent effort must go into the development, parallel to the condemned patterns, of new systems coherent with man's needs. Arcology is, in short, an efficient plumbing system for contemporary society.

589

4. Arcology and dimension

The squandering in land, time, energy, and the wealth of megalopolis and suburbia, now well entangled in their increasing contradictions, is rejected as obsolete. With arcology there are two conditions: (1) immense nature: extensive, kind, and brutal, the reservoir of life; and (2) the man-made: dense, organized, powerful, and serving man well. With the third dimension, the vertical, no longer a limitless sea of housing in a choked system of dim vitality, man is reinstated as the measure of things and primarily as the compassionate measure of himself and nature.

5. Arcology and scale

Scale is that characterization that makes the performance effort congruous with the aim.

The configuration that makes it impossible for the hungry man to sit at the bountiful table is a configuration that is not human. Dimension, proportions, and visual grasp are subordinate categories made human or unhuman by the amount of real reaching power they offer to the individual. A building or a city are out of scale with the people they serve when the function they promise is put out of the realm of the possible.

Arcology is both dimensionally (1 cubic kilometer as against 400 square miles) and functionally on the human scale without loss of its awesome force, indeed almost because of it.

6. Arcology and distance

Distance is a tax on reaching power. By the aberration of the car, such a tax is starving our culture. The car is dividing things more and more by scattering them all over. Then one finds that it becomes more and more difficult to reach them one by one, impossible to reach them all in one. Acceleration-deceleration, natural sluggishness, and the antiswiftness inherent to scatterization make high speed urban transportation a perpetual illusion.

In arcology, distances are measured again by walks and in minutes. Within it the car is nonsensical. It has nowhere to go.

7. Arcology and land conservation

The compactness of arcology gives back to farming and to land conservation 90 per cent or more of the land that megalopolis and suburbia are engulfing in their sprawl. To be a city dweller and a country man at one and the same time, to be able to partake fully of both city and country life, will make the arcology a place in which man will want to live. The creation of truly lovable cities is the only lasting solution for land conservation.

8. Arcology and natural resources

The reserves of ores and fuels are not infinite. The squandering of such collective capital wealth, while proclaiming the sacredness of exclusive and personal possession, is irrational, to say the least. Chemistry and biochemistry might find a magnificent future for such resources. By then most of these will be reduced to the second-rate pockets that will have escaped man's greed. The frugal character of arcology moves consumption toward the use of the earth's income rather than the exhaustion of its capital.

9. Arcology and industry

The destructive bite of the car on the U.S. economy and life will not last another fifteen years, nor will the Pentagon's ravenous hunger for war hardware. The car will follow the horse to the pastures of sport and eccentricity. War hardware will destroy us or will be destroyed by us.

There is the colossal and challenging task of punctuating the earth's landscape with a humane, beautiful "culturescape." Each arcology will be an industry in itself with its original standardizations, its automated systems, a cybernetic organism growing of its own volition. It will be an industry turned forward instead of backward.

10. Arcology and pollution

We are concerned with the immediate menaces of pollution, but the long-term consequences escape us. These may well reach into our genetic structure as well as into the total geophysical and biochemical balance of the planet.

In arcology the ratio of efficiency to energy becomes many times greater, thus pollution will be manyfold smaller. Pollution is a direct function of wastefulness. The elimination of wastefulness is the elimination of pollution.

11. Arcology and climate

For both extremes of heat and cold, as for any intermediate condition, the compactness of arcology makes it a most workable system. Instead of sealing the outside out, conditioning will extend to the ground, space, and the air enveloping the structure. The climate of the arcology, not a sealed cell but an open city, will be a tamed facsimile of the regional climate.

12. Arcology and waste

As a sprawled-out man 2,000 square feet in area and 3 inches tall can work only on paper, if at all, so possibly can our megalopoly and suburbias work only on paper. They will never truly and substantially work for real. They are not real. They are utopian. Arcology can be a congruous system and, as such, an optimum system for the full and complex logistics of individual and social life.

13. Arcology and cost

The initial cost of research and experimentation is by necessity high. A radical turn is never inexpensive. The actual planning and production cost of an arcology would be a fraction of the cost of our gigantic dwarfs for equal population, but not equal fullness, of life.

14. Arcology and obsolescence

Flexibility and dynamism cannot be found where there is built-in obsolescence (a downgraded system is by nature inflexible). These are to be found where the full flow of life runs throughout a structure. If the tempo of obsolescence has the same beat as individual growth—childhood, youth, maturity, age—the individual himself is obsolete. The precariousness of his significance will destroy him. Arcology is a mirror of man's identity and a support to his doings.

15. Arcology and underdeveloped countries

With arcology comes the possibility of leaping beyond the mechanical age into the cybernetic culture and thus the chance of avoiding the robotization of men, the blight of the environment, the slavery of the car, the starvation of culture, all scourges of our Western success story.

16. Arcology and leisure

A cybernetic system of immediate feedback with information, communication, transportation, and transfer quickened by shrunken distances, is an organism for true leisure.

For many, if not most, of the citizens such leisure will be voluntary work at the enrichment of the city, starting from one's own home and reaching throughout the intrastructure of the whole city. This will be a totally new challenge for artists, performers, craftsmen, and the engaged citizenry.

17. Arcology and segregation

Segregation concerns not only ethnics and religions. It concerns activities and all age levels as well as it concerns, and stills, life itself. A social pattern is influenced, if not directed, by the physical pattern that shelters it. In a one-container system are the best premises for a nonsegregated culture. The care for oneself will tend to be care for the whole.

18. Arcology, aggression, and guilt

Aggression and guilt are in good proportion a bridge of a sort connecting meaninglessness to meaningfulness. Therefore a better bridge must be found. If man is really in need of risk and violence, if frustration and guilt are really tearing society asunder, then the awesomeness of arcology and the complexity of its construction are positive alternatives to war, social strife, and squalor.

19. Arcology and medical care

In arcology there is interchangeability and diffusion of functions because the obstacles of time and space are minimized, miniaturized. As all of arcology can be called a marketplace, all of it a learning organism, all of it a productive mechanism and a playground, so in a true sense arcology can be considered a total medical-care system. Home nursing becomes as feasible and as professional as hospital care, but far less costly and far more personal. Nurses and doctors move from home to home, as from ward to ward, making the family doctor real again. Infirmaries, clinics, and hospitals are always at walking distance, leaving no pockets of indifference (if not those maliciously wanted) that might be maliciously ignored.

20. Arcology and survival

To pinpoint an orbital warhead on a square mile or so is a feat for the not-too-distant future. Evacuation in arcology can be almost instantaneous; its vast underground structure for foundations, anchorages, and automated industries will be good emergency systems. Arcology is the coherent expression of a faith in man, and as such it is beyond the survival platform.

21. Arcology and the underground

Man must refute underground living. He is a biological animal of sun, air, light, and seasons. He is an aesthetic animal, and his senses are more and more oriented toward a usefulness of purely aesthetic worth.

The underground is ideal for automated production in need of technologically sophisticated environment: pressure, vacuum, radiation, heat, cold, rare atmospheres, and so forth. (It is also ideal for sense-less and senseless man.)

22. Arcology and spaces

Man has been experiencing what one might call flat spaces. It is congruous with the space age itself that man acquaints himself and lives with the deep spaces an arcology creates.

As man lives intensely on the horizontal, the density of his societies can only be achieved vertically.

23. Arcology and space

If we are destined to a "space" life of some sort, this life will be miniaturized by necessity. In arcology are the elements of interiorization, living inside instead of on top, and of compactness. In this sense arcology is a space architecture as much as it is a land and sea architecture.

24. Arcology and the sacred

Limitless energies in limitless spaces for limitless time are the scattered ingredients by which nature works. For man to succeed, he must make tight bundles of that minimal portion of them allowed to him so that his own infinity—the infinite complexity of his compassionate and aesthetic universe—can blossom.

Life is literally in the thick of things. Its sacramentality is in the awesome power concealed in its "densified" fragility.

25. Arcology and geriatrics

One of the ravages of "mobility," or at least directly accountable to it, is the institutionalized ghetto for the elderly. Following the generalized scattering of things and thoughts, the family has broken down into four main fragments: the young, the parents, the grandparents, and the anonymous relative. Aging being common to all (the lucky ones), all will have a taste of the tragic segregation of the aged; the insurance company and social security will not do, lest man become or remain marketable goods.

The implications of "arcological life" are the most favorable for reintegration of the different age groups and thus for the knitting of family strands.

26. Arcology and play

The playground is the act of condescending to playfulness in a habitat where grimness, ugliness, and danger are endemic and offer the last measure of unconcern in an adult world gone sour. The playground is segregative. The absence of children in the so-called respectable public places is disheartening. The child has reason to become irresponsible and destructive, caged, as he is, away from the "other world."

Arcology is an "environmental toy." As a miniaturized universe it offers unending elements for surprise and stimulation. There will not be fenced-in playgrounds. The whole city is the place where the child is acting out the learning process, one aspect of which is play.

27. Arcology and youth

The rift between youth and the holders of power, from the home up to the nation's policy makers, parallels the schism that exists between the preaching and the doing of the elders. The flow of hypocrisy is constant and perhaps irresistible. The revolt is at times blind, at times cynical, but it is a matter of survival within the limits of self-respect. If mere survival is to be dislodged by hopefulness, a form of things to come has to be suggested that will not drift away in the sea of the faceless, the irrelevant, and the expedient. As the god of the past "ill-serves" imperfect man and technology may yet cancel his humaneness, a step toward realism at the expense of powerful but conservative, if not reactionary, "practicality" is what the young may need most.

Arcology is a container where ideas and vision can meet man in his quest for a structure for living and not just an amorphous container for depersonalized survival.

28. Arcology, the practical and the real

The function of the practical is to instrumentalize the real. The function of the real is to dictate why, what, where, and when the practical is to operate. This antimaterialistic tenet is lost in the feverish idolatry of the feasible and the license of "free" enterprise. Most of what is feasible is irrelevant or unreal. It is not real because it does not converge with the aims of free man. The practical is no longer the specially tempered tip of a willfully driven utensil but is instead a vain, aimless, and squalid façade imposed upon the well burdened train of the real. The real is to be sought by the skill of the practical. The practical is a subskill whenever it is enthroned on the idol's chair. Arcology rejects as totally unreal the practicality of such a bigoted position.

29. Arcology and identification

The capacity of suburbia and megalopolis for unending sprawl, the amorphism caused by the lack of structuralization, the blurring of everything into the countless makes the identification of the individual as difficult as the identification of the environment. What one reflects in, one is or one tends to become. Arcology is physical identification. The whole of it is at grasp and unmistakable, while the detail in its secretiveness can be unlimited and ever changing.

30. Arcology and culture

To be exposed early in life to the complex workings of the individual and of society, to have a substantial reach for all those things and institutions that make metropolitan life rewarding, to be able at the same time to seek and be in the midst of nature, to enjoy the limitless and meaningful variety the life of society may produce for itself and the individual are all built-in characteristics of arcology. Arcology is the largest cultural whole physically available to men day in and day out.

31. Arcology and aesthetics

The beauty of nature is achieved in the awesome reservoirs of space and time where things are hammered out in the order that probability dictates, justly, rationally, impassionately. The genesis of man-made beauty, the aesthetic, is of a different nature. It is not incidental to man's action but is the very essence of man himself. By necessity it has to be frugal. It does away with probability and predictability. It is synthetic and transfigurative. It is never irrational because it is always superrational. It cannot simply be just, because it must also be compassionate.

With the aesthetogenesis of nature, man reaches into the structure of reality and forms a new universe in his own image. Arcology can be one of these forms. Arcology is essentially an aesthetocompassionate phenomenon.

32. Arcology and politics

The long involvements of the generations that have produced today's cities constitute such tightly interwoven interests that the hopes are very dim for a really purposeful renewal.

What has been the living cause has become very much that which takes life away. Too many things in our cities are spent cartridges, too little is of a nonbrittle nature. Even doodling around any of the city's many problems tends to weaken this or that interest or this or that group. And doodling seems to be what at best we do with them. An urban culture is per se the nth power of complexity. The burden of a not-too-glorious past may be just the amount of ballast that will not allow the take-off.

33. Arcology and miniaturization

In its evolution from matter to mind, the real has been submitted to numerous phases of miniaturization so as to fit more things into smaller spaces in shorter times. This process, from haphazardness and dislocation to co-ordination and fitness, has been mandatory because each successive form of reality carried in itself a greater degree of complexity. Any higher organism contains more performances than a chunk of the unlimited universe light years thick, and it ticks on a time clock immensely swifter. This miniaturization process may well be one of the fundamental rules of evolution. Now that the inquietude of man is turned to the construction of the superorganism, which society is, a new phase of miniaturization is imperative. Arcology is a step toward it.

Arcological miniaturization will cause the scale of the earth to "expand" and will also make feasible the migration of man to the seas and orbital lands. The orbital lands will also function as transformers on the earth's climate. The population explosion will then have different meanings. Both terrestrial and extraterrestrial towns and cities will be arcological.

34. Arcology and symmetry

There are, among others, the following three kinds of symmetry: structural symmetry, functional symmetry, and formal symmetry. Structural symmetry is probably observed throughout the universe. It is the necessary balancing of stresses that finds its patterns around points, lines, planes, and spaces of symmetry.

Functional symmetry is observed very clearly in any organism, be it monocellular or highly composite. Functional symmetry is the direct solution to the constant wavering of the energy balances composing the living organism and its nonsymmetrical behavior. Without such symmetry the organism would be constantly lopsided, that is to say, unfit for life. Formal symmetry might well be the imprint of all other kinds of symmetry into the mind and the sensitivity of man. Even if the impositions of structure and function were lifted, impositions that result in formal symmetry, there would still linger in man the need for a visual and in general sensorial symmetry.

The greater the symmetry, the greater the vitality of the performance. Arcology is not an exception, especially when one considers the enormous structural and functional complexity involved. It is to be noted that arcology is never symmetrical for the individual user. In other words, the individual user is always eccentric to the whole: symmetry in the whole, singularity in the parts.

35. Arcology and mobility

Structure defines a certain configuration suited to a particular set of performances. Urban planning supposedly defines that structure which channels, contains, and swiftens the performances of society.

Mobility in society does not reside in migratory waves but in the minute and perpetual shifting of bodies, functions, relationships, and mental processes of the body-social. To suppose that lack of structure favors mobility is tantamount to saying that a disintegrating corpse can function as a living body. To suppose furthermore that tenuity can favor mobility is like saying that nature was foolish in inventing almost exclusively three-dimensional organisms.

The explicit structurality of arcology and its three-dimensional congruence are, at least potentially, the basis for full and pragmatic mobility. In

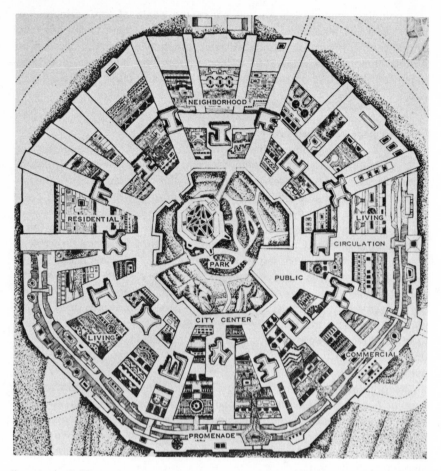

". . . to host life, work, education, culture, leisure, and health for hundreds of thousands. . . ."

arcology coercive mobility is unnecessary—the kind of mobility, commuting for instance, that orders and pushes people and things around. (The penalty for noncooperation is the loss of man's source of livelihood.) Unburdened of coercive mobility, free and functional mobility obtains the necessary elbow room for the full display of its dynamics.

36. Arcology and the biological

An animal is an organism of one mind. The city is an organism of one thousand minds. This is the most significant difference between a biological organism and the city. Furthermore, those one thousand minds do not stay put. They are eminently peripatetic, but in clusters of three or four or so (the family) they tend to define a territoriality that is more static (the home). What confronts the planner is the organization of the body to the satisfaction of the thousand minds. One may say that while an inner center, the brain, is the center to which the body renders service biologically, urbanistically the epidermis made up of a thousand brains is the "center" to which the body is dedicated.

The mental processes of the biological entity are centralized and interiorized; the mental processes of the city are diffuse and epidermal. While the skin is prevalently a defensive and containing device for the animal body, for the city it is eminently a casual, ontological structure. The miniaturizing implosion of the social body is thus accompanied by a micro-explosion of the thousand brains toward the periphery of the miniaturized organism. The mental, installed within its biological receptacle (the individual), places itself in the skin where its senses can capture both the natural vastness of the outer and the man-made miniaturization of the inner. This is a description of arcology.

37. Arcology and cybernation

The urban organism has a new tool on hand. It can delegate to a non-biological brain some of its labors. This nonbiological brain can be collectivized and can be interiorized because it does not belong to a body, to any body. Then the parallel between the biological and the urban is modified. In the biological, the brain and the body are single and almost certainly spatially coincidental. In the urban organism, the brain may be imagined as split: one part is the group of the single brains, each belonging to individuals; the other part is the collectivized nonbiological brain ideally centered in the organism.

In the urban organism, the mind remains in independent but correlated parcels divided spatially and coincidental with the parceled brains, the whole forming the mental or thinking skin of the city. In the function of the urban organism the implosion of the whole performance is paralleled by the parceling of the mind-brain toward the skin, leaving in the "cranial box" a shadow brain which is mechanically and chemically composed and not biologically developed. Such a centralized brain cares for the collective and instrumental functions while individual minds govern the pluralism inherent in the whole organism. Arcology is such an organism.

ALVIN FEINMAN
November Sunday Morning

And the light, a wakened heyday of air
Tuned low and clear and wide,
A radiance now that would emblaze
And veil the most golden horn
Or any entering to a sudden clearing
To a standing, astonished, revealed . . .

That the actual streets I loitered in
Lay lit like fields, or narrow channels
About to open to a burning river;
All brick and window vivid and calm
As though composed in a rigid water
No random traffic would dispel . . .

As now through the park, and across
The chill nailed colors of the roofs,
And on near trees stripped bare,
Corrected in the scant remaining leaf
To their severe essential elegance,
Light is the all-exacting good,

That dry, forever, virile stream
That wipes each thing to what it is,
The whole, collage and stone, cleansed
To its proper pastoral . . .
                                      I sit
And smoke, and linger out desire.

WILLIAM CARLOS WILLIAMS
Perpetuum Mobile: The City

   —a dream
we dreamed
   each
separately
   we two

of love
   and of
desire—

that fused
in the night—

in the distance
   over
the meadows
   by day
impossible—
   The city
disappeared
   when
we arrived—

   A dream
a little false

toward which
   now
we stand
   and stare
transfixed—

All at once
        in the east
rising!

        All white!

        small
as a flower—

a locust cluster
a shad bush
        blossoming

Over the swamps
        a wild
magnolia bud—
        greenish
white
a northern
        flower—
And so
        we live
        looking—

At night
        it wakes
On the black
        sky—

a dream
        toward which
we love—
at night
        more
than a little
        false—

We have bred
we have dug
we have figured up
our costs
we have bought
an old rug—

We batter at our
unsatisfactory
            brilliance—

There is no end
            to desire—

Let us break
            through
and go there—

in
            vain!

—delectable
            amusement:

Milling about—

Money! in
armored trucks—
Two men
            walking
at two paces from
            each other
their right hands
            at the hip—
on the butt of
an automatic—
till they themselves
hold up the bank
and themselves
            drive off
for themselves
            the money
in an armored car—

            For love!

Carefully
            carefully tying
carefully

            selected
wisps of long

dark hair
        wisp
by wisp
upon the stubs
of his kinky wool—
For two hours
        they worked—
        until
he coiled
        the thick
knot upon
that whorish
        head—

Dragged
        insensible
upon his face
by the lines—

—a running horse
    For love.

Their eyes
        blown out—

—for love, for love!

Neither the rain
Nor the storm—
can keep them

        for love!

from the daily
accomplishment
        of their
appointed rounds—

Guzzling
the creamy foods
        while
out of sight
        in
the sub-cellar—
the waste fat

the old vegetable
      chucked down
a chute
      the foulest
sink in the world—

And go
on the out-tide
ten thousands
      cots
floating to sea
      like weed
that held back
the pristine ships—

And fattened there
an eel
in the water pipe—

     No end—

There!

     There!

There!

     —a dream
of lights
     hiding

the iron reason
     and stone
a settled
     cloud—

City

     whose stars
of matchless
     splendor—

     and
in bright-edged

clouds
the moon—

bring

silence

breathlessly—

Tearful city
on a summer's day
the hard grey
dwindling
in a wall of
rain—

farewell!

Glossary of Authors

A. R. AMMONS (1926–   ), poet and teacher of English at Cornell University, has written *Ommateum* (1955), *Corsons Inlet* (1965), and *Northfield Poems* (1966).

SHERWOOD ANDERSON (1876–1941), midwestern American writer, is best known for his stories in *Winesburg, Ohio* (1919) in which he portrays the boredom and loneliness of the small town while recalling the sense of vitality once present in rural life.

MARY ANTIN (1881–1948) wrote often of her experiences as an immigrant in America. She is the author of *The Promised Land* (1912).

DONALD BARTHELME (1931–   ) is a young, highly inventive fiction writer whose stories appear often in *The New Yorker*. His collections include *Come Back, Dr. Caligari* (1964) and *City Life* (1970). He has written one novel, *Snow White* (1967).

SAUL BELLOW (1915–   ) is Canadian born, grew up in Chicago, and was educated at midwestern universities. He is currently a member of the faculty at the University of Chicago. As the author of *Dangling Man* (1944), *The Victim* (1947), *The Adventures of Augie March* (1953), *Seize the Day* (1956), *Henderson the Rain King* (1959), and *Herzog,* National Book Award winner in 1964, Mr. Bellow deals primarily with urban themes, the plight and responsibility of the individual confronted by mass society.

KENNETH E. BOULDING (1910–   ), Professor of Economics at the University of Michigan, is the author of *The Image* (1964).

WILLIAM S. BURROUGHS was born in St. Louis in 1914. *The Soft Machine* (1961), *Naked Lunch* (1962), and *Nova Express* (1964) are among his best-known works. Burroughs documents the horror of drug addiction; his style the brilliance of contemporary language. The novels seem like futuristic hallucination, grounded in false aspects of current American life: the abuse of power, violence, materialistic obsession, intolerance, and hypocrisy.

ROBERT COOVER (1935–   ) is the author of the 1966 William Faulkner Award novel, *The Origin of the Brunists*. Coover has taught at Bard College and the University of Iowa. He has also published a second novel, *The Universal Baseball Association, Inc., J. Henry Waugh, Prop.* (1968), and a collection of short writings, *Pricksongs and Descants* (1970).

HART CRANE (1899–1932), American poet who lived most of his life in Cleveland and in the urban intellectual and artistic atmosphere of Greenwich Village. His works include *White Buildings* (1926) and *The Bridge* (1930). Crane's poetry reflects his turbulent personal life and his hope for the redemption of himself and of "the broken city."

FRED DAVIS (1925–   ), sociologist, is the author of *The Nursing Profession: Five Sociological Essays* (1966).

ST. CLAIR DRAKE (1911–   ), educator and anthropologist, is the author of *Black Metropolis* (1945) and *Race Relations in a Time of Rapid Social Change* (1966).

THEODORE DREISER (1871–1945), leading American novelist in the early decades of the twentieth century, wrote often of New York and Chicago. His novels include *Sister Carrie* (1900), *The Financier* (1912), and *The American Tragedy* (1925). Dreiser's characters are driven by desire for wealth, sex, power; the city is a magnet attracting them to promised pleasure. They soon discover, however, their helplessness against the inner force of their own desire and the outer force of the overpowering city.

WILLIAM E. B. DU BOIS (1868–1963), distinguished writer and historian, was a founder of the National Association for the Advancement of Colored People and editor of its journal, *Crisis.* Du Bois was educated at Harvard and taught economics, history, and sociology for many years at Atlanta University. His many books include *The Souls of Black Folk* (1903) and *Black Reconstruction* (1935). Du Bois was outspoken in his criticism of the injustice perpetrated against blacks both in this country and in the emerging African nations. This criticism, his Marxist leanings, and his joining the American Communist Party in 1961 led to inevitable conflict with the U.S. Government. He left America and settled in Ghana until his death.

ALAN DUGAN was born in Brooklyn, New York, in 1923. He is the author of *Poems* (1961), *Poems 2* (1963), and *Poems 3* (1967). His first collection won the Yale Younger Poets Award in 1961, and both the National Book Award for Poetry and the Pulitzer Prize in 1962.

ROBERT DUNCAN was born in 1919 in Oakland, California. His works include *Selected Poems 1942–50* (1959) and *Opening of the Field* (1960).

RALPH ELLISON was born in 1914 in Oklahoma City, and majored in music at Tuskegee Institute from 1933 to 1936 when he came to New York to study sculpture. He has written short stories, articles, reviews, and criticism, in addition to his first novel, *Invisible Man,* which won the National Book Award for Fiction in 1953.

ALVIN FEINMAN (1929–   ), a poet who teaches at Bennington College in Vermont, is the author of *Preambles and Other Poems* (1964).

F. SCOTT FITZGERALD (1896–1940), American writer of the 1920's and the Jazz Age, is best known for *The Great Gatsby* (1925). Other books include *This Side of Paradise* (1920), *The Beautiful and the Damned* (1922), and *Tender is the Night* (1934). Fitzgerald was born in St. Paul, Minnesota, educated at Princeton, lived in New York, Hollywood, the French Riviera. His novels deal with the contradictions of wealth and sophistication, and document the pleasure and loneliness of the "beautiful" people of the decade. The Fitzgerald myth persists; the tragi-comedy of his novels and of his personal life is not entirely absent from our own time.

ROBERT FROST (1874–1963), perhaps the best-known and most widely read of modern American poets, deals mainly with themes and settings of New England rural life. Read against the backdrop of the city, Frost's poems stand as a powerful, if momentary, stay against the confusion of urban life. His many volumes include *A Boy's Will* (1913), *North of Boston* (1914), and *Collected Poems* (1930).

KENNETH GANGEMI (1940–   ) is a young poet living in New York. He has published a short novel, *Olt* (1969), and a collection of poetry, *Lydia* (1970).

ALAN GINSBERG was born in 1926, the son of the lyric poet, Louis Ginsberg. He is an eternal itinerant, having lived in Texas, Denver, Harlem, Mexico, San Francisco, Tangier, throughout Europe, and around again. His writings include *Howl and Other Poems* (1956), *Kaddish* (1961), and *Reality Sandwiches* (1963). Ginsberg emerged in association with Jack Kerouac and Gregory Corso, part of San Francisco's Beat Generation; however, his unrepressed style has survived the cultural fickleness of the last fifteen years, and Ginsberg remains today a highly visible, audible personality and poet.

PAUL GOODMAN (1911–   ) is a novelist, poet, critic, and sociologist. His contribution to the latter discipline includes *Growing Up Absurd* (1960), *Communitas* (1947), and *The Community of Scholars* (1962). He has also published several volumes of literary criticism and a novel, *The Empire City* (1959).

PERCIVAL GOODMAN (1904–   ) is on the architecture faculty at Columbia University and a practicing architect in New York. He was educated at the École des Beaux Arts in Paris. He collaborated with his brother, Paul, on *Communitas* (1947), an early and influential book dealing with the planning of cities.

ELIEZER GREENBERG (1896–   ), poet and translator, has co-edited with Irving Howe *The Treasury of Yiddish Stories* (1954) and *The Treasury of Yiddish Poetry* (1969).

NATHANIEL HAWTHORNE (1804–1864) is best known for *Twice-Told Tales* (1837), *The House of the Seven Gables* (1851), and *The Scarlet Letter* (1850). Hawthorne deals with the past history and legend of early nineteenth-century America, portraying the narrowness and hypocrisy of the Puritan vision and the psychology and secret guilt of its victims.

JOHN HOLLANDER (1929–   ) poet and writer, editor and critic, teaches at the City University of New York and is the author of *A Crackling of Thorns,* winner of the Yale Younger Poets Award for 1958. Hollander has published many reviews and scholarly articles in addition to *Movie-going and Other Poems* (1962), *Visions from the Ramble* (1965), and *The Quest of the Gole* (1966).

J. B. JACKSON, founder and until recently editor of *Landscape Magazine,* has written extensively on art, architecture, city planning, and anthropology as an expression of his interest in the inter-disciplinary study sometimes known as human or cultural geography.

SARAH ORNE JEWETT (1949–1909) lived and wrote in South Berwick, Maine. She is the author of *A Country Doctor* (1884), *Strangers and Wayfarers* (1890), *The Country of the Pointed Firs* (1896), and *Deephaven* (1877). She writes best of the environment and the quiet lives of the inhabitants of her native Maine.

LEROI JONES was born in 1934, graduated from high school in Newark, New Jersey, and, at age nineteen, from Howard University. He has published several volumes of poetry, including *The Dead Lecturer* (1964), a novel, *The System of Dante's Hell* (1965), a book of criticism, *Home: Social Essays* (1966), and several one-act plays. Most recently, Jones has been active in politics in Newark.

ALFRED KAZIN (1915–   ), writer and critic, is the author of *On Native Grounds* (1942), *A Walker in the City* (1951), and *Starting Out in the Thirties* (1965).

GALWAY KINNEL was born in Rhode Island in 1927 and has taught at many American universities. He is currently at the University of Iowa. In 1962 he received an award from the Institute of Arts and Letters, and a year later, a Guggenheim Fellowship. His collections include *What a Kingdom it Was* (1960), *Flower Herding on Mount Monadnock* (1964), *Black Light* (1966), and *Body Rags* (1967).

LE CORBUSIER (1887–1965), along with Frank Lloyd Wright and Walter Gropius, was in the forefront of the archtecture of this century. His buildings and his book *The Radiant City* (1935) remain a major influence upon architects and city-planners. His most familiar building is the church, Notre-Dame du Haut, in Ronchamps, France. Other publications are *Toward a New Architecture* (1927), *The City of Tomorrow* (1929), and *When the Cathedrals were White* (1947), an analysis and plan for the architecture of the city of New York.

ELIOT LIEBOW, Project Director, Adolescent Process Section, Mental Health Study Center, National Institute of Mental health, is the author of *Tally's Corner* (1967).

ROBERT LOWELL was born in Boston in 1917 and is one of America's most respected poets. His collections include *Lord Weary's Castle* (1946), *Life Studies,* winner of the national Book Award for Poetry in 1960, *Imitations* (1962), and *For the Union Dead* (1964). His most recent publication is *Notebook 1967–68* (1969), a series of poetic fragments relating to the events of those tumultuous years: the death of Martin Luther King, Jr. and Robert Kennedy, the Democratic convention in Chicago, and the Vietnam war.

NORMAN MAILER (1923–   ), novelist, journalist, and filmmaker, is one of the few American writers who also follow a career as public figures. Among other performances, Mailer ran for Mayor of the city of New York in 1968. His books include *The Naked and the Dead* (1948), *The Barbary Shore* (1951), *The Deer Park* (1955), *Advertisements for Myself* (1959), and *Armies of the Night* and *Miami and the Seige of Chicago* in 1968.

MALCOLM X (1925–1965) was born in Detroit and educated in the ghetto streets of Roxbury, Massachusetts, and Harlem. He became an early follower of Elijah Muhammed, the founder of the Black Muslims, and later Elijah's most energetic and trusted organizer and lieutenant. A break between Malcolm and Elijah split the black nationalist movement. Following a pilgrimage to the Holy City of Mecca, Malcolm returned to New York; where he was assassinated addressing a rally. Malcolm's significance is far greater than the international publicity he brought to the black cause in America. He was a symbol, both living and dead, of black identity in white America, of manhood, individuality, and true equality.

MARSHALL MCLUHAN (1911–   ), Canadian writer and professor, has been an extremely influential student of the mass media and their impact upon society. His books include *The Mechanical Bride* (1951), *The Gutenberg Galaxy* (1962), *Understanding Media* (1964), *The Medium is the Message* (1967), and *From Cliché to Archetype* (1970).

JACK MCMANIS (1920–   ) teaches English at the Pennsylvania State University. He co-edited with Harold Holden the poems of Samuel Greenberg, and has published his own verse in many journals.

JAMES ALAN MCPHERSON was born in 1943 and is the author of a collection of short stories, *Hue and Cry* (1969). He is an Associate Editor and frequent contributor to *The Atlantic.*

JAMES MERRILL was born in New York in 1926. He is the author of *First Poems* (1951), *Selected Poems* (1961), *Water Street* (1962), and a novel, *The (Diblos) Notebook* (1965).

JOSEPHINE MILES (1911–   ), Professor of English at the University of California at Berkeley, is well known as both a poet and a critic-scholar. Her books include *Eras and Modes in English Poetry* (1957) and *Poems, 1930–60* (1960).

HENRY MILLER (1891–   ), for many years before World War II a famous American expatriate writer in France, has written extensively of the life of cities. New York and Paris are the most prominent places in his best-known books, *Tropic of Cancer* (1934), *Tropic of Capricorn* (1961), and *Black Spring* (1936). Miller's writing is primarily autobiographical, was long banned in America as pornographic, and has had a strong influence on certain contemporary writers and poets.

N. SCOTT MOMADAY (1932–   ), a native American Kiowa indian, teaches English at the University of California at Berkeley. His books include *The Way to*

Rainy Mountain (1969) and *House Made of Dawn,* the Pulitzer Prize for Fiction in 1968.

LEWIS MUMFORD (1895–   ) is famous internationally for his distinguished histories and criticisms of cities, of technology and art, and of architecture and city-planning. His many works include *Sticks and Stones* (1924), *Technics and Civilization* (1934), *The City in History* (1961), *The Myth of the Machine* (1967), and *The Pentagon of Power* (1970). For almost fifty years, Mumford has argued persuasively for human uses of the machine and eloquently against allowing technology to divert us from the goal of human perfection.

FLANNERY O'CONNOR (1925–1964) was born in Savannah, Georgia, and is the author of *Wise Blood* (1952), *A Good Man Is Hard To Find* (1955), *The Violent Bear It Away* (1960), and *Everything That Rises Must Converge* (1965). Miss O'Connor wrote of her native South, captured its charm and humor as well as its terror and violence, and instilled in her writing always her strong sense of personal faith.

ROBERT E. PARK (1864–1944), a leading member of the University of Chicago sociology department in the early years of this century, and a founder of the ecological school of urban sociology, gained much of his knowledge of cities and race relations as a newspaper reporter in Minneapolis, Chicago, and Detroit. He received his Ph.D. from Harvard in 1904, and served as personal secretary to Booker T. Washington before beginning his teaching career. His principal work is *The City: Suggestions for the Study of the Urban Environment* (1925).

ANN PETRY was born in Old Saybrook, Connecticut, in 1911 and attended the University of Connecticut. After moving to Harlem, she worked for several social agencies and was a reporter for *The People's Voice.* Her first novel, *The Street* (1946), was written on a Houghton Mifflin Literary Fellowship. Her other books are *The Country Place* (1947), *The Drugstore Cat* (1949), *The Narrows* (1953), *Harriet Tubman: Conductor on the Underground Railroad* (1955), and *Tituba of Salem Village* (1965).

EDGAR ALLAN POE (1809–1949), American writer and poet best known for stories of terror such as "The Fall of the House of Usher" and stories of mystery and crime such as "Murders in the Rue Morgue," spent much of his career as an editor in New York and Philadelphia. His contribution to literature was an indirect one, for through the fascination his poetry had for Baudelaire and Mallarmé his was the strongest original influence on the French Symbolist poets.

FRED POWLEDGE is a young, free-lance journalist living in New York. His articles have appeared in *Life, New York,* and *Harper's.*

MURIEL RUKEYSER (1913–   ) is a well-known New York poet. She has published *Theory of Flight,* winner of the Yale Younger Poets Award in 1935, *Selected Poems* (1951), and *Speed of Darkness* (1968), as well as children's books, plays, filmscripts, and translations of the poetry of Gunnar Ekelof and Octavio Paz.

JEAN-PAUL SARTRE was born in Paris in 1905. After graduating from the École Normale Supérieure in 1929 with a doctorate in philosophy, he taught in Le Havre, Lyon, and Paris. In 1964 he was awarded the Nobel Prize for Literature. His philosophical writings include *Psychology of the Imagination* (1940), *Being and Nothingness* (1943), and *Existentialism* (1946). He has written autobiography, *The Words* (1964), and biography, *Saint Genet* (1952), plays, *The Flies* (1943), *No Exit* (1947), *The Victors* (1947), and *The Respectful Prostitute* (1947), novels, *Nausea* (1938) and *The Age of Reason* (1947), as well as literary and political essays. Sartre has long been considered a foremost spokesman for existentialist philosophy. Most recently, he has been active as a supporter of the radical French student movement.

LOUIS SIMPSON, born in 1923, is a former editor and professor at the University of California at Berkeley. His works include *At the End of the Open Road,* winner of the Pulitzer Prize for Poetry in 1964, and *Selected Poems* (1965).

PAOLI SOLERI is an Italian architect now working in the United States. He is a former student of Frank Lloyd Wright. Soleri lives and works at Arcosanti, his workshop in Arizona, where he is attempting to construct the first major example of an "arcology."

WALLACE STEGNER (1909–   ) is the author of many novels, among them *The Big Rock Candy Mountain* (1943) and *Wolf Willow* (1962). He is Professor of English and Director of the Creative Writing Program at Stanford University. Stegner is also known as a lifelong conservationist.

STAN STEINER is the author of *The New Indians* (1968) and *The Chicanos* (1970), studies of the history, culture, and contemporary plight of two ethnic minorities in the United States.

STEPHEN THERNSTROM (1934–   ), Professor of History at the University of California at Los Angeles, is the author of *Progress and Poverty* (1964) and editor of *Nineteenth-Century Cities* (1970).

HENRY DAVID THOREAU (1817–1862), poet and essayist, graduated from Harvard in 1837 and tried teaching without success. His famous *Walden: or, Life in the Woods,* inspired by his two-year stay in a cabin outside Concord, Massachusetts, was published in 1854. It was preceeded in 1849 by *A Week on the Concord and Merrimack Rivers* and by his essay of the same year, *On the Duty of Civil Disobedience,* one of the many contributions he made to the anti-slavery campaign.

NATHANAEL WEST (1904–1940), writer and satirist, produced several novels, *The Dream Life of Balso Snell* (1931), *Miss Lonelyhearts* (1933), *A Cool Million* (1934), and *Day of the Locust* (1939). West's work was not well known during his lifetime and he was forced to live in Hollywood writing film scripts. He died at thirty-six in an automobile accident. In the content and tone of West's novels lie the antecedents of the current "black humorists," such as Thomas Pynchon and Kurt Vonnegut.

WALT WHITMAN (1819–1892) was brought up in Brooklyn, left school early and worked as an office boy and printer's devil, taught in country schools, and finally took up journalism in New York. A pamphlet of twelve poems entitled *Leaves of Grass* appeared in 1855 and was subsequently revised several times with more poems added to each new edition. Other writings include *Specimen Days* (1842) and *Democratic Vistas* (1871). Whitman has had great influence on contemporary poets; he is a strikingly urban poet, a celebrant of the texture of city life.

WILLIAM CARLOS WILLIAMS (1883–1963) was a practicing physician in Rutherford, New Jersey, the town of his birth, for more than thirty years. After medical school, internship, and travel abroad, Williams was content to remain in Rutherford with his patients and poetry. He was twenty-six when his first small volume of poems was published by a local printer; in the years that followed he produced nearly forty books of prose and poetry, including *Autobiography* (1951) and a collection of short stories, *The Farmer's Daughter* (1961). Perhaps his greatest work is *Paterson* (1946–1958), an epic poem dramatizing Paterson, New Jersey, and evoking his vision of America and modern man.

LLOYD ZIMPEL (1931–   ) is a San Francisco poet who has won several prizes for his short stories.

Glossary of Photographers

BERENICE ABBOTT (1898–   ) originally studied sculpture, but in 1923 she turned to photography and became assistant to Man Ray in Paris. In 1929 she returned to the United States and began her important documentation of New York City. Much of this work during the thirties was done under the auspices of the Federal Art Project, and was published in *Changing New York* (1939). The most recent book of her photographs, *Berenice Abbott: Photographs,* was published in 1970.

ANSEL ADAMS (1902–   ) is the foremost photographer of the American landscape. His work has been widely published and exhibited since his first important one-man show in 1932. He is the author, with Nancy Newhall, of *This Is the American Earth* (1960), the first and most significant of the Sierra Club portfolio publications. Nancy Newhall has also written the first of a two-part biography entitled *The Eloquent Light* (1963).

ROBERT ADAMS (1937–   ) is Assistant Professor of English at Colorado College. He is the author of *White Churches of the Plains* (1970), and his photographs have appeared in such publications as *The American West* and *Art in America*.

DIANE ARBUS (1923–   ) was born in New York and studied photography with Lisette Model. She began her professional career as a fashion photographer, but in recent years has largely abandoned commerical photography in order to pursue her personal work. She was the recipient of Guggenheim Fellowships in 1963 and 1966. Her first major exhibition was at The Museum of Modern Art in 1967, and her photographs frequently appear in such publications as *Esquire* and *New York Magazine*.

DONALD BLUMBERG (1935–   ) is Associate Professor of Art, teaching photography and film, at the State University of New York at Buffalo. A portfolio of his photographs was published in the volume *The Persistence of Vision* (1967).

NEAL BOENZI (1925–   ) is a staff photographer for *The New York Times*. His photographs were most recently exhibited in the exhibition "May 2–May 9" at The Museum of Modern Art.

HARRY CALLAHAN (1912–   ) now on the faculty of the Rhode Island School of Design, is one of the most influential American photographers and teachers. His photographs have been widely exhibited in this country and abroad, and two volumes of his work have been published, *Photographs Harry Callahan* (1964) and *Harry Callahan* (1967), with a text by Sherman Paul.

PAUL CAPONIGRO (1932–   ) first studied music, but in 1952 turned to photography. He studied with Benjamin Chin and Minor White, and now teaches private workshops himself. One volume of his photographs has been published, *Paul Caponigro* (1967), and in addition his work has frequently appeared in such publications as *Aperture* and *Contemporary Photographer*.

BRUCE DAVIDSON (1933–) is a member of the Magnum Photos group. His sensitive documentation of the American social landscape has placed him at the forefront of this movement. His most recent work was a two-year concentrated study of one block in Harlem. Some of these photographs have been published in *East 100th Street* (1970), and several were exhibited at The Museum of Modern Art and in the American pavilion at the Osaka World's Fair. In 1970 he was voted Photographer of the Year by the American Society of Magazine Photographers.

WILLIAM EGGLESTON (1939–) was born in Memphis and grew up in Mississippi. A self-taught photographer, he devotes himself wholly to photography and to the study of the music of J. S. Bach.

WALKER EVANS (1903–) since the publication of his *American Photographs* (1938) and *Let Us Now Praise Famous Men* (1941), has been one of this country's most influential artists. From his work, which in concentration and focus is centered in the mid- and late thirties, has come the contemporary movement of social realist photography. He had his first one-man show at The Museum of Modern Art in 1934, and this same institution gave Evans a retrospective exhibition in 1971.

ANDREAS FEININGER (1906–) a member of a distinguished family of artists, first studied and practiced architecture. He later worked as an architectural and industrial photographer in Sweden and then, in 1943, joined the staff of *Life* magazine. He is the author of numerous books on the practice of photography, including *The Complete Photographer* (1968), and several volumes of his photographs have been published, including *The Face of New York* (1954) and *Changing America* (1955).

STEVEN FOSTER (1945–) a graduate of the Rochester Institute of Technology, also studied with Nathan Lyons. At present he is completing graduate studies at the University of New Mexico.

ROBERT FRANK (1924–) was born in Zurich and began photographing seriously in 1942. Following a period as a still photographer for a Zurich film company, he came to the United States in 1947 where he photographed fashion for *Harper's Bazaar* and received encouragement from Alexey Brodovitch. In 1955 he became the first European photographer to receive a Guggenheim Fellowship. Extensive travels in the United States led to the book *The Americans* (1959), which has since become one of the most fundamental publications in the field of photography as a tool of social commentary. Since 1958 he has been primarily involved with making films.

LEE FRIEDLANDER (1934–) began photographing at the age of fourteen and later studied under Edward Kaminski. In recent years he has worked as a freelance photographer, living near New York. He received Guggenheim Fellowships for photography in 1960 and 1962, and in 1966 he was artist in residence at the University of Minnesota. In 1970 he taught at the University of California at Los Angeles. He is the author of *Self Portrait* (1970), and portfolios of his photographs have appeared in *Toward a Social Landscape* (1966) and *12 Photographers of the American Social Landscape* (1967), in addition to numerous periodicals.

LEWIS W. HINE (1874–1940) was a powerful force in the development of the American social consciousness through his photographs of Ellis Island immigrants and for the National Child Labor Committee. His photographs, which transcend common reportage, appeared in numerous reform publications and in his own books. His work has most recently been published in a critical biography by Judith Maria Gutman titled *Lewis W. Hine* (1967).

YASUHIRO ISHIMOTO (1921–   ) was born in San Francisco. He spent his childhood in Japan and then entered the University of California in 1941. During World War II he was interned at Amach, Colorado. In 1952 he graduated from the Institute of Design in Chicago where he studied photography with Harry Callahan and Aaron Siskind. In 1953 he went to Japan where he is now a photographer and teacher. In 1958 he returned to the United States to photograph for a few years in Chicago. These photographs were published in Japan in 1969 under the title *Chicago, Chicago.* He is also the author of *Someday Somewhere* (1958) and a book of architectural photographs, *Katsura* (1960).

RUDOLPH JANU (1934–   ) was born in Chicago and began photographing in 1959. He is now a free-lance photographer in New York. A portfolio of his work appears in *12 Photographers of the American Social Landscape* (1967) as well as in numerous periodicals, including *Art in America, Esquire, Fortune,* and *Horizon.*

FRANCES BENJAMIN JOHNSTON (1864–1952) opened a photographic studio in Washington, D.C. in 1890. She enjoyed a high position in Washington social life and through her portraits, interiors, architectural studies, and photographs of works of art she became known as the unofficial "photographer of the American court." For the Paris Exposition of 1900 she was commissioned by the Hampton Institute to produce a portfolio of photographs to show all aspects of the school. A copy of this folio of original photographic prints was later acquired by The Museum of Modern Art which published selections from it as *The Hampton Album* (1966).

GERTRUDE KÄSEBIER (1852–1934) was one of the earliest and most successful female professional photographers. She maintained a studio in New York from about 1897 to 1926. A woman of broad interests, her more personal and pictorial work was published by Alfred Stieglitz in the first issue of *Camera Work.* She was deeply interested in the American Indian and she made several trips to the north central plains to photograph them. She also documented the Indians who were members of Buffalo Bill's troupe. A group of these photographs was published in *Everybody's Magazine* in 1901.

ANDRÉ KERTÉSZ (1896–   ) was born in Budapest. From 1925 to 1936 he lived in Paris, establishing himself as one of the pioneers of miniature camera photography. In 1936 he moved to New York, and in 1944 became an American citizen. His work has since been widely exhibited and published, including *Paris* (1934), *André Kertész Photographer* (1964), and *André Kertész* (1966). His photographs were most recently shown in the American pavilion at the Osaka World's Fair in 1970.

GEORGE KRAUSE (1937–   ) is a free-lance photographer living in Philadelphia. In addition to his professional assignments his work has been published in numerous periodicals, including *Art In America, Camera, Contemporary Photographer, Harper's Bazaar,* and *Infinity.*

HELEN LEVITT was born in New York and began photographing in 1936. She was awarded a Museum of Modern Art Fellowship for photography in 1946 and Guggenheim Fellowships in 1959 and 1960. In the early forties she photographed in Harlem, producing a remarkable and sensitive documentary study which did not achieve publication until 1965 in the book *A Way of Seeing,* with an introduction written several years earlier by James Agee.

ELAINE MAYES (1938–   ) studied photography at the San Francisco Art Institute. She has worked as a free-lance photographer in San Francisco for six years and taught photography at the University of Minnesota for two years beginning in 1968. A portfolio of her San Francisco photographs has appeared in *Aperture.*

RAY K. METZKER (1931–   ) a graduate of Beloit College and the Institute of Design, Chicago, now teaches at the Philadelphia College of Art. A photographer who for several years has focused on the more graphic and visual aspects of the urban landscape, his work has been published in such periodicals as *Aperture, Camera,* and *Creative Camera.*

JOEL MEYEROWITZ (1938–   ) studied painting at Ohio State University. His interest in photography developed in the early sixties, when he worked as an art director in New York. In 1965 he left commerical art to devote himself wholly to photography. His work was most recently exhibited in the American pavilion at the Osaka World's Fair in 1970.

DUANE MICHALS (1932–   ) has been a free-lance photographer in New York since 1961. Portfolios of his photographs have been published in *Toward a Social Landscape* (1966) and *12 Photographers of the American Social* Landscape (1967). He is also the author of *Sequences* (1970).

KEN OHARA (1942–   ) was born in Tokyo, Japan and studied art at Nihon University. In 1962 he came to the United States and later worked for three years as an assistant to the photographer Hiro. In 1970 he published the book *One,* a remarkable volume of some five hundred close-up portraits taken of anonymous people on the streets of New York.

TIMOTHY O'SULLIVAN (1840?–1882) documented the Civil War and, afterward, the exploration surveys of the American West. The most comprehensive publication of his work is in James D. Horan's *Timothy O'Sullivan* (1966).

TOD PAPAGEORGE (1940–   ) a graduate of the University of New Hampshire in English Literature, studied photography with Garry Winogrand in New York. He was the recipient of a Guggenheim Fellowship for photography in 1970.

GEORGE READ was an American daguerreotypist active in Philadelphia about 1842.

JACOB RIIS (1849–1914), a Danish immigrant, arrived in New York penniless in 1870 and lived in semi-poverty for some seven years. Almost haphazardly he drifted into newspaper work, and by 1886 he was a seasoned reporter and photographer for the *New York Tribune.* He combined words and pictures in several books and publications calling for social and economic reform, the most famous of which, *How the Other Half Lives,* was published in 1890. An anthology of his writings and photographs was published in 1968 titled *Jacob Riis Revisited.*

JOHN RUNK (1878–1964) was the owner and maker of a collection of historical photographs documenting the area surrounding Stillwater, Minnesota.

ED RUSCHA (1937–   ) born in Oklahoma, is now a successful painter and printmaker in Los Angeles. He has produced a series of highly influential books of casually taken photographs of aspects of the southern California urban landscape, including *Twentysix Gasoline Stations* (1962), *Some Los Angeles Apartments* (1965), *On the Sunset Strip* (1966), and *Thirtyfour Parking Lots* (1967).

STEVE SALMIERI (1945–   ) studied at the School of Visual Arts in New York where he is now a free-lance photographer. His photographs have been published in *Art In America* and *Camera,* as well as in numerous studies of social issues prepared by the First National City Bank.

WILLIAM SHEW (1830?–1903?) was an American daguerreotypist and student of Samuel F. B. Morse. He opened his own studio in Boston in 1845, but moved to San Francisco in 1850 where he maintained a studio through 1903.

STEPHEN SHORE (1947–   ) began photographing at the age of nine and is essentially self-taught. He has recently studied with Minor White and at the New School for Social Research with Lisette Model. His work forms a substantial portion of the book *Andy Warhol* (1968), and other photographs appear in *Art in America* and the catalogue *Foto-Portret* (1970).

ART SINSABAUGH (1924–   ) Professor of Art at the University of Illinois, graduated from the Institute of Design in Chicago where he studied under Moholy-Nagy and Harry Callahan. His highly influential photographs of the rural and urban landscape, which he began in the early fifties, have been widely exhibited and published, including a volume of photographs with accompanying prose by Sherwood Anderson, published in 1964, and a portfolio in *The Photographer and the American Landscape* (1963). He received a Guggenheim Fellowship for photography in 1969.

W. EUGENE SMITH (1918–   ) the foremost American photo-journalist of his generation, defined the highest level of accomplishment in the area of the photo-essay in his work for *Life* magazine. His "Country Doctor" (1948), "Spanish Village" (1951), and "A Man of Mercy" (1954) are landmark essays. Now a free-lance photographer in New York, he earlier spent several years documenting Pittsburgh. A retrospective volume of his photographs, *W. Eugene Smith,* was published in 1970.

NORMAN SNYDER (1936–   ) is a free-lance photographer in New York whose subway photographs were published in *Du* in 1970.

ALBERT SANDS SOUTHWORTH (1811–1894) and JOSIAH JOHNSON HAWES (1808–1901) were partners in a Boston gallery of photography. Two of the most successful and pictorially significant daguerreotype artists of their day, they are noted for their portraits of prominent early nineteenth-century political and social figures.

JOHN SPENCE (1943–   ) was born in Abilene, Texas and graduated from the University of Nebraska. In 1970 he taught photography at the University of Connecticut. At present he is completing graduate studies in photography at Nebraska. His photographs have been published in *Motive.*

RALPH STEINER (1899–   ) graduated from the Clarence H. White School of Photography in New York. For several years he was a highly influential still photographer. With Willard Van Dyke, he directed and photographed the motion picture *The City,* which was first shown at the 1939 World's Fair. In recent years he has devoted himself to film-making.

ALFRED STIEGLITZ (1864–1946) is considered the major figure in American photography. As an artist he made photographs which, in effect, defined the very nature of the medium, and as a publisher and gallery-owner from 1902 to 1946 he materially encouraged the work of many younger photographers. Reproductions of several of his photographs and a bibliography of his publications are found in *Alfred Stieglitz* (1960) and *Alfred Stieglitz: Photographer* (1965).

PAUL STRAND (1890–   ) began his first photography under the guidance of Lewis W. Hine with whom he studied at the Ethnical Culture School in New York. An intimate of Stieglitz, Strand has carried forward in his own work the concepts of interpretative vision first articulated by Stieglitz. In 1950 Strand, together with Nancy Newhall, published *Time in New England,* a book which many feel is the most successful combination of words and photographs yet to appear. He has since published several volumes, each on a country or locale, including *La France de Profil* (1952), *Un Paese* (1955), *Tir A 'Mhurain* (1962), and *Living Egypt* (1969).

ALWYN SCOTT TURNER (1936–   ) was born in Leonard, Texas and was raised in Detroit. Formerly a newspaper photographer, he now devotes himself to his personal work. In 1970 he published a volume titled *Photographs of the Detroit People.*

JERRY N. UELSMANN (1934–   ) is Professor of Art at the University of Florida. A major artist utilizing the complex techniques of photo-montage, his work has been widely exhibited and published. The most recent volume of his photographs, titled *Jerry N. Uelsmann,* was published in 1970 and includes an introduction and notes by Peter C. Bunnell.

PAUL VANDERBILT (1905–   ) studied art history under Paul Sachs at Harvard University. After working in the museum and library fields, he went to the Library of Congress in 1947, becoming Chief of the Prints and Photographs Division. Since 1954 he has been Curator of Iconographic Collections at the State Historical Society of Wisconsin. He has worked as a serious photographer of rural and small town life in Wisconsin only during the past decade. His photographs have been published in *The Photographer and the American Landscape* (1963) and most recently exhibited in the American pavilion at the Osaka World's Fair in 1970.

ROBERT WALCH (1942–   ) a free-lance photographer in New York, studied at the Rochester Institute of Technology. For some years he has been working on a set of photographs depicting the Pennsylvania Dutch culture.

WEEGEE (1899–1968), whose real name was Arthur Fellig, was for many years a newspaper photographer in New York who pictured some of the darkest but most vital aspects of urban life. His work is influential in defining that particular iconography and style of the large-city tabloid of thirty years ago. He wrote a number of books, the most important of which was *Naked City* (1945).

BRETT WESTON (1911–   ) the son of Edward Weston, has established himself as a major artist in the straightforward tradition of photography. His work is dramatically different in style from that of his father, although his technique is the same. While not particularly known for his work in urban areas, his photographs made in New York during and after World War II display his masterful translation of the city's scale. His photographs have been widely published, including *Brett Weston: Photographs* (1956) and in a catalogue of the same title in 1966.

EDWARD WESTON (1886–1958) one of the most influential photographers in the history of the medium, is with Stieglitz the other pivotal figure in American photography in this century. For over forty years he demonstrated that the most common of subjects, approached with the most straightforward of techniques, could be made beautifully new. For a sampling of his work, which has been well published and exhibited, and bibliographic information see Nancy Newhall's *Edward Weston* (1965).

MINOR WHITE (1908–   ), an influential photographer and teacher, has enlarged upon the work of both Stieglitz and Edward Weston. He is on the faculty of the Massachusetts Institute of Technology and conducts numerous private workshops. Since 1952 he has edited and published *Aperture,* a quarterly of photography. His work, previously known only through exhibitions and the publication of original print portfolios, has recently been published, together with his writings, in *Mirrors Messages and Manifestations* (1969).

GARRY WINOGRAND (1928–   ) born in New York, began photographing while in the Air Force during World War II. After the War he studied with Alexey Brodovitch at the New School for Social Research. Winogrand has since worked as a free-lance photographer in New York. In 1969 The Museum of Modern Art published his book *The Animals,* and a portfolio of his photographs is reproduced in *Toward a Social Landscape* (1966).